THE PAPERS OF
DAVID SETTLE REID

David Settle Reid (1813-1891) of Rockingham County became governor of North Carolina in 1851 after serving in the state Senate and the United States House of Representatives. His gubernatorial campaign of 1848, though unsuccessful, introduced the issue of free suffrage and signaled the resurgence of the state Democratic party. This portrait probably dates to the period between 1843 and 1847 when Reid was a member of the House of Representatives. Photograph courtesy of the Library of Congress.

The Papers of David Settle Reid

VOLUME I

1829-1852

LINDLEY S. BUTLER, *Editor*

Assisted by PATRICIA R. JOHNSON, E. T. MALONE, JR., and ANN WARD LITTLE

DEPARTMENT OF CULTURAL RESOURCES
DIVISION OF ARCHIVES AND HISTORY
RALEIGH, NORTH CAROLINA

1993

ISBN 0-86526-249-7

for *Lucile Reid Fagg*

CONTENTS

ILLUSTRATIONS

FOREWORD

The publication of Volume I of *The Papers of David Settle Reid* opens an important vista on North Carolina's nineteenth-century political culture. Curiously, over the years prominent Whig statesman have received the lion's share of the volumes of papers published by the North Carolina Division of Archives and History. The eighth and final volume of *The Papers of William Alexander Graham* has been completed, and during the 1950s the then Department of Archives and History published five volumes of *The Papers of Willie Person Mangum.*

This first volume of Reid papers shows how the Democrats were able to capture control of the state after fifteen years of Whig ascendancy. Indeed, Reid's campaigns for governor sparked fierce debate because of his advocacy of "free suffrage"—the removal of a fifty-acre property qualification to vote for state senators. Reid's papers give valuable insight not only into the issues dividing Whigs and Democrats but also into the rough-and-tumble campaign style of the second party system at mid-century.

Dr. Lindley S. Butler, historian-in-residence at Rockingham Community College and editor of this volume, received his graduate training under Hugh T. Lefler at the University of North Carolina at Chapel Hill. In addition to publishing various studies on the colonial and Revoluntionary period in North Carolina, he has conducted a vigorous county history program in Rockingham County. With Alan D. Watson, he is also the coeditor of *The North Carolina Experience: An Interpretive and Documentary History* (Chapel Hill: University of North Carolina Press, 1984).

Dr. Butler has received the able assistance of various members of the Historical Publications Section's staff. Trudy M. Rayfield prepared the manuscript for typesetting by encoding it on a microcomputer. Lisa D. Bailey performed the proofreading. Patricia R. Johnson, a former staff member, began the initial in-house editing, but E. T. Malone, Jr., completed it. He verified transcriptions of documents, edited footnotes to conform to the section's style, prepared appendixes, located several valuable additional documents, and conducted further research to annotate numerous references in the documents. Ann W. Little compiled the index. The North Carolina Literary and Historical Association also provided timely financial aid to allow a search for two possible Reid letters in Britain's Public Record Office.

A second volume of Reid papers, now in preparation, will conclude the series.

Jeffrey J. Crow
Historical Publications Administrator

July, 1993

PREFACE

The bulk of the papers of David Settle Reid are located in two major collections in the North Carolina Archives: the David S. Reid Papers, consisting of nearly 850 letters, circulars, and miscellaneous documents; and Governor Reid's letter books and official papers. There are Reid letters and papers (approximately 300 items) in the Rockingham County Historical Collection of the Rockingham Community College Library, and Duke University library has a small group of about 75 items. With the exception of his four years as governor, David Reid regrettably did not retain copies of his correspondence; consequently, his papers consist primarily of letters written to him. A few letters which he wrote to family members are extant, and a search of various repositories has yielded scattered letters written by Reid. Only in the period when he was governor are his papers nearly complete. For other years—especially after 1860—the letters are sparse.

Unless otherwise noted, all of the letters published in this volume are autograph letters signed. Regardless of their significance, previously published letters and documents are calendared and not republished here. Because of their relative inaccessability some letters published in contemporary newspapers have been included. The intent of this edition is to reproduce the letters as written except that obvious slips of the pen have been corrected and the salutation and closing have been omitted unless they are an integral part of the letter. Insofar as possible spelling, capitalization, and punctuation have been reproduced as originally written. Given the inconsistencies of nineteenth century grammar and spelling and the vagaries of the penmanship of diverse correspondants, an editor is obliged to interpret considerably, and any errors of interpretation are mine alone. Words added to the manuscripts for the purpose of clarification are italicized in brackets, but additions are minimal. A few inferred readings of difficult handwriting are bracketed in roman type. An attempt has been made to identify all correspondants and persons mentioned in the papers, as well as geographic references. However, identification of individuals, especially when only a common last name was used, was not always possible.

Since some of the letters received by Reid were trivial or repetitious, a number of letters have been excluded. The excluded documents have been calendared. This format allows the reader to grasp an overview of the existing Reid papers without the burden of needless repetition. Letters and papers published in this collection were selected because they chronicle significant or interesting events in Reid's personal career or his era; they furnish insight into the political attitudes of Reid, his acquaintances, and the period; or they illustrate important steps in the maturation of Reid as a political leader.

Any scholar is always indebted to others for his work. I particularly want to thank Dr. Thornton W. Mitchell, former State Archivist, and his capable staff, who in many ways made my task easier, especially Ms. Ellen McGrew who prepared the excellent calendar of the governor's letters and papers. Much of the transcription and typing of the letters was done by the staff of the Historical Publications Section of the Division of Archives and History. Former Section Chief Memory F. Mitchell gently prodded this project and offered encouragement and advice over the years. E. T. Malone, Jr., of the Historical Publications Section provided significant editorial assistance in the latter stages of the project. The staffs of the Southern Historical Collection at the University of North Carolina library, the manuscript collection of the Duke University library, the Rockingham Community College library, and the Reidsville Public Library have been helpful. Mrs. Lucile Reid Fagg of Eden, granddaughter of Governor Reid, has been of inestimable value to this project, continually unearthing new family papers and artifacts and willingly sharing them. Without her aid and enthusiasm this volume would be the poorer. My wife, T, has encouraged me, typed portions of the letters and the manuscript, and given her invaluable editorial advice.

I am deeply indebted to the National Endowment for the Humanities for the fellowship that enabled me to initiate this project and complete much of the basic research and transcription of the documents.

Lindley S. Butler
Wentworth

CHRONOLOGICAL LISTS OF THE PAPERS OF DAVID SETTLE REID 1829-1852 PRINTED IN THIS VOLUME

LETTERS WRITTEN BY DAVID SETTLE REID

Place	Date	Written to
Reidsville	June 15, 1839	William Stringer
Reidsville	February 17, 1840	Beverly Daniel
Rockingham County	September 28, 1840	Larkin Stowe and Committee
Rockingham County	May 19, 1843	R. P. Cardwell and others
Washington, D.C.	January 14, 1844	Reuben Reid
Washington, D.C.	March 4, 1844	Hamilton Brown
Washington, D.C.	April 12, 1844	John C. Spencer
Washington, D.C.	January 19, 1845	Frances R. Adams
Washington, D.C.	February 9, 1845	Reuben H. Reid
Wentworth	May 1, 1845	R. P. Williamson and Committee
Wilkesboro	August 5, 1845	Reuben Reid
Reidsville	November 19, 1846	E. W. Hubard
Washington, D.C.	December 16, 1846	Jesse Albert Waugh
Reidsville	April 26, 1847	James K. Polk
Salem	June 19, 1850	William Lander
Reidsville	June 22, 1850	Robert Strange and Committee
Reidsville	June 24, 1850	William W. Holden
Reidsville	October 5, 1850	Whitmel Stallings and others
Reidsville	December 2, 1850	Elizabeth Waugh
Reidsville	December 4, 1850	Elizabeth Waugh
Raleigh	March 21, 1851	George B. Mathew
Raleigh	August 23, 1851	Jacob Siler
Raleigh	September 24, 1851	Jacob Siler
Raleigh	October 22, 1851	William H. Thomas
Raleigh	March 22, 1852	Jacob Siler
Raleigh	May 20, 1852	Jacob Siler
Greenville	May 30, 1852	Henrietta S. Reid
Fayetteville	June 7, 1852	Henrietta S. Reid
Lenoir	July 11, 1852	Henrietta S. Reid
Marion	July 16, 1852	Henrietta S. Reid
Burnsville	July 26, 1852	Henrietta S. Reid
Franklin	August 1, 1852	Henrietta S. Reid
Murphy	August 4, 1852	Henrietta S. Reid
Raleigh	August 29, 1852	Henrietta S. Reid
Raleigh	September 8, 1852	Thomas Settle

LETTERS WRITTEN TO DAVID SETTLE REID

Place	Date	Written by
Greensboro	March 29, 1829	John M. Morehead
Clarksburg, Kentucky	July 28, 1830	Joseph C. Reid
Orange Court House, Virginia	July 16, 1835	James Roach

Talbotton, Georgia	May 20, 1836	William Scott
Carthage	July 15, 1836	John A. D. McNeill
Rockingham Springs	July 30, 1836	John J. Wright
Raleigh	August 28, 1836	Joseph B. Hinton
Chesnut Grove, South Carolina	September 11, 1836	James A. Lewis
[Rockingham County]	July 31, 1837	Thomas W. Wariner
Chapel Hill	August 13, 1838	John H. Dillard
Troublesome	December 12, 1838	Samuel F. Adams
Rockingham County	January 19, 1839	Richard P. Cardwell
Richmond, Virginia	March 5, 1839	Samuel F. Adams
[Rockingham County]	[1839]	Richard C. Stubblefield
Madison	August 9, 1840	John M. Rose
Anderson's Store	September 5, 1840	Quinton Anderson
Albrights	September 12, 1840	William Montgomery
Caswell County	March 31, 1841	Bedford Brown
Kinston	September 19, 1841	Thomas Settle
Hitchcockville, Connecticut	February 15, 1842	James Phelps
Washington, D.C.	February 17, 1842	Romulus M. Saunders
Caswell County	September 20, 1842	Bedford Brown
Hitchcockville, Connecticut	September 20, 1842	James Phelps
Rockford	May 9, 1843	Richard P. Cardwell and others
Rockford	December 23, 1843	William P. Dobson
Troublesome	February 26, 1844	Samuel F. Adams
Rockingham County	March 20, 1844	Weldon E. Wright
Reidsville	April 10, 1844	Reuben Reid
Good Spring	April 11, 1844	Augustine Henry Shepperd
Bethania	April 15, 1844	George F. Wilson
Surry County	April, 1844	Andrew J. Folger
Milton	May 12, 1844	John T. Garland
Milton	May 16, 1844	Barzillai Graves
Baltimore, Maryland	May 29, 1844	John Hill
Jefferson	May 31, 1844	Roderick Murchison
Madison	June 3, 1844	Peter Scales
Reidsville	June 6, 1844	Reuben Reid
Hitchcockville, Connecticut	June 12, 1844	James Phelps
Pontotoc, Mississippi	July 13, 1844	C. A. Bradford
Rawlinsburg	July 29, 1844	Robert P. Williamson
Jefferson	August 27, 1844	Joseph W. Hampton
Raleigh	October 30, 1844	William W. Holden
Essex, Connecticut	November 27, 1844	James Phelps
[Rockingham County]	December 8, 1844	L. P. Wright
Milton	January 11, 1845	Barzillai Graves
Essex, Connecticut	January 24, 1845	James Phelps
Rockingham County	January 28, 1845	Joseph W. Neal
Rockingham County	January 31, 1845	Daniel W. Courts
Milton	February 7, 1845	Nathaniel Henry McCain
Germanton	February 16, 1845	Archibald R. Ruffin
Greensboro	March 4, 1845	A. C. Lindsey
Wentworth	April 30, 1845	Robert P. Williamson and Committee

Raleigh	May 24, 1845	William W. Holden
Essex, Connecticut	June 27, 1845	James Phelps
Jefferson	July 9, 1845	Roderick Murchison
Richmond, Virginia	October 16, 1845	William Scott
Essex, Connecticut	November 25, 1845	James Phelps
Hamilton	December 14, 1845	Jesse Cooper
Wentworth	December 24, 1845	Weldon E. Wright
Chesnut Grove, South Carolina	January 6, 1846	James A. Lewis
Raleigh	January 8, 1846	J. Julius Wheeden
Troublesome	January 11, 1846	Samuel F. Adams
Brown's Store	January 15, 1846	Calvin Graves
New York	January 16, 1846	Lemuel Sawyer
Raleigh	January 21, 1846	Louis D. Henry
Milton	January 22, 1846	John T. Garland
Telmont	January 30, 1846	Andrew J. Folger
Beattysford	February 4, 1846	John Hill Wheeler
Red House	February 21, 1846	James W. Jeffreys
Davie County	February 23, 1846	Lucius Quintus Cincinnatus Butler
Stokes County	March 1, 1846	John Hill
Reidsville	March 8, 1846	Reuben Reid
Person County	March 9, 1846	James E. Williamson
Raleigh	March 20, 1846	William W. Holden
Rockingham County	May 6, 1846	Daniel E. Guerrant
Rockingham County	May 6, 1846	Daniel E. Guerrant
Wilkesboro	May 27, 1846	William C. Emmett
Troublesome	June 18, 1846	Samuel F. Adams
[Surry County]	June 20, 1846	John H. Dobson
Wentworth	June 20, 1846	Thomas B. Wheeler [with enclosure]
Yanceyville	June 22, 1846	William Brown
Troublesome	June 30, 1846	Samuel F. Adams
Philadelphia	July 19, 1846	Lucien B. Chase
Stone Mountain, Georgia	July 20, 1846	Weldon E. Wright
Reidsville	July 28, 1846	Joseph W. Neal
Davie County	January 28,1847	Lucius Quintus Cincinnatus Butler
Raleigh	January 28, 1847	William W. Gray
Milton	February 18, 1847	Nathaniel J. Palmer
Greensborough	February 19, 1847	Wilson S. Hill
Reidsville	February 21, 1847	Elias Dodson
Raleigh	March 7, 1847	James C. Dobbin
Gaston	March 24, 1847	Stephen A. Douglas
Essex, Connecticut	April 15, 1847	James Phelps
Beattiesford	April 19, 1847	John Hill Wheeler
Falling Creek	April 20, 1847	Curtis H. Brogden
Essex, Connecticut	October 1, 1847	James Phelps
Raleigh	December 8, 1847	William W. Holden
Saltillo, Mexico	January 31, 1848	Patrick M. Henry
Greensboro	April 16, 1848	Robert P. Dick
Kinston	April 17, 1848	William B. Gulick
Raleigh	April 19, 1848	William W. Holden
Newbern	May 30, 1848	William B. Gulick
Fayetteville	June 16, 1848	James C. Dobbin

Raleigh	June 23, 1848	William W. Holden
New Castle	June 30, 1848	Leland Martin
Hillsborough	July 26, 1848	E. G. Gray
Raleigh	August 6, 1848	William W. Holden
Leakesville	July 31, 1849	Thomas W. Keen
Washington, D.C.	May 26, 1850	Stephen A. Douglas
Raleigh	June 1,1850	William W. Holden
Raleigh	June 15, 1850	Robert Strange and Commitee
Goldsboro	June 17, 1850	S. A. Andrews
Greensboro	June 20, 1850	Robert P. Dick
Raleigh	July 4, 1850	Samuel F. Adams
Raleigh	July 7, 1850	William W. Holden
Raleigh	July 10, 1850	William W. Holden
New Berne	July 11, 1850	Samuel F. Adams
Reidsville	July 17, 1850	Hugh K. Reid
Raleigh	July 19, 1850	William W. Holden
Raleigh	July 24, 1850	William W. Holden
Fayetteville	July 29, 1850	James C. Dobbin
Raleigh	August 7, 1850	William W. Holden
Gatesville	September 6, 1850	Whitmel Stallings and others
Marion	November 5, 1850	John M. Dick
Raleigh	December 1, 1850	William W. Holden
Franklin	December 11, 1850	Ezekial Dowdle
Washington, D.C.	December 20, 1850	George Talcott
[Iredell County]	January 3, 1851	Charles R. Jones
[Raleigh]	January 6, 1851	John A. Gilmer
[Raleigh]	January 7, 1851	William W. Holden
Sulphur Springs	January 9, 1851	Reuben Deaver
Dayton, Ohio	January 10, 1851	George W. Houk
Rutherfordton	January 10, 1851	Thomas A. Hayden
[Raleigh]	January 17, 1851	Charles Manly [with enclosure]
[Raleigh]	[February 2, 1851]	Asa Biggs
Plymouth	February 3, 1851	Hezekiah G. Spruill
Beattiesford	February 7, 1851	John Hill Wheeler
Chapel Hill	February 8, 1851	William H. Miller
Chapel Hill	February 10, 1851	Elisha Mitchell
[Chapel Hill]	February 12, 1851	Albert M. Shipp
Macon County	February 17, 1851	Jacob Siler
Murphey	February 18, 1851	E. P. Sharp
Albany, New York	February 19, 1851	Ebenezer Emmons
Rutherfordton	February 20, 1851	John Gray Bynum
Albany, New York	February 27, 1851	Ebenezer Emmons
Fayetteville	February 27, 1851	James C. Dobbin
New York	March 10, 1851	John Hill Wheeler
Washington, D.C.	March 13, 1851	William H. Thomas
Charleston, South Carolina	March 13, 1851	George B. Mathew [with enclosure]
Locust Hill	March 18, 1851	Calvin Graves
Bracket Town	March 26, 1851	John F. Hoke
Charleston, South Carolina	March 27, 1851	George B. Mathew
Beattiesford	March 30, 1851	John Hill Wheeler

Wilmington	April 14, 1851	Daniel Dickson
Fayetteville	April 17, 1851	Duncan G. MacRae
Asheville	April 18, 1851	Newton Coleman
Lincolnton	April 18, 1851	Burton Craige
Eagle Mills	April 21, 1851	Andrew Baggarly
Aquone	April 26, 1851	Nimrod S. Jarrett
Murfreesboro	April 28, 1851	Samuel J. Wheeler
Goldsboro	April 28, 1851	William B. Gulick
Rutherfordton	May 3, 1851	Frank I. Wilson
Marion	May 9, 1851	Thomas Settle
Murphy	May 13, 1851	George W. Hayes
Franklin	May 19, 1851	David W. Siler
Raleigh	May 28, 1851	Thomas Settle, Jr.
Fayetteville	June 27, 1851	Duncan G. MacRae
Greensboro	June 30, 1851	John M. Dick
Rutherfordton	August 9, 1851	Thomas A. Hayden
Washington, D.C.	August 30, 1851	Robert J. Powell
Enfield	September 5, 1851	L. H. B. Whitaker
Franklin	September 10, 1851	William H. Thomas
Asheville	September 12, 1851	Ezra McCall Gates
Haywood County	September 16, 1851	Robert Henry
Wayne County	September 27, 1851	William K. Lane
Albany, New York	October 4, 1851	Ebenezer Emmons
Yanceyville	October 8, 1851	Samuel P. Hill
Albany, New York	October 22, 1851	Ebenezer Emmons
Wilmington	October 22, 1851	George Aaron
Weldon	November 3, 1851	John O. Campbell
Rutherfordton	November 28, 1851	Frank I. Wilson
Albany, New York	December 11, 1851	Ebenezer Emmons
Columbia,	December 17, 1851	William Glazer
[Caswell County]	December 30, 1851	Calvin Graves
Robeson County	January 2, 1852	Thomas J. Mims
[Randolph County]	January 10, 1852	Braxton Craven
Chapel Hill	January 15, 1852	Elisha Mitchell
Washington, D.C.	January 22, 1852	John R. J. Daniel
Aquone	February 2, 1852	Nimrod S. Jarrett
Weston, Missouri	February 3, 1852	Abraham Featherman
Fayetteville	February 6, 1852	Ebenezer Emmons
Locust Hill	February 14, 1852	Calvin Graves
Aquone	February 17, 1852	Nimrod S. Jarrett
Person County	February 26, 1852	C. H. Jordan
Goldsborough	March 6, 1852	Ebenezer Emmons
Fayetteville	March 8, 1852	James C. Dobbin
Chapel Hill	March 11, 1852	Henry R. Shorter
Chapel Hill	March 15, 1852	David L. Swain
Newberne	March 21, 1852	Ebenezer Emmons
Washington, D.C.	March 22, 1852	Henry K. Craig
Newberne	March 28, 1852	Ebenezer Emmons
Aquone	March 29, 1852	Nimrod S. Jarrett
Fayetteville	March 29, 1852	Archibald M. Campbell
Milton	March 30, 1852	Nathaniel J. Palmer
Yanceyville	April 3, 1852	Samuel P. Hill

Nash County	April 3, 1852	Calvin R. Finch
Washington, D.C.	April 4, 1852	Orlando B. Ficklin
Elizabeth City	April 22, 1852	Robert R. Heath
Fayetteville	May, 3, 1852	J. B. Ferguson
Locust Hill	May 3, 1852	Calvin Graves
Plymouth	May 19, 1852	Joseph C. Norcom
Washington, D.C.	May 19, 1852	Abraham W. Venable
Gatesville	May 20, 1852	Willis F. Riddick
Enfield	May 24, 1852	Spier Whitaker
Halifax	May 27, 1852	William B. Pope
Raleigh	June 8, 1852	Romulus M. Saunders
Rockingham County	July 16, 1852	Thomas Settle
Washington, D.C.	July 18, 1852	Abraham W. Venable
Raleigh	July 22, 1852	Daniel W. Courts
Raleigh	August 10, 1852	William W. Holden
Williamston	August 23, 1852	Asa Biggs
Fayetteville	August 28, 1852	Jesse G. Shepherd
Williamston	August 31, 1852	Thomas Settle
Philadelphia	October 2, 1852	Sarah J. Hale
Greensboro	November 29, 1852	James R. McLean
Washington, D.C.	December 13, 1852	John E. Kendall
Washington, D.C.	December 14, 1852	Robert J. Powell
Yanceyville	December 28, 1852	Samuel P. Hill

MISCELLANEOUS DOCUMENTS

Item	Date	Place
David S. Reid, Philip J. Irion, and Blake W. Braswell to the Freemen of Rockingham County	December 22, 1835	[Raleigh]
Remarks of David S. Reid in the North Carolina Senate	[January 6, 1837]	Raleigh
David S. Reid and Philip J. Irion to the Voters of Rockingham County	January 23, 1837	Raleigh
Circular of David S. Reid to His Constitutents	March 7, 1845	Washington, D.C.
Speech by David S. Reid on the Oregon Question	[February 7, 1846]	Washington, D.C.
Circular of David S. Reid to His Constituents	March 31, 1847	Washington, D.C.

David S. Reid to the Democratic Party of North Carolina	May 25, 1850	Rockingham County
David S. Reid to the People of North Carolina	June 28, 1850	Reidsville
Inaugural Address of David S. Reid to the General Assembly	January 1, 1851	[Raleigh]
Message from His Excellency, Gov. David S. Reid to the General Assembly Relative to Putting Under Contract the Western Turnpike	January 14, 1851	Raleigh
Opposition View of "FREE SUFFRAGE REID"	January 30, 1852	Raleigh
David S. Reid to Council of State [draft]	May 19, 1852	Raleigh
Obituary of Ann Augusta Holden	June 25, 1852	Raleigh
A Whig Satire Directed at David S. Reid	July 9, 1852	Raleigh
Special Message of David S. Reid to the General Assembly	October 4, 1852	Raleigh
Biennial Message of David S. Reid to the General Assembly	October 14, 1852	Raleigh
Second Inaugural Address of David S. Reid to the General Assembly	December 22, 1852	Raleigh
Poem by William W. Holden	[December 1852]	Raleigh

MISCELLANEOUS LETTERS

Written by	Date	Written to
Anonymous Farmer, Rockingham County	September 14, 1840	Thomas Loring, Raleigh
J. Julius Wheeden, Raleigh	March 21, 1846	Reuben Reid, Reidsville

Martha Martin Douglas, Quincy, Illinois	September 3, 1847	Elizabeth G. Settle, Reidsville
George B. Mathew Charleston, South Carolina	March 13, 1851	David L. Swain, Chapel Hill
William W. Holden, Raleigh	June 26, 1852	Henrietta S. Reid, Raleigh
Matt W. Ransom, Franklinton	July 5, 1852	Daniel Shine Hill Louisburg
Samuel J. Person, Wilmington	July 6, 1852	Thomas D. S. McDowell Bladen County
Thomas Settle, Jr. Richmond Hill	September 23, 1852	Henrietta S. Reid Rockingham County
Fanny Settle, Rockingham County	September 30, 1852	Thomas Settle, Jr., Richmond Hill

ABBREVIATIONS USED TO DESIGNATE REPOSITORIES OF REID PAPERS

A&H-AB	Mrs. Albert Bauman Collection, Division of Archives and History, North Carolina Department of Cultural Resources
A&H-DSR	David S. Reid Papers, Division of Archives and History, North Carolina Department of Cultural Resources
A&H-GLB	Governors' Letter Books, David S. Reid, Division of Archives and History, North Carolina Department of Cultural Resources
A&H-GP	Governors' Papers, David S. Reid, Division of Archives and History, North Carolina Department of Cultural Resources
A&H-GAR	General Assembly Records, Archives, Division of Archives and History, North Carolina Department of Cultural Resources
A&H-mn	Microfilmed newspapers collection, Division of Archives and History, North Carolina Department of Cultural Resources
Duke-DSR	David S. Reid Papers, Manuscript Department, Duke University
Duke-RBR	Rare Book Room, Duke University
Duke-WHT	William H. Thomas Papers, Manuscript Department, Duke University
Duke-WWH	William W. Holden Papers, Manuscript Department, Duke University
LC-JKP	James K. Polk Papers (microfilm copy in the University of North Carolina Library, Chapel Hill), Library of Congress

NCC	North Carolina Collection, University of North Carolina at Chapel Hill
RCC	Rockingham County Historical Collection, Rockingham Community College, Wentworth, North Carolina
RF	Reid Family Papers, in possession of Mrs. Lucile Reid Fagg, Eden, North Carolina
UC-SAD	Stephen A. Douglas Papers, Manuscript Collections, University of Chicago Library, Chicago
UNC-BF	Battle Family Papers, Southern Historical Collection, University of North Carolina at Chapel Hill
UNC-CIG	Charles Iverson Graves Papers, Southern Historical Collection, University of North Carolina at Chapel Hill
UNC-CP	Clingman-Puryear Papers, Southern Historical Collection, University of North Carolina at Chapel Hill
UNC-CHW	Calvin H. Wiley Papers, Southern Historical Collection, University of North Carolina at Chapel Hill
UNC-H	Hubard Family Papers, Southern Historical Collection, University of North Carolina at Chapel Hill
UNC-HB	Hamilton Brown Papers, Southern Historical Collection, University of North Carolina at Chapel Hill
UNC-JHD	John Henry Dillard Letters, Southern Historical Collection, University of North Carolina at Chapel Hill

UNC-JP	Jones-Patterson Papers, Southern Historical Collection, University of North Carolina at Chapel Hill
UNC-JS	Jacob Siler Papers, Southern Historical Collection, University of North Carolina at Chapel Hill
UNC-MWR	Matthew Whitaker Ransom Papers, Southern Historical Collection, University of North Carolina at Chapel Hill
UNC-SR	Scott-Reid Family Papers, Southern Historical Collection, University of North Carolina at Chapel Hill
UNC-TMcD	Thomas D. S. McDowell Papers, Southern Historical Collection, University of North Carolina at Chapel Hill
UNC-TS	Thomas Settle Papers, Southern Historical Collection, University of North Carolina at Chapel Hill.

BIOGRAPHICAL SKETCH*

At New Bern, North Carolina, on May 10, 1848, the first joint debate of the gubernatorial campaign opened with speeches by candidates Charles Manly, Whig, and David Settle Reid, Democrat. Reid astonished his opponent when without warning he raised the issue of free suffrage, by advocating abolition of the last property qualification on voting in the state. A vestige of the 1776 constitution, the fifty-acre freehold requirement for citizens voting for state senators had been retained by the Constitutional Convention of 1835 but was now considered by many North Carolinians to be archaic and undemocratic. Reid characterized the suffrage restriction as an "odious distinction between voters in our State, as a relic of aristocracy borrowed from another country, that was neither suited to our country or to the spirit of the age in which we live. . . ."[1] The clearly unsettled Manly asked for time to consider his position on the issue and the next day roundly attacked free suffrage, which subsequently became the key issue of the election.

Reid narrowly lost the race by 854 votes, the closest gubernatorial election in the state's history, but he had sounded the death knell for the complacent Whig party. In the next election he decisively defeated Manly, becoming the first popularly elected Democratic governor of North Carolina. The progressive leadership provided by the youthful Reid and his close ally William W. Holden, editor of the influential *North-Carolina Standard*, established the Democratic party ascendancy that has dominated state politics from 1850 until the present.

Serving half a century on the local, state, and national levels, Reid was a prominent political figure in the antebellum public life of North Carolina. His career began in 1829 when at the age of sixteen he was appointed the first postmaster of Reidsville. When he was just twenty-two years old he was elected colonel of the county militia regiment and defeated a well-known and experienced Whig for a seat in the state Senate. After four terms as senator he was elected to the United States House of Representatives for two terms. Following two terms as governor of the state, he served in the United States Senate. A member of the state Constitutional Conventions of 1861 and 1875, he played a key role in the latter meeting in arranging the compromise that made it possible for the convention to be organized.

Although involved throughout his life in partisan political conflict, Reid earned and retained the respect of the people of North Carolina by his strength of character and his advocacy of free suffrage. A contemporary historian, John Hill Wheeler, wrote in an early biographical sketch, "There are few men in the State who enjoy more of the respect, regard, and the affection of the people than Governor Reid, for unaffected simplicity of character, stern integrity, and unsullied purity of life. . . . No one who knows him, or who has observed his long, successful and brilliant career, can ever doubt where to find him—the unwavering supporter of popular rights and democratic principles."[2]

The strong character observed by Wheeler was molded in the rolling hills of the northern piedmont border county of Rockingham where Reid's family has lived for more than two hundred years. Near the end of the American Revolution, David Reid's paternal grandfather, Hugh Reid of Baltimore County, Maryland, moved south with his family and on August 16, 1782, purchased 550 acres on Hogan's Creek in northern Guilford County, the area that became Rockingham County in 1785. A native of Chester County, Pennsylvania, Hugh Reid had married Jemima Carmen in Maryland on March 13, 1770. The Reids had five sons and three daughters: John, William, Joseph, Elisha, Reuben, Sarah, Mary, and Jemima. Hugh Reid remained a farmer of moderate means, accumulating some additional land and one slave by 1815.[3]

David Reid's maternal great-grandfather Josiah Settle of Pantherskin Run, Loudoun County, Virginia, came to northern Guilford County before 1779, when he received a state grant dated November 13 for 300 acres on Pruett's Fork of Hogan's Creek. By 1786 his eldest son David had married Rhoda Mullins of Rockingham County, the daughter of Thomas Mullins, who was an elder of Lickfork Primitive Baptist Church. As early as October, 1783, David Settle began acquiring land on Hogan's Creek, and by 1815 he had a plantation of 1,200 acres with six slaves. The children of David and Rhoda Settle were John, Thomas, Frances, Elizabeth, Mary, Josiah, Benjamin, Lucinda, and Matilda. The Settles and Reids were near neighbors and attended Lickfork Church. Eventually the two families were united by the marriage after April 11, 1812, of Reuben Reid and Elizabeth Williams Settle.[4]

The marriages of three of David Settle's children, that of Elizabeth to Reuben Reid, Mary to Robert Martin, and Thomas to Henrietta Graves, created a remarkable North Carolina political dynasty. In the three succeeding generations, descendants of these marriages and their in-laws included a presidential candidate, Stephen A. Douglas; two United States senators, Stephen Douglas and David S. Reid; four United States congressmen, Stephen Douglas, David Reid, Thomas Settle, Sr., and Thomas Settle III; a governor, David Reid; and two state Supreme Court justices, Thomas Settle, Jr., and Robert M. Douglas. In addition to holding important national and state positions, these men served in numerous local and state offices, including the state legislature and the superior court. Thomas Settle and Thomas Settle, Jr., are the only father and son ever to be speaker of the state House of Commons. No other family in the state and few in the nation can match this record of distinguished public service and political leadership. The influence of the Settle-Reid-Martin dynasty certainly contributed to the rise of David S. Reid as a politician, although successive generations served three different political parties—Whigs, Democrats, and Republicans.

A year after the marriage of Reuben and Elizabeth Reid, a son, whom they named David Settle Reid, was born on April 19, 1813. The following year the Reids moved two miles west of their farm on Hogan's Creek and on May 30, 1814, purchased 204 acres on a ridge between Wolf Island and Little Troublesome creeks. The Reids settled in a log house on the property near the main road from Danville, Virginia, to the south. Although he retained his Hogan's Creek farm, Reuben Reid soon opened a store at his house. The Reid family eventually consisted of three sons—David Settle, Hugh Kearns, and Reuben Hunt—and four daughters—Frances, Rhoda, Henrietta, and Annie C. With only one slave to help with the farming, the Reid children were involved in farm work and the store at an early age.[5]

Young David Reid began full-time work at the age of twelve and had scant opportunity for a formal education. According to family tradition, he did attend for a time the plantation school of his wealthy uncle, Thomas Settle, who served in the United States Congress from 1817 to 1821. Essentially self-educated, Reid began purchasing a variety of books and study aids such as a dictionary, classical grammars, and an English course entitled *The Synopsis; or, Self Instructor of English Grammar*. His letters exhibit a mastery of grammar and spelling and a concise style that would be a credit to any self-educated person in any era. One clue to his achievement is found in the advice that he sent in 1873 to his son Thomas, a student at Wake Forest College:

> Application and industry will accomplish much; without them nothing. Time can never be recalled. When a man accustoms himself once to habits of application, labor and research become sources of substantial happiness. . . . The earlier these habits are cultivated the sooner they are acquired, for without them man defeats the great end for which he was created.[6]

Reid's personal library, containing over 350 volumes, reflected a wide range of interests. Not unexpected were the numerous books in the fields of law and history. There were several sets of English and world history, but Reid's chief interest was American history. He had the standard histories of North Carolina by John H. Wheeler and Francis Hawks, George Bancroft's American history, *Democracy in America* by Alexis de Tocqueville, sets of diplomatic correspondence, congressional debates and reports, and the collected works of Thomas Jefferson, Alexander Hamilton, and John Adams. Among the numerous biographies in his library were John Marshall's *George Washington*, Richard H. Lee's *Arthur Lee*, and the lives of Benjamin Franklin, Nathaniel Macon, Lewis Cass, the Marquis de Lafayette, and Zachary Taylor. Literature was represented by such standards as the works of John Milton, the poems of Robert Burns, Walter Scott's Waverly novels, and many other titles. In the miscellaneous category fell classical literature, religion, philosophy, economics, travel accounts, and two narratives on Arctic exploration.[7]

In 1825, when he was twelve, David Reid moved to Wentworth and began clerking in the store of his uncle, Robert Martin; he remained there for four years. He attempted to secure a position in the Leaksville store of John M. Morehead, but Morehead replied that he had ample staff. When the family store required more help, David returned home and worked with his father for the next decade.[8] He had matured into a young man, small in stature and weighing about one hundred and twenty pounds. Always neat, he had handsome, delicate features highlighted with black hair and blue eyes. Although he never lost the diminutive "little Davy," throughout his political career he waged strenuous campaigns that indicated a strong physical constitution.[9]

With the addition of his son as a clerk Reuben Reid felt that he could apply for a post office, and on October 24, 1829, the postal service authorized a new office, which was named Reidsville. The sixteen-year-old youth David was appointed postmaster. The Reid store was now a regular stop on the main north-south stage route, which increased business considerably. David Reid served as postmaster until succeeded by his father in 1835.[10] The fortunes of Reuben Reid had improved over the years, and by 1840 he had seven slaves, several hundred acres of land, and a thriving business. He became a justice of the peace by 1831 and served in this office until his death twenty-one years later.[11]

Besides clerking for his father and running the post office, David Reid began to acquire land on which he produced tobacco. His first recorded purchase, from his father, was on August 1, 1834, for 248 acres in three tracts on Little Troublesome and Hogan's creeks. In 1841 and 1842 he bought two other tracts of 329 acres on Hogan's Creek, which gave him a total of 577 acres. By 1840 he had three slaves, one of whom he inherited from his grandfather David Settle. The others were possibly acquired from his brother-in-law Samuel F. Adams, who was a slave trader. Reid apparently was an investing partner with Adams, but there is no evidence that he actively engaged in the slave trade.[12]

Reid's political career began in 1835 when at the age of twenty-two he was elected a state Senator and also colonel of the county militia regiment. Holding either one of these offices at that age would be unusual, but to be elected to both positions in his first year of politics was an indication of the esteem of his fellow citizens. Militia duty, a serious obligation for each citizen in an era of few taxes, was in effect universal military service, requiring each able-bodied adult male (unless exempted) to be enrolled. Rockingham County had two regiments; Reid's command, which he held for seven years, was the sixty-seventh. As colonel he was responsible for mustering the regiment and the various companies when called and ensuring that the companies were properly equipped and armed. In 1837 Reid ran for major general of the Ninth Division but was defeated by Joseph Winston. Reid considered his militia service important and resigned in November, 1842, only because he had been elected to the United States Congress. His superior officer, Brig. Gen. John M. Logan, upon forwarding Reid's resignation to the governor, commented that he had been "an excellent officer."[13]

At an early age Reid was launched into politics, which dominated his life for the next twenty-five years. The political milieu of his native county at the birth of the republic was Antifederalist, and the county's state convention delegates had solidly opposed the ratification of the Federal constitution. The inheritors of the Antifederalist tradition, the Jeffersonian Republicans, dominated early county politics, and this trend continued with the Jacksonian Democratic party. Despite the influence of his uncle Thomas Settle, a leading Whig, Reid imbibed the ideals of Thomas Jefferson and could identify his own life with that of Andrew Jackson, a self-made man. Reid consistently lived and expounded the principles of Jeffersonian Republicanism and Jacksonian Democracy, never once swerving from his chosen path in his long political career.

Reid's political debut came in 1835 when he defeated Thomas Blackwell, a veteran Whig legislator, for a seat in the state Senate. The *Danville Observer* commented on this campaign that,

> Mr. Read was quite young and unknown to the people before the canvass, while Mr. Blackwell was one of the oldest and most respectable citizens of the county; and had the advantage of having represented the county several years. But his *White whigism* was fatal to him. He was beaten by an untrained colt.[14]

Unopposed in his second campaign the following year, Reid faced strong Whig challenges from planter aristocrats Thomas S. Gallaway and William Fewell in 1838 and 1840 but won convincingly in each election, compiling a wider margin every time. The "untrained colt," no longer the unknown of his maiden campaign, was asked to address the county Democratic convention in May, 1836. After effective service in the Senate he became an established figure in the state party organization, taking an active leadership role in the convention of 1840 and serving on the state committee.[15]

In the turbulent antebellum years national issues dominated North Carolina state politics. The controversial policies of President Andrew Jackson and his successor, Martin Van Buren, concerning the national bank, the distribution of surplus federal revenue, and the sale of public land generated Whig-inspired condemnations in the state Senate. The Panic of 1837 was believed by the Whigs to be related directly to Democratic fiscal policy. An earlier United States Senate censure of Jackson over his war on the national bank had been expunged from the record, but North Carolina Whigs in this period sought to have the "expunging resolution" rescinded. Reid, an ardent Jacksonian, found himself at the center of the various state Senate floor fights on these issues, especially in the 1840 session, which had a Whig majority.

In his four terms in the state Senate Reid developed into an adroit legislator and party leader. As a freshman he served only on one standing committee, the Committee on Privileges and Elections, and a few ad hoc committees, but through successive terms he became a member of the important Education and Literary Fund Committee and numerous essential joint and select committees, ranging from military affairs to agriculture. In his last term he took a daily leadership role in committee work and parliamentary maneuvering.[16]

Resolutions on the revenue derived from the sale of the public domain became a bitter point of contention between the two parties in the Assembly of 1835. Reid, viewing the issue as one that should be decided in Congress and not in the state legislature, proposed that the resolutions be postponed, but his motion lost.[17] A circular published by Reid and his Democratic colleagues in the House of Commons, Philip J. Irion and Blake W. Braswell, delineated their position on the legislation and the issues of the session. The Rockingham County legislators directed attention to the need for tax reform, reapportionment of representation, and support for common schools.[18]

In his second term, the session of 1836-1837, Reid again served on the Committee on Privileges and Elections and was thrust into the position of voting against his uncle Thomas Settle, who was running for the United States Senate against Democrat Robert Strange. Settle lost by just two votes, and the outcome might have been reversed if Reid had been influenced more by his family ties than by party principle. The election did not affect the close personal relationship of the two men; in fact Settle had not sought his party's nomination and was content to remain on the superior court bench.[19] Later in the session on January 6, 1837, Reid made a major speech opposing the banking privileges being sought in an act of incorporation for the Louisville, Cincinnati, and Charleston Railroad, but the measure passed.[20]

The major partisan controversy of the 1838-1839 legislative session centered on the resolutions introduced by the Whig leader Kenneth Rayner which condemned the United States Senate for expunging a resolution of censure of President Jackson from Congressional records. Reid with other Democrats opposed the Rayner resolutions and a reporter recorded that on December 27

> Mr. Reid of Rockingham, took the floor, and entertained the Senate for some length of time with his remarks against the resolutions, with that eloquence and animation which that gentleman has displayed on former occasions when matters touching the interests and welfare of his constitutents and State were involved.[21]

Reid offered amendments to the resolutions that would force the Whigs to agree to allow the legislature to instruct the state's United States senators. This principle the Whigs had formerly bitterly opposed, and the Whig majority voted the amendments down. The Rayner resolutions passed but for the time being were ignored by the Democratic Senators—Bedford Brown and Robert Strange.[22]

In his last two terms Reid was on the Education and Literary Fund Committee in the period when the first public schools in the state were established. Because of his own limited educational experiences as a youth, Reid was a strong supporter of public education. Acts creating public or common schools were passed in 1839 and 1841, and the first school in the state opened its door on January 20, 1840, in Rockingham County.[23]

The election of 1840 was a debacle for the North Carolina Democrats. Not only was there a Whig governor and a Whig legislative majority, but also for the first time a Whig, William Henry Harrison, occupied the White House. It was obvious to the party leadership that fresh candidates were needed, so in 1841 Bedford Brown urged Reid to run for Congress in the ninth district, which consisted of Caswell, Rockingham, Guilford, and Stokes counties. Reid responded to the challenge, taking on Augustine H. Shepperd of Stokes County, who had served six terms in Congress (1827-1839). Shepperd's established support in a district that had a Whig majority spelled defeat for Reid, although he lost by only a few hundred votes.[24]

Following his defeat Reid spent the next year reading law, and by April, 1843, he had passed the bar exam and was practicing.[25] He had had a taste of politics, however, and when the General Assembly, now under a Democratic majority, reapportioned congressional districts in 1843, Rockingham County was placed in the third district with enough Democratic counties so that Reid felt that he had a good chance in the new district. Consequently, he responded favorably when county meetings began to nominate him. His opponent, Anderson Mitchell of Wilkes County, had served in the last Congress from another district but was well known in the third. In the election the Democrats lost the gubernatorial race but retained their legislative majority. Reid won his seat in Congress by 368 out of some 8,000 votes cast.[26]

David S. Reid took his oath as a representative in the United States Congress on December 4, 1843.[27] The leading issues of the day in Washington were the reduction of the tariff and territorial expansion, specifically the annexation of Texas, which had been a republic since 1836, and the dispute between Great Britain and the United States over control of the Oregon country. The Democrats were now adamant expansionists, whereas the Whigs opposed expansion with equal fervor. The Texas and Oregon questions were the focus of the presidential election of 1844, which brought the victory of Democrat James K. Polk of Tennessee over Henry Clay.

A number of letters to Reid from his constituents reflected the Democratic view. A. J. Folger of Surry County wrote, "Oregon and Texas are the general topic of Conversation here, the people are generally in favor of annexation of both of them to our Government."[28] John T. Garland, a Democrat of Milton, reported, "There is quite a strong Texas current with us. . . ."[29] A dutiful party man, Reid supported the administration, advancing arguments in favor of the annexation of Texas and the possession of Oregon in a circular to his constituents of March 7, 1845. The Mexican claim on Texas, which led to war in 1846, was rejected by Reid, who wrote:

> Texas never did belong to Mexico: she acquired her freedom from Spain by revolution, as Mexico herself did; and when she entered the Mexican confederation, it was as an equal, retaining her sovereignty as a State. When she rebelled against Santa Anna's despotism, a sanguinary revolution ensued, by which she completely defeated the Mexican forces, and fully established and declared her independence.[30]

The daily activities of a congressman, Reid discovered, were much more mundane than consideration of clashes on the Mexican border or a potential confrontation with Great Britain in Oregon. Shortly after his arrival in Washington he wrote his father that

> I am pretty constantly engaged. In the morning I write letters, glance over the Papers, visit the Departments on business for my constituents, and attend Committees. At 12 oclock the House meets and we generally sit till 4 or 5 oclock. . . . Congress is engaged at work, but nothing of much importance has been done.[31]

Most of his correspondence with his constituents concerned pension claims, postal affairs and appointments, and such personal business matters as paying bills, newspaper subscriptions, and collecting debts.[32] Although this correspondence at first glance may appear trivial, the letters to and from the postmasters of the district reveal the key communication link between a congressman and his constituents. Reid's background as a postmaster and his service on the House Committee on the Post Office and Post Roads[33] gave him a multitude of contacts and involved him directly in party patronage. The post office in that era was the largest federal department, and the rural postmaster had a pivotal role in the flow of information. Through no conscious plan, Reid constructed a broad political base out of his background, experiences, and acquaintances. As a result, his congressional seat might have been safe for many years beyond his initial two terms if the Whigs in the next legislature had not gerrymandered him out.

Perhaps the most important acquaintance that Reid made in Washington was with another new congressman—Stephen A. Douglas of Illinois. Assigned adjacent seats on the floor of Congress, Reid and Douglas, the same age and both small in stature, soon became close friends. During a visit to Washington by Reid's uncle Robert Martin, a wealthy planter, and his family, Reid introduced Douglas to his attractive cousin Martha Martin. Encouraged by his friend, Douglas promptly began a courtship, which led to his marriage in Rockingham County on April 7, 1847.[34] The relationship between Reid and Douglas probably reinforced their democratic ideals and may have influenced the maturation of Reid's stand on free suffrage and Douglas's "popular sovereignty" position. After the death of his wife in 1853, Douglas became the guardian of the slave property of his sons, and this firsthand encounter with slavery tempered his antislavery stance and contributed to his emergence as a national figure.

In 1845 the Whigs sought to recover the third district, which they derisively labeled the "Shoe-string district," from the Democrats with a major effort behind their candidate, Alexander B. McMillan, of Ashe County, an experienced state legislator. Describing the strenuous campaign, one of Reid's supporters wrote in July, "I presume by this time that you have *warm* times in Surry both as to weather & Politicks—but I hope you have no grounds to be discouraged or to fear the result of the present contest."[35] When Reid defeated McMillan by a larger majority than in the previous election the *Greensborough Patriot* lamented: "Reid, Loco Foco, has left McMillan, Whig, a long way behind as was expected. When the Legislature cut *that* 'Shoe-string,' they knew where the *thick parts of the leather lay*."[36]

When Reid returned to Washington, the annexation of Texas had been accomplished, but there remained a war to be fought with Mexico to secure the new state. The Oregon question was still unsettled, and the Democrats sought to reduce the tariff, a goal achieved in 1846. Most of Reid's constituents did not believe that there would be a war over Oregon. Samuel F. Adams, his brother-in-law, expressed the opinion that "we shall have no war although the chances are decidedly in favor of it unless Mr. Polk falls back again on the 49th degree. . . ,"[37] and the astute Calvin Graves of Caswell County observed

> now that Texas is Ours. The project would be too perilous for England. The Annexation of Texas has closed and sealed the question of war between these Powers through all time.[38]

The Oregon question was the one leading issue on which Reid made a major address in Congress, urging the administration to secure Oregon even if it meant war with Great Britain.[39]

As the Whigs increased their criticism of the Mexican War, Reid correspondingly stepped up his defense of the administration, writing in December, 1846, that

> [the Whigs] allege that it is a war of the Presidents own, & that it is an unjust and unconstitutional [war]; and they do this in the face of the facts that the Mexican Government shed the *first blood, declared war first*, and they (the Whigs) themselves *voted for the declaration of war against Mexico.*[40]

In his circular to the district of March 31, 1847, Reid listed the "many outrages" of Mexico against the United States prior to the war, most of which were seizures of ships.[41]

In 1846 the Whig majority in the legislature restructured the congressional districts, hoping to reduce the number of Democrats in Washington. Rockingham County was placed in the fourth district with Guilford, Stokes, Randolph, and Davidson counties, which created an overwhelming Whig electorate. The *North-Carolina Standard* railed against the "Raynermander," but it was to no avail.[42] Realizing that he had no chance in the new district, Reid declined to run; and in his circular of March, 1847, he bade his constituents farewell. He had been seriously ill that winter, and much of the time he was attended by his friend Stephen Douglas.[43] At the end of the session in March, he was not reluctant to turn toward home to his farm and law practice. He little suspected that even greater political opportunities awaited him.

This brief interlude in his political career gave Reid an opportunity for reflection and consideration of both his religious beliefs and the possibility of marriage. During his illness the noted Baptist missionary Elias Dodson, a friend of the family, attempted to convert Reid. Even though his parents and in-laws were Baptist and his personal beliefs were shaped by the Baptists, there is no evidence that Reid ever formally joined a church. He was a daily Bible reader, and he attended the Baptist church wherever he was living, whether in Reidsville, Raleigh, or Washington. There are occasional indications from his letters that reveal that he was a deeply religious man.[44]

Reid's personal letters to his family and friends disclose a sensitive young man with a romantic inclination, but he had long since resigned himself to bachelorhood. He wrote Edmund W. Hubard, a friend and colleague in Congress, upon the occasion of Hubard's marriage in 1846, "I am glad you are going to marry, both on *your own account and my own*, for it is just what every sensible bachelor ought to do; but I regret to say that I am yet in a state of *single wretchedness, and so likely to remain.*"[45] Over the next several years, however, his first cousin Henrietta Williams Settle, the daughter of Thomas Settle, began to attract him and awaken in him a deep, tender, and lasting love. Henrietta, eleven years his junior, was petite, delicate of feature, and had dark hair and eyes. The family tradition is that she would not marry him until he was elected governor, and indeed they did not marry until December 19, 1850, about a month after the election results were known. Part of Henrietta's dowry was a 700-acre plantation south of the Dan River in the center of the county where they soon erected a plain two-story frame house, which became the Reid home for the next twenty years.[46]

In 1846 when Greene Caldwell declined the Democratic nomination for governor, in the scramble for an alternate David Reid's name was proposed by both John J. Wheeden, a close associate of William W. Holden, the editor of the *North-Carolina Standard*, and John H. Wheeler, a party stalwart best known for his state histories.[47] At the time Reid was in Congress and the nomination went to James B. Shepard; nevertheless, it was obvious that Reid was under consideration by the party leaders, and in 1848 he was available. William W. Holden, editor of the *Standard* since 1842, had made his publication the most influential Democratic newspaper in the state. At the apogee of party leadership Holden had an immediate affinity for Reid, who represented a younger, more progressive outlook in the party. The two men established an intimate friendship that did not cool until the trials of Reconstruction.[48] Holden would name his youngest daughter, born in 1852, Henrietta Reid, and personal notes in the Reid correspondence attest to the warmth of the relationship. The two men were so closely identified that the Whig press would characterize Reid, who was not well known statewide, as a mere pawn of their longtime adversary Holden.[49]

The Democratic state convention met in Raleigh on April 12 with the noted guest speakers Stephen A. Douglas of Illinois and Sam Houston of Texas. The nominating committee had several Reid supporters on it—Holden, James B. Shepard, W. K. Lane, and Robert P. Dick—and Reid was finally nominated in Holden's words as a "forlorn hope." Upon receipt of the nomination Reid initially declined in a letter to be published in the *Standard.* Prompted by Wheeden, Holden held the letter and implored Reid to reconsider. Reid then accepted the nomination and traveled to Raleigh to meet with the party leaders where he stated his plan to campaign on the issue of free suffrage. There was some dissension, but Reid received approval for his issue and left for New Bern.[50]

A persistent Greensboro tradition credits Stephen A. Douglas with originating the idea of free suffrage in a meeting there with Reid, but both Douglas and Reid denied this.[51] Reid stated in the 1850 campaign that

> my attention was directed to the inequality and injustice of this feature of our Constitution even before I became a voter. . . . Many years ago, while a member of the Legislature, I determined at one time to present the subject to the consideration of that body, but met with no encouragement from those to whom I communicated my intention. . . . The time and state of public opinion then appeared unpropitious, and I abandoned my determination.[52]

Reducing suffrage qualifications was a well-established Democratic dogma and had been articulated by Reid's Connecticut friend James Phelps, who wrote him in 1842 that to "abridge the right of citizenship and encumber the elective franchise with qualifications excepting only infamy of character, non-residence, and minority, and 'you lay the axe at the root' of free and equal privilege. . . ."[53]

The Whigs never quite recovered from the surprise that Reid unleashed at New Bern, and they never could believe that free suffrage would be the issue that would end their dominance of the state. James Bryan, a Whig, reported to William A. Graham during the campaign, "I think your fears as to the ruinous progress of Mr. Reid's demagoguical doctrine of free Suffrage in the East are rather groundless; they are a *brutum fulmen* in this quarter."[54] The Whig press ranted that advocates of free suffrage desired the "desececration of the Bible and the abolition of Matrimony" as well as women's suffrage.[55] The Whigs had dominated the state with a fragile party structure forged in the limited constitutional reforms of 1835 that bound the westerners, who sought equal representation, and the eastern conservatives. This brittle alliance had survived by emphasizing national issues in the campaigns at the expense of state issues, but strains had begun to appear when the Whig opposition to the Mexican War tainted them with disloyalty and the festering slavery question began to gain momentum. When Reid injected the volatile free suffrage question in the 1848 campaign, the Whigs started to unravel, and the far more cohesive Democrats sensed the possibility of victory. Conservatives in both parties realized that free suffrage opened the door to the more radical constitutional reforms of abolition of property qualifications for officeholders and legislative representation determined by the white population rather than the Federal basis (the white population and three-fifths of the slaves). The Democratic leadership, which was backed by a secure organization, was so hungry for victory that it was willing to take the risk of following Reid with his free suffrage proposal. Although the Whigs carried the state house, the legislature, and the Presidency, Manly's narrow defeat of Reid was viewed as a moral victory for the Democrats.[56]

In 1850 the Democrats had never been more sure of victory, but Reid gave the party some anxious moments when he again declined to run in a letter that was finally made public in the *Standard* on the eve of the state convention. Holden convinced Reid that he was the only Democrat who could win, and when the convention unanimously nominated him on June 15, Reid accepted.[57] Reid's campaign position in favor of free suffrage, improvements in the public schools, a responsible system of internal improvements, and a defense of southern rights was published in a lengthy address in June. The slavery question was foremost at the time and Reid urged that "*the South should take a firm stand in defence of her rights*," although he did not approve of the Nashville Convention, which was rumored to be considering the question of secession.[58]

Governor Manly, hoping to undermine Reid by demonstrating that he was not committed to any constitutional reform beyond the limited free suffrage issue, proposed a discussion of changing the legislative apportionment on the federal basis of population to the white basis in a debate at Wentworth, the county seat of Reid's home county. Although he was not advocating a change, the local Democrats informed Holden that Manly had favored the white basis, a position popular in the west but an anathema to the slaveholding east. Holden attacked Manly by accusing him of supporting the white basis. Manly vainly tried to explain that he did not advocate a change in representation, but Holden and Reid pilloried him on this issue which became the decisive factor in his defeat.[59] The Whigs countered by accusing Reid of having voted as a Congressman for the Wilmot Proviso which would have limited the expansion of slavery. While the slavery and southern rights issue might have diverted attention from free suffrage, the accusation was so patently absurd that Reid heatedly replied in debate that "it was false and false as hell which he [Manly] pocketed without much resentment."[60] Despite the desperate Whig efforts to discredit Reid he won the election by 2,743 votes, sweeping a Democratic majority into both houses of the General Assembly.[61]

According to the traditional view, the Democratic victory of 1850, which was to establish the party as the dominant political force in the state for the next century and a quarter was wrought from the vigorous, progressive leadership embodied in Holden and Reid, the party's harmonious position on the slavery question which now loomed so ominously, and the popularity of free suffrage. In the words of historian William K. Boyd, Reid was responsible for "a victory which marked a revolution in party politics."[62] Never again would national issues predominate state politics to the extent that they had earlier in the century. Never again would the Whigs elect a governor, and in the coming decade the party would disintegrate under the pressure of the slavery agitation. With the exception of the troubled and unusual Civil War-Reconstruction period, only three governors of North Carolina since 1850 have not been Democrats.

In recent years historians have turned to North Carolina antebellum politics, broadening the traditional interpretation of the Democratic victory which was largely based on Holden's analysis, and have found the free suffage issue to be far more complex than a political campaign based on a limited constitutional reform. In his study of the second party system Marc Kruman argues that no real political revolution occurred in 1850 because the Whigs continued until the Civil War to poll a substantial vote, despite the collapse of the national party, and the Democrats held only a slight majority.[63] Paul Escott credits Reid and Holden with arousing class consciousness with the free suffrage issue that appealed to yeoman farmers and craftsmen, cutting across party lines.[64] Engendering a broad emotional response in the electorate, free suffrage introduced constitutional reform into state politics, and it remained in the forefront, supplanting national issues in the state, until transcended by the burgeoning secession crisis.

The most comprehensive study of North Carolina politics in the 1850s is the work of Thomas Jeffrey. Although Jeffrey agrees with earlier scholars that free suffrage altered state political life by substituting a local issue for national issues, he contends that the importance of free suffrage was its impact on the Whigs rather than any ideological change among the Democrats. The Whigs were no more aristocratic than the Democrats, but by seizing an issue that symbolized the growth of democracy, Reid and Holden were able to pin the aristocratic label on the Whigs. Damaged by the charge of aristocracy, the Whig leadership found that it could not exorcise this image, which drove a sectional wedge into their party, alienating east from west. Free suffrage was not the sole issue that caused the gradual floundering of the North Carolina Whigs; slavery and the national sectional conflict also contributed heavily, but free suffrage was the beginning of the end for the Whigs.[65] Lesser opponents might have been outmaneuvered, but the astute Reid and the brilliant Holden formed a political team that seldom if ever has been equaled in the state's history.

On January 1, 1851, David S. Reid took the oath of office as governor of North Carolina in the Capitol building; immediately following the ceremony he delivered his inaugural address, which enunciated his plans for the administration. Major portions of the speech were devoted to the burgeoning slavery crisis, internal improvements, public education, and free suffrage. Stating that he was loyal to the Union, Reid firmly declared that the state did not owe allegiance to a Union that threatened to overthrow the Constitution and to suppress the rights of the states. He asserted "*that the encroachments of the North on the domestic institutions of the South, have already proceeded to the farthest allowable point*," and he urged the General Assembly to provide for the defense of the state if necessary. On internal improvements Reid pledged to back a "judicious" system that would not encumber the state with a large public debt. He called for increased support of the public schools. The remainder of his address was centered on legislative action for constitutional amendments for free suffrage and election of judges for limited terms.[66]

There were three sessions of the General Assembly while Reid was governor—the first ending in January, 1851, the second in the fall of 1852, and the third beginning in November, 1854, just before he left office. The governor's first priority was the constitutional amendment for free suffrage. A majority of the legislators advocated the removal of the land qualification, but they differed on whether the amendment should be achieved by legislative action or a constitutional convention. Reid favored the legislative route, and after considerable debate the administration-sponsored amendment finally passed both houses by the necessary majority, clearing its first hurdle. In the next session the amendment failed to pass the Senate by one vote, causing consternation in the party when Speaker Weldon N. Edwards, a

Democrat, refused to cast a vote for the measure.[67] Although Reid would be denied the satisfaction of seeing the free suffrage amendment passed in his administration, in subsequent legislative sessions it was approved and became part of the Constitution in 1857.

Internal improvements legislation emphasized chartering plank roads and railroads and amending the charters of existing transportation companies. Presiding over the Board of Internal Improvements, Governor Reid had administrative responsibility for the state's interest in the various railroads, navigation, and plank road companies. Construction on the western turnpike from Salisbury to Georgia was begun under the direction of Nimrod S. Jarrett, and the sale of Cherokee lands provided funds for a survey of a western railroad from Salisbury to Tennessee. Two questions concerning the former Indian land in western North Carolina were settled by granting monetary relief to purchasers of this land and by confirming the titles of Cherokee Indians who had remained in the state.[68]

Governor Reid recommended to the General Assembly that the office of state superintendent of public schools be established. The legislature responded by authorizing that post and by passing legislation to improve the administrative organization of the public school system. The legislature chose Calvin H. Wiley of Guilford County as the first superintendent of common schools, and under his capable guidance the state system of public education improved dramatically over the next decade. In his biennial message to the General Assembly on October 4, 1852, the governor proposed an increase in taxation for support of the common schools, saying, "I can imagine no object for which an increase in taxation would be more justifiable and commendable. Contributions for public education have been aptly compared to vapor drawn from the earth, not to exhaust, but to be returned in fertilizing showers."[69]

Another farsighted action taken that affected the state's future was the approval of a state geological and agricultural survey. The governor was to appoint the director of the survey, who was to conduct a county-by-county examination of the natural resources of the state. After a lengthy search and on strong endorsement of the governor of New York, Reid appointed Professor Ebenezer Emmons, who had been in charge of a similar survey in New York. The ensuing correspondence between Emmons and the governor demonstrated the personal interest that Reid had in the survey. The letters furnished considerable information about the state and generally were published in the *Standard* and other newspapers.[70]

The first year of Governor Reid's administration was under the shadow of the renewed controversy over slavery and the developing Compromise of 1850. The assembly received resolutions from the

Nashville Convention that were moderate in tone while upholding the institution of slavery and demanding equal access to the territories. A legislative committee, formed to consider the resolutions, caused some concern when its members voted to endorse the right of secession. The final committee report, which was written by the majority, was a compromise and recommended that the state acquiesce to the provisions of the Compromise of 1850.[71]

In his biennial message, Reid reminded the General Assembly that the energetic program of internal improvements had strained the existing tax system based on land and a poll tax. The governor suggested a tax based on the value of a person's estate, stating,

> Persons and property being the principal objects of taxation they should bear a fair and just relation to each other, in a system of revenue. It is believed that, after excepting slaves, each person's estate, real and personal, including money, whether at interest or not, ought to be taxed alike, according to value. This would require every person to contribute in proportion to the value of his or her estate, and would equalize the public burden between the various classes upon principles of justice.[72]

The governor's tax reform proposal provided for the taxing of income earned by professional men and in other employment and allowed an exemption for those persons having an estate of less than $150. Obviously tax reform would have an important effect on the future of the state, but the governor was too far ahead of the thinking of the assembly. The assembly took no action on the measure in that session, although ad valorem taxation became one of the major political issues in the next few years.

The active, successful, and popular leadership of Governor Reid in his first term ensured his nomination for a second term in 1852. The Democrats were unified and well organized. At the convention in Raleigh, Reid was nominated by acclamation in a dramatic scene described by a delegate:

> the party from the mountains to the seaboard had but one choice for the gubernatorial office, he [James Dobbin] would move that the Convention nominate David S. Reid by acclamation. The speaker's voice was drowned amid a spontaneous burst of enthusastic [*sic*] applause which literally shook the walls of the old Capital. . . . Every sentence that fell from the lips of the eloquent speaker was received with unbounded applause; and when the question was put to a vote, it was received with a perfect hurricane of enthusiasm.[73]

The Whigs were divided on the question of a state constitutional convention, and the party platform as finally drafted satisfied neither faction. The Whig nominee, John Kerr of Caswell County, met Reid in a grueling series of statewide debates that began on May 31 and ended on August 4. When the vote was tallied Reid had increased his majority to 5,564, but the Whigs had gained control of the House of Commons, making it unlikely that free suffrage would pass in the coming session.[74]

The momentum begun in Governor Reid's first term on railroad development, turnpikes, and the public schools continued. The Democrats were now totally converted to internal improvements, causing Holden to boast in the *Standard* that "the Democrats have shown themselves competent to lead in this matter, and under their auspices the State has done more in four years to develop her resources of all kinds, than had been done during fourteen years of whig rule."[75]

The lull on the slavery question following the passage of the Compromise of 1850 ended in January, 1854, when Stephen A. Douglas introduced in the Senate the Kansas-Nebraska Bill, which would replace the Missouri Compromise by allowing the new territories to decide for themselves on the institution of slavery. When the bill finally passed, most North Carolinians considered it a victory for the South, potentially opening up new slave territory. Reid expressed his pleasure to Douglas, saying,

> I would have written you long ago informing you of the proud satisfaction experienced by your friends in this state, and in the South generally, in consequence of your course on the Nebraska question had I not known that you had the most *unmistakable* assurances of that fact. Your course has been statesmanlike and patriotic and I hope the American people will not forget it.[76]

In his biennial message to the General Assembly on November 20, 1854, which was to be his last speech as governor, Reid reviewed the achievements in the areas of public education and internal improvements. He urged increasing support for the common schools and eloquently expressed the role of public education in a free society:

> There is no subject more worthy of favorable consideration than Common Schools. The greatness of a State depends upon her people. . . . The education of the masses of the people is the best security for the rights of persons and property; and, in a free government, where intelligence and virtue are the two passports to fame and distinction, it places the poor and obscure upon an equality with the rich and powerful, and will prove the best means of perpetuating the blessings of liberty.[77]

The failure of the free suffrage amendment to pass the last session of the assembly had been a disappointment to the governor, particularly since the amendment had to start over in its legislative course. To Reid a suffrage qualification that denied the right to vote to 50,000 free white men was "so palpably wrong, that the time will come when the fact that it had ever had a place in the Constitution, will be regarded with profound astonishment. No system of free government can be based upon the supposition that the people are politically corrupt, and incapable of exercising the right of suffrage."[78] Although the amendment failed in this session, it did pass in the next two sessions of the General Assembly by the required majority, and on August 6, 1857, the free suffrage amendment was overwhelmingly ratified by the people of North Carolina. Historian John S. Bassett, in a study of the free suffrage movement, regarded it as "the greatest purely political victory ever won in the State. It was a great triumph for liberty and human equality."[79]

Now at the close of his administration David Reid must have had mixed feelings about his achievements. Although he had failed to secure the free suffrage amendment, his efforts had earned the measure broad popular support and the commitment of his party. The Democrats, with Thomas Bragg as the candidate, had won the election of 1854 and would be in power at least two more years. At the time Reid little realized that he had influenced the political party structure of North Carolina. There was much to be done, yet much had been accomplished in internal improvements, the public schools, and the geologic survey.

The Raleigh years were a pleasant interlude for the growing Reid family. Friends and relatives visited frequently, but more important was the beginning of his own family. Just a month after the election of 1852, on September 10, a son, David Settle Reid, Jr., was born; and on April 1, 1854, the Reids had a second son, Thomas Settle Reid. The chief personal loss to Reid in this period was the death of his father, Reuben Reid, on June 22, 1852.[80]

Because of partisan wrangling the General Assembly had failed to elect a United States senator in 1852 so that in 1854 there were two vacancies. In June Governor Reid had written Douglas that "it is probable I shall never again be a candidate for any thing; certainly not for a seat in the House of Representatives at the next election, I am perfectly content to retire to private life for the remainder of my days. I am not a candidate for the Senate."[81] However, the governor did not rule out the possibility of a nomination when the legislature met. From several nominees the General Assembly elected Reid and Asa Biggs United States senators on November 24, 1854. Reid was informed that he was elected to the term that had begun on March 4, 1853. He accepted the post and delivered the executive authority to the Speaker of the Senate Warren Winslow.[82]

Within three weeks, on December 11, David Reid had taken the oath as the United States senator from North Carolina. Since he was entering the last session of the Thirty-third Congress, the committees were already organized, but a place was found for him on the select Committee on the Transcontinental Railroad. The session was about half over when he received word from home that Henrietta was ill, and he forthwith returned to his family.[83]

The Thirty-fourth Congress opened in December, 1855, and its third session terminated in March, 1857. In the organization of the Senate, Reid was appointed to three minor committees: Indian Affairs, Revolutionary Claims, and the District of Columbia.[84] Because his wife was about to give birth to a child, he did not reach Washington until February, which was well into the session. A daughter, Carrie Settle Reid, was born on January 24, 1856, but she was destined to live only eighteen months, dying the following year on August 18.[85] The letters from Reid to his family indicate that he was much more concerned about them than the business on hand in Washington.

The leading national issue during this period was the continuing controversy over the Kansas-Nebraska Act. Stephen Douglas at first had been praised for his "popular sovereignty" stand. However, when the proslavery and abolitionist factions established two different territorial governments, Douglas and the northern Democrats backed the free state of Lecompton's (Kansas) constitution. Southerners took this to be a betrayal by Douglas. Reid was concerned over the southern mistrust of his longtime friend and relative, but the slavery question was sweeping reason aside. In this session both Reid and his colleague Asa Biggs responded to the heated debate over the admission of Kansas with strong southern rights speeches. Reiterating that the North was forcing southerners to emancipate their slaves against their will, Reid declared that "whenever a majority of the people of the northern States become prepared to endorse the doctrine [of emancipation] . . . this Union cannot last an hour longer. We simply ask you to let us alone as we let you alone."[86]

In December, 1857, the Thirty-fifth Congress began and ran in two sessions, closing in March, 1859. Reid was appointed to the Commerce Committee and was named chairman of the Committee on Patents and the Patent Office.[87] He traveled home in December to bring Henrietta back to Washington, and early in January while on the return trip in Richmond, Virginia, he fell seriously ill with pneumonia. His recovery took nearly four months, and then he returned to his home rather than to the Capital. His friends kept him informed of the Kansas debate and reassured him that his single vote would not be needed in the Senate. At one point the debate in the House of Representatives degenerated into a free-for-all which Senator Biggs described as "disgraceful," although fights in Congress were not that unusual. In May, 1858, the Reids finally made it to Washington, staying until the end of the session in June.[88]

Though Reid was still held in high esteem by the general public, his illness, his remoteness from the party's internal political maneuvering, and his unacceptability to the party's states' rights radicals had made his reelection to the Senate uncertain. As confidant William J. Yates stated, "the large majority of our party in the State has caused too many of our men to desire office."[89] Asa Biggs accepted an appointment as a federal district judge in May, 1858, and Thomas L. Clingman, an ex-Whig and ardent secessionist, had been appointed to complete the term. William W. Holden had unsuccessfully contested John W. Ellis, a judge from Salisbury, to be the successor of Thomas Bragg in the governor's mansion. Some observers believed that all of these moves were related to a conspiracy to retire Reid.[90] Whether the conspiracy was true or not, at least two ambitious party leaders, Holden and Bragg, were without office in 1858, and the retirement of Reid, the elder statesman, would create a vacancy. In the coming session of the General Assembly Clingman and Reid both desired reelection. Although amply warned by his friends to go to Raleigh before the Democratic caucus, Reid did not really believe that he was being threatened until it was too late. Even Weldon Edwards, no ally of Reid, was disgusted by the treachery within the party, and told Thomas Ruffin that

> I pray for the defeat of all political Combinations—I mean of *Politicians*, and I stand ready to commission any one, altho his escutcheon may be tarnished by the stain of that miserable Humbug "free suffrage," as it is called—who will assist to accomplish so desirable an end. The efforts to squeeze Reid out will I fear, succeed.[91]

Clingman had carefully arranged his own election and apparently was supporting the election of Bragg for the other Senate seat. When Holden entered the race, he said as an opponent of Bragg, even the Whig press could not believe what was happening. The *Raleigh Register* reported that

> it will be asked, what is to become of Mr. Reid? Aye, "there's the rub," and most extraordinary it is that in an overwhelmingly Democratic Legislature, there should be any rub at all—that there should be any doubt about the reelection of a man who has done so much for the cause of Democracy in North Carolina.[92]

The result of the first ballot was Bragg 40, Holden 36, and Reid 18; on the second ballot, Reid's supporters, angry with Holden's treachery, voted for Bragg, giving him the victory with 58 votes. The *Register* could not resist gloating over the downfall of its old nemesis by commenting that "When the train went westward on Wednesday morning, it certainly carried off a 'bruised Reed.' "[93]

There was one more session of the Senate before Reid left the political scene. He departed immediately for Washington but took little interest in the work of Congress. Characteristic of the consoling letters he received from his friends was the one written by Governor John W. Ellis, who reminded Reid that the people of North Carolina supported him even if some politicians did not. Ellis wrote: "Few men in this country have retained so large a share of public confidence after so long a service in distinguished positions."[94] Within a month the governor offered to appoint Reid as a commissioner of the survey of the Virginia-North Carolina boundary, but he declined.[95]

When Congress adjourned in March, Reid journeyed home to his plantation near Pleasantville, where he hoped to devote his time to his family, his law practice, and to farming. On December 16, 1859, the Reids had their last child, a son, Reuben David Reid. The Dan River tract of 700 acres, valued at $10,000, was a tobacco plantation, producing 7,000 pounds in 1860. For consumption on the farm Reid grew wheat, corn, oats, peas, potatoes, and yams. In 1860 he had twenty-two slaves, half of whom were children; of the adult slaves, of whom there were six females and five males, the eldest was only twenty-eight. The farm livestock included 3 horses, 3 mules, 6 milk cows, 4 beef cattle, and 43 hogs.[96]

The "calm which precedes the great political storm in 1860" described by Reid a year earlier was over, and his friend John Wheeler reported from Washington in January, 1860, that the "country was never in such a crisis." Selected to represent his county in the Democratic state convention in Raleigh in March, 1860, Reid was elected presiding officer. Governor Ellis was renominated but faced a tough campaign against Whig candidate John Pool, who had taken a lesson from Reid by identifying a popular issue, ad valorem taxation. Although the Whigs lost, if the nation had not become engulfed in war their party might have recovered in the state.[97]

The split of the Democratic party at the convention in Charleston, South Carolina, in April, 1860, which resulted temporarily in no nomination and split the then-dominant national political party, contributed to the election of Abraham Lincoln and secession. Stephen Douglas received the nomination at a rump convention in Baltimore, but most North Carolinians supported the candidacy of John C. Breckinridge of Kentucky, the radical southern candidate. Lincoln's election was an alarming event to the majority of North Carolinians who still preferred to remain in the Union. The secession of South Carolina and six other southern states, beginning in December, 1860, and continuing through February, 1861, led to a compromise proposal in the United States Senate presented by John J. Crittenden and to a call for a peace convention by the state of Virginia. In late January, 1861, the General Assembly elected Reid, Thomas Ruffin, Daniel M. Barringer, John M. Morehead, and George Davis as commissioners to the Washington Peace Conference.[98]

The peace conference opened on February 4 and submitted its resolutions, which were based on the Crittenden Resolutions, to Congress on February 27. On the eve of the conference Sen. Thomas Bragg met with the delegation and recorded that Reid was the strongest pro-southern delegate. He said that Reid "seemed not to be willing to accept of anything, except equal rights in all territories—and indeed to take nothing that would not satisfy the seceding States, for without their return he thinks we would not be safe in the Union."[99] Reid's uncompromising position was amply demonstrated in the convention where he made firm statements on southern rights and the protection of slavery. At one point, just prior to an important vote, he rose from his seat and said:

> I came here disposed to agree upon terms that would be mutually satisfactory to both sections of the Union. I would agree to any fair terms now, but the propositions contained in the report of the majority, as that report now stands, can never receive my assent.[100]

There were seven resolutions passed by the conference, but Reid voted for only the third and fourth, which among other things forbade congressional interference with slavery and the domestic slave trade, protected slavery in the District of Columbia, and strengthened the fugitive slave law.[101] When the resolutions were rejected by the Senate most North Carolinians lost hope for compromise.

While the peace conference was under way, back in North Carolina there was a campaign on the question of holding a convention for the purpose of considering secession. Reid was nominated to be a delegate from Rockingham County and won election. The convention was defeated because the clear majority of the delegates were Unionist. In a letter of acceptance to the county committee Reid clarified his position on the sectional crisis:

> I have ever cherished a sincere desire for the preservation of the Union according to the letter and spirit of the Federal Constitution. But circumstances have arisen to excite a well founded distrust on the part of the Southern States that their rights and institutions will not be respected by the Northern States.[102]

North Carolina's ambivalent attitude toward secession ended in April with the attack on Fort Sumter, Lincoln's call for troops, and the secession of Virginia. Another convention election was authorized by the legislature, and when the Constitutional Convention convened in Raleigh on May 20, 1861, secessionists dominated. Reid was appointed to the committee that drafted the ordinance of secession, which was adopted the first day. This action was followed immediately by ratification of the provisional constitution of the Confederate States of America. Over the next twelve months the convention met in three additional sessions for the purpose of further amending the state constitution. Reid attended all but the last session, taking an active role in proposing amendments and serving on committees.[103]

Although he had been a consistent defender of southern rights, David Reid always had been moderate in tone and did not embrace secession until he believed that the North left no alternative. Once North Carolina left the Union, however, Reid became a staunch defender of the Confederacy and the war effort. When the newly elected governor, Zebulon B. Vance, requested his advice, Reid unequivocally answered:

> The present struggle for independence is paramount to all other questions—life, liberty, property, and all that is dear to freemen depend upon it—and party prejudices and all minor differences should be sacrificed upon the alter [*sic*] of the Common Cause. *We are right and the enemy wrong*; re-Union with the North by the Consent of the people is impossible. Urge the vigorous prosecution of the War, and invoke the fortitude and patriotism of the people to meet the crisis like freemen. . . .[104]

Possibly for family or health reasons Reid did not serve the Confederacy in any official capacity; nevertheless, he consistently supported the war effort and agreed in 1863 to be on a committee of prominent citizens to draft an address to the people of the state encouraging the war and condemning those who opposed it.[105]

In the postwar years Governor Reid remained in political retirement except for his service in the 1875 Constitutional Convention. His law practice prospered, and he continued to farm the Dan River plantation. In 1870 the plantation produced only 1,000 pounds of tobacco but quantities of wheat, oats, corn, potatoes, yams, honey, and butter for consumption on the farm. There was little change in the livestock except that fifteen sheep had been added and were producing some wool. Two black families were living on the place—one domestic servant and one farm laborer.[106]

The Reids spent two tranquil decades on the plantation, which was just a few miles northwest of Wentworth and convenient to the court, until the tragic death of their eldest son, David S. Reid, Jr., on August 7, 1871. In the family memory the death is associated with a swim in the river and a fever, possibly typhoid. The Reids could not bear to be reminded of this sorrow and soon moved to Wentworth, never returning to the plantation to live. In 1877 following the graduation of his son Thomas from the law school at Richmond Hill, Reid established a partnership with an office in Reidsville handled by his son and his office in Wentworth.[107]

Several times during the turbulent Reconstruction period Governor Reid rendered valuable service to North Carolina. In 1869 and 1870 at the height of the Ku Klux Klan violence Governor William Holden responded by declaring martial law in a number of counties and occupying them with a special militia force commanded by Col. George W. Kirk. The Klan terror in Rockingham County escalated in the spring of 1869 with numerous beatings and the torture of blacks. Reid deplored what he perceived as the corruption and misrule of the Republican regime, but he was shocked by the Klan's program of intimidation, assault, and murder. With his fundamental faith in democracy, Reid believed the only acceptable cure for the Republicans was to beat them by legal, constitutional means—at the ballot box. When he joined his relative Thomas Settle, a Republican judge, in publically denouncing the Klan, he did so at the risk of his life, but his influence was such that the local Klan disbanded in the next few months. The following year he addressed an open letter to the people of the state, calling on them to reject violence and to rally in the next election to rid the state of the corruption-tainted Republicans.[108]

In 1875 Governor Reid was elected delegate from Rockingham County to the state Constitutional Convention. At the convention many of his supporters wanted him to be the presiding officer, but realizing that he was not acceptable to the Republicans, he nominated Dr. Edward Ransom of Tyrrell County. The vote was tied, and after thirteen ballots Reid finally persuaded Ransom to vote for himself so that the convention could be organized. Reid was considered to be the leader of the Conservative faction. The Wilmington *Daily Journal* commented on his key role in the convention, declaring that the governor was "entirely too useful upon the floor to be permitted to occupy the chair. It is really a pleasure to see how orderly and smoothly and harmoniously everything proceeds under his lead."[109] The convention presented thirty amendments to the 1868 constitution, primarily on the judicial system.

In May, 1881, Governor Reid suffered a severe stroke which left him permanently crippled and confined to a wheelchair. The Reids moved from Wentworth to the new home of their son Thomas in Reidsville. Over the next decade the governor lived a confined life, occasionally hearing from old friends and adversaries. Over the decade the governor's health declined, and on June 18, 1891, early in the morning, he died in his sleep.[110]

The key to the political success of David S. Reid was his personality and character. A contemporary, Andrew J. Boyd of Reidsville, wrote at the time of his death:

> He had a stronger hold upon the masses than any man I have ever known. His habits and tastes were plain and simple. He was always pleasant in the social circle, and easy of approach. The humblest citizen of the land could at all times gain his attention and consideration, and he was exceedingly courteous in his manners to all.[111]

A North Carolina historian in a biographical sketch of Reid characterized him as the "wisest and most resourceful leader" of the Democratic party in the antebellum period.[112]

David Reid never lost his simple democratic faith in the intelligence and honesty of the common man, and the people of North Carolina never lost their trust in his integrity and wisdom. He was a living example of what a man could accomplish with basic intelligence, willingness to work, and ambition. Governor Reid held most of the important political offices that the citizens of the state could bestow. His concept of public office was that he was a temporary servant of the people, and he never strayed from this democratic vision of public trust in a lifetime of public service. For this the people of North Carolina have honored his memory. There could not have been a more appropriate ending to his epitaph, which states, "above all a true and honest man."

***A portion of this sketch has been previously published and is used with permission. See Lindley S. Butler, "David S. Reid, 1813-1850: The Making of a Governor," *The Journal of Rockingham County History and Genealogy, IV*, (June, 1979), 1-21, hereinafter cited as Butler, "Reid."**

NOTES

[1]*Newbern Republican*, quoted in *North-Carolina Standard* (Raleigh), May 24, 1848, hereinafter cited as *North-Carolina Standard.*

[2]John Hill Wheeler, *Reminiscences and Memoirs of North Carolina and Eminent North Carolinians* (Baltimore: Genealogical Publishing Company, reprint edition, 1966), 391, hereinafter cited as Wheeler, *Reminiscences.*

[3]Guilford County Deeds, Office of the Register of Deeds, Greensboro, Book II, 274, hereinafter cited as Guilford County Deeds; Rockingham County Tax List, 1815, Treasurer's and Comptroller's Papers, Archives, Division of Archives and History, Raleigh, hereinafter cited as 1815 Tax List; Hugh Reid Scott, "Family History of William Scott and his wife Rhoda (Settle Reid) Scott," microfilm copy of unpublished manuscript, 1921, Southern Historical Collection, University of North Carolina at Chapel Hill, hereinafter cited as Scott, "Family History"; Hugh Reid Scott, "Concerning Many of the Families of Rockingham County and Their Lateral Connections who Attained Both State and National Prominence, Among whom were the Reids, Settles, Martins, and others of the Earliest Settlers in the County," unpublished manuscript, Reidsville Public Library, 1954, 1-2, 19, hereinafter cited as Scott, "Families and Connections." Hugh Reid was born May 20, 1745, and died on September 8, 1822. Jemima Carmen Reid was born July 2, 1742, and died September 4, 1822.

[4]By 1790 Josiah Settle had six slaves. He died about 1800. David Settle was born in Virginia on October 25, 1758, and died in Rockingham County on April 3, 1833. Rhoda Mullins Settle was born November 21, 1768, and died in Rockingham County in 1852. Reuben Reid was born March 12, 1787, in Rockingham County and died there on June 22, 1852. Elizabeth Settle Reid was born on January 1, 1794, in Rockingham County and died there August 19, 1870. Guilford County Deeds, II, 156; III, 172-173; 1815 Tax List; Rockingham County Marriage Bonds, Office of the Register of Deeds, Wentworth; Rockingham County Wills, Office of the Clerk of Superior Court, Wentworth, B, 73; Settle Family Cemetery, near Reidsville; First Baptist Church Cemetery, Reidsville; Scott, "Family History"; Scott, "Families and Connections"; William Emmett Reese, *The Settle-Suttle Family*, edited by Fannie Lu Camp Fisher (Carrollton, Georgia: Privately printed, 1974), 166, 168, 347, 348, 678, hereinafter cited as Reese and Fisher, *Settle Family.*

[5]Greenview Cemetery, Reidsville; Rockingham County Deeds, Office of the Register of Deeds, Rockingham County Courthouse, Wentworth, Book P, 229, hereinafter cited as Rockingham County Deeds; "Family Record," Reuben David Reid Bible, in possession of Mrs. Lucile Reid Fagg, Eden; Scott, "Families and Connections"; Fourth Census of the United States, 1820: Rockingham County, North Carolina, Population Schedule, 604, microfilm of National Archives manuscript copy, Learning Resources Center, Rockingham Community College, Wentworth, hereinafter cited as Fourth Census, 1820, with appropriate county, schedule, and page number. Hugh Kearns Reid (1817-1897) married Caroline Graves and after her death Caroline Settle, the sister of David Reid's future wife. Hugh Reid had four children by his first wife. Frances E. Reid (1819-1854) married Samuel F. Adams of Rockingham County and had seven children. Rhoda Settle Reid (1822-1865) married William Scott of Rockingham County and had six children. Of the children of Reuben Reid who did not have any descendants, Reuben Hunt (1834-1849) did not marry; Henrietta (1824-1868) married George Price of Pittsylvania County, Virginia; and Annie C. (born 1831) married Ansalem Reid of Rockingham Coun-

ty. A daughter Beulah died in 1815 when just a few months old. Reese and Fisher, *Settle Family*, 679-680; First Baptist Church Cemetery, Reidsville

[6]David S. Reid to Thomas S. Reid, May 6, 1873, Private Collections, David S. Reid Papers, PC 1, Archives, Division of Archives and History, Raleigh, hereinafter cited as Reid Papers, PC 1, State Archives. The earliest known use of Reid's signature is on a deed of his father's, dated 1823, which he witnessed. Rockingham County Deeds, X, 253.

[7]Most of the Reid library was given by the family to the North Carolina Museum of History in Raleigh in 1975, when the museum purchased the documented collection of furniture made by Milton cabinetmaker Thomas Day for David Reid. The library is on partial display in the present governor's office. "Preliminary Inventory of the David S. Reid Book Collection," North Carolina Museum of History, Raleigh, 1975.

[8]Scott, "Families and Connections," 6; John M. Morehead to David S. Reid, March 29, 1829, Reid Papers, PC 1, State Archives; Reid Store Account Book, David S. Reid Papers, Duke University Library, Durham, hereinafter cited as Reid Papers, Duke; H. S. D. Rawlin to David S. Reid, August 22, 1832, Reid Papers, PC 1, State Archives; *North-Carolina Standard*, July 10, 1850.

[9]Scott, "Family History"; *Webster's Dollar Weekly* (Reidsville), June 23, 1891, hereinafter cited as *Webster's Dollar Weekly*.

[10]"Records of Appointments of Postmasters, 1827-1929," Records of the Post Office Department, Record Group 28, National Archives and Records Service Microfilm, I, 379, 456; II, 98. In the Reid Papers, PC 1, State Archives, there are post office quarterly reports, receipts, and correspondence that relate to Reid's postmastership. The earliest document is a letter from Washington, D.C., dated January 18, 1831, concerning the postal route, and the last is a receipt dated January 1, 1836. Reid had to resign the position after his election to a militia colonelcy and to the state Senate. His father held postal appointments dated September 5, 1831, and September 5, 1836.

[11]Sixth Census of the United States, 1840: Rockingham County, North Carolina, Population Schedule, 17, microfilm of the National Archives manuscript copy, Learning Resources Center, Rockingham Community College, Wentworth, hereinafter cited as Sixth Census, 1840, with appropriate county, schedule, and page number; Rockingham County Deeds, P, 235; S, 252; T, 119; 2E, 109; 2n, 299; 20, 352; Rockingham County Court Minutes, North Carolina Archives Microfilm, Learning Resources Center, Rockingham Community College, August, 1831-August, 1852 passim, hereinafter cited as Rockingham County Court Minutes.

[12]Rockingham County Deeds, 2H, 235; 2L, 285, 504; Thomas W. Wariner to David S. Reid, July 31, 1837, Reid Papers, Duke; Rockingham County Court Minutes, May-August, 1833; Samuel F. Adams to David S. Reid, February 26, 1844, Reid Papers, Duke; Samuel F. Adams to David S. Reid, July 11, 1850, Reid Papers, PC 1, State Archives.

[13]Frederick Nash, James Iredell, and William H. Battle, *The Revised Statutes of the State of North Carolina* (Raleigh: Turner and Hughes, 1837), 392-419; Neal Bennett to David S. Reid, October 1, 1835, Reid Papers, PC 1, State Archives; David S. Reid to Richard Dobbs Spaight, November 6, 1836, Governors Papers, David S. Reid, Archives, Division of Archives and History, Raleigh, hereinafter cited as Governors Papers, Reid; Joseph Winston to Edward Dudley, July 27, 1837, Governors

Papers, Reid; "Commissions and Resignations, 1841- 1855," 11, Governors Office Records, Archives, Division of Archives and History, Raleigh, hereinafter cited as Governors Office Records; John M. Logan to John M. Morehead, November 17, 1842, Governors Papers, Reid.

[14]*North-Carolina Standard*, August 27, 1835; James Roach to David S. Reid, July 16, 1835, Reid Papers, PC 1, State Archives. Thomas Blackwell (1776-1856) served in the House of Commons, 1814-1816, 1820, and in the state Senate, 1822, 1824, and 1826. He had fourteen slaves in 1840. *Raleigh Register*, May 21, 1856; Sixth Census, 1840, Caswell County, Slave Schedule, 12; John L. Cheney, Jr. (ed.), *North Carolina Government, 1585-1979: A Narrative and Statistical History* ... (Raleigh: North Carolina Department of the Secretary of State, second, updated edition, 1981), 1251-1252, hereinafter cited as Cheney, *North Carolina Government*. The phrase "*White whigism*" refers to Hugh L. White (1773-1840) of Tennessee, who was an unsuccessful Whig candidate for president in 1836. Allen Johnson, Dumas Malone, and others (eds.), *Dictionary of American Biography* (New York: Charles Scribner's Sons, 20 volumes, 1928; index and updating supplements), X, 105-107, hereinafter cited as *DAB*.

[15]*North-Carolina Standard*, May 19, 1836, August 5, 1838, January 15, June 17, August 19, 1840. Both Thomas S. Gallaway and William Fewell were leading Dan River planters and slaveholders of Rockingham County. Gallaway, who had thirty-six slaves in 1840, lived south of Leaksville, and Fewell, who had twenty-two slaves in 1840, lived just south of Madison. Sixth Census, 1840, Rockingham County, Slave Schedule, 15, 29.

[16]*Journals of the Senate and House of Commons of the General Assembly of the State of North Carolina at the Session of 1835* (Raleigh: Philo White, 1836), 8, hereinafter cited as *Senate Journal, 1835*; *Journals of the Senate and House of Commons of the General Assembly of the State of North Carolina at its Session in 1836-37* (Raleigh: J. Gales & Sons, 1837), 20, 39, hereinafter cited as *Senate Journal, 1836-1837*; *Journals of the Senate and House of Commons of the General Assembly of the State of North Carolina at its Session in 1838-1839* (Raleigh: Thomas J. LeMay, 1839), 39, 44, hereinafter cited as *Senate Journal, 1838-1839*; *Journals of the Senate and House of Commons of the General Assembly of the State of North Carolina at its Session in 1840-41* (Raleigh: Thomas J. LeMay, 1841), 26, 31, 40, 51, 93, hereinafter cited as *Senate Journal, 1840-1841*.

[17]*Senate Journal, 1835*, 51, 54, 66-67; Clarence C. Norton, *The Democratic Party in Ante-Bellum North Carolina, 1835-1861* (Chapel Hill: University of North Carolina Press, 1930), 60-61, hereinafter cited as Norton, *Democratic Party*.

[18]David S. Reid, Philip J. Irion, and Blake W. Braswell, "To the Freemen of Rockingham County," December 22, 1835, Reid Papers, PC 1, State Archives. Philip Jacob Irion, originally from Bedford County, Virginia, settled in the Rockingham County region in 1784. He was in the House of Commons 1830-1837 and was elected major general of the Ninth Division, North Carolina Militia, December 30, 1834. Rockingham County Deeds, B, 63. "Resignations and Commissions, 1827-1836," Governors Office Records; Cheney, *North Carolina Government*, 1252. Blake W. Braswell was in the House of Commons, 1834-1839. Cheney, *North Carolina Government*, 1252.

[19]J. G. de Roulhac Hamilton and Max R. Williams (eds.), *The Papers of William Alexander Graham* (Raleigh: Division of Archives and History, Department of Cultural Resources, projected 8 volumes, 1957—), I, 468-469, hereinafter cited as Hamilton and Williams, *Graham Papers*. Thomas Settle (1789-1857), a Rockingham County attorney, was Reid's uncle and, later, his father-in-law. Settle was a member of

the House of Commons (1816, 1826-1829) and was elected speaker in 1827 and 1828. He served two terms in the United States House of Representatives (1817-1821). In 1832 he was elected to the state superior court bench, where he served for twenty-two years. He was a leading Whig after the party was founded. His wife was Henrietta Williams Graves (1799-1886) of Caswell County, the sister of Calvin Graves. *Biographical Directory of the American Congress, 1774-1971 . . .* (Washington: United States Government Printing Office, 1971), 1582, hereinafter cited as *Biographical Directory of Congress.*

[20]*North-Carolina Standard,* January 18, 1837; *Senate Journal, 1836-1837,* 169-170, 177.

[21]*North-Carolina Standard,* January 2, 1839.

[22]Norton, *Democratic Party,* 77-79; *Senate Journal, 1838-1839,* 154-158.

[23]*Senate Journal, 1840-1841,* 26; Guion G. Johnson, *Ante-Bellum North Carolina: A Social History* (Chapel Hill: University of North Carolina Press, 1937), 272-276, hereinafter cited as Johnson, *Ante-Bellum North Carolina*; Richard L. Zuber, *Jonathan Worth: A Biography of a Southern Unionist* (Chapel Hill: University of North Carolina Press, 1965), 48-52.

[24]*Greensborough Patriot,* April 20, May 4, 1841; *North-Carolina Standard,* May 26, 1841. Shepperd (1792-1864), an able lawyer, returnd to Congress, 1847-1851. *Biographical Directory of Congress,* 1592.

[25]*North-Carolina Standard,* April 19, 1843; Romulus M. Saunders to David S. Reid, February 17, 1842, Reid Papers, PC 1, State Archives; Legal Petition, May 22, 1843, Reid Papers, PC 1, State Archives.

[26]*Raleigh Register,* August 16, 1842, May 26, 1843; *North-Carolina Standard,* April 19, May 24, 31, August 25, 1843. Anderson Mitchell (1800-1876), an attorney, represented both Ashe and Wilkes counties during various terms in the North Carolina legislature from 1827 to 1855. He served in the United States House of Representatives (1842-1843). After he moved to Iredell County he was in the state constitutional convention (1861-1862) and served on the state superior court (1866-1876). Johnson J. Hayes, *The Land of Wilkes* (Wilkesboro: Wilkes County Historical Society, 1962), 85, 152, hereinafter cited as Hayes, *Land of Wilkes*; John Crouch, *Historical Sketches of Wilkes County* (Wilkesboro: *The Chronicle,* 1902), 107.

[27]*The Congressional Globe,* Twenty-eighth Congress, First Session, 1845 (Washington: United States Government Printing Office, 46 volumes [in 111], 1834-1873), XIII, 3, hereinafter cited as *Congressional Globe,* followed by number, session, years, volume, and page.

[28]A. J. Folger to David S. Reid, April, 1844, Reid Papers, PC 1, State Archives.

[29]John T. Garland to David S. Reid, May 12, 1844, Reid Papers, PC 1, State Archives.

[30]*Circular of Hon. David S. Reid to His Constituents* (Washington: n.p., March 7, 1845), North Carolina Collection, University of North Carolina Library, Chapel Hill.

[31]David S. Reid to Reuben Reid, January 14, 1844, Reid Papers, PC 1, State Archives.

[32]Just a sample of this correspondence in Reid Papers, PC 1, State Archives, is James R. Dodge, December 21, 1843; Ephrim Hough, December 25, 1843; W. W. Peden, January 1, 1844; and John J. Martin, January 22, 1844.

[33]*Congressional Globe*, Twenty-eighth Congress, First Session, 1845, XIII, 29.

[34]Robert W. Johannsen, *Stephen A. Douglas* (New York: Oxford University Press, 1973), 125, 207- 208, hereinafter cited as Johannsen, *Douglas*.

[35]Roderick Murchison to David S. Reid, July 9, 1845, Reid Papers, PC 1, State Archives; *North-Carolina Standard*, July 2, 1845.

[36]*North-Carolina Standard*, August 20, 1845; *Greensborough Patriot*, August 18, 30, 1845. Alexander B. McMillan of Ashe County was a delegate to the state constitutional convention of 1835. He served in the House of Commons (1821-1825, 1840-1841, 1850-1851) and the state Senate (1826-1828, 1844-1847). Reid defeated him for a congressional seat in the election of 1845. Cheney, *North Carolina Government*, 278, 280, 282, 283, 286, 288, 310, 313, 315, 318, 817.

[37]Samuel F. Adams to David S. Reid, January 11, 1846, Reid Papers, PC 1, State Archives.

[38]Calvin Graves to David S. Reid, January 15, 1846, Reid Papers, PC 1, State Archives.

[39]*Speech of Mr. Reid, of North Carolina, on the Oregon Question. Delivered in the House of Representatives, February 7, 1846* (Washington: Union Office, 1846).

[40]David S. Reid to J. A. Waugh, December 10, 1846, Jones-Patterson Papers, Southern Historical Collection, University of North Carolina Library, Chapel Hill.

[41]*Circular of Hon. David S. Reid of North Carolina, To His Constituents* (Washington: *Congressional Globe*, 1847), hereinafter cited as *Circular, 1847*.

[42]Norton, *Democratic Party*, 145-146; *North-Carolina Standard*, August 18, 1847; Cheney, *North Carolina Government*, 684.

[43]*Circular, 1847*; [Given name unavailable] Laurie to Willie P. Mangum, April 21, 1847, Henry T. Shanks (ed.), *The Papers of Willie Person Mangum* (Raleigh: State Department of Archives and History, 5 volumes, 1950-1956), V, 60-61, hereinafter cited as Shanks, *Mangum Papers*.

[44]Elias Dodson to David S. Reid, February 21, 1847, Reid Family Papers, Mrs. Lucile Reid Fagg, Eden, hereinafter cited as Reid Family Papers; David S. Reid to Henrietta S. Reid, February 6, 1859, Reid Papers, PC 1, State Archives; William V. H. Brown to David S. Reid, March 1, 1859, Reid Papers, PC 1, State Archives.

[45]David S. Reid to Edmund W. Hubard, November 19, 1846, Hubard Family Papers, Southern Historical Collection.

[46]*Charlotte Journal*, January 8, 1851. The marriage license was issued on December 12 in Rockingham County. Index to Marriages, Rockingham County, Archives, Division of Archives and History, Raleigh. Henrietta was born October 7, 1824, and died on March 2, 1913. Greenview Cemetery, Reidsville; Rockingham County Deeds, 2T, 326.

[47]William W. Holden to David S. Reid, May 24, 1845, Reid Papers, PC 1, State Archives; John H. Wheeler to David S. Reid, February 4, 1846, Reid Papers, PC 1, State Archives; John J. Wheeden to David S. Reid, January 8, 1846, Reid Papers, PC 1, State Archives.

[48]Norton, *Democratic Party*, 17-19; Johnson, *Ante-Bellum North Carolina*, 771; Edgar E. Folk, "W. W. Holden and the *North Carolina Standard*, 1843-1848: A Study in Political Journalism," *North Carolina Historical Review*, XIX (January, 1942), 22-47.

[49]William W. Holden to David S. Reid, August 24, 1852, Reid Papers, PC 1, State Archives; William W. Holden to David S. Reid, undated notes, David S. Reid Papers, Rockingham County Historical Collection, Rockingham Community College, Wentworth; Horace W. Raper, *William W. Holden: North Carolina's Political Enigma* (Chapel Hill and London: University of North Carolina Press, 1985), 9, 20, hereinafter cited as Raper, *Holden*. Other recent biographies of Holden are Edgar E. Folk and Bynum Shaw, *W. W. Holden: A Political Biography* (Winston-Salem: John F. Blair, 1982) and William C. Harris, *William Woods Holden: Firebrand of North Carolina Politics* (Baton Rouge: Louisiana State University Press, 1987).

[50]Norton, *Democratic Party*, 153-155; William W. Holden to David S. Reid, April 19, 1848, December 22, 1880, Reid Papers, PC 1, State Archives; *North-Carolina Standard*, April 19, 1848; W. W. Holden, *Memoirs of W. W. Holden* (Durham: Trinity College Historical Society [volume 2 of John Lawson Monographs], 1911), 3-4, hereinafter cited as Holden, *Memoirs*.

[51]Norton, *Democratic Party*, 131; J. G. de Roulhac Hamilton, *Party Politics in North Carolina, 1835-1860* (Chapel Hill: University of North Carolina Press, 1916), 118, hereinafter cited as Hamilton, *Party Politics; North-Carolina Standard*, July 26, 1848, July 6, 1850. Free suffrage is examined in John W. Carr, "The Manhood Suffrage Movement in North Carolina" (Durham: Trinity College Historical Society [Series XI of Historical Papers], 1915), 47-78, and in Paul Apperson Reid, *Gubernatorial Campaigns and Administrations of David S. Reid, 1848-1854* (Cullowhee: Western Carolina College, 1953), 6-8, hereinafter cited as Reid, *Gubernatorial Campaigns*.

[52]David S. Reid, "To the People of North Carolina," June 28, 1850, Broadside, Reid Family Papers, hereinafter cited as Reid, "To the People."

[53]James Phelps to David S. Reid, February 15, 1842, Reid Papers, PC 1, State Archives.

[54]James W. Bryan to William A. Graham, July 18, 1848, Hamilton and Williams, *Graham Papers*, III, 238.

[55]*Raleigh Register*, June 6, July 5, 1848.

[56]Thomas E. Jeffrey, " 'Free Suffrage' Revisited: Party Politics and Constitutional Reform in Antebellum North Carolina," *North Carolina Historical Review*, LIX (January, 1982), 25, 27-28, 32-33, 33-36, hereinafter cited as Jeffrey, "Revisited"; Thomas E. Jeffrey, "National Issues, Local Interests, and the Transformation of Antebellum North Carolina Politics," *Journal of Southern History*, L (February, 1984), 45-46, 49, 54, 60-61, hereinafter cited as Jeffrey, "National Issues."

[57]William W. Holden to David S. Reid, June 1, 1850, Reid Papers, PC 1, State Archives; *North-Carolina Standard*, June 12, July 3, 1850; Reid, *Gubernatorial Campaigns*, 22-23; Norton, *Democratic Party*, 157-158.

[58]Reid, "To the People"; Avery O. Craven, *The Growth of Southern Nationalism, 1848-1861*, Volume 6, *A History of the South* (Baton Rouge: Louisiana State University Press, 1953), 92-94, hereinafter cited as Craven, *Southern Nationalism*.

[59]Jeffrey, "Revisited," 38-41; Marc W. Kruman, *Parties and Politics in North Carolina, 1836-1865* (Baton Rouge and London: Louisiana State University Press, 1983), 93-94, hereinafter cited as Kruman, *Parties*; Reid, *Gubernatorial Campaigns*, 26-27.

[60]Samuel F. Adams to David S. Reid, July 11, 1850, Reid Papers, PC 1, State Archives. The Wilmot Proviso was an amendment to an appropriations bill forbidding slaves to enter any territory taken from Mexico. It was rejected in 1846. Craven, *Southern Nationalism*, 33-34.

[61]Reid, *Gubernatorial Campaigns*, 26-27, 32; Norton, *Democratic Party*, 164-165.

[62]William K. Boyd, *History of North Carolina, Volume II, The Federal Period, 1783-1860* (Chicago: Lewis Publishing Company, 1919), 292.

[63]Kruman, *Parties*, 151.

[64]Paul D. Escott, *Many Excellent People: Power and Privilege in North Carolina, 1850-1900* (Chapel Hill and London: University of North Carolina Press, 1985), 27-28.

[65]Jeffrey, "Revisited," 45-48; Jeffrey, "National Issues," 62-67. See also Thomas E. Jeffrey, *State Parties and National Politics: North Carolina, 1815-1861* (Athens: University of Georgia Press, 1989), chapters 8-9 passim.

[66]"Gov. Reid's Inaugural Address Delivered Before the Two Houses of the General Assembly of North Carolina. The 1st Day of January, 1851." Broadside, Reid Papers, PC 1, State Archives.

[67]Thomas E. Jeffrey, "Beyond 'Free Suffrage': North Carolina Parties and the Convention Movement of the 1850s," *North Carolina Historical Review*, LXII (October, 1985), 397-405, hereinafter cited as Jeffrey, "Beyond"; Cheney, *North Carolina Government*, 317, 319, 322, 822; Reid, *Gubernatorial Campaigns*, 38-40, 61. The legislative constitutional amending process was for the amendment to pass two successive legislative sessions (the first by a three-fifths vote and the second by a two-thirds vote) and then be submitted to the people for ratification.

[68]Reid, *Gubernatorial Campaigns*, 42, 47, 51-53, 56, 63; Minutes of the Board of Internal Improvements, 1851-1912, Governors Office Records, 142.

[69]David S. Reid, Biennial Message, October 14, 1852, *Legislative Documents, Executive*, 1852, Governors Letter Books, David S. Reid, Archives, Division of Archives and History, Raleigh, hereinafter cited as Biennial Message, October 14, 1852.

[70]Reid, *Gubernatorial Campaigns*, 45, 49-50; Ebenezer Emmons to David S. Reid, February 19, 1851, Governors Papers, Reid; *North-Carolina Standard*, February 11, April 21, 1852.

[71]Craven, *Southern Nationalism*, 95; William W. Holden to David S. Reid, December 1, 1850, Reid Papers, PC 1, State Archives.

[72]Biennial Message, October 14, 1852; Reid, *Gubernatorial Campaigns*, 65-66.

[73]*North-Carolina Standard*, June 2, 1852.

[74]Jeffrey, "Beyond," 409-410; Reid, *Gubernatorial Campaigns*, 74-76, 78-79, 85; *North-Carolina Standard*, June 30, July 28, September 15, 1852. John Kerr (1811-1879) was elected to the United States Congress, 1853-1855, but was better known as a judge of the state superior court. *Biographical Directory of Congress*, 1159.

[75]*North-Carolina Standard*, May 24, 1854.

[76]David S. Reid to Stephen A. Douglas, June 17, 1854, Stephen A. Douglas Papers, University of Chicago Library, Chicago, hereinafter cited as Douglas Papers, Chicago; Johannsen, *Douglas*, chapter 17.

[77]*Message of His Excellency Gov Reid, to the Legislature of North Carolina, Session 1854-'55, Executive Document #1* (Raleigh: W. W. Holden, 1854), hereinafter cited as *Message*, November 20, 1854.

[78]*Message*, November 20, 1854.

[79]John S. Bassett, "Suffrage in the State of North Carolina, 1776-1861," *Annual Report of the American Historical Association, 1895* (Washington, 1895), 284; Jeffrey, "Beyond," 411-413.

[80]David S. Reid to Thomas Settle, January 2, 1853, Reid Papers, PC 1, State Archives; Greenview Cemetery, Reidsville; First Baptist Church Cemetery, Reidsville.

[81]David S. Reid to Stephen A. Douglas, June 17, 1854, Douglas Papers, Chicago.

[82]*The Democratic Pioneer* (Elizabeth City), November 28, 1854; Reid, *Gubernatorial Campaigns*, 113-114.

[83]*Congressional Directory for the Second Session of the Thirty-Third Congress of the United States of America* (Washington: G. S. Gideon, 1855), 27, hereinafter cited as *Congressional Directory for the Second Session of the Thirty-third Congress*; Asa Biggs to David S. Reid, February 2, 1855, Reid Papers, PC 1, State Archives.

[84]*Congressional Directory for the First Session of the Thirty-fourth Congress of the United States of America* (Washington: G. S. Gideon, 1856), 25, hereinafter cited as *Congressional Directory for the First Session of the Thirty-fourth Congress.*

[85]Greenview Cemetery, Reidsville; Asa Biggs to David S. Reid, January 21, 1856, Reid Papers, PC 1, State Archives.

[86]*Appendix to the Congressional Globe Thirty-fourth Congress, First Session*, 1856, 792-794; Norton, *Democratic Party*, 194; J. Carlyle Sitterson, *The Secession Movement in North Carolina* (Chapel Hill: University of North Carolina Press, 1939), 145, hereinafter cited as Sitterson, *Secession*; David S. Reid to Henrietta Settle Reid, December 11, 1857, Reid Papers, PC 1, State Archives.

[87]*Congressional Directory for the Second Session of the Thirty-Fifth Congress of the United States of America* (Washington, D.C.: Government Printing Office, 1859), 19, 20, hereinafter cited as *Congressional Directory of the Second Session of the Thirty-Fifth Congress.*

[88]Asa Biggs to David S. Reid, January 15, 1858; William B. Gulick to David S. Reid, February 7, 1858; Alfred M. Scales to David S. Reid, February 8, 1858; Asa Biggs to David S. Reid, February 8, 1858; William V. Geffroy to David S. Reid, March 9, 1858; David S. Reid to Minerva Telley, May 13, 1858; David S. Reid to Caroline L. Settle, May 27, 1858, Reid Papers, PC 1, State Archives.

[89]William J. Yates to David S. Reid, November 11, 1858, Reid Papers, PC 1, State Archives; William B. Kennedy, "David S. Reid, North Carolina Politician, 1813-1891" (unpublished master's thesis, Duke University, 1948), 89, hereinafter cited as Kennedy, "Reid."

[90]Norton, *Democratic Party*, 247; William V. Geffroy to David S. Reid, August 30, September 28, 1858, Reid Papers, PC 1, State Archives.

[91]Weldon N. Edwards to Thomas Ruffin, September 4, 1858, J. G. de Roulhac Hamilton (ed.), *The Papers of Thomas Ruffin* (Raleigh: North Carolina Historical Commission, 4 volumes, 1918-1920), II, 609-610, hereinafter cited as Hamilton, *Ruffin Papers*.

[92]Norton, *Democratic Party*, 247-248; *Raleigh Register*, November 17, 1858.

[93]*Raleigh Register*, December 1, 1858; Holden, *Memoirs*, 8. A perceptive analysis of this election is in Brian G. Walton, "Election to the United States Senate in North Carolina, 1835-1861," *North Carolina Historical Review*, LIII (April, 1976). In addition to the causes already stated, Walton mentions Reid's own indifference to the Senate as exhibited by his lack of interest in the election as well as his lack of achievement in Washington. His correspondence in this period reflects a boredom with Washington and a desire to be at home with his wife and children.

[94]Noble J. Tolbert (ed.), *The Papers of John Willis Ellis* (Raleigh: Department of Archives and History, 1964), I, 212-213, hereinafter cited as Tolbert, *Ellis Papers*.

[95]Tolbert, *Ellis Papers*, I, 217-218.

[96]Greenview Cemetery, Reidsville; Eighth Census of the United States, 1860: Rockingham County, North Carolina, Slave Schedule, 31, microfilm of National Archives manuscript copy, Learning Resources Center, Rockingham Community College, Wentworth, hereinafter cited as Eighth Census, 1860, with appropriate county, schedule, and page number; Eighth Census of the United States, 1860: Rockingham County, North Carolina, Agricultural Schedule, 15, microfilm copy of National Archives manuscript copy, Archives, Division of Archives and History, Raleigh.

[97]John H. Wheeler to David S. Reid, January 13, 1860, Reid Papers, PC 1, State Archives; Norton, *Democratic Party*, 235-236.

[98]Norton, *Democratic Party*, 253-255; Sitterson, *Secession*, 165, 168, 175, 180, 204-205, 208-209.

[99]Diary of Thomas Bragg, 40, Southern Historical Collection.

[100]L. E. Chittenden, *A Report of the Debates and Proceedings in the Secret Sessions of the Conference Convention, for Proposing Amendments to the Constitution of the United States, Held at Washington, D. C. in February, A. D. 1861* (New York: D. Appleton & Company, 1864), 434-435, hereinafter cited as Chittenden, *Peace Conference Debates*.

[101]Chittenden, *Peace Conference Debates*, 589-591; Sitterson, *Secession*, 230-231.

[102]David S. Reid to County Committee, February 18, 1861, William H. Thomas Papers, Manuscript Department, Duke; Sitterson, *Secession*, 211-213, 219, 223-224.

[103]*Journal of the Convention of the People of North Carolina Held on the 20th Day of May, A. D. 1861* (Raleigh: John W. Syme, 1862), 6, 7, 16, 19, 24, 25; *Journal of the Convention of the People of North Carolina, Third Session, Held in January and February, 1862* (Raleigh: John W. Syme, 1862), 7, 10, 57-58, 73, 96, 129; Sitterson, *Secession*, 232, 239-240, 243, 248. At that time May 20 was generally observed in North Carolina as Mecklenburg Declaration of Independence Day—the beginning of North Carolina's existence as a sovereign state; consequently, the date of the secession ordinance had symbolic significance to the whole state.

[104]David S. Reid to Zebulon B. Vance, September 2, 1862, Frontis W. Johnston (ed.), *The Papers of Zebulon Baird Vance* (Raleigh: State Department of Archives and History, 1963), I, 168, hereinafter cited as Johnston, *Vance Papers*.

[105]J. G. de Roulhac Hamilton, *Reconstruction in North Carolina* (New York: Columbia University Press [Volume 58 in *Studies in History, Economic and Public Law*], 1914), 48-49, hereinafter cited as Hamilton, *Reconstruction.*

[106]Ninth Census of the United States, 1870: Rockingham County, North Carolina, Agricultural Schedule, 5, microfilm copy of National Archives manuscript copy, Archives, Division of Archives and History, Raleigh; Ninth Census of the United States, 1870: Rockingham County, North Carolina, Population Schedule, 39, microfilm copy of National Archives manuscript copy, Rockingham County Historical Collection, Rockingham Community College, Wentworth, hereinafter cited as Ninth Census, 1870, with appropriate county, schedule, and page number.

[107]Greenview Cemetery, Reidsville; Kennedy, "Reid," 98; author's interview with Lucile Reid Fagg, Eden; David S. Reid to Thomas S. Reid, January 30, February 18, 1878, Reid Papers, Duke.

[108]Allen Trelease, *White Terror: The Ku Klux Klan Conspiracy and Southern Reconstruction* (New York: Harper and Row, 1971), 195. See Hamilton, *Reconstruction*, for background on the Kirk-Holden War. *Daily Sentinel* (Raleigh), July 26, 1870, hereinafter cited as *Daily Sentinel.*

[109]*Daily Journal* (Wilmington), September 10, 1875, hereinafter cited as *Daily Journal*; Hamilton, *Reconstruction*, 637, 642-643.

[110]William W. Holden to Henrietta S. Reid, May 29, 1881, Reid Family Papers; *Weekly Review* (Reidsville), June 24, 1891, hereinafter cited as *Weekly Review.*

[111]Andrew J. Boyd to Matthew W. Ransom, July 20, 1891, Matthew W. Ransom Papers, Southern Historical Collection.

[112]Joseph G. de Roulhac Hamilton, "David Settle Reid," *DAB*, XV, 476.

Settle-Reid-Martin Genealogical Chart

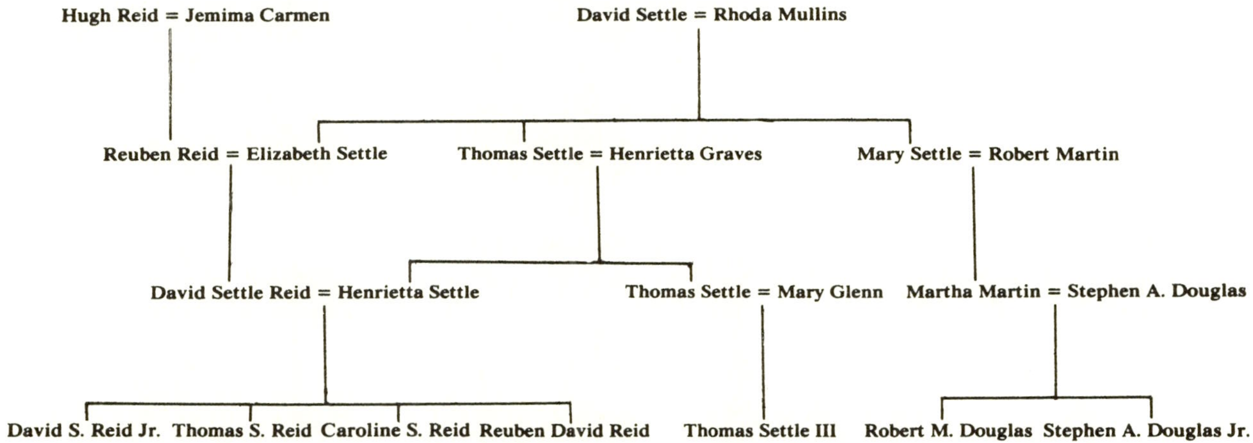

Reprinted from Lindley S. Butler's "David S. Reid, 1813-1850: The Making of a Governor," *Journal of Rockingham County History and Genealogy*, IV (June, 1979), 3.

Elizabeth Settle Reid (1794-1870), David S. Reid's mother, was a lifelong resident of Rockingham County. She married Reuben Reid (1787-1852) on May 12, 1812. Original photograph courtesy of Lucile Reid Fagg; copy from the files of the Division of Archives and History.

The Reuben Reid House, believed to have been built in the 1820s, was moved from Main Street around 1910. In 1980, the two-story frame structure was destroyed by the Reidsville municipal government to straighten Lindsey Street. This photograph, taken by E. F. Small in 1883, also shows a small log structure to the left. Copy from the files of the Division of Archives and History.

Henrietta Williams Graves (1799-1886) and Thomas Settle (1789-1857), David S. Reid's aunt and uncle, were married on September 21, 1820. In 1850, Reid married their daughter Henrietta. Thomas Settle represented Rockingham County in the state House of Commons and was a member of the United States House of Representatives. He served as a superior court judge from 1832 to 1854. Portraits courtesy of Lucile Reid Fagg; copies from the Rockingham Historical Collection of Rockingham Community College.

The William Garl Browne portraits of David S. Reid and his wife, Henrietta (1824-1913), painted during Reid's first term as governor, hang side by side in the home of their son Thomas in Reidsville. A reference to Browne's sketch of Governor Reid appears in William W. Holden's letter of December 1, 1850. Portraits owned by Reidsville Historic Properties Commission; photographs courtesy of the Division of Archives and History.

Hugh Kearns Reid (1817-1897), brother of David S. Reid, was a Reidsville farmer and merchant. He married Caroline H. Graves, daughter of Calvin Graves, on May 27, 1857. After her death, he married his first cousin Caroline L. Settle, Mrs. David S. Reid's sister. Photograph from Richard R. Saunders's *Open Doors and Closed Windows of the First Baptist Church of Reidsville, North Carolina* (Reidsville, 1948), 258.

Thomas Settle (1831-1888), first cousin and brother-in-law of David S. Reid, served as Reid's private secretary for a year during his first term as governor. Like his father, the elder Thomas Settle, he became an attorney, a state legislator, speaker of the House of Commons, and a judge. This portrait, now restored, hangs in the North Carolina Supreme Court Building. Photograph from the files of the Division of Archives and History.

1829

John M. Morehead[1] *to David S. Reid* A&H-DSR

Greensboro
March 29th 1829

I reply to yrs of 9th instant. I cannot now say whether we shall wish to get another Clerk at Leaksville. Col Corrigan,[2] and John M. Reynolds[3] will attend to the store and are both well acquainted with business: They will be capable of doing a great deal of business, more I fear than we shall have to do.

I should be glad if our business would urge us to the employment of another Clerk; whether it will or not is an experiment yet to try.

---

[1]John Motley Morehead (1796-1866) was governor of North Carolina from 1841 to 1845 and the first president of the North Carolina Railroad. He was reared in Rockingham County, where he purchased and inherited a considerable amount of property. He developed commercial and industrial interests in Leaksville. Burton Alva Konkle, *John Motley Morehead and the Development of North Carolina, 1796-1866* (Philadelphia: William J. Campbell, 1922), 103, 356, hereinafter cited as Konkle, *John Motley Morehead.*

[2]William A. Carrigan purchased a lot in Leaksville in 1820 and remained there as one of Morehead's business associates until 1837. He owned three slaves in 1830. Rockingham County Deeds, Book T, 273; Book HH, 60; Fifth Census of the United States, 1830: Rockingham County, North Carolina, Population Schedule, 278, microfilm of the National Archives manuscript copy, Learning Resources Center, Rockingham Community College, hereinafter cited as Fifth Census, 1830, with appropriate county, schedule, and page numbers.

[3]John M. Reynolds (1810-1860) of Leaksville was a business partner of Morehead. Beginning in 1836 there were numerous land transactions involving Reynolds and the partnership of Morehead and Reynolds. Dillard Family Cemetery, Eden; Rockingham County Wills, Book C, 335; Rockingham County Deeds, passim.

1830

Joseph C. Reid[1] *to David S. Reid* A&H-DSR

Clarksburg Lewis County Kentucky
Wednesday July 28th 1830

It is with pleasur I take my pen in hand to answer yours bearing date the 1st Inst. which give me great satisfaction to hear that you are well together with the rest of Our relations, I also send my Kind Respects to you, your Father and mother Brothers and sisters will please to except my most cincear love also any other of my friends who are within your cirquit or neighborhood and let them know that I am well in health. I also Return my thanks to you for the information you give respecting your Representatives in Congress, as well as those who are about to represent your county to the legislature. Our election comes on here on monday next for this state we have two that offers to the legislature and two for the senate, in this county one of each of Jackson[2] side of the question and the other two on the Adams[3] side of the question, or in other words the Jackson party is against the terriff internal improvement and domestic manufactries, and the adams party is for Adamses administration which is revers to that of Jackson but Jackson is at this time loosing ground very fast here he is even cursed by some of highest and greatest friends in this state, his ministration in many things is so repugnant to the well fair of the state of Kentucky that his best friends are abusing him. The state of Kentucky asked the united states for alone of money and the bill passed both houses and Jackson set his vetoe against it.[4] He has done what no other president did that was before him turned everyman out of office that was in his power and filled some of their places with Bankrups and would have none only those who are his friends and their qualifications not look at. What looks more like monarchy than this. The calling home all the ministers and fitting out new ones does not look like curtailing expences, and still to mend his credit he has cleared one man for Robbing the mail and hung another when they were bouth found guilty alike by the Juries. The people in philidelphia have raised in companies and have paid for all or some of the Jackson Signs and burned them and made the fire out of the long hickery poles that were hoisted up as Jackson standers.[5] It would take a quire of paper to relate all the accusations that he is accused with, in this state.

Please to write me again as soon as your election is over. The court of [t]his county has thought proper to appoint me clark to the election which will last three days at One dollar pr day.

With my cincear prayers for your well fair I subscribe my self your mose affectionate uncle

---

[1]Joseph C. Reid, Reid's uncle, in 1820 lived in Fleming County, Kentucky, which is adjacent to Lewis County. At that time he owned one slave. Fourth Census of the United States, 1820: Fleming County, Kentucky, Population Schedule, 41 (microfilm), Archives, Division of Archives and History, Raleigh, hereinafter cited as Fourth Census, 1820, Fleming County, Kentucky, with appropriate schedule and page number.

[2]Andrew Jackson (1767-1845) served as president of the United States from 1829 to 1837. He had originally been considered an advocate of states' rights, but during the nullification controversy he vowed to use force if necessary to uphold the law on collection of tariff duties. Born in South Carolina, he was also a lawyer, member of the United States House of Representatives (1796-1797), United States senator (1797, 1823-1825), Tennessee supreme court judge (1798-1804), Indian fighter (1813-1814), major general in the War of 1812, and military governor of Florida (1821). He is noted for expanding presidential power. Richard B. Morris, *Encyclopedia of American History* (New York: Harper and Row, 1965), 733-734, hereinafter cited as Morris, *Encyclopedia of American History*; Allen Johnson, Dumas Malone, and others (eds.), *Concise Dictionary of American Biography* (New York: Charles Scribner's Sons, 1964), 481-482, hereinafter cited as *CDAB*.

[3]John Quincy Adams (1767-1848) was president of the United States from 1825 to 1829. After his defeat by Andrew Jackson in 1828, Adams served in Congress for seventeen years. In 1836 he suggested that military authorities abolish slavery in the South in the event of war. He served also as a United States senator, minister to Russia and Great Britain, and secretary of state (1817-1825). *CDAB*, 6-7.

[4]In May, 1830, Jackson, in an effort to curtail construction of internal improvements with federal money, vetoed a bill passed by Congress, which would have authorized government subscription of stock for the Maysville, Washington, Paris, and Lexington Turnpike Road. Morris, *Encyclopedia of American History*, 169.

[5]Standard, in the sense of emblem or rallying point.

1835

James Roach[1] *to David S. Reid* A&H-DSR

Orange Ct. Ho. Virginia
July 16th 1835

After my [*torn*] to you I will just drop you a few [*torn*] you that at this time I am enjoying good [*torn*], negroes are much higher than I ever saw them and I have bought only three since I left home and it is verry uncertain whether I shall buy any more. I calculate remaining here a few days only and perhaps I will then go a little further. I doubt verry much whether I shall be at home to the Election but Success to you in your undertaking.

Nothing more but remain yours.

P.S. I have an idea of buying a few more for my own use, return home and quit the trade untill better time.

---

[1]James Roach (d. 1841) purchased 200 acres on Little Rockhouse Creek (now Roach Creek) in 1795. In 1830 he had one slave, and his son James Roach, Jr., had two slaves. Rockingham County Deeds, Book D, 135; Rockingham County Wills, Book B, 268; Fifth Census, 1830, Rockingham County, Population Schedule, 285-286; Irene B. Webster and Linda C. Vernon (eds.), *Early Families of the North Carolina Counties of Rockingham and Stokes with Revolutionary Service* (Madison: James Hunter Chapter, Daughters of the American Revolution, 1977), 99-100, hereinafter cited as Webster and Vernon, *Early Families.*

David S. Reid, Philip J. Irion, and Blake W. Braswell A&H-DSR

22 Dec. 1835

to the Freemen of Rockingham County

FELLOW CITIZENS: In returning home to resume our stations as private individuals among you, it will be expected of us to give you an account of the course we have pursued while in the discharge of our duties as your Representatives: this you know we can but partially do, in the limits of a small Circular. A large number of the acts passed are of a private nature, and not interesting to our countrymen; we hope it will be some apology for what we have done, when we inform you that the past Session of your Legislature has been the shortest one for many years.

At an early period of the Session, Resolutions respecting the Public Lands were introduced in the House of Commons; the same that were before the house the previous session. Your Representatives in that branch of the Legislature voted on them as they had heretofore done, with this difference, that a division of the question was obtained and each distinct proposition contained therein was separately put, which enabled them to vote for such propositions contained in them as they deemed expedient, and against such as they deemed inexpedient. These Resolutions finally passed the House of Commons by a majority of 16 votes, (showing a great change since the previous Session, they passed that house then by a majority of 58 votes.) These Resolutions were laid on the table in the Senate, your Senator voting in the affirmative.

Resolutions on the same subject (differing materially, from those introduced in the House of Commons) were introduced in the Senate. Your Senator moved and voted for the indefinite postponement of these Resolutions, not that he objected to the sentiments expressed in them, but because this was a National subject, and he believed that the time of the Legislature and the money of the people would be saved if they could be postponed. The Senate however, refused to postpone, and upon the passage of the resolutions, he voted for them, believing them preferable to those passed by the Commons. In acting upon this question we were influenced by what we believed to be the true principle of our Government, at the same time consistent with what we professed when you elected us.

An act has been passed authorizing the Treasurer to issue Cirtificates to the amount of $400,000, and the same to be sold and to pay the enstalments on so many of the Shares of the Capital Stock of the Bank of the State as remain unpaid for, by and in behalf of the State.

An act has passed making an appropriation for building the Capitol, and appropriating $75,000 for that purpose: we regretted to vote for this appropriation but we found no other alternative. A building of the most splendid and costly nature had been commenced, and was in a rapid course of completion. To have voted against this Bill the work would have ceased, and the building which has already cost $200,000, would have been of no use to the State. It is true that its cost and style does not correspond with the condition of our Treasury. In short, it cost too much money, but it had been commenced and we could not consent to throw it away: we are of the opinion that one half of the money would have built a Capitol that would have answered every purpose, but there is one thing that may be said about it, it will when finished compare with any building in the United States and do credit to the age in which it is built.

Resolutions were passed, denouncing the course of the Abolitionists, and asking other Slave holding States to unite with us in passing such laws as may be necessary, to suppress and prevent the circulation of any incendiary publications within any of the slave holding States,—that the citizens of the non-slave holding States have no right to interfere with our property; and tendering the thanks of this State to our brethren of the North, who have so magnanimously maintained our rights against the wild and deluded fanatics of those States.

Acts chartering various Rail Road Companies have passed, among which is one from Weldon by way of Danville to Evansham in Wythe county, Virginia, and one from Milton to Salisbury; both of these roads, if built, will in all probability pass through Rockingham: We are gratified to observe that an extraordinary spirit of improvement in this way is manifest in every section of the country, and we hope the day is not far distant, when North Carolina will present a great improvement in this respect.

During the past session, there were an unusual number of elections to be made by your legislature, and among the rest that of Governor. Knowing that this was the last election that would take place for that appointment by the legislature, and that hereafter he would be elected by you the people, we felt deeply interested in the election of some individual who would fill that important appointment with general satisfaction. We conferred this appointment on *Richard Dobbs Spaight*,[1] of Craven county, who is, and ever has been a genuine Republican, of the Jeffersonian order, and a devoted friend to the administration of General Andrew Jackson. J. M. Dick[2] and R. M. Saunders[3] were elected Superior Court Judges. The former Counsellors of State have been re-elected, all of which are understood to be true Democrats—among the number is Col. P. H. Dillard[4] of our own county.

We are sorry to say that our financial concerns present quite a gloomy aspect: this is attributed to our system of taxation, our system of representation, our system of legislation, misfortune and neglect. We would here call your attention particularly to our revenue system—it presents numerous defects. It was thought best not to attempt a revision of it until the next session of your legislature, in which body the different counties will be represented with a regard to population and taxation.

The Literary Fund set a part for Common Schools is gradually increasing; and we shall hail the period when this fund shall justify the accomplishment of the great and laudable purpose for which it was created, as the beginning of an incalculable blessing. We ought to adopt every opportunity that may offer for increasing and fostering this fund, for it will indeed be a happy era in the history of our country, when the blessings of education shall be dispersed throughout our state, and made accessable to the poorest and most obscure as well as the wealthy class of the community. It is a melancholy fact that thousands of our countrymen for the want of education have lived and died, obscure and unknown, who otherwise would have been bright ornaments to their country and polar stars in our horizon.

This being the last time that your legislature will assemble under the old Constitution, and under the new Constitution a great part of the private and unnecessary legislation which has consumed so much time heretofore, will be transferred to other and more appropriate tribunals, where all parties can be heard at their own expense. This being the last session that they could *frolic* at the public expense, they took advantage of it, and the consequence was that the legislature was crowded with bills to divorce, restore to credit, legitimate, &c. This species of legislation retarded the progress of more important measures, and greatly protracted the length of the session.

When we entered into your service as your representatives, it was to serve you honestly, and with this view, we were in favor adjourning as early as possible, and thereby save expense—we have endeavoured to attend to all appointments and other private matters for our county, where our agency has been necessary.

We take this opportunity to say that we have on all occasions endeavoured to promote the true principles upon which we conceive our government to be predicated, and exceedingly regret that we had not been better qualified to watch your interests and protect your rights. We should do our feelings great injustice, if we were not on this occasion to return you our thanks for the many manifestations of your kind liberality towards us on all occasions—we are under obligations to you that we can never repay—we feel interested with you in promoting the dignity and prosperity of our country, and as such we hope ever to be found.

May that great Ruler of the Universe who guides our course and presides over our destinies, direct and protect our country from any impending evil, and grant us a continuation of health, peace and prosperity.

---

[1]Richard Dobbs Spaight, Jr. (1796-1850), governor in 1835-1836, was the last governor elected by the General Assembly. He was defeated for reelection in 1836 by Edward B. Dudley. John L. Cheney, Jr. (ed.), *North Carolina Government, 1585-1979: A Narrative and Statistical History* . . . (Raleigh: North Carolina Department of the Secretary of State, second, updated edition, 1981), 161, hereinafter cited as Cheney, *North Carolina Government*; Samuel A. Ashe and others (eds.), *Biographical History of*

North Carolina: From Colonial Times to the Present (Greensboro: Charles L. Van Noppen, 8 volumes, 1905-1917), IV, 403-405, hereinafter cited as Ashe, *Biographical History*.

[2]John McClintock Dick (1791-1861) resided in Greensboro by 1811 and was a town commissioner in 1829. He was a state senator from Guilford County in 1819 and 1829-1832 and was a superior court judge from 1835 to 1861. Ethel S. Arnett, *Greensboro, North Carolina: The County Seat of Guilford* (Chapel Hill: University of North Carolina Press, 1955), 21, 25, hereinafter cited as Arnett, *Greensboro*; Cheney, *North Carolina Government*, 361, 370n, 1146.

[3]Romulus Mitchell Saunders (1791-1867) of Caswell County was a member of the House of Commons in 1815 and 1818-1820 and of the United States House of Representatives from 1821 to 1827 and from 1841 to 1845. He was a superior court judge from 1835 to 1840 and from 1852 to 1865. *Biographical Directory of Congress*, 1563-1564; Cheney, *North Carolina Government*, 274, 276, 361.

[4]Peter H. Dillard (d. 1847) of Rockingham County was colonel of the county militia regiment, resigning in November, 1831. He served two terms on the Council of State from December 24, 1834, to December 27, 1836. *Journal of the Senate of North Carolina, 1831*, 7, hereinafter cited as *N.C. Senate Journal, 1831*; Cheney, *North Carolina Government*, 175-176.

1836

William Scott[1] *to David S. Reid* RCC

Talbotton Georgia
May 20th 1836

I with pleasure take my pen in hand to wright a few lines to you, to Inform you that I Am well and a doing first rate—And do hope when thes few lines Comes to hand, that thay may find you InJoying the same Blesings—I can inform you that The creek Indians have be come verry house tile in this Country Thay have killed fifty pearsons In the creek nation—the govener of georgia has hordered Everry third man In this country to gow to the nation to kill the Indians—I had the good luck To Be left behind my self—Give my complements to your father And family, also give my love to all Inquiring friends—So I will come to A close—By making one Request of you that is to wright to me as soon As you Recd. Direct to Bellvew P. O Talbot County Georgia.

So I Remain as I Ever Shall yours Respectfully

[1]This letter was directed to Reid as postmaster. The letters "P.M." follow his name. William Scott (1813-1884) married Reid's sister Rhoda Settle Reid (1822-1865) in 1846. Reese and Fisher, *Settle Family*, 679.

John A. D. McNeill[1] *to David S. Reid* A&H-DSR

Carthage, Moore County N Carolina
July the 15th 1836

I received your verry welcome letter under date July 5th and was highly gratified in its perusal, in answer to it permit me as a preliminary introduction to tender you my best wishes for your present and future welfare.

As you have learnt, I am again a candidate for a seat in the house of Commons of our state legislature, and indulge a sanguine belief that I shall be Elected my Competitor is Josia Tyson[2] the Gentleman

I beat on the last year—Mr. Kelly[3] is a candidate for the senate his antagonist is a Mr Allen[4] of Montgomery County. they are boath anties. the opposition in this county are tolerable strong and are strugling for prieminance with the grasp of a dying man. I think they will be defeated.

I went out to raleigh on the 15th of June to the supreme Court and after undergoing a rigid examination obtained a license to practice law in the County Courts of this State—while in raleigh I attended the Episcopal Church and received now an then an occasional glance from the Eyes of the Fair ladies that ware in attendance but more perticularly from the Eyes of one whose looks spoke unutterable things and whose charms surpassed all others that ware there if I shall be so fortunate as to meet you at Raleigh in November next I will there Communicate to you her name and shew her to you besides—on leaving the church I felt that I had received an arrow from Cupids quiver which filled my bossom with more internal commotion than I ever experienced before, and I trust to providence ever shall Experience again—I always thought that I was invulnerable to many things, that I could Stare stern adversity in the face without emotion or realize the bountiful fruits of providence without any External Show, yet not withstanding all this I find I am far from being woman proof that a Cannonadeing from the Eyes of a pretty gall unmans me a little of the most, so much so that on beholding—this invincible fair I was bound exclaim in the words of the poet

> Guiltless of harm the Bright destroyer lives
> At random wounds nor knows the wound she gives.[5]

As I have no inclination to disguise the fact I must tell you in sober seriousness that I am getting verry tired of a Single life, profoundly impressed with the belief that there are many comforts and blessings attending the matrimonial state which are not enjoyed by those living in a state of single wrechedness. this is abundantly proven from the fact that even Adam himself, in paradise, amidst the glories of a new world found himself not completely blessed untill he had a wife—Confidentially speaking—as my unbiased opinion that the heart of man created for delight—would in a state of celebacy pine in lassitude or grow sour with mesanthropy long before the hand of time would silver his head with age. As I believe you know all these things I shall write no more about them.

In a few days I shall set out on my Electioneering Campaign which will end on the day of Election. I have been about but verry little since I saw you on my return home from the Assembly. I sought in to reading law and applied myself verry close untill I went to the Supreme Court.

I should like verry much to see you now or at any time and trust that I shall meet you on the 3d Monday in november next at the State house. I have not heard a syllable respecting our friend A. Moore[6] since we left Raleigh whether he is a candidate in Rutherford or not I have not heard.

there is nothing affords me so much satisfaction as to hear of the success of democratic principles. I think we will carry the day through out the State. My health has been good since I saw you. you can guess at my enjoyment, when I tell you that my time has been spent in reading Blackston & Coke upon littleton—Write to me imediatly after the Election let me hear all the news—I will write in return—whether beaten or not—nothing more only with sentiments of respt I am

[P.S.] I am like D Crocket.[7] I cross no t or dot no i.

---

[1]John A. D. McNeill of Carthage, Moore County, served in the House of Commons (1835, 1836, 1838). Because of severe illness, he resigned his seat on November 20, 1838, just four days after the session began. McNeill, who never married, died November 21, 1838, and left the bulk of his estate to his cousin Joseph L. Reid, who had cared for him during his last illness. Cheney, *North Carolina Government*, 352n, 1211; Will of John A. D. McNeill, November 20, 1838, Moore County Wills (microfilm), Book B, 121, Archives, Division of Archives and History, Raleigh, hereinafter cited as McNeill Will; *Fayetteville Observer*, November 28, 1838; *North-Carolina Standard*, November 28, 1838.

[2]Josiah Tyson of Moore County was in the state Senate (1819, 1826-1827, 1831-1833), and in the House of Commons (1813-1817, 1820-1822, 1824-1825, 1828-1829). Cheney, *North Carolina Government*, 1210-1211.

[3]John B. Kelly of Moore County was a delegate to the state Constitutional Convention of 1835 and was in the state Senate (1818, 1836-1837). Cheney, *North Carolina Government*, 817, 1210.

[4]James Allen of Montgomery County served in the House of Commons (1804-1806, 1827-1828). Cheney, *North Carolina Government*, 1208.

[5]From the 18th-century English satirical poem "On a Fan" by Alexander Pope. McNeill slightly misquoted the couplet, which actually reads: "Yet guiltless too this bright destroyer lives; / At random wounds, nor knows the wound she gives." Alexander Pope, *The Works of Alexander Pope* (Philadelphia: Davis, Porter & Coates, 1866), 351.

[6]Alanson W. Moore of Rutherford County served in the House of Commons (1833-1834) and the state Senate (1835). Cheney, *North Carolina Government*, 1264-1265.

[7]David Crockett (1786-1836), frontier humorist and Tennessee politician, was a militia colonel, state legislator, and United States congressman. His *Narrative* was published in 1834. After his defeat by Jackson forces in a congressional race, he went to Texas, where he died at the Alamo. Allen Johnson, Dumas Malone, and others (eds.), *Dictionary of American Biography* (New York: Charles Scribner's Sons, 20 volumes, 1928; index and updating supplements), IV, 555-556, hereinafter cited as *DAB*.

John J. Wright[1] *to David S. Reid* A&H-DSR

Rockingham Springs.
July 30th 1836.

In this part of the County you are apprised. our friends carry every Thing—Vanburren,[2] Johnson[3] & Speight we go for, the whigs & Bank men It seems are disposed to abuse our candidates particular Colo Johnson they talk free and slander Colo Johnson about his colord children &c do they Reflect that Colo Johnson is, a Gentleman and Statesman and Soldier, his pattriotizim caused him to [bleed] for his Country at the head of 1,000 vollentiers, which he raised in the last War. he is respected by all the offerces of our Goverment from the president of U States includeing his Cabinett the Senators of U States members of Congress even his political opponants: all respect him he has more laurels as a Statesman & soldier his constituants has kept him in there servise in the Councils of the nation, for thirty years; he is now placed by the Dimmocrat party of the nation by a convention which they Elected for that purpose as their candidate for the 2nd office in the Goverment.

(*The Journals of Congress will Shew the Fact*) Will the little whigs still abuse him and It dose appear strange when they are abuseing Colo Johnson, that the whigs are so warm for Genl Dudley[4] who was in favor of introduceing a much more Motley Race for our Society, It appears when Genl Dudley was a member of Congress he voted in favour of a polisey to give our fellow citzens a premium To Marry Indian Squaws—and It appears that he was willing to vote a way the public lands belonging to the people for that purpose and gave for Excuse for his vote that it woud Extinguish the Indian tribes in our Country, yes the whigs excuses Genl Dudly—for his motley crew and will vote for him altho he wanted our citizens to marry Indian Squaws with a breach clout to their back side and introduce a sosiety of half Savage for our sosiety and They will also vote for Genl Dudley altho when at the time that our Legislature passed the Electoral law of this state in favour of the genl Ticket Sistem Genl Dudley then a member of the legislature voted in favour of the Legislature appointing the electors in preferance to the Genl Ticket Sistem or district Sistem the Republican party in the legislature voteing in favour of Genl Ticket for the purpose of giveing our State her due weight In the Election of President & V President with other States of the Union as most of the States Elected their Electors, by Genl Ticket yes, Genl Dudley was in favour of Takeing the Election from the people & giveing into the hands of the legislature, Gov Speight has always bin a firm Republican has always bin able to put down the fedralists & nullifiers he goes for the present administration Van Burren & Johnson and agst the bank in haste

---

[1]John J. Wright, a Rockingham County planter, had in 1830 sixteen slaves. He lived near Rockingham Springs, also known as Lenox Castle, which was a mineral springs resort in the southeastern section of the county. He was a lieutenant colonel of the county militia in 1823. In the 1830s he owned a bar in Wentworth and was serving on committees appointed by the county court. Fifth Census, 1830, Rockingham County, Population Schedule, 289; Rockingham County Court Minutes, August, 1833; Roster of the General and Field Officers of the Militia of North Carolina, 1813-1842, Adjutant General's Office, Archives, Division of Archives and History, Raleigh, hereinafter cited as Militia Officer Roster.

[2]Martin Van Buren (1782-1862) of Kinderhook, New York, was vice-president under Andrew Jackson (1833-1837) and president from 1837 to 1841. In 1840 he was defeated in his bid for reelection by William Henry Harrison. *DAB*, XIX, 152-157.

[3]Richard Mentor Johnson (1780-1850) of Kentucky was a congressman, senator, and vice-president under Van Buren. During the War of 1812 he was a colonel in command of a regiment of Kentucky mounted riflemen. He was wounded in the Battle of the Thames in Canada, where he was credited with killing Tecumseh. He had two daughters by a mulatto mistress, Julia Chinn, whom he acquired as part of his father's estate. *DAB*, X, 114-116.

[4]Edward Bishop Dudley (1789-1855) of Wilmington served as the first president of the Wilmington and Weldon Railroad (1836-1837, 1841-1847) and was the first governor elected by the people, serving from 1836 to 1841. A member of Congress from 1829 to 1831, he voted for Indian removal legislation, which confirmed property ownership in mixed marriage situations. The intent of the legislation was removal of the Cherokee from the state rather than the creation of a mixed-breed people. *DAB*, V, 480-481; *Biographical Directory of Congress*, 832.

Joseph B. Hinton[1] *to David S. Reid* A&H-DSR

Raleigh, N.C.
August 28th, 1836.

Your kindness, I am sure, will excuse me for making the present call. Allow me to offer you my sincere congratulations upon your late successful canvass for the Senatorial honor of your District.

The honorable body of which you are a member, will have to elect a new Chief Clerk, and a new Reading Clerk also, at its next session; as the gentlemen who filled these offices at the last session, have accepted of appointments under the United States.

Some of my friends kindly urge me to become an applicant for one of those vacancies; and believing myself qualified to discharge the duties of either, to the entire satisfaction of the Senate, and that my business habits and moral deportment would be every way acceptable to that body, I have consented, and now most respectfully ask your friendly support.

I ask the favor, not as a political partizan, but as a freeman—a North Carolinian, who has rendered some service to the State; and in the hope that I shall be found to be, on trial, both honest and capable.

I would be thankful for either situation, but, perhaps, might be more useful to the Senate in the Chief Clerkship—as I have had much experience in similar duties, as Clerk of the County Court of my native county (Beaufort) for upwards of twenty years.

Those Senators with whom it was my pride and pleasure, a few years ago, to act in the Legislature, I am confident, will not be slow in giving me this token of their friendly recollections; and those with whom I have not had the happiness of personal relations, I hope, will not unkindly respond to this, *my first request* for office under the General Assembly.

In conclusion, I will add, should it be my good fortune to be the choice of the Senate, I shall endeavor to shew that its confidence has not been misplaced.[2]

P.S. I have remarked above, that it is not as a partisan, that I ask the favor of the Senate: because, if I should be elected, as I have much reason to believe I shall be, I wish to enter the office as the servant of the whole Senate and not merely of a part of it. Beside this, however, I may justly claim the support of Jackson Van Buren Senators, on the ground of my services to the party long before now. They have not forgotten that *my Resolutions* in the Senate, in Jany 1831, contributed not a little to the ruin of the combination then forming, to confine Genl. Jackson to a single term—and afterwards, as a Newspaper Editor,

I battled for the party. I did more, I plead, in its columns, in the eastern part of the State, the just claims of the people in the West, to the then proposed alterations in the State Constitution. This fact, will entitle me to a liberal support by the Western Senators.

---

[1]Joseph B. Hinton of Beaufort County was a state senator (1829-1833). In January, 1831, he introduced a resolution supporting Jackson's reelection. Hinton was not elected to either of the positions he referred to in this letter, and he held no other state office. Cheney, *North Carolina Government*, 292, 294, 298; Alice Barnwell Keith, William H. Masterson, and David T. Morgan (eds.), *The John Gray Blount Papers* (Raleigh: Division of Archives and History, Department of Cultural Resources, 4 volumes, 1952-1982), IV, 551-552, hereinafter cited as Keith and others, *Blount Papers*. The resolution is reproduced in the *Blount Papers*.

[2]The main body of this letter is a printed form letter; the postscript is directed to Reid personally.

James A. Lewis[1] *to David S. Reid* A&H-DSR

Chesnut Grove South Carolina
Sept 11th 1836

I take the present opportunity to write you a few lines to let you know that I have not forgotten you; although my long silence might have caused you to form a different opinion

Myself and family are in good health my little boy has not enjoyed as good health this summer as formerly but notwithstanding is as fine looking a little fellow as you will see

Mothers family are well Robert has gone to college I have received a letter from him since he got there and by its contents he seems entirely satisfied David Settle[2] starts for Rockingham [County] in the morning but in such a hurry that he will hardly take time to speak to his friends he leaves his wife and a little fellow he calls his son, here and doubtless it is for it is as like him as it can be and is a very fine looking child I dont want you to let him know that I said any thing in its favor because it will make him so saucy about it and he is enough so already Our crops of corn this season will be plentiful if not abundant our cotton has been greatly injured by the rain and is very late beginning to open it is impossible to form any estimate of the quantity that may be made this season but I would suppose that it will exceed last years crop.

Politicks in this District is at present at high water mark; and that means in South Carolina that every man is ready to fight for his Particular candidate Electioneering is carried to a most disgraceful height every candidate must have a bar well stored with all kinds of liquor or he stands no chance to be elected Dr. Dunevant[3] our former Senator and at present a candidate for that ofice keeps a free bar open to all who may wish to enter and partake of wine, french brandy rum, whiskey, or any other liquer that he chooses and that without money and without price only it is understood that if you do so it is expected that you will vote for the proprietor.

The contest in this district is different from what it was formerly The nullifiers[4] have got the ascendency so far that the Union party[5] cannot elect a man to any office they therefore stand aloof and look on only endeavoring to ferment the quarrel which has commenced with great violence amongst their opponents and which threatens to weaken that overbearing party so much that in a few years the Union party may triumph not so much in their own strength as in the weakness and Dissention of ther adversaries Major Eaves[6] opposes Dr. Dunevant and there are 6 candidates for the lower house whereas only 4 are eligible; Major Eaves is a nullifier and has neither talent nor any thing else to recommend him to the support of the people only that he is the only man of that party who would oppose Dunevant and so many have become so completely disgusted with the latter that they will vote for Eaves not because they love him more but because they hate they other worse; a praiseworthy motive truly, but it is one that actuates myself on the present occasion for there is no person in my knowledge whose person principles, or qualifications I hold in such supreme contempt as Major Eaves but my disgust at the course of the other both as a politician and partizan is so great that I am constrained to vote for the one as the only possible means of defeating the other The Electors who Elect the President, you are aware, are elected by the legislature in this state instead of by the People a serious attempt will probably be made to alter the law in that respect so that the people may have a hand in choosing the chief magistrate of this Republick, a privilege and a *right* which I am surprised the people of South Carolina have suffered themselves to be deprived of so long seeing that the sister states suffer the people to elect the President But it is evident that South Carolina is far more Aristocratick than any other state of this confederacy This state at the ensuing election will support Harrison[7] but if the People elected the Electors they would be nearly equally divided betwixt Harrison, White[8] and Van Buren Those about here opposed to Van Buren are crowing very much over the result of the Elections in your state Presaging By them that Van Buren is losing ground all over the country But because Dudley has beat Speight it does not follow as a corollary that White will beat Van Buren even in North Carolina

Pardon my intrusion of so much Politicks upon you at this time and write to me as soon as you have leisure

David Settle can tell you about the times here how that he has bought land; that negroes are most unreasonably high etc. etc.

Receive My hearty wishes for your welfare and Permit me to subscribe myself your friend

---

[1]James A. Lewis had settled in Chester County, South Carolina, by 1830 and was a militia captain by 1840. Fifth Census, 1830, Chester County, South Carolina, Population Schedule, 307; Sixth Census, 1840, Rockingham County, Population Schedule, 309.

[2]David Settle (b. 1804) of Rockingham County was Reid's cousin and the son of Benjamin Settle. He moved to Chester County and later to Mississippi, where he died. Reese and Fisher, *Settle Family*, 350.

[3]Dr. John Dunovant was in Chester County by 1830. Fifth Census, 1830, Chester County, South Carolina, Population Schedule, 286.

[4]State elections in October, 1832, resulted in a decisive victory in South Carolina for the nullification party, which opposed the federal Tariffs of 1828 and 1832. The state legislature called for a state convention which adopted on November 24, 1832, an Ordinance of Nullification by which South Carolina refused to obey the federal tariff law. Upon learning that a compromise tariff bill was in the making, South Carolina on January 21, 1833, suspended the ordinance of nullification, but nullification sentiment continued to run strong in the state. Morris, *Encyclopedia of American History*, 172.

[5]The Union party here refers not to a specific political party but to those people who were unionist in sentiment and opposed nullification.

[6]Major Nathaniel R. Eaves of Chester County. Sixth Census, 1840, Chester County, South Carolina, Population Schedule, 271.

[7]William Henry Harrison (1773-1841) of Virginia and Indiana was the ninth president of the United States, serving in 1841. He had previously served in Congress and had been a major figure in the War of 1812. *DAB*, IV, 348-351.

[8]Hugh L. White (1773-1840) of Tennessee was a state legislator, judge, and United States senator. Although he at one time had supported Jackson, he became the Whig presidential candidate in 1836. *DAB*, X, 105-107.

1837

Remarks of David S. Reid in the N.C. Senate[1] A&H-mn

[1837]
In Senate Jan. 6th.

REMARKS OF MR. REID.

On the Bill conferring Banking privileges on the Stockholders of the Charleston, Louisville and Cincinnatti Rail Road Company.
Mr. Speaker: —

I rise, sir, not to make a speech; but a sense of duty to my own feelings, and obligations to those whom I have the honor to represent, make it necessary that I should give some of the reasons which will influence me in recording my vote against the bill now under consideration. Aware, as I am, of the *censure* that awaits him who opposes any thing connected with this scheme of Internal Improvement, it makes it doubly necessary that those reasons should be given. To the grand project, the Charleston, Louisville and Cincinnatti Rail Road, I claim to be an advocate, and it has my hearty wishes for its accomplishment; and if proof of this is necessary, my vote will be found among those who first gave the act of incorporation its existence. This work is one of surpassing importance; it is a magnificent scheme, and none would go further, in the bounds of reason, in contributing his mite towards its completion, than the individual who addresses you. But, Sir, a Rail Road is one thing and a Bank is another; and it cannot follow that because I am friendly to the Road, that I must also vote for a Bank; I beg sir, that Senators will take this into consideration.

We are told that without extending banking privileges, this work must fail; with perfect respect for the opinions of others, I must say that I am inclined to doubt this position. This brings us to inquire if the road, when completed, will yield a profit to the share holders? If I am answered that it will not, it is the strongest argument against the work; I for one believe that the work will yield a handsome income to the stockholders, and if so, why heap a boon upon that which is already profitable? I may entertain towards banking institutions generally, a sensitive jealousy; but if I err, I wish to do so on the safe side.

Sir, the Bill now under consideration, proposes to charter a Bank with Twelve Millions of dollars as its capital. This, sir, is a much larger capital in proportion to the country in which it is intended to circulate, than the Bank of the United States ever had. The Bank of the United States was incorporated with a capital of thirty-five millions for the whole union; this was something like one and a half millions to each State; but this Bank is intended for three or four States, with a capital of Twelve Millions, which is three millions to each State—double the amount of the capital of the U. States Bank, in proportion to the territory in which it is to circulate its notes. It proposes, further, to issue a paper currency to the amount of twenty-four millions, and to establish in your State a branch; and, sir, I now ask what security have we, while only a small portion if any of the Road is built in this State, that the whole of this may not be put in circulation in this State, and thereby exclude the capital of our own citizens, and carry with it general consternation and ruin?

One clause in this bill makes it the duty of your Treasurer to receive the notes of this Bank in payment of public dues; this I object to, for I think it should be left discretionary with the Secretary to receive such money only, as would answer in the discharge of the debts the State may owe. Can the State, in the payment of her debts, compel any man to take this money? No, sir. The constitution prohibits it. Then does policy or justice say that we shall compel ourselves to receive that which we cannot compel others to take.

In addition to this, the bank is permitted to owe thirty-six millions—is permitted to deal in every thing, and more than this, the stock is conditionally exempt from taxation, while we tax the capital of our citizens unconditionally.

Sir, the Bank of the State of North Carolina was chartered at a time when we had no Bank, and the necessity for a Bank was as great at that time as I hope it will ever be again; and it is but fair to presume that she extended to this Bank as many privileges as policy dictates there should be extended to any. I would ask gentlemen to examine and compare the restrictions of this charter with the one now on your table. Ask yourself sir, how you will execute a process against or send a committee to Charleston or Cincinnatti, with authority to examine this Bank. I ask how will you reach the object?

I do not charge the friends of this bill or those under whose auspices it originated, with any improper motives. But, sir, it is now asked of us to grant this charter for the accomplishment of the Rail Road; but I fear, that when they wish it renewed, it will be urged as a matter of necessity, and I fear its power then cannot be withstood. There is another point that I would urge, to those who profess a desire to build up and foster a commercial city in our own State, and it is this: that this road carries the produce of the State to enrich and build up a city in another State; in regard to this it has but little influence upon me, for while I would by all means extend to our own towns all the encouragement in my power, it is the right and duty of the farmer to carry his produce to the nearest market where he can get most for it.

It appears that we are now about to grant to others what we have so often refused to our own citizens. We now have the use of a large sum of money under the deposit act of Congress, and it is to be disposed of or invested in some way, and shall we give others a Bank charter when we refuse it to ourselves. Will South Carolina give us banking privileges in her State to build us a central Rail Road? I should think not. I am entirely opposed to a State granting privileges, to the extent proposed in this bill, to any institution; but sir, if we are determined to grant such a Bank charter at all, why not grant it to a company to improve our own State; for I think that I hazard little in saying, that with such a charter as this, offered to our citizens, we could have a Rail Road from Beaufort to the mountains.

There is another consideration which ought to be taken into view; it is that sacred instrument, I allude to the Constitution of the United States, which declares *that no State* shall enter into any *compact or agreement* with another State, without the consent of Congress. Gentlemen, no doubt, differ with me in regard to this; but I am inclined to the opinion that the bill now under consideration comes in conflict with the Constitution.

Upon this important question I would ask Senators to reflect and pause before they act. I would ask how many of the freemen of the State there are, who know that there is such a bill before you; I would ask have we their sanction to the measure. It is a project that is novel in its character and if passed it may not only rule the currency, but may also seal the political *destiny* of our happy country. If we reject this bill, and upon experience and the will of the people, find that we have erred, we shall then possess the same power that we do now and the error may be amended; but pass the bill, and it is not like a statute to be repealed at pleasure—the power is gone— irrevocably gone, and then if you have erred, you can never amend it.

---

[1]This document appeared in the *North-Carolina Standard*, January 18, 1837.

David S. Reid and Philip J. Irion to the Voters of Rockingham County A&H-DSR

Raleigh
January 23, 1837.

Fellow Citizens:—Prompted by a sense of duty as well as custom, we attempt briefly to render you an account of the manner in which we have attempted to fill our station as your Representatives; together with a notice of some of the important subjects which claimed the attention of the Legislature. Although the Legislature was in session a little longer than usual, if we take into consideration the business *done*, it has perhaps been shorter than any previous one.

It will be recollected that at the session of 1833, the General Assembly passed an Act empowering three Commissioners to Revise and Digest the Public Statute Laws of this State; and in compliance therewith they reported the same at the past session comprising one hundred and fifteen Bills; each subject embraced in a separate bill, so that all former acts or laws on the particular subject were consolidated in one; all of which had to be read and passed three times in each House. The object of the Revision and re-enactment of the laws was to furnish them in a form so as to be understood by every individual. As the laws formerly stood, if you wished to know its bearings upon a particular subject, in many instances you would be subjected to the trouble of looking up and the expense of purchasing various law Books and Acts of Assembly and perhaps then not get the right ones. If the Commissioners have paid proper attention to the subject (to judge of this fact correctly, a man must be very familiar with the law) it cannot fail to aid every man in acquainting himself with the law to an extent which he could not otherwise conveniently do. We however doubted the propriety of acting upon this subject at the past session, for we believed that the work of the Commissioners would not loose any thing if laid aside till the next session; in the mean time its correctness might be better understood: another objection was that if the first session under the amended Constitution was a long one, that its length hereafter might be taken as a precedent and others might feel justified in sitting as long whether the public good required it or not. It would be illiberal to distrust those who may hereafter be the Representatives of the people, but when we see the powerful influence of example it can not be considered unkind to endeavor to avoid a bad one. It was thought best to act upon it, and after much time and great labor the task was performed.

Your Legislature was again called on to make an appropriation for the completion of the State Capitol; for this purpose $120,000 was app[rop]riated. It is thought that this sum will complete the Building and furnish it ready for the reception of the next Legislature, but, if we judge from former estimates there is reason even to doubt this. Altho' it is deemed amply sufficient. While it must be a matter of pride for the state to have a Capitol so splendid, we are sorry that her liberality has been so heavily taxed in its erection.

The Hon. Robert Strange[1] was elected to the United States Senate to fill the unexpired term of *Willie P. Mangum*[2] who resigned when he found he could not be re-elected. Mr. Strange was also elected for the next six years from the 4th March next: It is believed that in this gentleman we have one who is well qualified to represent the state in the station he occupies; his political *faith* and high moral and intellectual accomplishments are too well known to need comment on the present occasion. The following gentlemen were elected Judges of the Superior Court, Viz; Messrs. Frederick Nash,[3] J. D. Toomer,[4] Richmond M. Pearson[5] and John L. Bailey.[6] Daniel W. Courts,[7] Treasurer and William F. Collins,[8] Comptroller. Of the seven Councillers of State five are democrats, among that number Col. James Watt[9] of Rockingham is one. We thought perhaps it might not be amiss to use *checks* and *ballances* with a Whig Governor.

Application was made by the agent of South Carolina, for the passage of a Bill to confer Banking privileges on the Charleston, Louisville and Cincinatti Rail Road Company, with a capital of Twelve Millions of dollars, with permission to issue Twenty four millions of paper, to owe to the amount of Thirty six millions, to deal in every thing and to establish a Branch in each of the States of North Carolina, Tennessee and Kentucky; the principal Bank to be located in Charleston, S. C. &C. This bill had passed the Legislature of South Carolina and it was disired to get it enacted by the other states above mentioned. We regret exceedingly to be compelled to state that this Bill passed your Legislature, but such is the fact. Should the Bank be found an evil, which we fear will be the case, we have the Consolation to know that it was not Chartered by our Consent. The arguments for the Bank were based on the necessity for the Road and but for the name of its Connection with a popular project could not have received that support which passed it: we believe it could not have passed the Commons at all, but it was put on its passage in that House at a late period of the Session, when many members had left who were compelled home and else where. If the State was willing to grant Banking privileges to this extent to *any* company she ought Certainly to do so, to a Company that would build a road that could emphatically be called a North Carolina Road; for there can be but little doubt that with such a charter as this she could have got a Rail Road from the *Sea* to the *Mountains*. This subject was novel in its character and one upon [which] the views of the people had not been consulted, it differs from a common statute that you can repeal if found obnoxious for it *purports* to legislate away your right to do so for thirty one years. We endeavored to retain *indisputably* this right to the people by offering amendments to that effect to the bill, but its friends refused it for they dare not trust it with people, they knew they would object to it. The limits alloted to this Circular, preclude our objections to this Bank and we must leave the subject with the single remark that we believe the passage of its Charter *a bad job* for the State.

An act was passed which vests the election of all militia officers, in the Commissioned Officers of the respective divisions brigades and regiments, so that each division are to elect their Major General, each brigade their Brigadier General, &C. No officer is to be taken out of his county to vote. This Act also provides for the distribution among the Several Counties of the State a certain portion of the Public Arms, which will be sent to the respective counties at the public expense.

An act was passed making an appropriation for the Survey and Sale of a portion of the lands acquired by the late Treaty with the Cherokee Indians, it is thought that this tract of country will yield the state some four or five hundred thousand dollars.

Of all other subjects you perhaps feel most anxious to hear the result of the deliberations of the Legislature in regard to the Surplus Revenue alloted to the state under the deposit act of Congress; An act was passed desposing of this fund in the following manner: The sum of Three hundred thousand dollars to purchase the Scrip and pay the public debt the state owes at the north- One hundred thousand dollars that she owes the University is to be paid in Stock of the Bank of the State that now belongs to the state, Both of these appropriations are conditional for it is not certainly known that either of these debts can be paid now, inasmuch as this scrip is not redeemable till 1860, but it is presumed that they can be paid by substituting other 5 per cent stock in the place of ours. The Stock of the Cape Fear Bank is to be increased seven hundred thousand dollars,—three hundred thousand of which is to be subscribed by the State. Five hundred thousand dollars to drain *Lakes* and *Swamps* in the eastern part of the State; and two fifths of the Capital that is required to construct three Rail Roads viz. "The Wilmington and Raleigh Rail Road," "The Fayetteville and Yadkin Rail Road," and "The Central Rail Road," which extends from Beaufort to Fayetteville. It is provided that until the money shall be so expended, it shall be under the controul of the Governor and two others to be appointed by him with the advice and consent of the Council, who shall constitute the Board of Commissioners who are authorized to loan the same to companies or individuals to be paid semi anually with interest, &C. On this subject there were a variety of interests and views which rendered this subject as difficult to settle by the Legislature as it had heretofore been intricate and vexatious to the community.

We take the act of Congress on this subject to be what it is, and can view the sum of One Million Nine hundred and eleven thousand six hundred and seventy six dollars and fifty three cents which the State receives under this act, in no other light than a *deposite* and not a *gift*, and that the State pledges herself to refund it to the General Government when called for, upon the terms stipulated in the act. Perfectly aware that the past Legislature was looked to with considerable solicitude to give an impulse to some general system of Internal Improvement, but with our views on this subject, had objects presented themselves in which our Constituents could have been *immediately* interested we should have doubted much the propriety of investing the Surplus Revenue so as to put it beyond the reach of the State if called on for it, much less could we think of voting for a system so extravagant in its nature, but, extravagant as it is, it gives nothing to those we represent. Yes, the Surplus Revenue of which so much has been said and so many promises made, is disposed of before it is received; and altho' you do not directly participate in its benefits, if it is demanded by the General Government you will *participate* directly in its repayment. It was said that the money must be returned to the *people*, but where is it? The answer is you are bound for your part of it and still get *none*. The distribution of the Surplus Revenue is a hoax! It is a gross imposition on the people and the events of every day more fully demonstrate the fact! We are indeed sorry that more money was collected from the people than was necessary for the expenditures of an economical Government. But we were told that a surplus had unavoidably accrued in the Treasury and that it must be returned to the people and none were then to be found to contend that this as a principle was not unjust and dangerous in its tendency, but it is a lamentable fact that there are some now who propose it as a general system. Reduce the taxes you pay on your necessaries of life to the wants of the General Government and you have no surplus in your Treasury, but have it in your *pockets* subject to your own disposal: it is hoped that the number is few who will ask a boon from the National Treasury when it is perfectly obvious that for every dollar we get we must previously pay one and a half; this is well calculated to make the Treasury rich and the people poor, it is not believed that there are many who for *party devotion* will nurse a doctrine so inimical to the Constitution and dangerous to the Country: We have little hesitation in saying that time will confirm the correctness of the views we have so often repeated to you on this subject. It is hoped that it is not understood that we are opposed to Internal Improvement for such is not the fact, for we are devoted to it when Conducted upon principles of equity with an eye to all the great interests of the State, but Can not Consent to a system of *Log rolling*, more particularly with the *funds* of the *General Government*.

An act was passed establishing a new county out of a part of Rowan to be known by the name of *Davie*. A new Judicial District was established and instead of six, you now have seven Superior Court Judges; and their Salary is fixed at $1950 per anum each, subject to a deduction of $100 for every court they fail to attend. A great many other acts both of a public and private nature, (not to say any thing about the Revised Code) were passed and we do assure you that we felt ourselves compelled to say "*No*" no few times.

This may be the only opportunity we may have and we avail ourselves of it (we hope it will not be considered vain) to congratulate our County-men in the triumph of those political principles which we have indeavord to sustain, and which have met the sanction of so large a portion of you,—principles upon which we believed, depended in a great degree the prospects of our happy Republic: and it gives additional gratification to learn that the Senate of the United States has expunged from its Journals that unjust record of Censure against your President.

By your kindness we have been favored with a seat in your Legislature the last Session under the Old Constitution and the first one under the New Constitution, during which time party politics have raged to an extent seldom witnessed in our Government and in many instances personal respect and social feelings have been lost sight of—feelings have been enlisted with a zeal equaled only to love of liberty but we a[re] proud to state that our Country has spoken in a language not to be misunderstood that she is capable of self government. Harmony among ourselves, at peace abroad, prosperity at home; improvements in an Aggricultural Mechanical and Intellectual point of view now pervades our Country and points us *onward* in pursuit of the noble ends for which we were intended. Due encouragement to virtue and enterprise, a strict enforcement of the laws with proper industry and economy can not fail to bring us all the blessings which Heaven ever bestowed upon a nation, this should stimulate us in our domestic pursuits and gives us renewed confidence in our form of Government and additional energy in protecting our institutions and defending our rights.

We can not close our letter without again tendering to the Citizens of Rockingham our many obligations and lasting gratitude towards them. *One* of us at least must dissolve his political connection with you, and altho he may be *else where* he will ever feel a deep and abiding interest in his native state and particularly the county of his early days, at whose hands he has received so repeated expressions of confidence, and in his farewell, perhaps for ever, it gives him the highest gratification to know that he leaves you in domestic and political prosperity.[10]

In conclusion permit us to say that while acting as your representatives our feeble exertions have been devoted to what we believed best calculated to [redound] to our Country's good.

Your kindness towards us has formed in our affections for you a warm gratitude too indellible to be erased by the storms of life or the lapse of time.

---

[1]Robert Strange (1796-1854), a native of Virginia and an attorney, had moved to Fayetteville by 1815. He served in the House of Commons (1821-1823, 1826) and was lieutenant colonel of the county militia. In 1827 he was elected to the superior court bench and served until his election to the United States Senate as a Democrat, serving there from 1836 to 1840. *Biographical Directory of Congress*, 1667.

[2]Willie P. Mangum (1792-1861), an Orange County attorney, was a leading Whig on both state and national levels. He served as a state legislator, superior court judge, United States congressman (1823-1826), and United States senator (1831-1836, 1840-1853). Shanks, *Mangum Papers*, I, xv-xliii.

[3]Frederick Nash (1781-1858) of Hillsborough served in the House of Commons (1814-1817) and was speaker in the 1814 session. He served as a superior court judge (1819-1826, 1837-1844), as an associate justice of the state supreme court (1821, 1844, 1845-1852), and as chief justice (1852-1858). Cheney, *North Carolina Government*, 265, 360-361, 1227-1228; *DAB*, XIII, 387-388.

[4]John D. Toomer (d. 1856) of Fayetteville was a member of the House of Commons (1827) and the state Senate (1831-1833). He served as an associate justice of the state supreme court for six months in 1829 and as a superior court judge (1818-1819, 1837-1840). He was also a delegate to the Constitutional Convention of 1835. Cheney, *North Carolina Government*, 361, 817, 1106; Keith and others, *Blount Papers*, IV, 113n.

[5]Richmond Mumford Pearson (1805-1878) of Rowan and Yadkin counties was an attorney and a noted justice of the state supreme court. He served in the House of Commons (1829-1833) and in the superior court (1837-1848). He became an associate justice of the supreme court in 1849 and served until 1878, serving as chief justice after 1849. He conducted the state's best-known law school at his home, Richmond Hill. William B. Rutledge, Jr., *An Illustrated History of Yadkin County, 1850-1965* (Yadkinville: Privately printed, 1965), 81-83.

[6]John L. Bailey of Pasquotank County was a member of the House of Commons (1824-1825) and the state Senate (1827-1829, 1832-1833). He attended the Constitutional Convention of 1835 and served on the superior court bench from 1837 to 1863. Cheney, *North Carolina Government*, 361, 817, 1233-1234.

[7]Daniel William Courts (1800-1883) of Rockingham and Surry counties graduated from the state university in 1823 and served as a university trustee for twenty-nine years. He served in the House of Commons and the state Senate and was elected to two terms as state treasurer. William S. Powell (ed.), *Dictionary of North Carolina Biography* (Chapel Hill: University of North Carolina Press [projected multivolume series], 1979—), I, 443, hereinafter cited as Powell, *DNCB*.

[8]William F. Collins of Nash County served as the comptroller of the state from 1836 to 1851. Cheney, *North Carolina Government*, 182.

[9]James Watt (d. 1863), a Rockingham County planter and gristmill owner, served on the Council of State (1837-1839, 1843-1845). In 1830 he had twenty-four slaves. Cheney, *North Carolina Government*, 176-177; Rockingham County Wills, Book C, 391; Fifth Census, 1830, Rockingham County, Population Schedule, 293.

[10]The precise meaning of this "farewell," and to whom it refers, is uncertain. Reid returned to represent Rockingham County at the next session of the legislature, and Irion did not. However, as Irion was born in Virginia, he would not allude to North Carolina as his "native state."

Thomas W. Wariner[1] *to David S. Reid* Duke-DSR

[Rockingham County]
July the 31st, 1837

you and Mr Walker will not come for your Tobacco untill wednesday morning as Business Calls me from home on Tomorrow and not fail to come on wednesdy as I Shall Stay at home for the purpose of Delivering it and your Compliance will oblige your friend & sevnt

---

[1]Thomas W. Wariner (1792-1854) of Rockingham County purchased a farm on Wolf Island Creek in 1825, and there are numerous land transactions involving him in the 1830s. He owned two slaves in 1830. In 1840 and for several years thereafter he had a license to retail liquor and probably had a tavern or bar near his home. Fifth Census, 1830, Rockingham County, Population Schedule, 314; Rockingham County Deeds, Book Z, 227, passim; Rockingham County Court Minutes, August, 1840.

1838

John H. Dillard[1] *to David S. Reid* UNC-JHD

Chapel Hill
August 13th 1838

According to your request I avail myself of this, of the first opportunity, since I have been able to ascertain the result of the election in this county. I heard of the result on yesterday, by a person from Hillsborough, who is worthy to be believed. The news he brought was entirely contrary to the expectation of all whom I have seen. If the account he brought was a correct one, (and I have no doubt but that we have heard the true result, since I have not heard it contradicted) the result was as follows, Viz, Allison[2] elected to the Senate, Trollinger,[3] Stockard,[4] Graham,[5] and Sims[6] to the house of Commons. There is no doubt but that the above is a true account—Indeed since I took my seat to drop you this note, later accounts verify the above. There is a report in circulation about College that Aministration men have been elected in Wake without any difficulty. The report even says that every Whig candidate is left at home, though this is mere rumour brought to Chapel Hill by a citizen of Wake, who is supposed to be incapable of bringing the truth the distance of 25 miles; though there may be truth in this report. I have nothing more of interest to communicate. I wish you if you please to write me an account of the Rockingham election. I remain your Friend

[1]John Henry Dillard (1819-1896) of Rockingham County and Greensboro was educated at the University of North Carolina and at William and Mary. He practiced law in Patrick County, Virginia; but by 1846 he had returned to Rockingham County. He served as a captain in the Forty-fifth Regiment North Carolina Troops during the Civil War. After the war he moved to Greensboro and opened a law school in association with Judge Robert P. Dick. He served on the state supreme court from 1879 to 1881. John Hill Wheeler, *Reminiscences and Memoirs of North Carolina and Eminent North Carolinians* (Baltimore: Genealogical Publishing Company, Reprint Edition, 1966), 392-393, hereinafter cited as Wheeler, *Reminiscences*; Walter Clark, *History of the Supreme Court of North Carolina* (Raleigh: Reprint from the *North Carolina Booklet,* 1919), 20.

[2]Joseph Allison of Orange County served in the House of Commons (1830-1835) and the state Senate (1835, 1838-1839, 1842-1843). Cheney, *North Carolina Government,* 295-311 passim.

[3]Benjamin Tròllinger of Orange County was a member of the House of Commons (1838-1839) and the Council of State (1855-1857). Cheney, *North Carolina Government*, 178, 309.

[4]John Stockard of Orange County served in the House of Commons (1826-1831, 1833-1839, 1842-1843, 1848-1849). Cheney, *North Carolina Government*, 288-317 passim.

[5]William Alexander Graham (1804-1875), a Hillsborough attorney, was one of the leading Whigs in North Carolina's history. In addition to serving in both houses of the General Assembly, Graham was a United States senator (1840-1843), governor (1845-1849), secretary of the navy (1850-1852), and Confederate States senator (1864). In 1852 he was an unsuccessful candidate for vice-president. *Biographical Directory of Congress*, 965.

[6]Herbert Sims of Orange County served in the House of Commons from 1838 to 1839. Cheney, *North Carolina Government*, 309.

Samuel F. Adams[1] *to David S. Reid* A&H-DSR

Troublesome N.C.
Dec 12th 1838

I reached home last saturday in fine health and find all my family enjoying the same. I wrote to you from Montgomery Alebama and expected to have received a letter from you by the time I reached home but as yet no such has come to hand. Frances received a letter from you the day before I got home and I was glad to hear that you had enjoyed good health since you had been at Raleigh. I have made as good profits on the negroes which I carried out as any of us expected. I think we shall make this trip after paying all expenses $2000. negroes is not olny [*sic*] selling brisk but they are in Considerable demand throughout the States of South Carolina and Georgia and a good many could be sold in the section of Alebama in which I was at the prices which we sold at. but since I reached home I find there is a great rise in the price of negroes here since I left how this will opperate in the south I am unable to say as I dont think the people in south will stand a rise in the prices that they bought at last fall and summer Capt Mattock[2] has not bought a single negro since I left last fall he talks of starting in a few days to some of the upper counties of Virginia for the purpose of buying. we intend to buy again and that as soon as possible as I have before stated myself and family are all in very good health I have just returned home from Reidsville and your father mother and all the family are in very good health no complaint that I heard of Mr Scott requests me to say to you that himself and family are all well and that they each Individually and collectively send you their very best respects there is no news that I have heard of in either the neghborhood of Troublesome [or] Reidsville worthy of relation it appars from the letter which you wrote to Frances that you are progressing slowly with your legislative duties I saw your friend Maj Wright[3] today who appeared to be greatly pleased with certain resolutions which he said had been introduced by a certain Mr. Rainy[4] the only fault which the Maj found of them were that they suited him too well. on my return home seven miles this side of Columbus in Georgia I met a man who informed me that Hugh[5] was just a head of the stage in which I was traveling but he turned off another road before the stage overtook him and I did not see him but the man said he was well and hearty that was about the 28th Ultimo Frances sends her love and respects to you and I do the same.

---

[1] Samuel F. Adams (1807-1869) of Rockingham County was married to Reid's sister Frances (1819-1854). He farmed and engaged in slave trade; in 1850 he owned three slaves. Troublesome post office was located in the southern part of the county near the Troublesome Creek Ironworks. Reese and Fisher, *Settle Family*, 679; Rockingham County Deeds, Book HH, 324, 334, 345, 397; Seventh Census of the United States, 1850: Rockingham County, North Carolina, Slave Schedule, 112, microfilm copy of National Archives manuscript copy, Learning Resources Center, Rockingham Community College, Wentworth, hereinafter cited as Seventh Census, 1850, with appropriate county, schedule, and page numbers; First Baptist Church Cemetery, Reidsville.

[2]This probably refers to Charles Matlock, son of former Rockingham County sheriff John Matlock. In 1830 Charles Matlock owned one slave. Rockingham County Court Minutes, May, 1804, May, 1822; Fifth Census, 1830, Rockingham County, Population Schedule, 288.

[3]John J. Wright, previously identified, of Rockingham County.

[4]Kenneth Rayner (1808-1884), a leading Whig and an attorney from Hertford County, was a delegate to the Constitutional Convention of 1835, member of the House of Commons (1835, 1836, 1846, 1848, and 1850), state senator (1854), and United States congressman (1839-1845). Resolutions he introduced called for rescinding the "expunging resolution," which had removed from congressional records an earlier condemnation of President Andrew Jackson. The Rayner resolutions also criticized two Democratic policies: the subtreasury and surplus revenue distribution. The resolutions were intended to embarrass the Democrats by forcing Senators Robert Strange and Bedford Brown either to consent to the resolutions or resign. The senators refused to accept the resolutions as instructions and resigned just prior to the next legislative elections. The Whigs retained their domination of the General Assembly, and both Brown and Strange were defeated for reelection. Clarence C. Norton, *The Democratic Party in Ante-Bellum North Carolina, 1835-1861* (Chapel Hill: University of North Carolina Press, 1930), 77-78, hereinafter cited as Norton, *Democratic Party; Biographical Directory of Congress,* 1501.

[5] Hugh Kearns Reid (1817-1897) of Reidsville was Reid's brother. A farmer and merchant, he owned twenty-four slaves in 1860. His second wife was Caroline L. Settle, sister of Reid's wife, Henrietta. Reese and Fisher, *Settle Family*, 679; Eighth Census, 1860, Rockingham County, Slave Schedule, 11.

1839

Richard P. Cardwell[1] *to David S. Reid* A&H-DSR

Rockingham Cty N. Carolina
January the 19th 1839

I take this occasion to Drop you a few lines to let you know that I am well and also that I found my family enjoying good health on my arrival at home I have nothing of importance to communicate to you at present I have not been out much among the people but so fare as I have heard there has been no objection urged against our course in the legislature as yet those that I have conversed with seem to concur with us that little has been Done to better the condition of the State and not to be verry well pleased with what has been Done but fortunately for us all the measures I have heard any complaint of we opposed and I tell the whigs they should not complain for it was a good whig Legislature and they could pass any thing they pleased old Mr Searcy[2] says whig or the Devil they have done damed little good, you must write to me whether or no you have heard any more from Brown[3] & Strange[4] and what course they intend to persue you must write to me often, Remember me to the people of your neighbourhood and give my best Respects to your farther and mother and family and I remain your friend with sentiments of the highest respect

---

[1]Richard P. Cardwell (ca. 1795-1850), a farmer and native of Virginia, lived on Beaver Island Creek in western Rockingham County. He served in the House of Commons (1838, 1840, 1842). By 1840 he owned several hundred acres of land and nine slaves. Rockingham County Deeds, EE, 73; HH, 23; KK, 17; Cheney, *North Carolina Government*, 1258; Sixth Census, 1840, Rockingham County, Population Schedule, 128; Seventh Census, 1850, Rockingham County, Mortality Schedule, 567.

[2]Thomas Searcy was clerk of superior court in Rockingham County in the 1830s. In 1840 he had fourteen slaves. *North-Carolina Standard*, August 3, 1837; Sixth Census, 1840, Rockingham County, Population Schedule, 138.

[3]Bedford Brown (1795-1870) of Rose Hill plantation, Caswell County, was a member of the House of Commons and the state Senate. He was elected to the United States Senate in 1829 and served until 1840, when he resigned over the issue of legislative instruction. He returned to the state Senate in 1842 but left North Carolina the next year and lived out of the state until 1852. He was reelected to the state Senate in 1858 and 1860. *Biographical Directory of Congress*, 606.

[4]United States senator Robert Strange, previously identified.

Samuel F. Adams to David S. Reid A&H-DSR

Bell Tavern Richmond Va
March 5th. 1839

Your letter of the 5th Inst. requesting me to purchase for you the *secret debates in the Convention which framed the federal Constitution,*[1] has just been received and I have purchased the book as you desired; I could only find three or four copies in this place, it is, I am told, a late publication, and very much sought after.

I purchased last night at auction, for myself several books, consisting of the history of England, by Hume, Smollett, and Miller,[2] complete in four volumes, price $2.45 per volume: The works of Shakespear[3] complete in 2 volumes, elegently bound in calfskin, with gilt edges, price $1.20 per volume: American Oratory,[4] this work embraces a large collection of speeches delivered by the most eminent American Orators at different times, and uppon various subjects; and is said to be the best specimen of American Eloquence ever published: also the speeches of the celebrated Irish Orators, Philips, Curran, Grattan, and Emmett,[5] the price of each of these works was $1.40, together with a number of others of various kinds; such as Rollins Ancient history[6] complete in eight volumes, elegantly bound at 46 cents per volume, don Quixote,[7] Scottish Chiefs,[8] Children of the Abbey,[9] etc. etc.

I have bought eleven negros and shall start home tomorrow morning. I am very unwell with a bad cold have hear[d] nothing [of] Benj Settle[10]

---

[1]The full title of this book is *Secret Proceedings and Debates of the Convention Assembled at Philadelphia, in the Year 1787, for the Purpose of Forming the Constitution of the United States of America. . . .* Washington: Printed for G. Templeton, 1836. Carol Rinderknecht (comp.), *A Checklist of American Imprints for 1836* (Metuchen, N. J. & London: Scarecrow Press, 1986), 318, hereinafter cited as Rinderknecht, *American Imprints 1836.* There was also an 1833 edition, published in Cincinnati, Ohio, by A. Mygatt. Scott Bruntjen and Carol Rinderknecht Bruntjen (comps.), *A Checklist of American Imprints for 1833* (Metuchen, N. J. & London: Scarecrow Press, 1979), 449, hereinafter cited as Bruntjen and Bruntjen, *American Imprints 1833.* This book was not among those acquired by the state as part of the David S. Reid Book Collection for the North Carolina Museum of History, although the collection contains other volumes of congressional debates.

[2]*The History of England* by David Hume (1711-1776) was a standard work that had been continued, expanded, abridged, and revised by a number of historians, including Tobias George Smollett (1721-1771) and J. R. Miller, whose 4-volume edition was published sometime between 1820 and 1839 in Philadelphia by Thomas, Cowperthwait & Company. David S. Reid owned two other editions: *The History of England from the Invasion of Julius Caesar to the Revolution, In 1688,* by David Hume,

4 volumes, and *The History of England, from the Revolution in 1688, to the Death of George II* (designed as a continuation of Mr. Hume's history), by T[obias]. Smollett, 2 volumes, both editions published by E. Littell in Philadelphia, 1828; Albert M. Hyamson (comp.), *A Dictionary of Universal Biography of All Ages and of All Peoples* (London: George Routledge & Sons; New York: E. P. Dutton, 1916), 318, 607, hereinafter cited as Hyamson, *DUB*; O. A. Roorbach (comp.), *Bibliotheca Americana. Catalogue of American Publications, Including Reprints and Original Works from 1820 to 1852 . . .* (New York: Peter Smith, reprint, 1939), 274, hereinafter cited as Roorbach, *Bibliotheca Americana*; David S. Reid Book Collection.

[3]Although there were numerous American editions of the works of William Shakespeare, O. A. Roorbach does not report a calfskin-bound American edition between 1820 and 1852. Because Adams states that he bought the books he lists at auction, this may have been an older, used set or even an English edition. Roorbach, *Bibliotheca Americana*, 492-493. David S. Reid owned a different edition of Shakespeare, a 9-volume set published in 1812. David S. Reid Book Collection.

[4]This is probably a reference to *American Oratory; or Selections from the Speeches of Eminent Americans 1775-1826*. Compiled by "A Member of the Philadelphia Bar," it was published in Philadelphia by Desilver, Thomas & Company in 1836. Rinderknecht, *American Imprints 1836*, 12.

[5]Probably *Irish Eloquence. The Speeches of the Celebrated Irish Orators Philips, Curran and Grattan to Which Is Added, the Powerful Appeal of Robert Emmet, at the Close of His Trial for High Treason*. Selected by a Member of the Bar. Philadelphia: Desilver, Thomas & Co., 1836. Rinderknecht, *American Imprints 1836*, 211.

[6]This was another standard work, *The Ancient History of the Egyptians, Carthaginians, Assyrians, Babylonians, Medes, and Persians, Macedonians and Grecians*, by Charles Rollin (1661-1741), French educator and historian. Adams could have purchased any one of at least six 8-volume editions printed between 1831 and 1839 by various American publishers. All were simply reprintings of the revised and corrected 15th London edition. David S. Reid owned a 4-volume edition of this work, published in 1827. Hyamson, *DUB*, 555; Carol Rinderknecht (comp.), *A Checklist of American Imprints 1830-1839, Title Index* (Metuchen, N. J. & London: Scarecrow Press, 2 volumes, 1989), I, 64, hereinafter cited as Rinderknecht, *American Imprints 1830-1839, Index*, with appropriate volume and page number; David S. Reid Book Collection.

[7]*Don Quixote*, the classic tragi-comic chivalric work of Spanish author Miguel Cervantes (1547-1616), originally published in 1605, was first translated into English in 1612. The most recent translation available to Adams would have been that done by Tobias George Smollett in 1755. There were numerous American editions of this work, especially in the 1820s. W. N. Hargreaves-Mawdsley, *Everyman's Dictionary of European Writers* (London: J. M. Dent, 1968), 116; M. Frances Cooper (comp.), *A Checklist of American Imprints 1820-1829. Author Index, Corrections & Sources* (Metuchen, N. J.: Scarecrow Press, 1973), 80.

[8]*The Scottish Chiefs, A Romance*, by English-born writer Jane Porter (1776-1850), was originally published in 1810. The story of the life of William Wallace, it was popular with Scottish children. There were at least eight different American editions during the 1830s, so that it is impossible to tell which one Adams may have purchased. D. C. Browning (comp.), *Everyman's Dictionary of Literary Biography* (London: J. M. Dent, fifth edition with supplement, 1969), 544-545; Rinderknecht, *American Imprints 1830-1839, Index*, II, 704.

[9]*The Children of the Abbey*, originally published in 1798, was the "luridly sentimental" and highly popular third novel of Irish writer Regina Maria Roche (1764-1845). There were three American editions during the 1830s, all published by the J. and B. Williams Company of Exeter, New Hampshire. Stanley J. Kunitz and Howard Haycroft (eds.), *British Authors of the Nineteenth Century* (New York: H. W. Wilson, 1936), 525; Rinderknecht, *American Imprints 1830-1839, Index*, I, 179; Roorbach, *Bibliotheca Americana*, 160.

[10]Benjamin Settle (1806-1861) of Rockingham County was Reid's first cousin. He married Sarah Campbell in December, 1845, and was killed in Mississippi during the Civil War. Reese and Fisher, *Settle Family*, 350. See Weldon H. Wright to David S. Reid, December 24, 1845, Private Collections, David S. Reid Papers, PC 1, Archives, Division of Archives and History, Raleigh, hereinafter cited as Reid Papers, PC 1, State Archives.

David S. Reid to William Stringer[1] Duke-DSR

[Copy]

Reidsville, Rockingham Co.
June 15th, 1839.

I received yours of the 10th inst on yesterday I return you my thanks for the information you have furnished in relation to the present prospect of our party in this State, I hope the event may realize your expectations. In this district I think our prospect favorable, but I think the majority will be small, not more than 100 either way. If we can get a general turn out on the day of election, in the Counties of Rockingham Stokes and Caswell we may perhaps beat Shepperd[2] 300 votes. Where parties are so nearly balanced the result must be doubtful.

You are mistaken, when you say Branch[3] beat Dudley[4] 179 votes in this district. It occurs no doubt, from omiting *Guilford County* which belongs to this district and gives a whig *majority* of *from 12 to 1400 votes*. In 1837 Shepperd majority in that county was 1400. There is no doubt but Rockingham, Caswell and Stokes will each give Mr. Hill[5] a majority as they did in 1837.

You wish me to state when the musters take place in the several Counties composing this district. Upon this subject I am not sufficiently informed at present to answer you. In this county the Battalion musters will have been over before you could reach here. The Company musters will take place between this and the election but there is no regularity observed in the times for holding them, they often conflict, two or more happening on the same day. I presume the candidates will not attend many of them. I do not know any thing about the arrangements in Guilford and Stokes. In Caswell, I believe they have gatherings that take place and continue in regular order with a view to accomdate candidates and others who may choose to attend. I think it likely that the Candidates will not attend very many of these small gatherings. You would find it a very difficult matter to hire or buy a saddle Horse in this neighborhood at this season of the year. I have been trying to buy one my self but can not find a saddle horse for sale. I know of no place at this time where you would be certain to meet with the Candidates. You enquire whether I entend going round the Campaign myself. I do not. I may attend a few promenent gatherings in this County *where business may call me.*

If you conclude to visit this part of the State you must call on me, and be assured that it will afford me great pleasure to see you, Perhaps when you get here I can put you on the track of the Candidates

You wish me to state what are the grounds upon which Mr Hill expects to defeat Mr Shepperd. I have hastely written you a *Chapter* upon the subject which will afford you a view of some of the grounds upon which he *ought* to beat him. If Mr. Loring[6] thinks it can be of any service to our cause I have no objections to its appering in the Standard. As a politician Mr. Shepperds course is vulnerable, perhaps as much so as that any of politician in the State. he is not only so in relation to the subjects that I have mentioned, but upon many others.

Be so good as to remember me in terms of respect to my friend Mr. Loring

---

[1]William Stringer was in Raleigh in 1839, working for Thomas Loring, the publisher of the *North-Carolina Standard.* By 1846 Stringer had moved to Wilmington and was the copublisher of the *Commercial.* Guion G. Johnson, *Ante-Bellum North Carolina: A Social History* (Chapel Hill: University of North Carolina Press, 1937), 773, hereinafter cited as Johnson, *Ante-Bellum North Carolina.*

[2]Augustine Henry Shepperd (1792-1864) of Forsyth County was originally from Rockford, Surry County, where he practiced law. As a Democrat he was a member of the House of Commons (1822-1826) and the United States Congress (1827-1839). He broke with the Democratic party and returned to Congress as a Whig (1841-1843, 1847-1851). He defeated Reid in 1841 in Reid's first race for Congress. *Biographical Directory of Congress,* 1592.

[3]John Branch (1782-1863) of Halifax County was a state senator for several terms, governor of North Carolina (1817-1820), federal judge in Florida (1822), United States senator (1823-1829), secretary of the navy (1829-1831), United States congressman (1831-1833), and the last territorial governor of Florida (1844-1845). Originally a Jacksonian Democrat, he opposed Van Buren, a course that eventually led him to the Whig party. *Biographical Directory of Congress,* 588-589.

[4]Edward Bishop Dudley, previously identified.

[5]John Hill (1797-1861) of Germanton, Stokes County, was clerk of superior court for thirty years. He served in the House of Commons (1819-1823), the state Senate for several terms, and was elected as a Democrat to the United States Congress (1839-1841). He died in Raleigh while attending the state Secession Convention. *Biographical Directory of Congress*, 1053.

[6]Thomas Loring purchased the *North-Carolina Standard*, which became the state's leading Democratic newspaper, from Philo White in 1836. Friction with Democratic leaders led to Loring's sale of the *Standard* to William W. Holden in 1843. Loring subsequently defected to the Whig party. Norton, *Democratic Party*, 14, 17.

Militia Return from Richard C. Stubblefield[1] *to David S. Reid* A&H-DSR

[Rockingham County]
[1839]

Anual return of a company of militia attached to the Sixty- seventh Regiment of N.C. Militia under the command of R C Stubblefield, for the year 1839.

Captains	—	1
Leutenants	—	3
Ensigns	—	1
Musicians	—	2
Sergeants	—	1
Privates	—	80
		88
Swords	—	2
Drums	—	1
Fifes	—	1
Shot Guns	—	70

[1]Richard C. Stubblefield, a militia captain, lived in eastern Rockingham County on Wolf Island Creek. He was the son of Richard C. Stubblefield, Sr., who died in 1847. Will of Richard C. Stubblefield, Sr., July 30, 1844, Rockingham County Wills, Book C, 52 (microfilm), Archives, Division of Archives and History, Raleigh, hereinafter cited as Stubblefield Will.

1840

David S. Reid to Beverly Daniel[1] A&H-DSR
[Copy]

Reidsville, N.C.
Monday, Feb'y 17, 1840

Your letter of the 11th inst. was received on Saturday, but not in time for me to answer you by that days mail. Sensible of the Confidence you have been pleased to place in me in submitting to my judgement certain matters contained in your letter, I should prove recreant to my own sense of propriety were I not to be governed by Candor in my reply.

Having been requested some weeks ago to state to you the qualifications of Mr. Sharp[2] I confined myself to facts that I felt warranted in Stating; but in doing so, I had not the least idea of desparaging the claims of Col. Scales.[3] That letter was written with the understanding that the application for Col Scales had been *unfavorably* received and that another individual was about to receive the appointment. And that the object of my first letter may not be misconstrued, I feel it due to state that Col Scales is a gentleman of a liberal Education and his moral habits are certainly unquestionable: his Capacity—and application added to a tolerable acquaintance in the County will enable him to perform the duties of the appointment faithfully and efficiently. *I consider either of the gentlemen well qualified*: But I can not say "that the interest of the State, or the object of the law for taking the Census would be *more faithfully and effectually* accomplished by Substituting Mr Sharp in the place of Col Scales. After his name has been announced, Col Scales, who is a young man of nice sensibility, would no doubt feel much mortified if he were superseded

With these statements I decline to make a decision as to the distinction of the papers you enclosed me: if you desire that they should take effect, under *your Special instructions alone*, Shall I consider myself at liberty to give them a direction; otherwise they will be destroyed as you requested. I shall therefore retain them till I hear from you. My respects & best wishes. In haste.

P.S. You need have no doubts as to Col Scale's qualifications. I would like to be informed if either of the gentlemen knows that this matter has been submitted to me.

[1]Beverly Daniel of Wake County was adjutant general of North Carolina (1821-1840). Cheney, *North Carolina Government*, 183.

[2]Probably a reference to Hiram Sharp, captain of a militia district in Rockingham County in 1840. Rockingham County Court Minutes, May, 1839-February, 1840. Before township lines were surveyed in counties, militia districts—frequently designated by their captain's surnames—were utilized as federal census enumeration units. Hence the involvement of the state adjutant general in appointment of census takers.

[3]Peter Scales was appointed district census taker of Rockingham County in 1840. He was in the House of Commons (1842-1845), and in 1846 he was serving as justice of the peace. In 1840 he had ten slaves. Rockingham County Court Minutes, February, 1846; Sixth Census, 1840, Rockingham County, Population Schedule, 134; Cheney, *North Carolina Government*, 1258.

John M. Rose[1] *to David S. Reid* A&H-DSR

Head Quarters
Madison
9 Aug 1840

You are hereby commanded to parade the regt. under your command at Reidsville, on Wednesday the 14 Oct next at the hour of 10 o clk armed & equipt as the law directs for review & Inspection
By order of Brig Genl. S. A. Dalton[2]

[1]John M. Rose, a Madison merchant, was active in Whig politics in Rockingham County. He later moved to Fayetteville. Shanks, *Mangum Papers*, III, 46, 48.

[2]Samuel A. Dalton of Madison served in the militia during the War of 1812. He was brigadier general of the Eighth Brigade during the time Reid commanded the Sixty-seventh Regiment. Dalton was elected major general of the Ninth Division and received his commission January 22, 1841. In that same year he served on the county Democratic committee. Governors Office Records, "Commissions and Resignations, 1841-1855"; Committee to David S. Reid, April 30, 1845, Reid Papers PC 1, State Archives.

Quinton Anderson[1] *to David S. Reid* A&H-DSR

Anderson's Store N C.
5th Septemr 1840

Your very friendly letter of the 16th Ulto was receivd by last mail I cannot conjecture why it was long on its passage but may be the Van Buren mails are Slow under misfortune. I was pleased to see that Rockingham acted in her proper character and am pleased that Caswell has so Chaste a Sister.

but oh, the elections throughout the State how painful the reflection that every Department of the State Government is to be under the controul of Whigery and the Senators to congress both whigs Pity, pity, that this political paradise should be turned into a *Hell* but friend David Dont give up the Ship let us hope there is a redeeming spirit in the people.

I am under obligation to you for attending to the collection of my claim against Simpson[2]

Your claim against Noah Hall[3] is in process of collection and is believd to be safe

let me hear from you at your leisure hours.

---

[1]Quinton Anderson of Anderson's Store, Caswell County, was a merchant and postmaster from 1841 to 1854. A county justice, he also provided leadership in establishing public schools and in railroad development. During the October 1840 term of the Caswell County Court of Pleas and Quarter Sessions, Anderson served as a judge. William S. Powell, *When the Past Refused to Die: A History of Caswell County, North Carolina, 1777-1977* (Durham: Moore Publishing Company, 1977), 174, 314, 316, 373, 499, hereinafter cited as Powell, *Caswell County*; Minutes of the Caswell County Court of Pleas and Quarter Sessions, October Term, 1840, p. 153 (microfilm), Archives, Division of Archives and History, Raleigh.

[2]Mr. Simpson has not been identified, although he may be the same Simpson mentioned in a January 28, 1845, letter to Reid from Rockingham County resident Joseph W. Neal.

[3]Noah Hall was in 1840 a resident of Orange County. He may have lived in that portion of Orange from which Alamance County was created in 1849. Anderson's Store was located near what was in 1840 the Caswell-Orange county line. Sixth Census, 1840, Orange County, Population Schedule, 183; William S. Powell, *The North Carolina Gazetteer: A Dictionary of Tar Heel Places* (Chapel Hill: University of North Carolina Press, 1968), 5, hereinafter cited as Powell, *North Carolina Gazetteer*.

William Montgomery[1] *to David S. Reid* A&H-DSR

Albrights N. C.
Sept 12th 40.

I have an appointment to meet a large crowd of people at the Store of Jesse Thompson[2] in Guilford County, on the 26th Inst. to meet charges made against me by Js. Morehead[3] & G. Mendinghall[4] at that place during the late canvass, I expect to have the Ohio Journal there to show Harrisons vote to sell white men and women, and a certified copy of the Indiana selling law[5]; should be happy to see you there Mo & M will be there.

I intend to show some other of Harrisons votes Relative to Slavery, and show by the Journals of the 25th congress that the whigs voted for all the appropriations they complain of Gardeners Salary and all, Also that they have 3 times recorded there names against punishing those who plunder and steal the publick money, I shall want some assistance to Examine and read, & hope you will aid me, I have written Capt Berry[6] our Editor to come up and also Mr. Guinn.[7]

---

[1]William Montgomery (1789-1844) was a physician in Albrights, Orange County. As a Democrat he served in the state Senate (1824-1827, 1829-1834) and in the United States House of Representatives (1835-1841). *Biographical Directory of Congress*, 1347.

[2]The Whig newspaper in Greensboro reported a few days later: "A political discussion took place at Mr. Jesse Thompson's Store, in the northeastern part of this county on Saturday last, between the Hon. Wm. Montgomery and James T. Morehead, Esq." The reporter claimed that Morehead got the better of Dr. Montgomery, "who fell very far short of the expectations of a good many that went to hear him; and, taking his speech on Saturday as a sample of his abilities, the wonder seems to be, how he has ever managed to *navigate* among the people so well as he has." *Greensborough Patriot*, September 29, 1840.

[3]James Turner Morehead (1799-1875), brother of Governor John M. Morehead, was an attorney in Greensboro. A leading Whig politician, Morehead served five terms in the state Senate from 1835 to 1842 and was in Congress from 1851 to 1853. An 1819 graduate of the state university, he served there as a trustee from 1836 to 1868. *Biographical Directory of Congress*, 1354.

[4]George C. Mendenhall (d. 1860), an attorney from Guilford County, was in the state Senate (1833-1834) and the House of Commons (1828-1831, 1840-1843). Wheeler, *Reminiscences*, 192; Shanks, *Mangum Papers*, III, 408; Cheney, *North Carolina Government*, 1152-1153.

[5]While William Henry Harrison was territorial governor of Indiana, a law was passed permitting individuals to hire prisoners convicted of minor offences. Although the law explicitly forbade the hiring of whites by free blacks, Democrats erroneously interpreted the law as subjecting whites to a form of slavery. The law

was a practical measure in a sparsely populated territory; and considering the conditions in jails of that period, the law could be termed a reform. Norton, *Democratic Party*, 87-88.

[6]John Berry (1798-1870), an architect and builder from Hillsborough, was in 1840 a Democratic candidate for presidential elector from the 8th district, consisting of Person, Orange, and Granville counties. He later served as a state senator (1848-1852, 1864-1865, 1866-1867) and a delegate to the state constitutional conventions of 1861 and 1865. *North-Carolina Standard*, October 14, 1840; Hugh Lefler and Paul Wager (eds.), *Orange County—1752-1952* (Chapel Hill: Orange Printshop, 1953), 324, hereinafter cited as Lefler and Wager, *Orange County*; Cheney, *North Carolina Government*, 825, 832, 1227.

[7]Probably a reference to Littleton A. Gwynn of Yanceyville, who was in 1840 the Democratic candidate for presidential elector from the 5th district, which consisted of Rockingham, Stokes, and Caswell counties. Gwynn served also in 1840 as a district school superintendent. A trustee of the Dan River Institute, he was a member of the House of Commons (1830-1839), and a state senator (1844-1845). *Lincoln Republican* (Lincolnton), October 14, 1840, hereinafter cited as *Lincoln Republican*; Powell, *Caswell County*, 369, 373, 549, 550.

Anonymous Rockingham County Farmer to Thomas Loring[1] NCC

Rockingham County
Sept. 14*th*, 1840.

EDITORS' CORRESPONDENCE.

I am a farmer, and have never undertook to write any thing for the public eye before,[2] I wish you to say to the good people of this State, that the Democrats of old Rockingham are not dead yet, although they have been a little disappointed in the late election. On Tuesday of our August Court, we had Mr. Mebane,[3] the whig Elector to address us; the democratic Elector was not present owing to the death of his child.[4] Mr. Mebane addressed us at great length; he went on to say a good deal about the standing army, as he chose to call Mr. Poinsett's[5] plan for the re-organization of the Militia. From that he went to the Expenditures of the government; he dwelt loud and long upon the quills and penknifes, but forgot to tell the good people of Rockingham how many had been used under previous administrations; he next went to the Census. He said that Mr. *Van Buren* was a going to lay a direct tax, or he would not have had the statistical information taken in regard to the chickens and ducks. Oh, how inconsistent those whigs are. Mr. A. H. Sheppard[6] the late whig member of Congress from this district, voted for that information to be taken, and then behold they turn around and blame Van Buren for it. After this he said that Van Buren had received negro testimony against white men!—Shame to any party who would resort to such base falsehoods to deceive the people.[7] During his remarks he stated that he had been called a federalist. He finally came to a close by saying he hoped the people would vote for him, &c.

Loud calls were made for Col. David S. Reid; he stated that he had not expected to make a speech on the occasion, but as his friends had called on him he concluded to reply to Mr. Mebane, and I do assure you that I never heard a man get such a rattling in my life as friend Mebane got.—Well may old Rockingham be proud of such a son as Col. Reid. Mebane was obliged to acknowledge that the whigs did wrong sometimes.—I am of the opinion he will not come to Rockingham again soon; the whigs all stayed and heard Mebane, but when the Colonel began to salt him they began to dodge out of the Court House, one by one, till friend Mebane was left almost friendless in the hour of his trouble. Even Governor Morehead left. I assure you it did revive the democrats of old Rockingham, and they seem determined to do their duty in November.[8]

---

[1]Thomas Loring, previously identified, was editor (December 28, 1836-1843) of the *North-Carolina Standard*, in which this letter was published on October 7, 1840. Mary Wescott and Allene Ramage (comps.), *Bibliographical Contributions of the Duke University Libraries: A Checklist of United States Newspapers (And Weeklies before 1900) in the General Library* (Durham: Duke University, six parts, 1932-1937), part V, 622, hereinafter cited as Wescott and Ramage, *Duke Newspaper Checklist*, with appropriate part and page number.

[2]William W. Holden noted in his memoirs that the Democratic party in the early 1840s had not more than eight thousand members in the entire state, and that most of these were rural dwellers, in the lowest social classes. In contrast, the Whigs, he wrote, lived mainly in the towns and villages and possessed a large proportion of "the intelligence and all the decency," supporting the reforms of public education and internal improvements, whereas the Democrats tended to be "ignorant, awkward, and opposed to reform." Horace W. Raper, *William W. Holden: North Carolina's Political Enigma* (Chapel Hill: University of North Carolina Press, 1985), 10-11, hereinafter cited as Raper, *William W. Holden.*

[3]James Mebane of Caswell County was the Whig candidate for presidential elector for the Fifth District, which consisted of Rockingham, Caswell, and Stokes counties. He also spoke at the Whig festival at Yanceyville on October 1, 1840, which the Democratic press reported was a failure, attracting only 300 people, but which the Whig press countered by claiming that 1,500 were present. All fifteen Whig candidates for presidential elector were victorious in North Carolina in 1840. *Raleigh Register*, August 14, 1840; *North-Carolina Standard*, October 7, 1840; *Raleigh Star, and North Carolina Gazette*, November 4, 1840, hereinafter cited as *Raleigh Star*.

[4]Littleton Gwynn, previously identified, was the Democratic party candidate for presidential elector in 1840 for the Fifth District. *Lincoln Republican*, October 14, 1840.

[5]Joel Roberts Poinsett (1779-1851), a South Carolina congressman (1821-1825), resigned to enter diplomatic service and was minister to Mexico (1825-1829). Upon his return home, he openly sided with President Andrew Jackson during the Nullification controversy, formed a pro-Union militia and commanded it in Charleston. As a reward, he became secretary of war (1837-1841) in the Van Buren administration, during which time he attempted to reorganize the militia nationwide. He wrote articles on science, agriculture, manufacturing, and botany; the poinsettia is named for him. David C. Roller and Robert W. Twyman (eds.), *The Encyclopedia of Southern History* (Baton Rouge: Louisiana State University Press, 1979), 987, hereinafter cited as *Encyclopedia of Southern History*.

[6]Augustine Henry Shepperd, previously identified, of Surry County.

[7]Van Buren was referred to derisively in Whig newspapers as "the Negro Witness Chief." *Raleigh Star*, October 21, 1840.

[8]Democratic party candidates carried all major races in Rockingham County in 1840. David S. Reid was reelected to the state Senate, George D. Boyd and Richard P. Cardwell were elected to the House of Commons, gubernatorial candidate Romulus M. Saunders out-polled his Whig opponent John M. Morehead, 1000-533, and in the presidential race, Democrat Martin Van Buren defeated Whig opponent William H. Harrison, 905-547. Cheney, *North Carolina Government*, 310, 311, 1329, 1397.

David S. Reid to Larkin Stowe[1] and Committee of Invitations[2] A&H-mn

Rockingham County, (N. C.,)
Sept. 28th, 1840.

Your invitation to attend the celebration at King's Mountain battle ground, on the 7th of October was received yesterday. To be at such a place, among Democrats so true, and engaged in so great a cause would afford me the highest pleasure; but other engagements will not permit me to be there. The great issue to be decided by the people of the United States involves questions of paramount importance and it becomes every admirer of free Government to weigh well the consequences that may follow a defeat and overthrow of the Democratic Republican party. The subject is too serious to be treated lightly. That factious spirit which has ever been the bane of Republics, is making rapid strides in our happy and peaceful land. We behold a political party comprising every faction that has grown up since the formation of our government, arrayed in the same cause, acting in common concert, and with the most untiring zeal and indefatigable industry that ever characterized a political party in this or any other country. While the Democratic Republicans have been relying upon the correctness of their cause, for success, the leaders of the opposition under the name of "Whigs," have deceived and misled the unwary until their numbers have increased to an extent that they believe will enable them to seize the reins of Government; and in the execution of their designs, they seem as regardless of the means employed as they are of the welfare of the country or the perpetuity of our free institutions. They claim for the Federal Government powers which the States have never granted: They have attempted to subject the people to the rule of irresponsible corporations, and to sell their rights in the name of charters: They have been instrumental in burdening the country with Foreign debts: They have by a tariff endeavored to tax the *South* to carry on works of Internal Improvement unauthorised by the Constitution: They have, by brow-beating, and proposing enactments in Congress, attempted to restrain the liberty of speech: They have endeavored to destroy the great and inestimable right of suffrage, by substituting the will of a *Whig Governor* in the place of the votes of the freemen of a sovereign State: They are making common cause with the Abolitionists in the support of the same individual for the Presidency, and, by about one half of the whole whig party in Congress favoring the right of petition on the subject of slavery: They use every means in their power to embarrass the action of the Federal Government to bring our chief Magistrate into disrepute: They denounce our Government as a "Monarchy." They take the bold and aristocratic ground that the people have not the right to require their candidates to give public pledges and seem determined to use both fraud and force in accomplishing their purposes.—And to aid in the consummation of their designs, they present to us in the person of Wm: H. Harrison a Candidate for the Presidency. It does seem that if there had existed a doubt as to the identity of the leaders of the present whig party with the old Federalists, this nomination must have afforded the most convincing proof of the fact.—Gen. Harrison's speech in favour of the standing Army of the elder Adams, his own admissions, and other evidence upon the subject, shows that *he did not oppose the Black Cockade Federal Administration of old John Adams*, if they do not establish the fact that he positively did give his support to every leading measure of that Administration. From 1800 up to the election of John Q. Adams there was no Federal Administration for him to support. In 1825, we find him a warm supporter of the Administration of Mr. Adams, who it is notoriously known was nominated by, and received the support of the Federal party; and his election to the Presidency, through intrigue, against the known wishes of a majority of the people was openly denounced by the Republicans throughout the United States. Was Gen. Harrison with us then? No: He was found supporting the federal Administration of Mr. Adams and the fraud which had been perpetrated upon the elective franchise.—He continued his support of that Administration throughout, and was the warm advocate for Mr. Adam's [*sic*] election for a "*second term.*" Shortly before the close of that Administration he was rewarded with a little appointment on a Foreign mission, the duties of which he did not satisfactorily perform, and he was recalled by Gen. Jackson soon after his Administration commenced. For this act, Gen. Jackson was assailed by the whole Federal party, but was triumphantly sustained in it, by the Republican party, upon the ground that Gen. Harrison was UNFIT to discharge the duties of the appointment. But many of those who *then* pronounced him unfit to fill the little mission to Columbia, have since apostacised from the Republican ranks, and are *now* loudest in chanting the praises of the "Hero" of Tippecanoe!! Did we find him with the republican party in 1836?—No; no: He was then a candidate for the Presidency, run by the Federalists and Abolitionists of the north, with Francis Grainger, of New York, *an Abolitionist*! on the ticket with him a Candidate for the Vice Presidency. At that time no man that, I heard of, in N. C., had the temerity to advocate his claims to the Presidency, and it was considered by a Bank whig as "*rather personal*" for a democrat to make such an allusion! Has Gen. Harrison fought any battle or moved into a log cabin since that time? Strange to tell he has not! But why has this mighty change come over the leaders of that party? A disclosure of the proceedings of their midnight conclaves could answer this question, and present astounding facts to the people! "*An eloquent record*" has [been] manufactured to betray the honest; party discipline has been enforced, and the tourniquet of the money power has been screwed-up to the *last notch* to subdue the timid; and a blare of misguided enthusiasm, fed by falsehood and vituperation, has been kindled, to effect by Passion's storm what could not be done by Reason's calm. All these things, and many more, have been done to consummate their unhallowed designs. And the enemy up by success and ripe for the most ruthless proscription, are now perching upon the body politic, ready to seize with vulture fangs the vitals of the Constitution, and it becomes every true patriot to pause and reflect before it be too late! Every man owes a higher duty to himself and to his country, than to party. The contest is between Wm: H. Harrison and the factions of Federalism, on one side, and Martin Van Buren and the friends of the constitution and Equal Rights, on the other; and let us in the spirit of brothers, invoke those who have imbitered unfounded prejudices against Mr. Van Buren, to sacrifice them upon the altar of the common good, and aid us in rescuing the constitution and the Union from the impending danger. Let us not be dismayed, for the cause of Democracy, is founded upon the great and immutable principles of Truth and Justice.

---

[1]Larkin Stowe, a resident of Lincoln County, was chairman of the Committee of Invitations for the October 7, 1840, Democratic party celebration of the anniversary of the October 7, 1780, Revolutionary battle of King's Mountain. Stowe later served in the House of Commons (1842-1843), state Senate (1844-1847), and on the Council of State (1855). *Lincoln Republican*, October 14, 1840; Powell, *North Carolina Gazetteer*, 265; Cheney, *North Carolina Government*, 178, 312, 313, 315.

[2]The Committee of Invitations sent letters of invitation to a number of Democratic party leaders, several of whom delivered addresses at the King's Mountain celebration, which lasted two days. Letters received from Reid and others unable to attend were read aloud to the gathering, which voted that they be published. Stowe, as committee chairman, accordingly had the letters printed in his local Democratic party newspaper, the *Lincoln Republican*, published by Robert Williamson, Jr., in Lincolnton. The *North-Carolina Standard* in Raleigh carried an account of the meeting but did not reprint the letters of regret. *Lincoln Republican*, October 14, 1840; *North-Carolina Standard*, November 4, 1840.

1841

Bedford Brown to David S. Reid A&H-DSR

Caswell, N.C.
31st March 1841

I write you a line to Say, that I attended Court, this week and had an opportunity of ascertaining public Sentiment extensively, in regard, to who Should become the Candidate of the Democratic party, in this District, for Congress.

I can inform you, with the most entire candour that there is but one Sentiment, in favor of your being the candidate, among the Democratic party and public opinion, is the more completely united on your name, as Mr. Calvin Graves[1] positively declines. I think I may Say, if you are a candidate that you will receive a greater majority of votes than Mr. Hill did, in our County, by fifty or Sixty.

I earnestly trust that you will comply with the wishes of your friends and immediately declare yourself. Since Mr. Hill has declined, my belief is that you are the next Strongest in the District. If you are victorious the honor will be great, if defeated you will have fallen in a glorious cause and it will be more credit to you, to be defeated as the champion of liberty, than victory will confer on the adversary of popular rights. The madness of the federal party since they have come into power—their violation of every promise made by them—their precipitancy and insidious designs in calling an extra Session— their evident intention to carry the elections by *a Surprise* upon the people, will all form powerful topics to attack the new administration on and cannot fail, to aid your election. If you will consent to come out, do so promptly and immediately and go to Stokes Court and make a bold address to the people. I know that you have both the capacity and the firmness to meet the crisis and may effect much, by activity and public addresses.

Our County did not hold any public meeting, as it was believed if it took the lead, in nominating, that it would form a topic for federalism to make the charge of *Caswell dictation.*

The federalists will hold a District convention in Greensborough. This will not aid them, as it will be viewed as an attempt to dictate to the people. I again Say, if you can be prevailed on, to offer, *take the field immediately* as there is no time to lose. Any delay in doing so, would be a disadvantage, as the federal candidate Spoken of is personally known more extensively, in Stokes and Guilford than yourself.

I write in haste and am much and truly yours

[1]Calvin Graves (1804-1878), a Caswell County attorney, was the brother-in-law of Reid's uncle Thomas Settle. Graves served in the House of Commons (1840-1845) and was speaker for one term; he served in the state Senate (1846-1849), as speaker during his last term. He is noted for casting the tie-breaking vote for the North Carolina Railroad bill that ended his political career in 1849. He was a trustee of the University of North Carolina from 1844 to 1868 and served on the Board of Internal Improvements. Powell, *Caswell County*, 149-151.

Thomas Settle to David S. Reid A&H-DSR

Kinston Lenoir County N. Ca.
September 19th 1841

You will permit me to ask the favour of you to write to some friend of yours in the town of Germanton or its vicinity and ascertain whether lime can be procured there & the terms. If you will do so you will confer a great favour on me & communicate the result of the information to your Aunt Henrietta. I got to the commencement of my circuit in good time & have enjoyed tolorably good health since I have been down here. Hope you are all in good health. There is much confusion & speculation here in relation to the disolution of the late Cabinet. What may be the result to both or either of the two great political parties it is difficult no[w] to see.[1] I have written to your Aunt that I have written to you in relation to the lime I want & that when you get the desired information you will give the same to her. Let me hear from you how you are, how the family is & what they are doing in our neighbourhood

[1]On September 11, 1841, Tyler's cabinet, which he had inherited from the late president William Henry Harrison, resigned over the president's veto of the second bank bill. Secretary of State Daniel Webster was the only member of the cabinet who remained with the president. North Carolinian George E. Badger, who was secretary of the navy, resigned with the other cabinet members. Oliver Perry Chitwood, *John Tyler: Champion of the Old South* (New York: Russell and Russell, reprint, 1964), 272-273, hereinafter cited as Chitwood, *Tyler*.

Romulus Mitchell Saunders (1791-1867) of Caswell and Wake counties was a superior court judge and a member of the state House of Commons. In 1840, as Democratic candidate for governor, he was defeated by John Motley Morehead. Saunders served five terms in the United States House of Representatives between 1821 and 1845. Photograph from negative originally in the possession of M. Q. Plumblee.

Calvin Graves (1804-1878), a Caswell County attorney, was the brother-in-law of Reid's uncle, Thomas Settle. He served as speaker of the state House of Commons and Senate. Graves, a Democrat, was appointed to the Board of Internal Improvements by Whig governor John Manly. He continued to serve on the board during Reid's administrations. Engraving from John Livingston's *Portraits of Eminent Americans Now Living*... (New York: R. Craighead, Printer, 1854), facing 375.

Robert Strange (1796-1864), Fayetteville attorney, was a member of the state House of Commons, lieutenant colonel in the Cumberland County militia, and a state superior court judge. In 1840, four years after his election to the United States Senate, he and fellow Democrat Bedford Brown became locked in conflict with the Whig General Assembly. After resigning from the Senate in protest, they failed in their bids for reelection. Photograph of portrait from the Albert Barden Collection, Division of Archives and History.

Bedford Brown (1795-1870) of Caswell County served in both houses of the North Carolina General Assembly and in the United States Senate. In March 1841, shortly after his resignation from the Senate, Brown wrote Reid urging him to become a Democratic candidate for the House of Representatives. Copy of Matthew Brady photograph courtesy of the North Carolina Collection, University of North Carolina Library at Chapel Hill.

1842

James Phelps[1] *to David S. Reid* A&H-DSR

Hitchcockville[2] [Connecticut]
February 15th 1842

I have the pleasure to acknowledge the receipt of several newpapers, since I last saw you engaged in the arduous duties, and the high responsibilities of legislation at your Capitol[3]—I have also for a long time past, lived in the fond anticipation, that a communication from your pen was forthcoming, & speedily, but alas! every hope I have so anxiously indulged, and every pleasing anticipation of this so good fortune, has risen up in my mind but to be crushed by disappointment, and regret. "Hope deferred makes the heart sick," and is but poor and insufficient satisfaction, and I have therefore assumed the privilege, (may you not consider it presumption) to break the spell that has unhappily to me, interposed to arrest the course of that friendly correspondence which has been dearly esteemed on my part—I am aware it may be comparatively, and perhaps entirely, disinteresting, to you, on account of the discrepancy that prevails in the subject matter of our communications, arising necessarily in part from the differences in age and capacity by which we are separated, yet, I trust this apologetic preface will be in your estimation a sufficient atonement for my writing at this time—

Since I came from Carolina I have devoted most of my time to the prosecution of my studies preparatory to entering upon the Legal Profession, the last few months of which I have spent at New Haven in the enjoyment of the classic influences of "Old Yale" which are so liberally and so beneficially dispensed upon the minds of very many youth who have chosen for their avocation the flowery walks of Science—I left N. Haven a few days since at the solicitation of my friends on account of ill health, which I am so unwise as to imagine has been injured by too severe application—I have not however relinquished my studies, but continue to devote all the time and service to them which the state of my health will permit. I am occasionally driven to the unhappy reflection that I shall be compelled ultimately to an entire abandonment of my Books and the adoption of some other pursuit more congenial to my constitution if indeed there be any refuge of this character that will enable me to escape from what I sometimes fancy impending danger. I am sometimes harrased with the melancholy apprehension that my brightest prospects will soon be clouded by the rayless darkness of the sepulcher, and that I already behold the unerring premonitions of approaching dissolution—This may be but the offspring of diseased imagination—the creature of disordered fancy, which may God in mercy grant—But if it so be that my doom is written I can obey the awful summons with cheerful confidence in the goodness of God through Christ, and lay aside the vainly anticipated earthly land, for the Amaranth of immortality—Were my health and ability equal to my ambition, I would not despair of being one day entitled to the proud distinction of a constitutional Lawyer, which sounds in my ear with peculiar charms and which I recognize as one of the most honorable titles by which man can be distinguished, and is especially the child of republican institutions which we all revere—There are many such and an infinitely greater number more appropriately qualified for the humble occupation of "hewers of wood, and drawers of water"—

It is with feelings of gratitude to our countrymen, and especially to the sovereign Arbiter of nations, that I congratulate you upon the recent achievements of Democracy throughout the Union—The sacred principle was apparently almost extinguished by the disaster that attended the great campaign of 1840, yet its vitality survived that embittered contest from which it has arisen Phoenix like to its present proud ascendency. It was purged in that ordeal of every excrescence which had hitherto impeded its vigor, and prevented its more extentsive dissemination, and now stands forth arrayed in the purity and legitimacy of its true character. To this circumstance in no small degree may be justly attributed the conquering march of its resistless career. Its principles are akin to the great precepts inculcated by the true followers of Christ, and it is emphatically the political gospel of the world, seeking to elevate no man above his neighbor in point of privilege, but to establish the rights and the freedom of all upon a basis of Equality, This is the doctrine of consistent, unqualified, and universal, liberty in its broadest and most comprehensive signification, than which, none can be better adapted to the interest and welfare of our race. This I consider true Democracy & for such a principle do I contend. It is far better to be a "humble fisherman" under the protection of such a government, than to sit enthroned in princely splendor over millions of slaves—Take from the people the power to appoint their public Officers and to sit in solemn judgement upon their conduct, and you restrain at once their proper authority. Abridge the right of citizenship, and encumber the elective franchise with qualifications excepting only infamy of character, non-residence, and minority, and you "lay the axe at the root" of free and equal privilege, and deprive a portion of the people of the most exalted attributes of sovereignity—

Our State Election takes place the first Monday in April—Our enemies prevailed last year by a majority of 6,000 votes. The democratic State Convention has been holden and the candidates for State Offices put in nomination—The Ticket is by no means the most popular which might have been selected, which is a very unfortunate circumstance at this particular crisis—It is believed if a different set of candidates had been presented the party might prevail, and there is yet hope—The choice of a U.S. Senator devolves upon the Legislature to be chosen which increases the importance of the election. The chances of securing a majority of the Legislature are more favorable than for the election of State Officers, as our Cities give a large majority for the Whigs but send no more members to the Gen. Assembly than the smaller towns—Be assured our friends will do battle manfully—It is their paramount duty to strive to advance their principles with uncompromising zeal and unfaltering energy. I regret that my age prevents my participation but my sympathy is fully offered—It will be with the greatest satisfaction when the time does arrive, that enables me to avail myself of the freemen's oath and engage in the duties it enjoins, and when I prove recreant by a violation or disregard of what I consider the only correct principles of the science of free government, I shall desire to be branded with the degradation and infamy suited to the crime. I am encouraged to believe that this great political regeneration has been sufficiently efficacious in your district to secure your election in the next canvass. It is my heart's desire and prayer to Heaven that such may be the issue— It is an enviable distinction to be made the favorite of an enlightened party, and the recipient of their voluntary and undivided suffrage, though it be unsuccessful in effecting its object at the first trial. We know that retribution has visited our opponents elsewhere, and have good reason to believe it will extend even to benighted "Old Guilford"—Be not surprised however to hear that Connecticut is still "joined to her idols" and yet lingering in the wake of Federal Massachusetts—but hope better things than our being found in such company—I am very desirous of seeing you and once more taking up the hand [of] the friend of my earlier days—I feel myself under very many obligations for the kindness you have ever since our acquaintance, manifested towards me—The warmest obligations of a thankful heart are yours—I shall send if I ever have an opportunity a copy of C. J. Marshall's decisions on Constitutional questions[4] which have been hitherto discussed—An elegant and a valuable work to every politician—I hope I may have a chance to forward it as early as next fall—Mr Persons[5] is yet at Charlotte Mecklenburg County.

I do not know that I shall ever go to Carolina again If I do I will go to Rockingham assuredly—Mr Hodges[6] I suppose is at Milton but have not heard from him in a long time. Accept the best wishes of my Father[7] for your personal and political prosperity—also my respects to your Father's family and excuse the length and imperfections of this communication.

---

[1]James Phelps (1822-1900) was an attorney in Essex, Connecticut. Educated at local academies and at Trinity College and the law department at Yale, he served in the state House of Representatives (1853, 1854, 1856) and state Senate (1858, 1859), was a judge of the state superior court (1863-1873, 1885-1892), and served in Congress (1875-1883). He corresponded with Reid over a period of several years; they apparently met in Raleigh while Reid was in the state Senate and Phelps was visiting the state. *Biographical Directory of Congress*, 1452; *Penny Press* (Middletown, Connecticut), January 16, 1900, hereinafter cited as *Penny Press.*

[2]Hitchcockville (now Riverton) is in Litchfield County, Connecticut, where West Branch and Sandy Brook converge to form the Farmington River. After his second term as representative in Congress ended in 1839, Dr. Lancelot Phelps, James's father, engaged in agricultural and mercantile pursuits in Hitchcockville before moving to Colebrook, Connecticut, his former residence. *Biographical Directory of the United States Congress, Bicentennial Edition* . . . (Washington: United States Government Printing Office, 1989), 1642, hereinafter cited as *Biographical Directory of Congress, Bicentennial Edition.*

[3]Phelps is probably referring to the Assembly of 1840-1841, which was in session in Raleigh from November 16, 1840, to January 12, 1841, and in which Reid represented Rockingham County as a member of the Senate. Cheney, *North Carolina Government*, 309-310.

[4]Probably a reference to United States Supreme Court Justice John Marshall's 8-volume work, *Opinions on the Federal Constitution*, published by James Munroe & Company of Boston in 1839. Roorbach, *Bibliotheca Americana*, 347.

[5]Mr. Persons has not been identified. He may have been a bookstore owner or publisher's agent. For another reference to him, see James Phelps to David S. Reid, September 20, 1842.

[6]Mr. Hodges, likewise, has not been identified. He was apparently a person with whom both Phelps and Reid had some business dealings. For another reference to Hodges, see James Phelps to David S. Reid, June 12, 1844, which also mentions other correspondence, now lost. A number of persons named Hodges resided in Litchfield County, Connecticut, in 1850. Seventh Census, 1850, Litchfield County, Connecticut, Population Schedule, passim (microfilm), Archives, Division of Archives and History, Raleigh.

[7]Phelps's father, Dr. Lancelot Phelps (1784-1866), was a native of Windsor, Connecticut, a physician, farmer, and merchant who served in the state House of Representatives (1817, 1819-1821, 1824, 1827, and 1830) and served two terms in Congress (1835-1839), first as a Jacksonian and second as a Democrat. *Biographical Directory of Congress, Bicentennial Edition*, 1642; *Penny Press*, January 16, 1900.

Romulus M. Saunders to David S. Reid A&H-DSR

Ho. Rep.
Feb. 17—42'

I called to day on the Post Master General & learnt the matter of changing the rout to which yr. letter refers had been before the Dept about a month since—but was not adopted—I request to be informed if it should be reviewed—tho' there is not much danger of an increase—as every depart now stands more in need of a Capping off than of adding to their expenses—

We are getting on but slowly—the whigs talk of reform—the democrats stand ready to assist but some how they can never at the right point—

It is thought here yr. man Shepperd[1] has disgraced himself by serving on the comee. of foreign relations, after what has occured—he ought to be ashamd—

The times are rather inauspicious for the Law—tho' labor does every thing—Our friends ought to muster strong at Salisbury in May—The whigs say—Mr. Clay[2] is to be at their Convention in April—This to draw a crowd—

There is said to be a move for Van & old Dick in Misse[3]—all wrong—I go for a Southern man first—then for the next best—Van can't do for another Seat & old Dick—would play the nick with any party—

My respects to Judge Settle when you see him—tell him I hope to join him at Nash—

[1]Augustine Henry Shepperd, previously identified, of Forsyth County, the turncoat Democrat who, running as a Whig, defeated Reid in Reid's first try at election to Congress in 1841. Saunders may be alluding to the Whig administration's failure to force British authorities in Nassau to return slaves who mutinied aboard the American brig *Creole* in November 1841. Morris, *Encyclopedia of American History*, 185.

[2]Henry Clay (1777-1852) of Lexington, Kentucky, was the leading Whig presidential contender for three decades. He served his country in both houses of Congress, as speaker of the House, and as secretary of state. He ran unsuccessfully for president in 1824, 1832, and 1844. *DAB*, IV, 173-179.

[3]The phrase "Van and old Dick" refers to Martin Van Buren and Richard M. Johnson.

Bedford Brown to David S. Reid A&H-DSR

Caswell, N.C.
20th Sep. 1842

I avail myself of a few moments to write you a line by Dr. Williamson[1] who informs me that he expects to see you to day.

I am informed from several sources, that a plan has been formed by a portion of our party, to defeat my election this winter, if it can be effected. This plan has its origin among certain politicians during the late Session of Congress, at *Washington*. The *wires* were put actively in motion before the adjournment, (indeed I have been aware that they were secretly in motion for twelve months) and have been followed up by the most active measures since in various Counties of the State. The public will now begin to perceive why a certain politician (*Genl Saunders*) wrote a letter to the Salisbury Convention in May last (near *three years before the election*) coming out without Reserve for John C. Calhoun[2] as the Candidate of the Democratic party for President. The election for Senator to Congress is to take place this winter and it was important to *rub out old Jackson Van Buren* party impressions and throw himself at the head of *a new* party organization and rally it to his aid in effecting his views. I knew it then and it is now developing itself by active and insidious movements by an active Corps of letter writers who no doubt by *preconcert*, are trying to represent my election as out of the question and to urge the claims of Genl Saunders. I should have been willing to have retired from public life, but the vindictive violence of the federalists against me for years past and the persuasion of many esteemed friends that the vindication of my public character from *the censure* of the *Rayner Resolutions* required it, induced me in answer to inquiries from friends, to say that they were at liberty to use my name.

In regard to the presidential election my ground is this, *I am first of all for the cause—next* for the man whether *Van Buren or Calhoun* who can most successfully carry our party through the contest. *This*, I am afraid, though, does not go far enough to satisfy some *new comers* into our ranks who wish to *dictate* to the old Democracy everything. Mr. Henry[3] Mr Strange[4] and myself at the Salisbury Convention opposed the nomination of Mr. Calhoun by the Convention, which was strenuously urged in letters from Washington[5] and Fisher[6] and others acting with them in conjunction. We opposed it on the ground that it was too early and might do injury in our August election. *It was prevented* and I fear in doing so that among others I have sinned past forgiveness. I hope however, that some conciliatory course can be adopted in relation to these difficulties that threaten our party in the

State and therefore shall be cautious in giving utterance to the above remarks which I have so freely communicated to you as a friend who at the most difficult periods has sustained me.

I know that you can do much by correspondence with friends in the State. There is no time to be lost. The plans of those engaged in the scheme which I have mentioned are in active operation. *I write in confidence.*

---

[1]Robert Pogue Williamson (c. 1803-1849), a Rockingham County physician, was appointed postmaster at Rawlinsburg (Ruffin) in 1844. He was in the House of Commons (1842-1845). He died on October 6, 1849, in Rockingham County, of typhoid. Robert P. Williamson to David S. Reid, April 15, 1844, Reid Papers, PC 1, State Archives; Cheney, *North Carolina Government*, 314; *Milton Chronicle*, November 1, 1849.

[2]John C. Calhoun (1782-1850) of South Carolina was the leading southern statesman of the period. In addition to his long service in both houses of Congress, he was secretary of war (1817-1825), vice-president (1825-1832), and secretary of war (1844-1845). He was a leading candidate for president in 1824, although he did not receive the nomination. He always had a number of supporters in North Carolina. *DAB*, III, 411-419.

[3]Louis D. Henry (1788-1846), a native of New Jersey and a Princeton graduate, lived in Fayetteville. He served in the House of Commons (1821-1822, 1830-1832) and on the Council of State (1835). For a number of years he was a state leader in the Democratic party, and in 1842 he was the unsuccessful Democratic candidate for governor. John Hill Wheeler, *Historical Sketches of North Carolina from 1584 to 1851* (Baltimore: Regional Publishing Company, reprint edition, 1964), 129, hereinafter cited as Wheeler, *Sketches*.

[4]Robert Strange, previously identified, former Democratic United States senator from Fayetteville.

[5]William H. Washington (1813-1860), a native of Wayne County, was an attorney and had moved to New Bern by 1835. He was a Democratic representative in Congress (1841-1843), a member of the House of Commons (1844, 1846), and a member of the state Senate (1848, 1850, 1852). *Biographical Directory of Congress*, 1781.

[6]Charles Fisher (1789-1849) of Salisbury was in the state Senate (1818) and the House of Commons (1821-1836), serving as speaker of the House (1831-1832). He attended the state Constitutional Convention of 1835 and served in the United States House of Representatives (1819-1821, 1839-1841). *Biographical Directory of Congress*, 889.

James Phelps to David S. Reid A&H-DSR

Hitchcockville [Connecticut]
September 20th 1842

I send you by Mr Persons the Volume of "Chief Justice Marshall's Constitutional Opinions" which I desire you to accept as a simple testimonial of the sincere regard and undeviating friendship, of an humble individual happy for having received any assurance of the reciprocity of a sentiment so dear to man, and yet so rare—Disinterested friendship is the hallowed enclination of the soul, and archetype of the true divinity of human nature; and must have its origin in the finest sensibilities of the heart which are strikingly evinced in the observance of that sacred ordinance of the blessed Savior, "Love one another."

Our acquaintance has been comparatively limited yet to declare my conviction from its duration of your just right to receive my warmest attachment is saying far too little, and that higher gift is not awarded me of expressing my feelings in a manner adequate to their intensity, or of arraying them in the garb of beauty and sublimity so admirably suited to an occasion of the present character—I can only exhort you to a continuance in the career of honor and distinction you have so propitiously commenced and the satisfaction of having attained the goal of wise ambition cannot fail to be your fortune. You have already an abiding place in the affections of your fellow citizens which their kindness towards you will never suffer to abate, and as you cannot fail to remain worthy of their confidence, neither will you be called to experience their ingratitude—

It is improbable that I shall ever be allowed the pleasure of another personal interview yet, let us not only cherish, but perpetuate that kindly sentiment now operating in its fullest force, and with its holiest influences to bind in everlasting unison two kindred souls, allied even in their disproportion You will ever be remembered with the warmest gratitude so long as memory does her office, and in your own noble disposition I witness an imperishable evidence of the hospitality, the courtesy, the integrity, of the people of North Carolina—a people dear to me—not entirely, on account of the many demonstrations of personal regard which have been uniformly manifested towards me—but also in no small degree, for the reason of those interesting associations blended with her history with which also my young and happy days are inseparably connected—the period I have spent among the citizens of the "Old North State" is an epoch in my life fraught with many incidents of a pecularly pleasing and profitable character. At the early age of seventeen I entered upon her soil an unsophisticated youth, fresh from the "land of steady habits", from the bosom of a beloved and affectionate family, and from the midst of a society in which I had been reared from infancy, second to none in point of virtue, intelligence, and refinement, upon the face of the wide universe—Yes Sir, under these happy circumstances, and these so endearing associations, I left my home for a roving occupation in another, and a distant State, where it cannot be denied, temptations were too numerous, and too inviting for one so peculiarly situated, but—and it is with no ordinary satisfaction I can say it—I passed the alluring ordeal unscathed and uncorrupted by its dangerous, and when indulged, destroying, tendency—there is I can assure you (and you well must know) no higher source of pride, no noble consciousness of the immortal and triumphant destiny of men than to be enabled to recur to the trials of life overcome by a virtuous resolution, and to a series of inviting temptations, aligned and deprecated by an energy of character, and a manifestation of genuine morality too strong to be seduced and too indelibly impressed ever to be eradicated— this self-denial and self-reliance combined with the ordinary instinct of our race constitutes the real dignity of character, and the only legitimate nobility of nature. But to this important truth and these ennobling sensibilities I am convinced you are no stranger; and I give them utterance not for the purpose of affording instruction, but because they come crowding involuntarily upon my mind and afford a theme upon which I can reflect with rapture.

May you realize that professional success commensurate with your most ardent expectations, and fill to overflowing the measure of political distinction you so well deserve, and which your friends so fondly hope for you, and in after time when you shall have ascended, as I trust you may, to a high seat in the Councils of this nation, may your stedfast republican principles and statesmanlike ability, earn for, and secure to you, the welcome and enduring plaudit of "well done good and faithful servant" which shall burst from the hearts of your countrymen and be echoed to the remotest borders of the land—*We may not meet again on earth* to exchange the joyful greeting the heart-felt congratulations of separated friends—painful reflection! yet partially mitigated by the redeeming consolation that we shall be permitted to behold each other face to face when a "ransomed universe shall come up to Zion wih songs and evrlasting joy." Then will the different nations and societies of earth now separated in feeling in interests and in language be united in our "living head", and the entire family of man present the spectacle of an unbounded, an undivided fraternity—and then be realized the mellennial harvest, and we become emphatically that "happy people whose God is Jehovah"!

1843

R. P. Cardwell, Lytle Hickerson,[1] *George Bower,*[2] A&H-mn *Solomon Graves,*[3] *and Solomon Transou*[4] *to David S. Reid*

Rockford, N.C.
May 9th, 1843.

The undersigned, Committee, appointed to address you in behalf of the Democratic Convention of the Third Congressional District of North Carolina, held at this place on the present instant, take great pleasure in announcing to you, that you have been *unanimously* nominated by said Convention as a suitable person to represent the principles of the democratic party in the next Congress of the United States.

We trust that the feelings and wishes of those whom we represent may be gratified by your acceptance of the nomination, and that your answer to this communication may be given as soon as your convenience will allow.[5]

---

[1]Lytle Hickerson of Wilkes County was a district commissioner for the public schools and was on the county school board in 1848. Hayes, *Land of Wilkes*, 134-135.

[2]George Bower (1788-1861), a Jefferson merchant and farmer, was one of the first trustees of the local Methodist church in 1847. He served in the state Senate (1812-1817, 1848-1855) and the House of Commons (1842-1843) and was a delegate to the state Constitutional Convention of 1835. John Preston Arthur, *Western North Carolina: A History, 1790-1913* (Raleigh: Edwards and Broughton, 1914; Spartanburg: The Reprint Company, 1973), 164-165, hereinafter cited as Arthur, *Western North Carolina*; Arthur L. Fletcher, *Ashe County: A History* (Jefferson: Ashe County Research Association, 1963), 87, 88, 167, hereinafter cited as Fletcher, *Ashe County*; Cheney, *North Carolina Government*, 817, 1053.

[3]Solomon Graves, Jr. (1784-1862), attorney, native of Virginia, lived in Caswell County and later in Surry County, which he represented in the House of Commons (1818-1819) and the state Senate (1820-1824). He was a trustee of the state university (1821-1860). Powell, *Caswell County*, 159, 324, 352; Cheney, *North Carolina Government*, 1279-1280; Kemp P. Battle, *History of the University of North Carolina from Its Beginning to the Death of President Swain, 1789-1868*, Volume I; *From 1868-1912*, Volume II (Raleigh: Edwards and Broughton, 2 volumes, 1907, 1912), I, 823, hereinafter cited as Battle, *History of the University*; R. D. W. Connor (comp. and ed.), *A Manual of North Carolina . . . 1913* (Raleigh: North Carolina Historical Commission, 1913), 542, hereinafter cited as Connor, *North Carolina Manual*.

[4]Solomon Transou, a planter from the Yadkin River valley, moved from the Moravian community of Bethania in 1840. He maintained his contact with the church, and his home was a popular stop for ministers in the region. Adelaide L. Fries, Douglas LeTell Rights, Minnie J. Smith, and Kenneth G. Hamilton (eds.), *Records of the Moravians in North Carolina* (Raleigh: North Carolina Historical Commission, 11 volumes, 1922-1969), IX, 4436, 4561, 4804, 4922, hereinafter cited as Fries and others, *Moravian Records*.

[5]This letter appeared in the *North-Carolina Standard*, May 31, 1843.

David S. Reid to R. P. Cardwell, Lytle Hickerson, George Bower, Solomon Graves, and Solomon Transou[1]

A&H-mn

Rockingham Co., N.C.
May 19th, 1843.

Your letter informing me of my nomination by the Democratic Republican Convention assembled in Rockford, on the 9th instant, as a candidate for a seat in the House of Representatives of the next Congress from the third district, was not received until yesterday.

Believing that I did not possess the experience to enable me to be eminently useful if elected to the station for which your kind partiality has prompted you to nominate me, and being anxious to devote my time to other pursuits, I sincerely desired that the nomination should be conferred on some individual possessing more leisure and ability than myself. But, inasmuch as the nomination is the emanation of the spontaneous choice of my Fellow-Citizens, I have only to say that if they believe I can aid them in rescuing the country from the devestating wreck of the political storm by which it was overrun in 1840, and in bringing the Government back again on the good old Republican tack, duty to the country as well as to myself, will not permit me to withhold either my name or exertions towards the consummation of such a desirable object.

Please accept for yourselves and for those you represent, my profound and grateful acknowledgements for the honor you have done me.

---

[1]This letter appeared in the *North-Carolina Standard*, May 31, 1843.

William P. Dobson[1] *to David S. Reid* A&H-DSR

Rockford
Decr. 23d 1843

I was from home when your Letter reached this place or I should have attended to It before you left

I inclose you names and Post offices to send Letters at the rise of Congress I have underscored some names to whome you may send speeches or any Document you may wish to send I wish this Congress being democratic to make as much display as possable on the subject of econemy and retrenchment, I am in a perfect Bustle as I start tomorrow 500 miles to try to Collect from a man in Georgia $800. which I am bound to pay as securety If I live I shall be back in six weeks and shall be glad to hear from you present my best respects to Genl Saunders I would rather Annex Texes to our goverment than let Great Brittain have any hold there I think this govement should take a bold stand as respects the Oregan in hast I am yours

---

[1]William P. Dobson of Rockford, Surry County, was a delegate to the state Constitutional Convention of 1835 and served in the state Senate (1830-1835, 1836-1837, 1842-1843). Cheney, *North Carolina Government*, 818, 1279.

1844

David S. Reid to Reuben Reid[1] A&H-DSR

Washington city, D.C.
Sunday evening, January 14, 1844.

Your letter of the 9th instant which brings me the welcome intelegence that all are well, has been received this evening. This is the second letter I have received from *you* since I left home. The other one was backed in the handwriting of Sister Henrietta, and neither that nor the one received this evening was sealed. If wafers are to be had—and I presume they can—I would much prefer that you would seal your letters, for they pass through a great many hands before I get them. I received one letter from mother. If you enclosed me the letter that I told you to give to Smith I have never received it. Though the letter which I requested you to enclose to me is of no account, still I should have liked to have received yours, and do not like the idea of failing to get any of my letters. I am receiving a larger or smaller number of letters from North Carolina every day—many of them containing sums of money for me to pay over to persons here—and I have heard no complaint that any has failed to reach me, except yours; though I now fear that others may also have failed. I have written you every sabbath since I reached here, and several times during the week besides.

I am pretty constantly engaged. In the morning I write letters, glance over the Papers, visit the Departments on business for my constituents, and attend Committees. At 12 Oclock the House meets and we generally sit till 4 or 5 Oclock. After we adjourn, we dine, generally about sunset, and then our mass assembles in the Parlour and we talk over matters and things for a while. I then go to my Room & read and write letters till 7 Oclock, when we again assemble in the Parlour and take tea, and after chatting a while I go to my Room and commence my writing which I continue till bed time, unless I have some party to attend, and when that is the case I go to a party a 8 oclock and spend the evening in eating good things and in conversation with fashionable & distiguished gentlemen and ladies. When we are invited to dine out the regular hour in Washington is 5 oclock.

Since I have reached here I think my health has been as good as it ever was. I am better dressed, and perhaps look as well as you ever saw me. But amidst all the [*torn*]ity and splendour here I hope I do not forget home and my constituents, Congress is engaged at work, but nothing of much importance has been done. Tell mother that I hope to dine with her next May. Give my respects to mother, Rhoda, Henrietta, Ann, & Reuben & to sister Frances & her family when you see them; also to the neighbours generally, and accept for yourself the respects & best wish of Your affectionate son

There is a gentleman in this city from Mississippi who informs me that Mr. Scott came on the Rail Road with him to Weldon, and that he left him there on his way to Raleigh. I do not know whether he was going home, but suppose he was.

---

[1]Reuben Reid (1787-1852), a Rockingham County farmer and merchant, was Reid's father. He served as a county justice (1831-1852) and was the postmaster of Reidsville from 1836 until his death. He had seventeen slaves in 1850. The sisters of David S. Reid mentioned here were Henrietta (1824-1868), who married George Price of Danville; Annie C. (1831-1889), who married her cousin Ansalem Reid; and Rhoda S. (1822-1865), who married William Scott. Reese and Fisher, *Settle Family*, 679-680; Seventh Census, 1850, Rockingham County, Slave Schedule, 112; Scott, "Family History," 2; Settle Family Cemetery.

Samuel F. Adams to David S. Reid Duke-DSR

Troublesome, N.C.
Feb. 26 1844

your favour of the 18th Inst is just received. I am glad to hear that you enjoy good health myself and family are all well and they were all well at fathers this morning although it is extremely sickly in the neighborhood Mrs. Boyd[1] is at the point of death it is not supposed she can live a number of persons have died both black and white John Reid Esqr[2] has had a very severe attack but has got almost well. I arived at home a week ago yesterday and shall start to the south tomorrow I have not determined where I shall go but I think to Alabama I understand negro men are selling in that state from $900 - $1000 and all others in proportion if so we shall do well on this trip as I received a letter today from Richmond informing me that men were worth $700 there which is at least $100 on the head higher than when I left I believe I know of no news that would be interesting to you you may not be surprised if you hear of a runaway marraige in this section one of the parties lives in the neighborhood of wentworth and the other in the neighborhood of Maj Wrights I expect you will be surprised to hear this but it is a certain fact I have undoubted information that both parties have agreed to consumate the matter by an arrangement of that kind and is only awaiting an opportunity to carry it in to effect (and as one of the Parties Interestid is now in Mississippi) they think that will not be long wanting Francis [*sic*] & the children send you their best love and affection I am with high respect your affectionate Brother

N.B. James Patrick[3] died about a week ago his children are all at Mr. Martins.

---

[1]Minerva Hill Boyd (1808-1844) was the wife of George D. Boyd, who was a leading planter, merchant, and state senator from Rockingham County. Powell, *DNCB*, I, 201.

[2]John Reid (Reed) (1777-1844) of the Haw River section of Rockingham County was Reid's uncle. He had been a clerk of the county and in 1830 owned eight slaves. Scott, "Family History," 2; Fifth Census, 1830, Rockingham County, Population Schedule, 284; *Cemetery Records of Rockingham and Stokes Counties, North Carolina* (Madison: James Hunter Chapter, Daughters of the American Revolution, 1978), 129, hereinafter cited as *Cemetery Records*.

[3]James Patrick, Jr., a Rockingham County mill owner, had married Reid's aunt Matilda Settle in 1828. Patrick was a county justice and had eight slaves in 1840. Robert W. Carter, Jr., "Mills in Simpsonville Township," Part I, *Journal of Rockingham County History and Genealogy*, III (April, 1978), 7-9.

David S. Reid to Hamilton Brown[1] UNC-HB

Ho. Reps.
Washington City,
March 4, 1844.

I have the honour to acknowledge the receipt of your letter recommending John T. Finley[2] for the appointment of Postmaster at Wilkesboro. Immediately on its reception I laid the case before the Postmaster General and he consented to appoint *Mr. Finley* as you will perceive from the enclosed letter.[3] I hope that the appointment will give general satisfaction.

A terrible accident occured here last Wednesday, which caused the death of the Hon. Mr. Upshur,[4] Secretary of State, the Hon. Mr. Gilmer,[5] Secretary of the Navy, Hon. Mr. Gardner,[6] formerly a member of Congress from N. York, Commodore Kennon,[7] and Virgil Maxcy,[8] late Chargé de Affairs to Belgium. This awful catastrophe happened in the following manner: Capt. Stockton[9] of the Steam ship *Princeton* gave a splendid entertainment on board of the ship which was attended by a large number of ladies and gentlemen, among them the President of the U. States, the heads of Departments, a number of members of Congress & others. There was a large Cannon on board which it required *thirty pounds* of powder to load & which carried a ball weighing 225 pounds. In firing this Gun it bursted at the breech killing the persons I have mentioned, besides wounding several others. Col. Benton[10] was knocked down, but I hope is not seriously injured. Nicholas Biddle[11] died a few days ago. Mr. Frick[12] a member of the House died in this city on friday last.

The vote has been taken on the twenty-first Rule & for the present the Rule is retained. I can not now say when we shall adjourn, I hope it will be a shorter session than usual.

Please give my respects to Maj. Emmett,[13] Syney Stokes,[14] Mr. Gwyn,[15] Maj. Hickerson[16] and my acquaintances in your part of the County, generally. My respects to Col. Mitchell.[17] In haste.

---

[1]Hamilton Brown (1786-1870) of Wilkesboro was sheriff of Wilkes County (1816-1818), a county justice by 1820, and colonel of the county militia by 1823. Hayes, *Land of Wilkes*, 80, 88, 163.

[2]John Tate Finley (1817-1896) of Wilkesboro was one of the founders of the local Presbyterian church (1837) and a brother-in-law of James B. Gordon, Confederate cavalry general. Hayes, *Land of Wilkes*, 123, 158.

[3]This letter could not be located.

[4]Abel Parker Upshur (1790-1844) of Northampton County, Virginia, served in the House of Delegates and on the state general court (1826-1841). He was named secretary of the navy by President Tyler in 1841 and succeeded Daniel Webster as secretary of state in 1843. *DAB*, XIX, 127-128.

[5]Thomas Walker Gilmer (1802-1844), an Albemarle County, Virginia, attorney, served in the state legislature and was elected governor of Virginia in 1840. He resigned to run for Congress and was elected to the House of Representatives (1841-1844). He was named secretary of the navy just prior to the *Princeton* accident. *DAB*, VII, 308- 309.

[6]David Gardiner, a state legislator from New York, was the father of Julia Gardiner, who married President Tyler in June, 1844. Chitwood, *Tyler*, 399-400.

[7]Beverly Kennon entered the United States Navy as a midshipman in 1809. He was promoted to captain by 1837. Edward W. Callahan, *List of Officers of the Navy of the United States and the Marine Corps from 1775 to 1900* (New York: L. R. Hamersly and Company, 1901), 311, hereinafter cited as Callahan, *Navy Officers*.

[8]Virgil Maxcy (1785-1844), originally from Massachusetts, was a Baltimore attorney. He served as solicitor for the United States Treasury (1830-1837) and was chargé d'affaires of the United States missions in Brussels and the Hague. *DAB*, XII, 434-435.

[9]R. F. Stockton, commander of the *Princeton*, was a personal friend of President Tyler. He became a midshipman in 1811 and rose to the rank of captain by 1838.

Stockton had important commands during the Mexican War and had a key role in the conquest of California. He left the navy in 1850. Chitwood, *Tyler*, 320, 431; Callahan, *Navy Officers*, 524.

[10]Thomas Hart Benton (1782-1858), a North Carolina native, was a St. Louis attorney and editor. In the War of 1812 he had been a lieutenant colonel in the army. He served in the United States Senate (1821-1851) and House of Representatives (1853-1855). *Biographical Directory of Congress*, 546; *DAB*, II, 210-213.

[11]Nicholas Biddle (1786-1844) of Philadelphia had been a director and president of the Bank of the United States. He was President Jackson's chief antagonist in the controversy over the president's veto of the bank charter. *DAB*, II, 243-245.

[12]Henry Frick (1795-1844), a Milton, Pennsylvania, editor, had been a state legislator and was serving his first term in the United States House of Representatives. *Biographical Directory of Congress*, 917.

[13]William C. Emmett of Wilkes County was in the House of Commons (1831-1832). Hayes, *Land of Wilkes*, 84-85.

[14]Montfort Sidney Stokes (1810-1862), of Wilkes County, was the son of Governor Montfort Stokes. He was educated at the United States Naval Academy. After several years in the navy he returned to Wilkes County, where he served as a county justice. He was a major during the Mexican War period, and during the Civil War he was colonel of the First Regiment North Carolina Troops. He was mortally wounded at Mechanicsville in 1862. Hayes, *Land of Wilkes*, 62, 89, 106, 153, 155; J. G. de Roulhac Hamilton and Max R. Williams (eds.), *The Papers of William Alexander Graham* (Raleigh: Division of Archives and History, Department of Cultural Resources, projected 8 volumes, 1957—), III, 216, hereinafter cited as Hamilton and Williams, *Graham Papers*.

[15]James Gwyn of Wilkesboro was a vestryman of St. Paul's Episcopal Church, Wilkesboro, in 1858 when it was admitted to membership as a parish in the Episcopal Diocese of North Carolina. He also served as a county justice in 1862. Hayes, *Land of Wilkes*, 89, 100.

[16]Lytle Hickerson, previously identified.

[17]Anderson Mitchell, previously identified.

Weldon E. Wright[1] *to David S. Reid* A&H-DSR

Rockingham Co NC
March 20h '44

I have delayed writing to you longer than I expected when I received your letter; on account of pressing engagements. The Sickness in this part of the country is still raging, though somewhat less severe The people begin to see the necessity of sending for a physician in time, & I have recently found no difficulty in relieving the cases, more particularly since I got the hang of the disease I had all the first cases that were in the country & it being altogether a new disease, I lost four or five Cases before Christmas; but have succeded ever since & have lost but one case since christmas, having attended at least one hundred & fifty or two hundred cases. After my first cases I fell into a plan of treatment of relieving them in the first stage without any difficulty and being so well pleased with its success, I concluded to publish my views for the benefit of the community. You will find my essay on the disease in the Danville Reporter a copy of which I send you: You will see that Doct Atkinson in an editorial has niggled it by reccommending dracham doses of calomel in congestion, which I am convinced would prostrate the patient with this disease. He has certainly acted very unwisely in recommending a treatment for a disease that he has never seen & knows nothing about. I have writen him a letter on the subject with directions to publish it.

Colonel! When I herd of the explosion of the gun in the Princeton I trembled for your fate till I heard from you Why do you not write to me sometimes? I imagine that you think me not worthy of consideration as an intimate friend: though I am doing you injustice to think that your station would put you above your old friends, I must attribute it to the right case; your pressing engagements: but I do think that you could find time to write a few lines to one who has always loved you as a brother, & for whom you have always (from first acquaintance) expressed such friendship. You have no idea how I want to see you, & have a good old social fireside chat: for I feel almost alone without an intimate friend whith [*sic*] whom to associate, though my professional engagements in which I begin to delight more keep my mind in a good & lively condition. And besides this I am cut off entirely from seeing my dear [*blank*] in whose society above all others I delight: though I have received a kind & affectionate letter from her since I last wrote to you. Politicks are very dull in this county: I scarcely ever hear the subject mentioned. Your views on that subject expressed in your last letter are entirely correct.

There is one Subject Colonel! which above all others should engage our attention in this time of death & destruction; that is our duty to our creator. He warns us daily by death on every hand: & we ought to hold ourselves in readiness for we know not when we shall be called

I believe that I have no other news of interest. Your father's family are all well. As ever your devoted friend

---

[1]Weldon E. Wright (d. 1850), a Rockingham County physician, was a local Democratic leader, serving on the county committee. Committee to David S. Reid, April 30, 1845, Reid Papers, PC 1, State Archives.

Reuben Reid to David S. Reid RCC

Rockingham county N C
Reidsville Apl 10th 1844

again I Rite to you to inform you that we are all well. I Recd yours of the 31 March and was glad to here you was well. You complain of not riting. I did not Rite as Soon in that weak by two days as usal and it did not get on as Soon by Some days as you could See as I Saw mr Alfred Ellington[1] afew days after I Rote, on his way to Philadelpa he told me that he would certinly Call and See you in the corse of a weak made me fail in answering yours of the Request to know how your Mother was geting. mr Ellington come to take the Hack saw us all up and well. I Recd a lette from Hugh[2] dated 30 Mch from Madison Ga Stating that mr Scott[3] had arrivd the day befor with 21 negroes from Richmond va and he him self had one on hand makeing 22 on hand he also Rote that mr Adams[4] and Capt Matlock[5] had past hough Ga and mr Adams had Rote to him he had not Sold any nor did not know Where he Should Station for th Purpose of Selling. Frances and the children is well. all the famaly desiers to be Remembred to you I Remain your loving Father.

P S I hav not been cald on for any money yet and hav no peticular us for any that i know of at this time.

---

[1]This Alfred Ellington was likely a relative of Reuben Reid's brother-in-law, Dr. John W. Ellington, who was married in 1830 to Lucinda Settle, sister of Elizabeth Williams Settle Reid. Reese and Fisher, *Settle Family*, 688. Alfred Ellington did not reside in Rockingham County in 1840 or 1850, however. Sixth Census, 1840, Rockingham County, Population Schedule; Seventh Census, 1850, Rockingham County, Population Schedule.

[2]Hugh Kearns Reid, brother of David S. Reid, previously identified.

[3]William Scott, brother-in-law of David S. Reid, previously identified.

[4]Samuel F. Adams, brother-in-law of David S. Reid, previously identified.

[5]Charles Matlock, previously identified.

A. H. Shepperd to David S. Reid A&H-DSR

Good Spring
Apl 11 1844

You see I am here again. Please forward the enclosed to my friend in George Town: I have concluded to have my books shiped to Petersburg to the care of "Head & Robbins" The proper direction will be to myself Salem NC to the Care of Head & Robbins Petersburg Va" Mr Robinson[1] has a box to be shiped also Please write him to send it over or contrear and get it to send with the balance. Heretofore the Post Master or a Messenger has attended to the marking & forwarding: if this practice is changed please get it done, & whatever expense you are at in getting my goods under way I will pay you most Cheerfully when you return among us—The boxes should be well secured against injury etc.—See our Friend French[2] & request him to ascertain why my Documents of the last session of the last Congress have not been sent—but two volumes of reports have come to hand—surely there were more

I am without news but few have gone from this part of the State to meet Mr Clay at Raligh I presum a very large proportion will be from the Eastern part of the State—this is the week of our Superior Court Judge Dick presideng—nothing of interest—& but few people in attendance—It is the busiest season with the farmers

How comes on the Texas question—Is it true that its annexation will be seriously urged by Capt Tyler[3] & his cabinet I have no means of knowing what the people think of the matter but for myself I can say that it is the most impudent & meschievous project that has been hatched for many years

[1]Mr. Robinson has not been identified.

[2]Mr. French has not been identified.

[3]John Tyler (1790-1862), an attorney from Charles City County, Virginia, was a militia captain in 1813. In addition to his service in the United States Congress and as governor of Virginia, he was elected vice-president on the Whig ticket in 1840. Upon the death of President William Henry Harrison a month after the inauguration, Tyler succeeded to the presidency. According to his biographer, the title "captain" was one of derision used by his enemies. *Biographical Directory of Congress*, 1737; Chitwood, *Tyler*, 30.

David S. Reid to John C. Spencer[1] Duke-DSR
[copy]

Ho. Rep's,
Washington,
April 12, 1844

Will you do me the favour to furnish me a certified copy of the quantity of *Public lands actually received* by each State under the Distribution act passed by the twenty-seventh Congress? Also the quantity which each State had received under prior donations which went to make up the quantity to which such State was entitled under said act?

I have not deemed it necessary to call for this information by a Resolution of the House but it is proper to state that I ask it with a view to use it publicly if I think proper so to do.

[1]John C. Spencer (1788-1855), a New York attorney, served as a state legislator and as a representative in Congress (1817-1819). A Democrat, he was appointed by President Tyler to the cabinet posts of secretary of war (1841-1843) and secretary of the treasury (1843-1844). *DAB*, XVII, 449-450.

George F. Wilson[1] *to David S. Reid* A&H-DSR

Bethania
Apr. 15. 1844

Again I trouble You with a few more Dollars to pay for Globes, Enclosed You have four Dollars to pay for the 2 Copies of the Weekly Globe. 1 Copy to be Sent to E. Hunter Vienna P. Office Stokes county N.C.—1 Copy to be sent to D. Reynolds Salem P. Office Stokes County N.C.

I return You many thanks for attending to the request in my other communication, and will repay you the 75 c when we meet. News is now circulating here that clay did not arrive in Raleigh at the time of the greate preperation, And that Many of our Blue *lights*[2] have been disappointed I should be glad to accommodate my pollitical friends in being a candidate this Summer, but it seem impossible. and even if I should so much *disregard* their *interest*, as to gratify them, It will or would be to their *injury* and a loss, of that seat for which I should be [*torn*]ng. They will (the feds,) unite stronger against *me* than any other man in *the* county and my friends will not go as Strong for me, as for *others*, because I have no *compromise*, with, or *mercy* for *feds*. We want Mr. V Buren's cours[e] on the Missouri question and [h]is course in relation to the Tariff in 1828, and in relation to the last war.—And we want also the course of Mr. Clay—the whole subject of the Adams Allience,[3] and the charges that were made by Adams, which Clay said were not true, and that he would expose them &c

Turning out and putting in scheme we want in short hand. Expenses, defalcatione &c. I am sorry to see Conn. go again for federalism. I hope the great boddy of the Democrats will go for a reduction of the Tariff. Anexation of Texas, and for holding on fast on to the *Oregon*. I see the feds oppose it. that is good, is equal to opposeing the last war. American feeling is fast leaving our land,—We seem sliding fast down to an Aristocracy. why will not the people see, and do accordingly. where is the Spirits of our forefathers? why liberty, so little valued, so little sought for, and so little cared for. Duncan[4] made, a very good examination of the Same Old Coon—but take the matter of the Speech I have seen more Able one from him.—It is said, here by the feds that our Clingman[5] used Duncan up,

---

[1]George F. Wilson lived in Bethania, Forsyth County, formed in 1849 from Stokes County. Seventh Census, 1850, Forsyth County, Population Schedule, 268; Powell, *North Carolina Gazetteer*, 178.

[2]"Blue Lights" was a nickname given to American Federalists by their political opponents during the War of 1812, when the Federalists were accused of signaling traitorously with blue lights to British warships. Democrats delighted in passing on this derogatory label to the Whigs, whom they identified as latter-day Federalists similarly deficient in military enthusiasm. William W. Holden gleefully reprinted the following comments from the *Old Dominion* (Portsmouth, Virginia): "*Colored Lights*. The *Raleigh Register* informs us that on the evening of Friday and Saturday, during Mr. Clay's sojourn in that city, the party used *colored lights* to illuminate it. This is quite natural. The same party used *blue lights* in old Connecticut, during the war, to give signals to the enemy." *North-Carolina Standard*, May 1, 1844.

[3]Adams Alliance refers to the "corrupt bargain" that John Quincy Adams and Henry Clay made in the disputed election of 1824. Andrew Jackson led in electoral votes but did not have a majority; consequently, the election was to be decided in the House of Representatives. Clay gave his support to Adams, who was elected president, and Clay became secretary of state. Jackson's supporters always believed that the election was unfairly decided by Clay's deal. See Albert R. Newsome, *The Presidential Election of 1824 in North Carolina* (Chapel Hill: University of North Carolina Press, 1939).

[4]Alexander Duncan (1788-1853), a Cincinnati physician, was a state legislator and Whig representative in the United States Congress (1837-1841, 1843-1845). *Biographical Directory of Congress*, 834.

[5]Thomas Lanier Clingman (1812-1897), an Asheville attorney, was a member of the House of Commons (1835-1836) and the state Senate (1840). As a Whig he served in the United States House of Representatives (1843-1845). After losing an election, Clingman became a Democrat and served six additional terms in the House (1847-1858). He was appointed to the United States Senate in 1858 to complete the term of Asa Biggs, who had resigned; Clingman remained in the Senate until North Carolina withdrew from the Union. He was appointed Confederate brigadier general in 1862. *Biographical Directory of Congress*, 708; Wheeler, *Reminiscences*, 72-75; *DAB*, IV, 220-221.

A. J. Folger[1] *to David S. Reid* A&H-DSR

Surry County N.C.
April. 1844

I received your Communication in due time, I have not Conversed with my friend Mr. Patterson[2] since, On the account of his absence from home, But I know it does not matter, for previous to me giving my Consent for a petition to be got up, for the establishment of a post office at my house, I saw Mr Patterson and endeavoured to get his Consent, to have one started for him, But he told me that it was out of the question for him to attend to an office on the grounds of his being assistant County Surveyor, and gon from home almost continually which I know to be the fact and I would Still have you to erase out my name, and put Mr Patterson's in the place of mine, if he could possibly attend to the matter, for I do not want to act as a post master, it will be a great [d]eal of trouble and Expence, for no proffit, But in complyance with the wishes of my neighbours, and for their benifit, I am willing to act, yet if, Mr. Patterson will make araingements so he can act, I will with sattisfaction have the office moved to his house if I can, as the distance is Short, between my house and his, as he is one of the finist kind of men, and every way worthey of filling any office that the people may want him to fill

The distance to nearest postoffice is 6 miles any direction, the Stage runs by my house, From this to Mount airy is 6 Miles, to Thoms Creek 9 to Esqr Carsons[3] in, Stokes 13 or 14 to Rocford 18, and to every place a desperate bad road, The reason why Mr. Pattersons name was not on the petition I sent you, was because it was never presented to him, when my friends sent it to me it was full, Consequently I did not present it to any one, If Mr Patterson was at home I would have him to write you a line, But as above Stated I know it will not matter, and as the time may be short that you will remain at Washington I thought best to write immediately, yet if you think best, I will get Mr Patterson to write on his return home

I am glad to se that you are endeavouring to make an alteration in the Whig tariff and I also trust that Mr. Haywood[4] Bill will pass both branches of Congress, though I have some objections to the bill, But not enough to make me vote against it, ware I a member of Congress. The Oregon and Texas are the general topic of Conversation here, the people are generally in favour of the annexation of both of them to our Government. My opinion is, that if we can get a new set of candidates out in our county this year, that we can make a clean sweep of Clay and, Federalism In fact my notion is, that but few counties in our State will send a whig representation to the next legislature, And I apprehend no fears in regard to our next Goviner and legislature being purely democratic, But I trust that you, and the rest of the Democratic members of Congress, will spare no pains, and disregard all trouble, in distributing public documents among your constiants, I am confident that all the people wants, (to save their bleeding County, from the tiranical grasp of aristocratical whiggery) is correct information

Though I am extreemely Sorry to se S. Carolina act in the manner she does yet I hope for the best. do you think the friends of Mr. Calhoun will (from what you se of them in Congress) go for Mr Van Buren, or will they act as they did in 1836 thro their votes away, let me no soon, relative to the matter I have written on, and if We get a post office, or if we do not, as soon as I hear from you, I will, (if you wish it) giv you the names of my neighbours, so you may send letters or documents to them at any time when it suits your convenience

---

[1]Andrew J. Folger was the first postmaster of the Tilmont post office, established June 20, 1844, in Surry County and discontinued December 30, 1847. By 1850 Folger was a resident of Forsyth County. Lemuel Johnson and Phil H. Perkinson, *North Carolina Post Office Catalog, by County* (Raleigh: By the Authors, 1984), 234, hereinafter cited as Johnson and Perkinson, *Post Office Catalog*; Seventh Census, 1850, Forsyth County, Population Schedule, 268.

[2]Possibly Joshua Patterson, a farmer who was 54 years old in 1844. He was appointed on November 4, 1842, to serve on a jury "to lay off and alott" a Surry County widow's dowry lands. There were eleven male heads of households named Patterson in Surry County in 1850. Jury appointment, November 4, 1842, Surry County Deeds, Office of the Register of Deeds, Surry County Courthouse, Dobson, Book 3, pp. 3-4, hereinafter cited as Surry County Deeds; Seventh Census, 1850, Surry County, Population Schedule, 4, 7, 53, 54, 63, 82, 93, 98, 145, 146.

[3]Probably Jacob Carson, a middle-aged farmer residing in Stokes County in 1840. The only other head of household with the same surname in Stokes in 1840 was Virlen Carson, a farmer under 30 years of age. Sixth Census, 1840, Stokes County, Population Schedule, 187.

[4]William Henry Haywood, Jr. (1801-1852), a Raleigh attorney, was a graduate of the state university. He served in the House of Commons (1831, 1834-1836) and was speaker of the House in his last two terms. He was elected to the United States Senate, commencing his term in 1843. Haywood resigned from the Senate in 1846, when he could not follow the state legislature's instructions to support a Democratic downward revision of the tariff. *Biographical Directory of Congress*, 1032; Norton, *Democratic Party*, 120; Cheney, *North Carolina Government*, 297, 303-305, 307, 308, 683, 685, 745n.

John T. Garland[1] *to David S. Reid* A&H-DSR

Milton
May 12. 1844

Please accept my thanks for documents & speeches[2] remitted me this session tho not a professed politician, I cannot but feel a deep concern at the progress & prospect of things at Washington; I percieve that the annual report of the Commissioner of Patents, Ellsworth has been recently laid before you; as it is represented to contain much important information to the agricultural community & I suppose intended for grautitous distributions, I would be glad if it imports with your convenience to have a copy.

The May term of our Sup. Court is just over, I have seen & conversed with many of our mutual political freinds since the result of the Virg. election & since the reception of Mr V. Burens Texas letter[3]: I must in candor say, there is quite a feeling of dispondencey in our ranks, & quite an apprehensive distrust of Mr V. Burens present availibility; tho we concede that the nomination at Baltimore was strictly due him & have anticipated no other result yet after the late indication we all would go into the canvass with no enthusiasm & with every anticipation of defeat: There is quite a strong Texas current with us & if it be not a violation of national faith & honor, nine in ten of our population will vote the annexation, for my own part I should hold the national honor like individual honor sacred, but I cannot say in this case that any bad faith could be rightfully ascribed to us; I regard Texas as soverign & independent de Facto, as well as de jure she has been so for 8 years past & no man now believes that Mexico either can or ever will reconquer it. We had better annex where we can, it is indispensable to the security of the whi[tes] & equally essential to the ultimate preservation of the blacks; Providence is colonising the blacks in that direction & the Texas door must be kept open, it is the safety valve to the South & stern & inexorable necessity proclaims that it must & shall be kept open it is evident that the Treaty will be rejected, whether a joint resolution for the annexation will be more successful I cannot say. I would incur many hazards, even to the "imminent deadly breach" sooner than it should directly or indirectly, commercially or politically become the dependent instrument of that only nation on Earth G. Britain that desires & contemplates our ruin & dissolution I overlook all mere questions of the balance of political power in our confederacy, all monied calculations in this great national question not that they are not important in themselves & vastly influential in their consequences, but they are still vastly subordinate & transitory, to the great & vital question of security, of life, liberty & happiness; this is from everlasting to everlasting [I] fear there is a jealous personal [*torn*] among the leading political aspirants at Washington that will sacrifice our most important interests at the shrine of selfish ambition, would that we had another hero of the hermitage to inspire some confidence at home, some respect abroad, what effect the nomination of Cass,[4] Stewart,[5] or Johnson[6] would have I am unable to declare, Mr V Buren would please the *reading politicians*, but for success in the coming contest it requires an individual whose prominent developments & bold chivalry of character would rouse & excite into enthusiastic action the dormant patriotism of the masses; excuse this hasty & disultory communication; I fear an abortive nomination at Baltimore, our friends should deliberate free from personal committals & present us the most *available*

---

[1]John T. Garland of Milton, Caswell County, was the largest slaveholder in his county in 1860. He was active in banking, educational, and political affairs of his community. Powell, *Caswell County*, 114, 334, 364, 369, 499; Cheney, *North Carolina Government*, 1089.

[2]Other persons in the Milton community were not so pleased with Reid's mailings. Whig editor C. N. B. Evans of the *Milton Chronicle* wrote in its May 22, 1844, number: "LOOK OUT FOR 'PISEN!' Last Sunday's Mail from Washington City, (via Halifax C. H., Va.,) brought about two bushels of packages franked by the Hon. D. S. REID—all bound for the maridian of Rockingham and the upper part of this county. What the character of these pamphlets is we cannot exactly say, but they 'smelt of poisen' and we are inclined to the belief they are 'Kendall Tracts,' or, what is equally filthy and vile, Dr. Duncan's speech.

"Our gentlemanly little representative, should bear in mind that 'David' slew 'Goliath' with a stone—not mud, or 'carrion with engendered grubs.' We say *gentlemanly*, because in all the private relations of life *David* S. Reid is a gentleman; as a politician, however, we believe David is not as fair and clever as he might and ought to be. We hope, for Mr. R's own credit-sake, that he has not polluted his hands with infamous tracts of that 'lying caitiff'—that inky cutthroat—that pen-stabbing footpad—that prying, pilfering, prostituted pander, *Amos Kendall*. As for Duncan's disgusting nostrum speech, Mr. Reid may be excusable for handling the thing provided he touches it only with a pair of tongs, and sends it only to the vulgar and base."

[3]When Van Buren had been Jackson's political heir, he was considered the natural choice for the Democratic presidential nomination in 1844. His southern critics, however, obtained a letter from Jackson (published March 22, 1843, in the Richmond *Enquirer*) advocating the annexation of Texas. Van Buren, who had made a pact with potential Whig opponent Clay to ignore the annexation issue in the upcoming election, responded with a letter in the Washington *Globe* dated April 20, 1843, in which he maintained that annexation was unfeasible because it could lead to war with Mexico. This stand alienated Jackson and the South and was a major factor in Van Buren's failure to receive the nomination. The Democrats nominated James K. Polk, who won the election. Morris, *Encyclopedia of American History*, 189-190.

[4]Lewis Cass (1782-1866), a native of New Hampshire, was an attorney in Ohio and later settled in Detroit. He served as a brigadier general in the army (1813), governor of Michigan Territory (1813-1831), secretary of war (1831-1836), minister to France (1836-1842), United States senator (1845-1848, 1849-1857), and secretary of state (1857-1860). Cass received the Democratic nomination for president in 1848 but lost the election to Zachery Taylor. *DAB*, III, 562-564.

[5]Charles Stewart (d. 1869), a commodore in the United States Navy, was promoted as a candidate for the Democratic presidential nomination in 1844 by friends in Philadelphia. He was one of several candidates proposed as alternatives to Van Buren, but he received only a scattering of votes in the convention. Charles G. Sellers, *James K. Polk, Continentalist, 1843-1846* (Princeton: Princeton University Press, 1966), 46, 83, 89, hereinafter cited as Sellers, *Polk*.

[6]Richard Mentor Johnson, previously identified.

Barzillai Graves[1] *to David S. Reid* A&H-DSR

Near Milton N C
May 16th 1844

My affliction during the spring has kept me from writing to you and other friends as often as I desired.

I have been crippled by a fall from a fence and my right hand is stiffened with something like Rheumatism so that I write with pain, but irksome as the task is I cannot lay still and let the Federal Whigs go on in their own way rejoicing. The Standard of Raleigh will convey to you the news of some of the proceedings of old Caswell, you will there see that we are aroused on the subject of Democracy and determined to do our duty in support of our Principles and our Candidates, and the better to inable us to go on we have formed a Democratic Association at Yanceyville and auxiliary associations in each Captains Company District throughout the County and appointed committees of Vigilence to pursue and use all honourable means to aid our great and good cause—Who is to be the Nominees by the Baltimore convention, or rather the National Convention which is to meet at Baltimore on the 27th instant is the question asked by every one we meet now a days in this region of Country Great anxiety, and increasing anxiety is now manifested since Messrs Van Buren and Clay have come forwards in oposition to the annexation of Texas So far as my limited opportunity inables me to judge they have lost and are continuing to lose popularity in all the Southern country—the current in favor of anexation is runing Mountain high and the people are cut, or split up into parties, each contending for his favorite candidate for President, and that we are sorry to see is the case with the members of Congress—Great divisions seem to be fashionable where unanamity should prevail, the effects of which are to be dreaded and regreted.

I think the knowing ones about here who would prefer Van B. to all other men for the Presidency fear he cannot rally and lead his party to victory in the coming contest—R. M. Johnson is often spoken of here as the strongest Democrat in the Union—and although he may not be equal to others on point of intellect he it is thought is sufficiently qualified, aided as he will be by an able Cabinett of his own selection to discharge the important duties of that great and responsible office—A man of sufficient qualifications that can succeed and triumph over Fed'l Whigery and Clay we think is far preferable to one that would run unsuccessfully and lose the race and thereby fix upon the Country, Clay, his detestable Federal Principles and a Fifty Million National Bank—We though as a party will go for the nominee with the exception of a few who do not duly appreciate the subject—from this expression you must not understand me to say that some will break off and go to Clay—it is not so—The oposition of Col Benton to the anexation of Texas to the Union astonishes a great many of his devoted friends Buchanan[2] or Cass would get the vote of the Democratic Party in the South if it is true that they will go for anexation—Upon that point I am inclined to believe the election will mainly turn in the South—I beg you to accept my sincere thanks for a Document and a good speech you now and then send me—that of Doct Duncan with the Coon appended is greatly sought for and is doing good among the thinking, reflecting community.[3]

It seems that I am compelled to meddle with Politics once in a while and I have not the means to take any Newspaper except the NC Standard and that furnishes but little of what is going on only in our State—You must know from this circumstance that a little help from you and other friends will greatly assist me in preparing to meet the Feds hereabouts

The Hon Messrs Walter Coles,[4] Jacob Thompson,[5] Wylie P. Mangum and others used to send me Speeches, Papers and Documents but have now forsaken me—I fear I have incured their displeasure or is it because I have grown too old to busy myself in such matters that I am thus neglected—I know Sir that no one is under the least obligation to send me even a syllable but every one is bound to support his cause just in that way he sees cause to persue—It is rumored here that the Democratic members of Congress have held a caucus and ascertained that Mr Van Buren is to be, or should be droped by the National Convention and that Com Stewart will probably get the nominat'n.

I am glad to learn that the dreadful disease that has prevailed with such fatality in your neighborhood in Rockingham has in a great degree subsided and the health of the people restored—Will you please to send me a line so soon as you hear from the National Convention and let me know who are the nominees for Pres. & Vice Pres.

---

[1]Barzillai Graves of Caswell County served in the House of Commons (1813, 1818-1822, 1832-1833) and the state Senate (1814-1815). He was an elder in Bush Arbor Primitive Baptist Church and served on the county public school committee. In 1845 he unsuccessfully attempted to establish a Democratic paper in Milton to compete with the Whig *Milton Chronicle*. Cheney, *North Carolina Government*, 1088-1089; Powell, *Caswell County*, 340, 377, 403, 457, 511.

[2]James Buchanan (1791-1868), a Lancaster, Pennsylvania, attorney, served as a state legislator, United States congressman and senator, minister to Great Britain and Russia, secretary of state, and president of the United States (1857-1861). *DAB*, III, 207-214.

[3]See note 2 following John T. Garland to David S. Reid, May 12, 1844, in this volume for a local Whig's reaction to this same speech.

[4]Walter Coles (1790-1857), a planter from Pittsylvania County, Virginia, was an infantry captain in the War of 1812, a state legislator, and a representative in the United States Congress (1835-1845). *Biographical Directory of Congress*, 721.

[5]Jacob Thompson (1810-1885), a native of Leasburg, Caswell County, graduated from the state university and became an attorney. He settled in Pontotoc, Mississippi, in 1835 and served as United States congressman (1839-1851) and secretary of the interior (1857-1861). During the Civil War he was a special agent for the Confederacy to Canada. *Biographical Directory of Congress*, 1708.

John Hill to David S. Reid A&H-DSR

Baltimore
29th May 1844

As I am situated here, I have no chance of writing a letter to you which would reach you with the news sooner than the news papers of this place.

You must therefore not expect me to write any more until I get home.

The result of the several ballotings you will have seen. Mr Van Buren is the choice of a majority of the Convention. But I fear & think that intrigue & management will defeat him.

The vote of our State has been given different ways with a view to effect a compromise. We were willing to give all the gentlemen voted for a fair chance. But in future we must act as we think best. I think we should stand up to the man of our preference & fall with him if he should fall.

A great deal of electioneering was going on last night & no one can tell how we shall stand this morning. A new man may be put forward or otherwise a great change in the result of the last ballot take place.[1]

---

[1]The Democratic National Convention opened on Monday, May 27, 1844, in Baltimore. Voting began the next day, during which there were seven ballots in which no candidate could gain enough support to obtain the nomination. The eleven members of the North Carolina delegation voted as follows: 1st ballot—Van Buren 2, Cass 4, Johnson 5; 2nd ballot—Cass 5, Johnson 5; 3rd ballot—Johnson 11; 4th ballot—Cass 11; 5th ballot—Cass 7, Johnson 4; 6th ballot—Cass 7, Johnson 4; 7th ballot—Van Buren 2, Cass 7, Johnson, 2. Wednesday morning, May 29, as Hill predicted, a new candidate, James K. Polk, was introduced. On the 8th ballot the North Carolina vote was Van Buren 2, Cass 8, and Calhoun, 1. On the 9th ballot, James K. Polk was unanimously nominated as the Democratic party's candidate for president of the United States. North Carolina delegates, by congressional district, were: 1st District—[*information unavailable*]; 2nd District—Burton Craige, Romulus M. Saunders, alternate; 3rd District—John Hill; 4th District— Walter F. Leake, Neil Nicholson, alternate; 5th District—Robert Strange, Josiah O. Watson, alternate; 6th District—Gabriel Holmes; 7th District—Weldon N. Edwards, Sydney Smith, alternate; 8th District—William A. Bloom, H. S. Clark, alternate; 9th District—[*information unavailable*]. Louis D. Henry of Wake, chairman of the Democratic State and Central Committee, and Charles Fisher of Rowan were at-large delegates. Saunders called the Convention to order, and Watson, although an alternate, also attended the sessions. *North-Carolina Standard*, April 24, May 27, 1844; *Baltimore Republican*, reprinted in the *North-Carolina Standard*, June 5, 1844.

Roderick Murchison[1] *to David S. Reid* A&H-DSR

Jefferson N C
May 31st 1844

Your esteemed favor of 14th Inst came duly to hand—I am sorry that Gen. McKay's[2] Bill to modify the Tariff has received its *quietus*. How goes the Annexation Treaty?

Before this time you know at Washington who our candidates are for the Presidency & Vice pres—we will here the same here in a few days—I do hope however that our party will harmonise & cordially support the nominees—our candidates in Ashe are for Commons T. Witcher[3] (Dem.) no oppos yet) Senate Surry & Ashe Wm P. Dobson of Surry—no opposition yet—but one expected—for Sheriff Geo W. Reeves[4] & E C Bartlett[5] Esq.

There is an old gentleman in this neighborhood Capt Daniel Dickson, who wishes you to inquire in Washington for Benjamin Chambers—who is a step son of Dickson who says he has not heard from him in many years—if you find out Chambers—please say to him that his mother (Mrs. Dickson) is getting old and very infirm and that she says she is extremely anxious to see him before she dies—and at any rate she wishes him to write to her—the old gentleman further requests that Mr. C. may be informed that he (Mr. D.) and family are all well and although old and decl[in]ing he still makes a compitency to subsist on

I hope you will not consider the old gentleman troublesome—he was a warm supporter of you last summer—

Let me hear from you often as convnt

P.S. Mr. Chambers is or formerly was an engraver by trade & resided in Washington but I think he married in N. Y.

---

[1]Roderick Murchison, a Jefferson, Ashe County, merchant, was a partner in the mercantile firm of Waugh, Poe, and Murchison. He was appointed postmaster of Jefferson in 1834. Fletcher, *Ashe County*, 89; Records of the Appointments of Postmasters, Records of the Post Office Department, Record Group 28, National Archives and Records Service Microfilm.

[2]James Iver McKay (1793-1853), a Goldsboro attorney, served in the United States House of Representatives (1831-1849). He was the United States district attorney for North Carolina in 1817, and from 1815 to 1830 he served several terms in the state Senate. As chairman of the House Ways and Means Committee, he was a leader in securing a downward revision of the tariff of 1842. His 1844 bill failed, but with administration backing he was able to get passage in 1846 of the lower Walker tariff. *Biographical Directory of Congress*, 1303; Norton, *Democratic Party*, 119-120, 124.

[3]Taliaferro Witcher of Ashe County was a Democrat in the House of Commons (1831-1835). Fletcher, *Ashe County*, 121.

[4]George W. Reeves of Jefferson was on a local public school committee (1879-1880). Fletcher, *Ashe County*, 188.

[5]E. C. Bartlett of Jefferson was the sheriff of the county, a town commissioner of Jefferson, and chairman of the Ashe County commissioners in 1872. Fletcher, *Ashe County*, 76, 88, 93.

Peter Scales to David S. Reid A&H-DSR

Madison
Rockingham County N Ca
June 3rd 1844

I have not heard from you for some time, if Congress continues in session, I hope you will favor me with a line, that I may know how our prospects are at Washington, I have just been informed that Col Polk[1] of Tenessee, has recieved the nomination of the Democratic convention for president and Silas Wright[2] of N York for vice president, If it be true we may flatter ourselves that the die is cast, and that Col Polk will be elected by a triumpant majority, The state of feeling here and in the whole South and South West is such on the Texas question that no individual who opposes that measure can posibly succeed, and Mr Clay you know has taken decided grounds against it,

A Convention assembled at our court house on Tuesday of May Court to nominate Candidates to Represent Rockingham County in the next Legislature, who nominated Geo D. Boyd[3] in the Senate, and Dr R P Wiliamson & myself in the Commons, Our old friend Cardwell[4] was there and addressed the Convention in a few feeling and pertinent remarks, declining a nomination which the Convention was disposed to give him by acclamation. It was generally understood that the Candidates would address the people on Thursday, but Mr Boyd was too unwell to attend, Dr Williamson also did not attend, but both of them wrote to D W Courts Esqr saying that they would accept the nomination, I made a few remarks to the people saying that I woul also accept without any intention of makeing a speece [speech] but to the surprise of every Democrat in the house, Wm R Walker[5] Esqr anounced himself as a candidate in a party speech of about an hour in which he declared himself in favor of a Bank, protective tariff, Distribution, and all the other measures of the whig party, I replied to him in a speech of about the same length in which I so completely entangled him, that he attempted a rejoinder, but made an entire failure

I must ask the favor of you to procure me the following papers a coppy of Mr Serjant's life of Mr Clay,[6] (as I understand it is writen for a northern atmosphere), Mr Badger's address to the people of N Carolina in 1828 on the subject of Mr Clays bargain, the address of the Whig Convention of Virginia in 1840 (in which they deny that Genl Harison was a Bank man) and the address of the whig members of Congress in which they assert that the Bankrupt law was a whig measure, your compliance with the above request and if you would be kind enough to furnish me with any other documents that you may think useful, will confer a great favor on your friend and Obt Servt

PS—Please ascertain what Niles Register of Debates[7]; from its establishment to the present time can be procured for

Also please procure for me P.—Mr Galatin's work, entitled, "Suggestions on the Banks an Currency of the several United States in reference principally to the suspension of specie payment"[8]

Also a work by Nathan Appleton, Entitled "Remarks on Currency and Banking, haveing reference to the present derangement of the circulating medium in the United States["][9]

And also a "Treatise on Currency & Banking["] by Condy Raquet [*sic*][10]

---

[1]James Knox Polk (1795-1849), a Columbia, Tennessee, attorney and North Carolina native, was a state legislator, governor of Tennessee, and member of the United States House of Representatives. He was president of the United States from 1845 to 1849. *DAB*, XV, 34-39.

[2]Silas Wright (1775-1847), a New York attorney, was a state legislator, member of both houses of Congress, and governor of New York (1844-1846). In 1844 he declined a nomination on the Democratic ticket as vice-president, and the nomination went to George M. Dallas, who was elected. *DAB*, XX, 565-567.

[3]George D. Boyd (1797-1886), a Rockingham County planter and merchant, was a local Democratic leader, justice of the peace, member of the House of Commons in 1840, and a state senator seven terms from 1842 to 1858. Powell, *DNCB*, 201.

[4]Richard P. Cardwell, previously identified.

[5]William Richmond Walker, originally from Caswell County and an 1838 graduate of the University of North Carolina, was an attorney in Wentworth. A Whig in a Democratic county, Walker was defeated in his attempt to win a seat in the House of Commons. Hamilton and Williams, *Graham Papers*, II, 12, 300-303.

[6]Epes Sargent (1813-1880), a native of Massachusetts, was Washington correspondent for the *Boston Daily Atlas* in the early 1830s. Sargent's *Life and Public Service of Henry Clay* was published in 1842 in New York by Greeley & McElrath. *DAB*, XVI, 356-357.

[7]*Niles's Register* was a weekly journal published (1811-1849) in Baltimore by Hezekiah Niles (d. 1839) and continued by his son William Ogden Niles. The journal was considered so valuable a source of information concerning American history

that the first 32 volumes, covering 1812-1827, were reprinted. The journal at its conclusion comprised 76 volumes. James Grant Wilson and John Fiske (eds.), *Appleton's Cyclopaedia of American Biography* (New York: D. Appleton and Co., 6 volumes and supplements, 1888), IV, 521, hereinafter cited as *ACAB* with appropriate volume and page number.

[8]Probably the standard work by Albert Gallatin (1761-1849), *Considerations on the Currency and Banking System of the United States* (Philadelphia: Carey & Lea, 1831). Scot Bruntjen and Carol Bruntjen (comps.), *A Checklist of American Imprints for 1831* (Metuchen, N. J.: Scarecrow Press, 1975), 127, hereinafter cited as Bruntjen and Bruntjen, *American Imprints 1831.*

[9]Nathan Appleton, *Remarks on Currency and Banking Having Reference to the Present Derangement of the Circulating Medium in the United States* (Boston: n.p., 1841; 2nd ed., C. C. Little, 1841). Frances W. Gregory, *Nathan Appleton Merchant and Entrepreneur 1779-1861* (Charlottesville: University of Virginia Press, 1975), 321.

[10]Condy Raguet (1784-1842) wrote *A Treatise on Currency and Banking . . .* (Philadelphia: Grigg and Elliott, 1839). Carol Rinderknecht (comp.), *A Checklist of American Imprints for 1839* (Metuchen, N. J. & London: Scarecrow Press, 1988), 223, hereinafter cited as Rinderknecht, *American Imprints 1839.*

Reuben Reid to David S. Reid A&H-DSR

Reidsville NC
June 6th 1844

I again in form you that we are all well hopin that you are enjoying the Same blessing yours to Roday[1] has come to hand and we were all glad to here of your good health I hav nothing very Strange to tell you at presant Hugh[2] & Mr Adams[3] has both got home & in good health and made very good trips we hav fine Seasons Crops of corn looks well amost too much rain I fear for the wheat crop all the famaly desires there love to you Frances[4] & the children is well Hugh says he will rite to you in a few days I remain your loving Father.

---

[1]Rhoda Reid, previously identified, was David S. Reid's sister. She was married in 1846 to William Scott. Reese and Fisher, *Settle Family*, 679.

[2]Hugh Kearns Reid, previously identified, brother of David S. Reid.

[3]Samuel F. Adams, previously identified, brother-in-law of David S. Reid.

[4]Frances Adams, previously identified, was wife of Samuel F. Adams. She was also a sister of David S. Reid.

James Phelps to David S. Reid A&H-DSR

Hitchcockville [Connecticut]
June 12th 1844

I have just reached here on business, from Essex, and shall return in a very few days—I found your letter of the 31st May in this office—In relation to the business of Mr Hodges about which we have given you too much trouble, I understand from him (Hodges) that he has recently written you which letter you probably received soon after the date of yours to me[1]—He says he instructed you to sell the scrip for what it is worth etc—You will therefore be guided by his direction in the matter—The money belongs to him and by his request, I consented, though reluctantly, to burden you with the disposition of it—

In regard to the Democratic nominations made at Baltimore—I think they are having a good effect—are generally received with enthusiasm which indicates a thorough union of the party and a rally at the polls that will greatly endanger the success of the Federalists—The Tyler men at present seem to be possessed with the reckless and foolhardy determination of persisting in their project of reviving a ticket in favor of their great exemplear but I think they will before election see the utter hopelessness of his reelection and the folly of presuming that he can carry even a single State—they are only plunging the classes into the bosom of Democracy by their obstinacy—With the accession of their little disaffected strength I believe we should be completely united—I have written you two or three times without receiving an answer until the present, but as you are soon to be released on [parole][2] I hope you will have more time to spend in writing to your friends—Write me at Essex if possible before leaving Washington—

[1]Further identification of Hodges has not been possible. The letter that James Phelps mentions, from Hodges to Reid, written in early June, 1844, does not survive. See also James Phelps to David S. Reid, February 15, 1842. Reid Papers, PC 1, State Archives.

[2]This is a jocular allusion to the approaching recess of the first session of the Twenty-eighth Congress, which took place on June 17, 1844. The second session began December 2, 1844, and concluded March 3, 1845. *Biographical Directory of Congress, Bicentennial Edition*, 134, 136.

C. A. Bradford[1] *to David S. Reid* A&H-DSR

Pontotoc Misspi
July 13. 1844.

Some ten days have elapsed since I reached home from Washington, and I have been busy in collecting the evidences of public sentiment in this State relative to the propects of Gov. Polk. The vote of Misspi is just as certain as that of any other state in the Union, and our majority will be larger than has ever been given in the State before. I think it cannot be less than 5000. The truth is, the contest affords no amusement. The whigs know & feel that they are defeated here and make no show of battle. They never even express a hope of the State except in jest or bravado. They will not bet even when immense odds is offered them.

From Tennessee we have frequent accounts, and they are most cheering. I name one. The probate Court clerk of an adjoining County, *a whig*, and a few years ago, a Tennesseean, has just returned from a visit to that State. He was here buying land a day or two since, and gave it as his decided opinion that Polk would have got that State without the Texas question, but with it, he expected to see "a very large gap" in the race. He is a frank plain spoken and respectable man, and like few whigs, free from the influnce of party drill, hence his candor. Other accounts corroborate this, fully. We shall certainly get Tennessee. Louisiana too, is just as safe as Misspi. So a very respectable whig from that State, but not a noisy politician, admitted to me yesterday.

May I ask the favor of you to give me your *candid* opinion of the prospects in North Carolina? Will Mr Hoke[2] be elected Gov? If so, may we then count on the State for Polk? I see the editorials of the Standard are in the best temper and spirit, but they may be written for effect and not be truly felt. I shall be pleased to hear from you at your earliest convenience.

Our friend Thompson[3] came very near losing his little Son last week. The child, you know, took the whooping cough at Washn. and on the journey down the river, he took cold, which was succeeded by violent fever. They were obliged to lie by on the way and for a time the physicians despaired of him. But the little fellow has weathered the storm and is now convalescent.

What information have you of an extra session? Will there be one?

---

[1]C. A. Bradford, a resident of Pontotoc, Mississippi, was apparently originally from North Carolina. Pontotoc County was organized on February 9, 1836, out

of the Chickasaw Cession. Bradford was living there by 1840. Sixth Census, 1840, Pontotoc County, Mississippi, 147.

[2]Michael Hoke (1810-1844), an attorney from Lincoln County, was a member of the House of Commons (1834-1842). He ran as a Democrat for governor in 1844 but lost to William A. Graham. Hoke died within a month after the election. Wheeler, *Reminiscences*, 245.

[3]Jacob Thompson, previously identified, was also a resident of Pontotoc and a North Carolina native.

Robert P. Williamson to David S. Reid A&H-DSR

Rawlinsburg
July the 29th 1844

I thank you for your kind information—I had observed that difficulty in the Constitution to my being eligible to a seat in the legislature—I have resigned my office[1] some weeks past & to make it still more certain I have [*illegible*] it to the dep[artment] again.

I regret my health is still delicate—I have a very unpleasant swimming in my head growing out I think a deranged stomach which makes it very unpleasant to encounter the sun & even to take much exercise—I have it in contemplation to attend the C House at Leaksville or wherever you or my friend Boyd[2] may deem best—Please to write me upon return mail without fail as I may wish to start Wensday evening—Please to consult Boyd & let me know by the return mail

I must press upon you the importance of urging the texas question—it is founded in justice & reason and accords well with popular sentiment—Col. Brown's[3] sentiments met with no response from the people—he is a devoted admirer of Colo Benton[4] very great authority when he is right—But upon this question I think he is inconsistent as well as wrong.

I thank you kindly for your interposition in my behalf & hope it will be in my power to return the kind office.

---

[1]Robert P. Williamson previously identified, had been appointed postmaster at Rawlinsburg (Ruffin) in Rockingham County. He was successful in his bid for reelection to the House of Commons, serving in the session of 1844-45, which began on November 18, 1844. Cheney, *North Carolina Government*, 313-314.

[2]George D. Boyd, previously identified, a Rockingham County politician.

[3]Bedford Brown, previously identified.

[4]Thomas Hart Benton, previously identified.

Joseph W. Hampton[1] *to David S. Reid* A&H-DSR

Jefferson, Ashe
27th Aug. 1844

I take the liberty, at the request of several of our friends in this County, to drop you a line, suggesting the importance of your visiting Ashe some time previous to the ensuing election. I have been here about two weeks, on a visit for my health, and find our friends in fine spirits, notwithstanding their recent defeat. And I have no doubt a speech or two in this County, would restore our ascendency. The late elections here were carried by stratagem, based on a local question—that of a division of the County—and not by a political change. Col. Bower[2] leaves in a few days for the North, and will return here by the Superior Court, and requests me to say to you, that he would be very glad (as would the entire Democracy of the County) to see you here at that time (7th Octr.) He also suggests that as you come over, have an appointment to address the people at Gap Civil, the Saturday previous to Court, and he will meet you there, or if he cannot be there, Col. Murchison[3] will. I think this is an opportunity now offered to make a very favorable impression in this County. I have succeeded in circulating over a hundred copies of my paper (the Jeffersonian) in this County, and shall probably be enabled to circulate more before I leave, as the people, Whigs as well as Democrats, seem anxious to read

Sending you my warmest respects, and prayers for the success of our cause,

---

[1]Joseph W. Hampton of Jefferson, Ashe County, published a Democratic newspaper, the *Jeffersonian.* In 1835 he was coeditor of the *Western Carolinian* of Salisbury. Johnson, *Ante-Bellum North Carolina,* 770n.

[2]George Bower, previously identified.

[3]Roderick Murchison, previously identified.

William W. Holden[1] *to David S. Reid* A&H-DSR

Raleigh
Oct 30, 1844

Yours of the 26th has been received. The tickets have been sent as you requested and I hope they will reach you in good time.

Your letter in reply to mine enclosing the forged letter was received. I hold this forgery over the head of its author, and justice to Dr. Williamson may yet call it out. I wrote to the P.M. at Wentworth, who informed me that he knew no one by the name of "Thomas A. H. Hughes."

The democrats hereabouts are wide awake and full of enthusiasm. Listen for *thunder* from Edgecomb! From all quarters we have assurances of an increased vote. Orange will poll a powerful vote. So our friends there inform me. Wake will also do her duty, and Cumberland promises 500 majority for Polk and Dallas.[2] Indeed the Cape Fear counties are all ready and panting for action. Upon the whole we have much cause to hope for N. Carolina. I may be too sanguine, but it does seem to me that the election of Col. Polk is placed beyond a reasonable doubt.

Be pleased to send me all the returns you can get, as soon as possible.

---

[1]William Woods Holden (1818-1892), an Orange County native, was a leading antebellum Democratic publisher and editor. Although he began his journalistic career with the Whig Raleigh *Star*, he was offered the editorship of the Democratic *North-Carolina Standard* in 1843. He switched parties, and under his leadership the *Standard* became one of the most influential papers in the state and was a factor in the rejuvenation of the Democratic party. He represented Wake County for a term in the House of Commons (1846-1847). Holden became a close friend and supporter of Reid and was instrumental in persuading Reid to take the gubernatorial nomination in 1848. After the Civil War, Holden helped to found the Republican party in North Carolina. He was appointed provisional governor in May, 1865, by the occupational commander but was defeated in the fall election. Elected governor in 1868, Holden had a controversial administration and was impeached by a conservative legislature and removed from office in 1871. Powell, *DNCB*, III, 169-171; Cheney, *North Carolina Government*, 189n, 316, 433n.

[2]George M. Dallas (1792-1864), an attorney from Philadelphia, was the vice-presidential candidate on the Democratic ticket. He had previously served in the diplomatic corps and in Congress. *Biographical Directory of Congress*, 772.

James Phelps to David S. Reid A&H-DSR

Essex Conn.
Wednesday Evening
Nov 27th 1844—

I trust you will hold me excusable for troubling you with a short communication at this time in view of the recent triumphant achievement of the Democracy of the country as evinced in the brilliant success of Mr Polk, and the galling discomfiture of Henry Clay—

This is indeed a most truly gratifying result and one which has cast our everlasting veil over the prospects of the Whigs of this section of the Union—They could not be made before this election to doubt but that their favorite hobby Protection would receive the sanction of the people as a principle of just and equitable and saving national policy, not for a moment suspecting that the grossness of the imposition covered as it was by an outside garb of affluent plausibility would be detected—In this as in every other thing they placed a false estimate upon the intelligence of the great mass of the people and instead of deceiving others were themselves most disastrously duped—thanks to the discrimination and integrity of the majority who have decided to confer no special immunity upon our New England capitalists, and to protect them only equally, and in common with other deserving interests of the nation—You of the South cannot readily imagine the influence which the cry of protection against foreign pauper labor, has in our manufacturing community which in many neighborhoods is literally composed of lords and their dependents—and consequently do not realize the tremendous odds against which the gallant spirits which compose the true neutral democracy of a few of the Northern States have been arrayed— Every imaginable species of bribery, coercion, intimidation, and downright Oppression have been extensively resorted to, to swell the vote of the Clay Electoral ticket, and thereby give countenance to the unjust unequal, arbitrary, and anti-republican doctrine of high duties for the mere purpose of affording exclusive protection to a particular class of citizens, and the very one's above all others best capable of sustaining themselves—Our friends in this state standing in the very midst of ten thousand looms and spindles, took their position in the canvass upon the broad platform of principle, and maintained it with unshrinking firmness—With proverbial sincerity they proclaimed exactly the same views in regard to the justice and expediency of the protection policy as were advocated by their noble-hearted brethren of the Southern States—this was the great question at issue here—the struggle was one of principle and the righteousness of the republican faith above proved the rock of our political salvation—True the power and influence of the unscrupulous Capitalists assisted by corruption and oppression gave our adversaries a temporary advantage in the manufacturing states, which however would not have been gained but for the means put in requisition for its accomplishment—Had every man been left entirely free to have voted as he chose, the result in this state, though it might perhaps have been the same in effect, yet the relative strength of parties would have been vastly different. As it is their glorious consummation is attained, and all is emphatically well—The result is such as cannot fail to inspire the patriot's soul with emotions of thanksgiving and light up his countenance with the kindling beam of gladness—The public morals have been sustained—virtue has triumphed over vice—democracy over federalism, and the honor of the nation has been vindicated—This was the political death struggle of the leprous demagogue and thanks to Heaven his last hope has perished—the blood of Munda[1] crying from the earth has been partially avenged, and the punishment of the "embodiment"[2] like that of the murderer of old "already greater than he can bear"[3]—this country and its institutions has passed through the most mighty violent and fearful trial in the history of her civil progress from the days of the Constitution. And we are yet a free and happy people—May we always so fortunately escape the dangers that encompass us—

My Examination took place last month and I am happy to be able to inform you resulted in an honorable acquittal—I am now an attorney counsellor in all the Courts of this state—The examination was conducted by all the members of this County Bar and was protracted and extensive lasting several hours and covering almost every branch of the science—I am not aware that I missed a single question through the entire course—

My dear Colonel may I ask of you the favor of sending me a copy of the tariff bill now in force and also a copy of the act [*illegible*] by Mr McKay?[4] If you have them at hand and can spare them as well as not you will very much oblige me by sending them—They will be of much service to me in the spring campaign—If possible I intend to be present at the Inauguration Do write me when you have leisure—In haste truly your friend &c

---

[1]Probably Munda, a city in Spain, site of a battle in 45 B.C. in which the forces of Caesar defeated the sons of the popular former Roman consul Pompey, capturing and putting one of them to death. Agents of Caesar had three years earlier murdered Pompey as he stepped off a boat in Egypt. In his consulship, Pompey had openly broken with the aristocracy and had become a great popular hero. Thus Phelps's allusion to "the blood of Munda crying from the earth" having been partially avenged. This early defeat of a "democratic" leader by a tyrant, Phelps

suggested, was at least partly compensated for by the victory of the Democratic candidate, Polk, over Henry Clay, whom Phelps considered a foe of democracy. Sir William Smith, *Smaller Classical Dictionary* (New York: E. P. Dutton, revised edition, 1958), 194, 234-235, hereinafter cited as Smith, *Smaller Classical Dictionary*.

[2]Phelps refers to Clay as the "embodiment," apparently of an unspecified tyrant such as Julius Caesar, who caused the death of Pompey, a protodemocratic Roman consul who rose from humble origins. The imperious and arrogant actions of Henry Clay during 1841 and 1842 led him to be called "dictator" by his enemies and even by some of his friends. Smith, *Smaller Classical Dictionary*, 234; Clement Eaton, *Henry Clay and the Art of American Politics* (Boston: Little, Brown, 1957), 147, hereinafter cited as Eaton, *Henry Clay*.

[3]The punishment alluded to here appears to be Clay's loss in the 1844 presidential election, about which he was particularly bitter. Phelps again metaphorically compares Clay's defeat to the reverses of guilty Caesar, who first suffered from remorse at causing the death of Pompey and later was himself assassinated. The reference to a murderer's punishment being "already greater than he can bear" is from an unidentified literary work, possibly the *Pharsalia* of the Latin poet Lucan, who was an admirer of Pompey.

[4]Congressman James Iver McKay, previously identified, Democrat of North Carolina. See Roderick Murchison to David S. Reid, May 31, 1844, note 2, for reference to his bill.

L. P. Wright[1] *to David S. Reid* A&H-DSR

[Rockingham County]
Decr 8th 1844

I drop you a line to let you see that I am well and hope these few lines, will find you the same.—after our glorious Political tryumph I thought I would like to talk with you a little.—I think there is no Doubt but we have lost 2 or 3 States by the principle of Betting and Tenness Certain I have ascertained that on the nomination of Polk there was some $50000 Betted in the state that Polk would not get the state well you know last year the whigs had 3800 Maj. well the whigs was on one side of every Bet of Course.—and every whig had his whig relations which would Stand up to him to keep him from loosing while otherwise they might have changed and of course this prevented many changes in our favour and no Doubt but some Democrats voted for the whigs of thier relation to keep them from loosing—so that betting has hurt us the worst this year—and Col I am in hopes you will get a Bill before the house to prevent if possible the principle of Betting on Elections Especially on the President and Membrs of Congress for it Certainly does in some degree Defeat the will of the people and

I hope you will try to fix the Prsd Election to take all over the Union the same day—we only lost it the last session by one in the Senate. Give it another trial this winter perhaps it will take I would like very much to hear from you when ever Convenient—

---

[1]L. P. Wright was a farmer from Rockingham County. In 1850 he had one slave. Seventh Census, 1850, Rockingham County, Slave Schedule, 104.

1845

Barzillai Graves to David S. Reid A&H-DSR

Near Milton
January 11th 1845

I wrote you a month ago on the subject of the removal of the P. M. at Milton stating that a Petition had gone to the Genl P. Office for that purpose—I am informed the P. M. Genl has the matter before him—My object in addressing you formerly and now, is to request you to interfere and have the decission of the P. M Genl suspended for a while—I stated to you, and now repeat that the Petition bears not the name of an influential or leading character about Milton and all agree that it is useless to remove one Whig and make way for a successor of a great deal more violence and he the brother in law to the Editor of the dirty Milton Chronicle and no doubt acting with him—I am making and have partly concluded arrangements to establish a Democratic Printing Press in Milton which, when it goes into operation will support the New Administration and the cause of Democracy with all the power my partner and myself possess I would have communicated my intentions to you sooner but wanted a little time to act and reflect on the (to me a new) subject. Mr. Palmer[1] will probably be in Washington City by the time you get this and altho he is friendly & promises me assistance in my undertaking I wish you to keep the contents of this from him—None deny but that he ought to be removed for many reasons which might be enumerated and which are not set forth in the Petition and I shall not state in this way—Prefering to treat him respectfully—I therefore repeat that this is in confidence & request you to use it so. The profits of the P Office at Milton is supposed to be $300 and that added to the Printing Office would greatly assist a poor fellow in advocating the cause of Democracy—By the first of March or sooner I, with the assistance of an experienced partner expect to have the Printing Press in operation and publish a Weekly Newspaper devoted to the old fashioned Republican principles[2] Please help me. I have written to Mr Haywood[3] & Mr Saunders[4] with whom I desire you to confer

Any thing from you directed to Red House Post office will be thankfully accepted.

P S. January 13th. Since writing the above I learn that a recommendation has gone on in favour of Mr. George Wilson[5] as P M. He is a clever young man worthy the appointment, and a good Democrat. I should prefer him to any young man in Milton but so anxious am I to get the Printing Press in operation and devote its columns to the cause of Democracy that I must say I fear its profits would be doubtful in sustaining it unaided by the Post Office. With the assistance of that Office a Press has always done well in Milton—without it bad. If the matter cannot be postponed I expect my partner or assistant could remove to Milton & commence business in the course of two or three weeks but we prefer acting more at leisure and hope that if Palmer is removed a little time can consistently be given as to prepare for both Offices

---

[1]Nathaniel J. Palmer (d. 1854), a Milton publisher, established the *Milton Spectator* (later the *Milton Chronicle*) in 1831. He was postmaster of Milton from 1831 to 1848, and in 1849 C. N. B. Evans was appointed postmaster there. In 1853 Palmer bought the *North Carolina Democrat* and moved it from Hillsborough to Milton. Powell, *Caswell County*, 377, 402-403, 404, 557; *Raleigh Star*, October 24, 1849.

[2]In February, 1845, C. N. B. Evans, who owned the *Milton Chronicle* (formerly the *Milton Spectator*) wrote Senator Willie P. Mangum that Graves had plans to publish a Democratic paper called the *Milton Banner*, but this plan apparently never reached fruition. Powell, *Caswell County*, 402-403.

[3]William Henry Haywood, Jr., previously identified.

[4]Romulus Mitchell Saunders, previously identified.

[5]George W. Wilson (b. 1822) was a resident of Yanceyville Township, Caswell County, by 1850, where he was employed as a clerk. Seventh Census, 1850, Caswell County, Population Schedule, 231.

David S. Reid to Frances R. Adams[1] UNC-SR

Washington City, D.C.
January 19, 1845.

It affords me pleasure to have it in my power to again inform you of my uninterrupted good health. Providence has been propicious to me in this as well as in many other respects. I often think of what you said to me when we parted. My habits and conduct here are very much the same as they are at home; but I fear I have not that Religion which seems to make you so happy.

In my last letter I informed you that there was a duel on hand between Clingman and Yancy.[2] They exchanged shots, and nobody was hit, whereupon the matter was settled and they returned to their seats in the House and have behaved very well ever since. I am anxious to see you all. My love to the Children. In haste.

---

[1]Sister of David S. Reid.

[2]William Lowndes Yancey (1814-1863), an attorney from Montgomery, Alabama, served in the United States House of Representatives (1844-1846). He was an active secessionist and served the Confederacy as an agent in Europe and as a senator. The duel between Yancey and Congressman Thomas L. Clingman was precipitated when, during a debate in Congress in January, 1845, Clingman accused the Democrats of having used unfair political tactics during the 1844 presidential campaign. Yancey responded by questioning Clingman's honor; Clingman then challenged Yancey to a duel. The duel, which took place near Bladensburg, Maryland, was finally settled by seconds. *Biographical Directory of Congress*, 1855; Shanks, *Mangum Papers*, 253n.

James Phelps to David S. Reid A&H-DSR

Essex Connecticut
January 24th 1845

I received your letter in due time and the valuable documents you were so kind as to send me for which I thank you very much—Since the receipt of your letter I have been absent considerable, and unwell a portion of the time with a severe cold which has prevented me from writing you, and I have an opportunity now to say but a few words—I am at much loss even as are all "*the people*" to know what Congress is going to effect in the progress of the present session—It appears somewhat doubtful whether Annexation or the Postage Bill will be gone through with before the close of Mr Tyler's term.

I suppose you will of course be a candidate for re-election and if so of course again successful. This is my sincere wish unless in your judgment you could further advance your honor and interest, the welfare of your constituents, and the glory of Democracy by some other course—Knowing your numerous and responsible representative duties I feel unwilling to urge you to write me but be assured whenever you can find leisure and inclination I should be most heartily gratified by hearing from you—

As for myself personally, I have gone so far in life as to become induced to prepare to enter upon the new and interesting scenes of domestic life—I have made a "*contract*" of marriage which is however yet "*Executory*" but will be probably consummated ere the present year

shall have rolled with its burden into the bosom of eternity—I am confidently anticipating the enjoyment of much pleasure from this new relation which advances the crowning blessing of life.
"The only bliss of Paradise"
"Which has survived the fall"—
to lonely wayward and despairing man—

The clangor of preparation for another political campaign is already ringing in our camp notwithstanding the din of the last great battle of the Union has scarcely died upon the ear—I think we shall be able to redeem ourselves partially at best in this State—We expect to lose two or three of our Congressmen but hope to gain the State ticket and the Legislature—The election of the one will devolve upon the others in consequence of the failure of a popular choice—

Joseph W. Neal[1] *to David S. Reid* A&H-DSR

Rockingham County N. C
January 28th 1845

Your letter of the 8th Inst was [*faded*] mail in which you say that Mr. Cassell[2] desires Mr. Simpsons[3] deed to the property I sold him sent on

In reply to which I can only say that I Expected it had been sent on before this you can say to him that I had it Executed on the part of Mr. Simpson at the time I did mine and sent it on to Hamburg[4] to Mr. Simpson and requested him to forward it to Washington to Mr. Birch[5] for Mr. Cassell when he should get the necessary Certificates to it. I Suppose he has neglected it though not from any design to misput Mr. Cassell in any way as he sanctioned the terms of the sale by a letter I recd from him before it was Closed. I am now at this time Expecting him here Every day and as soon as he arrives I will see that his deed is Completed and sent on or if any thing occurs that he dont Come as soon as I am aware of it I will write to him that the trade has been Closed and to send on his deed Immediately

Doct Scales[6] & William Bethell[7] have arrived holme from Louisiana are much pleased with the Cuntry say they have purchased Land near Pinckney Bethell[8] 1000 acres for $25000—and setled their negros on it—Doct MCain[9] hired his out in Mississippi for high prices Nothing new or Interesting have occured with us since I rote you last there is a good deal of sickness & Death in the Cuntry there is a litle spur in the Tobacco market which seems to Encourage the people some otherwise business is dull and Languid though some of us Looking forward with hopes of an Improvement soon

our Legislature adjourned after several weeks siting and done but litle Except to make some provision by borrowing to meet present demands uppon the State I think the old North State is Likely not to be a verry desirable holme for the riseing generation as its authorities have not and never will have the Courage to Levy taxes to pay its debts as long as they Can practice the Expedient of the Spendthrift which all Experience show will succeed only for a time

write to me soon I hope texas will be annexed though I Confess I fear it will not

---

[1]Joseph W. Neal, a Rockingham County planter, served in the House of Commons (1846-1847, 1854-1855). In 1860 he was one of the county's largest slaveholders with seventy-nine slaves. Cheney, *North Carolina Government*, 316, 323; Eighth Census, 1860, Rockingham County, Slave Schedule, 6.

[2]Mr. Cassell has not been identified.

[3]Possibly James Simpson, who was in 1840 a resident of Franklin County, Mississippi, where the village of Hamburg is located. Simpson was probably a former resident of the Rockingham County, North Carolina, vicinity. Sixth Census, 1840, Franklin County, Mississippi, 165.

[4]Hamburg is a village in Franklin County, Mississippi, about twenty miles east of Natchez.

[5]Mr. Birch has not been identified.

[6]Dr. Robert H. Scales (1805-1885) married Jane Watt Bethell, the sister of William D. Bethell. Marjorie Craig, "Family Records of Henrietta Alberta Ratlikke and Jasper Newton Craig" (Reidsville: Privately printed, 1955), unnumbered, hereinafter cited as Craig, "Family Records."

[7]William Decatur Bethell (1815-1888), a leading planter and landholder in Rockingham County, served in the state Senate (1848-1849). He was a director of the Bank of Yanceyville in 1852. Craig, "Family Records"; Cheney, *North Carolina Government*, 1257; Powell, *Caswell County*, 345.

[8]Pinckney Bethell was either the uncle or brother of William D. Bethell. Craig, "Family Records."

[9]Dr. McCain is probably a nephew of Robert H. Scales. Scales's sister Mary married Joseph McCain in 1807, and Dr. McCain is probably their son. Webster and Vernon, *Early Families*, 106.

Daniel W. Courts to David S. Reid A&H-DSR

Rockingham Co. N.C.
Jany 31st 1845

I have again taken up the case of Martin Miller[1] & intend to run it out. You may recollect that Mr Edwards[2] said in his answer that "the certificate of the Register of the Land office at Annapolis should be attained as to the evidence which the Archives of Maryland afford of his alledged service or that of his designated officers" Mr Edwards did not return the declaration & Miller died before his answer came so that I do not now know who he said were his officers. I have this day written to the Register & stated to him that you would forward to him in a day or two an extract from Millers declaration, Will you do me the favor to call at the office of Mr E & copy that part of the declaration which speaks of the nature of his service and the names of his officers & forward it to the Register. I have been talking to some more of Miller's neighbours who say they are confident of his having served in the revolution I almost reflect on myself for having let the matter sleep so long & his family suffering. You can say to Mr E that the most abundant testimony of the opinion of the neighbourhood can be procured in favor of the claim. I dont intend to cease till I get it The Whigs now speak of runing McMillan[3] of Ashe for Congress. I suppose they think if he is beaten it will make but little difference any way, the biger dogs I think are afraid to pitch in. I wish you would send me if you please a copy of the Presidents message with the accompanying documents, I have seen the first of course but I want to see the last I should like to have also a printed form of a power of attorney for drawing pension money I think Mr Edwards has them

How is Texas coming on & how was the matter between Clingman & Yancy settled, Did the latter succumb?

Let me hear from you

---

[1]Martin Miller (d. ca. 1844) was apparently a Maryland native and Revolutionary War veteran who had settled in Rockingham County.

[2]James L. Edwards (b. 1788), a native of Virginia, was commissioner of pensions in 1845. Created in the War Department in 1833, the office of Commissioner of Pensions became the Bureau of Pensions within the Interior Department in 1849. W. G. Leland, *Guide to the Archives of the Government of the United States in Washington* (Washington: Carnegie Institution, 2nd ed., rev., 1907), 209, hereinafter cited as Leland, *Guide to the Archives*; Seventh Census, 1850, District of Columbia, Population Schedule, 60; J. L. Edwards to David S. Reid, February 15, 1845, Reid Papers, PC 1, State Archives.

[3]Alexander B. McMillan, previously identified.

N. H. McCain[1] *to David S. Reid* A&H-DSR

Milton
Febry 7th. 1845

I desire to trouble you to make examination in some one of the offices at Washington for information of which I know so little myself, that I fear I shall not be able to aid you in directing your enquiries—I understand a Mr. Israel Johnson[2] (or Johnston) a soldier of the revolution who was killed in the battle of Guilford was entitled to a land bounty, that he obtained a grant for the same, which grant, if ever taken from the office, & it is said it was not, is now lost and the grant, or perhaps rather the land, was never located—If such be the facts and you can ascertain it upon examination will you do me the kindness to advise me of the same, and also what steps must be taken to enable his surviving friends to get the benefit of the same—

I see that your body has lashed Texas on, without her debt— How comes on the Canada petition? I trust you will use becoming prudence to steer clear of the dwelling mania—If, however, by an unforeseen accident, it should seize you, tarry in Washington until you are thoroughly cured; I should regret to see it spreading in this peaceable district whose representative you are—We have had a good deal of sickness and several deaths amongst us since you left us, the most of which I suppose you have heard of—You may not have heard of the death of John N. Watt[3] & the little daughter of our friend R. B. Watt[4] Esqr—Let me hear from you—

---

[1]Nathaniel Henry McCain (b. 1814) was an attorney who, like many other North Carolinians in the 1830s and 1840s, migrated to the fertile cotton lands of the Deep South states. Sometime in the late 1840s he moved to Lowndes County, Mississippi, and married Jane C. Topp, daughter of attorney John S. Topp, in whose household they were living at the time of the 1850 census. By 1860 McCain had abandoned the practice of law for full-time farming. He and Jane, by then parents of four children, had moved to Carroll County, Mississippi, and their combined real and personal estate was worth $50,000. Next door to them lived William A. McCain, also a North Carolina native and farmer, whose combined real and personal estate was worth $60,000. As half that amount was classified as personal estate, this is an indication that he was a large slave owner. He may be the Dr. McCain referred to in Joseph W. Neal to David S. Reid, January 28, 1845, as he was a resident of Mississippi prior to 1850. Seventh Census, 1850, Lowndes County, Mississippi, Population Schedule, 115, Carroll County, Mississippi, Population Schedule, 392; Eighth Census, 1860, Carroll County, Mississippi, Population Schedule, 18.

[2]There is no one named either Israel Johnson or Israel Johnston listed as having served as a soldier from North Carolina in the American Revolution. *Roster of Troops from North Carolina in the American Revolution* (Baltimore: Genealogical Publishing Company, reprint, 1967).

[3]John N. Watt probably died in January, 1845, in Rockingham County. His will, dated January 6, 1845, and witnessed by N. H. McCain and Robert B. Watt, was probated in February, 1845. Rockingham County Wills (microfilm), Book C, 21, Archives, Division of Archives and History, Raleigh, hereinafter cited as Watt Will.

[4]Mary Baily Watt, daughter of attorney Robert B. Watt, died in Rockingham County probably near to the time that John N. Watt died, in January, 1845, although her death was not reported in the *Raleigh Register* until March 11, 1845. Area newspapers reported many deaths from typhoid fever and pneumonia in the winter of 1844-1845.

David S. Reid to Reuben H. Reid[1] RCC

Washington City, D.C.,
February 9, 1845.

I have the honor to acknowledge the receipt of your letter of the 6th inst. It affords me very great pleasure to learn that you are all well. I am proud that my *youngest* brother *can* and *will* write to me. It is a good letter, but you did not write enough. I am pleased to hear that you are going to school, and that your school[2] is opened with prayer. My health never was better than at present.

Mr. Polk will probably be here this week, or at farthest the week after. The vote will be Counted and the result of the Presidential election declared on Wednesday next, and the new President will be inagurated on the 4th of March. A great many persons have already arrived in the City to attend the Inauguration.

We have had some very cold weather for several days past, and the ground is covered with snow, but it is not deep. I believe it is snowing at this time. I never suffer from cold weather here. In my chamber I keep my fire well regulated, the Capitol is heated by *flues* and altho' my seat is 20 yards from a fire I never get the least cold; and when I go out to walk the streets on business, or for exercise, I do not suffer from cold. I go so seldom to the parties that the ladies here tell me that they have no doubt but what I am engaged to be married at home.

The Oregon Bill has passed the House.

Give my love to father, mother, Rhoda, Henrietta,[3] and—yourself. It is now precisely 12 Oclock at night, and I have a letter to write to brother Hugh and one [to] Sister Frances and shall then be able to retire earlier than I have been able to do for some time. I suspect you sleep too much. Give my respects to the neighbours. *Good-by "Shab."* P S. Tell mother that to-day I have been to Church, read the Bible *some* in my room, and have super-scribed a good many Documents. I can not get a long without doing some work on the Sabbath.

---

[1]Reuben Hunt Reid (1834-1859) was twenty-one years younger than his brother David, who was the oldest of eight children born to Reuben and Elizabeth Reid. Reuben Hunt Reid, born when his mother was forty, was the last of the children. At the time this letter was written he was ten years old. Reese and Fisher, *Settle Family*, 679-680.

[2]Reuben probably was attending an academy or common school in or near Reidsville, to which this letter was addressed.

[3]Reid's sisters, previously identified.

Archibald R. Ruffin[1] *to David S. Reid* A&H-DSR

Germanton
Feby 16th 1845

I can only give you what is the common rumour in this and Surry County as to your next opponent altho I myself can give no credence to it McMillan[2] of Ashe is said to be your next opponent should the report turn out to be true it is conclusive evidence that your opponents despair of success and will make use of this *vain man* as their catspaw for it is well known they have many men in their ranks if they beleived there was any chance of success they would prefer to him should they actually run him it will in my estimation be a benefit to our cause. I can give you no news of a political character. There is great interest felt by many as to the result of the Texas question during this Session and from every thing I can learn or see I am induced to think the chances rather against annexation. I wrote to Mr Saunders[3] the other day relative to some appointment under Polk and referred him to you on the subject. Should there be any prospect of success in procuring an appointment which will require my residence in Washington will you be kind enough to inform me of the probable expence of a family consisting of 5 persons two grown the others children under six years old. Mrs. Nelson[4] requests if not asking too much at your hands that you will either send or bring her on your return home a parcel of garden seeds of such description as your judgement may select and in the event you display considerable skill in the selection will in return give you a strong recommendation among the girls.

[1]Archibald R. Ruffin (b. 1784), a native of Virginia, was an attorney living in Germanton, Stokes County. Seventh Census, 1850, Stokes County, Population Schedule, 106.

[2]Alexander B. McMillan, previously identified.

[3]Romulus Mitchell Saunders, previously identified.

[4]Possibly a reference to Susan S. Nelson, wife of Albert F. Nelson of Stokes County. He served one term (1842-1843) in the House of Commons. Stokes County adjoins Rockingham County on the west and was in the Ninth Congressional District in 1841 when Reid unsuccessfully challenged veteran Whig Congressman Augustine H. Shepperd. Stokes County Marriage Bonds; Cheney, *North Carolina Government*, 312, 670, 682-683. Nelson left no will in Stokes County, and he did not appear anywhere in North Carolina in the 1850 census, an indication that he may have moved to another state.

A. C. Lindsey[1] *to David S. Reid* A&H-DSR

Greensboro N C
March 4 - 1845

I suppose to day is a great day in Washington City.[2] I wish I was there altho I am a whig—but as you know a liberal one. I have not heard from you this winter by way of Letter I suppose you have been enjoying yourself so well that you could not or did not have time to think of a, poor, humble County Court Lawyer—but you are excusable if you have devoted part of your idle hours to the society of the ladies. I write you this, that you may inform the Editor of the Intilligencer to stop my paper after the expiration of the year. Settle my account with him and I will return it to you on your return

[1]A. C. Lindsey, an attorney from Greensboro, was living in Yanceyville by 1850. Seventh Census, 1850, Caswell County, Population Schedule, 177.

[2]Victorious Democratic presidential candidate James K. Polk was inaugurated in Washington on March 4, 1845.

Circular of David S. Reid to His Constituents NCC

Washington
March 7, 1845

TO THE VOTERS OF CASWELL, ROCKINGHAM, STOKES, SURRY, WILKES, AND ASHE.

FELLOW-CITIZENS: The term for which I was chosen your representative has expired; and I conform to the custom which has heretofore prevailed in our district, of noticing some of the subjects which have engaged the consideration of the last Congress. When I entered upon the duties assigned me, I entertained fears that I should not be able to discharge the trust with satisfaction to myself, or to those whose kind partiality had made me their representative; and now, after my duties have ceased, when I reflect upon the momentous and complicated questions upon which I have been called to act, I am free to say that those fears have not vanished. Embarrasing and perplexing as many of these questions were, I have avoided no responsibility. My conduct has been prompted solely by a desire to promote the honor and welfare of the country; and fully recognising the accountability of the representative to his constituents, I leave it with you to freely condemn whatever in my legislative course you find to be wrong, and to approve whatever you find in it to be right.

At the first session a bill was reported by the Committee of Ways and Means to modify the tariff of 1842. Although this bill did not provide for as great a reduction as I desired, yet I voted for it, because it was preferable to the present tariff. The southern and northern whigs, joined by a portion of the democrats from the North, voted against this bill, and defeated it in the House by a majority of six votes. Upon this important question, to many of you my views have been often and freely expressed. Subsequent reflection has not changed those views. A tariff is, in fact, a *tax bill*, and ought in detail to be so arranged as to equalize, as nearly as possible, the burdens to be borne by every section of the Union and by all classes, having due regard to the ability of each to contribute. I fancy that all who are opposed to conferring exclusive privileges upon a favored few will assent to the correctness of this position; and if it be right, then the tariff act of 1842 is clearly wrong, as all who impartially examine its operations will be able to discover.

To collect a duty on foreign importations sufficient to defray the legitimate expenditures of government is what no one objects to; but a tariff which taxes one class to enrich another, is unjust, and ought to be abandoned even by those for whose benefit it was enacted. We are told by those who favor this policy, that their object is to protect the American manufacturer against the pauper labor of European nations. When asked how they wish to effect their object, they allege that it is impossible for our manufacturers to compete with the cheap labor of foreigners, and that it is gross injustice to suffer their goods to be brought here and sold, to the exclusion of those manufactured at home. It is unnecessary to remark that if they were to succeed in keeping out all foreign articles, there would be nothing received at our custom-houses upon which to collect a duty, and the government would then have to resort to direct taxation to raise a revenue to defray its expenditures—a measure to which all are opposed.

The fact is, that although the duty on many articles is so high as to prevent their importation, yet the amount of importations under the present tariff for the year ending June 30, 1844, was one hundred and eight millions of dollars; and the question is not whether foreign merchandise shall be admitted into the country; but, after it is admitted, as it is under that act, whether we shall be compelled to pay a *high* or a *low* tax on it. It is contended by many of the friends of the measure that high duties do not enhance the price of the article to the consumer; and to maintain this position they point to the fact that many manufactured articles are lower now than they were some years ago; and, without proof, assume that the tariff is the cause. In this it is clear they are mistaken. But, suppose for the sake of argument, we assume that the tariff has made goods cheaper; and then see what will be the result. You know they tell us that the tariff protects the farmer and planter, as well as the manufacturer.

It is known to every one that, since the passage of the tariff act of 1842, the articles raised by the farmer and planter have fallen much more than the manufactured fabrics; so that, if the tariff is entitled to the credit, of causing the one to be lower, it must bear the blame of the great reduction in the price of the other. If their facts and arguments be untrue, *they prove nothing*; if true, *they prove the tariff to be wrong*. Some take the ground that because other countries lay heavy duties upon our products, we should retaliate by levying heavy duties on theirs; and contend that the consumer does not pay the duty, but that it is paid by the foreigner who sells us the article. Let us examine this position. The onerous duty on tobacco in England is often cited to justify the policy of retaliatory duties. Now, it is no doubt true, that if the duties on tobacco were repealed, it would leave the people there less tax to pay on article, which might enable them to buy and to consume more of it, and thereby increase the demand and raise the price to a limited extent. This would be true in regard to any other article in a similar situation in any country.

But if it were true that the planter who made the tobacco paid the duty, and not the British subject who consumes it; then a good crop of tobacco would ruin any of our planters, and the worst of it would be, that the more tobacco they made, the greater would be the ruin! To illustrate: suppose A raises four hogsheads of tobacco, which he sells for seventy-five dollars each, and they are exported to England, where they are consumed. The duty paid there, on these four hogsheads, would be at least three thousand dollars! Now, can it be pretended that A, whose tobacco was only worth three hundred dollars, has paid this British tax of three thousand dollars? The idea is preposterous. For A no more pays this tax than B, who sells the same quantity of the same article, and at the same price, to be consumed at home, and upon which the British duty is never levied. The consumer pays the duty; and those who insist on retaliating duties are in effect saying that because Great Britain taxes her subjects almost to starvation, to "retaliate," we must tax ourselves in the same way! The people, it is hoped, are not willing to give their sanction to any such system of retaliation.

Nothing is more fallacious than that the foreigner who brings the article to this country, and not the consumer, pays the duty. It must be recollected that we are only one of the great family of nations, and get the products of other countries by bidding as high a price as others are willing to give. If the duty on the foreign article is so high, when added to the price at which the foreigner is able to furnish it, that our people cannot afford to buy it, then the consequence is, that he seeks a market in another quarter, or employs his capital and labor in other pursuits. I will state an example to illustrate the iniquity of the present tariff. Under that act, undyed cotton goods, costing under 20 cents per yard, are valued at 20 cents per yard, and a duty of 30 per cent. charged thereon. The duty on goods costing 10 cents per yard is 6 cents per yard, or 60 per cent. It will be seen that he who consumes the *coarser article* is taxed 60 per cent.! while he who consumes the *finer article* is taxed 30 per cent.! But the injustice does not stop here. Suppose the farmer goes to the merchant and buys a dollar's worth of this foreign goods: in this case he pays 37½ cents of it to the treasury. But suppose he then buys a dollar's worth of the same kind of goods, differing in no respect except that it is of *domestic manufacture*, for which he pays the same price. Now upon this purchase he pays the tax of 37½ cents, or 6 cents per yard, as well as on the other, but with this important difference that in the former case the 37½ cents tax was paid to the treasury; in the latter, it goes into the pocket of the manufacturer. I do not pretend to assert that, upon every domestic article consumed, the price is enhanced the amount of the duty on the foreign article, for the duty, in many instances, greatly exceeds the value of the article, and in those cases it cannot be imported. When this is the case, the treasury derives no revenue from the article; and if the tariff affords it any protection, whatever it amounts to is all paid by the consumer to the manufacturer. But, as a general rule, where the duty is not so high as to prevent the importation of the article, then the amount of the duty is the amount of the tax paid by the consumer; and when paid on the foreign article it goes into the treasury; but when paid on the domestic article it goes to the manufacturer. In the case I have put, if there was no duty on the article, the foreigner would be able to sell his goods at 10 cents per yard, just as he now does; and to enable the American manufacturer to sell his goods, he would have to put them at the same price. But when the duty of 6 cents per yard is laid, it raises the price of the foreign article up to 16 cents, and that enables the American manufacturer, who pays no duty on his goods, to raise *his* price up to 16 cents, which he compels the consumer to pay. Thus it will be seen that the farmer, the planter, and the laborer, being the consumers, are not only made to bear the pricipal burden of supporting the government, but are also compelled to contribute millions as a bounty to the manufacturer. I will here remark, that I entertain no unjust hostility towards the manufacturing interest. On the contrary, I desire to see it left free to prosper and flourish with the other great interests of the country. But when it demands exclusive privileges, and exacts unjust contributions from the agricultural and laboring classes, it shall not receive my countenance or support to enable it to perpetrate such iniquity. It is a matter of some astonishment to see the mechanics in our southern towns and villages supporting the protective policy, and declaiming against those who oppose it, and alleging that the low price of foreign goods prevents them from selling their own manufactures, when, if they would but take the pains to inquire, they would ascertain the fact, that in nine cases out of ten, the article with which the merchant undersells them is manufactured, not in Europe, but in the northern and eastern States, and by the very men whom they seek to protect, and upon whom they endeavor to bestow additional bounties. The Secretary of the Treasury, in his last annual report to Congress, says:

"The existing rates of duties on imports and tonnage with the other sources of revenue, would, according to the best estimates, after keeping down the interest until the 1st of July, in the year 1853, and after paying the ordinary annual expenditures for the support of government, and after discharging the loan of $7,000,000, redeemable 1st July, 1853, leave an accumulated surplus of not less than $50,000,000; and the same rates and sources of revenue, if continued until the year

1863, would, after defraying the ordinary expenditures for the support of government, and discharging the principal and interest upon the debt then redeemable, leave an accumulated surplus in the treasury of not less than $112,000,000."

Thus, it will be seen, in addition to the objections already urged against the system, that a large surplus of revenue is anticipated; and this will have a tendency to produce corruption and extravagance in the expenditures of government.

Before dismissing this subject, I will allude to a vote which I gave shortly after the bill to modify the tariff was defeated. When that clause of the civil and diplomatic appropriation bill which made an appropriation for the purchase of stationery for the use of the House of Representatives was under consideration, a tariff member offered an amendment, requiring the stationery purchased to be of the growth and manufacture of the United States, provided the quality and terms were equal to that of the foreign article. It being the duty of the clerk to purchase the stationery of suitable quality, and at the lowest price, I saw no necessity for the amendment, and voted against it.

After my return home last summer, I found that, for this vote, myself and about twenty others were denounced in a pamphlet, written at the North, called "*The Whig Text Book*," as being inimical to American interests, and disposed to favor British policy! This denunciation was reiterated by some whig newspaper scribblers in my own State, who appeared to be regardless of every other consideration except that of pulling others down to the level of their own political depravity. Under the whig tariff act of 1842, the paper maker has a protection of from 30 to 90 per cent., while the article out of which paper is manufactured has a protection of only 6 per cent.! I then thought, and still believe, that if, after receiving this protection, the paper maker could not successfully manufacture the article, it was high time to stop legislating for his benefit, till we had done something for the other interests of the country. The amount of the purchase was inconsiderable; but it was the principle to which I objected. But few of my constituents are paper makers: they are all paper buyers; and, as their representative, I take this ground: if one of my constituents carries abroad, or sends, by his agent or merchant, (which amounts to the same,) his tobacco, cotton, wheat, beef, wool, or other article, and exchanges it for *paper, or any other commodity*, no matter where it was manufactured or what it be, it in fact becomes as much the product of his labor, as much the property of an American citizen, and as much entitled to the protection of the government, as though it had been manufactured by the farmer himself; and any act of the federal government giving a preference to the property of one citizen over another is unwise, unjust, and anti-republican.

The annexation of Texas—a question which has so earnestly agitated public sentiment—has at length been accomplished, so far as the action of Congress was concerned. It is believed by those conversant with public opinion in Texas that the terms proposed will be acceded to, and the union so anxiously desired finally consummated. This measure received my vote and cordial approbation. Had Texas been seperated from us by some great natural boundary, and occupied different relations towards this government, the question of annexation might have been a very different one. But a similarity of political institutions controlled by the same race of people, a proximity of territory, and an identity of interest, based upon mutual hopes and mutual fears, all conspired to make the measure desirable to both countries. And when Texas, with a patriotic magnanimity, proffered the Union every consideration of public policy, demanded our acceptance, and we have accordingly opened our arms to receive her; and she comes into the Union, not as a colony or dependent, but as a sister and an equal. To accomplish this great object, no sword has been unsheathed—no coercion threatened. But, confiding in the justice and good faith of our government, she will intertwine her fate with ours, and the act will afford the most beautiful commentary on the value of republican institutions that the world ever beheld.

The following are the joint resolutions passed on the subject:

JOINT RESOLUTION FOR ANNEXING TEXAS TO THE UNITED STATES.

Resolved by the Senate and House of Representatives of the United States of America in Congress assembled, That Congress doth consent that the territory properly included within, and rightfully belonging to, the republic of Texas, may be erected into a new State, to be called the State of Texas, with a republican form of government, to be adopted by the people of said republic, by deputies in convention assembled, with the consent of the existing government in order that the same may be admitted as one of the States of this Union.

SEC. 2. *And be it further resolved,* That the foregoing consent of Congress is given upon the following conditions, and with the following guaranties, to wit:

First. Said State to be formed, subject to the adjustment by this government of all questions of boundary that may arise with other governments; and the constitution thereof, with the proper evidence of its adoption by the people of said republic of Texas, shall be transmitted to the President of the United States, to be laid before Congress for its final action, on or before the first day of January, one thousand eight hundred and forty-six.

Second. Said State, when admitted into the Union, after ceding to the United States all public edifices, fortifications, barracks, ports and harbors, navy and navy yards, docks, magazines, arms, armaments, and all other property and means pertaining to the public defence, belonging to said republic of Texas, shall retain all the public funds, debts, taxes, and dues of every kind, which may belong to or be due or owing said republic; and shall also retain all the vacant and unappropriated lands lying within its limits, to be applied to the payment of the debts and liabilities of said republic of Texas; and the residue of said lands, after discharging said debts and liabilities to be disposed of as said State may direct; but in no event are said debts and liabilities to become a charge upon the government of the United States.

Third. New States, of convenient size, not exceeding four in number, in addition to said State of Texas, and having sufficient population, may hereafter, by the consent of said State, be formed out of the territory thereof, which shall be entitled to admission under the provisions of the federal constitution. And such States as may be formed out of that portion of said territory lying south of thirty-six degrees thirty minutes north latitude, commonly known as the Missouri compromise line, shall be admitted into the Union, with or without slavery, as the people of each State asking admission may desire. And in such State or States as shall be formed out of said territory north of said Missouri compromise line, slavery or involuntary servitude (except for crimes) shall be prohibited.

And be it further resolved, That if the President of the United States shall, in his judgment and discretion, deem it most advisable, instead of proceeding to submit the foregoing resolution to the republic of Texas, as an overture on the part of the United States for admission, to negotiate with that republic, then

Be it resolved, That a State, to be formed out of the present republic of Texas, with suitable extent and boundaries, and with two representatives in Congress until the next apportionment of representation shall be admitted into the Union by virtue of this act, on an equal footing with the existing States, as soon as the terms and conditions of such admission, and the cession of the remaining Texian territory to the United States shall be agreed upon by the governments of Texas and the United States.

SEC. 2. *And be it further enacted,* That the sum of one hundred thousand dollars be, and the same is hereby, appropriated to defray the expenses of missions and negotiations, to agree upon the terms of said admission and cession, either by treaty to be submitted to the Senate, or by articles to be submitted to the two Houses of Congress, as the President may direct.

That this government has the constitutional power to acquire foreign territory by *treaty* is generally conceded. Such has been the practice and construction of this government for upwards of forty years. Whether Congress can acquire such territory by act of legislation, is not material to the present purposes. That Congress has the express power to admit new States into the Union will be readily seen by referring to the following clause of the constitution:

"New States may be admitted by Congress into this Union; but no new State shall be formed or erected within the jurisdiction of any other State, nor any state be formed by the junction of two or more States or parts of States, without the consent of the legislatures of the States concerned, as well as of the Congress." Art. 4, sec. 3.

The power there is clearly expressed, that "New States may be admitted by the Congress into this Union," and there is no limitation or restriction on the power except that—

"No new State shall be formed or erected within the jurisdiction of any other State, nor any State be formed by the junction of two or more States, without the consent of the legislatures of the States concerned, as well as of the Congress."

And the admission of Texas as a State into the Union does not conflict with either of these. The proceedings of the convention which formed the constitution, show that this clause, as originally adopted, restricted the power to the erection of new States within the territory then belonging to the United States, but that it was finally changed so as to leave out this restriction. The constitution is plain; but if any doubt existed as to the construction of this clause, a case in point is to be found in the act admitting into the Union the State of Vermont which was not a party to the compact, and to all intents and purposes was an independent and *foreign state.*

Texas is of vast importance to the United States in a military point of view, and I regard annexation as the overthrow of a dangerous course of policy which Great Britain had conceived against this country. Had Texas maintained her separate existence as a nation, bordering upon us, as she does for so great a distance, in time of peace she would have been a troublesome neighbor, and in war she might have been a dangerous enemy. The similarity of her productions and the genius of her people would at least have made her our commercial rival. She would no doubt have monopolized the larger part of the cotton trade which we now possess, amounting to more than half of all the exports of the United States. Cultivating the friendship and commerce of those nations which afforded her a market for her cotton and other productions, she would have purchased her supplies of them, and not of us. But when she becomes a part of the Union, not withstanding she will supplant some of the States in the culture of cotton, which could occur any how, yet her trade will then be governed by our laws, and she cannot enter into any treaties or alliances to prejudice the interests of the United States. She will then afford a market to many of the States for their surplus of agricultural and manufactured articles; and thus the products of her fertile soil will not only enure to Texas, but will contribute to the wealth of all the States. Then the slightest insult offered from abroad to her most distant sister State would be considered as offered to herself; and when any internal commotion arises, she will unfurl the "stars and stripes," and plant herself on the constitution, to preserve our laws, and maintain this glorious Union.

It has been alleged that Texas belongs to Mexico, and that by annexation we should be robbing the latter of her territory. I have never viewed it in this light. Texas never did belong to Mexico: she acquired her freedom from Spain by revolution, as Mexico herself did; and when she entered the Mexican confederation, it was as an equal, retaining her sovereignty as a State. When she rebelled against Santa Anna's despotism, a sanguinary revolution ensued, by which she completely defeated the Mexican forces, and fully established and declared her independence. This was followed by an acknowledgment of her independence by the United States and the other principal nations of the world; and that independence she has maintained for about nine years. So we find that Texas established her freedom by the great and inalienable right of revolution, "inestimable to freemen, and formidable to tyrants only;" and, having thus established and maintained her liberty, she is free to do any act which pertains to the sovereignty of a nation. Instead of carrying out his boasted threats against Texas, Santa Anna has been driven from his own capital.

Policy points out the line of our duty; and to be deterred from it by the threats of Mexico or Great Britain, would evince such a disregard of our interests and of our national honor as has never characterized the conduct of our people. With this question Great Britain has no right to interfere in any way whatever. With Mexico the boundary of Texas will be a legitimate question of negotiation, and in its adjustment I have every reason to believe that this government will do her ample justice. The annexation of Texas, instead of involving us in war with either Mexico or Great Britain, will, in my opinion, do much to ultimately secure our *peace* with both. By adding to our wealth and increasing our strength, the acquisition of Texas will cause other nations to respect our rights and to cultivate our friendship. It will distribute the balance of power more equally among the different sections of the Union, and more effectually secure the domestic institutions of the South against that policy which was disclosed by the British Minister of Foreign Affairs when he avowed that it was the object of that government to use her influence to abolish slavery throughout the world.

It has been contended by some that annexation would jeopard the Union of the States. As essential as I regarded this measure to be, had I believed that it would endanger the existence of the Union, it could not have received my vote; for, if there is any one political consideration dearer to me than all others, except liberty itself, it is the preservation of this Union. That beautiful American sentiment: "The Union must be preserved; peaceably if we can—forcibly if we must," ought to be taught to every child as soon as it learns to lisp, that it may never be forgotten. But the annexation of Texas, instead of endangering the Union, will, in my opinion, promote its harmony and perpetuate its existence. Experience has shown that the Union is as secure with twenty-six States as it was under the original thirteen. It is a fact worthy of observation, that most of the questions which have threatened a dissolution of the Union arose in some of the *old States*, and that the admission of every new State has had a tendency to allay discord and to harmonize the government. Texas was once ours, but not lost by any act of her own. We therefore receive her, not as a prodigal who had wandered off, but as one unjustly discarded, and invite her to take a place among the great family of States, with the hope that, thus reunited, the ties of friendship and of union will remain forever.

A bill passed the House to organize a territorial government in Oregon, and directing the President of the United States to notify Great Britain of the intention of this government, at the end of one year, to abrogate the treaty of 1827, which provides for the joint occupancy of said territory. For this bill I voted, but it was lost in the Senate. France and Spain claimed Oregon by discovery, and the United States claims through them, as well as by her own discoveries, made by Captain Gray and others. As early as 1683, La Salle, a Frenchman, navigated the Mississippi from Canada to its mouth, by which France claimed the sovereignty of all that country watered by that river and its tributaries west of said river; and, upon the principle of continuity and contiguity, all the country not pre-occupied westward to the Pacific Ocean. The claim to the country west of the Mississippi extended from its mouth to at least the 49th degree of north latitude, and this claim was recognised by Great Britain in the treaty of Utrecht in 1713, and of Versailles in 1763. In 1803 this claim was transferred to the United States by France, in the purchase of Louisiana. In 1819, in the treaty by which we acquired Florida from Spain, the 42d degree of north latitude, from the source of the Arkansas river to the South Sea, is made the boundary between the United States and Mexico, which then belonged to Spain. In that treaty the king of Spain ceded to the United States "all his rights, claims, and pretensions, to any territory north of the said line." Oregon lies *north* of this line. The discoveries of this country by Spain, commencing as far back as 1543, and continuing up to 1775, are supposed by many to extend as far north as the 54th or 55th degree of latitude; and these discoveries in priority of time, and in every other respect, are, in my opinion, superior to those upon which the claim of Great Britain is founded. Nothing certain appears to have been known of Columbia river till discovered by Captain Gray, a citizen of the United States, who made a voyage to the northwest coast, under the direction of a company of fur traders. In April, 1792, Captain Gray fell in with the British ship "Discovery," commanded by Captain Vancouver, and informed him that he had discovered the mouth of a river in latitude 46 degrees and 10 minutes. He gave the river the name of his ship, the "Columbia," which name it now bears. This river waters Oregon. The law of nations gives the nation discovering a river the country watered by the principal stream and its tributaries.

The first actual exploration of the country is supposed to have been that made by Lewis and Clark in 1804. As early as 1808 the Missouri Fur company established trading posts on Lewis river; in 1810, the Pacific Fur company was formed under the auspices of John Jacob Astor, of New York, and in 1811, Astoria was established near the mouth of Columbia river. During the last war, this post, being unable to defend itself, was captured by the British in 1813. It remained in possession of them till 1818, when it was restored to the United States in conformity with a provision in the treaty of Ghent, stipulating that "all territory, places, and possessions whatever, taken by either party from the other during the war," (with certain exceptions,) "should be restored without delay." By the third article of the convention between the United States and Great Britain, signed October 20, 1818—

"It is agreed that any country that may be claimed by either party on the northwest coast of America westward of the Stony mountains," (now called Rocky mountains,) "shall, together with its harbors, bays, and creeks, and the navigation of all rivers within the same, be free and open for the term of ten years from the date of the signature of the present convention to the vessels, citizens, and subjects of the two powers; it being well understood that this agreement is not to be construed to the prejudice of any claim which either of the two high contracting parties may have to any part of said country, nor shall it be taken to affect the claims of any other power or State to any part of said country; the only object of the high contracting parties in that respect being to prevent disputes and differences amongst themselves."

Subsequently, in 1819, as before stated, the United States purchased the title of Spain to this territory, by which her title, if before doubtful, became full and complete. The joint occupancy under the convention of 1818 remained in force till it was renewed by the treaty of August 6, 1827, by which the convention of 1818 was continued without any limit as to time, but with the agreement that either party should have power at any time to abrogate the treaty upon giving the other one year's notice of their intention. This treaty is now in force, and thus the matter stands at the present time. The question has long been a subject of negotiation between the two countries, and it is perhaps to be regretted that it has not long since been adjusted.

Oregon is bounded on the west by the Pacific ocean, and on the east by the Rocky mountains. Its length is estimated at from 800 to 1,000 miles, and its average width at from 500 to 600 miles. It is at this time difficult to ascertain the value of this territory. That portion of it which borders on the mountains is high and cold, and is no doubt of little value, except its water-power, its pasturage, and perhaps for its minerals. In the middle part the climate is delightful, and it is said to contain large bodies of valuable land. As you leave the Columbia river the country breaks into beautiful prairies, covered with a luxuriant and nutritious grass, which lasts all the year. The Wallamette valley is represented to be about 150 miles wide, and is remarkably healthy. A writer who visited that country says:

"For producing hides, tallow and beef, it is superior to any part of North America."

That part of the country which borders on the ocean is said to produce wheat, rye, cotton, tobacco, and potatoes; and also oranges, lemons, figs and other fruits. The climate is very mild. Speaking of this country, a writer says:

"In beauty of scenery, fertility of soil, and other natural advantages, no portion of country surpasses that which is found on the Wallamette. The valleys of the Columbia and its tributaries are estimated to contain 350,000 square miles."

The British government has a number of posts in Oregon. It is represented that she is colonizing her subjects there, and extending her laws and jurisdiction over the territory, and making military preparations to maintain its possession. Believing that Oregon belongs to the United States, and knowing that my constituents were not willing to see their territory surrendered to gratify British ambition, I voted for the bill to extend the territorial jurisdiction of the United States over Oregon, and to conclude its joint occupancy after giving the notice required by the existing treaty.

An act was passed to reduce the rates of postage, and to change the post office laws in other respects. It goes into operation on the 1st July next. The rates of postage are reduced to 5 cents for every letter not exceeding half an ounce in weight, for any distance not exceeding 300 miles; and to 10 cents for all distances over 300 miles. It restricts the franking privilege of postmasters. They are permitted to charge the department, in the settlement of their accounts, with the postage of such letters as they *receive on the business of their office*, upon a verification on oath of their account for the same, and the "transmission of the letters charged as vouchers." Postmasters may frank letters *sent* by themselves which relate "exclusively to the business of their respective offices," and the postmaster is required to endorse on such letter, over his signature, the words, "Post office business." For every such endorsement falsely made, the postmaster making it forfeits three hundred dollars. The franking privilege is taken away from the officers of government, and the postage charged on the correspondence of their officers is to be paid by the government. In cases where the commissions of a postmaster do not exceed twenty-five dollars per annum, the Postmaster General may increase the commissions, provided they do not exceed 50 per cent, on letter postage. Newspapers may be sent through the mail to any point within thirty miles of the place where published, free of postage. There is a provision in the act to prevent private expresses; but, in my opinion, it will prove inadequate to the object. There is also a clause making an appropriation out of the treasury to supply the deficit in the post office revenue which will be caused by the reduction of postage. These are some of the details of the act. I voted against this act. It is probable that a reduction might have been made in the rates of postage which would not have diminished the amount of revenue; but the reduction made by this act is too great, and will have the effect of throwing the Post Office Department as a heavy charge on the general treasury, which has not been the case heretofore. The post office tax was the only one in which the North and the East bore their share equally with the South and the West. We would all like to have cheap postage; and if that were the only consideration involved, I would have voted for the act; but there were others which influenced me to oppose it. The reduction of postage will cause a diminution in the post office revenue, which must be supplied by the *general treasury*. The treasury collects the revenue which must supply this deficiency, by a duty levied on imports; so that the tax taken off of the *mail correspondence* will have to be collected on *salt, iron, sugar, blankets,* and other articles which we buy from the stores. The manufacturing States profit by this, because it aids the *protective* policy. I might add other objections, but deem it unnecessary at present.

An act was passed which requires the election of electors for President and Vice President to be held on the same day in all the States. This act received my vote. At the previous session I voted against a bill somewhat similar in its provisions, upon what I considered good and sufficient reasons. It was then but a short time till the presidential election; and to give the measure effect before that election would have required extra sessions of the legislatures in many States, and in some others an amendment to their constitutions, which, for want of time, could not be conveniently done before that election, I did not wish either to put the States to this inconvenience or to run the risk of having the election of President contested on account of informality. The States now have four years to conform their laws and constitutions to the act of Congress; and the reasons upon which my opposition to the bill was then based being removed, at the last session I voted for the law.

An act was passed to admit Florida and Iowa as States into the Union. With *Texas* we shall have twenty-nine States instead of twenty-six. The tide of emigration has been constantly westward, and we have now more than double the original number of States, and still we have a sufficient territory to make a great many more. The improvement of the country has been astonishing. The enterprise of our citizens knows no bounds; and although ambitious to attain distinctions, and acquire wealth, yet they are ardently attached to their country as they have shown on all great occasions which tested their patriotism. Providence has propitiously smiled on our country, and we look forward to the day when it will still be more prosperous and happy.

The estimated expenditures for the fiscal year ending June 30, 1845 including payments on account of the public debt, were $35,019,431.

The estimated receipts, means, and expenditures for the fiscal year commencing 1st July, 1845, and ending June 30th, in the year 1846, are as follows, viz:

Receipts.

From the customs for the four quarters	$30,030,302.00
From the sales of public lands	2,010,000.00
From the miscellaneous and contingent sources	120,000.00
Total of revenue	$32,160,302.00
Add estimated balance to be in the treasury on the 1st July, 1845, including the unexpended sum as before stated	8,504,929.43
Total of means for the service of the fiscal year ending 30th June, 1846	40,665,231.43

Expenditures

Expenditures during the year ending 30th June, 1846, as estimated at the several Departments of State, Treasury, Navy, and War, viz:

The balances of former appropriations which will be required to be expended in this year	$1,462,105.92
Permanent and indefinite appropriations	2,083,794.72
Specific appropriations asked for this year	24,647,884.18
Total of estimated expenditures	$28,193,784.82

That sum is composed of the following particulars:

For civil list, foreign intercourse, and miscellaneous	4,944,083.93
For army proper, &c	3,648,308.43
For fortifications, ordnance, arming militia, &c	4,845,736.75
For pensions	2,397,000.00
For Indian department	2,086,154.65
For naval establishment	9,411,656.34
For interest on public debt	860,844.72
	$28,193,784.82
Which sum of expenditures, deducted from the total of means before stated, gives an estimated balance of twelve million four hundred and seventy-one thousand four hundred and forty-six dollars and sixty-one cents to be in the treasury on the 1st day of July, 1846	$12,471,446.61

I regret to see such a tendency to extravagance in the expenditures of our government as sometimes takes place. I have voted against all appropriations which I considered of this character.

I regret to see such a tendency to extravagance in the expenditures of our government as sometimes takes place. I have voted against all appropriations which I considered of this character.

There are many other subjects to which I would like to allude, but must avail myself of some other opportunity of doing so.

The triumphant vindication of democratic republican principles, in the election of James K. Polk to the presidency, affords another evidence of the capacity of the people for self-government. I hope and believe that his talents and firmness will be found equal to the high station to which he has been called.

In conclusion, permit me to remark, that in the discharge of my duties as your representative, I have endeavored to conform my conduct to those principles upon which I was elected; but, warm as my attachments are to the democratic party, I trust that I have suffered no partisan feeling to cause me to lose sight of what I owed to my country. While I am not one of those who "prefer to count the dark spots in the sun to rejoicing in its glorious brightness," yet my short experience has convinced me that there are many abuses in our government that ought to be corrected, and to this end my course has been directed.

Please accept my warmest congratulations and best wishes, individually and collectively, for your political and domestic welfare; and for the confidence you so kindly reposed in me, permit me to tender you the homage of a grateful heart.

Robt. P. Williamson, W. E. Wright, Peter A. Cardwell,[1]*, Sam'l A. Dalton, Committee to David S. Reid*[2] A&H-mn

Wentworth,
April 30, 1845.

At a meeting recently held in the town of Wentworth, for the purpose of selecting a candidate to represent the Third District in the next Congress, the undersigned were appointed a Committee to inform you of your unanimous nomination by your democratic fellow-citizens of Rockingham county. From our confidence in your public services and in you as a man, it affords us great pleasure to perform the duty assigned us. We hope that you will respond to the wishes of your countrymen and numerous friends in the district by consenting to accept the nomination.

[1]Peter A. Cardwell (1800-1847) of Madison was a trustee of Spring Garden Presbyterian Church in 1837. Upon his death he bequeathed property for the town cemetery, and the remainder of his town property was sold to raise funds to build Madison Presbyterian Church, which is the oldest functioning church building in town. *Cemetery Records*; Rockingham County Wills, Book C, 55.

[2]This letter appeared in the *North-Carolina Standard*, May 28, 1845.

David S. Reid to R. P. Williamson, W. E. Wright, Peter A. Cardwell, and Samuel A. Dalton[1] A&H-mn

Wentworth, N.C.,
May 1, 1845.

I have received your letter of yesterday, informing me of my nomination by my fellow-citizens of Rockingham county for a seat in the next Congress. Similar meetings have been held in other counties of the district which have done me the same honor. I have invariably informed my constituents that I could not under any circumstances consent to be a candidate unless clearly satisfied that such was the general wish of the Democratic Republican party of the district. From public meetings which have been held in various parts of the district and other demonstrations of public sentiment, there appears to be but one opinion on the subject. Under these circumstances I do not feel at liberty to decline the nomination. My opinions are already known, but I shall avail myself of every suitable occasion during the canvass, to give my views on the great questions which agitate the public mind.

For repeated evidences of confidence and respect bestowed by my fellow-citizens, permit me through you, to tender them my deep sense of gratitude. Please accept my thanks for the friendly manner in which you express the wishes of those you represent.

---

[1]This letter appeared in the *North-Carolina Standard*, May 28, 1845.

William W. Holden to David S. Reid A&H-DSR

Raleigh
May 24, 1845.

Your esteemed favor of the 20th has been received. Mr. J. J. Wheeden,[1] my agent, who hands you this, you will find to be intelligent, gentlemanly, and a sterling democrat. He goes to collect for me, and to get all the Subscribers he can for the Standard. I am happy to say, that he is entitled to the fullest confidence. He is a good writer, and can give me weekly accounts of the discussions in your District, and you will oblige me by giving him, when convenient, the leads and main points in your speeches.

There is nothing of interest here. The late Texas news is good; but of course you get the Review, and know all about it. Things are just so with Clark[2] and Toole,[3] but I learn that Mr. C. will distance him, notwithstanding Mr. Stanly[4] has given in his adhesion to Mr. T. Stanly has personal spite against Clark.

Again thanking you for your kind words in behalf of the Standard, I remain

---

[1]J. Julius Wheeden, an aide to William W. Holden at the *North-Carolina Standard*, was assigned to help Reid in his campaign for Congress. Wheeden served as a second lieutenant during the Mexican War. He died in Raleigh on January 14, 1848. Johnstone Jones (comp.), *Roster of North Carolina Troops in the War wih Mexico* (Raleigh: Adjutant-General's Department, 1887), 46, hereinafter cited as Jones, *Mexican War Roster*; Wheeler, *Sketches*, 419.

[2]Henry Selby Clark (1809-1869), an attorney from Washington, Beaufort County, served as a Democrat in the House of Commons (1834-1836) and the United States House of Representatives (1845-1847). He also served as a trustee for the University of North Carolina (1834-1854). *Biographical Directory of Congress*, 697; Battle, *History of the University*, I, 824; Powell, *DNCB*, I, 374.

[3]Henry Irwin Toole (died 1850), a native of Edgecombe County, was an associate editor of the *North-Carolina Standard* in 1840 and was later editor of the Wilmington *Aurora*. A Democrat, he ran against Henry Selby Clark for Congress in 1845 but withdrew when a Whig entered the race. He lost another bid for Congress in 1847. Norton, *Democratic Party*, 16n, 145-146; *Raleigh Times*, January 3, 1851.

[4]Edward Stanly (1810-1872), a Whig attorney from Washington, Beaufort County, served in the United States House of Representatives (1837-1843, 1849-1853) and the House of Commons (1844-1846, 1848, 1849), as speaker in 1846. He was appointed to serve as military governor of North Carolina in 1862 and 1863. *Biographical Directory of Congress*, 1644.

James Phelps to David S. Reid A&H-DSR

Essex Conn
June 27th 1845

Your very welcome and interesting favor was received some time since and would have been answered sooner but for the fact that I was aware of the numerous and constantly pressing engagements which must from your situation necessarily crowd upon you. Since the receipt of yours the painful intelligence of the death of General Jackson has reached us and spread a deep and almost universal gloom throughout the Country. No man living could have passed away whose departure would have made a similar impression upon my mind. I have ever entertained towards him feelings of the most profound veneration and attachment which have arisen in consequence of the distinguished public services he has so signally rendered both in the Council and the field his Roman firmness of character—his unbending patriotism and integrity, and the unparalleled violence with which he has been assailed by unscrupulous political opponents. these in connection with his single hearted devotedness to his countrys highest good were noble traits in his character and won for him the affection of his friends the admiration of his countrymen and the glory of the world. But he has now followed in the way of all greatness. His memory is written in the hearts of his mourning fellow citizens. his greatness inscribed upon the pages of his country's history, and nothing save eternity can efface the record. I would that he might have been spared in the Providence of God to have seen the blessed light of another Independence morning when the dying declaration of the illustrious Jefferson, "nunc dimittis domina,["][1] might have fallen with peculiar appropriateness from his lips but it was not so directed. The funeral solemnities in New York were recently published and of such a character as to show most emphatically that no man ever had a deeper and stronger hold upon the gratitude and affection of the American people. The Procession was one of the grandest and most solemn and imposing ever witnessed upon this Continent and did infinite honor to the gallant Chieftain whose virtues it was intended to celebrate as well as to the assembled thousands whose sorrow led them to participate in this public manifestation of regret for the loss of an individual who had no superior.

I am now about erecting me a Dwelling House in this place which is to be hereafter the house of myself and the one I love even better than myself—It is to be completed in November and ready for the reception of a family. I am expecting to remain single however only until September at which time the most interesting period of my life will doubtless be duly celebrated. My dear Colonel I should be indeed happy if you could be present, And if you can not be at that time I hope you will at some time before long come to Connecticut. You shall be welcome under my roof as long as you will have a disposition to remain.

It seems from the tenor of your last communication that you too are seriously thinking of looking up a partner to share your joy and divide with you the sorrows of this life. I am glad to hear of your determination as you will receive thereby a more abundant store of happiness if you make such a choice as will be in your power to do. My Lady's regards to you—the "Carrier dove"[2] is not forgotten and the sweet Piano and the sweeter voices have done it justice.

---

[1]"Nunc dimittis domina" is the opening phrase of the Latin canticle that begins: "Lord, now lettest thou thy servant depart in peace, according to thy word. For mine eyes have seen thy salvation." A "nunc dimittis" is, generically, a request for permission to leave. The canticle, known as the Song of Simeon, is derived from Luke 2:29-32, in which the aged Simeon, having seen the child Jesus in the Temple, believes that he has beheld the predicted Christ and states that he is now ready to die.

[2]"The Carrier Dove," a ballad of three stanzas, begins with the lines "Fly away to my native land, sweet Dove." Composed by Daniel Johnson, it was a popular middle-nineteenth century sentimental song arranged for voices, piano, and guitar and was originally printed by the J. Andrews Company of New York. Reid apparently sent a copy of the sheet music to Phelps. Edwin Wolf II, *American Song Sheets, Slip Ballads, and Poetical Broadsides, 1850-1870: A Catalogue of the Collection of The Library*

Company of Philadelphia (Philadelphia: Library Company of Philadelphia, 1963), iii, 18; Minnie Earl Sears (ed.), *Song Index* (New York: H. W. Wilson, 1926), 89, 287; *Complete Catalogue of Sheet Music and Musical Work Published by the Board of Music Trade of the United States of America, 1870* (1871; New York: Da Capo, reprint, 1973), 19, 154, 261, 290.

Roderick Murchison to David S. Reid A&H-DSR

Jefferson, N.C.
July 9th 1845

I presume by this time that you have *warm* times in Surry both as to weather & Politicks—but I hope you have no grounds to be discouraged or to fear the result of the present contest—The Democrats have everything to encourage them—the whigs nothing except they claim that they have elected all the members to the next Congress from Va. but 14 & only lack 50 or 60 of having a majority on joint ballot in the Va Legislature[1] I hope you will stimulate Mr Dobson[2] & his friends in Surry to pay friend McM.[3] the debt of gratitude they owe him.

I expected that Mc would electioneere on the hobby[4] that he is a *farmer*—a pretty farmer & opposed to a *reduction* of the Tariff!—he makes more money by *shaving*[5] & speculating than he does by farming—& if you are a lawyer so were Col Mitchell[6]—& Hon Lewis Williams[7] (altho' the latter did not practice) and so are most perhaps *all* of the present whig candidates for Congress in N.C. except Col. Mc & Gen. Dockery.[8] As to Mc's pretended desire to reduce the publick expenditures by a reduction of the wages of members of Cong. etc—it is all intended as a gull trap and he is not sincere in it—why? because when I was a candidate I advocated the same measures—and he opposed me *might & main*

I have not learned anything discouraging here—not having heard a single complaint although Col Bower[9] says he is a little uneasy—and states he would not have You defeated for the best negro in Ashe Your friends appear sanguine & the whigs do not—I saw a young man a few days ago from McM's neighbourhood who says he is the only McMillan man he knows of in his vicinity of 12 or 15 voters—An Monday last at a reaping at John Ross' out of 14 reapers Mr R informs me there were 12 Reid men.

I was at Wilkesboro last Sunday & Dr Calloway[10] informed me of the appointments made for you both in Wilkes—which will conflict on one day with those made by us in Ashe—they have appointed for you to be at Jone's [Jones's] on Lewis fork in Wilkes on Sat. 26 & at Council's in Ashe on Mond. 28 you are aware that your appointmts Com[mence]. in Ashe at Councils on Sat 26th where I think you should be if you can—as I learn that is the day of an officer drill there & that it is not likely that many persons would come out again on monday: not wishing to dictate in the matter I would merely hint my opinion that you would make but little at Lewis' fork—for most of the people there will be at Wilkesboro to hear you at Court—and I think you would gain at Councils—as our party is said to be growing there—

As I am writing on some private business (about the purchase of cattle) to Esqr McMillan to Rockford—I will give him a list of your appointments for our County—so that he can not hereafter plead ignorance of them—& to which I refer you if necessary.

Wishing you a handsome majority (nothing under 500 will satisfy me) I am in haste

Confidential

P.S. Please write whenever you can spare time—but I hope you will, by all means be very industrious whenever you go to make friends—and you are not a slow hand at that.

I pay postage on this being doubtful whether or not the new law gives you the privelege of *receiving* letters free at present you can certainly *send* them free—can you also receive free?

---

[1]Murchison's sense of humor shines through in this letter. The Democrats, in other words, had won 14 out of Virginia's 15 congressional races. They had also a commanding majority in the state legislature. Of the 15 Virginians elected to the House of Representatives for the Twenty-Ninth Congress, whose first session began on December 1, 1845, only Robert M. T. Hunter was a Whig. *Biographical Directory of Congress, Bicentennial Edition*, 138, 142.

[2]William P. Dobson, of Surry County, previously identified.

[3]Alexander B. McMillan, of Ashe County, previously identified.

[4]Hobby horse, i.e., a topic to which one constantly reverts or harps on.

[5]"Shaving" in the sense of financial dealing, to discount a note at an exorbitant rate.

[6]Anderson Mitchell, previously identified.

[7]Lewis Williams (1782-1842), a native of Surry County, was an 1808 graduate of the University of North Carolina. He was in the state Senate (1813-1814) and in 1815 was elected to the United States House of Representatives, where he served until his death. He was known as "Father of the House." *Biographical Directory of Congress*, 1823.

[8]Alfred Dockery (1797-1875), a Richmond County planter, served in the House of Commons (1822), the state Constitutional Convention (1835), the state Senate

(1836-1844), and Congress (1845-1847, 1851-1853). He received the Whig nomination for governor in 1854 but was defeated. *Biographical Directory of Congress*, 817.

[9]George Bower, previously identified.

[10]Dr. James Calloway, a native of Ashe County, became a resident of Wilkesboro, Wilkes County. He served in the House of Commons from Ashe (1828-1832). In Wilkesboro he was active in St. Paul's Episcopal Church, a delegate to the state Constitutional Convention of 1861-1862, and on the Council of State (1862-1864). Hayes, *Land of Wilkes*, 81, 89, 125-126; Cheney, *North Carolina Government*, 179, 387, 1053.

David S. Reid to Reuben Reid A&H-DSR

Wilkesboro, N.C.
August 5, 1845.

I have to-day addressed the people at this place which winds up the Canvass. On tomorrow I shall leave here to attend some election precinct, but what place I shall attend I have not yet determined. Perhaps I shall go to Ashe. I shall not be at home till after the polls are Compared, which will be one week after the election. My health Continues remarkably good. I have not been the least sick since I left home. One more day and the election will be over. I am in good spirits. I hope I shall be elected, but we can not tell how these things will terminate. I hope, I shall do as well in Ashe as I expected. Some think that McMillan may beat me as much as 150 votes in Ashe. I shall not be surprised if he does not beat me that many. I hope I shall gain some in Wilkes. Mr. Wheeden[1] is yet with me and sends his respects to you all. I hope you are all well. I am anxious to see you all. I have stood the Campaign much better than any one could immagine from the labour I have performed. Give my love to Mother, brothers, and Sisters, and to brother Sam[2] & sister Fanny[3]: Also to the neighbours. In haste.

---

[1]J. Julius Wheeden, previously identified agent of the *North-Carolina Standard*.

[2]Samuel F. Adams, Reid's brother-in-law.

[3]Frances, Reid's sister and wife of Samuel F. Adams.

William Scott to David S. Reid RCC

Richmond Va.
October 16th 1845

According to promise I write you a few lines. I brought with me to this place six negroes and have sold them for a profet of two hundred and ninety five Dollars gross.

I shall take the cares[1] this evening bound for Newbern N.Carolina, at which place I exspect to find Hugh.[2] negroes have declined in this market for the last few days. Hugh was well when I left him a few days since.

Mr. Adams[3] is hear and has bought Eight negroes he is well &c. my health is first rate though It Is verry sickley in the lower part of N Carolina

Please give my Respects to your Father and family

In Hast verry Respectfully

N.B please write to me as soon as you Receve Direct Newbern NC

---

[1]The cars, i.e., travel by railroad.

[2]Hugh Kearns Reid, previously identified.

[3]Samuel F. Adams, previously identified.

James Phelps to David S. Reid A&H-DSR

Essex Conn
November 25th 1845

It has been a very long time since I have had the pleasure of hearing anything directly from you—so long that I have concluded to wait no farther before again venturing to trespass upon your notice—My last letter perhaps never reached you, as it was written previously to your last State Election—I had supposed that if it reached you, you would have given me in return some statement in reference to the late political ordeal through which you passed, as usual, unscathed & triumphant—I was very much rejoiced to learn through the public press of your very great success, which indicated most significantly on your part a resistless hold upon the attachment of the people in your District, and on theirs an abiding confidence in your ability, integrity & Democracy—These are tokens that must forever fill your heart with the livliest satisfaction and the warmest gratitude—There *must* be a proud conciousness of manly superiority attending a political and moral standing such as you possess, a distinction rarely possessed by one of your age. The most I fear for you is that you will be too soon satisfied, and yield the honorable course you are pursuing, to others less worthy than yourself—Do not abandon the advantage you have already acquired until you have accomplished everything in the way of public honor and political renown which lies in your power to attain with few and honorable exertions—You are now in the high road to preferment aye, distinguished preferment, which if abandoned may be lost forever—You cannot but be aware of the precariousness of political elevation, and as you now have it fully in your grasp do not I entreat of you relinquish it until it has crowned you with its highest and most unfading laurels—You will of course receive these remarks as the sincere wishes of a friend and the expression of his feelings void of flattery or any motive of a sinister or improper character—It is not for me to advise but implore you as a friend—

As for myself I remain pretty much "in status quo"—Am married,[1] to an amiable affectionate and agreeable wife and in the domestic line enjoy myself very much Indeed it is almost sufficient to charm me away from all participation in the strife and controversy of the political and I had almost said professional arena—But my profession I must pursue to make myself and her comfortable and happy in the possession and enjoyment of a worldly competence.

My time has for the past few months been almost entirely occupied with building a house and attending to my professional engagements which have not been few or small—But my house will be finished so as to enable me to be settled in the course of a few weeks, when I shall have more time to devote to my profession and to the pleasures of my fireside.—

So far as politics are concerned I am now placed in a strongly Federal town, so much so that it is unquestionably beyond redemption—The Senate District is also Whigs and the Congressional, very strongly so, as also the state—There is therefore but little inducement for me immersed in other duties and engagements as I am, to do more politically than to give a passing warning to our friends to stand firm—to cast back the falsehoods and calumies of our enemies in their teeth on all proper occasions, and to discharge my duty at the ballot box—I consider myself under a sacred obligation to do all this and as much more as is consistant under existing circumstances. The principles of Democracy are as dear to me as ever and so precious shall ever continue—They are the last to be sacraficed or abandoned, and I shall cling to them so long as I may live with the uncompromising determination of him who resolved to make the last entrenchment of liberty his grave"—[2]

I trust I shall hear from you at your earliest convenience, always mindful as I shall continue to be of your manifold and important duties as a representative of the People, and the solemn trust and responsibility confided to you by your constituents—

I shall be happy to be assured that you left your family and friends in the enjoyment of comfortable health—Please receive the compliments of my wife

[1]On September 30, 1845, James Phelps married Lydia Ingham, daughter of Samuel Ingham (1793-1881), an Essex, Connecticut, attorney and judge who served two terms in the United States House of Representatives, first as a Jacksonian and second as a Democrat (March 4, 1835-March 3, 1839). *Penny Press* (Middletown, Connecticut), January 16, 1900; *Biographical Directory of Congress, Bicentennial Edition*, 1244.

[2]This is probably a reference to Andrew Jackson, who had died on June 8. See Phelps's letter of June 27, 1845.

Jesse Cooper[1] *to David S. Reid* A&H-DSR

[Hamilton P.O., Martin County]
th 14 day of December 1845

it afords me grate pleashure to inform you that I am well hoping that my few lines may find you well. I feeal grateful to you for the Presedants Message the first and the oneley one as I understand That had reacht Hamilton post office and I shall at all times feeal thankfull to you for such papers and docements as you may think proper to send me. I feeal highly gratifyde with the Presedants vues as reguards the public lands he recommends to congrass the propiety of so modifying or reduceing the minimum price of the inferer Lands that is unsold down to fifty or sixty cents Pur acar for these lands that has been so long In market and cannot find any biddars for them and by so reduceing the price of them it would incourage a good hononst and Rugged fruntteair labour that was not afraid of the Indin[,] panter[,] nor bare to Settle on It and become owners of it and pay taxes for Them it would be agrate advantage to the States where these lands lies and also it would Be asorce of revenew to the Janeral Goverment and at the same time that the pre-emption Law should be so modifyde as to prevent Speculaters and capitalist from turning them out of their new exspected homes and that They should have the lands at the goverment price Disegarding whasoever impovements which they might have made on them I am also vary much plasd at the vues that the presedant has taken on thouse menaral lands belonging to the Janeral Govrment. It is now under the athorety of the war Department and is least out and conducted By agants and clarkes and ahost of other petty officars Costin the goverment fourtimes the amount of what she receives why not then repeal the Law and place them under the Janeral land office Those agants and clarkes and petty tinkers that Is amaking themselves rich out of the goverment and instead of the goverment receaving any benifit For the last four yeares they have cost the goverment $19.756.37 more than they made I vary much like the Presedants vues on the Tariff Law and in fact I see nothing in his Message But what I think was vary ably reasond So I come to a close hoping that you may have a Pleasent Sescion hoping by the inflewance and protecktion from his devine hands may Inable you to do grate good for your country and Spread lorrels over your heads that will allways Be reconized with the wormest of gratitude I am with respect yours Sinceare freind and obediant Searvent

---

[1]Jesse Cooper, a conservative Democrat, was a veteran legislator from Martin County. As a delegate, with Asa Biggs, from Martin to the state Constitutional Convention of 1835, Cooper favored continuing to bar Catholics from holding public office. When the convention amended Article 32 so as to remove affirmation of Protestantism as a prerequisite for officeholding, he voted against endorsing the work of the convention. Cooper served in the House of Commons (1822, 1825-1831) and in the state Senate (1831-1832, 1833-1843). Cheney, *North Carolina Government*, 817, 1198, 1199; Harold J. Counihan, "The North Carolina Constitutional Convention of 1835: A Study in Jacksonian Democracy," *North Carolina Historical Review*, XLVI (October, 1969), 341n, 351, 360n, hereinafter cited as Counihan, "North Carolina Constitutional Convention of 1835."

Weldon E. Wright to David S. Reid A&H-DSR

Wentworth
Dec 24th 1845

According to promise when I left Washington; I will now give you the news, if I can think of any of importance as I write: but the times are so dull that I doubt whether I can atall interest you. The President's message has completely dumfounded the whigs at least most of them; though there are some who will try to pick something out of it; but every attempt has so completely failed that I believe that they have all concluded to say nothing pro or con. Among some of their attempts to detract from its merits, some have called it a war message, while others would say that it exibited cowardice, thereby contradicting the former assertion; thus their views clashed until no one will dare to express an opinion Col; I think it admirable; I take a delight in reading it to every one that will listen to me & also Secretary Walker's[1] report, I consider tip top. It is plain, decisive & powerfully & boldly argumentative. Such documents it does seem to me cannot be bettered by mortal man, viewing every existing circumstance in its proper light

Do not forget to send me the report of the commissioner of Patents & all other good documents. I wish you to send also a copy of Bunlecund's[2] [*sic*] articles on the tariff if they are printed in pamphlet form. My brotherinlaw Thomas L Lea[3] requested me to mention to you that he would like to have a copy of Bunlecund's [*sic*] numbers on the tariff & the report of the Commissioner of Patents.[4] I hope that you will do all you can for the repeal of the present odious tariff: for it does seem to me that if any man with common reason will read the President's message & the treasurers report on that subject & will not desire its repeal, Must be either blinded by prejudice in other words a *fool* or a grand rascal I presume that you have heard of your cousin Ben Settle's marriage to Miss Sarah Campbell, & Josiah Walker's to Miss Zilphy Young to come off either tonight or was last night.[5]

I have rather concluded to move my nigroes out to Georgia if I do not go myself, as it seems from present prospects that it is impossible to make a support here. I called at your fathers on my return & delivered your commands; as I passed I took a glance at old man Barne's[6] place & the thought of living on that poor place all alone sickened me at once & I have determined to try & do better. Give my respects to Mr Dobbins[7] & receive for yourself the kind regards of one of Your humble constituents

---

[1]Robert James Walker (1801-1869), an attorney from Philadelphia, moved to Natchez, Mississippi, in 1826. He served as a United States senator (1835-1845), secretary of the treasury (1845-1849), and territorial governor of Kansas. *Biographical Directory of Congress*, 1766.

[2]Bundlecund was the pseudonym of Edmund Burke (1809-1882) of New Hampshire, who wrote a series of essays on protectionism and the tariff. Burke was a newspaper editor before serving as a Democrat in Congress (1839-1845). He was commissioner of patents from 1846 until 1850. *Biographical Directory of Congress*, 628; John T. Garland to David S. Reid, January 22, 1846, Reid Papers, PC 1, State Archives.

[3]Thomas L. Lea (born circa 1806 in Caswell County) was a prosperous farmer in the Milton community of Caswell County. Several members of his extended family were active in the Democratic party, and Lea's oldest child, a son born in 1834, was named Calvin Graves Lea. Seventh Census, 1850, Caswell County, Population Schedule, 195; *North-Carolina Standard*, November 12, 1845.

[4]The Bundlecund essays had been generously praised by editor William W. Holden in a recent issue of the *North-Carolina Standard*, of which Wright and Lea were probably avid readers. Holden read the essays in the Washington *Union* and reported that they might soon be published in pamphlet form. "We hope it will be done. They would furnish to the people the most valuable matter on a subject too little understood," he noted, promising to reprint the essays in his own paper as the coming political election campaign progressed. *North-Carolina Standard*, December 3, 1845.

[5]A marriage bond for Josiah Walker and Zilpha A. Young was issued December 17, 1845, in Rockingham County, with Benjamin Settle as witness. Rockingham County Marriage Bonds.

[6]Samuel Barnes (born circa 1776), a native of Virginia, was a widowed farmer living in modest circumstances near the homes of Reuben Reid and Thomas Settle in Rockingham County. The valuation of his homestead at only $400 indicates that it was, in fact, a "poor place" compared to the farm of Wright's brother-in-law Thomas L. Lea, which was valued at $5,000. Seventh Census, 1850, Rockingham County, Population Schedule, 26; Seventh Census, 1850, Caswell County, Population Schedule, 195.

[7]James Cochrane Dobbin (1814-1857), a Fayetteville attorney, was a representative in Congress (1845-1847), a member of the House of Commons (1848, 1850, 1852), speaker of the House (1850), and secretary of the navy (1853-1857). *Biographical Directory of Congress*, 817.

1846

James A. Lewis to David S. Reid A&H-DSR

Chesnut Grove S. C.
Jany 6th 1846

I have to give you thanks for sending me the speech of the Hon. Lewis Cass "On the Defences of the country," apart from the information such a document is calculated to convey, there are other sources of pleasure arising there from which thrill the soul with delight "Viz that I am still held in remembrance by one whose opportunities of acquaintance were extremely transient, and although enjoying the honorable post of Representative of an intelligent community in the great councils of the nation, yet can bestow a passing thought on an humble individual, whose only claim to it is an identity of political principle and ardent wishes often breathed for your success and prosperity

I had seen a sketch of those remarks in some of the papers, together with the debate called forth by the resolutions, and remarks, in which Mangum[1] of your State and Archer[2] of Virginia at first shewed some disposition to be Anti-American, but which wound up by protestations of patriotism I was pleased to see Indeed from my intercourse with my fellow citizens and information obtained from the papers generally, all parties, every where look upon the prospect of a war with England with a determination to meet it in a manner, not only to sustain the cause and glory of America, but to inflict a chastisement on that arrogant and assuming Nation, which has never ceased to tease harrass and insult us on every occasion where their faithless diplomatic impudence can insinuate itself either in our domestic concerns, or foreign relations War is an evil as Cass truly observes, and in a war with England somebody would get hurt but I think the world would have cause to rejoice at the sound of the drum that would call the embattled hosts of freemen to meet the hostile invader. It would sound the Knell of Englands greatness, and millions of oppressed men in both hemispheres would feel their bonds relase at the first round exchanged betwixt England and America in hostility. Her vast naval armament may enable her to strike a severe blow at the commencement. Our coasts may suffer for a season till the young giant of the west rises in his might and under the lead of some future Jackson, cause the enemy to fly from our shores so fatal to the instruments of tyranny and despotism The Talented Polk is the man under whose auspices a war with England should be conducted, his prudence, his firmness and patriotism, which seem to have settled upon him as with Jackson's mantle, would ensure a triumphant termination to a contest looked anxiously upon by a sympathising world. Crowned heads and "Holy Alliances" in sympathy with England, but philanthropy and suffering humanity in every clime sending forth the most ardent prayers for our success. And that success would be certain No man in whose bosom beats an American heart would ever agree to lay down his arms, or sound the notes of peace until England with all her pomp and power would be entirely banished from our hemisphere and deprived of that insulting boast "that the sun never sets on her dominions" and that "she rides monarch of the seas" No, no If she does provoke a war let it come. She will find the same irrisistible foe in the son that she found in the sire, she will find the same deadly opposition to her claims to our territory, that our forefathers manifested to her usurpation of their political rights with this difference that formerly our fathers were willing to make peace without imposing restrictions upon her, but now she must give bond and security for her future good behaviour and as an earnest of her good faith suffer Canada and her west India possessions to enjoy the blessings of democracy to which every coast and island of this hemisphere is entitled and which they will ultimately possess.

There are rumors afloat that England is willing now to accept the 49th degree as the boundary. In accepting this she certainly shews the *back out* right smartly and as a matter of policy, it would perhaps be better for our Government to settle the dispute in that way it would diminish the chances of war and only procrastinate our possession, for as sure as the melting snows on the eastern slopes of the Rocky Mountains eventualy lose themselves in the gulph of Mexico just so sure will the stars and stripes wave in triumphant folds over every foot of land from the frozen regions of the north to the narrowest place of the isthmus dividing north from South America I like the tone of the presidents message throughout, it is thoroughly Democratick and speaks with authority the true principles of our government You are doubtless aware of the shortness of the provision crop in some of the Districts of our State. The destitution is great—distressing, and it requires all the energy we are capable of putting forth to keep our families from want. I have heard of famine in beleagured cities, in Arabian deserts, in poor miserable, oppressed, injured Ireland, but the waves of a continent-dividing Ocean separated me from the dreadful scenes, but it now threatens our own citizens, our own neighborhood, our own families, we will perhaps get along but some will suffer. God grant we never see the like again. David Settle and family are well,

I hear Ben[3] is married May he enjoy all the happiness of the wedded state, for he is a good fellow. Give my Respects to Capt Black[4] and accept my wishes for your prosperity

---

[1]Willie P. Mangum, previously identified, Whig, United States senator.

[2]William S. Archer (1789-1855), an attorney from Amelia County, Virginia, served in the Virginia state legislature and in both houses of Congress. *Biographical Directory of Congress*, 486.

[3]Ben Settle. See Weldon E. Wright to David S. Reid, December 24, 1845.

[4]Not identified.

J. Julius Wheeden to David S. Reid A&H-DSR

Raleigh
Jan. 8, 1846

Supposing that you feel some interest in the events of the day, I hasten to inform you of what has transpired.

Our convention met—Col. Bower, of Ashe, in the Chair—and a committee was appointed to prepose rules, &c. Hon. Louis D. Henry, of Wake, was chosen President, four vice presidents, and J. W. Hampton (of the "Jeffersonian") and W. W. Holden (of the "Standard") Secretarie.—The convention allowed the counties to vote according to their representation in the Ho of Commons—and adopted the two-thirds rule.

Mr. Henry made a powerful speech on taking the chair—it was such a speech as only Henry can make.

At an informal meeting, held this eving at 7 o'clock, nominations were made, to see who was the strongest man. Judge Strange nominated Walter F Leak,[1] other individuals nominatd D. W. Courts, Hon. Jas. J. McKay, Hon. Green W. Caldwell,[2] and I nominated you, but at the request of your friends (who anticipated a squabble between the others, and wished to retain you as a peace-maker) I withdrew you before balloting. Green W. Caldwell is the man! This being ascertained, he was unanimously chosen—and it was also unanimously resolved by the meeting that he shall be our next Governor. And I think he will.

I do not know who are from Rockingham—or whether there are any delegates, from that county. Courts was on his way, but was thrown from his buggy, and so disabled as to be obliged to remain in Hillsboro![3]

The Convention is a large one. Said to be larger than ever assembled on any similar occasion. The most perfect harmony prevails—and they are enthusiastic enough. We meet to-morrow.

Fisher[4] threw us all aback. If it was not his intention to run, he should have so stated before the time came for the meeting. I, however, am very glad that he did so even this late—for, with him, we should have been beaten, badly beaten. At least I think so.

I am very much obliged to you for your kind attention in sending documents.

Be pleased to request Mr. Dobbin[5] to put my name on his list. You can show him this, or at lease let him know how far things have progressed.

There is nothing new. I shall be glad to hear from you, at any time.

---

[1]Walter F. Leak (1799-1879), an attorney from Rockingham, Richmond County, was a member of the House of Commons (1831), the state Senate (1832), and the Constitutional Convention of 1861. Noble J. Tolbert (ed.), *The Papers of John Willis Ellis* (Raleigh: Department of Archives and History, 2 volumes, 1964), I, 61n, hereinafter cited as Tolbert, *Ellis Papers*.

[2]Greene W. Caldwell (1806-1864), a Charlotte physician and attorney, was an assistant surgeon in the United States Army in 1832. He was a member of the House of Commons (1836-1841), the state Senate (1849), and the United States House of Representatives (1841-1843). In 1846 he received the Democratic nomination for governor but declined to run. He was then serving as superintendent of the United States Branch Mint at Charlotte, having in January received United States Senate confirmation of his appointment. During the Mexican War he was a captain in the Third Dragoons (1847-1848). *Biographical Directory of Congress*, 648; *North-Carolina Standard*, January 17, 1844.

[3]See more detailed account of this incident in *North-Carolina Standard*, January 14, 1846.

[4]Former Congressman Charles Fisher (1789-1849) of Salisbury, previously identified.

[5]Congressman James Cochrane Dobbin of Fayetteville.

Samuel F. Adams to David S. Reid A&H-DSR

Troublesome N.C
January 11th, 1846

I received your very kind favour this morning, and I was truly glad to hear that you enjoyed good health; myself and family are all in good health, and they were all well at Fathers on yesterday. There is no news of importance in the neighborhood. I have not heard from Brother Hugh in several weeks.

I am in hopes we shall have no war although the chances are decidedly in favour of it unless Mr. Polk falls back again on the 49th degree if he does I think it will be accepted and there will be no war but if we attempt to take the whole of Oregan and a majority of Congress and the people so decide the sooner we go to fighting the better for it will have to be done certain before we get it. Please write to me when ever you have an opportunity Frances and the children send their best love to you also Henrietta[1] who is here at this time. I remain your affectionate brother.

[1]Probably Henrietta Reid (1824-1868), born in Pittsylvania County, Virginia, a younger sister of David S. Reid. Henrietta, who was five years younger than her sister Frances, married George Price but died without issue. Reese and Fisher, *Settle Family*, 679-680.

Calvin Graves to David S. Reid A&H-DSR

Brown's Store, Caswell NC.
15 Jany. 1846.

I acknowledge my indebtedness to you for your repeated favors during the present session, and confess my remisness in not answering you earlier, for really I have recently been so immerced in my domestic and agricultural engagements, and in attention to the Estate of my deceased Brother-in-law, William Graves,[1] whose death you have doubless seen announced, that I have had no opportunity to write you until now.—

The result of the deliberations of Our Convention at Raleigh, have reached you before now.—before the meeting of the Convention I had written to several of Our prominent friends in this State, unqualifiedly declining to allow my name to be presented to the Convention. This course I deemed to be due to myself, And to our Democratic friends, upon mature deliberation. It seems that Our Eastern friends were determined to have a Western man, whether or not G. W. Caldwell Esqr. will accept the nomination. I think somewhat doubtful.

Mr. Fishers[2] course, seems to me to be wholely indefensable, he must have been aware for several month past, that his friends, in his own region, had been especially active, in having his name prominently presented, and it does seem to me, that he ought to have announced his determination earlier, that Our democratic friends throughout the State, might look abroad, and settle upon some proper person, to lead Our forces in the Comeing Contest.

The result may not have been otherwise, than at present; the Selection may be a good one, but that affords no excuse to him, for, to say the least of it, (if I am correctly informed) the Convention adjourned without knowing whether or not, they really had a gubernatorial Candidate.—We shall however, soon know all about that matter.—

War or no war, that's the question? Will you allow me to answer it? Your position, the focus of political intelligence, foreign and domestic, is much more favorabl to the Solution of this question than mine, and yet I have a mind to "Shew mine Opinion"—There will be no war growing out of the Oregon question. It can't be, that England, will go to War with America. The limits of this sheet will not allow of my going at length into my reasons. I will therefore State Only One or two. Her statesmen are as sharpsighted, and as much given to forecast, as those of Any other Nation, they can but see what would be the final result—what would become of her American possessions? What of her Cotton Factories? What of the thousands of her subjects who are dependant upon that trade for their bread, their actual subsistance?—now that Texas is Ours. The project would be too perilous for England. The Annexation of Texas has closed and sealed the question of War between these Powers through all time. I may be wrong, but I hazard the prediction, that no man now living, will ever witness a war between England & America.

I have just seen the report of the personal explanatory discussion between Mr. Rhett[3] & Mr. Adams.[4]—John Quincy is surely the Oddest man living, having recently uttered sentiments which elicited much applause, he must needs next, bring upon himself the denunciations of an immense majority of the American people, and in the meantime invite the Obstinacy of the British government, in the Vain hope, that domestic fudes will Compel the American government to recede from the position which she has assumed.—

In Conclusion, let me say, I am extremely Anxious to visit Washington, during the Session, having however to settle the Estate of the late Wm. Graves, in addition to my Other engagements, I can not now tell how it may be.—Should I make the trip at all, it will have to be after Our April Court.—My respects to Col. Biggs[5] & other friends. We are all well.

[1]William Graves, of Yanceyville, died in late 1845, and his will was probated in January Court 1846 in Caswell County. He married his cousin, Ann L. Graves, sister of Calvin Graves and sister of Henrietta Graves Settle. Thus, he was an uncle of David S. Reid's future wife, Henrietta Williams Settle. Will of William Graves, October 6, 1833, Caswell County Wills (microfilm), Book P, 283, Archives, Division of Archives and History, Raleigh, hereinafter cited as William Graves Will.

[2]Former Congressman Charles Fisher, previously identified.

[3]Robert Barnwell Rhett (1800-1876), an attorney from Beaufort, South Carolina, was a state legislator, state attorney general, member of Congress (1837-1849), United States senator (1850-1852), and delegate to the Confederate Provisional Congress in 1861. *Biographical Directory of Congress*, 1512.

[4]John Quincy Adams, previously identified.

[5]Asa Biggs (1811-1878), a Williamston attorney, served as a member of the Constitutional Convention of 1835, the House of Commons (1840, 1842), the state Senate (1844, 1854), Congress (1845-1847), the United States Senate (1855-1858), and as a federal district judge (1858-1861). *Biographical Directory of Congress*, 553.

Lemuel Sawyer[1] to David S. Reid A&H-DSR

N. York
Jany. 16. 1846

A tedious indisposition has prevented my paying you a visit & congratulating you on your reelection. I supposed it as a matter of course, as you are a great favorite, with both sexes. I presume you have seen our fair friends at Miss Shonnards,[2] since your return to your seat, & if you have not brought a companion with you, Miss Eure[3] still live in hopes. A gentleman left here for Washington last May, by the name of Thomson,[4] whom I recommended to stop at Miss S—ds I understand he bore down upon the widow, & that Mrs. Bonny[5] showed him sufficient encouragement. He has made a long stay of it, I presume from the attraction of the affinities of the two homogeneous substances, which may finally unite, by the laws of love, if not of chimistry—

Should you have a copy of Leut. Fremonts[6] Journal to spare, I should take it as a great favour, if you will forward it to me, either by some traveller, if too heavy to Frank, or by dividing it into two parcels, should it be unbound.

The enclosed is a letter to Robert Rose[7] Esqr. of Galveston, Texas, which I know not how to forward from this, so as to reach him early. Perhaps if you direct it, by way of N. Orleans, till the regular mail is established, it will arrive safe.

Give my best respects to Miss Shonnard & the ladies of the family, & Mrs. Bonny & Miss Lee[8] when you see them.

---

[1]Lemuel Sawyer (1777-1852), an attorney and author from Elizabeth City, was a member of the House of Commons (1800, 1801), a representative in Congress (1807-1813, 1817-1823, 1825-1829); and from 1829 he was either a department clerk in Washington or resident of New York City. Sawyer, an eccentric personality, was the author of the first play by a North Carolinian with a North Carolina subject, *Blackbeard*, published in 1824. He was a congenial participant in the salon life of Washington parlors and boarding houses. Sawyer's *Auto-Biography* (1844) was filled with self-revelations that reviewers termed "embarrassingly frank" and "disreputable" episodes. When Sawyer returned home in June 1820 to campaign for reelection to Congress, his opponent Gen. James Iredell attacked Sawyer's personal habits. Sawyer wrote: "Some malicious personal enemy at Washington had been plying him [Iredell] with letters from that place, with charges and certificates to prove my previous connection with a woman of bad fame, which, though I am ashamed of confessing contained too much truth, yet I was not singular in that offense." Iredell's attempt to damage Sawyer backfired, however, as voters resented his tactics and reelected Sawyer. *Biographical Directory of Congress*, 1565; Lemuel Sawyer, *Auto-Biography* (New York: Published by the Author, 1844), 24, hereinafter cited as Sawyer, *Auto-Biography*; Richard Walser, assisted by E. T. Malone, Jr., *Literary North Carolina: A Historical Survey, Revised and Enlarged* (Raleigh: Division of Archives and History, North Carolina Department of Cultural Resources, 1986), 8, 44, hereinafter cited as Walser and Malone, *Literary North Carolina*.

[2]Miss Shonnard has not been identified.

[3]Miss Eure has not been identified.

[4]Mr. Thomson has not been identified.

[5]Mrs. Bonny has not been identified.

[6]John Charles Frémont (1813-1890), explorer, politician, and soldier, was born in Savannah, Georgia, and was raised in Charleston, South Carolina. He explored much of the West in the 1840s and with his wife published reports of those daring explorations, bringing him national attention and acclaim. Fremont married Jessie Benton, the daughter of Senator Thomas Hart Benton. Sawyer is probably requesting Frémont's second journal, published in 1845, a report of his exploration of the Oregon Trail and California. A detailed, vivid, and readable account, with much careful scientific observation, it showed that travel to Oregon was not unreasonably difficult and that the Northwest was fertile and desirable, thus reinforcing the impetus to expansion provided by James Knox Polk's presidential election. At the order of the United States Senate, 10,000 copies of Frémont's journal were printed. *CDAB*, 315-316; *DAB*, VII, 21.

[7]Robert Rose (born 1815), a native of Virginia, was a general land agent residing in Galveston, Texas, in 1850. Rose owned real estate valued at $110,000. Sawyer mentioned in 1844, ". . . if I could ever realize the costs of my investment in Texas land stock, the remainder of my days could be spent in the enjoyment of peace and comfort." Seventh Census, 1850, Galveston County, Texas, Population Schedule, 268; Sawyer, *Auto-Biography*, 44.

[8]Miss Lee has not been identified.

Louis D. Henry to David S. Reid A&H-DSR

Raleigh
Jany 21 1846.

I owe you many thanks for your Kindness in franking me Bundelcund[1] on the Tariff, & for other favors heretofore of the like kind, for which I have not made my acknowledgements, owing to some accident, & not to the want of a due sensibility to such favors. We look now to you & your colleagues at head quarters with deep interest & anxiety for all the news & alarming portents of the times. I am glad to hear that our representatives are going for the "Notice" to England; I view it as the most peaceable & decided action we can take, & the one that is most consistent with the treaty of Joint occupation, altho, the measure of protection & civil jurisdiction, is wholly proper & admissible, but merely sequent in its nature. I am also of the opinion, that England will not be disposed to go to war with us, unless she can delude France or the allied powers to join her, on the principle, that it is to be *Canning's*[2] *war of Opinion*, or monarchy vs democracy, which they may suppose from the growing consequence of this country must soon or late come on. Our policy ought to be, to keep England in the wrong, where she is now beyond all question, to do nothing that will or ought to be considered as legitimately, as an act of aggression. Such a course as *notice protection* & *colonization*, is perfectly peaceable & consistent. Should G Britain choose to consider them hostile, on her will fall the odium & responsibility of the aggressor. This will unite not merely all our party, or ought to do so, but will sustain the President & unite the country. The whigs are anxious to throw the responsibility on the President, but that is not fitting & is only a political "ruse," to throw blame on him, do as he may. Should England propose to us the 49° I think we are bound to accept it, as it would be consistent with the whole negotiation for the last 25 years, and would be approved by the world, & avoid a war, which we must all deprecate, & resort to only as the last alternative. While I look upon our title to Oregon as "clear & unquestionable" yet an honorable compromise to avoid War, we cannot reject, & our honor to the 49° would be saved, as it has always been our proposition. *We* would not recede, but *England* would, if that should be the compromise. I have not yet seen my friend Dobbins'[3] great speech, but have seen it highly lauded, which gives me very grateful feelings. I do not know therefore what positions he has taken, but I hope we concur in opinion

Show this letter to him, & tell him I thank him for the Document he sent me, & shall write him soon, altho, I am by habit a poor correspondent. He is enjoying the sunshine of laudation which he deserves, whilst I am here enjoying the "bitter fury" of the Whig press, for saying that I had no more confidence in Daniel Webster[4] than a sheep stealing dog. And who does not agree with me?

I would suggest that our democratic representatives hold a meeting, & take measures to flood the doubtful Districts in our State with documents, especially the West. We cannot like the whigs raise funds & circulate our Newspapers, & the work must be done by an effort of that kind at Washington, & especially *now*, whilst you can take the *start* at this new juncture of affairs.

Excuse my freedom of suggestions & opinions they may not be worth consideration, as I am a poor politician I fear, I speak out however as the crisis demands.

---

[1]Bundlecund, the pseudonym of political essayist Edmund Burke, previously identified.

[2]George Canning (1770-1827), an English statesman, entered Parliament in 1794. He served as foreign secretary from 1807 to 1809 and from 1822 to 1827 and played a major role in the Napoleonic conflict. "Canning's war of Opinion" probably refers to his political policy of trying to achieve a balance between the opposing principles of oligarchy and democracy. Canning began his career as a Whig but became a staunch Tory. Leslie Stephen and Sidney Lee (eds.), *Dictionary of National Biography* (New York: Macmillan and Co., 63 volumes, 1885-1901, index and supplements), VIII, 420-431, hereinafter cited as *DNB*.

[3]James Cochrane Dobbin, previously identified.

[4]Daniel Webster (1782-1852), an attorney from New Hampshire and Massachusetts, was a representative in Congress (1813-1817, 1823-1827), a United States senator (1827-1841, 1845-1850), and secretary of state (1841-1843, 1850-1852). *DAB*, XIX, 585-592.

John T. Garland to David S. Reid A&H-DSR

Milton,
Jan 22, 1846

I have to express to you my indebtedness for sundry papers & documents this session. I look with great eagerness for the forthcoming report of the Commissioner of the Patent office; the talent & research exhibited by Mr. Burke in his tariff essays under the signature of Bundlecund warrants the highest expectations of an instructive & highly interesting report on the agricultural improvements & statistics of the country; any thing within your reach at Washington throwing light on the subject of agriculture would be thankfully recd. It sometimes occurs that our foreign agents send home for distribution samples of seeds either wheat, grapes, or any thing suited to our soil & climate, might add new variety & profits to our pursuits as planters; you are aware that the planting interest in your district is at a very low ebb & to those who have the *inverted good fortune* to be in possession of many slaves, the burden of their support is becoming so intolerable that every one is looking to the southwest for a more permanent & profitable home; If in your intercourse & associations with the gentlemen from Texas, Louisana or elsewhere in that direction any very eligible & striking inducements for investments in sugar or cotton lands be presented, I should myself be glad to be informed, for at some period if I live I wish to transfer my slaves to a more productive region; I have an itching for some land speculation in Texas; can you put me on the right track; perhaps your superior information obtainable at Washington would enable you to give some useful admonetory hints, several gentlemen in this neighborhood would be willing to associate & even emigrate to Texas if convinced of the certainty of any very profitable investment there. There is some excitement & painful apprehension in relation to our Oregon controversy with England; tis hoped & believed that two nations placed at the head of the Christian & civilized world can surely settle their pretensions to a remote & unimportant tract of country without the intervention of the sword, twould be a stigma & blot upon the civilization of the ages if this thing cannot be honorably adjusted without recourse to arms; Mr. Calhouns present attitude in the Senate is gaining him golden opinions from each party in this section of country; I am afraid that many in our party are disposed to act precipitately in this business; their braggadocio vaporing & bullying war speeches in congress indicate neither wisdom nor good taste. I cannot myself predicate an opinion whether giving the notice & extending the jurisdiction of our laws over our citizens in Oregon will heighten the danger of a rupture or not; we have clearly that right under the treaty & it is therefore no cause of war; if then there be a clashing jurisdiction afterward Ive no objection to arbitration when that point is reached; nations should be slow, very slow to anger. Time, the great pacificator & physician in national maladies would cure most of the evils that the sword is called upon to rectify; if war must come let us be clearly in the right & the burden of its declaration be on the other side, but when once engaged; fight like Devils & Furies incarnate fight; that we should be making every requisite preparation for such an event is not to be doubted; like Rhett,[1] I dislike the ominous conjunction between Adams[2] & Giddings[3] on this subject rely upon it, there is a secret & bitter hostility to the south on this subject; the south has nothing to gain & much to hazard & lose in the present crisis, tis therefore all important that our representatives should be very wary & cautious just now & not allow the ad captandum [*sic*] war spirit of the north or west to drive them from their propr[iety]. Pardon these suggestions, they come from one who delighted at the acquisition of Texas, as the glorious result of democratic wisdom & achievment, without surrendering an inch of our just rights to Oregon, would prefer the wise inactivity of the sagaious statesman to the bullying & war stirring agatation of the demagouge one of the highest attainments with the physician is to know when to do nothing & so with the Politician. time alone can determine whether oregon would be an apt illustration of its truth just now.

NB. Please write me what will be the probable denounement in congress on this subject.

---

[1]Robert Barnwell Rhett, previously identified.

[2]John Quincy Adams, previously identified.

[3]Joshua R. Giddings (1795-1864), an Ohio attorney, was a state legislator and a member of the United States House of Representatives (1838-1859). Historian Charles Sellers describes Giddings as "the strongest anti-slavery Whig in Congress." Giddings later became a Republican. Sellers, *Polk*, 173; *Biographical Directory of Congress*, 942.

A. J. Folger to David S. Reid Duke-DSR

Telmont. NC.
Jan. 30th 1846

I wish you would do me the kindness to inquire of the, Hon. George. W. Hopkin,[1] if he knowes a man by the name of Wm Sturgis[2] a Methodist preacher, who I am informed lives in his Destrict, that is in western *Va*, and if he does know him get him to inform you whare Sturgis now lives, I have Claims against him amounting to about $300-00 and I am informed the gentleman is now good for the debt But I Cannot find any one that Can tell me whare his Circuit is now, he is on some Circuit preaching at this time—I would also be glad if Mr. Hopkins would reccomend some Suitable person to me in Western *Va*, who I Could get to attend to this matter for me, as it would be much better for me to pay some one to attend to it, than it would be for me to go over there, and incur the expence of the trip, & than possibly not find. Sturgis. the last account I have of him, he was riding the Circuit in Tazwell cty. which I think is in Mr. Hopkins's Dist If you will Comply with this request and then write me a line on the matter I will be much obliged to you for so doing I have just received the news in the Standard that the Hon. G. W. Caldwell possetively diclines accepting the nomination for Gov. by the late Democratic Convention this will be a great theme for Federal Whiggery to bark upon, I am truly Sorry to see such an anouncement yet we must put up with such things the best we Can, I have no idea who will be our Candidate, or whether we will have any

The difficulty betene our Goverment and England Seems to be creating a greateal of exitement in this Section, and from the presant tone of the Standard it Seams as though a greateal of Confusion is going on in Mexico as well as England I trust our Government will take a bold, firm, and honorable Stand in this matter. and Show to England and to the world that we are not to be driven from our rights, by the thretts of that power, or the dishonorable Schemes of Federalism in our own republic, What do you think will be the final ditermination of Congress on the Origon question and many other important subjects which now agitate that body

The removele of Major, Mcgee[3] from the Post office at Mt Airy I fear will Cause you to loose some friends, and on the other hand my impression is it will Cause you to gain some few. a change in that office was Compelled to take place, though I actually regreted to se it done on the account of, Mcgee, who is a perfect gentleman though I seriously fear an abandoned drunken ruined man, I do not think he has sean a Sober day in 3 months

Col. Wah[4] and Samuel. D. More[5] are entirely broken up and sold out, Wah will pay his debts, and Injure no man But More will ruin not less than 30 and than be indebt, (report says) not less than $25 thousand dollars, and among the men he will ruin is some of your best friends General. Graves[6] Henry Samuels[7] Jos. Haynes[8] and others, who I learn are determined to leave the County Shortly

I will keep a watch on Mr. Nance[9] and if he does any thing wrong in regard to distributing your documents, I will duly inform you of it, I hope he will do what is right, Pleas write me a line Soon, & giv me all the information wanted

In Conclusion I will say to you, that the people here look to Congress for a greateal this Session, and are watching their diliberations with intence anxiety

---

[1]George W. Hopkins (1804-1861), an attorney from Abingdon, Virginia, was a state legislator, circuit court judge, delegate to the state Constitutional Conven-

tion of 1850, and a representative in Congress (1835-1847, 1857-1859). *Biographical Directory of Congress*, 1074.

[2]William Sturgis was not, apparently, a minister ever assigned to the Surry Charge of Salisbury District. Minutes of the district showing appointments for 1814-1846 do not mention him. His place of residence at the time he incurred his debt to Folger is unknown. Ruth M. Minick, *Central Methodist Church, Mount Airy, North Carolina, Its Early Years, 1829-1900* (Elkin: Blackwell Printing Company, 1975), 4-5, hereinafter cited as Minick, *Central Methodist Church.*

[3]Daniel M. McGee (born 1810) was appointed postmaster of Mount Airy in Surry County on August 25, 1843. His successor's appointment was effective January 20, 1846. By 1850, McGee, a native of North Carolina, still lived in Surry County, where he was occupied as a clerk, unmarried, and owned no real estate. United States Postal Service, *Records of the Post Office Department, Record Group 28, Records of Appointments of Postmasters, 1825-1929* (Washington, D.C.: General Services Administration, National Archives and Records Service, 1961), 398, 470, hereinafter cited as *Records of Appointments of Postmasters*; Seventh Census, 1850, Surry County, Population Schedule, 356.

[4]Harrison M. Waugh (1804-1882), merchant, represented Surry County in the state Senate (1835) and House of Commons (1833-1835, 1860-1861, 1864-1867, and 1872-1874). He was a party in numerous law suits in Surry County in 1845-1846. Tombstone inscription, Dobson City Cemetery, Surry County; Cheney, *North Carolina Government*, 1279, 1280; Minutes of Surry County Court, 1845-1846 passim (microfilm), Archives, Division of Archives and History, Raleigh.

[5]Samuel D. Moore of Surry County was a planter, merchant, and hotel operator. He served twice as postmaster of Mount Airy, receiving appointments on July 20, 1838, and again on June 21, 1841. He served a little over one year during the second appointment, a successor replacing him on July 18, 1843. William Franklin Carter, Jr., and Carrie Young Carter, *Footprints in the "Hollows" or Surry County and Her People* (Elkin: Northwestern Regional Library, 1976), 79, hereinafter cited as Carter and Carter, *Footprints*; *Records of Appointments of Postmasters*, 398.

[6]Barzillai Graves (born 1782), previously identified, was a Caswell County farmer. By 1850, when he was 68, the census does not list him as owning any real estate, an indication that he may have suffered a financial reverse of the sort Folger suggests. Seventh Census, 1850, Caswell County, Population Schedule, 226.

[7]Henry Samuel, a native of North Carolina, was a Surry County farmer and head of a large family. In 1850 he owned real estate valued only at $250. Seventh Census, 1850, Surry County, Population Schedule, 290.

[8]Joseph Haynes (born 1794) was a farmer in Wilkes County. His real estate in 1850 was valued only at $150, perhaps an indication that he too may have experienced economic loss. Seventh Census, 1850, Wilkes County, Population Schedule, 321.

[9]William M. Nance was appointed January 20, 1846, to replace Daniel M. McGee as postmaster at Mount Airy. Nance was replaced briefly by Thomas V. Hamlin (appointed September 16, 1846) later in the year, but Hamlin served only about one month, and Nance was reappointed on October 13, 1846, serving after that time for two more years. *Records of Appointments of Postmasters*, 470, 471.

John H. Wheeler[1] *to David S. Reid* A&H-DSR

Beattysford
Catawba Co. N.C.
4th Feby 46

We are thrown as a party into a momentary confusion by the declining of Mr. Caldwell to run for Governor—This was not unexpected to some, and therefore many of us did not take an active part in his nomination in the Convention of the 8th ulto Under all the circumstances his course has been of necessity and prudence. What now is to be done?

In the west our boys are full of fight. "Man to the knife & knife to the hilt—" I believe very sincerely that we can defeat them with proper men and means. Our party (juding from the Congressional Elections) will come up to Lincolnton 2,500 votes ahead, and no whig can gain that clear majority distracted as their party is by the feuds between Graham & Clingman.[2] There is a sensible increase among the Democrats & a falling off from the Whigs. They have left as hopeless all the issues for which they battled in the canvass for Mr. Clay. Read their resolutions in the late Whig Convention on the 12th ulto. Not a word for a Bank, nothing about Texas, a Tariff for *revenue* with *incidental* protection and for Oregon! Oh what a falling off is here.

I think that if you will consent to allow your name that you could remain in Congress and take the mountain District in July & August without any inconvenience.

We will pledge ourselves to do all we can for you in this section & you can get at least fisher's[3] vote

Let me hear from you by return mail, as our superior court circuit commences next week when we wish to start the ball.

Remember me to friend Daniel[4] and Colo Biggs[5]

---

[1]John Hill Wheeler (1806-1882), an attorney, diplomat, and historian, was born in Murfreesboro and later lived near Charlotte. He was a member of the House of Commons (1827-1830, 1852), superintendent of the Charlotte branch of the United States Mint (1837-1841), state treasurer (1842-1843), and minister to Nicaragua (1854-1857). In 1851 he published *Historical Sketches of North Carolina.* Ashe, *Biographical History*, VII, 472-478.

[2]Thomas Lanier Clingman, previously identified, a congressman from western North Carolina, differed increasingly with the positions taken by the Raleigh faction of the Whig party, headed by William A. Graham. Clingman eventually joined the Democratic party.

[3]Charles Fisher, previously identified, supported western North Carolina interests. Powell, *DNCB*, II, 201.

[4]John R. J. Daniel (1802-1868), a Halifax attorney, was a member of the House of Commons (1832-1834), state attorney general (1834), and a representative in Congress (1841-1853). In 1860 he moved to Louisiana. *Biographical Directory of Congress*, 775.

[5]Asa Biggs, previously identified.

Speech by David S. Reid on the Oregon Question[1]

Duke-DSR

February 7, 1846

On the resolution of notice to Great Britain to abrogate the convention of joint occupancy relative to the Oregon territory

Mr. REID obtained the floor, and addressed the committee as follows:

Mr. CHAIRMAN: The importance of the question under consideration must plead my apology for trespassing on the patience of this House, while I give some of the considerations which will influence the vote I intend to give. Could I cherish the vanity that I could, at any time, have enlightened this body on any topic of legislation before it, such a hope would be utterly vain on this occasion, after the question before the House has undergone so full and able a discussion.

The question under consideration is, whether it is proper, at this time, to give the notice to Great Britain that the convention of 1818 and 1827, touching what is generally termed the joint occupancy by the two governments of the Oregon territory, should terminate at the expiration of twelve months. I believe that we have a good title to Oregon. We have acquired title to it by settlement and discovery; and if anything was wanted to make it complete, that was supplied by the acquisition of the claims of France and Spain. But I did not rise to discuss the title at this time; the task has already been performed with an ability which has satisfied the country. I must confess that I was astonished to hear the gentleman from Kentucky (MR. DAVIS[2]) take the ground that the constitution had transferred the power of giving such notice to the President of the United States; and that the executive had endeavored to avoid that responsibility by throwing it on the legislative department of this government. Surely the gentleman did not listen to the able speech of the gentleman from Ohio, (MR. THURMAN[3]) What is a treaty? It is the supreme law of the land, and can only be abrogated by an act of Congress, or by another treaty made in conformity to the constitution. And can the gentleman from Kentucky desire that the President shall take into his own hands the perogative of abrogating a supreme law of the land? If the Executive himself should claim such a power, how would the cry of usurpation ring from one end of the country to the other? He would be charged with an attempt to violate the constitution, and seize upon despotic power. The whole country would condemn such a course, and I fancy that even the gentleman from Kentucky, and his political friends, would raise the cry of usurpation! If the gentleman thinks that the notice is a war measure, and equivalent to a declaration of war, as some have insisted, then surely he will not assert that the President has power to give it without the legislative action of this government. The gentleman thought proper to deprecate the idea of connecting this question with the party politics of the day; but he departed from this course by heaping partisan abuse upon the president, and charging on him a design of involving the country in a war without consulting its welfare.

Does the gentleman believe that the interests of the country required the President to make the British government a more liberal offer than he did? If not, then, how could he charge the President with an attempt to plunge the country into an unjust and unnecessary war? For myself, I believe that offer was too liberal; but we have been informed that it was refused, and withdrawn, and our title asserted to the whole of Oregon. Some of the gentleman's political friends say that "the President cannot be kicked into a war," while the gentleman himself insists that the President is too anxious for war. Whether the gentleman has met this question in the elevated spirit of a statesman, I leave to this House and to the country to judge.

I know not, sir, whether the giving of this notice will produce war; I am sure that it will not be a just cause of war; but I deny that it is a war measure. It ought not to be so considered here, for it is not so regarded even in Great Britain. The giving the notice is provided for in the convention of 1827; it is peaceable in its character, and does not prevent negotiation; but still so fruitful are the imaginations of some gentlemen that they cannot speak of it in any other light than as a war measure. The friends of this measure have not advocated it as a war measure; it has only been so characterized by those who oppose it.

In giving the notice, the only legitimate inquiry for an American statesman is, whether this question ought to be settled as early as practicable, or delayed for an indefinite period of time. The convictions of my mind are decidedly in favor of the former course. Let us examine this point. For the purpose of postponing the adjustment of the Oregon dispute, it was agreed in the third article of the convention between the United States and Great Britain, signed October 20, 1818, that—

"Any country that may be claimed by either party on the northwest coast of America, westward of the Stony mountains, (now called Rocky mountains,) shall together with its harbors, bays, and creeks, and the navigation of all rivers within the same, be free and open for the term of ten years from the date of the signature of the present convention, to the vessels, citizens, and subjects of the two powers; it being well understood that this agreement is not to be construed to the prejudice of any claim which either of the two high contracting parties may have to any part of said country, nor shall it be taken to affect the claims of any other power or state to any part of said country, the only object of the high contracting parties, in that respect, being to prevent disputes and differences among themselves."

This convention remained in force till it was renewed by the convention signed at London, August 6, 1827, which provided:

"ART. 1. All the provisions of the third article of the convention concluded between the United States of America and his Majesty the King of the United Kingdom of Great Britain and Ireland, on the 20th day of Oct., 1818, shall be, and they are hereby, further indefinitely extended and continued in force, in the same manner as if all the provisions of the said article were herein specifically recited.

"ART. 2. It shall be competent, however, for either of the contracting parties, in case either should think fit, at any time after the 20th October, 1828, on giving due notice of twelve months to the other contracting party, to annul and abrogate this convention; and it shall, in such case, be accordingly entirely annulled and abrogated, after the expiration of the said term of notice.

"ART. 3. Nothing contained in this convention or in the third article of the convention of the 20th October, 1818, hereby continued in force, shall be construed to impair, or in any manner affect, the claims which either of the contracting parties may have to any part of the country westward of the Stony or Rocky mountains."

From 1818, up to the present time, repeated efforts have been made to settle by negotiation the dispute between the two countries in regard to this territory; but Great Britain has always refused to propose such terms as this country could accept, without a sacrifice of her rights. In this condition the question stands at the present moment; and it might so remain, but for the change of circumstances which will in a short time render it both impracticable and impossible. While the country was only used for hunting, fishing, and fur-trading, there was but little difficulty between the two governments in relation to their conflicting claims, and it was not indispensably necessary to adjust them. But things have changed. Within a few years thousands of our industrious and enterprising citizens have gone with their families to that country to engage in agricultural, mechanical, and other pursuits of civilized life, and they are now cultivating the soil, and earning for themselves permanent homes, and an inheritance for their children. Does any one suppose that we have arrived at such perfection in the science of government as to justify the hope that two distinct races of people, each governed by a different code of laws, and owing allegiance to governments totally differing in their character, can settle and occupy the same territory, and maintain peaceable relations towards each other? Such a hope is illusive. Why then should we indulge further delay, when every moment we live this question becomes more difficult to settle? When a dispute arises between two neighbors as to the boundary of their lands, the dispute may often be easily adjusted at first; but if they once drive their fencestakes, cut their ditches, and build their houses on the disputed territory, a friendly settlement of the boundary becomes almost impossible. So it will be in regard to Oregon. This territory is now regarded as greatly more valuable than it was in 1818; and if you wait ten years longer, its estimation will no doubt be more than quadrupled. Is it not important, then, that this question should be settled as early as practicable? In view of all this, I ask, is it not our duty to take such measures as will facilitate the decision of this question? For one, I believe the country is ours to 54^{0} 40', but the extent of our title is not the question now under consideration; and all who believe that we have rights in Oregon, no matter to what extent, so they be greater than the British government has offered to concede, ought to vote for this measure.

The President of the United States, in his annual message at the opening of the present session of Congress, says:

"The extraordinary and wholly inadmissible demands of the British government, and the rejection of the proposition made in deference alone to what had been done by my predecessors, and the implied obligation which their acts seemed to impose, afford satisfactory evidence that no compromise which the United States ought to accept can be effected. With this conviction, the proposition of compromise, which had been made and rejected, was, by my direction, subsequently withdrawn, and our title to the whole Oregon territory asserted, and, as is believed, maintained by irrefragable facts and arguments.

"The civilized world will see in these proceedings a spirit of liberal concession on the part of the United States; and this government will be relieved from all responsibility which may follow the failure to settle the controversy.

"All attempts at compromise having failed, it becomes the duty of Congress to consider what measures it may be proper to adopt for the security and protection of our citizens now inhabiting, or who may hereafter inhabit Oregon, and for the maintenance of our just title to that territory. In adopting measures for this purpose, care should be taken that nothing be done to violate the stipulations of the convention of 1827, which is still in force. The faith of treaties, in their letter and spirit, has ever been, and, I trust, will ever be, scrupulously observed by the United States. Under that convention a year's notice is required to be given by either party to the other, before the joint occupancy shall terminate, and before either can rightfully assert or exercise exclusive jurisdiction over any portion of the territory. This notice it would, in my judgment, be proper to give; and I recommend that provision be made by law for giving it accordingly, and terminating, in this manner, the convention of the sixth of August, 1827."

Now, sir, in the face of these facts, can we shrink from giving the notice? Some gentlemen take it for granted that this measure will cut off all negotiation; but they are mistaken. It only carries out what public opinion has declared, and what the true policy of the country requires. If further negotiation shall be necessary or proper, then this notice in no wise prevents it; if further negotiation is unnecessary or improper, it is our imperative duty to give the notice. Passing this measure, then, will not prevent our government from doing anything that ought to be done, while it will untie our hands and leave us free to pursue such measures as the interests of the country demand. In doing these things, we must observe our national faith, and violate no treaty stipulation. At the last session of Congress, a bill to organize a Territorial government in Oregon passed this House by a vote of 140 to 59. This bill contained a section providing for the giving of the notice, in the following words:

"Sec. 43. *And be it further enacted,* That the President of the United States be, and he is hereby, required to cause due notice to be given to the British government of the desire and intention of the government of the United States to annul and abrogate the convention with Great Britain relative to territory on the northwest coast of America, concluded August 6, 1827, agreeably to the provisions of the 2d article of that convention: *Provided,* that nothing in this act contained shall be so construed or carried into effect by any of the officers or citizens of the United States, as to interfere in any way with any right which any of the subjects of Great Britain may have in the territory herein mentioned, as provided for in the convention aforesaid, until the expiration of twelve months after notice shall be given, as above provided, by the President of the United States."

Sir, I voted for this bill then, as did a very large majority of the members of the House, but it did not pass the Senate. Was it considered a war measure then? No, sir; and why should it be considered so now? Without a knowledge of the views of my constituents, I voted for the bill then, and they sustained me; but in giving the same vote now, I not only believe that I am doing right, but feel sure that I am obeying the will of those who sent me here. I repudiate the idea that this is a war measure. It is merely proof of our anxiety to settle the question, and of our determination to maintain our rights in that territory, and repel those who trespass on them. But while I repeat that this is no war measure, I would not be understood as saying that this country will not take such further steps as may be necessary to secure our rights in Oregon. The territory is ours, and we must not part with it. Sir, the time has ceased with us when we can act in that spirit of forbearance to Great Britain which characterized the conduct of the patriarch Abraham, when he said to Lot, "If thou wilt take the left hand, then I will go to the right; or if thou depart to the right hand, then I will go to the left." That might have been possible once when very little value was attached to territory. But not so now with us. We need all the territory we have, and ought not under any circumstances to part with any portion that we possess. But highly as we prize territory, we do not propose to take any that does not belong to us.

Sir, I am aware some gentlemen, who do not appreciate the importance of Oregon, represent it as a distant strip of land of but little value; and they ask, are we going to fight for that? I tell such gentlemen that Oregon is of vast importance to this country and that its loss would be deeply felt and sorely regretted to the latest moment of the existence of this great republic? Because Oregon is at a great distance from this Capitol, shall we treat her as the Roman empire once treated the island of Britain—clip her off, and tell her to take care of herself? Britain was once a part of the Roman empire; but that government thought her of so little value that they cast her off, and told the people if they could defend themselves against their enemies, good and well, let them do it; the Roman eagle would no longer take them under its wings. On this strip of country, thus severed—which is infinitely smaller than Oregon—is planted that mighty government, whose invincibility has this day been so eloquently described! It is the nation inhabiting this territory which now struggles for the conquest of the world, and carries terror with her name to the most distant parts of the earth! This teaches us the increasing importance of territory, and is a warning to us to guard against the loss of any part of our country, or of any portion of our people. It is quite natural for us to suppose, that, under any circumstances, Oregon is destined to be a part of our confederacy, but it may perhaps turn out otherwise. I here express the hope, and cherish the belief, that she will never be a British colony; that that country will be a republic, inhabited by freemen, I believe almost certain; but whether she is destined to remain a part of this confederacy, or to become a separate and distinct republic, depends upon the policy pursued towards her by this government. If we now refuse her protection, may she not hereafter scorn our proffer of reunion and refuse to be received by us as a State? The case of Texas was different. Texas was a distinct and independent nation, and we were under no obligations to protect her people or territory till she became a part of this Union. But we are under very different obligations to the people of Oregon, because we own the territory, and it is settled by our own citizens. If we leave her in the moment of her struggles to shift for herself by withdrawing our protection, will she hereafter, when she has established her right to the soil, come and ask to be again incorporated into this Union? I believe not. I must here remark that I would be the last man on this floor, or in this country, to claim a single inch of territory which I did not believe to be ours; but, on the other hand, I say with equal determination that I will never consent to the surrender of an inch that is our own—I care not where it lies, or what may be its value—to gratify the ambition of Great Britain or any other government upon the earth. We boast of being a great and glorious republic; but what constitutes a great government? It is the justice of its laws—the preservation of its rights—and the protection of its citizens. I care not how wealthy or powerful a nation may be; as soon as she ceases to preserve her rights and to protect her citizens she ceases to be great and is destined to fall. If we ever surrender any portion of our territory to Great Britain, gentlemen may rest assured that it will be but the beginning of surrenders; she will never be satisfied with demanding. Peace is our policy. We do not seek a war with Great Britain; but if she declares war against us for defending our right to Oregon, we shall stand justified in the eyes of the world, and every American heart, and every American arm will be found on the side of their country. Sir, the country is in favor of notice, and for maintaining our right to the territory. Even in North Carolina Oregon is stronger than any political party; and, as an evidence of this, I will refer to the fact that my whig colleague from *Lumber river* (Mr. DOCKERY[4]) publicly proclaimed during the canvass, that, before he would surrender any part of Oregon he would march barefoot over prickly pears to fight for it. I repeat that the "Old North State" is for Oregon.

Mr. DOCKERY rose, and asked his colleague to give him leave to explain. His colleague (Mr. REID) knew more of the geography of his State than to speak of him as his colleague from Lumber River district. The remark to which the gentleman alluded was, that he was ready to contend for all to which we had a valid title. I said that there were in Oregon British rights and American rights; and that, when the line was run, I would defend our soil to the utmost extremity; and what he had said about marching over prickly pears was said in that connexion. He had said that, when our rights were determined, then he would be ready to fight for them, though he had to march barefoot over prickly pears.

Mr. REID. Where does my colleague think our rights extend to?

Mr. DOCKERY. Just where the gentleman's favorite President settled it in his negotiations. A laugh.

Mr. REID. Then the gentleman is with the President, and the President says, "our title to the *whole of Oregon* has been asserted, and, as is believed, maintained by irrefragable facts and arguments." The gentleman's location arose from this connexion: him and myself were members of the legislature at the same time; he had a favorite project for the improvement of Lumber river, and from his zeal in favor of the measure, he became associated in my mind with the name of the river, so that I thought *Lumber river* certainly must run through his district. (A laugh.)

Mr. DOCKERY. The gentleman mistakes the nature of my patriotism. He thinks that a man's patriotism must be confined to his own district. Now, I am willing to improve North Carolina in any part of it; and just so I feel in regard to the United States.

Mr. REID resumed. I am happy to hear of the gentleman's partiotism, and I shall be still more so, if, when it comes to the vote, he shall show that his patriotism, which has already reached Lumber river, is found *sufficiently expanded to extend to Oregon*! I hope that we shall look on this as a great national question. My feelings are with the South—my destiny is with her's; but I will suffer no local or sectional views to influence my course on this important measure. It was with extreme reluctance that I heard the remark made by a member on this floor, that whatever might be the fate of this question, he should have the consolation to know that he had not followed in the lead of the gentleman from Massachusetts, (Mr. ADAMS.) I regret that it should be thought necessary to invoke existing prejudices against an individual to operate against a great national measure.

But, sir, in reply to that remark, I might, with equal propriety, say that we who support the notice will have the consolation to know that we are not following in the lead of Great Britain. But such a declaration would not be an argument for or against the notice. It has been said that the member from Ohio (Mr. GIDDINGS) is for the notice, and that he is actuated by motives unworthy of a statesman. But even this shall not deter me from giving my vote for a measure which I believe to be right. I might as well be told, because one of the chosen twelve was a traitor, and betrayed the Savior, that therefore I must reject Christianity. I follow in the lead of no man. I go for my country. We are told that we must not act lest a war ensue. Has it come to this that our government can carry out no important measure connected with her domestic or foreign policy without the cry of war being raised and held up as a terror over us? War and ruin panics have alternately prevailed ever since the commencement of our government, and if we wait for them to cease before we act we shall never do anything. If we attempt to procure indemnity for spoliations on the property of our citizens by a foreign country, the war cry is raised!—if we attempt to annex Texas, war in all its horrors is depicted as the consequence!—and when we attempt to assert our claim to Oregon, we are told an unjust and sanguinary war will be inevitable! The horrors of war have been described in so vivid and forcible a manner that one might almost imagine that they saw the British steamers darting from point to point along our coast—that they heard the thundering of British cannon, and beheld our cities with their temples of justice and their temples of religion wrapt in flames! But in the midst of this gloomy picture, the reflection rises in my mind, that whatever may have been the devasting effects of past wars, it is nevertheless certain a portion of mankind are so constituted that they grieve much about wars that never happen; and such, I hope, is the character of the lamentations of the gentlemen we have heard on this occasion. I am for peace; I love peace; I appreciate its effects upon commerce; and, above all, I admire its happy influences in a moral and political point of view. But while I say this, I must be permitted to remark, that I would scorn the idea of a peace that had to be purchased at the sacrifice of the interests and the honor of my country. The territory claimed by Great Britain on this continent, is greater in extent than our own with Oregon included; and ought we to surrender to that government any portion of our soil? No, sir; we have none to spare. It has been with deep regret that I have heard remarks on this floor more disparaging to our claim to Oregon than anything that I have ever seen in the correspondence of the British minister himself. It has always been unfortunate for this country that in all of her controversies with foreign governments, sentiments have been uttered here which were calculated to mislead other countries in relation to the state of public opinion in the United States, and thereby to render the subject of dispute the more difficult to adjust. Such, I fear, will be the case in the present controversy. Sir, it is time we had learned to stand on our own feet. Great Britain is, year after year, by the force of her diplomacy, and the power of her sword, bringing nation after nation to bow to power and dominion, until her possessions dot your map over a considerable portion of the globe. With our love of liberty, we could not withhold our sympathy from those whose misfortune it has been, from time to time, to fall within her grasp; but we have stood by and beheld all these things in silence, adhering to the policy not to interfere in foreign disputes in which our own safety does not require us to take part. But when she comes upon our own shores, and seeks to possess herself of a part of our territory, every consideration of interest and of patriotism requires that we should resist her arrogant demands in the spirit of freemen who know their rights and dare maintain them. If the preservation of our rights did not require it, such a course would then be absolutely necessary even to command the respect of Great Britain herself. In all the pictures that have been drawn of the horrid results of war, gentlemen have taken it for granted that we are to bear all the loss and make all the sacrifices, and that Great Britain has nothing to lose. But such is not the fact. Disastrous as such a conflict might prove to us, she has more to fear from it than ourselves. She cannot but foresee that the prosecution of a war against the United States would lead to a dismemberment of nearly all of her colonial possessions, and, perhaps, ultimately to an entire dissolution of her form of government. She has her domestic feuds and her immense debt; she has a commerce to suffer as well as ourselves; and the loss of our trade will injure her more than the loss of her trade can injure us. The defenceless condition of the United States has been frequently alluded to; and the gentleman from Alabama (Mr. YANCEY) said that there were perhaps no United States soliders in his own State at this time. I learned almost my first lesson on this Oregon question from that noble State. At the last session of Congress she sent to this House a resolution, passed by her legislature, in the following words:

Resolved, That the true policy of the United States requires that the joint occupancy of Oregon by the United States and England should cease; and resolved, that the title of the United States to the territory of Oregon is clear and indisputable.

This was the language of that gallant State one year ago. But, sir, Alabama has soldiers—citizen soldiers—the best in the world. Let a British soldier set his foot on Alabama's consecrated soil, and then we shall see where the soldiers are. Sir, "it takes time to discipline the slaves of despotism, but every man is a soldier when he combats tyranny." Our policy forbids the keeping of large standing armies in time of peace, but we depend on our citizen soldiery, who are the safest reliance. Sound the alarm that the invaders are at hand, and the question will not be whom can you urge to meet them, but whom can you hold back from the conflict? Tell me not of the want of soldiers to defend our country. Our citizen soldiers fight, not for pay, but for the rights of their country; and when they have achieved the victory their patriotism deserves, they lay aside their armour—they put off their martial character and retire to the bosom of their families, and tell their deeds to inspire the rising generation with the same patriotic ardor. These, Mr. Chairman, are our soldiers, and they will be found equal to any emergency. Let not Great Britain calculate on dissensions among ourselves, for when the first blow shall be struck, whether it be in the North or in the South, all local distinctions will be forgotten. We shall alone remember that we are citizens of the same republic; and the South will be ready to fly to the rescue of the North, and the North will be found defending the institutions and the rights of the South. But it has been said that our navy is not so large as that of Great Britain. It is true that she has a large navy, and out-numbers us in steamships; but it is equally true that our situation is infinitely better than it was at the commencement of the last war. Our resources are greater, and the facilities for commanding them vastly increased. The efficiency of the British navy has been greatly exaggerated. She has laid out millions in building fleets which the improvements in modern warfare have rendered next to useless. These improvements are constantly going on, and have already reached a point which renders a large portion of the vast navy of Great Britain on which she has lavished such immense sums utterly unavailable in a war with the United States. If we need fleets we can build them; and it is better for us that we have not exhausted our resources in the construction of a large navy, which would now be unfit for service. During the last war our gallant little navy won for herself enduring fame; and I undertake to say that when the emergency shall again arise, she will fully maintain that high character to which her noble deeds so justly entitle her. In conclusion, permit me to remark, that while I respect the opinions, and do not arraign the motives of those who differ from me on this question, no act of mine shall ever sanction the surrender of any portion of our territory, without a just equivalent. Entertaining the opinions I do, if I were to act otherwise, I should feel that I had not faithfully performed the high and responsible duty which I owe to my constituents, and to my country. Let us pass the notice, and follow it up by giving bounties of land to such of our citizens as may go there to brave the hardships and privations of a frontier life. Let us extend the laws and protection of the United States over the territory. Do these things, and my word for it, these brave pioneers will do much towards protecting themselves. We shall then prove to the world that we regard the great principle that the protection of our laws shall extend to every citizen of this republic, and that we are determined that our rights shall be respected all over the earth. It is natural that there should exist among a free people, some differences of opinion as to the best mode of accomplishing any end; but on this great question, let us present to England, to Europe, and to the world an undivided front, and this will ensure us peace, if peace is attainable.

[1]This speech was delivered in the House of Representatives and was printed at the *Union* office.

[2]Garrett Davis (1801-1872), an attorney from Paris, Kentucky, was a state legislator, a representative in Congress (1839-1847), and a United States senator (1861-1872). *Biographical Directory of Congress*, 782.

[3]Allen G. Thurman (1813-1895), an attorney from Ross County, Ohio, was a representative in Congress (1845-1847), a justice of the Ohio Supreme Court (1851-1856), a United States senator (1869-1881), and Democratic candidate for vice-president in 1888. *Biographical Directory of Congress*, 1714.

[4]Alfred Dockery, previously identified, lived in Richmond County, west of what one would ordinarily refer to as "Lumber River"—the Robeson County area. Powell, *DNCB*, II, 87.

James W. Jeffreys[1] *to David S. Reid* A&H-DSR

Red House N C
Feby 21st 1846

I have been requested by Richard J. Smith Esq.[2] Doct J. Comer,[3] William Smith[4] & others to address you and request you to send a map of Origon. They desired me to say that if the map of Oregon should cost you anything, we will pay the amt of costs on your return home.

I was much gratified to see your vote recorded for the notice and also much pleased to see that you advocated the measure by a speech before the house.

I[t] gives me much pleasure to assure you that your course in Congress thus far meets the warmest expectations of your friends in Caswell. It is with pride I make this announcement to you.

We have the utmost Confidence in your vote that the notice to be given. I have read almost every speech that has been printed. I hope you will give us your speech. It would give you additional popularity if possible in your district. I do not say this to flatter you. A number of your political friends converse together at my office *three times per week* to discuss over the affairs of the nation, and where your political course is spoken of in the highest terms. Public expectation and anxiety is very high relative to our foreign relations. We all believe that there shall [be] no war. But Sir permit me to say go for the honor and rights of your Country, and your course will be approved by your friends in this district. I have the utmost confidence in Col Polk. I know him well. I lived with him at Chapel Hill in the same room near twelve months. We were intimate and cordial friends. I received from him a letter sometime before he was elected. It would give me great pleasure to see him once more. Polk is a great man. I was confident when at Chapel Hill he would distinguish himself. He was a most laboreous student at college and carried with triumph the first honours in his class. He laid down excellent precepts and examples while at College, and I have endeavoured to adhere to them ever since. He was very ambitious but in a laudable way, and There is recorded in the archives at Chapel Hill in the Dialectic Society room more able essays and compositions than any other young man up to the time he graduated.

Please to present my warmest respects to him, when an opportunity offers, as I understood he made some very marked inquiries of me from Mr Wesley Jones of Wake a short time since.

I hope to be in Washington City in May next on my way to attend the General Asembly of the Presbyterian Church which will convene in Philadelphia in May when I shall do myself the pleasure to call on my friend Col Polk.

I would thank you to send me a copy of Col Allen's[5] able speech and any others that you may think proper.

We should be pleased to receive the able report of the Sect of the Treasury—if you can conveniently get a copy.

P.S. Since I wrote the above I have read a part of Mr. Hinnagon[6] speech in the Senate.

Will you be so good as to procure a copy and forward it.

---

[1]James W. Jeffreys, a planter and manufacturer from Red House, was a member of the Milton Jockey Club in 1830, a mail contractor, and a patron of Hyco Academy in 1834. Powell, *Caswell County*, 160, 174, 358, 497-498.

[2]Richard J. Smith was a planter and owned a flour mill in Caswell County. In 1860 he had forty-four slaves. Powell, *Caswell County*, 114, 118.

[3]John Comer was a physician in Red House, Caswell County. Powell, *Caswell County*, 398.

[4]This is probably the William Smith of Caswell County who was a commissioner of the Yanceyville and Milton Railroad in 1866. Powell, *Caswell County*, 503.

[5]William Allen (1803-1879), a native of Edenton, became an attorney in Chillicothe, Ohio. He was a representative in Congress (1833-1835), a United States senator (1837-1849), and governor of Ohio (1874-1876). *Biographical Directory of Congress*, 473.

[6]Edward A. Hannegan (1807-1859), an attorney from Covington, Indiana, was a state legislator, a representative in Congress (1833-1837), a United States senator (1843-1849), and minister to Prussia (1849-1850). *Biographical Directory of Congress*, 1003.

L. Q. C. Butler[1] *to David S. Reid* A&H-DSR

County Line
Davie [County] N.C.
23 Feb. 1846

I had the honor yesterday to receive yours of the 4th. Inst. together with the Weekly Union[2], and herewith I send you your money with my thanks for your pomt [*sic*] attention to my request I also received 16 Nos. of the message[3], &c they are excellent papers, and are read with much interest here; they are the plainest on the tariff of any productions which I have seen; against those papers there can be no rising up on the part of Whiggery, they are as silent now as toads in August!

I handed them out some in this Dist. and some in yours.

Mr. Barringer[4] does not find it conveneint [*sic*] or expedient to send us those papers, the reason is plain; he preaches a different doctrine;—but I think his days are numbered, he only got in this time by the skin of his teeth. Any thing which you may think fit at any time to mail to me will be read with int. and hand out in your Dist. as I have land in Ashe & some business in surry very frequently

I am very glad to receive your communications

If any of the Histories of Oregon are mailable I would be very glad of one and mail the money to you for it. I will promise to trouble you no more with my perhaps improper requests

---

[1]Lucius Quintus Cincinnatus Butler, an early resident and well-known eccentric of the County Line community, operated a gold mine with the aid of his two slaves. James W. Wall, *History of Davie County in the Forks of the Yadkin* (Mocksville: Davie County Historical Publishing Association, 1969), 290, hereinafter cited as Wall, *History of Davie County*.

[2]The *Weekly Union* was a political newspaper founded (at the request of President James K. Polk) May 10, 1845, in Washington, D.C., by Thomas Ritchie and John P. Heiss, as an organ of the Democratic administration. Westcott and Ramage, *Duke Newspaper Checklist*, part I, 54.

[3]The *Message* has not been identified. See also William W. Holden to David S. Reid, December 8, 1847, below, and note 9.

[4]Daniel Moreau Barringer (1806-1873), a Cabarrus County attorney, was a member of the House of Commons (1829-1834, 1840, 1842, 1854), delegate to the Constitutional Convention of 1835, Whig representative in Congress (1843-1849), minister to Spain (1849-1853), and delegate to the Washington Peace Conference in 1861. *Biographical Directory of Congress*, 520.

John Hill to David S. Reid A&H-DSR

Home.
Stokes Co. N.C.
March 1st. 1846

For several days past we have had exceedingly bad weather, and as it is yet too cold to go out, especially for one not in good health, I have concluded to remind you of *old lang signe* &c.

As to the Country news, there is none of interest. But little is said on politicks much as you all seem to be excited in Congress.

I see that you made a *flaming* speech on the Oregon resolutions respecting notice &c.

I hope the Senate will also act speedily on the subject, and let the Country & the World know what is to be done.

The firm & independent stand which the President & his friends have taken in defence of our national rights will no doubt, meet with a hearty approval from a large majority of the American people, be the result what it may. Yet it is to be hoped that the difficulty may be adjusted without war, as it can & probably will be.

Some time since I received a letter from the Hon'bl Mr. Brinkerhooff[1] of the house of Reps. enquiring about the character & servises of the late Col. John Armstrong formerly of this county.

I have not been able to give him the desired information, but would refer him to Albert Moore of Giles County Tennessee, Lynnville, who married one of his grand daughters & who can no doubt afford him the necessary information.

Be pleased to let him know of Mr Moore and his address. I fear I shall ask more of you than I ought, But Mrs Hill desires me to say to you, that she would be glad, through you, to know something about a Mr P. T. McKinny of Newton Indiana.

He administered on the estate of John Crawford an half uncle to my wife, in which we have some small interest, but altho, he has several times written to us about the matter, he seems to delay in closing the business of the estate.

We should be glad to know whether he is a man who can be relied on, as we have not heard from him since October 1844, when he wrote that he would be able to settle the business or effect the sale of Lands &c by the time Polk was elected president.

If you can let us know something about him by enquiring of the Representative of his District, without inconvenience, we shall thank you.

One other thing also. Some months ago I enclosed Mr Duvals printed letter concerning my fathers revolutionary servises & claims &c.

Did you ever receive it, & if so, have you got any reply from the proper Department?

In the event of war with England, I should like to be a recruiting officer, but I do not know whether I could muster up courage enough to face the enimy—

[1]Henry R. Brinkerhoff (1787-1844), a planter from New York and Huron County, Ohio, was a militia captain in the War of 1812 and became a major general of the New York militia in 1824. He represented Ohio in Congress (1843-1844). *Biographical Directory of Congress*, 598.

Reuben Reid to David S. Reid RF

Reidsville N C
Sunday Evening March 8th 1846

I again Send you a few loines to in form you that we are all well through the merces of a kind providanc we hav Seen the winter months pass and it has been a very cold one her up to this tim and I do hope that you are enjoying the Saim blessing I do not know thing that would be newes to you I would be very glad to see you but knowing that it is not conveniant I get along as usal I hav not Rote to you in Some time myself but know that you ar rittin to by Sum of the famaly regular we hav not had any letter from you in two weaks I think it is in consequence of the weather the roads has been all mos impasable here and I Expect it is worse to the North your Mother Brother and Sister Send there love to you please Except my best from your Father

---

James E. Williamson[1] *to David S. Reid* A&H-DSR

Person Coty No Ca.
March 9th 46

You may be somewhat serprised at recing a letter from me at this place, but I avail myself of the present leisure moment while watching at the bedside of my fatherinlaw to address a few lines to you partly on business and partly to elicit from you some of the news of the city. I have now been some three or four days in attendance on Mr Williams[2] who is laboring under a disease which I apprehend must prove fatal in some short time; the disease is anurism or in otherwords enlargement of the great bloodvessels leading from the heart which is finally to rupture and close the scene. I have heard of the unpleasant meeting of Messrs. Pleasants and Richie[3] and look upon it as a very unfortunate circumstance, for the individuals themselves as well as the two great political parties, in our country, for I fear from what I see and hear, that the matter which is [entirely] between the individuals themselves, will be made a party matter, and that much evil is to grow out of it. I was much pleased however to see that Mr. Richie, was not the chalenger and that he protested against the mode of settling the dispute, proposed by Mr. P. giving at the same time good and substantial reasons for his objection. I see that the Oregon Question has been acted on in your house, and has passed by an overwhelming majority on first view of that subject. I was opposed to the U.S. giving the notice, but after, reflecting and hearing some of the arguments in its favor I became fully satisfied that, that was the only mode by which the disputed question could be settled, for England never would give the notice so long as her citizens were protected in the country, and permitted, to carry on trade with the natives and enjoy all the advantages of the country under the treaty of 18 - and 28 - The democratic party in our section of county are unanimous in favour of the notice and yet are for peace if it can be procured without a sacrifise of the honour and dignity of the country. They go for Oregon to 54-40—if it is ours—but are willing for a compromise at 49 with "*honour bright*" rather than a war at this time I was very much pleased to see the secretary of state, take the stand he did in his negotiations with Mr. Pacherham[4] and hope he will be sustained in his positions as they are clear, and self evident to every person at all conversant with the matter. What are you doing with the Tariff, all eyes are turned in that direction, and expectation is tiptoe to know what course the house and senate will take in relation to the same. The policy, about to be pursued in England on the subject of their Tariff as set forth by L. R. P. must have some weight with the leading politicians in this county, and I hope will levy about; such a reduction in our Tariff as is proposed in president P. message to our congress, but I find I must stop politics.

I have an individual matter in which I should be glad to get your assistance provided it can be done without too much trouble to you, sometime in the year 36 or 37 or there abouts, a man became indebted to me several hundred dollars. and left this county, for Florida and I understand he is living in Tallahassee and has become responsible.

In the year 40 or 41 - the note was enclosed to the post master at that place with directions to collect it, and nothing has been heard from it since, Now the trouble that I wish to impose on you is to see Mr. Brockenborough[5] the Representative from that District and ascertain from him if he knows a man in Tallahassee by the name of McKinney as he is the man, and to know who was Post master at that place from 1838 to 1843. and to what attorney I can address a letter in that place in whom full confidence can be placed. if no attorney what gentleman of good character, you may think this a small matter to be troubling a member of congress about, but some four or five hundred dollars is no small matter to a poor man any assistance you can give me in this matter will be duly appreciated by your humble servant

Should you want any other information to make the thing understood let me know immediately

---

[1]James E. Williamson, a Caswell County physician and planter, was one of the organizers of the state medical society in 1849. A resident of Locust Hill (formerly Brown's Store), he was part owner of a flour mill and a member of the state agricultural society in 1856. Powell, *Caswell County*, 118, 164-165, 477; Powell, *North Carolina Gazetteer*, 295.

[2]John W. Williams did not die until 1852. His daughter, Minerva B. Williams, was married to Dr. James E. Williamson on September 22, 1830, in Person County. John W. Williams represented Person County at the 1835 Constitutional Convention. He was well known to David S. Reid, having served three terms with Reid in the state Senate, 1835, 1838-1839, and 1840-1841. Williams served a fourth term in 1842-1843. Cheney, *North Carolina Government*, 817, 1241; Will of John W. Williams, October 21, 1848, Person County Wills (microfilm), Book 17, p. 21, Archives, Division of Archives and History, Raleigh, hereinafter cited as Williams Will.

[3]John Hampden Pleasants (1797-1846), a Whig journalist from Virginia, founded the *Richmond Whig* in 1824 and edited it until his death in 1846. Thomas Ritchie, Jr. (d. 1854), was the son of the prominent Democrat journalist Thomas Ritchie of Virginia. The elder Ritchie had edited the influential Richmond *Enquirer* from 1804 until 1845, at which time he moved to Washington to edit the Washington *Union*, turning the Richmond paper over to his sons William and Thomas, Jr. When Thomas Ritchie, Jr., accused Pleasants of abolitionist leanings, Pleasants challenged him to a duel. During the duel, Pleasants was mortally wounded, and he died two days later. *DAB*, XV, 7; Charles Henry Ambler, *Thomas Ritchie: A Study in Virginia Politics* (Richmond: Bell Book and Stationery Co., 1913), 297-298.

[4]Richard Pakenham (1797-1868), English diplomat, began a career in the Foreign Office in 1817. He was minister to Mexico from 1835 to 1843, when he was appointed minister to the United States. He negotiated both the Oregon boundary question and questions regarding British interests in the Republic of Texas. He returned to Europe in 1847 and later served as minister to Portugal. *DNB*, XLIII, 85.

[5]William H. Brockenbrough (1812-1850), an attorney from Tallahassee, Florida, was a state legislator, United States district attorney, and a representative in Congress (1846-1847). *Biographical Directory of Congress*, 600.

William W. Holden to David S. Reid A&H-DSR

Raleigh
March 20. 1846

You will have seen, by the Standard, that the Committee have at length decided, and that Mr. Shepard[1] is the Nominee. Mr. Leak,[2] who is desirous of running, was fairly treated by the Committee, his name having been most respectfully considered; but now, that a majority has declared against him, he surely cannot be so selfish and unmanageble as to attempt to plunge the party into the perils of schism and division. Indeed, while the matter was under consideration, he wrote letters to me, which were, to say the least, offensive in their tone; but all this has been passed over, for the sake of harmony; and last night I wrote to him in the kindest manner, informing him of the action of the Committee, and that I should support Mr. Shepard, as I would have supported him, had he been the Nominee. I hope he may be induced to yield; but if he holds on, he cannot get 100 democrats to back him.

Mr. Shepard is in high spirits. He will start in a few days for the East, and will canvass vigorously until the day of election. He will attend Gov. G. in the East and in the West upon the Rail Road debts— and in the East I feel confident he will make heavy inroads upon the Whig party. Consider, if you please, that in 1840 William A. Graham beat William B. Shepard[3] for Senator; consider the feeling then aroused in the East against Gov. Graham, and the strong personal popularity of W. B. Shepard, and the certainty that he will not oppose his brother, and the probability rather that he will support him; consider also, that this is a section of the state where our friend Biggs[4] set the ball so gloriously in motion; and consider that in Tyrrell and Craven our Candidate has Whig relatives[5] of great influence, and who will doubtless favor him considerably and you will have some idea of his strength in the East. Besides, he is a bold and vigorous young man, full of enthusiasm and bent on success.

I will write more at length hereafter. I hope you will do all you can for him in your District. Your Oregon Speech will appear in the next Standard. Please let me hear from you.

---

[1]James B. Shepard (1815-1871) of Wake County was a member of the state Senate (1842) and the House of Commons (1844) and was the unsuccessful Democratic candidate for governor in 1846. One of Holden's friends and advisors, he helped influence Reid to run for governor in 1848. Tolbert, *Ellis Papers*, I, 61n; W. W. Holden, *Memoirs of W. W. Holden* (Durham: Trinity College Historical Society, 1911), 3-4, hereinafter cited as Holden, *Memoirs*.

[2]Walter F. Leak, previously identified.

[3]William Biddle Shepard (1799-1852), older brother of James B. Shepard, was an attorney and banker from Elizabeth City, a representative in Congress (1829-1837), state senator (1838-1840, 1848-1850), and trustee of the University of North Carolina (1838-1852). A native of New Bern, he was a powerful public speaker. *Biographical Directory of Congress*, 1591; Ashe, *Biographical History*, VII, 424-427.

[4]Asa Biggs, previously identified, of Martin County.

[5]James B. Shepard and William Biddle Shepard were the sons of William Shepard and Mary Blount of New Bern. Their maternal grandfather, Frederick Blount (1778-1823) was a New Bern physician, and through blood or marriage the Shepards were related to the Pettigrew, Harvey, Biddle, Sumner, Haywood, and other prominent families. Powell, *DNCB*, I, 177-184 passim.

J. Julius Wheeden to Reuben Reid Duke-DSR

Raleigh, N. C.
March 21, 1846

You will doubtless be surprised to receive a letter from me, having so long neglected writing to you. But it is never too late to do well.

As you will have seen, the Democratic State Committee have made a nomination for Governor.

You, sir, are an old soldier in the cause of democracy, and your actions carry with them a weight and influence: and for this reason I take the liberty of suggesting to you the propriety of holding a meeting and approving the nomination, at the same time resolving and calling upon all true democrats to sustain it.

Among other reasons why this should be done, is this! The whig press are industriously circulating the report that Mr. Leake, of Richmond county, has declared himself a candidate independent of the action of the committees. If this be true, we should sustain the committee, appointed by the largest convention which has ever assembled in our State, and which represented every portion of the State, in their action. And if the report be false then the course which I have suggested can have no bad effect.

If it is ever expected to elect a democratic Governor, now is the time. In this you will agree with me, I have no doubt. Then let us make every exertion consistent with honor—hold meetings— talk with and among the people, and if we are not successful we shall know that we deserved to be.

Mr. Shepard is yet a young man—He enters the campaign with a bright prospect, and I am sure, from my personal knowledge of the man, that if every member of the party shall perform his part as well as Mr. S. will, we shall have a democratic Governor.

I ought to have written to you before now, and I really am ashamed that I have not. Be pleased to mention me to Mrs. Reid, Miss Rhoda, Miss Henrietta, and your other daughters. Also, to H. K. Reid and Reuben. It would afford me a great pleasure to visit your hospitable mansion this Spring or Summer, but I do not know that I shall be able to do so. My respects also to Mr. Adams[1] and wife, and Mr. Settle.[2]

In reference to the meeting I have taken the liberty to suggest, if it meets your approval, and you think proper, it would be well to hold a meeting in your vicinity as well as at the Court House.

Let me hear from you soon, and you will much oblige

---

[1]Samuel F. Adams, previously identified, son-in-law of Reuben Reid.

[2]Thomas Settle, previously identified, brother-in-law of Reuben Reid.

Daniel E. Guerrant[1] *to David S. Reid* A&H-DSR

Rockingham [County] N. C.
May 6th 1846

I herewith inclose to you my Power of Attorney executed to you to impower you to draw the money that You stated Mr Wm Roach of Orange Va: had deposited in washington for me your attention to this matter will much oblige me besides paying you for your trouble, please let me know whether the Power will answer or not and if it will not, What other evidences they want for Indemfication—I saw your Father yesterday at Court his family and the people of our county Generally are well—The Candidates for the county Declared themselves on yesterday Boyd[2] in the Senate Daniel W. Courts & Joseph W. Neal Esqr in the Commons, Samuel C. Edwards[3] for Sheriff—Court Adjourned on Last night and the Bar with others of wentworth Repaired for greensborough to the widding of Ex Governor Moreheads Second Daughter and Mr Avory[4] it was said on the court green that this Act would bring about a perfect union in the political ranks[5]—Excuse my Jests I am too full of them—I am under many obligations to you for your attention to this matter of mine and remain your sincere friend

[1]Daniel E. Guerrant, a Rockingham County planter, was a justice of the peace. In 1850 he had ten slaves. Rockingham County Court Minutes, February, 1846, February, 1848; Seventh Census, 1850, Rockingham County, Slave Schedule, 99-100.

[2]George D. Boyd, previously identified.

[3]Samuel C. Edwards was sheriff and a justice of the peace of Rockingham County. Governors Office Records, "Commissions and Resignations, 1841-1855"; Rockingham County Court Minutes, May, 1843, February, 1846.

[4]John M. Morehead's daughter Mary C. was married to W. Waightstill Avery in May, 1846. Konkle, *John Motley Morehead*, 177, 399.

[5]Morehead was a Whig and Avery a Democrat.

Daniel E. Guerrant to David S. Reid A&H-DSR

Rockingham [County] N. C.
may 6th/46

I received yours of the 24th April informing me that the money due me from mr. Wm Roach of Orange Va. was deposited in the hands of his representative to be paid to you acording to our agreement but that he would not pay it until you were possesed of a Lawfull Power of Atterney from me, You thought you had had one but you only had my blank receipt—I will obtain a Power for you the fourth monday in this month and send it on fourthwith Your attention to the matter has been and will be thankfully received besides remunerating you for your trouble.

I Left your Fathers this morning and they were all well and the health of the People arr generally well.

You say the Oregan question has passed both Houses of Congress I wish it may be the best but I fear it will create dificulties—In Haste—

William C. Emmett to David S. Reid A&H-DSR

Wilkesboro N.C.
May 27. '46

I hope you will excuse the liberty I take in addressing you unceremoniously but I think short apologys best in these piping times of war.[1] I see Sir that Congress has passed a Law authorising the President to raise 50,000 men and the field and staff officers to be appointed by the President and to be taken from the States in which the men shall be raised and as I have a prediliction for a military life and as I have had considerable experience in deciplining troops and as to the discharge of the dutys connected with a camp or garrison I think I could discharge in a manner—calculated to render satisfaction to all who might be connected in the service with me I have therefore come to the conclusion to request you to propose me for an appointment in the army if in the infantry I would like the appointment of Majr. or Lieut Colonel or if any other Service an appointment equal to those or I would accept an appointment connected with the quarter masters department the dutys of which I have frequently discharged, or any other department of the Service that would be respectable I solicet the appointment as much for employment as any thing else I am entirely disengaged and could enter on the discharge of any dutys assigned me at short notice Should you think that there is any probability of your being able to succeed in securing me an appointment and any recommendation should be necessary please to inform me and I will attend to it

I am well satisfyed that in any move you may make in my behalf you will be assisted by your colleagues[2] Genl. Daniel Col. Barringer Mr. Dobbin, and Senator Haywood and I think the President himself will be disposed to do some thing for me—I have fought the battles of the democratic party all my life—and it is the first time I have ever asked for any thing from the government or any one else

[1]The United States declared war on Mexico, May 13, 1846.

[2]This is a reference to some of the other members of the North Carolina congressional delegation: John R. J. Daniel of Halifax, Daniel Moreau Barringer of Concord, James C. Dobbin of Fayetteville, and William H. Haywood, Jr., of Raleigh. The military ranks by which the writer refers to Daniel and Barringer are presumably state militia grades. *Biographical Directory of Congress, Bicentennial Edition*, 140.

Samuel F. Adams to David S. Reid A&H-DSR

Troublesome N.C.
June 18th 1846

I have just received your letter of the 10th. Inst., also the Union of the 9th. and the speech of Genl. Cass delivered on the 1st, for which I have to return you my thanks Myself and family are all in very good health. There is no news in this country worthy of communicating; the Regimental parade came off last saturday, and about forty volunteers turned out, and I think perhaps thirty of them will stand up to it, the ballance, I think it highly proberable, will back out. R. P. Cardwell[1] and some thirty others have volunteered in the upper end of the county, and some in the neighbourhood of Grogans: they think when they all get together they will make out one company from this county, but my impression is, that none of those that have volunteered in this county, ever expect to be called into service, and if they are I think some of them will be like *Marshall Tureen*, prefer taking a hasty plate of soup at home, to fighting the mexicans. I presume the whigs throughout the Union are greatly mortified at the course Genl. Scott[2] has thought proper to pursue, there certainly is nothing in the correspondence between him and the secetary of war to justify it. If there was an undercurrent at Washington, (as he intimates) attempting to injure his Political, or Military standing before the country, the course he has pursued, is, presisely the one, they would have desired him to adopt. He should have hastened to Mexico—assumed the command of the army, and he would have had abundant opportunities of putting a stop to the fire of his enemies at Washington: if he in reality has any there. But instead of pursuing that course, he sits down over a plate of soup, and commences a correspondence with the secratary of war, (about nothing, for I cannot perceive the necessity of a single line from him, to the secraty of war, except to ask for definite instructions, and put out for Mexico as fast as steam could carry him) in which, I think he casts very imprudent, and improper, reflections upon the President, for if there is, any meaning in language, that is the only inference that can be drawn from certain portions of his letter of the 21st May, notwithstanding his sebsequent denial of it, and also of his special pleading to get out of it. and it may be asked, what cause he had to complain of the president; none that I can see, except, his having conferred uppon him an important command, by which, with proper energy on his part, he might have covered himself with glory. by pursuing the couse he has, he has completely verified, the predictions of those enemies that he was so fearful of firing uppon his rear, that he was not the man, to send to Mexico. my impression is, that Genl. Scott is not the man to fight either Mexicans, or Indians, at any rate he has been peculiarly unfortunate in all of his southern campaigns. If nothing comes out in his favour more than has been published in the corispondence, he certainly is, Politically dead: for I presume there will be but one opinion, and that is, that he did not wish to go to Mexico. whether he was actuated by fears of meeting the Mexicans in his front, or the fire of enemies in his rear, or that he prefered remaining in Washington and taking soup at his ease and let others do the fighting—he having heretofore acquired sufficient laurels, to carry him into the Presidency, will be for the people to decide, and also to draw their own inference from the corispondence as published. I have read Genl. Cass's[3] speech, and think it a very able one, much better than I would have supposed (after reading Col Benton's) would have been made upon the Subject, and it has proved, that Genl. Cass, is an able debator. nevertheless, I still adhere to my original opinion, that Old Bulion[4] has borne off the palm of victory. This I suppose does not meet your views, as I know you are in favour of 54-40, and I believe, opposed to any compromise short of that line, you must excuse the length of this letter, it is much longer than I intended when I commenced writing. please accept my best respects and well wishes.

---

[1]Richard P. Cardwell, previously identified.

[2]Winfield Scott (1786-1866), a Virginian, became the nation's top professional soldier in the antebellum period. During the War of 1812 he rose rapidly in rank to brigadier general, and by 1841 he had become the commanding general of the army. In the Mexican War he led the invasion of Mexico that resulted in the capture of Mexico City and the end of the war. In 1852 he unsuccessfully ran for president. Scott, a staunch Whig, had few friends in the Polk administration and received much criticism on his seeming delay in preparing his strategy for the Mexican War. On May 25, 1846, the secretary of war sent Scott a letter informing him he would not be sent to the front. Scott was not in his office to receive the letter but was out eating "a hasty plate of soup" (not taking time enough from his duties for a regular meal), as he explained in a note to the secretary when he returned to his office. This note was published by national newspapers, and Scott's phrase was apparently interpreted to mean he was reluctant to fight. When the Civil War broke out, Scott served as commander of the Union army until his retirement in November, 1861. *DAB*, XVI, 505-511; K. Jack Bauer, *The Mexican War, 1846-1848* (New York: Macmillan, 1974), 73-74; Winfield Scott, *Memoirs of Lieut.-General Scott. LL.D.* (New York: Sheldon, 1864), 385.

[3]Lewis Cass, previously identified, Democratic senator from Michigan.

[4]"Old Bullion" was a nickname given Senator Thomas Hart Benton for his influence on banking and currency during the Jackson administration. Powell, *DNCB*, I, 140.

John H. Dobson[1] *to David S. Reid* A&H-DSR

Home
[Surry County]
June 20th 1846

my family ar all well presant & home [*sic*] you the same

knowing that you ar alwayes willing to heare of whigs being on the fence all most reddy to tumbel of on the side of democracy and nothing wanted but a littell attention from Headquarters I will prosede to fire you a fuw names Isaac Conrad[2] Huntsville Grimes Holcome[3] Doct Dozier[4] Dowel Town

Mr Douglas[5] on the army apreproation Bill will doo to start with They will be worth bating for we have made a Compay of volunteers on the North side of the Rivir for Mexico they have tryed on the south side & failed the war with Mexico is popular in this Country thoug the Whiggs throad Cold water at the start

we hav Nominated Candidates Democrats—R MClane James Sheaks & Charles Whitlock Esqrs Whiggs—R Porer Enoch Hunt & Hue Guyn[6]

I hope we shall be abell to Carry our ticket

---

[1]John H. Dobson was a resident of Surry County. Carter and Carter, *Footprints*, 46.

[2]Isaac Conrad (born 1801) was a prosperous farmer residing in 1850 in southern Surry County. Seventh Census, 1850, Surry County, Population Schedule, 250.

[3]Grimes Holcom (born 1803) was a well-to-do farmer, also residing in southern Surry. Seventh Census, 1850, Surry County, Population Schedule, 216.

[4]Nathan B. Dozier (born 1822), a native of South Carolina, was a physician living in southern Surry County. Seventh Census, 1850, Surry County, Population Schedule, 220.

[5]Stephen Arnold Douglas (1813-1861), an attorney from Springfield and Chicago, Illinois, was a state legislator, representative in Congress (1843-1847) and United States senator (1847-1861). He was the unsuccessful Democratic candidate for president in 1860. He and Reid became warm friends when they were freshman congressmen, and through Reid he met his first wife, Martha D. Martin of Rockingham County. *DAB*, V, 397-403; Robert W. Johannsen, *Stephen A. Douglas* (New York: Oxford University Press, 1973), 207-208, hereinafter cited as Johannsen, *Douglas*.

[6]In 1846 the successful candidates for the House of Commons from Surry County were Whigs Richard C. Puryear and Hugh Gwynn and Democrat James Sheek. Richard C. Puryear served in the state Senate (1840-1841) and the House of Commons (1838-1839, 1844-1847, 1852). James Sheek was in the House of Commons (1846-1851). Charles Whitlock served in the House of Commons (1854-1855). J. R. McLean served in the House of Commons (1850-1851). Cheney, *North Carolina Government*, 1273-1274.

Asa Biggs (1811-1878), a Williamston attorney, represented Martin County in both houses of the General Assembly. From 1845 to 1847, he was a Democratic member of the United States House of Representatives. Unsuccessful in his bid for reelection, he became a member of the commission to revise state statutes. In 1855, he was elected to the United States Senate. Biggs served in the Senate with Reid until May 1858, when he resigned to become a federal district judge. Photograph of portrait courtesy of the Division of Archives and History.

Thomas Lanier Clingman (1812-1897), best known as a senator and Confederate general, was elected to the United States House of Representatives in 1843 as a Whig. While serving his first term in Congress, Clingman became involved in a duel with Democrat William L. Yancey. Reid, also a freshman in Congress, described the incident in a letter to his sister on January 19, 1845. In 1858, after switching to the Democratic party, Clingman was appointed to complete the unexpired term of Asa Biggs. Later that year, he defeated Reid in his bid for reelection to the United States Senate. Photograph of William Garl Browne portrait, located at the University of North Carolina at Chapel Hill, from the files of the Division of Archives and History.

James Cochrane Dobbin (1814-1857), a Cumberland County Democrat, served with Reid in the Twenty-ninth Congress. He was speaker of the state House of Commons during Reid's first term as governor. Portrait by Eastman Johnson owned by the Philanthropic Society, University of North Carolina at Chapel Hill; photograph courtesy of the Division of Archives and History.

Martha Drennen Martin (1828-1853), Reid's first cousin, and Stephen Arnold Douglas (1813-1863) were married on April 7, 1847. Martha met the Illinois politician during a visit in Washington, while Reid and Douglas were serving in the House of Representatives. Photograph of Mrs. Douglas from Saunders's *Open Doors and Closed Windows*, 260; photograph of Mr. Douglas provided by the Library of Congress.

This engraving of the United States Capitol, published in N. P. Willis's *American Scenery: or Land, Lake and River* (London: 1840), portrays the building as it appeared in the 1840s. Major renovations in the 1850s and 1860s added two wings to the structure and enlarged the dome. Photograph from the files of the Division of Archives and History.

T. B. Wheeler[1] *to David S. Reid* A&H-DSR
[with enclosure]

Wentworth
20th June 1846

Inclosed you will find a copy of a matter which took place on yesterday between Conl. Martin[2] and myself you will see how it is to be decided & please procure anything & everything necessary to arrive at the truth of the matter August Court is the time we expect to have it settled. I suppose you will be at Home by that time.

Rumour says here the Oregon question is Settled at 49 all seem satisfied but most of us are fifty four men. I have nothing Interesting to write you. Wright's Suit against me was not tried at last court.[3]

We have an abundunce of rain & much damage is done by high water both to Crops & lands I learn Col. Shober[4] is dead James B. Shepperd[5] has been with us & we are well pleased with him. he used up his Political enimies in fine Style

Please write me on the receipt of this & give me your views about the matter between Martin & myself

[Enclosure]

Articles of agreement between T. B. Wheeler & Robert Martin to Wit Wheeler bets Martin that the Country between the Neuces and Rio Grande belonged to Texas before Genl. Taylor invaded it & that it was represented in the Congress of Texas by a resident of the country and agree to leave the question to Col. D. S. Reid & John Kerr[6] Esqs & if they do not agree are authorised to choose an umpire. the said Wheeler & Martin have placed two hundred dollars each in the hands of James D. Ellington[7] & do hereby authorise him to hand it over to the party in favor of Whom it may be decided Witness our hands this 19th June 1846

Test. A. W. Ellington[8] T. B. Wheeler

Ro. Martin

---

[1]Thomas B. Wheeler (d. 1857), a Rockingham County planter, in 1850 owned seven slaves, land on Troublesome Creek, a tavern in Wentworth, and lots in Leaksville. He served as clerk of the county court in the 1840s. Seventh Census, 1850, Rockingham County, Slave Schedule, 99-100; Rockingham County Wills, Book C, 252; Rockingham County Court Minutes, February, 1846.

[2]Robert Martin (1784-1848), a leading Rockingham County planter, was married to Reid's aunt Mary Settle. He served as a Whig in the House of Commons (1822-1826) and the state Senate (1829-1835). Martin owned extensive land holdings and a number of slaves in Lawrence County, Mississippi. He was the father-in-law of Stephen A. Douglas of Illinois. Lindley S. Butler, "Robert Martin" (unpublished biographical sketch), hereinafter cited as Butler, "Robert Martin."

[3]At the next county court session, in the civil case of Nathan Wright vs. T. B. Wheeler, a jury that included Reid's uncle Josiah Settle found judgment of non-suit. Rockingham County Court Minutes, August, 1846.

[4]Emmanuel Schober (d. June 14, 1846), of Salem, was a postmaster, Moravian elder, member of the Aufseher Collegium, and a community leader. He was responsible for the incorporation of the town fire department in 1843, and he apparently was a justice of the peace. He was a trustee of the University of North Carolina (1827-1846). Fries and others, *Moravian Records*, IX, 4410, 4457, 4534-4535, 4580, 4600, 4676, 4717-4719, 4728, 4831, 4840, 4893; Battle, *History of the University*, I, 824.

[5]James B. Shepard, Democratic candidate for governor, previously identified.

[6]John Kerr (1811-1879) was an attorney from Yanceyville and Reidsville. In 1852 as a Whig he lost the gubernatorial election to Reid. Kerr served as a representative in Congress (1853-1855), member of the House of Commons (1858, 1860), and superior court judge (1862, 1874-1879). He was a trustee of both Wake Forest College and the University of North Carolina. *Biographical Directory of Congress*, 1159.

[7, 8]James D. Ellington and A. W. Ellington were residents of Rockingham County in 1846 and were probably relatives of Reid's uncle John Waddell Ellington. Rockingham County Court Minutes, 1846 passim.

William Brown[1] *to David S. Reid* A&H-DSR

Yanceyville, Caswell, N C
June 22 1846

I have been remiss in not acknowledging my obligations to you, for your kindness in sending me a speech, or document occasionally. I have read with much interest and pleasure your first effort in the National legislature, on the Oregon notice resolutions, and permit me to say to you, that I regard it as a lucid and forcible exposition of your views on that highly important and much agitated subject, and was well received by your constituents hereabouts. I was quite amused at the little rencounter, (as given in your speech) between yourself and your redoubtable colleague, Genl. D.[2] who had arrogated to himself in a speech in our State legislature, being from Lumber River district, the possession of such a rare combination of *talents* and *virtues*, as to fit him peculiarly for the representation of an enlightened constituency; the Genl. however met with a sad discomfiture in the conflict with you. The speech of Mr. Jones[3] of Ga. which you sent me, is also a very sensible and cogent view of the question, the vote however has been taken long since, and the resolutions passed by a large majority, with Genl. D's name recorded as the only negative vote in the No Ca. delegation, for which I hope his constituents will hold him duly accountable.

Col. Benton,[4] and Genl. Cass[5] I perceive, have had a very excited discussion on this subject, in which the former, sustains fully his high reputation as a debater, a lawyer, & statesman. I hope however, that the day is not distant when it will be announced to the American people, and to the world, that this vexed question is adjusted. The war with Mexico, however, is the engrossing or more prominent topic with us at this time, and Caswell has in readiness for the service only 80 volunteers, while her neighbor Orange has near 500. It was a trite remark of the venerable Macon,[6] that we should have a war once in thirty years in order to unite parties, and strengthen the bonds of Union, tho' the whig party are endeavoring to make political Capital of this war, and say they have contended that Mexico had virtually declared war, ten years ago, and that our party had desired it, but we tell them that the public history of the whole matter will show that Mexico has acted in bad faith, has violated her treaty stipulations, and that on the part of the administration and the Country, it is a just, a righteous war. It is indeed to be regretted that she had the weakness, the folly to invade the U.S. as we have lost gallant & valuable officers & soldiers, and I fear may more without according Mexico any thing; but may result in the conquest of her whole territory. Genl. Taylor[7] has certainly conducted the war so far with great skill and judgement, and I was pleased to see that the Senate had unanimously promoted him to the grade of Brevet Major.Genl. I hear that Genl. Scott[8] in his correspondence with the war department indulges in much personal pique, but I really think it would have been more becoming to have submitted with as good a grace as he could to the Executive & Senate stance—

We had Mr. Shepard[9] with us a few days ago, when he addressed quite a large meeting here for the parties gain: He made a strong & forcible speech, and brings with all its weight upon Mr. Graham's[10] head the charge of bidding the whole amt. of the Secured loan of the State to the Ral & Gaston R. Road Company viz $303,000 at the first bid when he might have bought the Road Co. for it as he says, it being subject afterwards to the first mortgage for ½ million. S. says Badger[11]—himself does not deny this, & that Graham refuses to answer the question. Mr. S. Seems to indulge a hope of success, indeed appears quite Sanguine, from the great gains in the several districts. He has improved greatly as a speaker, is very frank, fearless, & bold, and made a very decidedly favorable impression here—and handled G. with gloves off tho' in quite a discreet, dignified manner. He has canvassed the East and is now winding his way in the West. Mr. G. may follow in his wake, but has not been in Caswell as yet. They had a warm conflict in Hillsboro' in which it is said S. had decidedly the advantage. Our canvass for the legislature will begin in a few days, and I should glory in it if by the force of principles and truth, we could redeem the old North State from the thraldom of Federalism, both in the legislative and Executive branches, in the former I feel sanguine of success, and the latter would exhibit Trust and interesting change in that department of our State government—We have three candidates for the Commons, viz Col. Jas. K. Lea,[12] Doct. McMullin[13] and our plain out and out democratic citizen Capt Rich. Jones[14]: all democrats, of course. Calvin Graves for Senate without opposition, Mr. Gynn[15] having declined—I am sorry to see that the great advocate & champion of southern interests Mr. Calhoun voted against the prosecution of the war, at least against the bill as passed for that object. I should suppose that it would be almost political suicide in the South, with him. It must be a period of intense interest and excitment in Washington at this time; the Oregon negotiation approaching a crisis, the movements & fate of the army in Mexico, and the exciting legislation connected therewith all conspire to make it a deeply interesting [epoch] in the history of our Country. A letter from brother Bedford[16] a short time since says all are well, but has not settled permanently as yet. I perceive that the 25 July is spoken of in the Senate for adjournment. You will have had a protracted Session of it indeed—I have written you in great haste, Dear Col., and fear you cannot decypher this desultary script. I fear you will find it a painful imposition. Our state has to deplore the loss of L. D. Henry of Raleigh whose death you have doubtless seen published—Thus are our prominent men rapidly passing off. I hope dear Col. to see you ere long among your constituents, when they can say to you well done good and faithful servant. I know your time is most [compressed], but a hurried line on the prominent topics at Washington, would be thankfully received by your friend.

P. S. I hope the advocates of free trade will stand firm on the vote on the forthcoming Tariff bill of Genl McKay—

P. S. The late heavy rains have done much damage to the crops by freshets Swept off many mill dams, & bridges in Rockingham & this County

---

[1]William Brown, a Yanceyville tobacco trader, was involved in a plank road company in 1855. Powell, *Caswell County*, 128, 494.

[2]Alfred Dockery, previously identified.

[3]Seaborn Jones (1788-1864), a Columbus, Georgia, attorney, was a representative in Congress (1833-1835, 1845-1847). *Biographical Directory of Congress*, 1139-1140.

[4]Thomas Hart Benton, previously identified.

[5]Lewis Cass, previously identified.

[6]Nathaniel Macon (1757-1837), a Warren County planter, was a representative in Congress (1791-1815), speaker of the House (1801-1807), and a United States senator (1815-1828). He was the foremost Jeffersonian Republican of North Carolina during his lifetime. *Biographical Directory of Congress*, 1250-1251.

[7]Zachary Taylor (1784-1850), a native of Virginia, began his military career in 1808. He served effectively in Indian campaigns and rose to the rank of colonel by 1832. After a success in the Seminole War he was brevetted brigadier general. When Texas was annexed he had command of the border army and won major victories in the Mexican War. In 1848 he received the Whig nomination for president and was elected. *DAB*, XVIII, 349-354.

[8]Winfield Scott, previously identified.

[9]James B. Shepard, previously identified.

[10]William A. Graham, previously identified.

[11]George E. Badger (1795-1866), an attorney from New Bern and Raleigh, was a member of the House of Commons (1816), a superior court judge (1820-1825), and briefly secretary of the navy, appointed by President Harrison. From 1846 to 1855 he served in the United States Senate. Ashe, *Biographical History*, VII, 35-44.

[12]James K. Lea was a Yanceyville tobacco manufacturer. He served in the House of Commons (1844-1847). Powell, *Caswell County*, 128, 551.

[13]John B. McMullen was in the House of Commons (1846-1849). Powell, *Caswell County*, 551.

[14]Richard Jones was a member of the House of Commons (1846-1849). Powell, *Caswell County*, 551.

[15]Littleton A. Gwynn of Yanceyville, previously identified.

[16]Bedford Brown, previously identified, brother of William Brown. Hurt by his failure to win election in 1842 to the United States Senate, Bedford Brown had moved in 1844 from North Carolina to Missouri, where he settled at Fayette in Howard County. Houston G. Jones, "Bedford Brown: State Rights Unionist. Part II: The Conciliator," *North Carolina Historical Review*, XXXII (1955), 486-488.

Samuel F. Adams to David S. Reid A&H-DSR

Troublesome N. C.
June 30th 1846

I have just received your favour of the 21st Inst. I was truly glad to hear that you are still blessed with a continuation of good health. Myself and family, are all in very good health. There is no news in this section worthy of relation. The settlement of the Oregon dispute, seems to give, general satisfaction, but my information uppon the subject is very limited, and only extends to this imediate neighbourhood. I am fearfull there will be a failure in the effort that is making to raise a company of Volunteers in this county, there was a sufficent number turned out in both regments to form one company, but they do not seem disposed to act in unity, and I think it doubtfull if they can raise a full company in either regment unless they will all come together please write to me whenever you have liesure to do so. Francis and the children send their best love and respects to you, and be pleased to accept the same from myself

---

L. B. Chase[1] *to David S. Reid* A&H-DSR
[Private]

Philadelphia
Sunday July 19 1846

From recent indications I am of the opinion that the senate will vote upon the tariff bill Earlier than I supposed, when I left Washington. It is *possible* the senate may amend the bill, making it necessary for our house to act upon it. When I left it was with the understanding that I had paired off with Delano[2] until Thursday morning. I was informed that he wished to pair off although I did not see him myself.

I told Trumbo[3] of Kentucky that I would not vote until next Thursday, he remarked that he would pledge Mr Delano not to vote until that time. So the matter stood. If the bill should be sent to our house before Thursday, *Delano not voting* there is no reason for me to return before that time; and I should not return in all probality [*sic*] until the last of this week If however it is returned thursday or after that day I must be in Washington We shall not leave here for Cape May until Tuesday at 8 o'clock A.M. If you can get this time enough to advise me of the State of affairs *before we leave*, do so. If not try and have a letter for me at Cape May by Tuesday at the time of my arrival there *& you will greatly oblige me*

I am enjoying myself exceedingly since I have been in this city; we might possible leave tomorrow, but that poor cousin Lucy, wishes to remain another day.

I hope you are Still at your post attending to the affairs of the Nation, as long as you are not, with us. Suppose you just run down to Cape May and I will go with you to Washington.

P.S. Please drop me a line at both places *here* and at the *Cape*, for fear we should not get off as soon as I Expect

[1]Lucien B. Chase (1817-1864), a Clarksville, Tennessee, attorney, was a Democratic representative in Congress (1845-1849). A native of Vermont, he had moved to Tennessee in 1838; in 1849 he moved to New York, and he eventually returned to his Vermont hometown, where he died. *Biographical Directory of Congress*, 684.

[2]Columbus Delano (1809-1896), an attorney from Mount Vernon, Ohio, was a Whig representative in Congress (1845-1847). He became active in the Republican party as a state legislator and was again elected to Congress (1865-1867, 1868-1869). He was secretary of the interior under President U. S. Grant (1870-1875). *Biographical Directory of Congress*, 796.

[3]Andrew Trumbo (1797-1871), an attorney in Owingsville, Kentucky, and later Frankfort, was a Whig representative in Congress (1845-1847). *Biographical Directory of Congress*, 1730.

Weldon E. Wright to David S. Reid A&H-DSR

Stone Mountain
De Kalb Co Ga
July 20th 1846

I received your very kind letter of May 5. & have delayed writing until now on account of my pressing engagements. My practice has been very extensive Since I came here & besides I was appointed to deliver the 4 of July oration on the Stone Mountain, which I did before five or ten thousand people: indeed I never saw such a crowd together before In the performance of the duty, I am happy to See the public prints of Augusta & Marietta & many others whose editors were present, teaming with applause to the orator of the day

I done better than I ever did in a speech in my life

But I claim nothing more to myself than the discharge of my duty entirely satisfactory to all

The[re] were persons here from all parts of the state & we had other speeches from several distinguished men

We have a great deal of company here at this time & indeed there is always a crowd here to see the mountain, which is very pleasant to me, as I can form acquaintances from all sections.

I am much pleased with the exchange that I have made in my location Col! do write to me often & do not wait for me to write every time; you certainly must know I am much pleased I am to hear from you. My feelings towards you can never change; and even now, (although it has been so long since I saw you) your examples and kind admonitions are always before me. There is not a day that rolls over my head, but that I think of you & when, I make a move or am about to do any thing: I invariably think to myself would the Col do this, and in this way avoid many stumps.

I have made you my patern, and Find great advantage from it; but you must not think the less of me for it Look upon me as one younger than yourself & lack experience

We are to have a great agricultural meeting here the 5 of August, called by several distinguished men of South Carolina Ga & Alabama & Tennessee. At which we expect an immense crowd

Tell some of our members of Congress we would be pleased to see them here if it is possible for them to leave Washington

I have received a very flattering letter from my *lady love* since I have been here, but have not answered it as yet. I may meet with you in NC next fall. of course you will not speak of this to any one

I shall expect a letter from you by the returning mail

Joseph W. Neal To David S. Reid A&H-DSR

Reidsville. N.C.
July 28, 1846

I recd yours informing me that Mr. Wallack had Closed the transaction with Mr Parker[1] and had sent you a Check for the payment made—you will please to draw the money and bring it to me when you return holme

Myself and fellow Candidates have been Canvasing the County and shall perhaps get through by the 1st of August we have no opposition as yet—Ex Goveornor Morehead felt himself Called on to reply to us at Leaksville a few days since for the purpose as he said of Defending his friend Goveornor Graham—on the Rail Road subject,

I saw a letter yesterday from Mr. Shepherd[2] he thinks his Election is Certain

I rote to Mr Cassel[3] requesting him to Call on you before you leave and pay off his Bond

our nieghbours & friends are generally well—In great haste I Conclude—your humble Servt

---

[1]Mr. Wallack and Mr. Parker have not been identified.

[2]James B. Shepard, at the time of this writing the Democratic candidate for governor.

[3]Mr. Cassel has not been identified, but see also reference to a Mr. Cassell in Joseph W. Neal to David S. Reid, January 28, 1845, supra.

David S. Reid to E. W. Hubard[1] UNC-H

Reidsville, N.C.
November 19, 1846

I have the honor to acknowledge the receipt of your letters requesting me to be present at your wedding. A few days after we seperated last summer I had a severe attack of billious fever, and I have not yet sufficiently regained my strength to bear the slightest exposure. I had flattered myself till within a few days past that it would be in my power to make one of your party, but I now feel so feeble that I fear that I can not leave home early enough to be with you. The 26th is on the week of Rockingham Court and if my health will permit, (but I fear it will not) I ought to be there; but, if able, I would willingly miss that court to be at *your wedding*. Oh! how painful the reflection that I must forego the pleasure of being present on such an interesting occasion! If I can not get there be pleased to make the necessary apology for me; and when your lady love becomes Mrs. H., ask her to sing you the "*Carrier Dove*,"[2] *for my sake*. I hope to have the pleasure of making her acquaintance this winter. If you see any single lady that you think *I would suit*, do take her on to Washington. Hubard, I am glad you are going to marry, both on *your own account, and my own*, for it is just what every sensible bachelor ought to do; but I regret to say that I am yet in a state of *single wretchedness, and so likely to remain*. May I not however, hope, that you who I have heretofore found so invincible, now that you are no longer in the field of competition, will have the magnanimity to give me the weight of your influence, and that for the future I may be a more successful adventurer among the ladies. We shall see. Be pleased to accept my congratulations and best wishes.

---

[1]Edmund W. Hubard (1806-1878), a planter from Buckingham County, Virginia, was a representative in Congress (1841-1847). He served as a colonel in the Confederate militia in 1864. *Biographical Directory of Congress*, 1086.

[2]The "Carrier Dove" must have been a favorite song of Reid's, as he seems also to have sent the sheet music for it to another correspondent, James Phelps of Essex, Connecticut. See James Phelps to David S. Reid, June 27, 1845, supra.

David S. Reid to Jesse Albert Waugh[1] UNC-JP

House Representatives,
Washington, Dec. 16, 1846.

I have the honor to acknowledge the receipt of your letter of the 5th instant. I have not had the name of Mr. Webb[2] or any one else placed on the list of applicants for a Cadetship at West Point, for the reason that I shall not have the appointment of one during my term of service as a member of Congress, and there are a number of applicants between whom I should dislike to decide unless an appointment could be made. I have ordered the direction of the "Union" to be changed agreeably to your request. I have already asked Mr. Lumpkin[3] for the money he owes your brother oftener than I would have done if the debt had been due to myself; and besides your brother Col. Waugh[4] wrote me insinuating that *I* had not treated him properly about it. Under these circumstances you may judge that I feel a delecacy in asking Mr. Lumpkin for it again, particularly as I fear that I have already incured his displeasure as well as that of Col. Waugh. But be this as it may, if you will send me the receipt—with such instructions as you give—I will hand it over to an attorney or collector.

I enclose you the letter of the Treasury answering your enquiry about the interest on the description of Treasury notes mentioned in your letter. Nothing of importance has yet been done in Congress. The whigs appear to be disposed to assail the Administration with all the bitterness that usually characterises that party. They allege that it is a war of the Presidents own, & that it is an unjust and unconstitutional; and they do this in the face of the facts that the Mexican Government shed the *first blood, & declared war first,* and they (the whigs) themselves *voted for the declaration of war against Mexico.* I think they will not make any thing by assailing the President on the war question—I am sure they ought not. The whigs are determined to re-district the state and prevent us from sending a democrat from our district to Congress. So far as I am individually concerned I can part with a seat in Congress without a single regret, but a loss of political strength and a severance of the relations between myself and the democrats of the third Congressional district who have so nobly stood by me through good and through evil report, is, to me, a matter of profound regret, They may *legislate* me out of Congress, but thank God they can not deprive me of the love and gratitude I owe to my friends, nor can they legislate away the confidence those friends have in me. My respects & best wishes. In haste.

P.S. I do hope that N. Carolina will not fail to raise a Regiment.

[1]Jesse Albert Waugh (born 1810) of Waughtown served in the House of Commons from Stokes County (1850-1852) and from Forsyth County (1854-1857), and as a state senator from Forsyth (1860-1861). He was on the Council of State (1858-1860). His father, James Waugh (1768-1844), represented Wilkes County in the state Senate (1812-1813). By 1870 Jesse Albert Waugh was still residing in Forsyth County. Cheney, *North Carolina Government*, 179, 193, 1135, 1275, 1311; John Nichols, *Directory of the General Assembly of the State of North Carolina, for the Session Commencing November 19, 1860* (Raleigh: John Nichols, 1860), 21; *People's Press* (Salem), August 10, 1860, hereinafter cited as *People's Press*; tombstone inscription, Salem Moravian Cemetery, Forsyth County; Ninth Census, 1870, Forsyth County, 343.

[2]Probably James C. Webb (born 1831), nephew of Jesse Albert Waugh and son of Waugh's sister Susan Lafayette Waugh and Horatio Webb of Jackson County, Georgia. After the death of her husband in the 1840s, Susan Webb returned to Forsyth County with her children. James C. Webb of Forsyth County enlisted at age thiry on May 22, 1861, in Company D, 21st Regiment, North Carolina Troops. Mustered in as a private, he was promoted to first sergeant. He was wounded at Gettysburg, returned to duty, and was later captured on April 6, 1865, near Sayler's Creek, Virginia. *Western Carolinian* (Salisbury), November 30, 1824, hereinafter cited as *Western Carolinian*; Seventh Census, 1850, Forsyth County, Population Schedule, 45; Louis H. Manarin and Weymouth T. Jordan, Jr. (eds.), *North Carolina Troops, 1861-1865: A Roster* (Raleigh: Division of Archives and History, Department of Cultural Resources, projected multivolume series, 1966—), VI, 573, hereinafter cited as Manarin and Jordan, *North Carolina Troops*; Sixth Census, 1840, Jackson County, Georgia, Population Schedule, 25.

[3]Mr. Lumpkin has not been identified, although he may have been prior to 1846 a resident of Surry County.

[4]This is likely a reference to Harrison M. Waugh (1804-1882), previously identified, who was Jesse Albert Waugh's brother-in-law, having married Jesse's younger sister Mary Maria Waugh (1814-1842). Will of Harrison M. Waugh, July 20, 1882, Surry County Wills (microfilm), Book 6, p. 177, Archives, Division of Archives and History, Raleigh, hereinafter cited as Harrison M. Waugh Will; Wilkes County Marriage Bonds.

1847

L. Q. C. Butler to David S. Reid A&H-DSR

County Line
Davie County N. Ca.
28th Jan. 1847.

You are entitled to my thanks for favouring me with the President's Message at So early a period. I read it with much interest, it is conclusive on the Mexican War:

The *modern* Whig party are now as they were under an other name, in days of old, opposed to a just war: In the former volunteering when they did not expect to be called they were brave fellows, very forward in volunteering, Saying they would whip the Mexicans and then whip Jas. K. Polk for making the war: and boasted loudly on some of the Whig Counties' being so forward in volunteering! but now, since a call is actually made these Same whig counties have not only refused to volunteer, but have used all sorts of means to prevent others from doing so; saying that the yellow fever was in the army, that the soldiers were badly treated, &c. Old Iredell that whole souled whig county offers but 8 volunteers:—The Whigs wish the honour without the trouble, they are valient men untried!

Enclosed I send a dollar for the Weekly Union 6 months; have it forwarded to me at County Line Davie County N.C. if you please. I was much pleased with Capt Freemont's Report which you sent me last Session.

William W. Gray[1] *to David S. Reid* A&H-DSR

Raleigh,
Jan. 28th 1847

I have seen it stated in some Newspaper, that a publication would issue from the Press, containing a History of the many Insults, Depredations, Grievances, &c &c inflicted upon us by Mexico, previous to commencement of the present War between the two Nations.

If such a Work has appeared, will you be so obliging as to send me a copy, and I will pay you therefor, on your arrival here a few weeks hence.

Governor Graham's Military appointments, appear to be very unpopular, even with many of his Whig friends, Gales's[2] assertions to the contrary, notwithstanding.

Some 25 volunteers, from this place have gone to Wilmington, and enrolled themselves in one of the Companies received.—The Regiment, however, was not quite full on the 26th instant, so I have been informed by the Adjutant General of the State; who will leave here in the morning for Wilmington.

I fear that I shall not be able to visit Washington before the 4th of March, when Congress will be compelled to adjourn.—If there be an extra session however, I shall endeavor to see the seat of Government; but, I sincerely hope there will be no necessity for an extra meeting; for the Administration has already many very bitter enemies, I discover, without the new members.

A son of mine, now 20, was very desirous to volunteer, but I could not reconcile it to my feelings to permit him to march under Officers who have so shamefully vilified the Administration and the War.—As they despise War, they might hate the soldier.

My oldest son, however, I very much fear will get to Mexico, as he was in New Orleans on the 29th. December, with several thousand boxes of the Ointment,[3] and designed, he said, to reach Texas, if not Mexico.

A son of Robert H. Gray, (my brother) of Lynchburg, is in Capt Carrington's company in the City of Richmond; which will soon embark for the Rio Grande, I presume, unless some emergency shall call him more directly to the seat of War.—Your indebted friend,

P.S. I shall be thankful for any Document, which you may deem interesting. Should you meet with my old friend, Thos. Ritchie, Esqr,[4] inform him, that I am yet in existence, and hope to see him once more; but at this time, I am much afflicted with rheumatism, chills, fevers, &c.

---

[1]William W. Gray (born 1788), printer, was a native of Virginia and resident of Raleigh as late as 1850. Seventh Census, 1850, Wake County, Population Schedule, 267.

[2]Seaton Gales (1828-1878) was editor of the Raleigh *Register* (1848-1858) and associate editor of the Raleigh *Sentinel* (1866-1869). During the Civil War he was a major in the Confederate army. Hamilton and Williams, *Graham Papers*, III, 314n.

[3]It has not been possible to identify this item, except to speculate that it must have been some sort of patent medicine. There was no "Gray's Ointment" or other such popular remedy that could be associated with the Gray family advertised in

the *Standard* at the time this letter was written. *North-Carolina Standard*, October, 1846-March, 1847, passim.

[4]A reference to the elder Thomas Ritchie, previously identified, editor from 1804 to 1845 of the *Richmond Enquirer* and, after that time, of the Democratic *Weekly Union* in the nation's capital.

Nathaniel J. Palmer to David S. Reid A&H-DSR

Milton, N.C.
Feb. 18th 1847

As the bill to raise ten additional Regiments has passed, I have thought it probable that the Secretary of War would be calling to give Mr. Whitfield[1] a Commission and authorize him to raise a Company of Regulars. I have but little doubt that he could proceed with the requisite authority and the means furnished to pay the bounty. I would give him all the assistance I could. Do the best you can for him.[2]

[1]This is probably William A. Whitfield of Milton, who had been a trustee, along with Nathaniel J. Palmer, in 1844 of the Milton Female Institute. Powell, *Caswell County*, 369.

[2]Apparently, Palmer's expectation was not fulfilled, as there is no record of any military commission having been issued to Whitfield during the years 1847-1850. Governors Office Records, "Commissions and Resignations, 1841-1855."

Wilson S. Hill[1] to David S. Reid A&H-DSR

Greensborough N C
Feb 19, 1847,

I am induced to wright you this letter to let you know my Freind J R, McLain[2] & A C, Lindsay[3] has gon on to Baltimore as I understand To Setle a mater of honor in the event the cival athority Should interfear with them you will confer a favour on me and the rest of the McLains Freinds to give him any assistance in the way of *Bail*

Please Send me Some of Judge Douglass Speaches in vindicating the President on the charge of conspring to injure General Taylor in the estimation of the people

Yours in great haste
P S, Judge Dick[4] wishes the Same favour for Robert McLains freind

---

[1]Wilson S. Hill of Greensboro was postmaster (1845-1849) and a member of the Council of State (1850-1851, 1852-1854). Arnett, *Greensboro*, 419; Cheney, *North Carolina Government*, 178.

[2]James Robert McLean, a Greensboro attorney, was a district attorney in the 1840s and was a representative in the Confederate States Congress (1862-1864). Cheney, *North Carolina Government*, 388; Rockingham County Court Minutes, February, 1846.

[3]A. C. Lindsey (born 1815) resided in Caswell County where in 1850 he was a teacher, probably at the Dan River Institute in Yanceyville. His wife, the former Elizabeth L. Graves, may have been related to Reid, as Reid's brother Hugh and two of his uncles, Thomas and Josiah Settle, all married women whose surname was Graves. Seventh Census, 1850, Caswell County, Population Schedule, 177; Caswell County Marriage Bonds; Powell, *Caswell County*, 370.

[4]John McClintock Dick, previously identified.

Elias Dodson[1] to David S. Reid RF

Reidsville N.C.
Feb 21 1847

I am now at your father's house & your relations are all well excepting little Elizebeth Adams.[2] She has been ill ever since Tuesday & is now better She had a small attack of the pleurisy

I was thankful for your restoration to health.[3] But if you had died from your illness how different would have been your condition from it now is. The gospel would have gone out of date & would have afforded as little benifit to you as if it had never been published Since your recovery the glorious prize of a happy immortality is still held out to you on they same terms on which they were offered to Abraham, Isaiah & Paul. The goodness of God at this time should make upon your mind a deep impression I hope that you will prepare speedily to meet God so that, if another spell should occur & prove fatal, you may meet beyond the tomb a smiling God & dwell with him in heaven forever

The obligations of the gospel are like all other obligations, they are imperative

Many persons believe that repentance & faith depend on *feeling*

If several debts of $15 or 20$ each are against a man the court never gives judgment in the following word. He may [pay] them if he *feels* like doing so. If the court were to give such a judgment the man *would never* pay his debts Many from their *actions* seem to presume that the court of heaven to pass such a decree But they will find that the obligations of heaven are as *binding* as those of earth

Again these matters should not be considered *secondary* in importance. Jesus Christ has said *First* seek the kingdom of God & his righteousness & all these things shall be added to you

Excuses are frequently made but no excuse should ever be offered which will not be received in the final day What will this world avail us 100 years from this time?

There are several reasons for which you should seek the Lord

1 Christ has died for you

2 You have a pious mother & pious sisters who have *deep* anxiety for your spiritual welfare

3 Many of of your relations are now in heaven

Don't say I have too much business to attend to & must postpone this subject. Recollect that David the King had much *civil* & *military* business to call his attention yet a more pious man scarcely ever lived.

I hope I shall [have] good news from you in a short time. I expect to be at your father's in one month from the present time & hope I shall [have] a letter from you when I come there again

I wish you to give the enclosed letter to Professor Ruggles[4] of the Columbian College. Don't sent it to him but give it to him from your own hand as I wish him to become acquainted with you. If he is not there give it to President Bacon.[5]

When you see Professor Ruggles you will see one of the best mathematicians in the United States

---

[1]Elias Dodson (1807-1882), Baptist minister and missionary, was educated at the College of William and Mary. He was ordained in 1838 and became a missionary for the General Association of Virginia. In 1844 he was appointed missionary for the North Carolina State Baptist Convention in the Beulah Association. He was the co-organizer and a pastor at Hogan's Creek Baptist Church, the family church of the Settles, Reids, and Martins. Richard R. Saunders, *Open Doors and Closed Windows of the First Baptist Church of Reidsville, North Carolina* (Reidsville: First Baptist Church Centennial Committee, 1948), 256-259.

[2]Elizabeth Adams (born circa 1843) was about four years old at the time this letter was written. Reid's niece, she was a daughter of Samuel F. Adams and Reid's sister Frances. The Adams family lived at Troublesome, several miles west of Reidsville, until about 1846-1847 when they moved next door to Reid's parents in Rockingham County. Seventh Census, 1850, Rockingham County, Population Schedule, 26.

[3]Reid's health problems, in fact, persisted beyond this date. On March 12, "Halifax," the Washington correspondent for the *Standard*, reported: "The Hon.

D. S. Reid . . . has been quite ill at his lodgings in this city for some days past, though I am happy to write you that he is better this evening." On March 19 the same writer noted: "I am happy to be able to write you that the Hon. D. S. Reid is rapidly recovering from his late serious attack of pneumonia." *North-Carolina Standard*, March 17, 24, 1847.

[4]William Ruggles (1797-1877), an educator, was born in Rochester, Massachusetts. He graduated from Brown University in 1822 and became a tutor at Columbian College. Named chairman of mathematics and natural philosophy in 1827, Ruggles remained there until his death. *ACAB*, V, 345.

[5]Joel Smith Bacon (1802-1869) from New York graduated from Hamilton College in 1826. He became the president of Georgetown College, Kentucky, in 1830, and three years later he assumed a professorship at his alma mater. In 1841 he was named the third president of Columbian College and served there until 1854. *National Cyclopedia of American Biography* (New York: James T. White and Company, 63 volumes, index and supplements, 1888-1984), V, 152, hereinafter cited as *NCAB*.

James C. Dobbin to David S. Reid A&H-DSR

Raleigh
Sunday Evening
March 7. 1847

After a tedious & uncomfortable journey we arrived here yesterday about 12. o'clock—We were detained at one point on the road about two hours—the locomotive ran off the track—no injury was sustained. My children are quite well. Mrs Dobbin[1] was much fatigued by the journey—but is really better than I feared she would be. We think of leaving for Fayetteville in the morning. I have seen Clark[2] & assured him of his appointment. The President must therefore make the appointment by all means. As to the Lieutenancy business—I have had two or three interviews with your friend Mr Disbrow[3] who thinks with Mr Clark as Captn & himself as Lieut—the thing would be done up in some style. I mentioned to him the chief & only difficulty in his way & I expressed the apprehension that there would be some complaint if so many were appointed from Raleigh. I have not seen Jones[4] yet. I will drop you a line from Fayetteville. Disbow says he would compr- for 2nd Lieutenancy. All I can say is that I will find no fault if he is appointed. Exercise your own Judgt. He is a good military disciplinarian I learn. No line to say more.

---

[1]Louisa Holmes Dobbin (died 1848), native of Sampson County, was married to Dobbin in 1838. During her last illness she was nursed by Dorothea Dix, who

had come to North Carolina to crusade for better treatment for the insane. Mrs. Dobbin urged her husband to aid this effort, and although it was unpopular with his party he strongly supported legislation that led to establishment of a state hospital for the insane. Powell, *DNCB*, II, 82-83.

[2]William J. Clarke, a Raleigh attorney, was a graduate of the University of North Carolina. In 1847 he was appointed captain of Company I, Twelfth Regiment, United States Infantry, and served in Mexico, where he was wounded. He was promoted to major for gallantry at National Bridge and Cerro Gordo. He was elected comptroller of the state and served from 1851 to 1855. In 1861 he became colonel of the Twenty-fourth North Carolina Volunteers and served throughout the war. Wheeler, *Sketches*, 419, 421; Cheney, *North Carolina Government*, 182; Jones, *Mexican War Roster*, 46; Francis B. Heitman, *Historical Register and Dictionary of the United States Army from Its Organization September 29, 1789 to March 2, 1983* (Washington: Government Printing Office, 2 volumes, 1983), I, 306, hereinafter cited as Heitman, *Historical Register and Dictionary of the Army.*

[3]Likely a reference to Lewis Dishbough (born 1799), a physician who by 1850 was living in Onslow County. Clarke was appointed company commander on April 9, 1847, but Dishbough's effort to obtain a commision was unsuccessful. Seventh Census, 1850, Onslow County, Population Schedule, 117; Jones, *Mexican War Roster*, 46.

[4]Probably a reference to Wesley Jones of Wake County.

Stephen A. Douglas to David S. Reid A&H-DSR

Gaston N C
March 24th 1847
7 oclock P M

I congratulate you that you did not conclude to come with me. Last night about 12 oclock the cars ran off the track in the swamp between Petersburg & the junction. No person was injured by the accident, but the baggage car was broken to pieces, and we found ourselves in the same mud hole at sun rise this morning. At last the conductor succeeded in getting another baggage car from a neighboring depot & got to this place about eleven or twelve oclock today. The Raleigh train had left, and this gave an opportunity of spending the day on the banks of the Roanoke and witnessing all the attractions of the city of Gaston. We have hope of getting away from here tomarrow morning, if the cars don't run off again tonight. We have a jolly set of fellows in company, and besides had a good appetite for of breakfast when we got here today. Tell Mrs Wimsat[1] that, if we did not have birds, we had shad & *frogs* in abundance. I shall sleep well tonight & be ready for an early start in the morning.

[1]Charlotte Wimsatt (born 1810), wife of Washington, D.C., fourth ward landlord Joseph Wimsatt. Apparently, Douglas and Reid sometimes boarded with or took meals at the Wimsatts'. Douglas's note is addressed to Reid "at Mrs. Wimsatt's." Seventh Census, 1850, Washington, D.C., Population Schedule, 222.

Circular of David S. Reid to His Constituents A&H-DSR
NCC

Washington City
March 31, 1847

TO MY CONSTITUENTS

FELLOW-CITIZENS: The term for which I was elected your Representative has expired, and I conform to the custom which has heretofore prevailed in our district, of noticing some of the questions which have engaged the consideration of the Congress which has just terminated. The duties of a Representative, at all times arduous and responsible, have been unusually so during the twenty-ninth Congress. I have met this responsibility by giving my support to such measures as I conceived the interests of the country demanded, leaving it with you to approve or condemn my course, as the convictions of your judgment may dictate. Knowing, as I do, that you are not governed by the partisan considerations which so often divide and distract our councils in Congress, I will not entertain a doubt but that you will arrive at just and patriotic conclusions in regard to the great questions which agitate the public mind.

The elections of 1844 brought the present Administration into power, and whether for good or for evil, a majority of my constituents, like myself, share the responsibility of the act. In this election, the only triumph we claimed was the just expectation of having the Government administered upon correct principles. In this, I think, the Executive has not disappointed us. One of the reforms to which we stood pledged was the modification of the tariff act of 1842. This unjust act was not only enriching one portion of the Union while it was impoverishing the other, but it was also taxing a large class of our citizens to contribute to the wealth of a favored few. It was, therefore, eminently desirable that this onerous system should be changed; and, after a hard struggle, we succeeded in passing the act of 1846.

It is not to be expected that this act is perfect, and it may, from time to time, require such slight modifications as experience or a change of circumstances may suggest; but, upon the whole, the act of 1846 may be considered as favorable to the agricultural classes as any tariff that has been in operation since the principle of protection has been seriously urged in this country. The predictions of the opponents of this act, that it would fail to produce revenue—that it would break down domestic manufacturers—that it would have a deleterious effect on all the great productive interests, instead of being verified by the experience of the country, have, thus far, proved to be fallacious and unfounded; and no matter what may be said of its effects, if its principles are faithfully carried out, it cannot fail to give additional prosperity to the agricultural interests of this country, by relieving them from many of the unjust burdens they have heretofore borne. It is not to be expected that any tariff will yield a sufficient amount of revenue to meet the demands of the treasury when the country is engaged in an expensive war with a foreign nation. To raise these extraordinary supplies, it becomes necessary to resort to direct taxation, or to an increase of the duty on such articles of foreign importation as will bear it, or to loans. Direct taxation is not only odious among the people, but it is an inconvenient and dangerous mode of collecting revenue by the Federal Government, and I would never resort to it unless it became an act of positive and indispensable necessity. In this opinion, I fancy, most of us agree. With a view to increase the revenue, during the war, the President recommended to Congress to impose a small increase of duty on iron and coal, and on certain descriptions of cotton goods, to reduce the price of public lands which have been in market for a number of years, and to impose a duty of 20 per cent on tea and coffee. I have always been in favor of a just revenue duty; and experience has more thoroughly confirmed me in the opinion, that a fair and reasonable graduation in the price of the public lands which have been in market for a series of years, is but an act of justice to the settler, and to the States in which such lands lie. Lands which, it is believed, can never be sold at the present Government price, would find purchasers in the poorer class of citizens desirous of procuring homes for themselves and their families; and the revenue derivable from the sales of the public lands would be increased by such reduction. Tea and coffee being articles used by all classes, and in all sections of the Union, they were long subject to a duty, and would no doubt have so remained to this day but for the fact that a duty on these articles affords no "*protection*"—it gives no boon to the manufacturer. The proposition to impose a duty on these articles did not prevail, but it received my vote. A system of taxation operating with perfect equality, is, perhaps, unattainable; but the statesman who regards the interests of his country, and the citizen who is devoted to his Government, will be satisfied with the nearest approach to this equality; and I am not sure but the same amount of revenue can be raised as easily and with as much equality upon tea and coffee as in any other way. In giving the vote to impose a duty on these articles, I expected to be assailed by demagogues and partisans, who care but little for the good of the country. If it comports with their sense of duty, I am willing it should be so; and I am free to say, that if the proposition had been to impose a duty on these articles to be expended for some unnecessary object, that then the complaint might be well-founded. But if this proposition had prevailed, I am sure I do not mistake the patriotism of my constituents when I say, that, instead of complaining of my vote to impose the duty, they would have congratulated themselves that they were contributing their means for the pay and support of the brave soldiers who have volunteered their services and left their homes to defend the rights and honor of our country in a foreign land. If there is one to be found who would grudgingly sip his tea and coffee under so moderate a contribution for the support of our gallant sons who are fighting a merciless foe, I would scorn approbation from the lips or sympathy from the heart of such an individual.

The independent treasury act has been passed, and is in operation; and although the time for its commencement is unpropitious, yet is is hoped that the predictions of its enemies will fail, and that the experiment will prove that the Government can manage its fiscal affairs without the aid of banks.

As the war with Mexico is a subject of deep interest to the whole country, I will advert to it. Although for years there had existed other good and sufficient causes for the United States to declare war against Mexico, yet I am free to admit that its commencement at the time it occurred, grew out of circumstances connected with the annexation of Texas. I am equally free to say, that if annexation had not taken place, a war with Mexico, growing out of other causes, would have been inevitable at no very distant period. In support of this opinion, I will state a few of the many outrages committed by Mexico against the United States prior to the commencement of the war. They are believed to be correct.

"No. 9.—BRIG CATO.—This vessel was boarded at Alvarado, on the 26th of August, 1824, by some twenty men, who rifled her of $2,701 in specie, and of numerous other articles. After threatening the life of the captain, and wounding two of the crew, they set the vessel adrift by cutting her chain cable, which with the anchor, were lost. The claim in this case is for $5,544."

"No. 13.—BRIG DELIGHT of Philadelphia.—A DOUBLE CLAIM.—This vessel in March, 1835, touched at San Blas, where the officers of the custom-house compelled the conveyance of her cargo over a mile to the custom-house stores, and its reshipment. The damage to the owners was estimated at $3,716.48. The same vessel entered the port of Sisal, in September, of the same year, where she was seized by the collector with an armed force, part of her cargo forced on shore, her hatches broken open, and the cargo taken to the custom-house. Estimate of damages arising from the condemnation and sale of the cargo, &c., $15,692.50."

"No. 14.—SCHOONER FAIR AMERICAN, of Baltimore.—This vessel arrived at Refugio, January 4th, 1826, was admitted to entry, landed her cargo under permit, and in part removed it to town, when the whole was seized by the Mexican authorities, and confiscated and sold. The Mexican consul at Baltimore afterwards requested of his Government that the property might be restored, and the owner indemnified. Mr. Wilson's claim for damages is $50,225.21."

"No. 27—JOHN BALDWIN, an American citizen, complains of gross outrageous treatment at the hands of the alcalde of Minotitlan, in Guazcualco. He asserts that the alcalde was interested in a suit which was brought against him by one of his creatures. Some altercation occurring at the proceedings before the alcalde, he was ordered to the stocks. He refused to submit, and, in attempting to escape, was shot at, and severely injured by a fall. He was captured, made to stand in the stocks, and afterwards imprisoned. The Mexican government were informed subsequently that the United States government 'would regard this a national question.' The reply of the Mexican Executive was, that it was a matter of judicial investigation," &c.

"No. 28.—SCHOONER TOPAZ.—The master of this vessel contracted, in 1832, to transport one hundred and fifty Mexican soldiers from Matamoros to Galveston. During the passage, the master and mate were killed by the Mexican officers, and the crew were forced to run the vessel into Anahuac. Here THEY were imprisoned, on a charge of killing their captain and mate, and attempts were made by the officers above mentioned to make them confess to that crime. They were at last liberated, on their agreement to be bound to the officers to serve them for three years. One of them subsequently escaped to the United States, and testified to the facts above stated. He states that the Mexican officers divided the captain's money between them. He thinks he had three of four thousand dollars."

"No. 40.—The schooner Harriet Elizabeth was stranded near Matagorda, in 1835. While in this situation she was fired upon by a Mexican schooner, and her captain, crew, and passengers carried to Matamoros and imprisoned."

"No. 42.—The brig Jane and four other vessels were detained at Matamoros, in 1836, countrary to express treaty stipulations."

"No. 44.—Mr. Coleman, acting counsul of the United States at Tabasco, was summoned before the authorities, in 1836, and publicly insulted and ill-treated, because he refused to legalize certain documents, the result of which would be to defraud."

"No. 45.—The schooner Aurora was stranded on the coast of Mexico in 1836. A part of the cargo was landed by the crew, when it was immediately taken possession of by an armed body of Mexicans. On the crew remonstrating against these proceedings, they were insulted, maltreated, and the mate seriously injured."

"No. 47.—It was proposed to sell the brig *Fourth of July* to the Mexican Government; but while the negotiation was going on, she was taken possession of by the Mexican authorities and the Mexican flag hoisted."

"No. 49.—In 1836, William Hallett and Zalmon Hall, citizens of the United States, were arrested in the streets of Matamoros by an armed force, who struck one of them on the face, and took both to the principal barrack. Here they were confined, while a guard was placed at the door of the house of the American consul to prevent his interference in the matter. The house was searched for the consul himself, and much of his property was stolen."

"No. 51.—The American citizens at Tampico having requested that a man-of-war might be sent for their protection, Lieut. Osborne, with a boat's crew from the revenue cutter Jefferson, proceeded there, when he was arrested by the authorities, carried off, and examined. On his return, he learned that his crew had also been arrested, and held for a long time in confinement."

"No. 53.—THE SCHOONER WILLIAM A. TURNER, of which James O'Flaherty was master, was seized off Sisal, in 1834, by an armed Mexican force. The vessel was released after Captain O'Flaherty had given bonds for her value. In 1836 his vessel was again seized, himself confined, liberated, and, after entering into bonds for $1,200, his vessel released. Soon after, the vessel was again seized, and the captain confined in the cabin, from whence he was sent as a prisoner to Tabasco."

"No. 67.—MARY HUGHES, WIDOW OF GEORGE HUGHES, MASTER OF THE BRIG 'JOHN,' of New York.—The brig 'John,' lying at anchor in the river Tabasco in 1832, was boarded and captured by an armed force, on a pretext altogether unfounded. Captain Hughes was knocked down, cruelly beaten with the buts of the muskets of the boarding party, carried off and imprisoned, and the cargo and stores of the vessel plundered. Captan Hughes subsequently died from the wounds received on this occasion."

"Mary Hughes claims reparation thereof."

"No. 68.—JAMES COCHRANE, engineer of the steamer Hidalgo, was impressed into the Mexican service, together with the boat in

1832—cruelly and ignominiously treated, and compelled to do duty as engineer for two months."

"No. 70.—CLAIM OF SAMUEL BALDWIN.—Mr. B., a citizen of the United States, settled in Mexico some years since, and had acquired considerable property. On the most frivolous pretext, he was seized and thrown into the public prison with the vilest criminals. While there, additional charges were fabricated against him; he was loaded with irons, poison was given him in his coffee, and he endured the most unparalleled sufferings from the brutal treatment of one Gomez, his jailor. From Acayuacan, where these barbarities were committed. Mr. B. was sent to Vera Cruz, and cast into a wet and filthy jail in the Castle of San Juan d'Ulloa."

"No. 71—CLAIMS OF HENRY B. HORTON, WALTER W. ADAM, AND JAMES KELLEY.—The claimants, (seamen on board the American barque 'Roger Williams,') having been paid off and discharged at Monterey, California, in 1840, were waiting for an opportunity to return home, when they, together with other Americans, were seized, and conducted to prison. They obtained their release, but were a second time arrested, robbed, and cast into jail, no cause for their commitment ever having been assigned."

"No. 72.—CLAIM OF WILLIAM LORD ETHERIDGE THOMPSON.—Thompson, an American seaman, was wrecked near San Blas, in 1838. In 1840, he was twice arrested, and thrown into prison—no cause whatever being assigned for his detention in either case. After suffering the most cruel treatment, he was released; but found, on his return to the farm where he had labored since his shipwreck in 1838, that all his property had been taken from him.

"No redress has ever been granted by the Mexican Government."

"No. 74.—CLAIMS OF ISAAC GRAHAM, WILLIAM CHURCH, JOSEPH L. MAJORS, CHARLES BROWN, AND OTHER.—These Americans, with six others, were seized in California, where they were engaged in business, in April, 1840, by the Mexican authorities, without any just cause or provocation, and thrown into prison. It also appears that at the time of his arrest, the House of Mr. Graham was surrounded, fired into, and $36,000 in specie plundered therefrom."

"No. 75.—CLAIMS OF A. C. BREDALL, OF NEW ORLEANS—1st. The schooner Lodi, with a valuable cargo of lawful goods, both belonging to Mr. Bredall, sailed from New Orleans in May, 1838, bound for Matamoros, in Mexico. On her arrival there, without any allegation of offence committed or contemplated, she was seized, her cargo landed, exposed, and pillaged."

"2nd. In 1843, Mr. Bredall arrived at Vera Cruz with passports granted him by the Mexican consul at New Orleans. He presented them to the proper authorities, but was arrested and imprisoned on the charge of a design upon the life of General Santa Ana. During his detention, he suffered the most wanton, cruel, and humiliating indignities and privations; and upon his release, he reached New Orleans in a helpless and shattered condition; his constitution broken, his hearing destroyed, and sinking under a hopeless consumption. IT IS PROPER TO REMARK THAT THE BRITISH MINISTER DEMANDED AND OBTAINED LIBERAL DAMAGES ON BEHALF OF THREE BRITISH SUBJECTS WHO WERE IMPRISONED WITH MR. BREDALL."

"No. 81.—CLAIM OF CAPTAIN JONAS P. LEVY.—1st. In 1843, the store of the claimant, with all its contents, was forcibly taken possession of with the connivance of the public authorities, and never returned. Amount of property lost, $6,846.02. Reparation has been refused from the commission of the outrage to the present time.

"2d. This claim is for illegal duties extorted from Captain Levy by the collector of the port of Laguna in 1843, under false pretences, amounting to $513.89.

"3d. The third claim is for goods belonging to the claimant and his brother, thrown overboard by the captain of the steamboat Petrita, amounting to $7,483.25 for which relief has been denied by the Mexican Government.

"4th. Captain L. also claims reparation for being imprisoned after the commencement of hostilities between the United States and Mexico, in direct violation of the treaty, providing for the occurrence of such an event, and for being compelled to leave Mexico, without time to arrange his business, also in violation of treaty stipulations."

The conduct of Mexico towards the United States called forth the following strong language from Mr. Forsyth, Secretary of State, in a letter to the Mexican Minister of Foreign Affairs, in 1837:

"These wrongs of a character which cannot be tolerated by any Government imbued with a just self-respect, with a proper regard for the opinions of other nations, or with an enlightened concern for the permanent welfare or [*sic*] those portions of its people who may be interested in foreign commerce. Treasure belonging to citizens of the United States has been seized by Mexican officers, in its transit from the capital to the coast. Vessels of the United States have been captured, detained, and condemned upon the most frivolous pretexts. Duties have been exacted from others, notoriously against law, or without law. Others have been employed, and in some instances ruined, in the Mexican service, without compensation to the owners. CITIZENS OF THE UNITED STATES HAVE BEEN IMPRISONED FOR LONG PERIODS OF TIME, WITHOUT BEING INFORMED OF THE OFFENCES WITH WHICH THEY WERE CHARGED. OTHERS HAVE BEEN MURDERED AND ROBBED BY MEXICAN OFFICERS, ON THE HIGH SEAS, WITHOUT ANY ATTEMPT TO BRING THE GUILTY TO JUSTICE."

It was in reference to outrages of this character, that General Jackson used the following emphatic language in regard to Mexico: "*That the length of time since some of the injuries have been committed, the repeated and unavailing applications for redress, the wanton character of some of the outrages upon the property and persons of our citizens, upon the officers and flag of the United States, independent of recent insults to this Government and people by the late extraordinary Mexican Minister, WOULD JUSTIFY, IN THE EYES OF ALL NATIONS, IMMEDIATE WAR.*"

The sum of two millions twenty-six thousand one hundred and thirty-nine dollars and sixty-eight cents, of these claims, were liquidated; but Mexico has refused to pay the instalments as they have become due, agreeably to her promise. The remaining claims have not yet been liquidated.

Thus it will be seen that we had borne insult after insult, and outrage after outrage, from Mexico. The peaceful injunction which we are commanded to obey, does not go farther than to require that, when we are smitten upon one cheeck, we turn the other. We had even gone further than this for the sake of maintaining peace with Mexico. But when she came on our soil and shed the blood of our citizens, every consideration of honor, of justice, and of patriotism, required that we should repel her. The right of Texas to annex herself to the United States has been too often demonstrated to need anything from me on this point. Texas had been one of the States of the Mexican confederacy, and was an equal of the other States, but did not belong any more to them than they belonged to her. In the revolution of 1836, she successfully resisted the usurpations of Santa Ana, and at the time of annexation, had for nine years maintained her independence as a separate and distinct sovereign State. Mexico had even herself acknowledged her independence during this time, and proposed to do so again upon the condition that Texas would not annex herself to the United States. For one, I am free to admit that I did not believe that Mexico would declare war against the United States in consequence of the annexation of Texas; and I am now inclined to the opinion, that if certain politicians and newspapers in the United States had not promulgated sentiments calculated to deceive and mislead Mexico in relation to the state of public opinion in this country, that she would not have declared war against the United States in consequence of annexation. It has been alleged that the war with Mexico was brought about by the President, without the sanction of the constitutional authority of the Government. The Governor of North Carolina, in his last annual message, in alluding to the Mexican war, says:

"In this posture of affairs, without consultation with Congress, though in session, by the authority of the Executive, as military commander merely, our army was made to take possession of the whole territory in question. Resistence was attempted, hostilities ensued, and we are thus involved in war on a point of honor—the constitutional department of our own Government never having authorized an appeal to force for the country in dispute, nor defined any objects, for the attainment of which, it should be waged. While our arms are signalized by victories worthy of the nation's renown, and the spirit of the people is ready to uphold the honor of our flag at any sacrifice, it still remains a momentous question, under our institutions, whether Congress can be superseded in the power to make war, and the authority given to the Executive, only to effectuate the will of the Legislature, can be used to determine and settle the policy of the country, in matters of boundary, or any other."

This assertion was followed by the declaration of the Whig members of the Legislature, that the war with Mexico existed by the action of the Executive and the subsequent sanction of Congress. Thus it will be seen that an effort has been made to throw the responsibility of the war upon the Executive, and not upon Mexico. I cannot envy the patriotism of the man, who, when his country is engaged in a foreign war, will seek to hide the wrongs of the enemy, by attacking the President who is endeavoring to maintain the rights and honor of the country. Suppose the President had erred—which I do not admit—does justice or patriotism require that that error should be heralded from one end of the country to the other, while the wrongs, the bloody wrongs, perpetrated by Mexico are passed over in silence? Why has this spirit manifested itself? Is it because the President is a Democrat? Or is it because Mexico is against our country. Let us advert to the facts, and see how they stand. Texas was lawfully annexed, and became one of the States of this Union. The President proposed to treat with Mexico in relation to the boundary, but Mexico rejected our minister, and refused to treat, declaring that she would invade Texas. The Constitution of the United States declares, that "the President shall be commander-in-chief of the army and navy of the United States," and that "he shall take care that the laws be faithfully executed." The army of the United States was removed towards the point where an attack from Mexico was apprehended. For if, after the declaration of Mexico, the President had permitted her army to have invaded Texas, destroying the lives and property of our citizens, without using every effort to repel such invasions, he would not have discharged his duty as commander-in-chief of the army of the United States, nor would he have discharged the further duty imposed on him by the Constitution, of taking care that the laws be faithfully executed. If a foreign enemy were marching an army to invade our country, and even private citizens were, on their own responsibility, to assemble at the point of invasion to defend their lives and their property, I could not take it upon myself to say that they had done wrong, or that they were the authors of the war, or that they had violated the Constitution; and much less can I undertake to say that the President, who is commander-in-chief of the army of the United States, and whose duty it is to "take care that the laws be faithfully executed," either violated the Constitution of the United States, or became responsible for the war, by marching the army to a point at which the country was about to be invaded. It has been said that removing the army from Corpus Christi to the Rio Grande produced the war; but it must be recollected that Corpus Christi is on the west side of the Nueces, and no one pretends that there is any difference between our claim to the territory on the west bank of the Neuces and to that on the east bank of the Rio Grande. At the time of annexation, Texas claimed to the Rio Grande, and that stream has always been regarded as the ancient boundary between Texas and Mexico, particularly the lower Rio Grande, which was occupied by our army. But it must be borne in mind, that Mexico not only claims the country lying between the Nueces and the Rio Grande, but she claims the *whole of Texas*; and she has never pretended that her claim to that part of the territory lying between the Nueces and the Rio Grande differed in any respect from her claim to the rest of Texas. Such distinction is only made by the enemies of the war in this country, for Mexico herself has never demanded of us anything less than the whole of Texas. I cannot well imagine how any one can oppose the war, unless such person is in favor of the surrender of the whole of Texas; and I cannot believe that any individual, whose mind is not warped by party madness, or whose feelings are not alienated from his country, could be in favor of such a surrender. It has been asserted, that this war was brought about by the action of the Executive; and by this it is either meant that the President is in the wrong and Mexico in the right, or that, although the war was right, yet the President ought to have suffered the Mexicans to cross the Rio Grande and murder our people, and take possession of the country, without resistence, until the news could have travelled two thousand miles to Washington, and until Congress could make a formal declaration of war and have sent it back to the scene of action. Suppose the President had not ordered the army to move until all this had taken place, what a burst of indignation would have rung from one end of this republic to the other! Even at the time that war was declared by the United States against Mexico, it was denied by many of those who now say the President caused the war, that war existed at all; for they took the ground that the acts of hostility which had been perpetrated by the Mexican army would not be recognised as a war by that Government; but when brought to vote directly on the declaration of war, only fourteen members voted against it in the House of Representatives; all the Whig members from North Carolina as well as the Democrats, voting in the affirmative. The preamble to that declaration of war asserts, that "whereas, by the act of the republic of Mexico, a state of war exists between that Government and the United States: Be it enacted," &c. Thus it will be seen, that while the Whigs in Congress, on the 13th May, 1846, declared that the war existed *by the act of Mexico*, the Whigs in our State Legislature, in less than one year thereafter, declared that the war existed *by the action of the Executive*! In asserting that the war existed by the action of the Executive, they were either mistaken or willfully wrong. How do the facts stand? The President proposed to treat in relation to the boundary, but *Mexico refused, and claimed the whole of Texas*. Mexico declared war against the United States, and proceeded to execute the declaration by crossing the Rio Grande, and shedding the blood of our citizens before a blow was struck by the army of the United States. After it has been shown that Mexico first declared war and was the first to shed blood, how can it be charged that the war was brought about by the action of the President? As well might the highwayman charge his own guilt upon his faultness victim. I have been pained to see the opposition that has manifested itself to the war. I have already adverted to the course of the Governor and the Whig members of the Legislature, as being calculated to disparage the war. The Greensboro' Patriot, a paper of high standing among the Whig party, on the 28th of November, 1846, in the same number which contained the Governor's message, published a communication, from which I take the following anti-war and un-patriotic sentiments. Read them:

"Pause—I call upon you as American citizens, as freemen, not to lend you[r] countenance, much less your aid, to gross violations of your Constitution.

"Whigs of North Carolina: this is the President's war, not the people's war. He is not the man of your choice. You are not bound to support him 'right or wrong'—only when right. The sage of Ashland, the man of your choice, two years before the event, foretold that war would ensue from the annexation of Texas. The President proclaimed in his message its annexation, and glorified himself upon it, as a bloodless achievement—and a short half year found the ensanguined plains of Palo Alto and Resaca de la Palma reeking with the blood of the slain, and a soldier's grave closing over the remains of the heroic Ringgold. Shortsighted man! What delusion possessed you? Had the giddy height to which you had been so unexpectedly raised addled your brain and destroyed your vision? Can you now tell what countless woes you will inflict on your country before another year rolls round? Are you able now to tell what you intend to do with you[r] twenty thousand volunteers? or where they will be six months hence?

"Democrats of North Carolina; you lent your aid to place this dizzy man on his tottering pinnacle. If you believe you were right, now is the time to show it. He calls upon you now to join his standard—now is his time of need; surely you will not desert him! Wheel horses of Edgecombe come to the rescue; a long pull and a strong pull! Game cocks of Nash, on with your gyves; give an everlasting flutter and show your pluck! Ye braves of old Martin, rush to the command of your lieutenant—colonel, and pluck bright honor from the swarthy ranchero! Will the trumpet voice of Sleepy Creek's orator be stilled, and Wayne's courageous Democracy be deaf to the call of their leader? Will the Unterrified of Caswell, and Rockingham, and Stokes, and Mecklenburg, with their noisy chieftains, turn away their ears unheeding from the alarum? Surely not.

"Democrats: your gallant leader—not your country, nor your country's interests—calls you to the tented field 'DURING THE WAR.' Make your testamentary dispositions, and obey the call. Surely you will not have others to follow him whom you have appointed and decline to follow yourselves! Can you decline?—will you falter? The slightest hesitation will be construed into an abandonment of your chieftain, for self preservation and your country's interests. What Democrats dare do this? 'Traitor, coward, turn and flee'— like Haywood.

"*Citizens: Rashness is not patriotism—the fear of the charge of cowardice, is not bravery—sustaining your President right or wrong, is not prudence—to abandon your wives and children 'during the war' is not affection—to desire to kill a distant people who are fighting for their country, their homes and their firesides, is unchristian.*

"BEWARE, THAT THE WICKEDNESS OF THE RULERS DOES NOT FALL UPON THE PEOPLE!"

The Patriot of the same day endorsed this communication in the following editorial article:

"We admire the straight forward honesty and boldness of the annexed communication. Its sentiments are those of the bluff candid citizen, unhackneyed in the paths of political trickery, who has no faculty to perceive how that which is morally wrong can be metamorphosed into political righteousness. The burlesque appeal, which it contains, to the Democrats, is perhaps too tart and sarcastic—especially as to those among them who have been deceived and who honestly disapprove of Mr. Polk's war measure; but for those who yet approve—let them take it! Let the fearful responsibility of treasure and of blood rest where it belongs— upon the shoulders of Mr. Polk and approving friends!"

Although the Democratic counties of Edgecombe, Martin, Caswell, Rockingham, Wayne, Mecklenburg, and Stokes, were taunted in this communication, yet, when the hour of trial came, they were not found wanting. They nobly volunteered their services, thereby showing that their Democracy is not of that kind which flinches in the hour of their country's need. Opposition to this war has not been confined to North Carolina alone. It has been denounced on the floor of Congress as "unholy, unrighteous, and damnable." The New York Tribune, a leading Whig paper, uses the following language in regard to the war:

"WHAT MEANS THIS WAR?—The House of Representatives has virtually declared war against Mexico. What is implied in that?

"It means that, so far as our Government can effect it, the laws of heaven are suspended, and those of hell established in their stead. It means that the commandments are to be read and obeyed by our people thus: Thou *shalt* kill Mexicans; thou *shalt* steal from them, hate them, burn their houses, ravage their fields, and fire red-hot cannon balls into towns swarming with their wives and children. It means that we are to stop producing food, clothing, and comforts, and turn to making swords, bullets, chain-shots, shells, and all the devilish enginery of human carnage. It means that we are to exhaust our treasury, multiply taxes, incur public debts, and mortgage the sweat and blood of honest labor for untold years to come. It means security, quiet, and gladness, are to be driven from earth and ocean, and their places usurped by butchery, rape, devastation, and horror. It means that improvement is to be arrested, the blessed arts of peace neglected, and the world recede toward the midnight of barbarism."

The State Journal, a leading Whig paper in Ohio, adopts the following language in condemning the war:

"Mr. Polk and his advisers, *who have brought this war upon us*, begin to report of the *madness and folly* that have characterized their proceeding. They are anxious to throw upon Mexico the responsibility of bringing about the war. They would represent our Government as kind and forbearing, under long-continued provocations and agressions. They would proclaim Mexico the agressor, and charge upon her the butchery of American citizens on American soil."

"The Whigs were willing, to a man, to vote means to defend our soil, and rescue our gallant army, endangered by the WEAKNESS AND WICKEDNESS OF THE PRESIDENT, but they were not willing to expose the country to all the horrors of a protracted war by declaring the war already commenced, when they had received no official notice that the war-making power of Mexico had authorized an assault. If the blood of gallant men is to be spilled; if the treasury is to be impoverished, our vessels plundered and scuttled, and their crews butchered; if our coast is to be exposed, and the nation made to feel the horrors of war; they wished the country to remember who brought about these things."

Governor Bebb[1] of Ohio, who is a Whig, in his inaugural, says:

"And how with the Constitution of the United States in our hands, proclaiming that Congress alone shall have power to declare war, can we behold a President of the United States trample that sacred instrument in the dust, deliberately, and without the advice of Congress, then in session, involve the country in a foreign war of conquest, and yet not dare give utterance to our indignant condemnation of his unconstitutional acts? Where is the man who does not know and feel that this Mexican war is a *Presidential* war;—a war which, before its commencement, Congress would not have declared?—a war begun without adequate cause, and without any great, justifiable, and commensurate object, compatible with the interests and integrity of the Union."

These are only a few of the many instances in which the war has been denounced and bitterly assailed, by Whig presses and Whig politicians. Strange and unnatural as such sentiments may appear, yet they are not without precedent. During the last war, kindred sentiments and similar denunciations came from the Federal party. Persons were violently abused, even for loaning their money to the Government, to enable it to prosecute the war. I will give a few examples to show the bitterness with which the Federal party of that day opposed the war of 1812:

"It is very grateful to find that the universal sentiment is, that any man who lends his money to the Government at the present time will forfeit all claim to common honesty and common courtesy among all true friends to the country. God forbid that any Federalist should ever hold up his hand to pay Federalists for money lent to the present rulers; and Federalists can judge whether Democrats will tax their constituents to pay interest to Federalists."—*Boston Gazette, April* 14, 1814.

"No peace will ever be made till the people say there shall be no war. If the rich men continue to furnish money, war will continue till the mountains are melted with blood—till every field in America is white with the bones of the people."—*Discourse delivered at Byfield, April* 7, 1814, *by Elijah Parish, D.D.*

"Give ear no longer to the syren voice of Democracy and Jeffersonian liberty. It is a cursed delusion, adopted by traitors, and recommended by sycophants. Jefferson—a man who, with the dagger of public confidence, first gave the stab to your liberties."—*Extract from a circular handbill, published at Newburyport.*

"Let no considerations whatever, my brethren, deter you, at all times, and in all places, from execrating the present war. It is a war unjust, foolish, and ruinous. It is unjust, because Great Britain has offered us every concession short of what she conceives would be her ruin. AS MR. MADISON HAS DECLARED THE WAR, LET MR. MADISON CARRY IT ON.;"—*Discourse of Rev. J. S. J. Gardiner, Rector of Trinity Church, Boston, July* 23, 1812.

"If, at the command of weak or wicked rulers, they undertake an unjust war, each man who volunteers his services in such a cause, or loans his money for its support, or by his conversations, his writings, or any other mode of influence, encourages its prosecution, that man is an accomplice in the wickedness, loads his conscience with the blackest crimes, brings the guilt of blood upon his soul, and in the sight of God and his law, is a murderer."—*Discourse of the Rev. David Osgood, delivered June* 27, 1812.

A report of the Massachusetts Legislature in 1814, declared that "the war, so fertile in calamities, was waged with the worse possible views, and carried on in the worse possible manner, forming a union of weakness and wickedness which defies for a parallel the annals of the world." It is unnecessary to trace the parallel further between the Federalists during the last war and the Whigs who oppose the present war. Public sentiment has long since consigned the opposers of the last war to the condemnation they justly deserved; and the day is not far distant when the opponents of the *present war* will share the same fate.

No one can dread the consequences resulting from war more than myself, nor would any one more highly appreciate the blessings of peace; but with all my love of peace, I can never consent that the rights and honor of my country shall be compromitted [*sic*], and that a foreign nation shall invade our territory, and murder our citizens, without repelling the aggression as becomes a great and free people. Believing Mexico to be in the wrong, and my own country to be in the right, I voted for such supplies of men and money as were deemed necessary to enable the Executive to prosecute the war to an honorable termination. As an encouragement to our soldiers, we passed an act giving to each one who volunteered for five years or during the war, one hundred and sixty acres of bounty land. In voting to sustain the war, I believed I was *acting right*, and at the same time *executing the will of my constitutents*. If, in this, I was mistaken, I have only to say, that while I hold a public trust, I never will refuse to raise men to defend my country against the attacks of a foreign enemy, nor will I refuse to vote to raise money to feed and clothe our soldiers while they are exposing their lives in defence of the rights and honor of our country. Were I to refuse to vote for such supplies I should feel that I had not only forfeited the confidence of my constituents, but also my claim to the name of a citizen of this Republic.

The battles of Pala Alto, Resaca de la Palma, Monterey, and Buena Vista, have shown our soldiers to be worthy of their country. Their daring deeds and invincible courage will teach other nations that our rights are not be assailed with impunity; and their brilliant victories and gallant achievements will have an imperishable place in the memory of their grateful countrymen.

The limits of this circular will not permit me to allude to many other subjects which were acted on during the last Congress. Upon all of these questions I have voted in such a way as I believed best calculated to promote the welfare of the country, and at the same time in accordance with the principles upon which I was elected. By the act of the last Legislature, re-districting the State, I am precluded from being again elected from the district I have heretofore represented. Of this unprecedented act of the Legislature, it is not my purpose now to speak. Being thrown into a district which contains an overwhelming Whig majority, I am spared the necessity of saying whether I would or would not accept a reelection to Congress. To be separated from any portion of a constituency like mine, who have supported me under the most trying circumstances, and have shown me so many acts of kindness, is to me a matter of deep regret. But so far as a seat in Congress is concerned, I can in truth say, that I can part with it with but one regret; and that is, that I have not possessed the ability to discharge in a more satisfactory manner to myself the responsible trust confided to me as your Representative. The relation which has existed between us for the last four years is, by the act of the Legislature, severed and dissolved; yet it is a high consolation to me to know that I have not been legislated out of the *confidence* of my constituents. Although divided into three districts, we shall remain united in feeling, and stand ready to use our exertions to maintain and perpetuate our free institutions.

This address has been delayed in consequence of severe indisposition, which has kept me confined in Washington since the adjournment of Congress, and even now I feel too feeble to write, but I am rapidly regaining my strength, and hope to be able to set out for home in a few days.

In taking my leave of you to resume my place in private life, I avail myself of this occasion, as it may be the last that may offer, to tender to you my profound acknowledgements for the generous confidence you have reposed in me. Your many acts of kindness and friendship towards me, are appreciated, and shall be gratefully remembered to the latest period of my life. I hope that Providence may avert every impending evil, and restore an honorable peace to the country, and give to each of you prosperity and happiness.

---

[1]William Bebb (1802-1873), a Rockford, Ohio, attorney, was Whig governor of Ohio from 1846 to 1849. During his administration the legislature passed a resolution that condemned the war and the leadership of President Polk. Robert Sobel and John Raimo (eds.), *Biographical Directory of the Governors of the United States, 1789-1978* (Westport, Conn.: Meckler Books, 4 volumes, 1978), III, 1204, hereinafter cited as Sobel and Raimo, *Biographical Directory of Governors*.

James Phelps to David S. Reid A&H-DSR

Essex Conn
April 15th 1847

I received a few days since, under your official frank a copy of your Circular to your Constituents, and since that, I have the pleasure to acknowledge the receipt of the Rep of the Com on Foreign Relations, upon the subject of the War with Mexico—I am of course highly gratified to receive these additional testimonials of your remembrance, and regard. The spirit of friendship & esteem in which they have their origin, is gratefully appreciated, and treasured up with feelings of the amplest reciprocity—

I am disappointed and chagrined, at learning through the medium of your able circular, that the Legislature of North Carolina has piratically deprived you of the prospect, or possibility, of again serving your constituents by a separation or transposition of the Counties comprising your district, in such a manner, as to change its political character, and hitch it to the Car of Federalism, so long at least, as the present dominant party retains the ascendency in the State—This act of partisan legislative usurpation, while it robs your constituents of the honorable exertion of an esteemed and faithful representative, has not indeed, defrauded you of their "confidence" and good opinion. This valuable possession, which I know it has long been your fortune to enjoy, is not within the reach of political ambition, chicanery or malevolence—Rank & station may be lost and gained, amid the political changes and revolutions incident to civil government, but the attachment and respect of friends, if sincerely cherished are not changed with them—Honor, love, obedience, troops of friends, where acquired by integrity and merit, are not suffered to be swept away in the fierce strife of contending principles and parties—They remain a consolation and a blessing in adversity and defeat—The election in this State as you are aware, has gone against us, and against the country—The issue was fully understood to hinge upon the justice of the war, and the propriety of vindicating upon the battle field, the rights and honour of the republic, against every species of outrage, crime & violation of good faith, which one government could possibly perpetrate upon another, through a long continued and uninterrupted career of perfidy and aggression—The democratic party without division, espoused with ardor the only American side of the question, and yet we were defeated—

The truth is, the Hartford Convention[1] spirit of the last war is still brooding over New England, and appears to find something there, so, congenial to its nature that it can probably never be entirely eradicated—The federal party are the same now, as then, and all human influences would prove entirely impotent, in an attempt to so transform them, as that they would not intentionally & naturally commit the crime of treason against this country, whenever it should unfortunately become involved in war, however just, necessary, or defensive— This is their real character, "rooted and grounded" in them, and must inevitably produce its legitimate results—

We are looking with confidence to Virginia. the "mother of Presidents & statesmen" and the nursery of revolutionary patriotism, for a different account—I am strongly encouraged by my good opinion of Southern character, chivalry, patriotism, & honor, generally to believe that in Virginia & elsewhere the policy of the Administration especially in reference to the war, will be strongly sustained, and treason and its abettors receive a just rebuke.—If it shall be so my soul, will leap with pride and exaltation in recognition of the fact, that the *whole* of our glorious Union is not degraded by the foul contamination, which has set its damning seal upon Connecticut—Under such circumstances, I could without regret, turn my back upon the free, proud, populous, flourishing & powerful North, the place of my nativity, the home of my connexions and the graves of my fathers, and choose my habitation in the honest, patriotic, chivalrous, warm hearted, hospitable and republican South—even though it had faults of a grave character—We at the North generally, unfortunately regard your system of bondage, viewed as an abstract question of human rights—and a small portion of us, unqualifiedly condemn everything identified with slavery—This is entirely erroneous, unreasonable, and absurd, and countenanced but by very few among us—My own views with regard to the South, its institutions, and its interest, are extremely liberal—I know something of her people their manners, customs, motives, and character, and I know that God's image no where exists nobler, or more perfect—Yet, I could wish, *for her own sake*, as well as for the name of freedom, that she might be rid of slavery—But place the bloodiest most brutal and degrading garb upon the institution, for which insane and fanatical abilitionism contend—acknowledge the tardiness of the South in agricultural, mechanical, manufacturing, commercial & common educational improvement & reform compared with the North, and at the same time be able to shield me from the sinking [*sic*] odium of participating in a treasonable opposition to the union in time of war, and from the imputation of "rendering aid and comfort to the enemy" and she stands an infinitely more honourable spectacle before the world, than her boasting traitorous, ally of the North—An individual cannot among honest men, long enjoy an enviable reputation, however exalted his rank, and talent, if he is destitute of the ordinary emotions of patriotism—It is what makes the freeman—So in government—It is the vital principle of liberty—the highest, noblest, attribute of genuine republicanism. Despotisms and Monarchies, can exist without it—indeed it is antagonistical to their nature; but it is the life blood of republics; the sublime characteristic of free, enlightened, popular Sovereignty—They can no more be separated, and the true genius of freedom preserved, than the glorious Sun be stricken from the heavens, and light & heat, generated by the Earth—The one is as anomalous, and utterly subversive of the principles of political—as would be the other, strange, and repugnant to the demonstrable truths, and axioms of natural science.—

I earnestly hope when this reaches you, it will find you completely restored in health—I can not believe you will not return to Congress, but if you do not may prosperity, happiness, and long life attend you—Would to God I could see you, but will it ever be? When shall I hear from you? Remember me most respectfully to your family, and be assured that I still remain, Truly & sincerely Your Friend

---

[1]The Hartford Convention was a meeting at Hartford, Connecticut, of twenty-six New England Federalists who felt that New England was unduly suffering because of the War of 1812, westward expansion, and commercial restrictions. Dominated by moderates, the convention was called by the Massachusetts legislature and included delegates from Massachusetts, Connecticut, Rhode Island, Vermont, and New Hampshire. It lasted from December 15, 1814, to January 5, 1815. Meeting in secret sessions, the delegates recommended interstate military and federal financial aid for defending their states against the British; protection from unconstitutional conscription; and limitations on southern political power, commercial embargoes and trade restrictions, declarations of war, admission of new states into the Union, and officeholding by naturalized citizens. The convention adjourned with the intention of reconvening in six months. However the delegates were forced to abandon their efforts in the face of public ridicule brought on by the immediate end of the war and the secrecy in which the meetings had been held. Opponents of the convention went so far as to accuse the delegates of conspiracy and treason. Wayne Andrews, *Concise Dictionary of American History* (New York: Charles Scribner's Sons, 1962), 422, hereinafter cited as Andrews, *Concise Dictionary of American History*.

John Hill Wheeler to David S. Reid A&H-DSR

Beattiesford NC
19th Apr '47

I learned from Mr James Graham[1] who stopped at my House on his return from Congress with great pain your dangerous illness at Washg; with unaffected sincerity I prayed that your life might be preserved, for future good & usefulness and I rejoice sincerely that you are again restored to health, to home, and friends.

I received last mail your circular to your constituents. The plain detail of grievances that our nation has received from Mexico will do much good. It will prove that had Texas never been annexed, an appeal to arms would have been rendered unavoidable, had our nation been true to herself, her honour and to justice; and it puts to flight the idea that the position of our troops at Rio Grande was the cause of war. The severe rebuke it gives Gov. Graham and his allies in "giving aid & comfort" to our enemies and proving by history, the close analogy between the former course of the federalist during the War of '12 and the course of the present Whig party, cannot fail to do us much good in the State. Be pleased to Send me a few copies, if you have some to spare, I think that I can make them tell. In this part of our State, the frosts and snows of winter are gone, and the heat of politics begins to move the waters. In a letter from Buncombe Judge Dick last week informs me that Clingman is already on the stump, so is Genl Bynum,[2] two or three others will run. Our friend Graham with his characteristic caution has not yet come out. Bynum takes ground *for the War*, and sustains the President. If he is discreet, and sober, this will cause some trouble; as it must rally the Demos around him. Some idea was intertained that Avery[3] would run; but Judge Dick thought not. I go tomorrow to Catawba Superior Court, where I shall learn more of these movements. So much for politics & the public. To one who is so kind a friend, it may not be uninteresting to hear that I reached home safely in about a week after I left you, and embosomed in the quiet joys of "wife children & friends" I have not been but once from home, since I arrived, and that time only by necessity (as Comr. to receive the Pubic Buildings of Catawba)—Mrs. W.[4] or Ellen as I call her expresses great curiosity to see *Col R* You know my communicative temper and we often laugh over my descriptions of our frequent little *tete* a *tetes* at Washg, and she wishes to know the gentleman who as Col Townes[5] says is, so popular at Washg. that "the whole ward belonged to him"—I hope that some day or other she will have that pleasure. We have fresh fish every day and a plenty of hooks and lines. She admires my clothes & thanks you for them.

Much as I love home, I am obliged to leave again for a few weeks, on a call of honour. Not to meet Guion at Gaston[6] or So. Ca. or to "Scare the soul of any frightened adversary"—but last mail brought me a note from the wife of Judge Saunders who commences her note by "the flattering unction" that I am *the only man* who without hesitation or gainsay that she can call upon to do her kindness, and that I must accompany her next week to New York & see her safe on board of the Havre packet of the 5th prox! What could I do? Why I could but say, by to day mail, that I should serve her; and that my life was occasionally blesst with opportunities of making others satisfied & happy. While at Raleigh I was almost an inmate of the family—& my wife says that I ought not to hestitate; altho' she thinks that there are some at Raleigh who should have discharged this duty. I mention this, more to show you that if your reply is delayed from this point, that you will know the reason. You can however reply to this directed to Washington City where I shall be on the 1st en route for New York & shall return home as fast [as] steam cars and stages can bring me.

By this unexpected movement, I miss the great Convention at Charlotte on 27th inst. for a Rail Rd to Camden—to which I was appointed a delegate. I shall however submit my views *in writing* as from Knox Walker[7] reports at the Senate. If you write to Washg direct it "care of Revd. OB. Brown[8] and you can aid me in respect to a young friend Junius B. Wheeler[9] now 18 years old, tall (5 feet 7) a native of NC intelligent & active, has been prepared for college. He is my ward & Brother. His mind has become inflamed with a desire for military fame, & has got Maj Henry W. Conner[10] & others to recommend him as a 2d. Leutenant in the 12th Regt. Infantry. He has offered his services to Capt. Clarke as a *private* which shows his determination, & Clarke has expressed his pleasure at this. So far as I am concerned I should prefer his going to college but he is old enough to judge for himself. Be so good as to enclose to me an expression of your wishes to Washg. in a letter to the Prest.

Our friend Tate[11] at Asheville, Judge Dick is very attentive & gives much satisfaction.

Let me hear from you at Washg

---

[1]James Graham (1793-1851), an attorney from Rutherfordton, was a member of the House of Commons (1822-1824, 1828-1829), and a representative in Congress (1833-1843, 1845-1847). *Biographical Directory of Congress*, 964.

[2]John Gray Bynum (1813-1857), an attorney from Rutherfordton, became a major general of the Fourth Division of the state militia in 1844. He served in the state Senate (1840, 1850, 1852) and the House of Commons (1854). He was a trustee of the University of North Carolina (1854-1857). Clarence W. Griffin, *History of Old Tryon and Rutherford Counties North Carolina 1730-1936* (Spartanburg: The Reprint Company, reprint edition, 1977), 227, hereinafter cited as Griffin, *Old Tryon and Rutherford*.

[3]William Waightstill Avery (1816-1864), an attorney from Burke County, was a member of the House of Commons (1842-1843, 1850-1852) and the state Senate (1856, 1860), serving as speaker in 1856. He was a member of the provisional Confederate Congress (1861-1862). He was killed during the Civil War in a skirmish with Union marauders led by Colonel George Kirk. *DAB*, I, 445-446; Cheney, *North Carolina Government*, 323, 1073-1074.

[4]Ellen Oldmixon Sully Wheeler (1816-1896), Wheeler's second wife, was a daughter of Thomas Sully, the noted portraitist from Philadelphia. Wheeler, *Reminiscences*, x; George C. Groce and David H. Wallace, *The New-York Historical Society's Dictionary of Artists in America, 1564-1860* (New Haven: Yale University Press, 1957), 614.

[5]This is possibly George Washington Bonaparte Towns (1801-1854) from Georgia, who served as a representative in Congress (1835-1839, 1846-1847) and as governor of Georgia (1847-1851). *Biographical Directory of Congress*, 1723.

[6]A figurative reference to dueling. Antebellum affairs of honor were frequently conducted near Gaston on the banks of the Roanoke River near the Virginia state line, or near the South Carolina line.

[7]James Knox Walker was a nephew of President James Knox Polk and served in Washington as his private secretary. He frequently carried written messages from the president to Capitol Hill for the Congress. Sellers, *Polk*, II, 190, 339.

[8]O. B. Brown, a minister from Georgetown, D.C., was the father of Wheeler's first wife, Mary Brown. Wheeler described her as being "one of the most accomplished and literary ladies of her day." Wheeler, *Reminiscences*, ix.

[9]Junius B. Wheeler (d. 1886) did volunteer as a private in Company I, Twelfth Regiment, United States Infantry; and by December, 1847, he was promoted to second lieutenant and transferred to the Eleventh Infantry. In 1851 he entered the United States Military Academy. Upon graduation in 1855 he joined the Second Cavalry, but within a year he became an engineer. During the Civil War he remained in the United States Army, eventually retiring with the rank of colonel in 1884. Wheeler, *Sketches*, 420; Jones, *Mexican War Roster*, 49.

[10]Henry W. Conner (1793-1866), a planter from Iredell and Lincoln counties, served as a major and aide-de-camp to General Joseph Graham in the campaign against the Creek nation in 1814. He was a representative in Congress (1821-1841) and a state senator (1848-1850). *Biographical Directory of Congress*, 730; Wheeler, *Sketches*, 82.

[11]Ezra M. Tate was postmaster of Asheville from 1847 to 1849. F. A. Sondley, *A History of Buncombe County, North Carolina* (Spartanburg: The Reprint Company, reprint edition, 1977), 800, hereinafter cited as Sondley, *Buncombe County*.

C. H. Brogden[1] *to David S. Reid* A&H-DSR

Falling Creek, Wayne County
April 20th, 1847.

I have the pleasure to acknowledge the receipt of a paphlet [*sic*] copy of your circular address to your constituents. It is the best document of the kind I have met with, and is, in my opinion, peculiarly suited to the times. The Whigs are *estopped* from controverting the unenviable position they occupy before the country in relation to the war; because, in the language of the good book, "out of their own mouths do they stand condemed." "He that is not for us, is against us," and he that is not for the country, is against the country. It is proved in your address, from the most incontestible *whig authorities*, that the Mexican War is violently condemed by the Whigs, and that they have justified the enemy ever since the first commencement of hostilities, notwithstanding the horrid massacres perpetrated on our countrymen long before the United States took up arms against perfidiou[s] Mexico. Those whigs who still oppose a vigorous and energetic prosecution of the war in order to bring it to a speedy termination, are doing greater injury to this country than if they were in *Mexico* in arms against the American forces. It is not to be disguised that in the present dangerous emergency of our country, there are some whose overheated ambition against the principles and policy of Mr. Polk's administration, are prompting them to a course portentous with evil to the destinies of their own country.

In their infatuated efforts to place their own country in the wrong, the urgent necessities of this country seem to be either entirely overlooked by them, or very improperly and strangely disregarded, in the wholly unjustifiable pursuit of a course well calculated to paralyze their own government. Nothing can contribute more effectually to enfeeble the arm of our government than the dangerous heresy, so illiberally propagated by the Whigs, that the war in which we are now engaged is unconstitutional and unjust.

When the calamities of a ruthless war are hovering over our country the concurrent energies of all parties are required to prosecute it to a successful termination. But there are those who are disposed to retard the action of our government, and to interpose every possible obstacle in the way of its efforts to accomplish this desirable object. They do not even occupy a neutral position in the present critical emergancy of our country; but, actuated by the settled and obvious purpose of avenging their malice against the Republican party, they are pursuing a course which must inevitably encourage the enemy. I discovered from the proceedings of the last session of Congress that Mr. Webster submitted resolutions, in the Senate, declaring that the existing war with Mexico ought not to be prosecuted for the acquisition of territory to form new states to be added to this Union.

This proposition of Mr. Webster is in perfect accordance with the doctrine avowed by the Whigs in the last State Legislature, that the war with Mexico was a war of *aggression and plunder*, made under the pretence of extending the "area of freedom." *The "Mexican Preamble"* attached to the appropriation[2] made at the last session of the Legislature, in aid of the Volunteer Regiment from this State, has placed North Carolina in an untrue position in regard to the war. But that infamous preamble was forced over the heads of the minority notwithstanding all our efforts to wipe out that foul stigma upon the State. For the favor you conferred by sending me a copy of your circular, be pleased to accept the assurance of my regard.

---

[1]Curtis Hooks Brogden (1816-1901), a Wayne County farmer, was a member of the House of Commons (1838-1851, 1886-1888) and the state Senate (1852-1856). During the 1852 gubernatorial campaign he was a major supporter of David S. Reid and was caricatured in one Whig newspaper's parody of a Democratic party election celebration: "Corporal Curtis H. Brogden, of Wayne, is hereby authorized to act as eleventh assistant Marshal. It is thought by the Governor and his council, that this individual will look best in the Georgia uniform, which is said to be nothing more than a shirt collar and a pair of spurs. But for decency's sake, he is advised to procure a large sash of orange colored cambric to cover some of the greatest of his deformities—upon which he must have inscribed in German black letter, this Resolution: 'Resolved, That the committe on constitutional Reform be requested to inquire into the expediency of so amending the constitution of the State as to allow the people to elect a Lieutenant Governor, Comptroller, Treasurer, and every and all the officers now known or that may ever hereafter be known to the State, by the people at the ballot box. What constitutes a State? Not high raised battlements or labored mound, thick walls or moated gates; not cities proud with spires of beauty crowned; nor bays or broad armed ports, where laughing at the storm rich navies ride; nor starred or spangled *courts*, where low-browed baseness wafts perfume to pride;—No men, high-minded men; these constitute a State.'" [Hidden within the resolution are allusions to the names of various Democratic party functionaries.] Brogden served as comptroller of the state from 1857 to 1867. After the Civil War he left the Democratic party to become a Republican, serving in the state Senate (1868-1872), as lieutenant governor (1872-1874), and as governor (1874-1877) on the death of Tod R. Caldwell. He served as a representative in Congress from 1877 to 1879, where he advocated pensions for Mexican War veterans. Powell, *DNCB*, I, 601; *Raleigh Times*, July 9, 1852.

[2]John R. Gilliam had introduced a resolution to appropriate $10,000 to help pay expenses for volunteer troops. The preamble to which Brogden objected began "Whereas, by the action of the Executive and the subsequent action of Congress, this Republic is involved in a foreign war. . . ." Hamilton and Williams, *Graham Papers*, III, 173n.

David S. Reid to James K. Polk LC-JKP

Reidsville, N.C,
April 26, 1847.

I promised to write you in relation to the time of the Commencement at the University of N.C.—It takes place on the first thursday in June. Great preparations are being made for your reception, and your friends will be delighted to see you there. *You ought to be sure not to disappoint them in this respect.*

I have regained my health and I feel like quite another man since my return among my native hills.

We have given your friend Judge Douglass a wife[1] in my county and he has just left for Illinois.

Please present my kindest regards to Mrs. Polk[2] and Miss Rucker,[3] and to Col. Walker & lady,[4] & accept the same for yourself.

---

[1]Martha Drennen Martin (1828-1853), the daughter of planter Robert Martin of Rockingham County, married Stephen A. Douglas of Illinois on April 7, 1847, in her home. The couple had met through the auspices of Reid, Martha Martin's cousin. Lindley S. Butler, "Robert Martin" (unpublished biographical sketch); Johannsen, *Douglas*, 207-208, 381-382.

[2]Sarah Childress Polk was married to James K. Polk on January 1, 1824. Sellers, *Polk*, I, 74-76, 92-93.

[3]A reference either to Johanna Lucinda Rucker (1822-1856) or Sarah Polk Rucker (1825-1850), sisters, both of Murfreesboro, Tennessee, and nieces of Mrs. Polk, who spent much time in the White House when their aunt was First Lady. They were daughters of Dr. William Reed Rucker, a native of Lynchburg, Virginia, and his wife Susan Childress, Mrs. Polk's only sister. Sudie Rucker Wood (comp.), *The Rucker Family Genealogy* (Richmond: Old Dominion Press, 1932), 124, 125; Allan Nevins (ed.), *Polk: The Diary of a President 1845-1849* (New York: Capricorn Books, reprint edition, 1968), 235, hereinafter cited as Nevins, *Polk*.

[4]J. Knox Walker, previously identified, Polk's private secretary. Mrs. Walker, who was "strikingly beautiful," was Mrs. Polk's social aide. Nevins, *Polk*, 235; Sellers, *Polk*, II, 190, 301, 308, 339.

Martha Martin Douglas to Elizabeth G. Settle[1] RCC

Quincy, Ills.
3rd Sept. 1847

I expect you will be somewhat surprised at receiving a letter from me, & indeed I am myself astonished at opening a correspondence with you:—for you, who are at home, & have, comparatively, little to engage your attention, ought to write two letters to my one: Moreover, your letters could never be uninteresting to me, (as mine might be to you) coming as they would from the midst of a circle of friends, & from the vicinity of my former home. Indeed, I had almost forgotten that I had any friends in N. Carolina, until reminded of them by my dear Parents,[2] whom I had the pleasure of seeing about a week since. We went down to St. Louis to meet them, & they returned with us to this State:—& after paying us a short visit they left for Carolina. When they left home my Father did not intend to remain with us more than a week, but my Mother expected to stay until we started for Washington, & then join my Father at some convenient point & go with him to Mississippi;— father being compelled to go South this winter, (not having gone last year,) & it being impossible for my Mother to remain in the state alone for that length of time. Besides they would be nearer to me in Mi. than they would be were they to remain in Illinois. Though it gave me great pleasure to see them, yet it grieved me much to find my Father in such indifferent health. He became unwell in two or three days after leaving home, & continued quite indisposed until within a day of his departure from this place. This was the cause of Mother's returning with him; for she could not think of letting him take so long a journey alone & unwell.[3]

And now would you not like to know something of the place & country in which I am living? Well, we have been staying this summer in Quincy, a town, or rather city of near six thousand inhabitants, situated on a high bluff on the Mississippi one hundred & fifty miles above St. Louis. It is regularly laid out, with a public square in the centre, has fine side walks, many handsome shade trees, & is surrounded by one of the finest & most highly cultivated countries that the sun ever shone upon. Really the country, for four or five miles back of town, appears to me to be a perfect garden-spot. It is prairie, gently undulating, & is principally owned by first-class farmers. I must not forget to add that there are ten churches in Q.; so you may see that even in a moral point of view it will not suffer in comparison with the towns, of the same size, in the old states.

In the month of June we took a trip to the Falls of St. Anthony, the head of navigation on the Miss:, & I suppose it useless to add, that I was highly pleased. I will not attempt to give you a description of the "Falls" or of the country through which we passed; suffice it to say, that we had to travel some eight hundred miles before reaching the "Falls," through every variety of country, & every grade of civilization, from the refined "pale face" to the savage red man. We stopped at the principal places on the river long enough to take a stroll round, and look at every thing of consequence. We stopped at two or three *Indian Villages*, & I can now say that my curiosity with respect to that race of people, is now fully gratified. For I saw quite enough of the Indians in their wild untutored state. Since then we have travelled considerably thro' this State, & visited most of the important places in it.

We will leave this place in a few days, for Chicago, which, as you may know, is the largest town in Illinois. From thence we will go to

N. York, to visit Mrs. Granger,[4] Judge Douglas' Mother; & then on to N. Carolina to see my Parents. At that time, cousin Elizabeth, I hope to have the pleasure of seeing *you*. And may I not expect the pleasure of your company this winter, in Washington? I should be very much pleased to take you & your sisters on with us, as we go from Carolina directly on to W. I know you would be much pleased with a sojourn of a few weeks in that City, & I know you would have many friends there would do every thing in their power to render your time agreeable. Judge Douglas sends his kind regards & begs me to say to you that *he* would be much pleased to see you in W. this winter.

How are you all getting on in your part of the country? Do write to me soon & let me know how you are and what you employ yourself about. If you write before I see you, you must direct your letter to me at "*Manchester Centre, Ontario Cty: N. York*". I think I have written enough for one time & must now try & overcome the impetus that has been impelling me forward. I would thank you to remember me affectionately to all my relations; I need not mention them by name, for I feel that I like them all equally well; though I must confess that I am under greater obligations to "*Cousin Davie*"[5] than almost any one else. You will present my kindest regards with those of Judge D. to him. Tell uncle Josiah[6] that I will try & get him to move to this country for I think it would exactly suit him. Moreover, it would be a gratification to us to have him near us.

Tell Grand-Mother[7] that I think of her very often & wish to see her very much, & that she must go up & see my Mother on her return.

Kind respects, if you please to your parents & sisters, and brothers. I believe I have now gotten through with love, respects, regards etc. etc. and it only remains for me to say Good-bye.

---

[1]Elizabeth G. Settle (1842-1848) was a daughter of Thomas and Henrietta Graves Settle. Only five years old at the time this letter was written, she was Martha Martin Douglas's first cousin. Reese and Fisher, *Settle Family*, 676.

[2]Robert Martin, Jr., previously identified, and Mary Settle Martin (1798-1860), who was a sister of Thomas Settle. Mary Settle Martin was David S. Reid's aunt. Her will, dated Nov. 17, 1857, was probated in Rockingham County Court of August, 1860. It lists as legatees grandsons Robert Martin Douglas and Stephen A. Douglas [Jr.]. Executors were Richard A. Ellington and Thomas Settle [Jr.], and the will was witnessed by W. M. Ellington and David S. Reid. Reese and Fisher, *Settle Family*, 681; Will of Mary [Settle] Martin, Rockingham County Wills, Book C, 334.

[3]Robert Martin, Jr., died in Rockingham County on May 25, 1848. Reese and Fisher, *Settle Family*, 681.

[4]Sarah Fisk, of Brandon, Vermont, married Stephen Arnold Douglass, a physician, in 1811. He died in 1813, only a little more than two months after the birth of their son, Stephen, who as an adult spelled his surname with only one "s." In

November 1830 she was married to Gehazi Granger of Ontario County, New York, and was still living when her son died in 1861. Johannsen, *Douglas*, 6, 11, 873.

[5]This is a reference to David S. Reid's important role in bringing about Martha's marriage to Stephen A. Douglas.

[6]Josiah Settle (1799-1869), brother to Elizabeth's father and Martha's mother, later moved to Ohio. Reese and Fisher, *Settle Family*, 686.

[7]Rhoda Mullins Settle (1768-1852). Reese and Fisher, *Settle Family*, 347.

James Phelps to David S. Reid A&H-DSR

Essex Conn.
October 1st. 1847

I saw it announced while you was at Washington perhaps a year since, that yourself among others, had left your seat in Congress, and gone home to raise a Regiment for the war in Mexico. This announcement was made in the New York papers probably upon the authority of their correspondents at Washington, and no doubt orginated in some rumor at W. & perhaps in a serious contemplation of your own at that time indulged—The announcement however was ill founded and erroneous. We have just received intelligence, (which perhaps may not be confirmed) that the armistace entered into by the respective Commanders in Chief of the opposing armies has been terminated, in consequence of a failure to obtain just and satisfactory terms to constitute the basis of an equitable treaty between the two governments, and therefore a prosecution of the war is the inevitable consequence. If this is true, it is reasonable to conclude that additional requisitions will be made by the President upon, the States, or some of them, in which event I think North Carolina may be called upon to furnish one or more additional regiments for the service of the Country—This being the case I have regarded it as not very improbable that you might be the commander of one of them, being out of public employment, and perhaps somewhat ambitious to go to the rescue of the Country, and at the same time blend with the civic laurel, the chaplet of military and patriotic renown— This train of ideas and possibilities has occurred to me and I write this letter for the purpose of soliciting in such a realization of my speculations, a place in your staff, where I could in a humble measure share your privations, dangers, and as the case might be, triumphs and achievement—Under such circumstances, I should be willing to go, while at the same time, I am not sure that I am not altogether drawing my bow at random, inasmuch as the project may never have been entertained by you— There may yet be a place, & I trust there will, & if there is not, the course I have laid down may not be pursued, so that there are a thousand ways in which my fine spun plans may fail of consummation—Yet if it should transpire I would be highly gratified to become a soldier—Connecticut is a small state & far North, & therefore will in scarcely any event be called on for a Regt.

And now, what particular harm would there be in your writing me a letter informing me of what you have been, are, and are expecting to be doing, how you enjoy yourself in private life, and especially, the very interesting excuse you can have, for not answering the several letters I have written you within the last twelve month—I say very interesting, because I am deeply interested to know what it can be—I recollect, in perhaps the last communication I received from you, you regretted that I was married, because my letter writing would be terminated; rather assuming that correspondence and domestic life were entirely out of the question—Have you allowed this principle to apply to yourself? I have sometimes half suspected you had consummated the nuptial, or rather hymenial act, and thus cut yourself off from the intercourse of the rest of the race—This however I shall not settle down upon as a fixed fact, until I receive some confirmation of it—

I was very sorry to hear of your illness during the latter part of your life at Washington, and trust you are long since completely restored—I should be much pleased to hear of the health, happiness, & prosperity of your father's family, and desire you to express to them my warmest wishes in that behalf And now my dear Sir, accept for yourself, the high consideration and respect of an humble individual, who has long regarded you as a sincere friend—Please do me the favor to excuse the very great haste in which this is written, and believe me Truly your friend &c

---

William W. Holden to David S. Reid A&H-DSR

Raleigh,
Dec. 8, 1847.

Yours of the 26th was duly received. I was glad to hear from you, and was much pleased with the Resolutions of the Rockingham Meeting.[1] We shall expect you, by all means, at the Convention.

The general impression among our friends seems to be, that January, or even Feberary, would be too early March or April has been mentioned; and I find, on reference to the Almanac, that fewer Courts will be in session about the 1st of April than any month in the year. Besides, the weather will then be clear and favorable for travelling. The Whigs will probably hold their Convention early in Februy. We always lose by long campaigns. The adversary has full time to rally.—to [bring] out his cross road politicians and merchants—to circulate his documents and "revolutionary Circulars"—and to put his presses two to one to ours—fully to war &c. A short campaign—a Chapultepec fight is the sort for us.

I see that the Whigs are getting pestered already, since Rayner begged off, on account of sick head-ache. and his Arkansas farm! The Roanoke Republican of a late date, give it to Gales[2] in fine style, on account of his cold and *business-like* notice of Col. Joyner[3]; Dr. Hill,[4] of Brunswick, is understood to be anxious to run; Gen. Dudley's[5] "great firmness of purpose and strength of intellect" inclines him the same way; and to cap the climax, I see that a writer in the last Wilmington Commercial gravely brings forward the Hon. Richard Hines![6] But after all the quarrelling, and snarling, and scrambling for an office which they have only by a pitiful four thousand majority, they will settle down on some one, and support him with a savage determination.

We ought to make our Convention as imposing and as powerful as possible. Let us kindle the fire here by the aid of strong hands and stout hearts, and keep it burning until Federalism is consumed.

I see that the Whigs of the House have done the deed! Winthrop,[7] a Wilmot Provisoist is the Speaker. I have not seen the vote, but I presume all our Whig Delegation voted for him. His is a base betrayal of the South, but they will be sustained here by the Register, Badger Clique; and I verily believe these men would support, for the two highest officers in the land, Webster and Corwin.[8]

I have not as yet seen the Message,[9] but we shall probably get it to-day.

Mr. French,[10] the former Clerk, is said to have been reelected.

Let me hear from you soon, and let me know, *in confidence*, what our friends in Rockingham think of a National Convention and the Presidency. When I get more time I will write you at length on this subject

---

[1]Reid presided at the Democratic party meeting held in Rockingham County, at the courthouse at Wentworth, on November 25, 1847. *North-Carolina Standard*, December 8, 1847.

[2]Seaton Gales, previously identified.

[3]Andrew Joyner, a leading Whig from Halifax County, was a state senator from 1835 to 1852, serving as speaker from 1838 to 1841. He was a trustee of the University of North Carolina from 1836 to 1856. Cheney, *North Carolina Government*, 308-309, 1150; Battle, *History of the University*, I, 824.

[4]Frederick Jones Hill, a physician from Brunswick County, was a member of the state Senate (1835), the House of Commons (1836-1841), and the Constitutional Convention of 1835. Cheney, *North Carolina Government*, 817, 1061-1062; Battle, *History of the University*, I, 824.

[5]Edward Bishop Dudley, previously identified.

[6]Richard Hines (d. 1851), a Raleigh attorney, was a member of the House of Commons in 1824 and a representative in Congress from 1825 to 1827. *Biographical Directory of Congress*, 1058.

[7]Robert C. Winthrop (1809-1894), an attorney from Boston, was a state legislator, a representative in Congress (1840-1850), speaker of the House (1847-1849), and a United States senator (1850-1851). *Biographical Directory of Congress*, 1838.

[8]Thomas Corwin (1794-1865), an attorney from Lebanon, Ohio, was a state legislator, a Whig representative to Congress (1831-1840), governor of Ohio (1840-1842), a United States senator (1845-1850), secretary of the treasury (1850-1853), a Republican congressman (1859-1861), and minister to Mexico (1861-1864). *Biographical Directory of Congress*, 740.

[9]It has not been possible to identify this newspaper. There was no paper called the *Message* being published in Washington, D.C., or in North Carolina in 1847. Wescott and Ramage, *Duke Newspaper Checklist*; H. G. Jones and Julius H. Avant, *Union List of North Carolina Newspapers 1751-1900* (Raleigh: State Department of Archives and History, 1963), hereinafter cited as Jones and Avant, *Union List of North Carolina Newspapers*.

[10]Benjamin B. French of New Hampshire was elected clerk of the House January 18, 1845, for the second session of the Twenty-Eighth Congress and reelected clerk on December 2, 1845, for the entire Twenty-Ninth Congress, March 4, 1845-March 3, 1847. Holden was mistaken regarding his reelection to the House clerkship. On December 8, 1847, Thomas J. Campbell of Tennessee was elected clerk of the House for the first session of the Thirtieth Congress. *Biographical Directory of Congress*, 137, 141, 145.

1848

Patrick M. Henry[1] *to David S. Reid* A&H-DSR

Saltillo, Mexico
January 31st 1848

I take the liberty of forwarding to you to day the Descriptive Rolls of all the deceased men of my company from Rockingham as well as that of Corporal Bouldin.[2] I hope you can find it convenient to become administrator for the whole, and if so I hope you will proceed immediately to procure for their heirs &c. the Bounties of the Government. *Col. Hancock,*[3] it seems, has become administrator of *Alexis Newnum,*[4] and it may therefore be necessary that you should hand over to him the Descriptive Roll of said Soldier. However, Sir, I hope you will undertake the management of the whole and that by immediate application you may be enabled to relieve some of the indigent families of the unfortunate men who have sacrificed their lives here.&c. The "Descriptive Roll and Clothing account" is the only paper that the Captain can afford, and through that the Admr. will find no difficulty—in obtaining the *Land Warrent* or *Treasury Scrip* as well as all other dues from the proper Sources in Washington &c. Poor *Bob* Wilson[5] is at last dead after having lingered out a tiresome existence. You will discover that I have lost some excellent men. I brought to Brazos some 94 men, yet by death, transfer, & discharge, my company is now reduced to 61 aggregate. *Richd Fitzgerald*[6] has also been brought up before a Board of Surgeons and will be discharged in a day or two. We need Recruits, but do not expect them until the State, as well as the whole country, comes to understand properly the character of Col. Paine[7] as an efficient officer, *even* should he remain in the service longer than will be heard the decision of the "Court of Inquiry" instituted on the account of him & Genl. Wool,[8] and which convenes here today. Said Court is composed of Excellent Officers, and will beyond doubt give to the country the very best and fairest report of his whole conduct. Those Officers are Colonels *Temple*[9] & *Tibbatts*[10] (10th & 16th Infy.) and Majr Cass[11] (3d Drag.) with Capt. Prentiss[12] as *Judge Advocate.* I tell you, Sir, that the services & efficiency of this much abused man are now well appreciated here, for all those who were formerly bitter against him, are now loudest in his praises—having seen so very clearly the good results of his discipline by presenting here the most orderly and respectable Regiment in the Service. But more anon.

The health of my company is now good, there not being more than 5 men now on the sick Report. Your acquaintances are all quite well. Before concluding this hasty communication, I desire, Sir, to say a few words on a Subject of deep interest to me—I am anxious to adopt for future life the profession of Arms; and having been already in the service sufficiently long to gain the approbation of all superior Officers with whom I have been in any way connected, they have *generally* united in bringing before the President and War Dept. my claims to, and desire for an office in the Regular Military Establishment of the United States after the conclusion of the War, or in one of the New Regular Regiments that may be raised by the Present Congress. I have a small family whom I am anxious to elevate, and to support whom the pay of a Majority in the army would be all sufficient; and would be glad to succeed in getting as high a station as my friends think I may deserve. By this mail I address the Hon. A. H. Shepperd[13] on the subject, and request you also as a *personal* friend, (if you can do so compatibly with your feelings) to address a letter to the Dept. on my behalf, or to the President as I know you can do some thing for me.&c.

By complying with this request you will much oblige me. By this mail I send on the recommendations of Genl. Wool and all the officers of high rank here &c. I shall write you again, Sir, in a week or two. My Respects to all friends in your neighborhood &c.

---

[1]Patrick M. Henry, a grandson of Revolutionary leader Patrick Henry of Virginia, was from Leaksville and taught in the local academy. The elder Patrick Henry had secured interest in the "Land of Eden" tract of William Byrd; consequently, three generations of his descendants lived in Leaksville. Patrick M. Henry raised a volunteer company, which was mustered in the First North Carolina Regiment as Company G. Captain Henry commanded this company from January, 1847, until July, 1848. After the war he secured a civil clerkship in Washington and left Leaksville in February, 1849. Rockingham County Deeds, Book EE, 92; Church of the Epiphany, Eden, Record Book, 47, 255, 313, 376, 377; Jones, *Mexican War Roster*, 27; Hamilton and Williams, *Graham Papers*, III, 176-177, 273-275. The editor is indebted to George A. Atkins of Eden for notes from the records of the Church of the Epiphany.

[2]Corporal John F. Bouldin of Company G, First North Carolina Volunteers, died in Mexico. Jones, *Mexican War Roster*, 28.

[3]E. W. Hancock of Rockingham County was a lieutenant in Company G. Before the war he had been a militia colonel and an important local Democratic leader, serving as secretary of the party county committee and of the county convention. *North-Carolina Standard*, October 23, 1844, March 10, December 1, 1847.

[4]Alexis Newnam of Rockingham County, a private in Company G, died in Mexico. Jones, *Mexican War Roster*, 28.

[5]Robert Wilson, a private in Company G, is listed in the company roster as being discharged early. Jones, *Mexican War Roster*, 29.

[6]Richard Fitzgerald, a private in Company G, is listed in the company roster as being discharged early. Jones, *Mexican War Roster*, 29.

[7]Robert Treat Paine (1812-1872), an Edenton attorney, owned a shipyard. He served in the House of Commons (1838-1842, 1844-1849) and was appointed by Governor Graham as colonel commanding the North Carolina Regiment. A strict disciplinarian, Paine was unpopular, and at one point there was a near mutiny in the regiment. The regiment was assigned the thankless and boring task of guarding supplies in an unhealthy region, which led to low morale and a high rate of illness and death. Paine served on the Mexican Claims Commission, and from 1855 to 1857 he served a term in the United States House of Representatives. In 1860 he moved to Texas and became a planter. *Biographical Directory of Congress*, 1421; William S. Hoffman, *North Carolina in the Mexican War, 1846-1848* (Raleigh: State Department of Archives and History, 1969), 16-17, 20-21.

[8]John E. Wool (d. 1869) of New York began his military career as a captain in the Thirteenth Infantry in 1812. In 1816 he was promoted to colonel, and in 1841 he became brigadier general. As brevet major general he served under General Zachary Taylor in the Mexican War and was cited for gallantry at the Battle of Buena Vista. He retired as a major general in 1863. Heitman, *Historical Register and Dictionary of the Army*, I, 1059-1060.

[9]Robert E. Temple (1809-1854) of Vermont was colonel of the United States Tenth Infantry. A graduate of the United States Military Academy, he entered the army as a second lieutenant in 1828. After the war he was an attorney in Albany, New York. Heitman, *Historical Register and Dictionary of the Army*, I, 950; Hamilton and Williams, *Graham Papers*, III, 274n.

[10]John W. Tibbatts (d. 1852) of Kentucky was colonel of the United States Sixteenth Infantry. Heitman, *Historical Register and Dictionary of the Army*, I, 960.

[11]Lewis Cass, Jr., of Ohio was the son of Lewis Cass, a prominent national Democratic leader. The younger Cass was a major of the Third Dragoons. Heitman, *Historical Register and Dictionary of the Army*, I, 289.

[12]James H. Prentiss (d. 1848) of Massachusetts was an 1830 graduate of the United States Military Academy and began his army career in the artillery. By 1846 he had been promoted to captain. Heitman, *Historical Register and Dictionary of the Army*, I, 805.

[13]Augustine Henry Shepperd, previously identified.

Robert P. Dick[1] *to David S. Reid* A&H-DSR

Greensboro
April 16th-48

By this mail, you will receive a letter from a Committee of the Democratic State Convention, informing you, that it is the wish of that Convention, that you should be the Candidate for Governor at the ensuing election.—I am fully aware that this nomination, so far from being agreeable to you, will place you in an unpleasant situation.—I was on the Committee that made the nomination, and I told *them* what I believed to be your *views* and *wishes*, I was satisfied that you did not desire the nomination, that it would be a great inconvenience and sacrifice, for you to accept; but that I did not believe that you would decline if it was the opinion [of] your friends that the interests of the *party* required your services.— The Committee were so decidedly of the opinion, that you was the most available Candidate then before them, that they would listen to none of my objections.—I should like very much to see you occupy the high position of Governor of N Ca. but I deamed it to be my duty to you, to state what I believed to be your views and wishes—On motion of Mr Lane[2] of Wayne, seconded by Mr Bascum[3] of Warren, your name was unnanimiously voted for.— The Nomination seemed to give general satisfaction. I sincerely hope that you will accept, as I know that your acceptance is much desired

The Party was in high hopes of success, as the nomination of Mr Manly[4] is not a popular one

When I left Raleigh I expected to have met with you at Guilford Court, forgetting that you was not a Superior Court attendant.—Many of the leading members of Convention requested me to confer with you personally on the subject, which I promised to do.—If you conclude to decline the nomination, I should like to see you before you do so, as I should like to give you my views on the subject. I can give you many *facts* with which you are unacquainted.—Come up to Guilford Court if you possibly can.—I will be by your Father's on the Friday before Rockingham Court, if I do not see you before, when I will give you a full account of "matters and things."

And now in conclusion, in behalf of the *Party* I would say "*Col*! please accept!—

Present my kindest regard to your family and be yourself assured of my highest esteem

---

[1]Robert Paine Dick (1823-1898), a Greensboro attorney and son of John M. Dick, was an 1843 graduate of the University of North Carolina. He was a delegate to the constitutional conventions of 1861 and 1865, member of the Council of State (1862-1863), state senator (1864), superior court judge (1865), United States district court judge (1865-1868, 1872-1898), and state supreme court justice (1868-1872). *DAB*, V, 287-288.

[2]William K. Lane, a Wayne County planter, was a county justice and a local Democratic leader. He was president of the Council of State (1850-1851) and a member of the state Senate (1856-1863). Cheney, *North Carolina Government*, 178, 1301; Frank A. Daniels, *History of Wayne County: Address at the Opening of Wayne County's New Court House* (N.p.: N.p., 1914), 28, 30.

[3]George D. Baskerville of Warren was the person to whom Dick was referring. Baskerville, Dick, Lane, James B. Shepard, William S. Ashe, T. G. Richardson, Henry Clark, Dr. Thomas V. Roberts, Richard Jones, Samuel J. Person, Dr. D. A. Montgomery, William W. Holden, editor of the *North-Carolina Standard*, and William H. Bayne, editor of the Fayetteville *North Carolinian*, were members of a 13-man resolutions committee that presented Reid's name in nomination to the 1848 Democratic State Convention in Raleigh. *North Carolinian* (Fayetteville), April 15, 22, 1848, hereinafter cited as *North Carolinian*.

[4]Charles Manly (1795-1871) of Chatham County, an 1814 graduate of the University of North Carolina, became an attorney and moved to Raleigh. After serving several terms as assistant clerk of the House of Commons, he was chief clerk from 1830 to 1846. Running as a Whig he defeated Reid for governor in 1848 and served until 1851. He was on the state university board of trustees from 1821 to 1868. Ashe, *Biographical History*, VI, 349-356.

William B. Gulick[1] *to David S. Reid* A&H-DSR

Kinston N. C.
April 17th 1848

You have no doubt been informed ere this, that you were unanimously chosen as the candidate for the office of Governor at the recent Democratic State Convention. On behalf of the delegation from Craven county I am requested to say that they hope you will accept this nomination; I also add my hope that you will see proper to do so. I may also add that your nomination is acceptable to every Democrat, with whom I have conversed from this part of the state. I shall myself exert all the influence I can in your favor. I have for more than a year been the Editor of the Republican at Newbern. I shall be happy to hear from you and my columns are at your command.

I saw Wm. K. Lane yesterday. He says he will canvass this district with you. You could not possibly go under better auspices. He thinks that you should accompany Mr. Manly through the State. We hope to see you and make your acquaintance at Newbern on the 10th prox., that being the appointment of Manly at that place. Although now in the minority, yet with a cause such as ours, and with Mr. Manly as the Whig Candidate, I think we may reasonably hope for success. At least we will try. Please to communicate with me immediately so that I can make the proper announcements in reference to the Canvass. Direct Newbern N. C.

[1]William B. Gulick was from New Jersey and an 1844 graduate of Princeton University. He was editor of the Goldsboro *Patriot and Republican* and the New Bern *Republican* in 1847 and 1848. In 1848 he was secretary of the state Democratic committee. In the 1850s he was a government clerk and served as Reid's secretary for a time. Wheeler, *Sketches*, 115; *North-Carolina Standard*, April 19, 1848; Joseph Holt to David S. Reid, January 1, 1859, Reid Papers, PC 1, State Archives.

William W. Holden to David S. Reid A&H-DSR

Raleigh,
April 19. 1848

I suppose, of course, that the Committee to inform you of your nomination have written you, and that ere this you have received their letter. I have just received a letter from our mutual friend, Dobbin,[1] of Cumberland. He is much pleased at your nomination. He feels assured that you will "run well," and he says he will "take care of you" in his part of the State. About a month ago I received a letter from Col. Biggs[2] expressing his desire to see you nominated, and, in addition to this, I *know* that your nomination has given universal satisfaction to the party. You will start with no enemies and no prejudicies to encounter, and, if you follow Manly up and hold him to the issues, you will defeat him.

We had a most enthusiastic Convention. The speech of Douglas was the greatest popular effort I ever heard, and Houston[3] sustained himself well. The view taken by Douglas of the boundary question is *unanswerable*. Have you a copy of his late speech on the subject in the Senate? You will find it very valuable.

You will see by the Register that Mr. Manly has made his Eastern appointments, and is about starting on his campaign. Of course you will follow him up as soon as possible. Now is the time to visit the East. We hope to see you here at the earliest day possible, when we can talk the matter over, and you can make your arrangements more fully.

You have hard work, but a brilliant path before you. If you succeed, you will achieve a reputation second to that of no man in the State, and the Union will know you; if you fail, you will fail with honor, and elevate yourself in the estimation of your party.

[1]James Cochrane Dobbin, previously identified.

[2]Asa Biggs, previously identified.

[3]Samuel Houston (1793-1863) of Tennessee became a founder of the state of Texas. He enlisted in the army in 1813 as a private and rose to the rank of lieutenant. After the war he was an attorney and served as a representative in Congress (1823-1827) and as governor of Tennessee (1827-1829). He went to Texas by 1833 and was commander of the Texas army at its victory at San Jacinto. He was president of Texas (1836-1838, 1841-1844), in the Texas congress, a United States senator (1846-1859), and governor of Texas (1859-1861). Morris, *Encyclopedia of American History*, 730. Houston was well acquainted with Reid when they were colleagues in the Senate during the 1850s.

William B. Gulick to David S. Reid A&H-DSR

Newbern N.C.
May 30th 1848.

I arrived at home too late to write to you at Louisburg, so I embrace this opportunity to write you at Raleigh. Nothing of any particular importance has transpired here. Your speech at Washington made a good impression; I remained there the whole week and heard the suffrage question talked about considerably. I have no doubt it will get you many votes in that county.

"Cass & Butler".[1] This is truly a glorious ticket and must run like a breeze. The Whigs say their only chance is General Taylor and that is no chance at all. A better ticket could not have been selected. Upon them the whole country can unite. With them the principles of Democracy are safe. We can elect them without New York, and it would be greater glory if we could do it. But it would be the greatest glory could we sway the Old North with our Reid and seccure the state to the Democracy.[2]

We are all working away here doing what we can. If the Whigs bring out the ticket it is rumored they will in this county we will have to work and no mistake; but I think we can carry it anyhow.

How do you get along. I see that Manly is to meet you at Louisburg. I think he is in rather bad quarters there to do anything. The Whigs held a meeting in Beaufort Co on Tuesday night after you spoke, but could not agree on candidates on account of the divisions in the party. I hope they will increase. Mr. Stanly wants to run in the Commons, but there are other candidates who will not be ruled off.

Write to me from Raleigh if you have time and inform me how you are getting along and how your health is. By the way have you made any inquiries in reference to the investment of the capital of the State Bank in U.S. stock? It will be a most potent engine. We have circulated it a little and its effects will be felt. Money is scarce here, the State Bank is contracting its circulation, and it would seem as if Mr. Cameron[3] was endeavoring to create a pressure in order to influence the elections or for some other object.

---

[1]William Orlando Butler (1791-1880), an attorney from Carrollton, Kentucky, was a graduate of Transylvania University. He was an army captain during the War of 1812, finally serving as an aide to General Andrew Jackson. He was a representative in Congress from 1839 to 1843 and was appointed major general of volunteers in the Mexican War. He was a delegate to the Peace Conference in Washington in 1861. *Biographical Directory of Congress*, 641.

[2]Lewis Cass of Michigan and Butler were nominated for president and vice-president, respectively, at the Democratic Convention in Baltimore in May, 1848. There was a split during the convention, with the seceding faction, the Barnburners, holding their own convention at Utica, New York, in June and nominating Martin Van Buren of New York for president. Whig Zachary Taylor won the election by a narrow margin. Morris, *Encyclopedia of American History*, 208-209.

[3]Duncan Cameron (1777-1853), a Hillsboro attorney, was in the House of Commons (1802, 1806-1807, 1812-1813), in the state Senate (1819, 1822-1823), a superior court judge (1814-1816), a trustee of the state university (1802-1838), and president of the state bank (1829-1848). Lefler and Wager, *Orange County*, 325; Cheney, *North Carolina Government*, 1220-1221.

James C. Dobbin to David S. Reid A&H-DSR

Fayetteville
June 16th 1848

I received a few lines from you dated Raleigh informing me of your contemplated departure Westward on the ensuing day. From a notice in the Standard I perceive you desire your correspondents to address you at Raleigh to the care of Holden. I avail myself of that suggestion to drop you a few lines hoping they may reach you thundering away in the mountains in the righteous cause. A few days before your letters reached me I had called Baynes[1] attention to your "equal suffrage" question and in his last he takes strong ground for it with a complimentary notice of yourself. We had a large ratification meeting here—hope you may see the proceedings. It was enthusiastic in the highest degree Judge Strange[2] and myself addressed the meeting. It passed off in fine style. You were properly noticed in the Resolutions and you will allow me to say that it gave me pleasure to make a speech for *you* in which I told the people that each Democrat would be personally & politically criminal if he did not vote for David S. Reid. I assure you you will get the full party vote here & in the adjoining counties and your equal suffrage question may help to swell the number. I am glad you followed Manly to the West. That Region of our State will be benefitted by your visit. Mr Manly may entertain & amuse the crowd with his declamatory eloquence & his anecdotes. but you are pursuing the true course—expose the *scarcity* of his arguments, the absurdity of the few he advances and then bring home to the people in the plainest manner—the triumphant operation of the Tariff of 46—bringing in Millions more of revenue than that of 1842—vindicate the Mexican War & then hold the Whigs responsible for the doings of the last legislature. Cass & Butler makes a strong ticket. It must be omnipotent in the North West & West. Cass is not obnoxious on the slavery question—but deserves our support for his independence in voting against the "Wilmot proviso" His tour north looks favourable. He was accompanied by Benton[,] Allen, Cobb[3] & others & magnificently received everywhere. Benton's coming out so strong is an agreeable surprize to our friends every where and it may have an effect in New York.

Taylor & Fillmore[4] is another attempt at Harrison hard cider humbugging and nothing else.

You see they are going to send me to the legislature. I have no opposition & consented reluctantly but will be happy to defend your gubernatorial action in the legislature & hope we may meet there

What think you of the next Legislature? Cant we gain in Orange Person Franklin & Halifax & elsewhere enough to make it a Democratic Legislature, Write me, my dear Sir, and let me know particularly of your prospects. Mrs Dobbins health is wretchedly bad & makes me very gloomy. She takes however much interest in your election & my boys shout for Cass Butler & Reid. They wanted you to come here very much & they remember you with much affection. Write to me at some leisure moment.

---

[1]William H. Bayne from Georgetown, D.C., was editor of the Fayetteville *North Carolinian* for eleven years prior to his death on August 22, 1851. In 1843 he commanded the Fayetteville Riflemen. Wheeler, *Sketches*, 114; John A. Oates, *The Story of Fayetteville and the Upper Cape Fear* (Fayetteville: Fayetteville Woman's Club, second edition, 1972), 113, hereinafter cited as Oates, *Fayetteville*; *Newbernian*, September 2, 1851.

[2]Robert Strange, previously identified.

[3]Howell Cobb (1815-1868), an attorney from Athens, Georgia, was a representative in Congress (1843-1851, 1855-1857), speaker of the House, governor of Georgia (1851-1853), and secretary of the treasury (1857-1860). He played an important role in organizing the Confederate government in the Montgomery con-

vention in 1861 and became a Confederate major general by 1863. *Biographical Directory of Congress*, 711.

[4]Millard Fillmore (1800-1874), an attorney from Buffalo, New York, was a state legislator, a member of the United States House of Representatives, vice-president in 1849, and president from 1850 to 1853, succeeding Taylor. In 1856 he was an unsuccessful candidate for president, running for the American party. Morris, *Encyclopedia of American History*, 707.

William W. Holden to David S. Reid A&H-DSR

Raleigh,
June 23. 1848

I have sent papers to you at different points, and hope you have received them.

Col. Biggs and Judge Strange have been here for a week, in attendance on the Supreme Court. They are both in high spirits, and think your chances of the best character. Biggs says his part of the State shall be thoroughly organized, and that the largest vote possible will be polled for you. The Suffrage question is still working well. We continue to hear of changes in your favor, but none for Manly. In Chatham I learn that you will gain—in Johnston, Greene, Franklin, Granville, Orange, and I *know* in Wake. I am doing all I can. Busbee[1] and McRae[2] are *thoroughly aroused*, and will do their duty. The truth is, the enthusiasm is all on our side. the attempt of the Feds here to get up extra feeling for Taylor, will signally fail. If we can only elect you, the State is sure for Cass & Butler. I send this letter to Asheville, and enclose a letter from Mr. Dobbin, the only one I have as yet received for you. Please write me from Asheville, and let me know at what point to address you hereafter.

Rest assured that we will do our best for you here. If you continue to gain you will defeat Manly. God grant it!

Your friends here send their respects and best wishes. Go ahead! Hoping to hear from you soon, and wishing you good health and success I am Truly Your Friend.

[1]Perrin Busbee (1816-1853) graduated from the University of North Carolina in 1837 and for a time was a reporter for the state supreme court. In 1843 he and Duncan McRae founded the *Democratic Signal*, a Raleigh newspaper, but within five months the paper was sold to William W. Holden. Daniel L. Grant, *Alumni History of the University of North Carolina* (Chapel Hill: General Alumni Association, 1929), 89, hereinafter cited as Grant, *Alumni History*; *Democratic Signal* (Raleigh), passim, hereinafter cited as *Democratic Signal.*

[2]Duncan Kirkland McRae (1820-1888) of Fayetteville was the coeditor of the Raleigh *Democratic Signal*, with Perrin Busbee. McRae was in the House of Commons (1842-1843), served as the consul to Paris (1853-1857), and was a delegate to the Constitutional Convention of 1865. Although he was a Democrat, he unsuccessfully ran as an Independent against John W. Ellis for governor in 1858. During the Civil War he served as colonel of the Fifth Regiment North Carolina Troops, state purchasing agent in Europe, and editor of the *Daily Confederate* (Raleigh). *Democratic Signal*, passim; Cheney, *North Carolina Government*, 312, 832; Oates, *Fayetteville*, 548-549; *DAB*, XII, 164-165.

L[eland] Martin[1] *to David S. Reid* A&H-DSR

New Castle N.C.
June 30th / 48

As I promised to write you after making all posible enquiries, about Lenoir. I am now glad of the opportunity of doing so. The Whigs in Lenoir Say you will get the full Dem-vote of that county. The Dems though [scarce] say you will get more than the party vote. Dr. Thos Jones who lives in the vally of the Yadkin (a strong whig) says you will get many whig votes on a/c of the "suffrage question" which from all I can learn will opperate in your favor every where—I trust it may—for I fully concur with you as to its Justness & propriety.—Every thing that can be done in Wilkes will be done. I have just written to Jas H Parks[2] Allen Gentry[3] C H Doughten[4] Jas M Gentry[5] and intend writing to other of your friends as I promised you in Ashe Co.

The Whigs throughout this section of country admire you as a man & honorable political debater. I am inclined to think your chance for Election is Equally as flatering as Mr Manly; Judging from opinions of men of both Parties.

I am Sir, with much Respect your friend And Obt. Servant

---

[1]This is probably Leland Martin, who lived in Wilkes County in 1850. Seventh Census, 1850, Wilkes County, Population Schedule, 286. New Castle was a community in Wilkes County.

[2]James H. Parks lived in Ashe County in 1850. Seventh Census, 1850, Ashe County, Population Schedule, 239.

[3]Allen Gentry represented Wilkes County in the House of Commons from 1854 to 1859. Fletcher, *Ashe County*, 122-123.

[4]C. H. Doughton lived in Ashe County in 1850. Seventh Census, 1850, Ashe County, Population Schedule, 249.

[5]James M. Gentry represented Wilkes County in the House of Commons from 1860 to 1864 and was a trustee of Jefferson Academy in 1861. Fletcher, *Ashe County*, 123, 302.

E. G. Gray[1] to David S. Reid A&H-DSR

Hillsborough
26th July 1848

Your friends here are in fine Spirits—we are Sanguine of your election & calculate on carrying this County for the Democrats I do think our Senator is almost certain and least 2 Commoners, though we are not willing to compromise for less than the whole 5

If you tie Manly in Orange you are elected—As Orange goes so goes the State—Many of your friends wish that you could be here next Monday there will be a considerable crowd here to see Ramonds Menagerie—I see Mr. Manly will be at Shallowford on Tuesday & your friends are anxious that you should attend that gathering & then would it not be well for you to come here on Thursday—no doubt Manly will be here there will be an immense crowd here that day but if you come to Shallowford as your friends all hope you will you can consult with your friends about it

"Free Suffrage" will not hurt you in Orange—Although all the whig Candidates have come out against it—but in such a way as to induce many of the ignorant to believe that they would go further & admit nonfreeholders to be jurors. but they do this to bring "free suffrage" into ridicule and our democratic candidates have not pinned them down to the point *for*, or *against*. I am certain you have gained on the whigs in this county

The mail is about closing I have not time to write more

P.S. Squire Nichols[2] is weeding a wide row

Mr Kirkland[3] a whig merchant of Chapel Hill is going for you Strong

[1]Elisha G. Gray (born 1805), a native of Orange County, was an unmarried clerk who lived at Andrew and Mary Murdock's boarding house in Hillsborough in 1850. Seventh Census, 1850, Orange County, Population Schedule, 176.

[2]Richard Nichols, a leading citizen of Hillsborough, was a town commissioner from 1835 and magistrate of the town police in 1844 and 1845. Lefler and Wager, *Orange County*, 368.

[3]Joseph Kirkland (born 1817), an Orange County native, was a merchant in Chapel Hill in 1850. Seventh Census, 1850, Orange County, Population Schedule, 162.

William W. Holden to David S. Reid A&H-DSR

Raleigh,
Aug 6, 1848.

The ball opens gloriously! If you have held up and gained in the Counties to be heard from in proportion to those given below, you are elected by a signal majority. Here are all we have as yet received:

	Reid	Manly
Wake	1293	991
Wayne	1089	260
Johnston	814	720
Lenoir	254 maj.	
Martin	546	339
Moore	499	294
Nash	900	65
Samson	692	530
Cumberland	1023	578
Franklin	638	290
Greene	100 maj.	
	7848	4067
	-4067	
	3781	
Hoke's majority in the	2821	
above Counties	960!	

What do you think of that? In Northampton you have beaten Manly—what maj. I know not.

Graham beat Hoke there about 150 votes. We have gained a Commoner and Senator in Northampton—one Commoner in Johnston—a Senator in Franklin—two Commoners in Orange—a Commoner in Person, and we have lost a member in Granville, and two in Halifax. We gave you a *gain* of 109 here in Wake. At the Raleigh box we gained 50, and at this box you got the *highest* vote ever given to any Candidate for Governor, and Manly the *lowest*. Wake, Wayne, Johnston, and Moore have done gloriously. The rumor is that Manly has *lost* 100 in Chatham. A Telegraphic dispatch from Mr. Dobbin informs us that you have gained in Robeson and Bladen. In 48 hours more we shall have enough to say with certainty. Many Whigs have give up. You never saw such long faces and heard such groaning! Free Suffrage—beg your pardon—*equal* suffrage is a humbug—is it?

You have no doubt lost some in Warren and Granville; but if you keep on as you have commenced, you are certainly elected.

I write in great haste, surrounded by excited and joyous friends. By the next Mail I will send you nearly all the returns.[1]

---

[1]See Appendix 1. Official Gubernatorial Election Returns by County, 1848, David S. Reid (Democrat) vs. Charles Manly (Whig).

1849

Thomas W. Keen[1] *to David S. Reid* A&H-DSR

Leakesville N.C.
July 31st—49

I have just Returned from Davidson & consequently concluded the canvass & I assure you that I have been agreably supprised at the state of things which I have found to exist in the upper counties infact they are so flattering that I think if the lower part of this county gives me a pretty good vote that the result will be exceedingly doubtful

It Remains to be seen whether the Democratic party is to be divided when the contest is between whig & democrats this election will show & I hope that it may not be the case not so much for my own sake as for the interest of the party for I am sure that after haveing sustained the defeat which befell us last fall that we should be constantly on the lookout

[1]Thomas William Keen (1823-1886), a Rockingham County physician, was a member of the House of Commons in 1848 and 1849 and served as a surgeon during the Civil War. After the war he moved to Salisbury and became a tobacco manufacturer. He eventually moved to Danville, Virginia, and served two terms in the Virginia House of Delegates. Lindley S. Butler and George A. Schweitzer, "Thomas W. Keen" (unpublished biographical sketch); Cheney, *North Carolina Government*, 317.

1850

David S. Reid to the Democractic Party of North Carolina[1] A&H-mn

Rockingham,
May 25, 1850.

Honorable mention has been made of my name at public Meetings in the various parts of the State, in connection with the nomination for the office of Governor at the ensuing election. Two years ago I was nominated by the Democratic Convention without being consulted in regard to my wishes on the subject. Under the peculiar circumstances attending my nomination, I then felt constrained to accept. Although defeated by a small majority, I did not feel in the least disparaged; and for the cordial and generous support I received, I take this occasion to tender to my numerous friends my most profound acknowledgements. Candor compels me to state, that the very flattering testimony of confidence and regard then bestowed upon me, would, under ordinary circumstances, impel me to make any personal sacrifice of interest or inclination to gratify the wishes of my friends. But I have never sought the nomination, and even if I desired to be Governor, I could not consent to be the candidate of a party for that distinguished office unless clearly satisfied that I was generally acceptable to such party. I believe that my nomination is not desirable to a portion of my fellow-citizens, without whose cordial and zealous aid my friends could not expect to elect me. Moreover, the time will be so short, from the holding of the Convention till the election, that it would not afford me an opportunity to do justice to myself or to the Democratic party in this important contest. Regarding, as I do, the harmony and success of the Democratic party, as being of more importance to the State than the mere gratification of my own personal wishes on the subject, I conceive it due alike to myself and to my friends to respectfully decline the nomination, and to request the Convention not to consider my name as one of those from among which the selection is to be made. To the kind friends, who desire my nomination, I trust this course will prove satisfactory.

In the last Canvass, I took the responsibility to urge to the consideration of the people of North Carolina the justice and policy of Equal Suffrage. I then predicted that, whatever might be my fate, the triumph of my views on this subject was certain. My opinions and motives in regard to this question were violently and ungenerously assailed. Time has, if possible, more fully confirmed the opinions I then expressed; and, when this great question of Constitutional Reform is consummated, (as it is destined to be at no distant day,) by which upwards of fifty thousand of the patriotic and intelligent men of North Carolina shall be enfranchised and restored to their rights at the ballot-box, I shall cheerfully abide the judgment of the people of my State as to the justice of the measure and the rectitude of my motives in advocating it.

I trust the Convention will be able to select some one to bear the standard of the party more successfully in the ensuing contest than it was my fortune to do in the last; and in this effort my friends may expect my hearty cooperation.

[1]This letter appeared in the *North-Carolina Standard*, June 12, 1850.

Stephen A. Douglas to David S. Reid A&H-DSR

Washington
May 26th 1850

I herewith enclose you the papers to which I refered in relation to the claim of John M Brooch against the estate of Robert Martin deceased.[1] They will undoubtedly be sufficient to defeat any claim he may set up and show besides a just claim against him for a considerable amount. I place them in your hands that you may be able to use them whenever occasion may require. I may hereafter mail them in Mississippi if Brooch shall set up a claim against the estate. I don't know when I will be able to come to N.C. again. I am anxious for Martha to return & bring my little Boy with her, but I cannot leave here at this time to come for I wish you could find it convenient to visit your old friends here & could induce Martha to come with you. Give my love to all of your family & believe truly yours

[1]Robert Martin, Jr., father-in-law of Stephen A. Douglas, died in Rockingham County on May 25, 1848. Reese and Fisher, *Settle Family*, 681.

William W. Holden to David S. Reid A&H-DSR

Raleigh,
June 1st. 1850.

Yours of May 25th was duly received by last night's mail; and you will receive this, if at home, on Tuesday morning.

I have read and *re-read* your confidential letter, but cannot, for my life, perceive that your reasons for declining are conclusive. So far as the Trusteeship is concerned, that argues but little. It is easy to understand how that was done. Hassell[1] was elected by his being an "iron-side" Baptist, and there being no such person in the Board, and the others were chosen because they were *here*, and they or their friends directly sought it. I know your friends, or those really your friends, stood by you. I regret that your name was ever brought forward for it; and if the result had been foreseen, it would not have been. But this, I repeat, proves nothing. You are the strongest man with the *masses* ever presented to the people, and the leaders *dare not* oppose you, or even appear indifferent. I know it.

Just look, if you please, at the condition of things. Both the Mountain Banner and the Asheville News, Whig papers, are *pledged against* Manly, and for "State Reform." Also, the Whigs of Buncombe, who have just had a meeting. In addition to this, I shall publish a communication next week, headed "who shall be the Nominee?" and pressing your name, from a well-informed Rutherford Democrat, who assures me that you will beat Manly in Rutherford 500 votes. John Gray Bynum is running for the Senate in that County *against* Manly; and in Halifax and Granville the Whigs are disorganized, and cannot get candidates. Besides, Clay has just attacked Taylor in the strongest terms, and Whigs in this State *must* devide between the two. Several Whig papers have already denounced Taylor; and next week the Raleigh Star will denounce Stanly,[2] the North State Whig and the Raleigh Times, in the fiercest terms. These things, altogether, may not indeed give you any *Whig* votes, but they *must* produce lukewarmness in the Whig ranks—divisions and hearthawings which cannot fail to *diminish* Manly's vote. For the last two months I have carefully kept back from the Standard all evidences of Manly's unpopularity, in the hope that he would be again the candidate; there is now no doubt that he will be; and I have all these evidences filed away, to be used as soon as he is nominated.

So far as the Central Road is concerned, you have taken in your letter to me, the *right ground, and the very ground which I have all along told our Friends you would take*. Allow me to assure you that though Raleigh is for the Road, *you* are the first choice of every Democrat here; and Maj Nixon,[3] B. B. Pruitt,[4] and others of our friends, who recognize the true ground in regard to the Rail Road *prefer* you. They say, and truly, that your election, under the circumstances, could not injure the Rail Road Democrats, who have nothing more to ask in the way of appropriations, while it would give confidence to the anti-Rail Road Democrats, because they could trust you on the subject. Gen. Saunders, I know, is warmly for you; and but a few days since he sent word to our friend D., by Judge Strange, not to think of running, for that he would be inevitably and disastrously defeated. All the Rail Road men ask of you is, what you have written me. I know it. I can speak for them; and besides, being for the Road, I have a right to require them, by every honorable consideration, to sustain you. They will do it, almost, if not quite unanimously. Again: If you will run you are obliged to get the same vote, at least, you got last year west of Raleigh, and I think you will increase it. *Eight or ten counties in the centre might have elected you before, by polling their full strength.* With you in the field, I shall call on these counties by name, point to the vote, and *prove* to them what they can do; and I will address every leading man in them in relation to his duty. These leading men know these facts, and they will be bound to do their duty towards you.

It is not necessary that you should stump the State at all. You have done it once. You are universally known as Manly's former competetor, *and as the author of Equal Suffrage.* All you will have to say, will be, that you and the Governor have already stumped the State once, and that, while you are willing to do it again, so far as the time will allow, *you await the movements of "His Excellency."* This will throw the blame on him of leaving his duties here.

In regard to the Nashville Convention, that is a dead question. *I knew, four weeks ago that you were opposed to it*; or rather that you thought it inexpedient now; but what of that? We are all for Union at the proper time; and in going for it I but yielded to the will of the majority, and did not dream of proscribing anyone. Saunders occupies the same position you do in regard to it, *and so does Strange now.* All you will have to do, in this regard, if you accept, is to endorse the Resolutions of the Convention. In regard to Clay's Compromise and Taylor's plan you need not advocate either; but you might say, if *compelled* to choose, that you would take Clay's plan. In your letter of acceptance, you might enforce Equal Suffrage—go for Judges, &c. by the People, and in regard to "State Reform" generally called for by the Buncombe Whigs, you might say that you were for "State Reform," and would if elected, cheerfully co-operate with the Assembly in bringing it about. *Manly could not say that, without considering his own party,* which has had the State government fourteen years.

You will see in the last Standard that a number of the counties have called upon you to take the field. *You are unquestionably the first choice of the party*. At our Meeting here, Mr. Shepard[5] offered a Resolution nominating you, which would have passed by acclamation; but Messrs. Busbee[6] and McRae[7] interposed. It was not withdrawn, however, until they had said that you were clearly entitled to the field, *and that they were for you, in perference to any one else*, provided you would consent to run. They opposed the Resolution on the ground that it would saver of Central dictation. If you run, Wake will do *better* for you than she did before.

I write the universal opinion of our friends here when I say you are, by far, the strongest man, and that your election is certain. I have not conversed with a single Democrat who speaks otherwise; and *Whigs* have told me you would certainly beat Manly. So far as I am concerned, I am for you against the world; and if you will consent to run, I will omit neither expense, nor labor, nor pains, so far as they will go, to ensure your success. I will publish the Standard twice a week from the Convention until the election, and labor for you, *with an assurance of triumph*, day and night.

I shall withhold your letter intended for publication, until I hear from you. If you receive this at home, you can write, me by return Mail. I shall also drop you a note to Chapil Hill, by some friend going to Commencement; but if you received this on Tuesday at Reidsville, you can reply so as to reach me, at farthest, on Sunday night, the 9th. That would be in time for the Standard of the 12th. But if you receive this Tuesday morning, and then start for Chapel Hill, *be sure to come to Raleigh before you return*. Should you utterly decline to run, I shall, of course, publish your letter with a heavy heart; but I sincerely hope you will reconsider the matter, and agree to take the field There are many things which I could tell you, if here, which would give strength to the view already advanced in this letter. All you have to do, as I wrote you before, is to allow us the use of your name, and to serve as governor. Messrs. Wilder,[8] Pruitt, Shepard, Nixon, and the entire party here, join me in this appeal.

Hoping for a favourable reply, but your friend always, happen what may,

P.S. The Wake Resolutions I drew myself. They embody the very views you take about the Central Road. No reasonable man can take any other view of it. It would be madness to make either the Central Road or the Nashville Convention a test. I have never done so; but directly the contrary.

During the last two months I have made it a point to converse with Democrats here from various parts of the State in regard to the governorship. I suppose I have talked with not less than fifty. They *all* assured me that *you* were the first choice of the party in their respective sections, and that your election is regarded as certain.

I have now given you facts, in a hurried and broken manner. Think over the matter most seriously, and do the best you can for your friends and your party.

But what if you are beaten? Is it a disgrace? And if the time for a canvass is limited, or if there is no canvass, that is not your fault; your party made it so. But if you succeed, as you must, what an honor for a young man to redeem poor old whig ridden North Carolina!

P.S. *again*. If you consent to run, you can so inform me, and I can announce the fact in the Standard of the 12th, that though you are not anxious about it, *you are in the hands of your friends*; and I can also authoritatively state the same to the members of the Convention.

I have seen several friends since writing this. They all concur with me in opinion. For the first time in fourteen years, the Democratic party would go into the contest with *confidence*. They did not have the confidence before, because they had been so often defeated, and did not know what you could do. This writing the Whig paper printed in Edenton has come to hand. The Editor in pressing W. B. Shepards nomination, says: "No nomination can be made that will be more unsatisfactory to the Whigs of the District than that of the present incumbent. It is not here necessary to explain the causes of the dissatisfaction—suffice it to say, *it exists*, and *that to no small extent*." This is one evidence out of dozens, East and West that I might give you.

---

[1]Cushing Biggs Hassell, a Baptist minister from Martin County, served as a trustee of the state university from 1848 to 1868. Reid's disappointment was temporary, as in January, 1851, he also was elected a trustee of the university. Battle, *History of the University*, I, 760, 825; *North-Carolina Standard*, January 15, 1851.

[2]Edward Stanly, previously identified, Whig congressman from Beaufort County, delivered a speech in the House on the slavery question, denouncing the Southern Rights Convention at Nashville, Tennessee, as a ruse to create alarm and excitement for partisan political purposes. He is reported to have said that if the citizens of Nashville would do their duty, when the convention delegates arrived, "They will drive every traitor into the Cumberland River." *Raleigh Star*, April 3, 1850, quoted in the *North-Carolina Standard*, May 1, 1850.

[3]Jerry Nixon of Raleigh was a political advisor and friend of Holden. Holden, *Memoirs*, 4.

[4]B. B. Pruitt was apparently a resident of Raleigh, but his name does not appear in the 1850 Census for Wake County.

[5]James B. Shepard, previously identified, was opposed to the Central Railroad but nevertheless called for party unity, speaking in a "noble spirit of conciliation and compromise" at the Wake County Democratic Convention on May 20, 1850. *North-Carolina Standard*, May 22, 1850.

[6]Perrin Busbee, previously identified.

[7]Duncan Kirkland McRae, previously identified.

[8]Gaston H. Wilder of Raleigh was a member of the House of Commons (1842-1847, 1852) and a state senator (1854-1857). In 1846 he was named paymaster of the North Carolina Volunteer Regiment and served in Mexico. Cheney, *North Carolina Government*, 1289-1290; Wheeler, *Sketches*, 418.

Robert Strange, G. W. Caldwell, James S. Battle,[1] *John S. Eaton,*[2] *and John Exum*[3] *to David S. Reid*[4] A&H-mn

Raleigh,
June 15, 1850.

At a Convention of the Democratic party of North Carolina, holden at this place on the 13th and 14th instant, the undersigned were appointed a committee to announce to you that you were unanimously and enthusiastically chosen as the Democratic candidate for the office of Governor of this State at the ensuing election.

We were desired to assure you that your acceptance of this nomination is most anxiously desired by the whole party, and that the sacrifices you have heretofore made in the service of your country, and the devotion you have shown to her true interests, inspire the confidence that you will make this additional sacrifice. It is confidently believed that under your lead the Democratic party will be successful in the ensuing contest; and it is the deliberate decision of the Convention that under no other leader could our hopes of victory be as strong, or the whole party rally to their standard with so much zeal and determination. Under this view of the subject, the Convention did not permit itself to doubt that your oft-tried patriotism would bring you to the rescue, at whatever cost.

Permit us to add our earnest individual solicitations to those of the Convention, and to assure you of the very high respect and esteem of Your friends and ob't servt's.

---

[1]James S. Battle (1786-1854) of Edgecombe County had attended the University of North Carolina and was a planter, local Democratic leader, and a justice of the peace. Battle, *History of the University*, I, 181; Wheeler, *Reminiscences*, 164; Grant, *Alumni History*, 39.

[2]John S. Eaton was a Democratic party leader who advocated internal improvements. Holden, *Memoirs*, 7.

[3]John Exum of Wayne County served in the state Senate from 1835 to 1850. Cheney, *North Carolina Government*, 1307.

[4]This letter appeared in the *North-Carolina Standard*, July 3, 1850.

S. A. Andrews[1] *to David S. Reid* A&H-DSR
[Private]

Goldsboro
17th June 1850

I have noticed an expression of yours in your letter dated 25 Ult.[2] to the Democratic party—which reads "I believe my nomination is not desirable" &c. Apprensive that the action of the primary meeting of this county may have had some agency in promoting your belief I hasten to explain to you the reason why your name was not inserted in our resolutions. *Rumors* had been long circulated that you did not intend to or wish to have your name before the convention. Therefore it was thought an expression of our wishes might have a disheartening effect upon any other who might receive the nomination—I drew the resolutions and you cannot doubt my attachment, nor let me assure you can you doubt any Democrat in Wayne County. Had your name been before the people then—now—or at any time, I do assure you there would be not a dissenting voice—Our sole hope & expectation of success has been & is in you—

Many of us feel a deep interest in the success of the No Car— R—R—But I assure you it will not weaken our party principles & attachments.

[1]S. A. Andrews was a Goldsboro physician. Apparently a close friend and political advisor to Reid, he was one of two men Reid consulted prior to injecting the free suffrage issue into the 1848 campaign for governor. Hamilton and Williams, *Graham Papers*, III, 164; Holden, *Memoirs*, 5.

[2]May 25, 1850.

David S. Reid to William Lander[1] A&H-mn

Salem
June 19, 1850

The Convention has nominated me, and I cannot decline a compliment so generously bestowed. You may therefore say to our friends, "All's right—and go ahead."[2]

[1]William Lander (1817-1868) was born in County Tipperary, Ireland, the year before his family immigrated to America, settling in piedmont North Carolina.

After attending Lincolnton Academy and Coker College in South Carolina, Lander studied law privately and was admitted to the North Carolina bar in 1839. He was elected in 1852 for one term to the state House of Commons. He seved briefly as county solicitor and was appointed Sixth District solicitor by Governor Reid on December 23, 1852. A Democrat, he became by 1861 an ardent secessionist and was elected in November 1861 to the Confederate Congress. Losing a bid for reelection to a peace candidate, Lander in 1863 resumed his law practice in Lincolnton, where he died. Ezra J. Warner and W. Buck Yearns, *Biographical Register of the Confederate Congress* (Baton Rouge: Louisiana State University Press, 1975), 146-147, hereinafter cited as Warner and Yearns, *Biographical Register of the Confederate Congress*; Governors Office Records, "Commissions and Resignations, 1841-1854."

[2]Reid apparently sent this same short message to a number of key supporters. From the *Lincoln Courier*, reprinted in the *Raleigh Register*, July 3, 1850.

Robert P. Dick to David S. Reid A&H-DSR

Greensboro
June 20th/50

I recd your letter from Salem and was much gratified to learn that you would accept the nomination.

I have written to various parts of the State communicating the fact, and soon the battle will be opened.

I regret that I cannot see you on Saturday but I will call by about Wednesday.—I *feel* that you can beat Manly, and I will tell you all the reasons why when I see you.—In haste

---

David S. Reid to Robert Strange, G. W. Caldwell, James S. Battle, John S. Eaton, and John Exum[1] A&H-mn

Reidsville, N. C.,
June 22, 1850.

In consequence of my absence from home I did not receive your letter of the 15th inst., informing me of my nomination by the Convention as the Democratic Candidate for Governor at the ensuing election, till yesterday evening.

A nomination so cordially and generously made, and so kindly and politely communicated, is irresistable, and I do not hesitate to accept. The bestowal of this additional mark of confidence calls forth the most grateful feelings of my heart.

I shall at once go into the canvass and devote myself to it until the election. I regret that the want of time will prevent me from canvassing many parts of the State which I desired to visit.

The history of the past affords me no cause to distrust my friends; they know their duty and they will perform it. If their efforts shall be crowned with success in electing me to fill the distinguished office for which I have been nominated, my earnest exertions shall be directed to the advancement of the prosperity and happiness of the people of the State, and to give to North Carolina that rank, influence, and consideration among the States of the Union to which she is justly entitled.

---

[1]This letter appeared in the *North-Carolina Standard,* July 3, 1850.

David S. Reid to William W. Holden[1] A&H-mn

Reidsville,
June 24, 1850.

The Raleigh Register of the 22d instant, in relation to my nomination, and my vote on the Bill to establish a Territorial government in Oregon, applies the following language to myself and the Democratic party:

"Yet they ask the people of North Carolina to cast their votes for a man who surrendered their rights and honor and opened the citadel to free soilers and abolitionists—aye, to sustain David S. Reid, whose name stands recorded upon the journals of the House of Representatives in favor of the same Bill with the Wilmot Proviso shining forth as its most prominent feature! What a monument of infamy to him is this vote, and what a monument of inconsistency of Locofoism is his nomination!"

Now I pronounce the charge that I have at any time or in any way voted for the Wilmot Proviso, *as utterly false.* I desire this architect, who intends to erect a monument of infamy to me, shall be branded with his true character, that the public may understand him.

When the bill to establish a Territorial Government for Oregon was before Congress, it contained a clause inhibiting slavery in that Territory. I had to vote for the bill with that provision, or against giving the people of that Territory a Government. Although I believed that in entering into the Missouri Compromise the South had conceded too much to the North, yet as that Compromise had long been acquiesced in, I did not feel disposed to disturb it; and being anxious to establish a Government for the protection of our citizens in that distant Territory, I, in company with a large number of Southern members, whom I know to be as ardently attached to the institutions of the South as any men in the Union, voted for the bill. Oregon lies north of the Missouri Compromise line, and the bill only inhibited slavery in that Territory. The Wilmot Proviso inhibits slavery in the Territory both north and south of that line. This I conceive to be a broad distinction. Why did not the Editor charge me with voting for the Wilmot Proviso in the annexation of Texas? The annexation Resolutions contained a Proviso inhibiting slavery in that part of Texas which lies north of the Missouri Compromise line. All the Democratic members from the South, and some of the Whigs, voted for these Resolutions with the Proviso, and they were approved by the Democratic party at the South. Yet, according to the Register, all who voted for or approved the annexation of Texas, were in favor of the Wilmot Proviso.

[1]This letter appeared in the *North-Carolina Standard*, July 3, 1850.

David S. Reid to the People of North Carolina[1] Duke-RBR

Reidsville,
June 28th 1850.

FELLOW-CITIZENS:

My name having been presented to you as a candidate for Governor, at the ensuing election is my apology for this address. As I do not claim the support of any man, against his honest convictions of duty to his country, I shall address myself to the reason and understanding of the people, and cheerfully abide their decision.

Believing that the great measures of public policy advocated by the Democratic party were calculated to promote the prosperity and welfare of the country, I have given to those measures my cordial support. If asked what these measures are, I may point to our statutes and the history of the country for an answer. I may point to the overthrow of a corrupt National Bank, and the establishment of the Constitutional Treasury; to the repeal of a ruinous Tariff system, and the enactment of the more liberal policy embraced in the act of 1846; and to the acquisition of large, valuable, and fertile Territories, destined to add wealth and strength to this great country. These, and other measures, I may point to, as proud monuments of the patriotism, the purity, and wisdom of Democratic policy. Although a Democrat, I owe no allegiance to party farther than the policy of such party is calculated to promote the good of the country.

The adjustment of the slavery question is a subject of deep interest to every portion of the Union, and more especially to the South, with whose fate our interests and destiny are inseparably intertwined. Long before my entrance into public life, the agitation of this subject led to what is familiarly known as the "Missouri Compromise." Although I believed that, in entering into that Compromise, the South had, for the sake of peace and harmony, conceded too much to the North, yet when I came into public life I was disposed to carry out that Compromise in good faith. We had a right to expect and to demand of the North, that she would, on her part, stand by the Compromise. But in this we have been sadly disappointed. A very large portion of the people of the North now seek to violate it, by demands incompatible with the interests, the safety, and the honor of the Southern States. The Territory of the United States was acquired by the common blood and common treasure of all the States; and to appropriate it to the use of some of the States, to the exclusion of others, would be a violation of every principle of justice and equality. Moreover, a vast amount of slave property is every year escaping into the Northern States, and most of those States, instead of faithfully carrying out the compromises of the Constitution, actually interpose legislation to prevent the recapture of fugitive slaves. In this way the South has lost millions. This grievance demands redress. The slavery question is of vital importance to us. To the North it is a mere abstract political question. To us, it is not only a question of right, involving an incalculable amount of private property, but the perpetuity of the Union, and, above all, the domestic quiet and security of ourselves and families. *The crisis demands that the South should take a firm stand in defence of her rights*. I have always been a Union man. I yield to no man in devotion to this glorious Union, and I desire to see it preserved and perpetuated to all time. After the enjoyment of civil and religious liberty, there is no object more desirable to me than the preservation of the Union. But the best and surest means in my humble opinion, to preserve and perpetuate the

Union, is for the South to take a firm and decided stand in favor of her rights, against the encroachments of the North.

I did not approve of the movement in favor of calling the Nashville Convention, yet a personal acquaintance with a large number of gentlemen, both Democrats and Whigs, who were in favor of that Convention, enables me to repel the charge that they were in favor of treason or disunion. They are gentlemen of elevated patriotism, and are ardently attached to the Union.

I hope that wise and salutary counsels may prevail, and that this distracting question may at once be settled upon principles of justice to the South.

While a member of Congress I endeavored to adhere to the principles of the Missouri Compromise; and when a bill was before that body to establish a Territorial Government for Oregon, containing a clause inhibiting slavery, *in that Territory*—being compelled to vote for the bill with that restriction or against extending the protection of our laws to that distant people—I voted for the bill, together with many Southern gentlemen. Some partizan Whig newspapers have seized on this pretext, and charged me with having voted for the Wilmot Proviso. This charge is untrue, for I am, and ever have been opposed to that Proviso, and have never voted for it at any time or in any way. The restriction in the Oregon bill applied to that Territory alone, all of which lies north of the Missouri Compromise line, whereas the Wilmot Proviso proposes to inhibit slavery both North and South of that line. I voted for the Resolutions annexing Texas, which contained a Proviso excluding slavery in all that part of Texas, North of the same line. These Resolutions were voted for by all the Democrats from the South, yet in doing so we did not vote for the Wilmot Proviso. While on this subject, it occurs to me that if these Whig partizans would spend more of their time in examining the opinions of their own candidates, and less in misrepresenting the opinions of Democratic candidates, it would be better for the country. Two years ago I cautioned them against voting for Gen. Taylor, without a public declaration of his opinions. They would not take my advice, but turned round and denounced Gen. Cass as a "Wilmot Proviso Abolitionist," and that too in the face of the fact that he had publicly declared his opinion to the contrary. Gen. Taylor was honored with the vote of North Carolina, and Gen. Cass was defeated. Since then, *who has done most for the South,* Gen. Cass or Gen. Taylor? Gen. Cass, although instructed by the Legislature of his State to vote for the Wilmot Proviso, boldly and eloquently appealed to the North to do us justice, and openly proclaimed that before he would vote to carry out the instructions to perpetrate this injustice upon the South, he would resign his seat in the Senate. His appeal to the people of his State was not in vain; for the same

Legislature assembled, and in a spirit of liberality highly creditable to themselves and still more complimentary to him, repealed those instructions. This is the same Gen. Cass who was charged in the late canvass with being a Wilmot Provision Abolitionist. How stands the case with Gen. Taylor? It affords me no pleasure to state that his course has not done justice to the South. You looked in vain to his Annual Message to Congress for any appeal to the North to give up your fugitive slaves, or to do you justice in relation to the question of slavery. But you will find that he recommends a miserable non-action policy, which is, in the end, to accomplish the very object of the Wilmot Proviso.

This plan has become the scheme of the Abolitionists at the North. Gen. Taylor's policy has already been denounced by the veteran statesman, Henry Clay, to whose eloquence many of you have delighted to listen, and around whose standard many of you have delighted to rally. Yet in the face of these facts, my competitor, Governor Manly, in a Speech delivered before the Whig Convention accepting the nomination, in speaking of the policy of Gen. Taylor, said:

"The Whig party of North Carolina, by a majority of 8000 votes, contributed to bring him into power, and we will be the last to desert the standard of the brave old soldier."

And again in the same Speech he says:

"The Whig party may well congratulate themselves and the Nation, in having at the head of affairs such a man, at such a tremendous crisis as the present."

For myself, I must say, that I cannot congratulate any portion of the people of my State upon having at the head of affairs a man who persists in a policy so deadly hostile to our dearest rights. In vain may we make avowals of our devotion to our interests, if we elect and support those who do not represent those interests. Is this bitter pill of destruction to be gilded with the popular name of a military chieftain? The question is not whether you will "desert the standard of a brave old soldier," but it is whether you will permit yourselves to be betrayed by the mischievous policy of Gen. Taylor and his Cabinet.

While I have opposed Internal Improvements by the Federal Government, yet I have always avowed myself the friend of a fair and judicious system of Internal Improvements by our State. But I have ever been opposed to such wild and extravagant schemes as were calculated to involve the State in a large debt, without the prospect of a return of adequate advantages to the people. That I may not be charged with concealment, nor my views misrepresented, I will state, that had I been a member of the last Legislature I would have voted against the bill, chartering the Central Rail Road. My objections would have been more particularly confined to the details of the bill. I do not assail those who voted for the bill, but I believe they were governed by high and honorable motives. The stock in that Road has been secured, and the charter has become the *irrepealable law* of the State, and this is no longer an open question.

The State is now largely interested in the Road. Under these circumstances as a citizen of the State, I desire to see the faithful execution of the law and the success of the enterprise. These views would govern my public conduct in regard to that subject.

I desire to see our system of Common Schools encouraged and improved, until it shall answer the laudable purpose for which it was established. This has ever been a subject in the success of which I have felt a deep interest. I voted with great pleasure for the first act ever passed by our Legislature to establish Common Schools. During the last canvass *in the West*, Gov. Manly assailed my vote on an amendment to that bill, to distribute the School fund according to *federal population*. Whether he will do so again, I know not. In his published Speech lately made before the Whig Convention, and which I presume was intended for circulation in the *East*, as well as in the *West*, I observe he does not make this point. I make this remark because the experience of the past has taught me what I have to expect for the future. I voted to distribute the School Fund according to federal population, because I thought that, upon the whole, it would be as satisfactory and as near right as any principle we could adopt. Since I gave that vote successive Legislatures have convened, and once, at least, a Whig Legislature has re-enacted the whole School law, and this principle of distribution still remains. For the part I acted, I think it has fallen to my lot to receive more than my share of abuse.

The views I expressed during the late canvass on the question of Equal Suffrage remain unchanged. Justice to myself and to the friends of this measure, requires a particular notice of a remark made by Gov. Manly in his late Speech, before the Whig Convention in Raleigh. In relation to the origin of that question, he uses the following language:

"Whence did it come? In vain was it sought for in the primary assemblies of our people. They had not spoken nor moved in the matter. The great lever of public opinion, the Press, had been silent. The Democratic Convention which had just been held, had *publicly* recommended no such rule of action for the guidance of their nominee. From what region then could it have proceeded? It was *conjectured* that it smelt of the *charnel house of the Washington City tactics*, and that it had been sent on *ready made* to frighten the Whigs of this State from their propriety, and to place them in a false position in the election of a Governor. What was conjecture *then*, has, in part, at least, become history *now*. It has been publicly asserted and admitted at Washington.

I am told, that it was gotten up and manufactured there and sent on for North Carolina use; quoted and signed and gloated over as the infallible Democratic thunder; as their patent exploding blunderbuss for demolishing every thing."

Again, in the same Speech, he says:

"It was not to equalize the voting rights of the 'people' of North Carolina; but to elect the Democratic candidate, Gen. Cass, to the Presidency, that 'set the ball in motion.' "

I am no stranger to the inventions of Gov. Manly's fruitful imagination. As to the charge that this question was started to elect Gen. Cass I have only to say, that I made several speeches in favor of Equal Suffrage before Gen. Cass was nominated. Gov. Manly must know this fact, for some of these speeches I made in his presence. The charge that this question "was gotten up and manufactured" elsewhere, and "sent on here," is totally untrue. I have frequently, in public speeches, and in private conversations in the presence of Gov. Manly, contradicted this and similar insinuations made by himself and others. It would seem strange that he still persists in such an illiberal course towards this measure and its friends. Perhaps when he made that speech he did not expect me to be a candidate again; but I do not think that justifies him. He says it "smelt" of "the charnel house tactics of Washington City," and in the last canvass he said it smelt of "*Abolitionism.*" No wonder this question of popular rights *smells bad* to Governor Manly, *who was a Federalist during the last War. Young* as he was, his prococious developments then but foreshadowed that in mature age he was to be the enemy of Equal Suffrage. It was not because it *smelt* of the "charnel house," that he opposed it, but because it was favorable to popular rights, and inconsistent with his notions of Government. It was too "levelling" and too "Agrarian" for him. He argued, that if the principle was carried out the poor men would make the laws, and divide the property of the rich among themselves. No wonder he does not like Equal Suffrage, for it came near doing for him in the last canvass what many of his friends fear it will do for him in this. Yes, fellow-citizens, I fancy, that the very worst smell, to him, of all that attaches itself to Equal Suffrage, is the *smell of defeat*; and in despite of all his abuse of the measure, the smell will be borne to him on every breeze till this great work is consummated.

I trust I shall be pardoned for alluding to the manner in which this subject was made an issue in the canvass of 1848, for I think the part I acted enables me to know more about this matter than any other human being upon the face of the earth. That some men were permitted to vote for the Senate and others were not, was no new discovery to me or to anybody else. At any rate, I well remember my attention was directed to the inequality and injustice of this feature of our Constitution even before I became a voter; and I presume there are but few men in the State who could not say as much. My attention was frequently called to the subject when a Candidate for the Senate, by persons who desired to vote for me, but expressed a regret that they could not do so for the want of the land qualification. Many years ago, while a member of the Legislature, I determined at one time to present the subject to the consideration of that body, but met with no encouragement from those to whom I communicated my intention. Occupying an humble position and possessing but little influence, I was fearful that a failure then might prove prejudicial to this question of Constitutional Reform, which, I believed, I could at some day convince the people they ought to adopt. The time and state of public opinion then appeared unpropitious, and I abandoned my determination. Early in the year 1848, I determined to press the subject to the consideration of the people of the State. As federal politics had governed almost every thing in our State for years, I foresaw that it would be difficult to procure for this subject that consideration which its importance demanded, unless it was adopted by one of the political parties. With this view I determined to attend the Democratic Convention to be held that Spring and urge its adoption as an issue; and that if the Convention would not adopt it, I would seek some suitable occasion to make a Speech on the subject in my own County, and write it out for publication; and that I would publish essays on the subject, urging the consideration of this question to the people. Ill health prevented me from attending the Convention. When I heard from that Convention, I was surprised to learn that I had been nominated for Governor. Before I received official information of my nomination I wrote Mr. Holden a letter stating that I should probably decline, but if I run I desired to make Equal Suffrage an issue. Believing the state of my health was such that a canvass of the State would be hazardous to my life, I subsequently wrote a letter declining the nomination. This letter was not published, and my friends prevailed upon me to withdraw it and to accept the nomination. The next day after I accepted I left home to meet my competitor, who was then engaged in the Canvass. Before leaving home I appraised some of my friends of my purpose to make this issue. When I reached Raleigh, I mentioned the subject to several of my friends there; and Mr. Holden assured me, if I carried out my intention, that the Standard would zealously advocate the measure. At Goldsborough I mentioned the subject to friends I met there. When I arrived at Newbern I consulted friends there on the subject, and Mr. Gulick promised me that the Republican would zealously advocate the measure. My friends will recollect that in all these conversations that to make this issue was a favorite object with me; and that these conversations and consultations on the subject were brought about by my own suggestions. I had no consultation or conversation on the subject of making this issue with any one living out of the State; neither did I receive from Washington City or elsewhere any suggestion, either written or oral, in relation to making the issue.

The Democratic party had nominated me without my knowledge or consent, and although they had not authorized me to make Equal Suffrage a question in the election, yet I believed they would sustain me if I did right; and I therefore took responsibility to put "that ball in motion" on the 10th of May, 1848. This is the way in which the subject was introduced into the canvass of 1848. Whether Gov. Manly's "thunder" is imported from the "charnel house tactics of Washington City," I know not, and I care not. If, however, I might be permitted to judge of this fact from his antiquated notions and uncompromising hostility to popular rights, I would sooner suspect that *his* "thunder" came from the "charnel house tactics" of ancient European monarchies. If he draws his supplies from this course, I do not wonder that a proposition to extend the right of suffrage came on him, as he says, "like a clap of thunder in a clear sky."

What is the dearest privilege of an American citizen? It is to exercise the great and inestimable right of suffrage. In advocating this reform I do not now, nor have I at any time, proposed to change the *basis* of Representation for either the Senate or House of Commons. Let that remain as it is. What I propose is, *to permit every man who is now entitled to vote for the Commons, to vote also for the Senate*. Is this right? I might call your attention to the fact that this odious distinction does not exist in any other States of this Union. As the Constitution now stands, a man cannot vote for the Senate unless he owns a freehold of fifty acres of land. This is unjust, even between landholder and landholder. One man owns fifty acres worth $25; he can vote for the Senate, while another may own one acre worth ten thousand dollars, yet the latter cannot vote for the Senate. It is still more unjust between those who own land, and those who do not. It is not to take the right of voting from the landholder, but it is to extend the right of suffrage to another meritorious and virtuous class of our own fellow-citizens. All experience has shown that the mere fact that a man owns land, does not make him more wise, more pure, or more patriotic. It is a slander upon the merits and character of this virtuous class of our citizens to say they would enact inequitous laws to plunder the landholders. There are many of our citizens who own property, and yet are not landholders; and no men would go farther to protect the rights of property of every description. A large portion of our enterprising young men, and of our industrious farmers and mechanics, do not own fifty acres of land. These men will never attempt to impose on the landed interest, because they intend, as soon as it is compatible with their convenience or ability, to possess themselves of land—not by the unholy means of plundering their neighbors, but by purchase with the proceeds of their honest industry. During the last canvass, while discussing this question *in the West*, Gov. Manly insisted that I could not be the friend of Equal Suffrage because I did not go for changing the *basis of Representation*, by which some of the Eastern Counties, having a less number of voters than some of the Western Counties, yet they had the same representation in the Legislature; and why, he would ask, did I not go for equalizing them? I do not know whether he intends to use this argument in the present canvass. I see, however, in his Speech lately made before the Whig Convention, and which I presume was published to be circulated *all over the State*, that he does not allude to this point. Our basis of Representation for one branch of the Legislature is taxation, for the other it is federal population. The Abolitionists at the North wish to destroy the basis of federal population upon which we are represented in Congress. I regard their course on the subject as mischievous and dangerous, and I should regard a similar movement in relation to our representation in the Legislature fraught with equal mischief and danger.

I presume there are at this day, fifty thousand of our free white citizens, of the age of twenty-one years, who cannot vote for the Senate. And why is it so? It is not because they are wanting in virtue, intelligence, or patriotism; but because of an arbitary feature in our Constitution which withholds from them one of their dearest rights. In vain may we boast of equal rights, while this feature remains in our Constitution. Although these men are not placed upon terms of equality at the ballot-box, yet, when taxes are to be paid, or when the rights and honor of the country are to be defended against the attacks of a foreign foe, these men—yes, these men are among the first to contribute their means and their blood to the cause of their country.

I would like to see the brave men who perilled their lives in the War against Mexico, received at the ballot-box upon terms of equality. Yes, I desire to see the grey-headed Revolutionary soldiers who stand tottering over the grave—the very men who fought for the liberty we enjoy, placed upon terms of equality when they come up to the ballot-box.

I am in favor of electing Judges by the people, and for a term less than for life; and I doubt not there are other Constitutional amendments of minor importance, that might well be made. But I do not wish to see this great question of Equal Suffrage clogged or loaded down with other things. I desire to see it stand on its own merits.

In defense of Equal Suffrage, I have had to encounter violent abuse, personal slanders, and bitter denunciations; yet I have stood by this great question in its inception and in its infancy, and I hope to have the proud satisfaction of rejoicing with you in its triumph. When fifty thousand of our intelligent and patriotic men shall be enfranchised and restored to their rights at the ballot-box, I do think we shall have cause to feel proud of such a glorious triumph. To-morrow, I start into the canvass, and the larger number of you I cannot see before the election. To you I commit the fate of this question.

In conclusion, permit me to repeat what I have said elsewhere, that the history of the past affords me no cause to distrust my friends. If their efforts shall be crowned with success, in electing me to the distinguished office for which I have been nominated, my earnest exertions shall be directed to the advancement of the prosperity and happiness of the people of the State, and to give to North Carolina that rank, influence, and consideration among the States of this Union, to which she is justly entitled.

[1]This letter appeared in the *North-Carolina Standard*, July 3, 1850.

Samuel F. Adams to David S. Reid A&H-DSR

Raleigh N. C
July 4th 1850

I pass this place today on my way to the eastern part of the State. my health is good—god grant yours may be the same. I left home the tuesday after you did, all was well when I left. I have heard but little said uppon the subject of politics thus far. your friends in this place are very sanguine that you will be elected, a number of whigs in this county they say, will not vote for Gov. Manly. I have seen the Register and times today of the third Inst, in which they reiterate the charge of the Wilmot Proviso, and amongst other things the Raleigh times, says, it is well know that Col Reid is an imense wealthy man, and consequently belongs to the Aristocracy and was never known to shake hands with a poor man. you may look out for all sorts of falsehoods—to be promulgated to injure your Election it is a death struggle with the party and they will stop at nothing whether it be true or false that will benefit the election of Manly I learn here that the two parties in craven have made a compromise and agreed to run Washington[1] in the senate and Jenkins[2] Whig and Stevenson[3] Dem in the commons, to which ticket both parties have pledged their support and agreed to run no opposition to any one of them I do not know that it is true if it be true it will be apt to cause a thin Election in that county as the people will not take the same interest in turning out. the object is said to be the extension of the central road to Newbern I do not expect to remain in the lower country more than three or four weeks if I can buy any negroes brother Hugh will come and meet me in ten days or two weeks and we will return home let me advise you to take care of yourself and save your strength as much as possible I will be in New Berne on Sunday evening from which place I will write to you at Morganton if you have leisure write to me at Kinston as I feel anxious to hear how you stood the canvass. my best wishes for your success.

---

[1]William H. Washington, previously identified, was a former Democratic congressman living in 1850 in New Bern.

[2]Alonzo T. Jenkins of Craven County was a Whig member of the House of Commons in 1850 and 1851. Cheney, *North Carolina Government*, 1110.

[3]George S. Stephenson of Craven County was a Democratic member of the House of Commons from 1848 to 1851. Cheney, *North Carolina Government*, 1110.

William W. Holden to David S. Reid A&H-DSR

Raleigh
July 7, 1850.

Your letters from Wentworth and Germanton were both received in due course of Mail. The infirmation that Manly had come out against the black basis,[1] astounded us all. I wrote forthwith to Bayne, Fulton,[2] Robinson,[3] and Gulick, and other friends. The Whig leaders in the East will deny it. I have written to Mr. Ruffin[4] at Wentworth, to have a statement of the fact made out and signed by Whigs and Democrats, for publication. If the people of the East Centre, and South, are convinced of the fact, Manly must lose thousands. Indeed, if he were to go to such Counties as Pitt, Beaufort, &c. and advocate the white basis he could not get one vote in ten in his own party. He must lose by it in the East, and it cannot affect you in the West. A baser demegogue than Charles Manly never lived. Give it to him.

Your address is well received. I have sent off a number of extra copies of the Standard containing it, and am now sending out the Address in all directions in handbill form. There are some ten Counties in this region that gave Mr. Polk 1000 votes more than they gave you. These votes you will get now. Manly's position on the basis will give you the full vote in Warren and other counties. Your friends here are all confident, and doing their duty. I have got Clarke, Shepard, Nixon and others to write to friends in all directions. The Feds are dismayed. They see the handwriting on the wall; and Manly's course on the basis question is regarded as evidence of his desperation. I shall *rake* him from this time forth in the hottest and heaviest style.

I learn that Clay has again denounced the President and cabinet as a "miserable cabal." and held them up to the general scorn. We have had no Northern Mail for two days, but as soon as I receive his Speech I will send it to you. You can exterminate Manly on his endorse[ment] of Taylor's "line of policy" and the New Mexican outrage. The Feds here do not pretend to defend Taylor. They denounce the Cabinet, and are silent about Taylor. "*Buna vista*" has lost its charm.

You will see that I have given it to Manly about his "negro Senators," and next Wednesday I shall have a list of charges against him which I shall keep standing.

Things are working admirably. You are obliged to beat him. There are Whigs here who give it up.

You ought to get 500 votes in Wilkes, now that our friend Stokes and the volunteers are back; and I think you must gain considerably, even on your last vote, from Caswell to Ashe. You will gain at least 100 in Person—100 in Orange and Alamance—100 in Warren, and also in Franklin, Edgecombe, Onslow &c.

I shall write you next at Morganton, and send to that point your papers, &c.

Our friend Avery[5] writes me that Manly has made a fatal mistake in not going to Rutherford. It is best for you not to go there. You might stir them up and make them vote against you. Let the medicine work.

With my best wishes for your health and success

---

[1]In response to Reid's stand on free suffrage, Manly proposed a constitutional convention that would have the power both to address the suffrage issue and to change the basis of representation in the House of Commons from federal to white population. This stand alienated eastern slave owners and created confusion in the party, and many party members believed it would weaken the South's political power. Reid, *Gubernatorial Campaigns*, 26.

[2]James Fulton was the editor of the *Wilmington Journal*, which had been founded by his brother David. Norton, *Democratic Party*, 20.

[3]William Robinson, a native of Ireland and a former teacher, was the editor of the Goldsboro *Patriot*. Wheeler, *Sketches*, 114.

[4]Thomas Ruffin, Jr. (1824-1889), son of noted state supreme court justice Thomas Ruffin, graduated from the state university in 1844 and read law. He opened a

practice in 1848 with John H. Dillard in Wentworth. In 1850 he was a member of the House of Commons from Rockingham County. In 1861 he was named to the superior court bench, but the next year he resigned to accept a commission as lieutenant colonel of the Thirteenth Regiment North Carolina Troops. In March, 1863, he was seriously wounded at the Battle of South Mountain and left the army for medical reasons. He served on the state supreme court from 1881 to 1883. Ashe, *Biographical History*, V, 360-366.

[5]William Waightstill Avery, previously identified, was an attorney in Morganton in Burke County, which adjoins Rutherford County. Powell, *DNCB*, I, 71.

William W. Holden to David S. Reid A&H-DSR

Raleigh.
July 10. 1850

Gen. Taylor died last night at 35 minutes past 10. His disease was Cholera Morbus. Of a truth "God rules in the earth as well as in the armies of Heaven"!

Fillmore, the Abolitionist, is now in the seat of Washington! I enclose you his famous Buffalo letter, in which he goes the full Abolition stripe. Gov. Manly will answer that he wrote a letter during the campaign, taking back his opinion in relation to the internal slave trade; but he only said that, as the Supreme Court had pronounced such a law unconstitutional, he yielded the right to enact it. He did not say that he had changed his mind and was *opposed* to such a law. On the other points, I am certain Gov. Manly cannot show that he ever said any thing. He is an Abolitionist; and not only that, but one of the *Champions* of Protection, and for a National Bank.

Manly's opposition to the Federal basis falls like a bomb shell on the middle and East. I wrote at once to Fulton, Gulick, Bayne, and Robinson; and you will see that I have put the points strongly in the Standard to-day. The Register evades and denies.—Your friends here are in the finest spirits. They regard your election as certain. Neither the Vagrant Law, (they used the same thing two years since,) nor the Oregon bill can affect you. The minds of the people are already made up. Manly also used the federal population matter against you two years since, and you nevertheless gained votes in the West!

The elements are getting hot here, but Whigism will collapse now.—now that blow after blow falls upon it, like an exploding steamboat.

Forward and onward! Your friends here will leave no effort untried, and you must succeed.

Samuel F. Adams to David S. Reid A&H-DSR

New Berne N.C.
July 11th. 50

I arrived here last night in good health. After leaving Raleigh I heard but little said about the Governors Election untill I reached Goldsboro, where there seemed to be more Interest taken in it. nothing has been heard at this point from the canvass as conducted by you and Gov. Manly in person great anxiety is manifested to know how you are getting along. Gulick of the Republican read to me a letter from Mr. Holden giving an account of the meetings at Wentworth and Germantown from which it seems you had a rough time of it at the latter place. I suppose Gulick has spoken of it, as I hear several saying that Manly charged you with voting for the Wilmot Proviso and that you told him it was false and false as hell which he pocketed without resentment. Holden tells Gulick to call on all Eastern Carolina to rise *en mass* and contradict Manly's ascertions that he never opposed Equal sufferage and also to expose his position on the basis of Representation in both branches of the Legislature as now established by the constitution uppon taxation and Federal population which Gulick says he will do in his next paper I have not seen the first whig or Democrat that pretends to say that you will not get every vote that you received at the last Election. W. S. Dunn[1] a strong Whig of Lenoir and a delegate to the whig convention informed me in a confidential conversation that it was admitted in the convention that Manly would lose 1000 votes by the defection of the Mountn Baner and the Rutherford whigs but that they could not get clear of him, to refuse to nominate him would have shown a weakness that would have amounted to defeat. the only fears that your friends entertain in the section of country through which I have traveled is, that in some parts there will not be sufficient excitement in the county elections to cause a general turnout, if the Democrats go the polls they will vote as they have heretofore done. The Wilmot Proviso is being used freely against you in this part of the state but it has no effect whatever no one pays any attention to it. It would seem from the energy and pertinacity with which they use it that it was considered by the whig convention the most effectual weapon they had to fight with, but you need fear nothing from its effects in this section as it is perfectly ridiculous and absurd for men who are sustaining the course and position of Stanly uppon the slavery question to attempt to make capital out of the vote you gave uppon the Oregon Bill containing a clause inhibiting slavery in that Teretory only. In the Newbernian which came out on yesterday is the following clause "are the Democrats snowed under in Craven, that they make so little stir about the governor's vote? Why are they not up and doing for their Wilmot Proviso, anti Newbern Rail Road *negro-trading* candidate" my attention was called to it by a freind, I this morning called uppon the Editor and Introduced myself as a friend of Col Reid's and called his attention to the paragraph in Italics and asked what Col Reid's friends were to understand he meant by negro-trading candidate, he seemed much excited and greatly agitated and commenced apologizing at once by saying that he was truly sorry he had let it appear in his paper as he had been called uppon by some half dozen political friends who informed him that the information uppon which he inserted it in his paper was eroneous and that he was truly sorry and had determined to contradict and correct it in his next paper before I called on him he said it was known to every one that Col Reid had a Brother who had been engaged in buying negroes in Eastern Carolina on speculation and that he had been informed by a whig on whose information he thought he could rely that Col Reid was Interested in the business that his Brother was engaged in, and that he did not wish to be understood as saying or intimating that the business of speculating on negroes was by any means disreputable, only that it was supposed to be unpopular with some persons and as such, supposing his information to be undoubted he thought it fair in a political contest to use it as he did but that as he was now convinced it was eroneous he would insert a paragraph in his next paper to which he would call special attention correcting and contradicting it. so much for that thrashing machine, I shall not remain dow[n] here more than a week longer when I shall leave for home. please accept my best wishes for your success.

P.S. Your adress came to hand in the Standard by the last mail your friends are well pleased with every part of it they laud it very high and say it is the very thing

---

[1]Walter Samuel Dunn, Jr. (1788-1850), a prosperous farmer, was a delegate from Lenoir County to the Whig State Convention in Raleigh, June 10, 1850. He died December 26, 1850. Seventh Census, 1850, Lenoir County, Population Schedule, 181; Mr. and Mrs. W. M. Creasy, *Dunn and Allied Families* (Raleigh: By the Authors, 1937), 4; *Raleigh Register*, June 19, 1850.

Hugh K. Reid to David S. Reid A&H-DSR

Reidsville N.C.
July 17, 1850

Yours of the 11th by Mr Neal[1] has been reced, and we were all very glad to hear you was improving. We are all well here, all well at Mr Adamses and Mr Scotts also. To day was muster at Reidsville and the candidates were all here Courts[2] led off for Reid free Sufferage &c. Ruffin[3] came next made a very good speech spoke for you and the measures you are for and it took very well He did what he was able for you and your election (he has roat to Holden) next came Kallam[4] he made a smug talk, then Squire Price[5] and told the people he was a candidate in the commons and was a democrat died in the wool and always expected to be, Cardwell,[6] Roberts,[7] Walker[8] and Patterson[9] told the people they were candidates for the office of Sheriff. The day went off quite smooth and I think the people are quite inthusiastic in your success.

Mr. Adams writes that the people are very inthusiastic in the east for you and the day he got to New Berne the Newbernian Whig paper came out in an artickle Saying are the Democrats of craven going for the abolitionist and *Negro Trader Reid.* Adams called on him to know what he ment by the artickle and he said he was sorry he let it be put in his paper and said, he was miss led by a whig hoo told him you was a pardner of mine he said that several whigs had called at the office before Adams did and told him he was mistaken about what he had published and he was going to correct it in his next paper. That he will do you some good no doubt as he will have to eat it up at once. I think your election is sure if you are understood throughout the state. Manly is growing weaker about here daily. Accept of my renew affections hoping for your good health and success

---

[1]Probably Joseph W. Neal, previously identified, wealthy Rockingham County planter and Democratic legislator.

[2]Veteran Democratic politician Daniel W. Courts, previously identified.

[3]Thomas Ruffin, Jr., previously identified, Democratic legislator.

[4]Horatio Kallam of Rockingham County served in the House of Commons (1850-1851) and as justice of the peace (1848). Cheney, *North Carolina Government,* 1258; Rockingham County Court Minutes, May, 1848.

[5]This was probably Allen Price, who was a county justice in 1850. Rockingham County Court Minutes, May, 1850.

[6]Probably Richard P. Cardwell, previously identified, former Democratic legislator.

[7]James Roberts was elected county sheriff in August. Rockingham County Court Minutes, August, 1850, 546.

[8]William Richmond Walker, previously identified, Whig attorney from Wentworth.

[9]Mr. Patterson has not been identified.

William W. Holden to David S. Reid A&H-DSR

Raleigh,
July 19, 1850.

I write you in haste, under high steam pressure. The Standard for to-morrow is just out, and I send you some copies by this Mail. I fear that my Foreman made a mistake, and sent the bundles of the 13th and 17th to the wrong places—the 17th to Morganton, and the 13th to Asheville. I have therefore sent you, to-day, a copy of the 17th; and I have written to the P.M. at Waynesville to forward to Franklin in case you pass the former place before these arrive.

Our friend Ivey[1] came down from Rockingham, just in time, last evening, bringing me the "Proofs against Manly on the basis matter. The Eastern Feds were denying and swearing—and it falls, of course, like a bomb-shell in ther midst. Manly must lose, to say the least, *hundreds* by it in the East. Leading Feds here admit his defeat in private conversation, and many of the Whig masses give it up.

The charge of Federalism against him stings his friends here, but I have *proved* it on him. If that was unpleasant, what will they say to the proof about the basis matter?

Go ahead! The glorious East will do her full duty. You will gain in Warren, alone, 200 votes—and the same in New Hanover, Samson [*sic*]. I have written largely to our friends, and expect to do more of it.

I could write you more, but the Mail is but to close. You shall hear from me again at Franklin by Sunday's Mail.

I regard your success as certain! Hurrah for—the "People's Candidate"!

[1]This is probably a reference to Stendon Ivey (b. 1816), a native of North Carolina, who was a teacher in Rockingham County in 1850. Seventh Census, 1850, Rockingham County, Population Schedule, 107.

William W. Holden to David S. Reid A&H-DSR

Raleigh,
July 24, 1850.

A *private* letter has been received from Gov. Manly, addressed to Mrs. Manly, in which he says: "Tell Chas. (meaning his son,) he may assure Robateau[1] (the Times Editor,) that the story about my having come out for white population as the basis for representation, is *false*. My views are set forth in my printed speech, and I take no course inconsistent with the positions and declarations therein made." This is taken, word for word, from the letter. You will see that in the Standard of to-day I have used it against him. His son called to get me to state that his father *denied*, and I took down the words. I considered it best to pursue this course, as they would have raised a terrible cry of *imposter*, and have gotten, perhaps, some sympathy in the surrounding counties; and I knew the letter had been received, and a denial would be made to-day in the Register. *His* denial, made in *this* way, makes the case much worse for him. It exposes him to the contempt of his friends everywhere; and it would do him no good now, even if his name were signed to it, with explanations. Ten to one against him—impartial men every where will decide against him.

If you get this in time you can use the words, quoted against him, at Murphy.

Your prospects are still brightening. *All* our friends here are firm in the belief that you will be elected. I have not the slightest doubt of it; and I should not be surprised if your majority were between four and five thousand. The enthusism for "Reid" is greater in this region than it was ever known to be before for any candidate. A few days, however, will decide.

I will send you the returns as fast as I receive them. Please send me all you get.

P.S. I have mailed to you a letter at Murphy. A request of James Fulton, Esq. of the Wilmington Journal. I presume it refers to the basis matter. He has the *proof*, however, [*illegible*] now, as it was in the Standard of the 20th. Now that Manly has denied, I have no doubt that our friend Ruffin will produce his "*fifty*" men to confirm his statement.

Gove. Manly's letter is dated Wilkesborough. If the election were only two weeks further off, you would beat him still more disastrously.

I learn that our friends in Chatham are betting *on your carrying that County*, and also on Gen. Cotten[2] being, the foremost man in the Commons!

Gen. Saunders is *raking* Manly on the basis question, and doing his best for you. The communication in today's Standard, signed "Marattoch" is from our friend Col. Biggs.[3] He says you will gain 75 in Martin. Hurrah!

---

[1]Charles C. Roboteau had been an apprentice on the Raleigh *Register*, the leading Whig newspaper in the state, and was in 1850 the editor of the *Raleigh Times*. Robert Neal Elliott, Jr., *The Raleigh Register, 1799-1863* (Chapel Hill: University of North Carolina Press, 1955), 112.

[2]Richard C. Cotten of Chatham County served in the House of Commons (1816-1818, 1822, 1824-1825, 1833-1837, 1850-1857) and as state adjutant general (1857-1859). Cheney, *North Carolina Government*, 183, 1094.

[3]Asa Biggs, previously identified.

James C. Dobbin to David S. Reid A&H-DSR

Fayetteville
July 29th 1850

I have just returned home after an arduous & thorough canvass of the whole of Cumberland. I have concluded merely in the winding up to drop you a line. The Battle has now *nearly* been fought. Three days more and our arms will be laid aside. I feel confident that you will hear good tidings from Cumberland. Ere this reaches you I suppose intelligence will begin to pour in upon you. Our vote for you here I think will be increased. I cannot resist the conviction that a triumph awaits us. The whigs are strong in this State tis true. But the Democrats are enthusiastic. The whigs seem cool. I never knew Democrats more zealous. Well my Dear Sir, whatever may be the result—allow me to express to you my thanks for your generous acceptance of the nomination & your ardent zeal in the attempt to redeem the State.

My family are well. My *boys* are the noisiest Reid *men* in Cumberland. It would do you good to witness their enthusiasm. With my sincere prayer for our triumph & best wishes for your happiness & the assurance that my mind will struggle for your triumph. I am your sincere friend

---

William W. Holden to David S. Reid A&H-DSR

Raleigh,
Aug 7.1850

You have swept evy [*sic*] thing before you. It is indeed a triumph, glorious and unprecedented. The Standard of to-day, which I have sent you to Salisbury, contains all the news up to this morning. The vot[e] in Craven, Onslow, Jones, and Person, is as follows:

	R.	M.
Craven	541	609
Onslow	715	186
Jones	182	221
Person	577	329

In Carteret Manly's maj. is about 60. You can cyphe[r] out the gains and losses for yourself

Your majority cannot, I think, fall below 3,000, and it may be 4,000. The Feds here are surprised and thunderstruck. We take it quietly, and just as if we expected it all along.

I should like to have time to write you more at length, but will do so when I think you have reached home.[1] I congratulate you on the very high position you now occupy.

---

[1]Reid was somewhat delayed in reaching home because of illness, according to a report published in the Lincolnton newspaper:

"This gallant democratic republican, Governor elect of this State, arrived in this place on Wednesday last [August 14, 1850]. His health, which had been much impaired by the labors of the campaign, and which was prostrated in the Mountains, by a severe attack of illness, is in a great measure restored.

"While his demeanor is as modest as ever, he wears with grace and dignity the laurels of the glorious victory which encircle his brow; enjoying his triumph with as much coolness as he bore his former defeat. Though grateful for such an unprecedented support from an intelligent people, his personal elevation seems not to have excited in him any other feeling than heartfelt gratification at the triumph of those republican principles which he has advocated with so much ability, ardor, and discretion. He expresses his views on national & State policy without reserve and, in a conversation with him, we learned enough to enable us to say, that should a majority of the members of the Legislature agree with him in opinion, (of which we have no doubt,) measures will be adopted calculated to promote the best interests of the State and to restore confidence among the people in the purity and patriotism of those who are necessarily chosen to make laws and execute them.

"Col. Reid rested a night and part of a day in Lincolnton, receiving the congratulations of many of our citizens, and winning the favorable opinion of all who approached him; and having called to see the new Cotton Factory of Messrs. Motz, Barrett & Co., and made kind enquiries about all the other factories in 'Old Lincoln,' which he would have visited, had time permitted, he left us with the best wishes of every individual of his own party and of all his unprejudiced opponents." *Lincoln Republican*, August 17, 1850, reprinted in the *Wilmington Journal*, August 30, 1850.

W. Stallings[1] *and Others to David S. Reid* A&H-mn

Gatesville, (N.C.)
Sept. 6, 1850.

The recent political battle so gloriously achieved by the Democratic Republican party of the old "North State" in the election of their nominee for Governor, and a handsome majority on joint ballot in the next Legislature, calls forth our warmest praise to those who, amid impending storms and tempests and surrounded by a destructive enemy, bore the toil, labor and fatigue of the day. And as your perseverence, energy, and untiring devotion to the great principles long and zealously contended for by the Democratic Republican party, assisted greatly in producing the victory above mentioned, we offer you our sincere thanks for the noble stand you occupied in favor of Free Suffrage; your able and satisfactory vindication of the justice and equality of the principle being conceded by patriots and philanthropists to be in unison with the spirit of the times and the genius of our institutions.

A large portion of the people of this county, being desirous of manifesting their respect for you and their joy and pride at your election to the high and responsible office of Chief Magistrate of our State, have appealed to us to inform you of their wish to tender you a public dinner, to be given at Gatesville, in October next, on such a day as may suit your convenience, which we hope you will designate in your reply.

Hoping it will be convenient for you to visit us and partake of the hospitality of our county, thus tendered to you, we beg leave to subscribe ourselves Your friends And obedient servants,

---

[1]Whitmel Stallings of Gates County was a delegate to the state Constitutional Convention of 1835, a member of the House of Commons (1831-1833, 1835, 1838-1841), the state Senate (1842-1847), and the Council of State (1851-1853). This letter appeared in the *North-Carolina Standard*, November 6, 1850, and was also signed by the following people: R. Gatling, Jno. Willey, C. E. Ballard, H. C. Willey, Wm. W. Hall, Wm. H. Harrell, Thos. P. Cherry, Ro. H. Ballard, Wm. G.

Daughtry, Wm. C. Cowper, Thos. G. Vaughan, Jas. K. Costen, R. H. McIntosh, Ro. B. Parker, and Sam'l J. Lowther. Cheney, *North Carolina Government*, 178, 817, 1142-1143.

David S. Reid to W. Stallings and Others[1] A&H-mn

Reidsville, (N.C.)
Oct. 5, 1850.

Your letter of the 6th ultimo, inviting me on behalf of a large portion of the people of Gates county to partake of a public dinner, at such time during the present month as may suit my convenience, was mis-sent, and did not reach me till to-day.

My arrangements are such that I have been under the necessity to decline similar invitations from my friends in other portions of the State, and for the same reason I am reluctantly compelled to forego the pleasure of partaking of the hospitality tendered by my fellow-citizens of Gates. My regret on this account is enhanced, from the fact that the names to your letter call to mind scenes and associations of "by gone days" upon which my memory delights to linger. I trust, however, that on some other occasion I may have the pleasure of meet friends in your country.

It is to the purity and patriotism of the people we are indebted for the late political triumph. For the part I have acted I have the satisfaction to know that I was prompted by considerations of public duty; and for the repeated marks of confidence and consideration bestowed upon me by my fellow-citizens throughout the State, I feel most profoundly grateful.

Identified, as I am, with North Carolina, and honored by her as I have been, I can but feel the deepest interest in her progress and destiny; that she may pursue such a course of policy as may advance the welfare and happiness of the people, is my most ardent desire. With my best wishes,

---

[1]This letter appeared in the *North-Carolina Standard*, November 6, 1850.

John M. Dick to David S. Reid RF

Marion
Novr the 5th 1850

I avail myself of the opportunity of writing to you by Mr Avery[1] and I hope this will find you enjoying good health—I have been requested by some of our democratic friends to mention to you the name of Col Robert H Penland[2] of Haywood County as a suitable person for Commissioner to let the contracts on the turnpike road from the Georgia line through the Counties of Cherokee Macon Haywood &c I took some pains to enquire into the qualifications of Penland and was assured by several persons that he would discharge the duties well—His name will be recommended to you by others of our democratic friends—You probably recollect Penland he lives on the road at Pidgeon River in Haywood County—And while on the subject of appointments for the west, if you conclude to remove Jacob Siler[3] from the office he now holds as the agent for the state in the management of the Cherokee lands, permit me to recommend to your favourable consideration Nimrod S. Jarrett[4] you know him I believe and stoped at his house Jarrett is a responsible man and I think quite as well qualified as Siler—and would certainly do more for the democratic cause than any other man in that region of Country—I think our cause is prospering gloriously in this region of Country Clingman is doing us a great deal of good—he is about as good a democrat as I want altho he retained the name of whig, and indeed he does us more good than if he was to come out as a democrat—The federal whigs all through his district are violently opposed to him but they cannot start a man of their party than [*sic*] can beat him & I think he will not have any opposition, he is more popular I think than he ever was—Genl Bynum has done our party a good deal of service and I would not be surprized if the whigs about Raleigh this winter do not drive him further off from them than ever—I had a talk with James Love[5] about the course he took towards you—His appology was, that he was under personal obligations to Manly but that hereafter he would go for you aganst any other whig—Perhaps it would be well for you to act towards his son as if nothing had happened, and I think thay will both stand firm the next time—Wm H Thomas[6] is doing a good deal for our Cause, and I think if our democratic friends will act prudently this winter we will have the state safe—I hope our friends will persue a prudent and moderate course with regard to the late proceedings of Congress so as to give the whigs no hold against us—There is a very strong attachment to the Union every where among the people and if the whigs could only get hold of something by which they could charge us with being disunionists they might make some Capital out of it—You are aware that the whigs in this part of the state charge you with being unfriendly to the west heretofore while you were in the Legislature—You will have it in your power to remove this impression The solvent purchasers of the Cherokee lands will petition the Legislature to have their lands valued in the same way that the lands purchased by insolvents were valued and then have the priviledge of taking them at valuation—This seems to me would be but an act of justice towards those men, they are surely more meritorious than men who refused to pay and threw the lands back on the state—If you take the same view of this subject that I do and your opinion was known to Thomas Hayes and others it would be of service to you, and our cause in that region—I hope and trust before two years rool [*sic*] round you will have a popularity all over the state that whigs cannot shake, for I am sure that a large majority of the people in Clingman district are now democrats if they only knew it, and they are daily becoming more so—I repeat if our friends are only prudent this winter the whigs can never rally successfully again in this state—Be pleased to accept my best wishes for your health & prosperity individually & politically

---

[1]William Waightstill Avery, previously identified.

[2]Robert H. Penland was an early settler of the Beaverdam section of Haywood County. W. C. Allen, *The Annals of Haywood County North Carolina* (Spartanburg: The Reprint Company, 1977), 174, hereinafter cited as Allen, *Annals of Haywood.*

[3]Jacob Siler (1795-1871), a surveyor and county justice from Macon County, was in the House of Commons in 1835 and from 1838 to 1841. He served as the state agent for Cherokee land claims and for construction of the western turnpike. Allen, *Annals of Haywood*, 435-436.

[4]Nimrod S. Jarrett (1800-1873) was a native of Buncombe County and had moved to Macon County by 1835. He was one of the first ginseng traders in North Carolina. In 1851 he was appointed an agent for construction of the western turnpike. Arthur, *Western North Carolina*, 176; Nimrod S. Jarrett to Reid, April 19, 1851, Governors Papers, Reid.

[5]James Robert Love (1798-1863) represented Haywood County in the House of Commons from 1820 to 1831. Allen, *Annals of Haywood*, 122-123, 305-306; Cheney, *North Carolina Government*, 277-295 passim.

[6]William Holland Thomas (1805-1893) of Haywood County by 1820 was a store clerk in Quallatown. Adopted into the Cherokee nation by Chief Yonaguska, Thomas served as chief after 1836. He worked for Indian causes in Washington and held land on their behalf. He served in the state Senate from 1848 to 1852 from Haywood County and from 1854 to 1861 from the newly formed Jackson County. He was a delegate to the Constitutional Convention of 1861-1862 and was a colonel of the Confederate army's Sixty-ninth Regiment, North Carolina Troops, also called Thomas's Legion. Allen, *Annals of Haywood*, 160-163, 306; Cheney, *North Carolina Government*, 824, 1157, 1171; Frontis W. Johnston (ed.), *The Papers of Zebulon Baird Vance* (Raleigh: State Department of Archives and History, 1963), 67n.

William W. Holden to David S. Reid A&H-DSR

Raleigh,
Dec. 1, 1850

No nominations have yet been made for Treasurer or Comptroller. The Caucus called on Friday night was not full, on account of the rain, and one is called to-morrow night to decide finally. Hinton[1] and Collins[2] will both get some Democratic votes! Clarke,[3] I think, is *certain* for Comptroller, and Wheeler is the strongest for Treasurer.[4] If he should be nominated he will be elected, though some of our friends—McLean among them—"swear" they will *not* support him. It is impossible to say *who* will be Treasurer.

The Slavery Committee[5] is still at work. I understand they have decided by a vote of 9 to 5 that a State has a right to secede. It is impossible to say what will be done on this question. Two things, however, are certain, if action is had—The late "adjustment" will *not* be opposed, and it will be emphatically answered that if the fugitive-slave law is not enforced, the State will take steps to dissolve. This question gathers danger every hour. Nothing but the Providence of God, which guided and shielded Washington, can save the present Union. I have just read the Message of the Governor of South Carolina. It is a calm, strong, *decided* document. He *despairs*, but he does not say that South Carolina will or ought to go off by herself. He speaks of her destiny as common with that of her southern sisters. He recommends a day of Meditation and Prayer to the Almighty, for blessings and guidance in the midst of troubles, which has been appointed by the Legislature! You will come into office at a time of general anxiety, and heavy, very heavy will be the responsibility which you must incur. I have no doubt you will acquit yourself well.

Next week the two Houses will get fairly under way. I will write you again by Wednesday's Mail.

Mr. Mc[Gowan][6] at my request, will send you in a day or so, copies of the Treasurer's and Comptroller's Reports.

I have seen the rough sketch of the next Governor at Mr. Brown's[7] room. It will be a good likeness. Brown cannot be surpassed.

If I should get a copy of the President's Message in time, I will send it to you by Wednesday's Mail.

---

[1]Charles Lewis Hinton (1793-1861) of Raleigh was an 1814 graduate of the University of North Carolina. He was a member of the House of Commons (1820-1821, 1832) and the state Senate (1827-1830, 1833). He was a trustee of the university from 1832 to 1860 and served on the executive committee. From 1839 to 1843 and 1845 to 1851 he served as state treasurer. Hamilton and Williams, *Graham Papers*, I, 497n; Battle, *History of the University*, I, 788, 824, 826.

[2]William F. Collins, previously identified, of Nash County, was defeated eighty-seven to seventy-three by William J. Clarke of Raleigh for the office of state comptroller by legislative vote of December 5, 1850. *North Carolina Standard*, December 7, 1850

[3]William John Clarke (1819-1886), a native of Raleigh, was an attorney, soldier, state official, educator, and poet. An 1841 graduate of the University of North Carolina, he was severely wounded in the Mexican War. He served as state comptroller from 1850 to 1855. In 1857 he moved to Texas and became president of the San Antonio and Mexican Gulf Railroad. After returning to North Carolina he served as a Confederate officer during the Civil War, and in 1864 he was wounded in battle, captured, and imprisoned. After the war he was a businessman and educator and served as a superior court judge from 1870 to 1874. He was instrumental in the formation of North Carolina's Republican party. Powell, *DNCB*, I, 381-382.

[4]On December 19, 1850, the legislature elected Daniel W. Courts of Rockingham County as state treasurer. He served from 1851 to 1862. *North-Carolina Standard*, December 21, 1850; Cheney, *North Carolina Government*, 181.

[5]As a result of the controversy surrounding the Compromise of 1850 several resolutions concerning slavery were submitted to the General Assembly when it convened in November, 1850. A Joint Select Committee on Negro Slavery was formed to consider the resolutions and to make a recommendation to the General Assembly. J. Carlyle Sitterson, *The Secession Movement in North Carolina* (Chapel Hill: University of North Carolina Press, 1939), 74-77, hereinafter cited as Sitterson, *Secession*.

[6]Patrick McGowan (born 1805), an Irish stonecutter, was the only man of that surname in Raleigh in 1850. Seventh Census, 1850, Wake County, Population Schedule, 259.

[7]William Garl Browne, Jr. (1823-1894), one of North Carolina's leading antebellum portraitists, arrived in America from Leicester, England, in 1837. His work was exhibited at the National Academy in 1840. He is credited with designing the first state flag of North Carolina in 1861. Laura McMillan (comp.), *The North Carolina Portrait Index* (Chapel Hill: University of North Carolina Press, 1963), 253. The portrait referred to here is still owned by descendants of Reid, and there is a matching one of Mrs. Reid.

David S. Reid to Elizabeth Waugh[1] UNC-JP

Reidsville, N.C.,
December 2d, 1850.

I some time since wrote you in relation to hiring your servant Henry,[2] but your answer came while I was absent in Raleigh. While there however I saw J. A. Waugh, Esq.[3] who told me what you had been offered for him. I told him that I thought the price too high, but that

I would give you seventy-five dollars for him for the ensuing year and clothe him, and requested him so to write you and say to you that I requested you to write me to this place immediately that I might know what to depend on. Henry told me he would like to live with me. I have confidence in him and for that reason I am particularly anxious to get him, and would give more for him than he is actually worth. If you think $75 is not enough I will give you $80. I shall leave here for Raleigh on the 20th December; and if you conclude to take my offer I do not care how soon I can get him. Indeed I wish I had him now. If he is hired to Mr. Butner[4] for the whole of the present year tell Henry that he may say to him that if he will let him off so that he may get here by the 10 or 15th of December that I will pay him more than a reasonable compensation for his services from then till Christmas. If he could not get here by the 15th then I would want him to go direct to Raleigh & get there as soon as he could.

PS. Please answer me immediately as I wish to know what to depend on, for if I do not get Henry I must make other arrangements

[1]Elizabeth Robinett Waugh (1788-1857), of Forsyth County, was the widow of former Wilkes County state Senator James Waugh. They were married in 1805 and by the 1820s were living in Stokes County, from which Forsyth was created in 1849. Elizabeth Waugh, a native of Virginia, in 1850 owned 17 slaves and 80 acres of land, valued at $2,000. She lived in a settlement called Waughtown. Seventh Census, 1850, Forsyth County, Population Schedule, 52, Agricultural Schedule, 241, Slave Schedule, 220; Marriage bond of James Waugh and Elizabeth Robinett, July 24, 1805, Wilkes County Marriage Bonds (microfilm), Archives, Division of Archives and History, Raleigh; *Western Democrat* (Charlotte), August 4, 1857.

[2]Henry Waugh was a slave belonging to Elizabeth Robinett Waugh. In her will dated November 13, 1854, and proved in September 1857, Mrs. Waugh devised Henry to her daughter Susan L. Webb of Salem. What happened to him after 1857 is unknown, but he was not a resident of Forsyth County at the time of the 1870 census. In 1860 Susan L. Webb owned 17 slaves, several of whom were men within Henry's probable age range. Her 22-year-old daughter Mary A. Webb, who resided in Susan's household, also owned a 45-year-old male slave in 1860. [NOTE: The federal slave censuses of 1850 and 1860 list the ages, sex, and color of slaves, but not their names. Hence, positive identifications can be obtained only from other documents that may have occasionally survived.] Elizabeth Waugh Will; Eighth Census, 1860, Forsyth County, Population Schedule, 752, Slave Schedule, 175-176; Ninth Census, 1870, Forsyth County, passim.

[3]Jesse Albert Waugh, previously identified, son of Elizabeth Robinett Waugh. Elizabeth Waugh Will.

[4]Probably John Butner, postmaster in 1843 at Old Town (formerly Bethabara) in central Forsyth County, whose residence was not a great distance from that of Mrs. Waugh. John Butner to David S. Reid, December 30, 1843, Reid Papers, PC 1, State Archives.

David S. Reid to Elizabeth Waugh UNC-JP

Reidsville, N.C.,
Decr. 4, 1850.

I have just received your letter of the 1st. inst. I will take Henry[1] for next year at 84$ tho' I think the price too high.

I wish you would do me the favor to get him off from Mr. Buttner[2] so that he can get here by the 15th or 16th of this month at farthest. I *shall have a special use for him here about that time*,[3] and tell Henry to try to get off and come. I will pay Mr. Butner more than a reasonable price for his time. If he can get off by that time, I want him *here*, if he can not I want him to go direct to Raleigh as soon as he can. Tell Henry to attend to this matter & try & come here by the 15th or 16th. In taking up your offer it is with the understanding that you pay tax and medical bills. In haste

---

[1]Henry Waugh, a slave, previously identified.

[2]John Butner, previously identified.

[3]The "special use" that Reid had in mind may have related to his wedding to his first cousin, Henrietta Williams Settle, on December 19, 1850.

E[zekial] Dowdle[1] to David S. Reid RF

Franklin, Macon County, N. C.
11th Decr 1850

You *will* recollect, that, in a conversation with you at J. R. Silers,[2] on your return home last summer, I intimated an opinion in relation to what I *then* thought ought to be the course of *our* party—in the event that we should *have* been successful—in the *then late* election, I mean in relation to proscription from office for opinions—*plytical*—I have thought on that subject *some* since—& the more I think on it—the more I am convinced—that I was then right—I know that it has been the *usual* custom with the *whigs*—to go it to the *Knife*—& too—I—*believe*—that the general policy in all the *states*—& with the *dominant* party in the general government too—*has been*—that when ever any party went down—all the important offices had to change hands, and that too—upon the principles—that to the *victors*— belong the spoils and it does strike me that *now* the *whigs* in N. C. have about as little to expect as—

any where—and yet it strikes me—that the better course would be—not to draw the strings too tight—And now by this time—you are wondering what I am driveing at; Then, this is it, Curiosity is beginning to prompt the *Wis*-a-*kers* to speculate upon who is to be the *new* agent in Western N.C. for the collection of Cherokee debts—*etc*—and here let me say— that from *my* knowledge of things here—If I were to give an opinion—& if my suggestion is worth any thing—I would not advise the removal of the *present* agent; There are many reasons which I might give, but the *narrow* limits of a *letter*—forbid my going into detail—This mutch however I will say—That *that* office like many others in N.C. was established for the benefit of the *Million*—and not for the *few*—as the *party*—It is a responsible and a troublesome office—The individual who now fills it has—*I believe*—been faithful and honest—he is—a *whig*— this I suppose you know—but it does strike me—that in putting off the harness from him—you will make it necessarily *rub* some honest and *innocent* persons—who cannot *well* help themselves—and too—in any other aspect of the case—It seems to me that—by a change *now* there is nothing to gain—not but there are other *men* who would make as faithful and as—honest agents as the present incumbent— but I have come to this conclusion by my self—and upon consultation with some of my *best* friends—I find them of the same opinion—If my suggestions & opinions are worth any thing—you have *them*—You *can*—as you doubtless *will*—take such course—as you *may* think *will* promote the *best interest* of *all N.C.*—and with that I am satisfied and remain to be—your ever *obt*

[1]Ezekial Dowdle (born 1805), native of Rutherford County, was in 1850 sheriff of Macon County. Unmarried at that time, Dowdle boarded in the household of Jesse R. Siler in Franklin, the county seat. Seventh Census, 1850, Macon County, Population Schedule, 327-328.

[2]Jesse R. Siler (born 1797), merchant, was a brother of Jacob Siler, previously identified, Whig political appointee. Seventh Census, 1850, Macon County, Population Schedule, 327-328; Arthur, *Western North Carolina*, 173.

George Talcott[1] *to David S. Reid* A&H-DSR

Ordnance Department
Washington,
Decr. 20th. 1850

In order that arrangements may be made to answer the calls of the State for arms to be issued in the next year, under the Law of 1808, for arming the Militia, you are respectfully requested to inform this Department what description of arms will be required by the State of North Carolina, for the year 1851.

The quota due to the State will be furnished in Muskets, or other small arms, or in field artillery, if practicable, of such patterns as are adopted in the U. States' Service, and, you will be pleased to state particularly whether the appropriate accoutrements, equipments, harness &c, will be required with the kind of arms that may be designated.

Be pleased also to say at what place, and to whom, the stores shall be delivered.

By the existing regulations, the arms can be delivered only at points within the State, that may be situated on naturally navigable water.

The annual distribution is usually made in the month of August, in each year, but the arms &c: may be furnished at an earlier date, if required.

The quota which will be due for the next year, it is supposed will amount to about 580 Muskets

[1]George Talcott (d. 1862) of Connecticut entered the army as second lieutenant in 1813, and by 1815 he had been promoted to captain in ordnance. He remained in the ordnance section throughout his military career, becoming lieutenant colonel of ordnance in 1832 and colonel in chief in 1848. For meritorious service in the Mexican War he was appointed brevet brigadier general. Heitman, *Historical Register and Dictionary of the Army*, I, 943.

William Woods Holden (1818-1892), editor and publisher of the *North-Carolina Standard*, was instrumental in persuading Reid to run for governor in 1848. A close personal friend and political ally, Holden played an active role in Reid's gubernatorial campaigns. His daughter Henrietta "Etta" Reid, born in 1852, was named for Reid's wife. Photograph from the Barden Collection, Division of Archives and History.

Charles Manly (1795-1871), a Chatham County attorney, served as assistant clerk and chief clerk of the state House of Commons. In 1848, as the Whig candidate for governor, he defeated David S. Reid. In their next contest, two years later, he was defeated by Reid. Photograph of portrait courtesy of the Division of Archives and History.

John Kerr (1811-1879), Caswell County attorney, was the Whig candidate for governor in 1852. After his defeat by Reid, he was elected to the United States House of Representatives and the state House of Commons. He served as a state superior court judge in 1862 and from 1874 to 1879. Photograph from Saunders's *Open Doors and Closed Windows*, 258, provided by the Division of Archives and History.

Daniel William Courts (1800-1883), a native of Virginia and active Democrat, represented Surry and Rockingham counties in the General Assembly. He served two terms as state treasurer, from 1837 to 1839 and from 1851 to 1862. Photograph from *Heritage of Rockingham County, 1983*, Charles Dyson Rodenbough, ed. (Wentworth: Rockingham County Historical Society, 1983), 218.

John Hill Wheeler (1806-1882), Democratic attorney and historian, represented Hertford and Lincoln counties in the North Carolina House of Commons and served one term as state treasurer. His work on *Historical Sketches of North Carolina, from 1584 to 1851* is mentioned in correspondence with Reid. Photograph of engraving from the files of the Division of Archives and History.

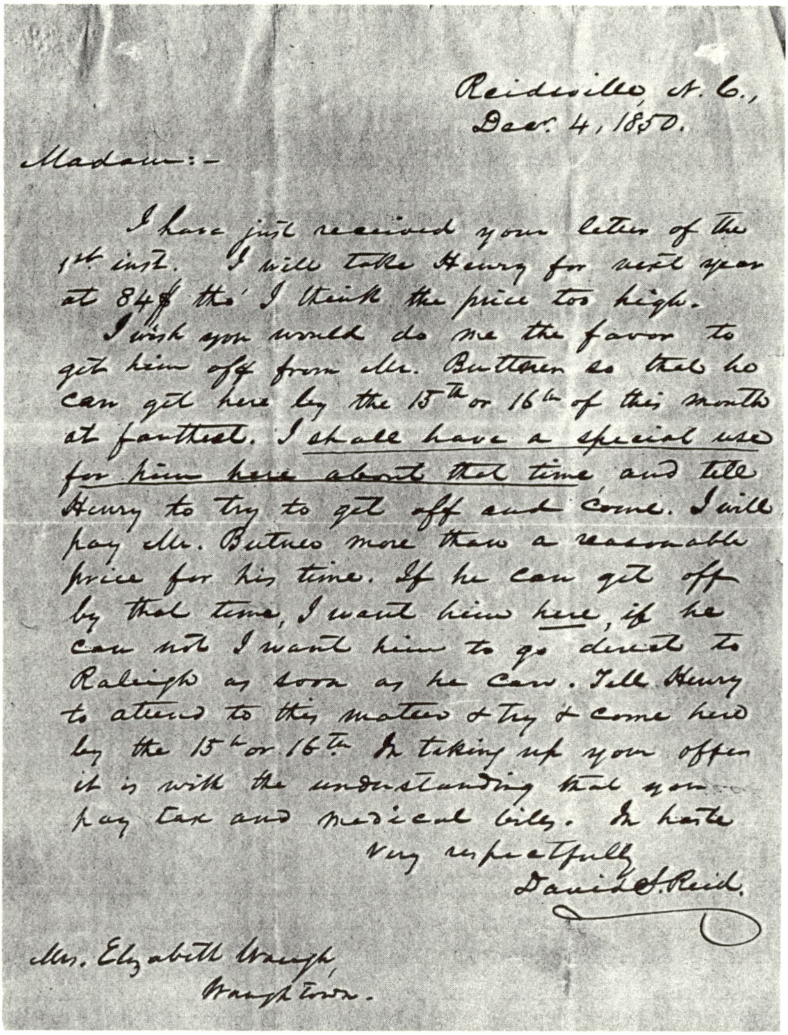

Reidsville, N.C.,
Dec. 4, 1850.

Madam:-

I have just received your letter of the 1st inst. I will take Henry for next year at 84$ tho' I think the price too high.

I wish you would do me the favor to get him off from Mr. Buttner so that he can get here by the 15th or 16th of this month at farthest. I shall have a special use for him here about that time and tell Henry to try to get off and come. I will pay Mr. Butner more than a reasonable price for his time. If he can get off by that time, I want him here, if he can not I want him to go direct to Raleigh as soon as he can. Tell Henry to attend to this matter & try & come here by the 15th or 16th. In taking up your offer it is with the understanding that you pay tax and medical bills. In haste

Very respectfully
David S. Reid.

Mrs. Elizabeth Waugh,
Waughtown.

This letter from David S. Reid to Elizabeth Waugh alludes to Reid's plans to marry Henrietta Settle on December 19, 1850. Photocopy courtesy of the Southern Historical Collection, University of North Carolina at Chapel Hill. Transcription on page 272.

1851

Inaugural Address of David S. Reid to the General Assembly A&H-DSR

[Raleigh]
January 1, 1851

Impressed with a deep sense of gratitude to my fellow citizens, I enter upon the duties of the station to which their kind partiality has called me, with the earnest invocation to Almighty God so to direct my official conduct as to promote the welfare, the prosperity, and the happiness of the people of the State. The duties of the Executive at all times delicate and responsible, are magnified by the importance of the crisis; and I should approach the fearful task assigned me with greater reluctance, were it not for the fact that I find myself surrounded by the Legislative authority of the State, confided to gentlemen whose wisdom and patriotism, I doubt not, will be found equal to the emergency.

The misguided fanaticism of Abolitionists at the North threatens the overthrow of the Constitution and a dissolution of the Union. The Slavery question is one of momentous importance to the Southern States of the Confederacy, involving an incalculable amount of property, as well as the domestic peace and security of our people. In the formation of the federal Constitution the institution of Slavery was recognized and provided for in a manner just and satisfactory to all the States. Subsequently, this question deeply agitated the country, and the South made concessions to the North and submitted to the Missouri compromise, with the assurance and expectation that this exciting element of political strife was to be forever put to rest. After availing herself of all the advantages derived under that compromise, the North urged exorbitant demands, which led to the enactment of the series of compromise measures passed by the present Congress, by which the South lost important rights by again making concessions to the North. The North, having availed herself of all the advantages under this compromise, does not cease to agitate the subject; and now threatens to repeal the only one of the measures which enured to the benefit of the South, accompanied, in many instances, by violent threats to disregard the Constitution and the laws, and to forcibly resist their execution.

We have not been indifferent to the encroachments that have been made on our rights, yet we have patiently suffered them with the hope they would not be again renewed. We now have just cause to fear that this hope was illusive. North Carolina, one of the last States to enter the Confederacy, yields to none of her sisters in ardent attachment to the Union. She would regard its dissolution as an awful calamity, which she would avoid at any sacrifice consistent with her rights and her safety. She came into the Union to be governed by the federal Constitution, and to secure herself against tyranny and oppression; and so long as the Constitution is faithfully adhered to and her rights respected, she will be among the last of the States to desert the Union. But she never gave her consent to enter into a Union which would overthrow the Constitution, violate her dearest rights, and manacle her with the fetters of oppression. To such a Union she owes no allegiance. A solemn sense of public duty impels me to declare, *that the encroachments of the North on the domestic institutions of the South, have already proceeded to the farthest allowable point.* Entertaining this opinion, I regard it as due to candor that we should make that fact known, that our brethren at the North may be fully informed that "we know our rights, and knowing, dare maintain them"; and that if they proceed in their aggressions, they must expect to meet the consequences.

In view of all the circumstances, I respectfully recommend to the General Assembly to provide—in the event of a contingency arrising to justify it—for taking the necessary steps to maintain the Constitution of the United States and the rights of this State; that we may co-operate with such other States as may determine to stand by a Union governed by the compromises of the Constitution. Pursuing this course, we shall feel a proud consciousness of the rectitude of our cause, and be justified in the estimation of all impartial minds; and then, if the awful calamity must come—which God forbid!—let the consequences fall upon those whose madness and folly have provoked it.

That the rights of the States may be respected, the Constitution preserved, and the Union, according to the Constitution, perpetuated, is my ardent wish; and the Legislature and the people of the State may rely upon my hearty co-operation in such measures as may tend to the consummation of these desirable objects.

It is well worthy of consideration whether our police regulations in relation to slaves and free persons of color are sufficient; and also, whether the public interest does not require further legislation to more effectually ensure the apprehension and conviction of persons who endeavor to excite slaves to rebellion or insurrection, or who kidnap or persuade them to leave their owners, and more especially in cases where such offenders flee to other States.

A judicious system of Internal Improvements by the State has ever been regarded as an object of importance worthy of the consideration and action of the General Assembly. Cheap transportation could not fail to add to the wealth and convenience of all classes of our citizens, and to the prosperity of the State. There are various objects which claim the consideration of the Legislature. Feeling a deep interest in the prosperity of every part of the State, and believing that the members of the General Assembly, residing as they do in the various Counties, will be fully prepared to give due consideration to the claims of every portion of the State, I do not feel myself called upon to decide between the peculiar merits of the many objects of public improvement which demand the patronage of the State. In carrying out a system of Internal Improvements a large expenditure of money is necessarily required, and it is not to be expected that a State can at once embark in all the schemes that are desirable. Works of this description should be undertaken with due caution in regard to their practicability and the adequacy of the means of the State to complete them. As a general rule, I think the Legislature which authorizes the construction of works of Internal Improvement ought, at the same time, to provide for raising the means for completion. Whether public opinion or the condition of the Treasury will justify the State at this time in embarking in other and new objects of improvement, and if so, to what extent, is a question which is submitted to the prudence and wisdom of the General Assembly. While a judicious system of Internal Improvements within the means and resources of the State, is desirable to all, yet a wild and extravagant one, involving the State in a large public debt without the prospect of a return of adequate advantages to the people, is to be deprecated. Such a system would, for a time at least, paralyze the spirit of improvement, and, with it, the prosperity of the State. The laws in force for carrying out works of Internal Improvement already provided for, and such others as the Legislature in its wisdom may hereafter provide for, so far as depends upon my action as Executive, shall be faithfully executed.

In a State like ours, where the popular voice directs and governs public affairs, education is a subject of general and paramount importance. It is therefore the policy of the State to foster and improve our system of Common Schools, so as to answer the laudable and beneficent purpose for which it is intended. In 1825, an act was passed setting apart certain sources of revenue for Common and convenient Schools, and providing for the distribution of its proceeds among the several Counties in proportion to the free white population in each, whenever in the opinion of the Legislature the same had sufficiently accumulated.[1] This fund did not sufficiently accumulate to put into operation a system of Common Schools, until the State received a considerable sum under the deposite act of Congress, the most of which sum, together with stocks belonging to the State, was transferred to, or invested for the use of, the Literary Fund. The State received this deposite from the General Government according to federal population, and the Assembly of 1836, which transferred these new acquisitions to the Literary Fund, expressly stipulated that they should be "subject at all times to the direction and control of the General Assembly." These accumulations had, in the opinion of the Legislature, sufficiently increased the fund to justify the commencement of a system of Common Schools; and in 1838, an act was accordingly passed. The act of 1840 provided that the nett annual income of the Literary Fund should be divided according to *federal population*. Since that time our School laws have been frequently revised and re-enacted, but every time retaining the principle of distribution according to federal population. Human ingenuity can devise no plan for the distribution of this fund that will not operate more favorably to some Counties than to others. Such a result is inseparable from the condition of the State; and it is believed that the present mode of distribution is, upon the whole, perhaps as just as any that could be adopted. The difference in the amount received by the larger number of Counties in the State, whether the distribution be according to federal or white population, would be very inconsiderable. Slaves are owned in every part of the State, and each County shares alike in the distribution in proportion to its federal population. Federal population is not made the basis of education, but of the distribution of the fund for that purpose. This principle of distribution has, in a commendable spirit of compromise, been time after time settled by the Legislature. Is the agitation of this question never to cease? The great inconvenience we have to encounter in relation to our system of Common Schools, I apprehend, is not to be found in the mode of distribution, but in the inadequacy of the fund and in the imperfect manner in which the Schools are regulated. And I submit whether, instead of continuing this agitation, which is calculated to array one portion of the State against the other, our attention may not be more properly directed to the enlargment of the fund and its proper investment, and to the improvement and better regulation of the Schools themselves.

The question of Equal Suffrage has for some time past engaged public attention, and it is believed that a large majority of the people demand this Constitutional reform. The subject embraces the plain proposition, whether the right to vote for the Senate shall be extended to such persons as are at present entitled to vote for the House of Commons. It is not doubted but such voters are fully competent to exercise the right of Suffrage in choosing both branches of the General Assembly. To withhold this invaluable privilege from those whom it is proposed to place upon terms of equality at the ballot box, upon the ground that if they enjoyed the right they might abuse it, is an unjust reflection upon their virtue and intelligence, and is denying the fundamental principle upon which all free governments are based. This question embraces no proposition to encroach on the rights of the landholder, but to extend to a numerous and meritorious class of our fellow citizens one of the dearest rights of American freemen. It is gratifying to know that this question of extending the right of Suffrage has not arrayed the landholders against the non-landholders, for such is the love of liberty and of equality among our people, that both classes are found actively co-operating in their efforts to carry out this question of Constitutional reform. Efforts have been made to connect with this question change of the basis of representation. I do not think that either justice or public policy demands such a change. The Convention of 1835, in a spirit of compromise and concession, adopted taxation as the basis for the Senate and federal population as the basis of representation for the House of Commons. The Abolitionists at the North wish to destroy the basis of federal population upon which we are represented in Congress. Their course on this subject is viewed as dangerous and mischievous; and I regard a similar movement in relation to our representation in the State Legislature, however well intended, as fraught with equal mischief and danger. The federal basis consists of three-fifths of the slaves added to the whole number of free persons. The white basis would wholly exclude the computation of slaves in representation. Persons other than voters are properly represented. Although federal population prevails as a basis, yet slaves do not vote, nor do white females and minors; still they are represented. Slaves, although property, are persons, and subject to legislation in that two- fold character.

Every county in the State is interested in the slave question, and the State should have but one voice on this important subject. Experience has but too recently shown us the sad consequesnce resulting from the agitation of the slavery question between the different States of the Union. Are these exciting scenes to be brought nearer home to us—to array one section of the State against another, and to destroy the good feeling, the peace and friendship which it is so desirable to cultivate between the various portions of the State? Let us forget that we are partizans, and bury this dangerous element of agitation, with the determination to unite our earnest exertions to promote the honor and prosperity of the State. Engrafting the white basis on Equal Suffrage would be an indirect, but a most certain and effectual mode of defeating the latter question. This must be obvious to every reflecting mind. Equal Suffrage, connected with a change of the basis, must fail; standing by itself, it must prevail. This amendment to the Constitution may be passed by the present and succeeding Legislatures, and submitted to the people for ratification in the manner provided in the Constitution, without incurring the expense of calling a Convention. In the initiatory step, it requires a larger number of the members of the Assembly to call a Convention than to pass the amendment. The Conventional mode of effecting this reform weakens the question, while the Legislative mode does not, and therefore the latter is preferable. It is believed that the success of this measure will be promoted by being submitted and voted upon as an isolated question, without being connected with any other Constitutional amendment.

The election of Judges and Justices of the Peace by the people, and for terms less than for life, are questions of Constitutional reform, which I recommend to the favorable consideration of the General Assembly. There are other amendments to the Constitution that have attracted public attention, to which, I doubt not, you will give that degree of consideration which their importance demands.

In conclusion, permit me to remark that the General Assembly may rely upon my hearty coo-poration in such measures as may tend to the prosperity and happiness of the people of the State.

[1]This was the Literary Fund Act, introduced by state Senator Charles Applewhite Hill of Franklin County. Powell, *DNCB*, III, 131-132.

Charles R. Jones[1] *to David S. Reid* A&H-GP

[Iredell County]
Head Quarters,
89th Regt. N.C. Militia
January 3, 1851.

His Excellency David S. Reid, Captain General,
Commander-in-Chief of the Militia of North Carolina

I have long felt the necessity of a well trained citizen-Soldiery in a Republican Government, such as ours; and at a time like the present, when our political horizon is black with portentious clouds of revolution, I think it the duty of every true patriot to prepare for the worst and use whatever of influence he may possess, for the good of our country, which we all so well love. With a view to events which may possibly transpire, I have labored for the past few months, to organize two volunteer companies in my Regiment, and I am happy to state that my efforts have proved successful to the utmost of my expectations; These two companies are now enrolled, organized, and equiped according to Law. Believing that you will take an interest in such matters, and feeling you will aid me all you can, I take pleasure in making application for arms for said companies; and I respectfully request that they be furnished with arms from the public arsenals, as provided by Law, &c. Enclosed I send you the certificate of Brig. Gen'l. C. W. Clarke,[2] commanding the Brigade of which my Regiment forms a part, as to the organization of a company of Riflemen. General Clarke writes me, that he has forwarded a communication to your predecessor, in regard to the organization of this company, and of a company of Light Infantry, concerning which I wrote him, enclosed in which communication, he forwarded to Gov. Manly his certificates of their organization and equipment, as required by Law.

I respectfully ask your excellency to have forwarded to my address a requisition on one of the public arsenals, (the nearest to this place) for the arms necessary for these two companies, to-wit: For Capt. Allen's comp'y of Lt. Infantry, *sixty bright muskets, complete; with bayonet-scabbards, cartridge- boxes, belts, buckles, plates, picks,* &c. For Capt. Wallace's company of Rifles, *sixty Rifles, (Hale's patent if possible) with bullet-pouches, powder-flasks, belts, plates, picks,* &c. and for the field-officers of the Regiment three pair of horseman's pistols, and holsters; with the necessary instructions for having executed to the State the bonds required by Law, of the commissioned officers of said companies, which bonds I will have faithfully executed as the Law requires.

I believe the prompt arming of these two companies will materially add to the military Spirit which I have been endeavoring to infuse into the minds of the people by whom I am surrounded. That the militia of some parts of Western Carolina, and this part in particular, needs a stimulus you will readily concede, and I hope you will help me to infuse a better spirit among the people in regard to military matters by granting me the arms I ask for, which I believe will have the effect. I hope that my efforts in organizing these two companies of volunteers, where none has heretofore existed, will meet with your approbation, and that you will forward as soon as convenient the necessary requisitions for arms, accoutrements, &c. &c.

---

[1]Charles R. Jones was a leading citizen of the Williamsburg community in Iredell County and colonel of the county militia regiment. Homer Keever, *Iredell: Piedmont County* (Statesville: Iredell County Bicentennial Commission, 1976), 181, hereinafter cited as Keever, *Iredell.*

[2]Cornelius W. Clarke of Lenoir, Caldwell County, was brigadier general of a state militia division. He served a term in the House of Commons in 1856 and 1857. C. W. Clarke to Reid, December 23, 1850, Reid Papers, PC 1, State Archives; Cheney, *North Carolina Government*, 324.

John A. Gilmer[1] *to David S. Reid* A&H-GP
[Private]

[Raleigh]
[Jany. 6th. 1851]

I intend to introduce a bill to make it the duty of the Keeper of the Capitol to work on and improve the public Square &c to be paid what his labor may be worth—that is his Salary. & a reasonable pay for the work he may do on the Square &c. Please make no appointment until the fate of my bill is known A good mechanic, would in this way cheaply in the course of two years beautify the Square &c—and attend to the Capitol also

[1]John A. Gilmer (1805-1868), a Greensboro attorney, served in the state Senate (1846-1856) and the United States Congress (1857-1861). In 1856 he was defeated as the Whig candidate for governor. *Biographical Directory of Congress*, 948.

William W. Holden to David S. Reid A&H-DSR

[Raleigh]
[Jan 7, 1851]
Monday Morning.

I ought to have written you last evening, according to your request.

You desired my opinion, finally, about the Boards. It seems to me, after some reflection, that it would be as good a plan as any to appoint Alfred Jones[1] and R. P. Dick[2] on the Litera[r]y Board, and put Mr. Bragg[3] on the other Board with Mr. Graves.[4] *Locality*, if the right sort of a man can be found, amounts to nothing. Dick and Bragg are both very suitable for these posts, and if you should prefer Dick, or any one else (a Democrat) from a distance, I know of no one of the Whigs of this County who would do better than Alfred Jones.

I have written this at your request, but hope you will do as it may seem best to you, without reference to my opinion. You know much more about the whole matter than I do, and have no doubt given to it a good deal of anxious consideration.

[1]Alfred Jones of Wake County served on the Council of State from 1830 to 1834. He was appointed in March, 1851, not to the Literary Board but instead as presi-

dent of the board of the Institution for the Deaf and Dumb. The Literary Board appointment, however, went to Wesley Jones of Wake County. Alfred Jones was named to the Literary Fund Board on February 20, 1853, during Reid's second term in office. Cheney, *North Carolina Government*, 175; *North-Carolina Standard*, February 5, 1851; *Wilmington Journal*, February 14, May 30, 1851; Governors Office Records, "Commissions and Resignations, 1841-1855."

[2]Robert Paine Dick, previously identified.

[3]Thomas Bragg (1810-1872), a native of Warren County, was an attorney in Jackson, Northampton County. He was a member of the House of Commons in 1842 and 1843, a delegate to several Democratic national conventions, and an 1851 appointee to the Board of Internal Improvements. He served as governor from 1855 to 1859 and was in the United States Senate from 1859 to 1861. He served as the Confederate States attorney general from 1861 to 1863. Sobel and Raimo, *Biographical Directory of Governors*, III, 1134-1135.

[4]Calvin Graves, previously identified, had been appointed to the Board of Internal Improvements in 1849 by Whig Governor Charles Manly. He was reappointed by Reid and served until 1854. Powell, *DNCB*, II, 343.

Reuben Deaver[1] *to David S. Reid* A&H-GP

Sulphur Springs N.C
9th Jany 1851

From our intimate conversation, held while you were with me last summer, I expected to *hear*, what I have already seen in the public print,[2] (and if it is in print it must be so) Therefore allow me to tender you the right hand of fellowship and wish you many long and happy days; for man (I think) is nothing without his better half—

I now insist, that some time during next summer I must have the honor of the Governor & *Governess* in my house at the same time, So as to show my Southern friends the marked difference between one Governor and his *Lady*, and two *Governors*.—

Private—Read when at Leasure

I have some knowledge, of the extent to which you were harassed, last summer while west of this place, *for appointments* &c. and I also recollect that yourself and I agreed on one particular, and that is this, that it is plain to be seen, that those men of Macon & Cherokee, want all the Cherokee Lands, or the proceeds expended in their own Country, and I think, that let the Law be passed as it may, for the building of the Turnpike, resurvey, and changing the mode of collecting the debts for land already sold, and give those men the controll, we will have neither road or money—to benifit the State, for if by management all the proceeds should be exhausted before the road reaches Asheville what benifit would it be to the State or the comunity west of Asheville—

I know that from reading the foregoing that you have already made up your mind, that I am taking more liberty with you than belongs to me, and at the same time expect to hear an *application* for appointment for myself; well I acknowledge *the corn*. I would like to be commissioner of the road; or should the Legislature Order another survey, I would willingly accept that office from your hands, although at less proffit I should feel bound to finish the work I had once began!

You have an idea of my capacity, and I think together with your own knowledge it would be nothing but right to enquire of others, but at the same time I beg you, not be misled by those men west of Haywood, as I have hinted above, I say west of Haywood for I am willing to refere you to Col. Love—but west of him I have doubts, and they are founded upon good reasons, and one of which no doubt you *will* see if not already, (viz), a man that takes it upon himself to travel over 300 miles, & bearing his own expence hunting Office that would pay poorly I think has some further Speculation in view, (I must here except candidates for Govr.) but yet my notion of a candidate & office hunting are as different as the moon & green cheese—

Upon the whole I will venture to sugest this idea, that you make all appointments (devolving on you) concerning the Cherokee Lands or Turnpike, east of Macon County.

I have thus spoken to you (Private) the same that I would tell you were you in my house at the dead hour of night, for so help me *God* I wish, and hope to see, your administration of State Affairs turn out different and more prosperous than for several years heretofore, and from the many applicants, I know you cannot satisfy all, Therefore I beg you, That upon your reflection you find that you have nothing to give me, I will be content, Satisfied, and unchanged.

I have written to several of my friends (some time past) to ask of you the appointment I now ask, simply for the reason that I disliked to trouble you with reading letters, but upon reflection I come to the conclusion, an office not worth asking for, was not worth having—

---

[1]In 1850 Reuben Deaver resided in Cherokee County; however, Sulpher Springs was a community in Buncombe County. Seventh Census, 1850, Cherokee County, Population Schedule, 64.

[2]Reid's marriage to Henrietta W. Settle, daughter of Thomas Settle, took place in Rockingham County on December 19, 1850, and was widely reported in state newspapers. *Raleigh Times*, January 3, 1851.

George W. Houk[1] *to David S. Reid* A&H-GP

Dayton O.
Jany 10th 51.

Please inform me whether there is not a provision in your statutes which allows a Jury Trial to a reclaimed fugitive Slave in case he sets up a claim in your State to his freedom. If so have the kindness in your answer to give me the language of the Section & a reference to the volume where it is to be found—Also the Section which provides for the punishment of kidnappers—

I wish to use these against the abolitionists whose infernal system of falsehood and misrepresentation is pursued with all the zeal of blind & traitorous fanaticism

An answer at your Earliest convenience will greatly oblige

[1]George W. Houk (1825-1894), an attorney from Dayton, Ohio, was a state legislator, a state Democratic leader, and a representative in Congress from 1891 to 1894. *Biographical Directory of Congress*, 1078.

Thomas A. Hayden[1] *to David S. Reid* A&H-DSR

Rutherfordton,
Jan. 10, 1851.

The materials used by me in the publication of the Mountain Banner were transfered to Mr Wilson[2] on the 22d October, 1850, At the time I proposed the sale, my terms were cash, when your proposition came, subscribing $250 payable in six months, Mills[3] & Carson[4] promising to pay up their subscription, I was unwilling to keep Wilson longer in suspence, and I accepted your terms. I do not now *dun* you, and I dislike to trouble you, knowing that weightier matters claim your attention, but my pecuniary embarrassments are of such a nature, that I feel like crying "Help—or I sink." If by any possibility you can make it convenient to pay the amount of your subscription *now*, I shall esteem it a favor, to be reciprocated, should opportunity offer; a check on Charleston or the North would suit.

Wilson is doing well—though the Democratic party has done but little to increase his circulation—he has lost no Whig subscribers,—

stir up the Leaders to his support—the Western Reserve is worthy of attention.

Write me at your leisure, that I, like the man of the Asheville Messenger may boast a letter from the "highest dignatary" of the State—Wishing you a prosperous Administration, and a never ending *honey-moon*, I am yours truly

---

[1]Thomas A. Hayden (1810-1851), originally from Florida, settled in Rutherfordton around 1830. He published the *Mountain Banner* from 1848 to 1851 and served as a justice of the peace and county coroner. Griffin, *Old Tryon and Rutherford*, 240n.

[2]Frank I. Wilson was an attorney and teacher in the local academy at Rutherfordton. He coedited the *Mountain Banner* from 1848 to 1851, when he became the owner, initially in partnership with Reid. In 1853 the *Mountain Banner* was moved to Salisbury, and the next year Wilson joined Holden on the *North-Carolina Standard* as associate editor. Griffin, *Old Tryon and Rutherford*, 241n.

[3]Probably Columbus Mills (1802-1882), a physician from Rutherford and Polk counties, who served in the state Senate (1846-1847, 1854-1857) and on the Council of State (1853-1855, 1859-1861). During the Civil War he served as a surgeon in the Sixteenth Regiment North Carolina Troops. He was instrumental in the formation of Polk County, and the county seat, Columbus, is named for him. Griffin, *Old Tryon and Rutherford*, 229; Cheney, *North Carolina Government*, 178-179, 1264; Sadie Smather Patton, *Sketches of Polk County History* (Spartanburg: The Reprint Company, 1976), 25-27, 46, 62. However, Ladson A. Mills represented Rutherford in the House of Commons during the 1852 Assembly and later in the state Senate (1858-1859), and William E. Mills served in the House of Commons (1838-1845). Cheney, *North Carolina Government*, 1264-1265.

[4]Possibly Joseph McDowell Carson of Rutherford County, who served in the House of Commons (1829-1830, 1835), and the state Senate (1832-1833, 1836-1839). Cheney, *North Carolina Government*, 1264-1265.

Message from His Excellency, Gov. David S. Reid to the General Assembly Relative to Putting Under Contract the Western Turnpike Road NCC

Executive Office,
Raleigh,
Jan. 14*th*, 1851.

Under the existing law, the Commissioner appointed to put under contract the Western Turnpike Road, is not authorized to let it out in contracts of less than one mile. A change of the law, so as to leave it to the discretion of the Commissioner to let the road in smaller contracts, would open competition to such as could not conveniently undertake a contract of one mile, and thereby cheapen the construction of the road, and at the same time facilitate its completion. I respectfully recommend, that the act be accordingly amended.[1]

I deem it my duty to recommend to your favorable consideration, the debtors to the State for the purchase of Cherokee lands. A knowledge of their embarrassed condition, constrains me to say that their situation presents a strong appeal to the General Assembly, for the passage of an act for their relief.

I also recommend that the legislature provide for the sale or entry of the unsold surveyed and unsurveyed Cherokee lands to *actual settlers* in limited quantities, and at reasonable prices, giving preemption rights to such persons as are settled on the lands. I feel confident, that justice to the people in that part of the State, where these lands are located as well as the true interests of the State at large, demand this course of policy[2].

---

[1]David Weimar Siler, a Whig member of the House of Commons from Macon County, introduced on January 14 a bill to amend the Western Turnpike act of 1848-1849. Referred to the Committee on Internal Improvements, it was reported out on January 27, read a second time and tabled, 61-27. *North-Carolina Standard*, January 22, 29, 1851.

[2]After much debate and complaints by the Whigs of Reid's "executive dictation," Public Act 29, entitled "An act to provide relief for purchasers of Cherokee lands, secure debts due to the State and authorize the sale of lands surrendered to the State under acts of 1844-5 and 1846-7," passed the state Senate by a 33-14 vote on January 23, 1851, and was concurred with by the House. The General Assembly of 1850-1851 also passed Resolution 53, "a resolution for the relief of certain purchasers of Cherokee lands, residing in Macon county." *North-Carolina Standard*, January 25, February 1, 5, 1851.

Charles Manly to David S. Reid A&H-DSR
[with enclosure]

[Raleigh]
Jan 17 51

In reply to your note of this evening, enclosing a copy of a Resolution of the Senate upon the subject of the School Fund & desiring to know where the information can be obtained that will enable you to answer the Senate's call I refer you to the ward or pigeon hole of the press in your office where the papers & correspondence of the two last years are deposited & which I think I pointed out to you. You will there find a package marked "Common Schools" which contains all the returns of the Superintendents referred to in the Report of the Literary Board. In that package is a list in my handwriting or that of Col. Settle[1] giving the names of the Counties & of the Superintendents who had made returns at that time.

Subsequently other returns were received, which do not appear in that list, but they are all in the same package tied up together with a red string.

The Senate's Resolution is herewith returned.

[Enclosure]

Resolved, That the Governor as President of the Literary Board be requested to inform the Senate in what Counties the School Fund, as mentioned in the Report of said Board, lies unemployed, and the name of the Chairman of the Board of Superintendant in each of said counties: also from what Counties no returns have been made by the Chairman of the Board of Superintendents and the names thereof.

[1]This appears to be a reference to Reid's uncle and father-in-law Thomas Settle, a Whig who had the confidence of retiring Governor Manly. Reid, however, as new governor was by law president of the Literary Board, and on March 31, 1851, he influenced the new board to elect his first cousin and private secretary Thomas Settle, Jr., as secretary of the Literary Fund Board. *State Board of Education: Literary Board Minutes, Letters, Reports, etc., 1848-1853*, volume 4, p. 302.

Asa Biggs to David S. Reid RF

[Raleigh]
[filed Feb. 2, 1851]

I leave this morning for home having obtained an opportunity to go down by private conveyance and as I shall not see you again I wish to say that I must beg leave to request that you will not nominate me as one of the Internal Improvement board.[1] Upon consideration of the matter it is more than probable that the duties of that board will conflict with my business at home so much as to render it impracticable for me to attend to it and if I were to accept I should desire to attend the meetings promptly: this coupled with the other reasons of which I have spoken to you induces me to decline, while it would afford me great pleasure to aid you in any part of your administration that might be desirable. I write in great haste and am as ever Truly yours,

[1]Reid's nominations for the Internal Improvements Board, confirmed by the Council of State, were Calvin Graves of Caswell County and Thomas Bragg, Jr., of Northampton County. *North-Carolina Standard*, February 5, 1851.

Hezekiah G. Spruill[1] *to David S. Reid* A&H-GP

Plymouth N.C.
Feby 3d 1851

I had the honor of addressing you a letter a few weeks since, making enquiry of you, of the proper way to secure a title to a small tract of State Lands, and address you, now to ask your attention to the subject.

It has been held that no title could be procured for Swamp Lands, by the ordinary course of Entry & Patent; but that the Literary Board would make title, when the Lands were surveyed & valued by disenterested persons.

The Land to which I refer, is not among the surveyed Lands, belonging to the state, nor is it located near the lands which have been drained. My object is to secure a title, and I am willing to have it surveyed & valued, or Enter & Patent, it; whichever course may be indicated by you.

I regret exceedingly that our General Assembly should have adjourned, without taking the proper Stand, upon the subject of Southern Rights—Rely upon it that the Doctrine of Secession, is the strong & popular doctrine in this State—it is the only position that the South can take to sustain itself; and it is a right which the people, will hold on to; No man can sustain himself before the People who will not admit the right of the oppressed states to secede—I had hoped for more independence, for less subserviency in the late Genl Assembly—by [which] I am disappointed—

[1]Hezekiah G. Spruill of Plymouth was a delegate from Tyrrell County to the Constitutional Convention of 1835 and served in the House of Commons (1831-1832) and the state Senate (1836-1843). Cheney, *North Carolina Government*, 818, 1289.

John H. Wheeler to David S. Reid A&H-GP

Beattiesford NC
7th Feb 51

Now that "the noise and confusion" of the Legislature is over, I trust that you will not consider the resuming of our correspondence as irregular or improper.

I could have wished that something had turned out different at the late session—but Shakespeare motto "All's well that ends well" is a good one, and I am entirely reconciled. Doubtless you noticed the laconic speech of G N Briggs[1] in yielding up the chair of state in Masstts. to his Demo successor It was in good taste, and to the point. I should have been most happy to have contributed my feeble aid to your successful administration of the Government of my native and beloved State. This one of the chief reasons why I desired to be reinstated to the position[2] from which I was removed by the Goths and vandals of 1844—But "no of this, Hal, 'an thou covert me" I think I hear you say. I will never allude to it again verbally or in writing, if I can help it.

I have noticed your reception by the Register. The illiberal and low attacks of that Press upon you only recoil upon his own party's head—for no one thinks them worthy of notice. I had intended to write an editorial for the Republican at Lincolnton. But I thought the game not worth the powder. I could not help saying to Genl. Bynum who was here the other day that I was surprized at his attack—He disclaimed the words of the Register and said that he never used the language towards you as that print had attributed to him.

I hope that you may have a pleasant time at Raleigh, but I fear you will realize that Shakespeare said more truth than poetry, when he declares "Uneasy tis the Head that wears a crown"

You must allow me to congratulate me [*sic*] on your marriage—which I suppose it true, as it is published—But you have the sin at your door, of making me say to the Ladies that you were in the market. But I like Tallyrand believed, that with lovers, sometimes as in politics "words are made to conceal our ideas."

That Book[3] is rapidly progressing although you predicted it would be sometime before it saw the light. I hope to publish it this Spring, as soon as I can make some extracts from the State Department Govr Swain's[4] collection, Col Force's[5] documents, Mr Bancroft[6] manuscripts and the Census returns.

It has received much more favour from various portions of the State than I had even hoped for or its merts deserve. This encourages me to make it worthy of its subject. I shall be down about the end of the month on my way north. In the interim I hope to hear from you,

Friend Holden owes me a letter—but I suppose such has been the confusion incident to the rising of the Assembly that he has neglected to write at the moment.

With my best wishes for your happiness in which Mrs. W. Cordially unites

---

[1]George Nixon Briggs (1796-1861), an attorney from Lanesboro, Massachusetts, was a Whig representative in Congress (1831-1843), governor of Massachusetts (1844-1851), and a judge of the state Court of Common Pleas. He was a founder of the Massachusetts state Republican party. Sobel and Raimo, *Biographical Directory of Governors*, II, 702-703.

[2]Wheeler was elected state treasurer in 1842. He was defeated in 1844 for the same office by Whig candidate Charles L. Hinton. The House of Commons on December 18, 1844, passed a resolution directing treasurer-elect Hinton to request departing treasurer Wheeler "to pay into the Treasury $81.00 (said to be a deficit) and in case of a failure directing the Attorney General to institute suit against Col. Wheeler." Democrats supported a motion to reconsider, but it was defeated 61-53 after strong debate the next day and remained a point of bitter contention for some time afterward. Ashe, *Biographical History*, VII, 474; *North-Carolina Standard*, December 24, 1844.

[3]This is a reference to Wheeler's forthcoming *Historical Sketches of North Carolina from 1584 to 1851*...(Philadelphia, 1851).

[4]David Lowry Swain (1801-1868), a native of Buncombe County, studied briefly at the university and became an attorney in 1823. He served in the House of Commons (1824-1830), as a judge of the superior court (1830-1832), and as governor (1832-1835). He was the first Whig and the youngest governor in the state's history. He was active in the state Constitutional Convention of 1835 and was then elected president of the state university, serving from 1835 to 1868. A founder of the North Carolina Historical Society, he was active in collecting colonial records. Ashe, *Biographical History*, I, 447-457; Sobel and Raimo, *Biographical Directory of Governors*, III, 1126-1127.

[5]Peter Force (1790-1868), was an archivist and historian from New York and Washington, D.C. In 1836 he served as the mayor of the District of Columbia. He is noted for his facsimile publication of historical documents in *American Archives*. *DAB*, VI, 512-513.

[6]George Bancroft (1800-1891), a historian and diplomat from Massachusetts and Washington, D.C., was an 1817 graduate of Harvard. His monumental ten-volume *History of the United States* was the first major history written of the country. He served as secretary of the navy (1845), minister to Great Britain (1846-1847), and minister to Prussia (1867-1874). *DAB*, I, 564-570.

William H. Miller[1] *to David S. Reid* A&H-GP

University of North Carolina
Feb 8th 1851

A number of Students connected with the University of North Carolina feeling desirous to form an Association to be called the "Southern Rights Association," and Learning from Gov Swain that it was contrary to the Laws of the Institution to establish a Society of any description therein, unless it be by consent of the Executive Committee. Therefore at a preliminary meeting of those Students wishing to form such a Body it was-Resolved—That the Secretary be authorized to correspond with Gov Reid upon the subject of the formation of a "Southern Rights Association" In accordance with the above Resolution I address you.

Trusting that you will, as soon as possible, lay this request before the Executive Committee, and forward to me their decision

[1]William H. Miller, a native of Virginia, was a student at the University of North Carolina in 1850 and 1851. Grant, *Alumni History*, 430.

Elisha Mitchell[1] *to David S. Reid* A&H-GP

University of N Ca.
Feby 10th 1851

I presume that in common with the other members of the Board[2] over whose deliberations you preside you may be willing to receive suggestions respectfully presented in relation to the best method of carrying into effect the act of the Legislature directing a Geological survey of North Carolina— the measures to be adopted and the men to be employed. Feeling, myself some interest in the success of the undertaking I venture to address to you a few lines respecting it and to state a fact or two in regard to which, it may without any discredit to them, be supposed, that the board are not very fully informed

The state is divided by a line running in a southwesterly direction from near where the Roanoke enters it from Virginia; to where the Pedee leaves it on the side of South Carolina, into two parts corresponding somewhat to each other in extent and wholly unlike in their Geological character. They require for their examination men of widely different scientific accomplishments. The person eminently qualified to take the part of the State lying on the Northwestern side of the line in hand; may, and very probably will be very indifferently fitted for an examination of the other.

There seems therefore to be no good method of providing that all parts of the state shall receive the attention of men well qualified for the undertaking, other than what was pursued in New York—where different sections of the state and different departments in those sections were given in charge to several individuals each of whom was held responsible for what had to be accomplished in his own particular line of duty and for nothing else.

It is desirable that the persons employed shall if possible be natives of the state so that whatever credit may be acquired by the successful prosecution of the enterprise may redound to the honour of North Carolina and be added to that of having directed the work and provided the funds to be employed in carrying it on.

My main object in writing then is simply this—before any appointments shall have been made and engagements entered into from which it will be impossible to recede—; to call your attention to a gentleman now occupying the place of Resident Surgeon in the New York Hospital—Dr. Frederic D Lente.[3]

This is a native of New Berne—a graduate of the University— and most favourably known amongst us here as a gentleman of talents industry and worth—as the fact of his having been appointed to fill the place just named also sufficiently testifies.

Besides having qualified himself for the practice of his profession by an earnest devotion of himself to the study of anatomy and surgery he has given a good deal of attention to one department of Natural history—that of Ornithology—and though not fully qualified at this moment to discharge the duties of Geologist, so far as the South Eastern or Seaboard portion of the State is concerned Yet his studies have for some years lain in that direction. He has been occupied with kindred pursuits so that it would be comparatively easy for him to prepare himself to do the thing well and if after having finished it—sufficient inducements could be held out to determine him to settle amongst us—the work might be expected still to go on after the labours of the persons officially engaged in it had been brought to a close.

I do not know that Dr Lente would consent to be employed in this business—having held no communication with him upon the subject. I do not know that he has been informed and is aware that the legislature have directed a survey to be made. But I do know that such occupation would be congenial to his taste and feelings and I think he would execute the work so creditably to himself and to North Carolina—so much better than any other person you would be likely to employ, that I should be pleased to hear that proposals having reference to it had been made to him.

I will trouble your Excellency no farther but am with much respect, your obedient servant

---

[1]Elisha Mitchell (1793-1857), a native of Connecticut, was a university professor of mathematics and then professor of chemistry, geology, and mineralogy. A Yale gradute of 1813, he went to Chapel Hill in 1817 and remained there the rest of his life. He fell to his death while verifying the highest peak east of the Mississippi River, Mount Mitchell, which bears his name. *DAB*, XIII, 45-46; Ashe, *Biographical History*, I, 384-391.

[2]Reid, as previously noted, served by virtue of his office as governor as president of the Literary Board, under whose jurisdiction the geological survey fell.

[3]Frederick Divoux Lente (1823-1883), a native of New Bern, received degrees from the Universityof North Carolina in 1845 and 1848. He was a surgeon at West Point Foundry, professor of gynecology at New York University, and assistant surgeon at Woman's Hospital in New York City. He was founder and president of the American Academy of Medicine. Grant, *Alumni History*, 362.

Albert M. Shipp[1] to David S. Reid A&H-GP

[Chapel Hill]
Feb. 12, 1851

I write to make application to the Executive Committee to authorize the sale of a small lot of about two acres owned by the Trustees of the University and lying directly opposite the one recently sold to Prof. Hubbard.[2] I desire to purchase said lot because mine without some additions, is too small and inconvenient. Gov. Swain with whom I have confered on this subject thinks the Trustees will not hesitate but readily grant my request. It will be gratifying to me if this matter can be acted upon at an early day so that, if successful in the application I make [*sic*] get immediate possession of the lot.

---

[1]Albert M. Shipp (1819-1887), from Lincoln County, graduated from the University of North Carolina in 1840 and became a Methodist minister and educator. He was the second president of Greensboro College (1847-1850), professor of history at the state university (1850-1859), president of Wofford College (1859-1875), and dean of the Theology Department at Vanderbilt University (1876-1886). Samuel B. Turrentine, *A Romance of Education* (Greensboro: Piedmont Press, 1946), 48-55.

[2]Fordyce M. Hubbard, a graduate of Williams College in Massachusetts, was an Episcopal clergyman and rector of Christ Church, New Bern. In 1848 he became professor of Latin at the state university and remained there for twenty years. He served as librarian from 1865 to 1868 and then as university chaplain. He later taught at St. John's College in New York. Battle, *History of the University*, I, 518, 784.

Jacob Siler to David S. Reid A&H-GP

Agency Office
Macon County N.C.
Feb. 17th. 1851

From a reliable sourse I learn that at the late Session of the Legislature a law passed that body for the relief of the solvant portion of debtors for Cherokee land—to carry out which law you are authorised to appoint three Commissioners unconnected with the sale of said lands and without wishing to dictate to you here let me respectfully recommend to your favourable consideration the name of Maj. E. Dowdle[1] of this County to make one of said three commissioners who from my knowledg of his business habits and prompness in business I am sattisfied would make a suitable commissioner and I also believe that his appointment to the office would give general satisfaction—

[1]Ezekial Dowdle, previously identified, was a Democrat and sheriff of Macon County in 1850. A bachelor at that time, he resided in the household of Siler's brother Jesse. Dowdle had written to Reid on December 11, 1850, requesting that Reid retain Jacob Siler, a Whig, as superintendent of the Western Turnpike, but Reid eventually deposed Siler and appointed Nimrod Jarrett to the position. Jesse Siler, T. P. Siler, H. G. Woodfin, J. M. Bryson, and sixteen other Macon County residents on February 15, 1851, petitioned Reid to appoint Dowdle and Mark Coleman as commissioners to value Cherokee lands. Governors Papers, Reid.

E. P. Sharp[1] *to David S. Reid* A&H-GP

Murphey N.C.
February 18th 1851

I have been in this Village for some days and say to you as a friend that the Citizens of Cherokee are well pleased with the part you taken in recommending the pasage of what is called the relief bill.

I hope you will give us, western men for commissioner, and amongst all the names that has been Segested to you I hope you will select Mark Coleman, Esqr[2] of Macon County I know him well and say to you that he is a warm friend of yours, as well as a gentleman of high standing in the Community and is well calculated to do equal Justice betwen the Cherokee Land purchasers and the State If you can consistantly confer the appointment on him, I do assure you that it will meet the approbation of many of your friends in this Country

I am Sir your friend & obedient Servant

---

[1]This may have been Eli Sharp, who lived in Buncombe County in 1850. Seventh Census, 1850, Buncombe County, Population Schedule, 221.

[2]Mark Coleman was an early settler of Macon County. Arthur, *Western North Carolina*, 173. Reid's eventual appointments, made on March 27, 1851, for commissioners to value Cherokee lands, went to Coleman, Henry Cansler of Lincoln County, and John McDowell of Rutherford County. Governors Office Records, "Commissions and Resignations, 1841-1855."

Ebenezer Emmons[1] *to David S. Reid* A&H-GP

Albany [New York]
Feb 19 1851

I was employed last Spring by a company of Gentlemen of the State to make a Geological examination of a Tract of Land in the Western part of North Carolina which gave me an opportunity of forming an acquaintance with several distinguished friends who feel an interest in scientific pursuits—Since my return several of these Gentlemen have solicited me to take measures which may secure my services in the then contemplated survey & which I am now informed has been ordered by the Legislature. I desire therefore to communicate with your Excellency upon the subject unless indeed the appointments have already been made or your views may be adverse to the employment of persons who are not residents of your State—

I have been employed by this State since 1836; first in the Geological survey & afterwards in the Agricultural survey—the results of which are published in 4 quarto vols. 3 of which are in the hands of one of the Gentlemen of the Senate—I should say however, that the last or 4 vol was not forwarded until near the close of the session & may not have been received as I have no acknowledgement of its safe arrival—I speak of those volumes as testimonials of the character of the work to which I have been devoted almost exclusively since 1836 though scarcely more so since, than previous to that time

[1]Ebenezer Emmons (1799-1863), a native of Massachusetts, became a physician, college professor, and state geologist of both New York and North Carolina. After graduation from Rensselaer Institute, he was a lecturer in chemistry at Williams College for two years and then returned to Rensselaer. He was named to the New York state geological survey in 1838 and later became professor of chemistry at Albany Medical School. In 1851 he was appointed to direct the North Carolina geological survey and continued as director until his death in Brunswick County. *DAB*, VI, 149.

John Gray Bynum to David S. Reid A&H-GP

Rutherfordton
Feb 20th 1851.

I have received a letter from Prof. Ebenezer Emmons of Albany New York, requesting me to present his name to your Excellency as a candidate for the appointment of Geological & Agricultural surveyor, and with a request that, if any recommendations were desired, that you would refer to Gov Marcy[1] or any of the distinguished individuals who have filled the office of Gov. of New York for the last ten years. Prof. Emmons was appointed by Gov Marcy ten years ago to conduct a similar survey of the State of New York. The bill which passed the Legislature I draw up according to his suggestions, and I am sure no individual could be found to carry out the objects of the act better than he will be able to do. Prof. Emmons was employed by a company in New York, who own some 300,000 acres of land in the counties of Rutherford, Buncombe, Henderson, McDowell Cleveland & Mecklenburg & Union to make a mineralogical survey, of their lands. He performed that duty last summer and some of his discoveries are of the greatest importance to the state. He has discovered the existence of gold ores, to an extent not heretofore suspected by our most scientific minds and which I think will show N.C to be the richest Gold Country in the Union. Those matters I personally know to be true. In addition to his Geological and mineralogical knowledge, he is a very iminent agriculturist and has for many years conducted the most scientific agricultural journal in the Union. His report of the survey of New York shows a most thorough acquaintance with all the soils, productions, fruits, trees &c of that state, all of which were thoroughly analised by him and the results given in his report, which I had the honor to lay before you while at Raleigh.

I am personally acquainted with Prof. Emmons. He is a man of the most untiring industry, and can perform more labor in a given time than any man I ever knew. I am aware that some objections have been razed to him in consequence of his being a Northern man He is not liable to the objection of being an opponent of our institutions. He was last summer, highly pleased with what he saw of our State, and pronounced the state superior in Agricultural resources to the State of New York.

I hope, sir, that you will not regard me as intrusive. Having drawn up the bill for the survey of the State, and taken a more active part in getting it through the Legislature than any one else, I have felt myself at liberty,—at the request of Prof E. to place his name before you, with the reasons which occur to me to be razed in his favor. I have no doubt but that your Excellency, after the several candidates should be presented to you, will give the appointment to him whom you reason will best carry out the objects had in view by the Legislature in passing the act.

---

[1]William L. Marcy (1786-1857), an attorney from Troy, New York, was the state comptroller (1823- 1829), a judge on the state supreme court (1829-1831), a United States senator (1831-1833), governor of New York (1833-1839), secretary of war (1845-1849), and secretary of state (1853-1859). Sobel and Raimo, *Biographical Directory of Governors*, III, 1076-1077.

Ebenezer Emmons to David S. Reid A&H-GP

Albany
Feb 27 1851

I have this moment received a letter from a Gentleman residing in the western part of N Carolina who is anxious or I may say, expresses a desire for my appointment to the Survey of your State, but wishes me to procure letters if it is convenient expressive of my freedom from abolitionism. Now, this is very well seeing that my doctrines on matters pertaining to slavery cannot be known, but my wife has just remarked, that if the gentleman & others refered to knew me as well as she does there would be no occasion for making enquiries upon this question—The facts in regard to my politics are just these; all my ancestors, as far as I ever knew them, were down right federalists, would be called perhaps blue federalists of the Caleb Strong[1] type; & yet I believe they were quite clever, State supporting, & church supporting men, I can even remember, When my fathers Apprentices & journey men (who was A Blacksmith) used to tease me by calling me a democrat!! But as I grew up, & came of age to act & vote for my self, I came out, sure enough a *democrat*; & I have voted for the democrats & represented the Democracy two years in the State Legislature of Massachusetts, my native State & So far from being an Abolitionist, I have always charged upon them the series of evils which have afflicted our common country for the last 20 years; & still I claim the highest respect & love for freedom & a strong desire that our human family should all sit under the tree of liberty & worship at her altars—My view of the interest of the slave, & the rights of the Planter are the antipodes of the Abolitionist—they agree entirely with those of Mr Marcy Mr Dickinson[2] Mr Dix[3]—In the sphere of life however in which I move, thse great questions never enter. I am partially acquainted with Mr Dickinson well acquainted with Mr Marcy & Genl Dix who are perhaps best known at the South—but so far as qualifications are concerned to carry out the wishes of the State in the survey it has ordered I must refer to my published works I am too old to ask any man to recommend me to a work of this kind if what I have done fails to bear testimony to my ability I have nothing farther to say; I have nothing to ask of friends—

---

[1]Caleb Strong (1745-1819) of Northampton, Massachusetts, was an attorney and a Federalist statesman. He helped draft the Massachusetts constitution (1779) and represented Massachusetts at the Federal Convention of 1787. He served as a United States senator (1789-1796) and as governor of Massachusetts (1800-1807, 1812-1816). *CDAB*, 1024.

[2]Daniel S. Dickinson (1800-1866), an attorney from New York, was a state legislator, Democratic lieutenant governor of New York, and a United States senator from 1844 to 1851. *Biographical Directory of Congress*, 809.

[3]John A. Dix (1798-1879), a soldier and an attorney from Cooperstown, New York, resigned from the army in 1828 as a captain and served as the New York adjutant general from 1831 to 1833. He was a Democratic member of the United States Senate from 1845 to 1849. He became a Republican and served briefly as secretary

of the treasury in 1861 and was then a major general in the army during the war. After the war he was minister to France and governor of New York from 1873 to 1875. *Biographical Directory of Congress*, 815.

James C. Dobbin to David S. Reid A&H-GP

Fayetteville
Feb 27. 1851

I have just returned from Robeson County Court. Rumours have reached us here that although certain names are particularly associated with the commission of revising the laws—yet the appointments have not been made & that you are still considering the matter. In conformity with the views of some of our friends as well as my own I have thought proper to suggest for your consideration the name of a brother Lawyer W Winslow Eqr[1] of our town.

He is admirably fitted for the place. The appointment would be a good one. It would not [be] in conformity with Mr Winslows feelings nor that of others here to put him in the position of an applicant preparing for the place. Nor would your friends desire to embarrass you! If you are not committed to others—you will I know pardon this liberty of suggesting that Mr Winslow is admirably fitted for the place

P.S. Remember me kindly to Mrs Reid.

[1]Warren Winslow (1810-1862), a Fayetteville attorney, graduated from the University of North Carolina in 1827. He was serving as speaker of the Senate in 1854, during his sole term in the legislature, when Reid resigned his gubernatorial office to become a United States senator. Winslow was acting governor in the month of December, until the governor-elect, Thomas Bragg, was inaugurated. Winslow was a representative in Congress from 1855 to 1861. Sobel and Raimo, *Biographical Directory of Governors*, III, 1134.

John H. Wheeler to David S. Reid A&H-GP

New York
10th March 51

I have taken much pleasure in examining Mr Bancroft's's[1] collection of Documents relative to the Colonial History of our State procured from a list published by the State, under my direction in 1843; Mr

Bancroft, while in England as our minister, received from me a list of the papers, in the offices of Board of Trade & Plantations in London, and has procured for his own use copies of the same.

He advised that your Excellency direct a correspondence to be opened with *Robert Lemon* Esq, State Paper Office, London, who will procure you *all the* papers at a cost of 3d. for every 70 words. In the interim, he offers most generously to my use copies of any matter that he has, relative to our State. In this employment I am now engaged here.

Hoping soon to see you and with my best regards I am very sincerely yours

---

[1]George Bancroft, previously identified.

William H. Thomas to David S. Reid A&H-DSR

Washington City
March 13. 1851.

The appropriation having been made by Congress as required by the Cherokee Treaty of 1846, the Commissioner of Indian Affairs has determined to take the opinion of the Attorney General upon the construction of both the Treaty and the law, before he makes any advances in their execution. This question will be submitted to the attorney General today and I shall be under the necessity of remaining here until the decision is made.

In the mean time, may I ask of you the favor to inform me if the appointment of an agent to superintend the construction of the Western Turnpike, and the commissioners to value Cherokee lands, have been made, and if made the names of the individuals who have received the appointments. Compliance will confer a favor on the undersigned

---

George B. Mathew[1] *to David S. Reid* A&H-GP
[with enclosure]

Consulate of North & S. Carolina
Charleston.
March 13. 1851

I beg to solicit your Excellency's intervention on behalf of a colored person, known by the name of Crace, who was, I am credibly informed, brought at an early age, (in 1838), from Jamaica to New Bern, and who is now in immediate danger of being, with her child, sold as a slave, as your Excellency will perceive by the annexed advertisement.

It has been my duty to communicate to Her B. Majesty's Minister at Washington, my appeal to your Excellency, for a postponement of any threatened steps, and for *due protection* to the girl, and her child, agst any designs, pending any requisite investigation, with a view to laying sufficient proof of her allegation before your Excellency—and I venture to assure myself of your Excellency's liberal & just interposition.

[Enclosure]

Newbern,
February 25th 1851.

NOTICE

WILLIAM M. ARCHER, in the month of April, A.D. 1838, came to this place bringing with him a negro girl, by the name of Grace, and having left said negro here, in pledge for a debt due to a citizen of this town, removed south in July A.D. 1838. Wm. M. Archer was heard from by letter, in which letter he advises his correspondent that the said negro Grace, is the property of his sister, M T Archer. As these persons have not been heard from since, this is to notify them, if they be living, that unless they appear at the expiration of one month, from this date, and prove their title and property in said negro, the said negro girl Grace, and her child, will be sold and the proceeds of said sale applied in payment of the said debt for which they are pawned and according to law.

N B Any information required, will be given by applying at the office of the Newbernian.

---

[1]George B. Mathew, British consul for North and South Carolina, resided in Charleston.

Ebenezer Emmons (1799-1863), a native of Massachusetts, was state geologist for New York and North Carolina. During 1851, discussions of his appointment appeared frequently in Reid's correspondence. Emmons directed North Carolina's Geological and Agricultural Survey from 1851 until his death in 1863. Portrait from the Williams College Archives in Williamston, Massachusetts.

William Holland Thomas (1805-1893), adopted member of the Cherokee nation, became a Cherokee chief, state senator, and a Confederate colonel. Describing himself as a "personal and political friend," Thomas corresponded with Reid on topics relating to western North Carolina: Whig intrigues, valuation of Cherokee lands, and development of the Western Turnpike. Photograph from the Barden Collection, Division of Archives and History.

David Lowry Swain (1801-1868), a Buncombe County Whig, was governor of North Carolina from 1832 to 1835. Reid corresponded with Swain during the years when Swain served as president of the University of North Carolina, from 1835 to 1868. Photograph of William Garl Browne portrait, located at the University of North Carolina, from the files of the Division of Archives and History.

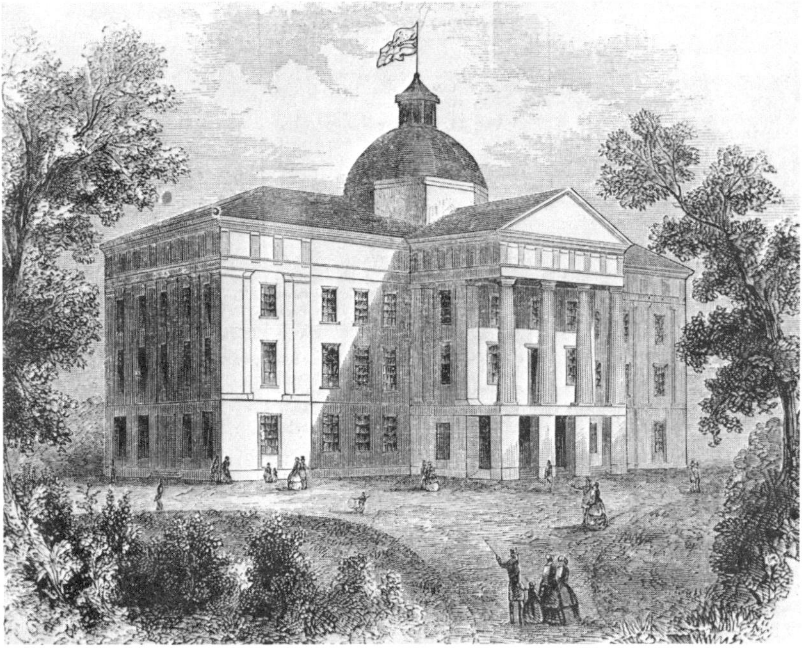

The exterior of the North Carolina Capitol has changed very little since its completion in 1840. This 1850s woodcut, though accurate in other respects, adds a cupola to the dome. Photograph of woodcut from the personal collection of John Sanders courtesy of the Division of Archives and History.

George B. Mathew to David L. Swain[1] A&H-GP

British Consultate
Charleston.
March 13, 1851.

I do myself the honor of addressing you, in consequence of a statement made to me with respect to a negro girl, named Grace, who is in danger of being sold, as a slave, with her child, at Newbern N. C., under an advertisement dated Feby. 25., which a correspondent states to me emanates from the agent of the N. C. College[2]—there appearing to be no doubt that she is a free British subject, brought at an early age from Jamaica to the U. States.

Pending the requisite negotiation on the subject, I venture to hope you will be pleased to instruct your agent to withhold any further proceedings.

[1]David L. Swain, previously identified, was at this time serving as president of the University of North Carolina.

[2]James W. Bryan (1805-1864), New Bern attorney and legislator, was an 1824 graduate of the University of North Carolina and a university trustee (1835-1856). He was, in 1851, escheator for Craven County. County escheators acted as agents for the university, which by state law received all unencumbered income derived from escheated properties. They reported annually to the trustee board treasurer, who served as principal escheator or escheator-general. Powell, *DNCB*, I, 255; Battle, *History of the University*, I, 622.

Calvin Graves to David S. Reid A&H-DSR

Locust Hill,
Caswell County No. Ca.
March 18th 1851

I have the honor to acknowledge the receipt, by yesterdays mail, of your Commission of the sixth of February, appointing me a Commissioner of Internal Improvements in North Carolina. I accept the Commission, and hereby tender you my acknowledgements for this token of your Confidence and regard.

In this Connection I beg leave to call your attention to the 21 Section of the Charter of the Fayetteville & Western Plank Road Company, by which you will perceive that it will be necessary for the Board of Int Imps. to meet and appoint a Proxy or Proxies, to represent the State's Stock in said Company, at the annual meeting of the Stockholders in Fayetteville; (which meeting, if I am rightly informed will be held on the 10th of April;) or for the members of the Board to meet on that Occasion in Fayetteville and represent the State in Person. Your predecessor adopted both plans on different Occasions.

If I mistake not there was some Legislation at the recent Session in relation to a change of route. What it was I have no means of knowing, perhas [*sic*] it refers some question relative to location, to the Stockholders in Annual meeting. It will be well to look to this thing, and shape your action accordingly. The Bye laws fix the time of Annual meetings.

It will be attended with great inconvenience to me to go to Fayetteville about the 10th of April. I hope it may suit the Convenience of Mr Bragg to be there. If not however, it will then be important to appoint two suitable persons as Proxies to represent the states Stock on that Occasion, for, the State Owning 3/5th of the Stock, she Controlls the Action.

I make these suggestions in view of the fact, that from your recent induction to Office, your attention may not have been Called to the matter.

I also Acknowledge the receipt of the Davidson papers, and will look into them.

Present me affectionately to Henrietta and Thomas[1]—and accept for your self assurances of Regard.

Betsey[2] & Caroline[3] send their love.

---

[1]Thomas Settle, Jr. (1831-1888), an attorney from Rockingham County, was Reid's brother-in-law and first cousin. A graduate of the state university in 1850, he became Reid's private secretary in January, 1851, serving a year. After attending the Richmond Hill Law School in 1852, he was admitted by the state supreme court in December, 1852, to practice law in the county courts and, in December, 1853, to practice law in the superior courts. He was a Democratic member of the House of Commons from 1854 to 1859 and speaker of the House in the last session. In the postwar period he was a founder of the state Republican party, state senator in 1865, speaker of the Senate, minister to Peru (1871-1872), an associate justice of the state supreme court (1868-1871, 1872-1876), and a federal district judge in Florida (1877-1888). In 1876 he was the Republican candidate for governor but was defeated in a notable campaign by Zebulon Vance. Lindley S. Butler, "Thomas Settle" (unpublished biographical sketch); *North Carolinian*, January 11, 1851; *North-Carolina Standard*, January 5, 1853, January 4, 1854.

[2]Elizabeth Graves was the wife of Calvin Graves of Caswell County and the daughter of John C. Lea. Ashe, *Biographical History*, II, 113.

[3]Caroline H. Graves was the daughter of Calvin Graves. She married David Reid's brother Hugh Kearns Reid on May 27, 1857. Reese and Fisher, *Settle Family*, 679.

David S. Reid to George B. Mathew A&H-GLB

Executive office,
Raleigh N.C.
March 21. 1851.

I have the honor to acknowledge the receipt of your communication of the 13th instant in relation to the Sale of colored persons advertised as Slaves in the town of Newbern in this State.

I know nothing of the case except what appears in your letter and the advertisement which accompanies it. The advertisement Sets forth that the negroes were left in pledge for money due a citizen of Newbern, and gives notice, if certain persons who claim them do not appear and prove title in one month from the 25 Feb. 1851. the negroes (Grace and her child) will be sold and the money applied to the payment of the debt for which they were pawned. No name even appears to the notice.

You do not say that they are free, but from your letter I infer such is the allegation. This is a case with which the Executive has no power to interfere. If the persons are Slaves they are subject to the laws regulating that kind of property and may be transfered by the owner. if they are free persons our Constitution, and laws afford them full and ample means of vindicating their rights as such. Our Courts are open to them and a sale or transfer will not preclude them from establishing their freedom.

Our trials are by jury—our laws are just and humane, and our judiciary pure and those persons have a remedy.

I must be permitted to remark that while North Carolina thus affords free persons most ample protection and will at all times be found ready to do justice to the citizens and subjects of other Governments, yet she entertains a sensitive jealousy in regard to any Foreign interference in relation to her municiple regulations concerning Negro Slavery.

John F. Hoke[1] *to David S. Reid* RF

Bracket Town
March 26th 1851

I have had a letter to you in contemplation for some time, and will now having leisure put it in execution. My Courts commence next week and unless I write at this moment I will not write soon. I write you free from embarassment as I know that you will be glad to hear anything of the sentiments of the western people. Since I have been at home I have mixed a good deal with the people of my County and find my course generally sustained in particular the votes on the states rights resolutions—And indeed the only vote that I find at all condemned is the vote I gave to distribute the school fund on the white basis principle. The convention men stand no chance. Our people do not think it just that the constitution should be altered in this way and they can not explain it satisfactorily why they voted against free suffrage—The argument of the people is that they ought to be gone for both if they were in earnest and honest. The great majority of them will never be returned, and the question is too strong for them to take ground against it in any shape. I have been in this district for some time and find very little feeling aroused among the people on it and the democrats very generally against the convention project—The circulation of Flemmings[2] speeches has been doing Avery great service in Burke & McDowel. They know Flemming so well that anything emenating from him is regarded with suspicion. The only thing much complained of at home is the tax bill—It does not affect me as I did not vote for it, and moreover told them that such a bill wd come at their next legislature—But let me suggest if it wd not be as well for Holden to have an article on that subject. I have been saying to them that we either had to borrow money to pay the interest of the state debt or lay a tax and that the former was a suicidal Course, only running the state deeper in; and that at last we wd have [to] pay out & that the sooner the better. A leader in the Standard on that subject wd Arm our people who read with the facts & arguments, and forestall the onset that will be made against the party on this account— The Geological Survey I find is popular and as we of the west feel a deeper interest in that than any other section of the State, I beg leave to speak of the appointment of the person to execute it. In primis I do not suppose you will appoint Dr Mitchel and therefore say nothing of him. Two others I hear spoken of Rodgers[3] of Maryland & Emmons of N York—The mineralogists in this part of the Country prefer the latter. They have examined the theories of both the Gentlemen & they think that Mr Emmons will be of the greatest service to us— To this may be added that he has been in this country & has become in fact acquainted with our localities & its structure—He is the man for us and will do good service & will have all our native talent in addition to his own—I spoke to Cansler[4] since I got home about the Cherokee County & he will go—if he is appointed

I hope this letter will find you & family in the same good favor & health as when I last saw you My wife joins me in regards to Mrs Reid and Miss Settle[5] if she is still with you

My respects to the young Secretary[6] & W. W. Holden

---

[1]John F. Hoke, an attorney from Lincoln County, graduated from the state university in 1841. He served as an army officer during the Mexican War. He was a state senator (1850-1855, 1862-1864), member of the House of Commons (1860-1861, 1865-1866), and state adjutant general (1861). Cheney, *North Carolina Government*, 183, 318-333 passim; Wheeler, *Sketches*, 246, 419.

[2]Samuel Flemming (1812-1851), a merchant from Burnsville, Yancey County, was a Democratic member of the House of Commons from Burke County and later from Yancey County. In October, 1851, as a result of a legal conflict, Flemming "cowhided" William W. Avery, also a Democrat and a Morganton attorney, in a Marion courtroom. On November 11, 1851, in the next court session, Avery shot and killed Flemming in the courtroom. Avery was found not guilty on a defense of temporary insanity. Edward W. Phifer, Jr., *Burke: The History of a North Carolina County, 1777-1920, with a Glimpse Beyond* (Morganton: Privately printed, 1977), 345-346, hereinafter cited as Phifer, *Burke*; W. Conard Gass, " 'The Misfortune of a High Minded and Honorable Gentleman': W. W. Avery and the Southern Code of Honor," *North Carolina Historical Review*, LVI (Summer, 1979), 278, 283.

[3]This could be either Henry Darwin Rogers (1808-1866) or his brother William Barton Rogers (1804-1882), both prominent geologists who had lectured at the Maryland Institute in Baltimore. *DAB*, XVI, 94-95, 115.

[4]Henry Cansler of Lincoln County was a delegate to the Constitutional Convention of 1835 and a member of the House of Commons (1831-1837, 1854-1855). In 1852 he served as chairman of the county Board of Superintendents of the Common Schools. He accepted his appointment in April, 1851, to the commission to value Cherokee lands. Cheney, *North Carolina Government*, 297-323, passim, 817; Comptroller's Account (1854), 9; Henry Cansler to David S. Reid, April 4, 1851, Governors Papers, Reid.

[5]Caroline L. Settle (1827-1905) was a sister of Henrietta S. Reid. On July 23, 1866, she became the second wife of David Reid's brother Hugh Kearns Reid. Reese and Fisher, *Settle Family*, 676.

[6]Thomas Settle, Jr., previously identified.

George B. Mathew to David S. Reid A&H-GP

H B M Consulate for
North & South Carolina
Charleston.
March 27. 1851.

I have the honor to acknowledge your Excellency's letter of the 21st. inst., respecting the negroes (Grace and her child) sought to be enslaved by parties residing at New Berne—

The reference made by your Excellency to the jealousy—(under the circumstances very natural)—with which any foreign interference in the Municipal regulations of N. Carolina, is viewed by her—leads me to apprehend that my last comn. did not with sufficient clearness express my meaning or the grounds upon which I had the honor of addressing your Excellency, which subsequent testimony of facts enables me more distinctly to do.

An English person of the name of Archer, accompanied by her brother, brought a young free girl with her from Jamaica to the United States—and the brother left her in charge of a Mr. Howland at New Berne—who alledges that she was so left as a *Slave Girl*—and who has for several years had her services.[1] It being *clear*, that Howland had, in no way, any property in the girl—the representative of the college[2] was induced by him to claim her and her child as "escheated" and to advertise her—When she was enabled thro' others to appeal to me, as a British subject.

Since I had the honor of writing to your Excellency, Miss Archer, now Mrs. Gouto, has been discovered, and bears unequivocal testimony to the above facts—

I regret to say, that notwithstanding due notice, Howland sold her & her child to a dealer—who was arrested with her on his way south.[3]

These being distinctly, and undoubtedly British subjects, I cannot hesitate in demanding your Excellencys protection in their behalf—thro' the sheriff, or other magistrates at New Berne.

Your Excellency's reference to the justice & humanity of the laws of N. Carolina, which I readily receive, assures me that they cannot, under any fraud of others, endanger the liberty of British subjects, whom it is my Special duty to protect, by a courteous appeal to the authorities of the State.

---

[1]Probably Solomon Howland (born 1791), a Craven County farmer who in 1850 owned six slaves, two of whom were young women who each had a small child—fitting the general description of Grace and her child. There were no free Negroes

named Archer in Craven County in 1850, and the census slave schedule did not include the names of either William M. Archer or M. T. Archer as slave owners. Thus, it appears that Howland may have already, in 1850, been claiming Grace as his property. Seventh Census, 1850, Craven County, Population Schedule, 314, Slave Schedule, pages unnumbered.

[2]James W. Bryan, previously identified, Craven County escheator, reported no 1851 escheat income to University of North Carolina trustee board treasurer Charles Manly, Reid's gubernatorial opponent during 1850. However, even though Grace and her child may have been declared "escheated property," if all the money from their sale went to the farmer Solomon Howland to compensate the alleged debt of Grace's owner to Howland, there would have been no funds payable to the university, as all the sale proceeds were thus encumbered. *Book for Escheats and Derelict Property in the State Opened with the Attorneys & Agents of the Board of Trustees of the University of North Carolina in the Several Counties*, 22, Business & Finance: Finance Division. Series 1: Historical Financial Books. Volume 22: 1850-1856, University of North Carolina Archives, University of North Carolina Library at Chapel Hill; *Treasurer's Annual Report to the Trustees of the University of North Carolina*, November 20, 1851, University of North Carolina Archives, University of North Carolina Library at Chapel Hill.

[3]Possibly Ansley Davis of Petersburg, Virginia, a slave trader who had an office at the New-Berne Hotel and who advertised that he was buying Negroes for resale in Louisiana and Georiga. *Eastern Carolina Republican* (New Bern), February 5, 1851.

John H. Wheeler to David S. Reid RF

[Private]

Beattiesford NC
30th March 51

The enclosed official letter be pleased to attend to & reply. I suppose that there will be no objection to your giving Mr Thomas[1] a commission as I assure you he is every way worthy.

I reached home, safely on Tuesday following the Sunday on which I left you, and found my family and all well. After leaving the hurried throughfares of New York and Phila, its ceaseless hurrying crowds, its bleak winds & snows, its desert country and naked streets, and land safely *at home*, with no noise but the prattle of my boys and the bleating of my flocks, with the country putting on its beautiful robes of spring and the gardens rich with flowers redolent with ordors [*sic*], I realize the cain[2] of Milton "—the wearied soul Is lapped in Elysium"[3] I have not been a mile from home since my arrival—so I can tell you but little news. I go however today to Iredell, next to Catawba, then Lincoln, Gaston, Mecklenburg &c.

Many friends have been to see me and among them our old Democratic Standard bearer Hon. Henry W. Conner[4]—not repeating remarks in bad faith, but for good, your name became the topic of conversation. He predicted that surrounded as you are at Raleigh, it would be singular if you did not yield to the influences around you. To this I replied that you had not been intimidated or swerved by their abuse and it was not likely that you would be seduced by their blanishments. For a more prudent man I rarely ever knew. "That very thing" replied he "will ruin him. He will not cut down the enemy or friends in disguise with such vigour that in another campaign he will succeed." If you knew Conner you would know that he is one of the most ultra men on earth—And his opinion of men and things though tinctured with Spartan severity, I often listen to with respect. He is your devoted friend and would do anything honourable to promote the success of democratic principles. I trust that you appreciate the act which communicates this—and believe that any wish on earth is uppermost in my heart, it is your successful and triumphant administration of the affairs of the State. I am in my religious opinions much of a Babtist. If the very hairs of our head are numbered, if not a sparrow falls to the ground without the consent of Omnipotence, are not the affairs and condition of a great State cannot escape his eye and supervision? I look up[on] the Defeat of Manly & the Whig Dynasty in North Carolina as an imediate "dispensation of Providence"; for with these uncrupulous means to carry out selfish and wicked measures, to what a fatal catastrophe would they have brought the good old master of us all! With prudence of our leaders, activity and vigilance of our friends, I hope, that the State is safe for 20 years. A travel on the circuit of a few weeks will give me much light as to the prospect before us. Doubtless the free basis as to the school fund will be very popular in the west, and if the matter *would stop at this point* we should not contend. But it opens the door, to that flood which is now sweeping Virginia, so that the *federal* basis of representation is not likely to be recognized in her convention now in session. For this question, we must be prepared.

So much for public matters. You were kind enough to say something about the Colonial Documents now in England. They ought to be procured and at an early day. Mr. Swain[5] has declined the matter, as he informed me. If I should be elected, I should go this summer—and finish in the shortest time the object for which I was sent—do nothing else think of nothing else, and return straight home. When in New York I copied from 10 to 5 o'clock documents for my work without leaving the room. The day I finished, I left New York. The appropriation would procure all that the printed Indexes call for, or the resolution requires. Let me know at an early day Your views upon this subject. It would aid the character of my Book which I propose at an early day to put to Press. Indeed I have now matter full enough for the two volumes. The documents procured can increase the value of another Edition. The work meets with much favour, far more that I had anticipated or I fear it merits. This fact will however cause me more assidously to labour to make it worthy of myself and its distinguished subject.

Mrs Wheeler presents her respects to Mrs Reid and hopes that you may visit us soon. She asked me a thousand questions about the lady who could fire the feelings of one who had so long devoted himself to public matters and so long resisted the charms of her sex.

---

[1]Mr. Thomas has not been identified, as the enclosure does not survive.

[2]Here Wheeler is using the word "cain" in a nineteenth century poetical sense, suggesting a type of pleasant compensation. His implied comparison of his own situation to that of the great English poet John Milton (1608-1674), who held public office during the Protectorate of Oliver Cromwell but was deposed when Charles II regained the throne in 1660, is suggestive of the exaggerated self-importance of which Wheeler was accused by his detractors. The Whig-dominated House of Commons in North Carolina removed Wheeler as state treasurer in 1844. When Wheeler was suggested as a Democratic candidate for governor in 1845, the Whig newspaper in Salisbury commented mercilessly: "Wouldn't it remind one of a monkey in *trowserloons* with red coat and cap on!" *North-Carolina Standard*, December 24, 1844; *Carolina Watchman* (Salisbury), November 29, 1845, hereinafter cited as *Carolina Watchman*.

[3]Elysium, synonymous with heaven or paradise, was the abode of the good after death in classical mythology.

[4]Henry W. Connor was previously identified.

[5]David Lowry Swain, previously identified.

Daniel Dickson[1] *to David S. Reid* A&H-GP

Wilmington NC
Apl 14, 1850 [1851]

I have been requested by several of our Democratic friends, to call your attention to an act, passed by the last Legislature, authorising a transfer to the Wilmington & Manchester Rail Road, of 2000 Shares of the Stock held by the State, in the Wilmington & Raleigh Rail Road Co we understand that the act provided that the W & Manchester Co shall not dispose of the Stock they receive from the State, at less than par—$100.

The act was passed about the close of the Session & those here, who feel an interest in Sustaining the Democratic party, knew nothing about it, until it had passed, or we Should have endeavored to have so guarded it, that the object which we think the originators (Whigs) had in view should have been prevented— we think the object is to curtail the vote of the state in the election of President & Directors & prevent Democrats from being appointed. We cannot see any benefit to be derived by the Manchester Co. taking a stock, which is so far below par & which, they cannot in good faith Sell. they may however not keep faith, but sell the Stock for what they can get.

For sometime after the passage of the act refered to, it appeared to be the opinion of most of the large share holders of the W & Manchester Stock, that the exchange would not be made, but, at a meeting in South Carolina in March last, they resolved to leave it discretionary with the directory what action to take on the Subject, this resolve was made after a speech from Genl McRae[2] favourable to the Exchange.

Genl McRae is Prest of our road & is no doubt desirous to keep the power in the present hands.

If after the Stock is transfd the State (as we think) has no power to compell the Manchester Compy to adhere to the proviso, would it not be proper for the officer who is authorised to make the transfer to refuse to do so until he is Satisfied that par can be obtained, we think so, as otherwise the object of the Legislature might be defeated.

Feeling satisfied that you have every desposition to aid us in this region, we respectfully ask you to give your serious consideration to this matter

The Manchester Co. have resolved to mortgage the road for $800.00—it is confidently believed that the Wilmington & R road will declare a dividend next fall

---

[1]Daniel Dickson of Wilmington represented the state with the Bank of Cape Fear and was interested in railroad development. Daniel Dickson to Reid, Wilmington, May 7, 1851, Reid Papers, PC 1, State Archives.

[2]Alexander McRae of Wilmington had been a solider in the War of 1812, and despite his advanced age, he served as a major in command of a battalion of heavy artillery at Fort Fisher during the Civil War. He was named superintendent of the Wilmington and Raleigh Railroad in 1836 and by 1847 was president of the company. This railroad was constructed to Weldon and became known as the Wilmington and Weldon Railroad. McRae was president until 1854. James Sprunt, *Chronicles of the Cape Fear River 1660-1916* (Raleigh: Edwards and Broughton, 1916), 127, 148, 150, 152, 302, 337, hereinafter cited as Sprunt, *Cape Fear*.

D. G. MacRae[1] *to David S. Reid* A&H-GP

Fayetteville N C
April 17th 1851.

I have made contracts with two of our mechanic's to add Eighteen feet to the rear of the State arsenal, so as to make the Entire building available for the storage of arms, as well as other munitions of war, for the sum appropriated by the last General Assembly *$600*—

They are to furnish all the material of Brick and Wood, and reshingle the roof—they are also to put the building in a safe and secure condition by closing up several unnecessary windows on the Ground floor—

As I have agreed to advance them money as they progress with the work, I respectfully submit to your Excellency if it would not be better to place the appropriation at my disposal at once.

The Brick mason has the walls nearly completed to the first story and I shall have to advance him one third of his contract tomorrow Evening, to Enable him to pay off his hands—for their weeks labour—

The addition will be 18 by 32 feet two stories high, walls of Brick—making the Building 32 by 40 feet—the whole to be covered with a new roof of best shingles.

---

[1]Duncan G. MacRae of Fayetteville was superintendent of the United States Arsenal, a town magistrate, and clerk of superior court. He was a promoter of railroads and plank roads and in 1889 wrote a historical sketch of Fayetteville. Oates, *Fayetteville*, 86, 94, 221, 317, 373, 519.

Newton Coleman[1] *to David S. Reid* A&H-DSR
[Confidential]

Asheville
April 18th 1851

There is a paper now published here, ("The Asheville Messenger",) which in the opinion of our political friends, is doing great injury to our party. We have upon calm and mature deliberation, determined to break it down.

Our causes of complaint are, that it has ever in all political matters, charged falsehood, fraud, and double-dealing, upon our party, and is now under the control of a few bitter whigs, actively engaged in endeavoring to break down the Hon T. L Clingman, who our party almost to a man, (for resons which will suggest themselves to you,) are determined to support, in the approaching election.

Our only means of breaking down such a paper, are, to withdraw our subscriptions from it. This we have determined to do. But this of itself, is not, in our opinion sufficient. That paper, has uniformly received the patronage of both the Federal and State administrations. The patronage of the Federal government, it will still continue to receive. Shall it still receive that of the State Governments. We hope not—and in the name of our party, I am authorized to request your Excellency to aid us in our attemp: to transfer the patronage of the State offices from the "Messenger," to the "News," a paper which is warmly cooperating with us in the election of Mr Clingman

---

[1]Newton Coleman of Asheville served in the House of Commons during the 1848-1849 session with Thomas W. Atkin. Both men represented Buncombe County. From 1843 to 1849 Atkin had been coeditor of the *Messenger*, but in 1849 he founded the *Asheville News*, which operated until 1883. The only issue surviving from 1851 is that of January 9, in which Atkin wrote regarding Reid's January 1 inauguration: "After the oath of office was administered, he delivered his address, which we have not yet received, and unlike some editors we know, we can't pass judgment on a thing until we see it. We wish Gov. Reid a prosperous and happy administration,—that he may be able so to steer the Ship of State as to avoid the breakers on the right hand and the left.—" This same number of the *News* noted that a rally in support of the Union was called by the opposing paper, the *Messenger*, and held on December 31, 1850, at the Buncombe County courthouse in Asheville. Atkin was present and introduced a resolution "approving the course of Mr. Clingman," which after debate was amended and passed. This issue also carried a brief account of Reid's marriage in December. Agents for the *News* in Macon County were Dr. H. G. Woodfin and J. T. Siler, two of the men who had signed a petition to Reid asking that Mark Coleman be appointed a commissioner to value Cherokee lands. Mark Coleman of Macon County was a brother of legislator David Coleman of Buncombe, but their relation to Newton Coleman is unclear. The effect of Newton Coleman's campaign against the *Messenger* is unknown, but it apparently ceased publication by late 1852. Only one issue of the *News* survives from 1852, that of October 28, and it carries Democratic Party campaign advertisements. Cheney, *North Carolina Government*, 317, 322, 324; Wescott and Ramage, *Duke Newspaper Checklist*, 476-477; Jones and Avant, *Union List of North Carolina Newspapers*, 4; *Asheville News*, January 9, 1851, October 28, 1852; Will of Mark Coleman, ca. 1817, Haywood County Wills, Archives, Division of Archives and History, Raleigh, hereinafter cited as Coleman Will.

Burton Craige[1] *to David S. Reid* RCC

Lincolnton,
April 18th 1851.

From the "Standard" I learned a few weeks ago that you had appointed "Charles McDowell of Rutherford one of the Commissioners to value Cherokee lands, and not knowing any such person living in "*Rutherford*", I concluded you meant "Charles McDowell[2] of Burke." A short time however after I saw that "*John*" & not "*Charles*" was appointed. This week I met Mr. Cansler[3] one of the comissioners who asked me how this was? He supposed there was a mistake. He said John McDowell[4] had been nearly blind for a long time, and was totally disqualified. It was then said by someone that Mr. John McDowell had taken out the letter addressed to *Chs.*—and had answered the same by declining the appointment himself, but had recommended his son,[5] a lad of sixteen, or eighteen years old. I know nothing of either of the Mr. McDowells of Rutherford, but Mr. Cansler who is a man of sense, and character says the appointment is too responsible to be divided with either of those gentlemen—the one being disqualified by reason of his infirmity & the other by reason of his youth, and inexperience. Of Mr. Charly McDowell of Burke he speaks in the highest terms—and I may venture to say if the others decline that his appointment will give satisfaction to every body up here as he is known to be a man of the most undoubted integrity, and a good judge of Mountain land.

We have had Wheeler[6] & Caldwell[7] both here this week. Wheeler is full of his book, and Caldwell I think would have no objection to a race for Congress. The Whigs are in trouble, and I think they will either settle down on "Guin"[8] or old "Deberry".[9]

In the mountain District Mr. Clingman[10] will have no opposition though Baxter[11] is talked of.

In our (the Salisbury) District J. P. Caldwell I am afraid will have no opposition.

The Convention Humbug is dying—will be dead unless it is galvinized by the Mo[r]ganton meeting.[12] The people care nothing about it. I am afraid however it will have one bad effect it will kill *all* amendments—Legislative or otherwise.

Be pleased to answer me at Salisbury where I now reside, and believe me most truly your friend & obt. sert.

---

[1]Francis Burton Craig (1811-1875), a Salisbury attorney, was an 1829 graduate of the state university and edited (1830-1833) the Salisbury *Western Carolinian.* An early supporter of the nullification doctrine, he served in the House of Commons (1832-1835), as a Democratic representative in Congress (1853-1861), as a delegate

to the state Constitutional Convention of 1861, and as a representative in the Confederate Congress (1861-1862). *Biographical Directory of Congress*, 748-749; Powell, *DNCB*, I, 453.

[2]Charles McDowell, Jr. (1785-1859), prosperous farmer of Burke County, was a local Whig leader and was recommended to replace John McDowell of Rutherford County on the board to value Cherokee land. He eventually accepted the appointment, but only after John McDowell resigned. Seventh Census, 1850, Burke County, Population Schedule, 402; Phifer, *Burke*, 323; Henry Cansler to David S. Reid, August 5, 1851, Governors Papers, Reid; Ashe, *Biographical History*, VII, 304; Henry Cansler to David S. Reid, September 13, 1851, Governors Letter Books, Reid.

[3]Henry Cansler, previously identified, of Lincoln County.

[4]John McDowell (1787-1855), farmer, of Rutherfordton served in the House of Commons (1820-1821) and on the Council of State (1824-1827). Under questionable circumstances, he accepted the appointment to the board to value Cherokee land but resigned by August, 1851, due to poor eyesight and ill health. He owned real estate in 1850 valued at $20,000. Griffin, *Old Tryon and Rutherford*, 171; John McDowell to David S. Reid, August 5, 1851, Governors Letter Books, Reid; Seventh Census, 1850, Rutherford County, Population Schedule, 356.

[5]John McDowell, Jr., was only twenty years old in 1851. At the time of the 1850 census, he was still living with his parents and had no occupation. Seventh Census, 1850, Rutherford County, Population Schedule, 356.

[6]John Hill Wheeler, previously identified, was the author of *Historical Sketches of North Carolina*, published in 1851. Walser and Malone, *Literary North Carolina*, 37.

[7]Joseph P. Caldwell (1808-1853), a Statesville attorney, was a state senator (1833-1834), a member of the House of Commons (1838-1844), and a Whig representative in Congress (1849-1853). *Biographical Directory of Congress*, 649.

[8]Possibly, Haywood Williams Guion, in 1840 publisher of the *Western Whig Banner* of Lincolnton. He married a daughter of Governor John Owen and was president of the Wilmington, Charlotte, and Rutherford Railroad. Powell, *DNCB*, II, 384; Wescott and Ramage, *Duke Newspaper Checklist*, 569.

[9]Edmund Deberry, a Whig of Montgomery County, served in the state Senate (1806-1811, 1813-1814, 1820-1822, 1826-1829) and as a representative in Congress, as a National-Republican (1829-1831) and as a Whig (1833-1845, 1849-1851). He declined to seek reelection in 1851. The eventual Whig nominee was Alfred Dockery of Richmond County, who won the election. Cheney, *North Carolina Government*, 678-681, 683, 686-687, 1207; *North-Carolina Standard*, April 30, 1851.

[10]Thomas Lanier Clingman, previously identified, was reelected to Congress in 1851 as a Whig. By the 1853 election he had switched to the Democratic party and was again reelected. Cheney, *North Carolina Government*, 687.

[11]John Baxter (1819-1886), Whig attorney and southern Unionist, represented first Rutherford County in the House of Commons (1842-1843) and then Henderson County (1846-1847, 1852, 1854-1855, 1856-1857). He was speaker of the House in 1852. In 1857 he moved to Tennessee. A Republican after the Civil War, he was appointed to a federal circuit court judgeship in 1877. Cheney, *North Carolina Government*, 312, 315, 321, 323-324; Powell, *DNCB*, I, 121.

[12]A meeting was held on April 30, 1851, in Morganton, during Burke County court week, to discuss holding a state southern rights convention. Sponsored

primarily by the Whig party, the gathering passed several resolutions, including one calling for the creation of a new political party, the Reform Republican party. Todd R. Caldwell presided. Democratic editors condemned the meeting as a guise to strengthen the Whig party. *Lincoln Republican*, probably of May 7, 1851, reprinted in the *North-Carolina Standard*, May 14, 1851.

Andrew Baggarly[1] *to David S. Reid* A&H-GP

Eagle Mills
Iredell County
April the 21st 1851

I hope you will not think it an imposition on your Excilency for me to inquire of you if you think their would be any Chance for me to obtain Aid in the State Legislature or of the State Funds by giving good and sufficient Surities For Ever or as Long as a payment might be Sett off—I would wish a few years to make payment by paying interest I applyed to the Legislature befoure the last—and the Sinate passed resolutions that if they hope me they would have Every body that It will be Sean in my Letter to Ex governor Graham the wishes of my heart, and this must be *recolected* That Their was never a Child Bornd and raised in the State nor in aney of the Southern States that have made the Start and Attempt that I have made Two it is strange for me to think of to See my State so Slow, I was poor but made the Start in Sept 1846 when I deturmined to doo all I could for the wellfair and improovement of my State. And by this means of persevearence it has redressed the agrievenses of the weddows & childrens cries of Some poor Children by means of active and dayly imployment. I have Sucseaded so far as to Have one Cotton factory now in opperation to Spin & weave course goods at the Eagle Mills, which seam to be well pleasing to all who se it. I have taken in a company with me but they Seam to not be willing to advance to my wishes therefour I wish Aid—And I wish to advance a Step at a time untill I arrive at Broad Cloth shall Tippit Casenett &c & flanel Tweeds Blancket-making & Cambrick & calico printing Spining and weaveing it all at a new place that I have Just purchased which is over 1 mile round from the Eagle Mills but right straight south is not moore than 3 to 5 Hundred yards, and a Butifull Location for building all to go by water and a never failing Stream, now if you Can consistaently with your wishes speak favourably on the Subject to a Source of Cappital I will return to you numberless thanks—or I am willing to form another company of our own country men My stock in Eagle Mills Manufactoring Company is so ready Sail that I have been offered the Cash for it repeatedly and at a percent premium but I would not take for it 100 percent—my stock now amt to 2500. dollars well I Estimate that my South Eagle Tract will be quite good to me for $6000. in a Short time. If you recolect me I stoped at your house on my travils to & from the North I have Lately returned from the north & I told them then what I had been trying to Doo and they told me that if we people of the South did go on and doo what I wished it—would breake them down if you be pleased to address me Direct to Eagle Mills &c &c

Iredell County NC or Post Master

[1]Andrew Baggarly was in Iredell County by the 1840s as a peddler, especially of clocks. In 1846 he purchased a mill site, which he named Eagle Mills, and rapidly established in partnership with other investors a sawmill, a gristmill, and a cotton factory, which produced both yarn and finished cloth. Although Baggarly lost his interest in the factory in 1859, it was still operating in 1860. Keever, *Iredell*, 145-146.

Nimrod S. Jarrett to David S. Reid A&H-GP

Aquone N.C.
26th Apl. 1851

By our last mail I wrote you acknowledging the receipt of com. &c,[1] and as I had but few minutes to write and was troubled with company at the time, I must now ask you to instruct me on several points, there was no mile marks set up in the Survey of the road and therefore it will have to be measurd so that all the nesesary marks may be set up to do this I must have two or three hands for a few days at a time and I shall need the assistance of one in Filling out Books and paper & perhaps some printing will have to be done how is all these continginses to be paid.

There is no spe[c]ific plan laid down in the act for the Building the road or Bridges, and I do not know whether Maj. Fox[2] has made out a plan in his work, if he did in all probability it is a verry *expansive* one, and if so must I be governed by it or not, if not I would then ask what plan is most advisable to Build the Bridges on, you know there is two general plans one is the cavern plane work pillow framd. and all of wood, the other is the Lattice plan covered and watherborded in, this will cost about four times as much mony as the first mentioned, and unless we had experienced workmen may not then stand.

The 9th Sec. of Sd. act requires that when there is 20 miles of road finished the Gov. of the state shall have Tole gates fixed thereon and a Tole collected &c. now it would seem from this that all undertakers should finish there lots about the same time, in order that the state may not be rouged out of the Tole, Suppose one or two men do not finish there lots in the time given, then those lots must be sold out to other persons and time given them to do the work, and that being the case the state will loose the Tole for four or six months, will it not be the better plan to take Bonds on all undertakers requiring them to finish their lots in a given time and in that way have 20 or 30 miles finished at the same time so that gates may be fixed thereon, If Bonds is to be taken I must have them printed, I make all those enquiries thus early that I may be prepared to proceed to business without delay when I receive the map and Books great anxiety prevails throughout this country about the road and all influential men are urging me to have the Bridges let out fourth with, and to have the worst parts of the road worked first I am of opinion that the mony due this fall will make 40 or more miles and that will take it from the georgia line to where I live or perhaps across the Nontigalee Mountain[3]

---

[1]A reference to Jarrett's commission of appointment as superintendent of the Western Turnpike.

[2]Moylan S. Fox was in charge of the survey for the Western Turnpike. Moylan S. Fox to Reid, August 6, 1851, Wilmington, Reid Papers, PC 1, State Archives.

[3]The Nantahala mountain range lies between the Great Smoky Mountains on the north and the Blue Ridge on the south. It extends across Macon and Swain counties. Powell, *North Carolina Gazetteer*, 345.

Samuel J. Wheeler[1] *to David S. Reid* A&H-GP

Murfreesboro
28th Apl 1851

Being unable to visit Raleigh at this time, I have requested Major Jones[2] (the bearer) to hand you our bond & receive for us the $3000. according to the act of the legislature. The bond is worth I should think $300,000: i.e. the corporation & surities are worth that amount or more—

I regret that I cannot visit you at this time, during my recent visit to Charleston, I learned some interesting facts relative to our revolutionary history—from old records in the Charleston Library, that I would like to communicate to you Our friends in S Carolina are in a state of intense excitement. Should the Secession Convention ever meet, South Carolina will certainly Secede, & then will we see a most unnatural Struggle; a fraticidal war: the friends of the Union will disentegrate themselves from the mass, with which they are now identified. Do you not understand Mr Elmore's[3] regret, expressed at Columbia, "that there would be no collision with federal authorities," A distinguished lawyer, & member of the last legislature, of S Carolina, remarked that a dark day was coming over his native state—

With kindest regards to Mrs R & family I am Yrs mo truly

---

[1]Samuel Jordan Wheeler (b. 1810), brother of John H. Wheeler, was a physician from Murfreesboro and later moved to Bertie County. He studied at Hertford Academy and Union College, Schenectady, New York, and was active in support of Chowan Female Institute, in Murfreesboro, which he served both as financial agent and teacher of anatomy and physiology. A native of Murfreesboro, he was also postmaster there for many years. Wheeler, *Reminiscences*, ii; Edgar V. McKnight and Oscar Creech, *A History of Chowan College* (Murfreesboro: Chowan College, 1964), 290, hereinafter cited as McKnight and Creech, *History of Chowan College*; Benjamin B. Winborne, *The Colonial and State Political History of Hertford County, N. C.* (Raleigh: Printed for the author by Edwards & Broughton, 1906), 137, hereinafter cited as Winborne, *History of Hertford County*; "Minutes, Board of Trustees, Chowan College, 1848-1961" (microfilm), Archives, Division of Archives and History, Raleigh, hereinafter cited as "Chowan College Board Minutes, 1848-1961."

[2]This is probably A. G. Jones, appointed by the board of trustees of Chowan Female Institute to receive $3,000 lent to the school by the president and directors of the state Literary Fund Board under the authorization of a resolution passed by the General Assembly of 1850-1851. "Chowan College Board Minutes, 1848-1961"; *North-Carolina Standard*, February 5, 1851.

[3]Franklin Harper Elmore (1799-1850), an attorney from Walterboro and Columbia, South Carolina, was a Democratic representative in Congress (1836-1839) and president of the Bank of South Carolina (1839-1850); he was appointed United States senator on April 11, 1850. *Biographical Directory of Congress*, 860.

William B. Gulick to David S. Reid RCC

Goldsboro; N. C.,
Apr. 28, 1851.

I have not heretofore improved your invitation to write to you, because I knew of nothing in this direction that I supposed would interest you. You have noticed, doubtless, that I have removed from New

Berne, and have become a denizen of the thriving village of Goldsboro. I can report that my prospects are pretty good here, and I hope, by dint of perseverance, to command success.[1]

I returned yesterdey from a short visit to Wilmington, and am sorry to have to inform you that the recent article in the Standard devoted to the Wilmington Journal is having an injurious effect in that quarter.[2] It is the general impression, but not without a number of exceptions, that you had no knowledge whatever of the writing and publication of the article alluded to, and that Mr. Holden is solely responsible for it. Such I believe to be the fact, but still an effort will be made by some to injure you by connecting you with it. I am also satisfied that Mr. Fulton[3] intended no censure whatever with regard to the appointment of Mr. Jones[4] as the representative of the State at the meeting of the Stockholders of the Fayetteville Plank Road Company; he is a consistent and true friend of yourself; but he believed that a more satisfactory appointment might have been made and expressed his opinion to that effect; and for this expression of his own opinion, he is taken to task by Mr. Holden in one of the most violent articles he has written in the last six months. Mr. Holden is overzealous in defending what required no defence. I do not agree with Mr. Fulton with regard to the propriety of the appointment of Mr. Jones, and told him so plainly; I consider the appointment of Mr. Jones a proper one, because he was *personally disinterested*; his being a Raleigh man or from a distance, is no objection whatever. But while I endorse fully, and shall sustain the appointment of Mr. Jones, I must protest against the manner in which Mr. Holden has noticed the remark of a brother Democratic Editor. Of course I am no party to this quarrel; but I deem it due to myself and my position as a Democratic Editor, enjoying an independent position, to repel the idea that I am to be dictated to by the central organ. While I shall always sustain Democratic principles & Democratic men with all my power, I consider myself as much the organ of public sentiment in my neighborhood as Mr. Holden is in his, and have the same right to my own opinion in all things. I consider Mr. Holden's article as offensively arrogant and dictatorial towards the provincial Democratic press, and, at the proper time, shall respectfully vindicate my position as an independent journalist.

The controversy between Messrs Fulton and Holden, I fear, will cause some difficulty, and perhaps lead to permanent misunderstanding. Mr. Fulton, however, cannot be driven to oppose, but will sustain you, in every thing he thinks right as an honest editor is bound to do. I conversed with a number of our friends at Wilmington on the subject and I found that the manner which characterizes Mr. H's article was unanimously condemned.

So much with regard to the Fayettevile Plank Road. I have written my own views and feelings with regard to the matter frankly and freely, confident that you will receive them as coming from one of your devoted friends & well wishers.

I wish also to write a word with respect to the meeting of the Stockholders of the Cape Fear Bank on the 5th Prox. It is the general impression at Wilmington that Gen. Saunders is to be appointed the State's proxy. At the present time there is much feeling against Raleigh, and particularly against Gen. Saunders[5] among the citizens of Wilmington, and I think the appointment of any other person would be more satisfactory than him. It will be extremely difficult however to satisfy them with the appointment of any person, and I have come to the conclusion that it will be to your interest and to the interest of the Democratic party for you to attend in person.[6] I most earnestly recommend a visit to Wilmington by you at the present time, if it is at all consistent with your other engagements. I am satisfied that *you in person* can satisfy all parties, and fear greatly that no other person can do so.

You must excuse this long letter but I could not write what I desired in shorter compass.

Give my particular respects to your excellent lady, and tell her to go to Wilmington with you.

I shall deem it an honor to hear from you at any time, and stand ready at all times to do what I can to promote your interests

I remain Your Obedient Servant

---

[1]William B. Gulick, previously identified, had published in New Bern a paper called the *Eastern Carolina Republican*; in late March, 1851, he moved the paper to Goldsboro and went into partnership with M. S. Richardson, changing the name of the newspaper in May, 1851, to the *Republican and Patriot*. Wescott and Ramage, *Duke Newspaper Checklist*, 536; *Eastern Carolina Republican* (New Bern), February 26, 1851; *Wilmington Journal*, March 14, 1851; *Eastern Carolina Republican* (Goldsboro), March 18, 1851.

[2]The article to which Gulick refers was published in the *North-Carolina Standard*, April 23, 1851.

[3]James Fulton, previously identified, was editor of the *Wilmington Journal*. He objected to the appointment of Wake County resident Wesley Jones because Fulton felt that it would "further fan the flames of sectional feelings" in the state. *Wilmington Journal*, April 18, 1851.

[4]Wesley Jones of Wake County, a member of the Literary Board, was selected on April 3, 1851, in Raleigh at a meeting of the Board of Internal Improvements, to serve as proxy for the state government at the April 10 meeting of the stockholders of the Fayetteville Plank Road Company in Fayetteville. He also served in the House of Commons (1828-1830, 1833-1835) and the state Senate (1850-1852). *Wilmington Journal*, April 18, 1851; *North-Carolina Standard*, April 23, 1851; Cheney, *North Carolina Government*, 318, 319, 1296.

[5]Citizens of Wilmington disliked Romulus M. Saunders's April 22, 1851, speech at Petersburg, Virginia, attempting to promote Virginia support for the Raleigh and Gaston Railroad by pointing out that it brought trade to Virginia markets, and that if the railroad failed the people of North Carolina "would be forced to build up a market within their own State." Saunders was condemned in Wilmington as part of the "Virginia garrison" in Raleigh. *Wilmington Journal*, May 2, 1851.

[6]Perhaps as a result of Gulick's advice, Reid did not choose Saunders but instead selected Daniel Dickson, previously identified, a resident of New Hanover County, as the state's proxy for the bank stockholders' meeting. *Wilmington Journal*, May 9, 1851.

Frank I. Wilson to David S. Reid A&H-DSR

Rutherfordton, N. C.
May 3d 1851

Your favor was received to-day, and I hasten to reply. Mr. [John] McDowell[1] does not reside in the village, and is only here occasionally. When the appointment came here to Charles McDowell[2] he [John] said that he supposed it was intended for him; but for fear of a mistake he would not decline beforehand, at the same time expressing his determination to decline provided the appointment was for him. He [John] is nearly blind, and wholly incapacitated thereby for the position. I presume he will be here in a few days; and I will see him on the subject.

Having given you what information I can in regard to the subject matter of your letter, I will claim your indulgence for a little while on other matters. I have been threatning to write to you for some weeks, but "the thief of time" has prevented me. I feel that I owe you an apology for my apparent neglect, but I assure you I have been very busy, and have had but little time for corresponding.

With the Banner I think I am doing a fair business. I have increased its issue from about 300, the number left me after the withdrawals when I took the press, to about 540, and as you see, I am getting a pretty good advertising custom. My most sincere thanks are due to Gen. Bynum and Co. for their proposed "Constitutional Reform Advocate," as they have thereby added nearly 100 names to my list. I was a little bothered at first to know the meaning of the new movement—the Convention movement; but I was not long kept in the dark and the people, both whigs and democrats, have sustained me with remarkable unanimity. Our members came home very unpopular, and still remain so. I was at a regimental muster a few weeks ago where

Col. Webb,[3] one of our Reps. endeavored to address the people, but out of a crowd of perhaps 500 I am certain he did not have 50 listeners; and when he concluded was replied to by a whig amid shouts and cheers.

The new paper proposed by Gen. Bynum[4] is dead—or rather never had an existence and never will. Of all the Prospectuses sent out but one has been returned and that had 3 names attached. Bynum has abandoned it, and *it is now said* that it is to be issued in Morganton, but by whom I have never heard. I look upon it as an "obsolete idea."

My course so far has, I think, met with general satisfaction. To induce the whigs to read was one prominent object, and I have been more successful than I could have reasonably anticipated. I have woke up 2 or 3 passengers that growled considerably, but none have yet bitten; and their opposition has been such as to be an advantage to me.

If I have luck in collecting I hope to be able to entirely disinthrall myself and refund the purchase money of the press and office in a short time. I have worked myself ever since I took posession of the office, and am now a pretty good printer. My expenses, exclusive of ink and paper; are only $13 a month; and my job work and advertising since I commenced have averaged about $40 a month.

Grateful for your assistance, & hoping to hear from you again soon.

P. S. I hope you will not be backward in making any suggestion you may think proper in regard to my course, editorially.

---

[1]John McDowell, previously identified.

[2]Charles McDowell, previously identified, of Burke County.

[3]Calvin J. Webb of Rutherford County served in the House of Commons from 1850 to 1852. Cheney, *North Carolina Government*, 1265.

[4]John Gray Bynum, previously identified Rutherfordton attorney and militia general, was married to Mary McDowell, daughter of the Charles McDowell, Jr., of Burke County, who was appointed by Reid in 1851 as one of the three commissioners to value Cherokee land. Ashe, *Biographical History*, VII, 304.

Thomas Settle to David S. Reid A&H-DSR

Marion
McDowell County N.Ca.
May 9th 1851

I had the pleasure on my arrival here on monday last to receive your letter of the 29th Ultimo directed to me at this place and I was much gratified to hear that you were all well and particularly to hear that Henrietta had entirely recovered. This is friday evening and I have gotten through all three Districts here for the first time in several years. If alive and well I shall start for Rutherford in the morning. I have not received a letter from home in the last two weeks The last was one dated the 14th Ultimo and received at Morganton. I cannot account for it and whether it is owing to the negligance of the Post Master or the failure of my family to write and communicate some unpleasant intelligence I cannot tell and I am left to the most unfavourable and gloomy conjectures and I am constantly writing home to get some information to relieve me from my most painful anxiety. I am in good health and getting on pleasantly with my judicial duties. I have had the disagreeable duty to perform here this week to pronounce the sentence of death on John Collins for the murder of William Jarrett some three years and six months since he was tried and convicted and his case went to the Superior Court where the Judge of the Court below was affirmed. He then broke Jail and made his escape and was about in the adjoining Counties and on the edge of South Carolina until three or four weeks since when he was arrested brought here and lodged in Jail. The sentence is to be executed some time in July. I postponed the execution of the sentence in order to give him a chance to apply for a Pardon You will have a Petition or Petitions presented to you to pardon him signed by most of the respectable men of this County.[1] I believe no one wishes him hung and they regret that he was arrested and brought back I will write you again on this subject. May the Lord bless you and yours is the prayer of your affectionate Father

P.S. Give my love to Henrietta and Thomas[2]

---

[1]Governor Reid pardoned John Collins of McDowell County on July 4, 1851, on condition that he leave the state immediately. *Wilmington Journal*, July 25, 1851.

[2]Thomas Settle, Jr., previously identified.

George W. Hayes[1] to David S. Reid A&H-GP

Murphy N.C.
May 13th 1851

Mr. Jacob Siler agent for Cherokee lands is now here granting preemption rights to those who have settled, vacant land and from the evidence before him it appears that there has been a fraud practised upon the state that is yet within the power of your Excellency to remedy I mean in the survey made for the State's [authority] under the act of the general assembly giving 3000 acres of land as a donation for iron works, the act of assembly only authorises the Jury to condem, such land as is *unfit for cultivation* and it appears here now that there are several tracts that were actually surveyed by the state prior to 1838 within their plot and survey, and not ploted out, that there is a great deal of good land fit for cultivation within the same that the lines have been run zig zag for the purpose of avoiding the Mountains and taking in the good land these facts can all easily be made appear by incontistable proof. The plats and certificates are on file in the secretarys office and I understand that the grant has not yet been issued I desire to have the matter stayed until we can give you proof on this subject. it is a most iniquitous proceeding and greatly to the prejudice of the poor occupants of this County as you must know that 3000 acres spun out in every shape on earth running with our small creeks and branches, takeing our coves, & excluding the mountains will cover a vast extent of Country—

I have with this mail written the atto general B F Moore[2] asking him to give this matter his early attention, and believing it will receive your immediate and prompt attention I remain my Dear [Sir] your Obt & humble Servt.

You will recolect that the time fixed for the preemption right will expire on 1st of October and that many citzens will loose their preemption rights unless this matter is settled an early day,

[1]George Washington Hayes of Murphy, Cherokee County, was a member of the House of Commons (1844-1851, 1860-1861). He served as a cavalry officer during the Civil War. Cheney, *North Carolina Government*, 1096; Tolbert, *Ellis Papers*, II, 812n.

[2]Bartholemew Figures Moore (1801-1878), an attorney from Halifax, was a Whig member of the House of Commons (1836-1846), state attorney general (1848-1851), and a member of the commission to revise the state statutes in 1851. He was a staunch Unionist and a leader in the 1865 Constitutional Convention. *DAB*, XII, 114-115.

David W. Siler[1] *to David S. Reid* A&H-GP

Franklin
May 19th 1851

Very soon after our interview in Raleigh I saw it stated in the papers that Mr McDowell[2] had declined the appointment as commissioner to value Cherokee land and I thought that it would be unnecessary to write the letter which you requested. I have been with the people of Macon and Cherokee to a considerable extent since my return. They are well pleased with the Relief extended to them by the legislature and they are looking with anxiety for the commissioners. These lands have given so much trouble to the legislature and to the Executive that it is a subject which we mention with reluctance. I told the people in Cherokee that you were showing a desposition to carry out the law and to secure their interest fully but that a little time will be required where there are so many laws to construe. The appointment of Capt Jarrett[3] is looked upon as being very judicious. He is anxious to commence the work on the Western Turn Pike. The people will continue in a state of anxiety and excitement untill the work of valuing the lands and of building the Turn Pike commences. The removal of the bonds is a matter about which you spoke in Raleigh. My Father[4] will be pleased to hear from you on that subject.

At the last session of the general assembly as is known to your Excellency a law was passed securing occupant rights to certain residents on vacant lands in Cherokee county. A few Cherokee Indians reside on such lands. And I am informed that attempts will be made by persons settling down by side these unfortunate people to turn them away from their last resting place among their native mountains I am not satisfied in an opinion as to whether Indians are persons capable of taking up land under the law of the last legislature. If your Excellency will do me the favor to advize me whether the benefits of this law can be extended to Cherokees it will be very thankfully received.

---

[1]David Weimar Siler (1822-1884), a farmer from Macon County, was a Whig member of the House of Commons (1850, 1856, 1860). Hamilton and Williams, *Graham Papers*, V, 194n.

[2]John McDowell, previously identified.

[3]Nimrod Jarrett, previously identified.

[4]Jacob Siler, previously identified.

Thomas Settle, Jr., to David S. Reid A&H-DSR

Raleigh
May 28. 1851.

I drop you a few lines by to days mail (which is the first since you left) merely to let you know that I am quite well and that every thing is going on straight.

Your negroes are all hearty and keep knocking away in the garden which looks remarkably well. I have felt considerable anxiety since you left, to know, both how you found Aunt Betsy[1] and Uncle Reuben,[2] and how you stood the trip, for I was almost afraid to see you start in such feeble health.

There is one thing to which I would call your attention, so that you may send out your letters immediately in case you should think it necessary to convene your council, in fact I believe it is a council appointment. I allude to the Attorny Generalship. The supreme Court meets on the 2d Monday in June, but I learn that they would willingly put off the State cases till the last of that month, so that you can convene your council immediately after commencement[3] if you think proper.

My love to all the family.

---

[1]Elizabeth Williams Settle Reid, mother of David S. Reid.

[2]Reuben Reid, father of David S. Reid.

[3]Reid traveled first to Rockingham County to visit his parents, who were seriously ill, and then to Chapel Hill to attend graduation exercises at the University of North Carolina, where he listened to recitations of seniors on June 3. Reid then scheduled a meeting of the Council of State in Raleigh for June 12 to appoint a new attorney general. *North-Carolina Standard,* May 28, June 4, 14, 1851.

Duncan G. McRae to Daniel W. Courts A&H-GP

Fayetteville
June 27th 1851

I want to call the Governors attention to a request made by the Officers and Members of the Fayetteville Independent Light Infantry Company in this place and to ask your assistance & influence to have their wishes gratified—

I understand they have made application for a Stand of Sixty Percussion Muskets Such as are now used in the Service of the United States—there are a large quantity of that discription of arms in the United States arsenal near this place, and I have no doubt that if the Governor would ask of the Secretary of War, an order would be given on the Commandant of that post for them—

Now it would take but a moment for the Gov. to make the demand—and as We have not received our quota of arms this year, the 60 Muskets might be deducted or taken in part of it.

I sent you with this letter a pamphlet containing the speeches delivered before the Independent Company—which will place you in possession of the Standing of that corp's. You will see that it will in August next celebrate its 58th Anniversary—that amongst its members are some of our most sterling men—and the influence they possess is very great a little kindness on the part of the Govr and an Effort to comply with their wishes would be felt and appreciated not only by them, but by the citizens generally—

They complain a little—but if the order could be had for the arms, so as to use them by the first of August—all their grievance would be forgotten—

Do my dear Courts ask the Governor to make the Effort and at once so that peace and quietness may be preserved in the Camp—and nothing lost by a seeming inattention to their wants.

The General Government might be appealed to Successfully on the ground that this Company is the only military protection the U S arsenal has.—And as we afford them our protection—it is as little as they could do to give us the arms to do it successfully with—

If the Govr. writes soon We can aid in the application by sending a petition to the secretary of War if it is deemed necessary.

Let me hear from you

You will understand why I write you & not the Gov.—He might consider it a public letter & so place it on record—I have been free to talk of the subject rather in a different light than I would were it to go on file—between ourselves they have considerable political influence which ought not to be overlooked.

John M. Dick to David S. Reid A&H-DSR

Greensboro
June 30th 1851

Having learned that you expect to visit this place on the 11th of July next I will be much gratified to have the pleasure of your company at my house during your residence here—I shall expect you, and shall endeavour to make you as comfortable as possible.

We are all alive on the subject of the rail road here and hope to meet a great number of our friends here on the 10th and 11th of July—Be pleased to present my respects to your Lady and to Mr. Settle[1]

[1]Thomas Settle, Jr., Reid's first cousin and secretary, previously identified.

Thomas A. Hayden to David S. Reid RCC

Rutherfordton,
Aug. 9, 1851.

The battle has been fought, and the victory won. Clingman has succeeded in this county—beating the Federal candidate Col Gaither[1] over 700 votes—his majority in the District will not fall short of 3000. The old Whig leaders are *wrathy*—they say *we* have all turned Democrats— one thing certain we are not Federalists. The Federalists worked hard for their candidate, but the people of Rutherford acknowledge no leaders—and will in future act for themselves. A few weeks ago I was over in Burke—the Gaither men then claimed Rutherford County by 400 majority. I asked for their authority. "Why your leaders—Bynum,[2] Logan,[3] Davis,[4] Baxters,[5] Shipp[6] and others"—I told them we had no leaders—or that we were all leaders—that I had conversed with nearly every man in the county—that with a full vote Clingman would get 1000 majority— under no circumstances less than 700—they thought me mad!—but the result shows who was right.

I understand that Mr John McDowell has forwarded his resignation as a Commissioner to value Cherokee Lands—if his successor has not yet been appointed—I would recommend Col. Wm. A. Tanner,[7] as a fit person for the appointment—true he is not a Democrat, but he is well qualified for the business, and his appointment would give general satisfaction—he supported you against Manly—and all the threats of the Federal party could not make him vote for Gaither—he is a true Southern man. There was a good deal of dissatisfaction when McD. was appointed, growing out of the fact that from his infirmities he was totally disqualified. If you intend to give the appointment to Rutherford Tanner is the man—

Excuse my intrusion, and believe me, yours truly.

---

[1]Burgess Sidney Gaither (b. 1807), a leading attorney and Whig politician from Burke County, was clerk of superior court, solicitor, a delegate to the Constitutional Convention of 1835, a state senator (1840, 1844), speaker of the Senate (1844-1845), superintendent of the United States Mint in Charlotte, and a representative in the Confederate States Congress (1862-1865). Phifer, *Burke*, 51-52, 77, 86, 145.

[2]John Gray Bynum, previously identified.

[3]Albert G. Logan (1811-1893), a farmer and cabinetmaker from Rutherford County, was a justice of the peace, a member of the House of Commons in 1848, and a soldier in the Confederate army. Griffin, *Old Tryon and Rutherford*, 229.

[4]Tolivar Davis (1810-1866), a planter from Rutherford County, was a local political leader and colonel of the county militia. He served in the House of Commons in 1844. Griffin, *Old Tryon and Rutherford*, 228.

[5]George Washington Baxter (d. 1854), a Rutherfordton attorney, had been deputy clerk of court and in 1846 was appointed county solicitor. Griffin, *Old Tryon and Rutherford*, 224.

[6]William Marcus Shipp (1819-1890), an attorney from Rutherfordton and Hendersonville, graduated from the state university in 1840. He served in the House of Commons (1854), the Constitutional Convention of 1861-1862, on the superior court (1863-1865, 1881-1882), and as state attorney general (1870-1873). He was a Confederate army captain during part of 1862 and 1863. Griffin, *Old Tryon and Rutherford*, 242; Cheney, *North Carolina Government*, 362, 427, 574, 824.

[7]William A. Tanner (1811-1890) of Rutherford County, was a justice of the peace (1845-1860), county treasurer of public buildings (1849-1853), and county coroner (1856-1860). Griffin, *Old Tryon and Rutherford*, 240.

David S. Reid to Jacob Siler UNC-JS

Executive Office,
Raleigh,
Aug: 23, 1851

Your letter of the 16th June was sent to the Attorney General, but in consequence of his absence I did not receive an answer till this evening. A copy of his letter I herewith enclose you. You will perceive that he asks more time to give his opinion. As soon as it is received I will communicate it to you, with such suggestions of my own as the case may seem to require. I will however remark that if the matter can be justly and properly settled without the delay necessarily incident to carrying it to the Supreme Court, I doubt not, it would greatly promote the convenience of all concerned.

Robert J. Powell[1] *to David S. Reid* A&H-GP

Washington, D.C.
30th August 1851

From a conversation last evening with Col. Wheeler[2] it seems that you and I misunderstood each other, relative to the Block for the Washington Monument—He understood that you were awaiting a letter from me, either in answer to one from yourself or in accordance with your verbal request when I was in Raleigh—If you have written me it has not come to hand—and as I understood it when I was in Raleigh, you would send the Block on to me in a few days, when I was to have the engraving done—These understandings however are of no moment—

Soon after my return home, I Saw Mr. Dougherty[3]—Superintendent of Workmen, on the Monument—He Said that on the reception of the Block, he would put it in the hands of Suitable Workmen, and charge the amount of their wages whilst engaged on it—You can immediately Send the Block to me—I will with much pleasure take charge of it and See that your instructions and wishes are fully carried out—with reference to which, please be full and explicit—

We have no news in this City—The Stories from Cuba are So contradictory that we know not what to believe[4]—

Can it be possible that the people of No Carolina will permit the Raleigh & Gaston R.R. to go down? I hope not—Yet from what I see and hear, I have fears on the Subject—

If the Raleigh & Gaston road be rebuilt, and the Central (or I believe North Carolina Railroad is the term used in the charter) be finished Say in three years from this time it may be Safely calculated, that with proper management the great Southern mail may be carried over that route, at a compensation of $250—or possibly $300—per mile per ann—If the Raleigh & Gaston road goes down there will be no possibility of getting that mail—the only mail carried will be the local mail at a compensation of not exceeding $100—per mile—making a difference of $150 or $200— per mile at the former rate an annual difference to the Central, in its income of about twenty five thousand dollars—and at the latter of about thirty five thousand dollars—This is a matter well worth consideration to those interested in the Central road—(by this name it ought to be called) This is computing the distance from Raleigh to Charlotte at about one hundred and Seventy five miles—

[1]Robert J. Powell, originally from North Carolina, was a physician and government clerk. By 1841 he was a clerk in the post office department. *Register of all the Officers and Agents, Civil, Military, and Naval, in the Service of the United States, from the Thirtieth September, 1841, to the Thirtieth September, 1843* (Washington: J. & B. S. Gideon, 1843), 2, hereinafter cited as *Register of Officers and Agents.*

[2]John Hill Wheeler, previously identified.

[3]William Dougherty (born circa 1815), native of Pennsylvania, a stonecutter living in the District of Columbia in 1850, is likely the person to whom Powell is referring. Seventh Census, 1850, District of Columbia, Population Schedule, 143 (microfilm), Archives, Division of Archives and History, Raleigh.

[4]Many southern volunteers interested in the annexation of Cuba were captured and imprisoned or executed by Spanish colonial authorities in Cuba following an unsuccessful invasion attempt in August, 1851, headed by Gen. Narciso Lopez, a leader of Spanish refugees in the United States. Morris, *Encyclopedia of American History*, 215.

L. H. B. Whitaker[1] *to David S. Reid* RF

[Private]

Enfield (Halifax Cty)
Sept 5, 1851

My acquaintance with you being limited, an apology may be necessary for this intrusion of my opinion on your attention at this time, which I hope will be found sufficient in the remarks below: The Annual meeting of the Stockholders of the Wilmington & Raleigh R R Co takes place on the 2nd Thursday in November next at Wilmington, at which time & place, the writer & he believes many of your personal & Political friends would be glad to see you & the Board connected with you, in the management & oversight of this work in attendance, that you may the better be made acquainted with the condition & prospects of the Road which at this time is believed to be more promising than at any time, since its completion, that the influence & patronage of the Road was at one time, brot to bear in advancing party purposes the writer believes, but this policy has been abandond or at any rate not carried out for the last 3 or 4 years and at this time the officers of the company are nearly equally divided between the two parties with the exception of the Directors (who are appointed by the Stock holders) who are all Whigs.

If however it should not suit your convenience to attend the Meeting I would most respectfully suggest that in the appointment of the States Proxy great care should be taken so as not only to give as little possible offence but advance the interest of the State as well [as those of] Stockholders. In submitting these remarks to the consideration of Your Excellency, I hope you will pardon my seemingly officiousness when I assure you that they proceed from an ardent wish to guard you in the course you may think proper to pursue. To the Principles of the Democratic party I yield to none in my devotion but do not believe that the Proscription policy is the best at all times & being the largest Stockholder (but one) on the Northern End of the Road. I feel some solicitude for the Welfare of the Road. With these considerations I hope they will be a sufficient apology for my troubling you. With sentiments of great regard

[1]L. H. B. Whitaker of Enfield, Halifax County, was postmaster of Enfield in 1843. In 1854 he was appointed a director of the Wilmington and Raleigh Railroad. Reid, *Gubernatorial Campaigns*, 91; *Register of Officers and Agents*, 283.

William H. Thomas to David S. Reid RF

Franklin N C
Sept 10, 1851

I attended the court last week at Cherokee, it was the first opportunity I have had of meeting the people since I returned home from Washington. With the legislation of last session a large majority of the Citizens are well pleased, I have found scarcely any—even among the Whigs—who do not admit the liberality of the democratic party towards the people of Cherokee. But the wire working Whig politicians are seeking every opportunity to prejudice the people against you, you are aware that all the lawyers in this section are whigs, and several of them politicians, they charge you with neglect in carrying out the laws of last session, that notwithstanding eight months have elapsed since the legislature adjourned, no portion of the lands, are yet valued and that the preemption rights have to be taken up against the first day of October, that the people will be deprived of the opportunity of taking up their lands by the delay in sending on commissioners. The political wire workers are telling the people that you will very likely not send on any commissioners at all for the purpose of defending the laws passed in their favor, your friends account for the delay in sending commissioners, and have exhausted their resources in furnishing excuses for the delay in sending them on—the mistake made in appointing a blind man &c, but if the commissioners can get on in time to value the lands to enable the people to take them up in this month as required by the act passed in their favor, discontent will soon be forgotten. The agent Capt N. S. Jarrett has put the Western Turnpike under contract from the Georgia line to within about 14 miles of this place, and it is in rapid progress of Construction. The lots first Sold are mostly nearly completed, and a small portion of them have been received. The first lots sold too high but they are making a splendid road where in a few years it will no doubt be planked, which can be done at a trifling expense. Several causes combined to make the first lots of the road sell high, as I am informed, at the time of the sale (I had not returned from Washington,) very few of the people knew any thing of the cost of constructing a road of the description required by the act. Even some persons who had come on from Burke to undertake building the road were of opinion that nothing would be made upon most of the contracts, and declined taking more than two or three of them. Another cause was that the leading men of the Country had warned the people against ruining themselves by bidding off the road so low as to cause them to sustain loss on their contracts, and by guarding against one extreme ran into another.

In the end I have no doubt when the lands are valued along the road, it will be valued much higher than it would, before the road was made. And in fact the road is made so far beyond the general expectation that I should not be astonished if what has been gained by high contracts would be lost by increased prices placed on the valuation. The last contracts are now being worked out and it will be found that most of them are rather lower than they should have been. The remainder of the road to Asheville I have no doubt will sell low, and should in my opinion be put under contract as fast as the bonds can be made available. This cannot be done until the valuation is made, and where the application has been made by the purchasers for the valuation of their lands, the agent cannot under the act for their relief pay out any of their bonds, he has to wait until the new bonds are given.

The Whig lawyers are endeavoring to influence the agent Mr. Siler, to submit several questions for the consideration of the Attorney General arising under the act of last session for the relief of the purchasers of Cherokee lands respecting which it would seem that not even a shadow of doubt could be entertained by any one, much less lawyers, One question of this character has I am informed been submitted with regard to interest upon the bonds of purchasers which accrues before the valuation is made and new bonds given, upon this subject I beg leave to submit a few remarks to show the absurdity of attempting to establish that the act is susceptible of two interpretations. The 1st section of the act provides that a board of valuation shall be appointed, whose duty it is to value the land. Upon the valuation being made all the payments that have been made are to be deducted from the valuation, and "for the *balance due* if *any*" new bonds shall be given payable in four annual enstalments. (Sec 5)

sec 6, Provides that upon the purchasers given new bonds, the agent is authorized to surender up "to the purchasers their heirs devizees or assignees all the bonds given to the state for said lands" When those bonds are given up and the new bonds received by the agent what has he got to recover interest upon or even to claim it on

After this provision of the law to one acquainted with the origin of the relief measure it seems strange any question should be raised about interest, and that any member of the senate should undertake to explain the intention of the Legislature to be in direct opposition to the language of the law, and that the Attorney General should recommend on that account the decision of the supreme court to settle the question, can only be accounted for by his having been recently appointed and acquainted with the duties of the office. I have a high opinion of his legal attainments but certainly should regret the adoption by you of the policy he has recommended. To refer a question to the supreme court to settle which the law itself settles and suspend thereby the construction of the Western Turnpike and keep the people in suspense the next two or three years could not fail to excite the dissatisfaction of the whole population west of the Blue Ridge. I mention these things as the personal and political friend of both your excellency and the Attorney General, and to guard you against being lead into error by your political opponents who are now arising to defeat both of you.

Capt Jarrett thus far fully answers the expectation of his friends in the discharge of his duty.

You will please excuse this long letter and attribute such excess as you may discover to the zeal of a personal and political friend

Ezra McCall Gates to David S. Reid A&H-GP

Asheville
12th. September 1851.

I was appointed by the last legislature a Justice of the Peace for Buncombe County, together with many others, six or eight, on the same commission. I was qualified to the duties of that office at last April Court, as was also some others; I think that each Justice should have a separate commission, and doubtless would have had each a commission but for the hurry consequent upon the close of the Legislature; if therefore it is practicable yet, to get a separate commission for myself, be pleased to fill up and forward one, as soon as you conveniently can, the date of the other commission is [*blank*] day of [*blank*][1]

N.B. The late Union humbug has been gloriously defeated in the late election, and the Southern States right party are growing stronger here, everyday. The Convention reform party are extinct. no man of the party now ever deigning to allude to it, the proposed Morganton Convention proving a total failure, also you perceive the Asheville News is almost as Republican in its columns as could be desired so that I think our cause for next year certain & sure. We have had and yet have many very many South Carolinians among us this season, the village and watering places having been crowded.

[1]There is no evidence, either in the Governors Office Records, "Commissions and Resignations, 1841-1855," or in the Buncombe County Court of Pleas and Quarter Sessions minutes of 1851, that Reid responded to this request.

Robert Henry[1] to David S. Reid RF

N. Ca. Haywood County
Septr 16th 1851

I have Considered that Gentlemen involved in as much business as you are Do not like to Read long prefaces therefore I make none. The Citizens of Cherokee County have been held in suspense since the time of the land sales to the present time, & wish to be Released from that State of suspense with respect to their lands. If they Cannot Get immediate relief that they may seek new homes, & leave their lands with their improvements to the State to Make its best of them; And I think that at a ready money sale the State Cannot Get more for them than the Value placed on them in the year 1836 including their improvements; as it is now known the exhausted State of those lands by the long cultivation by the Indians, which was not thought of by the purchasers at the time of the sale in 1836. No lasting improvements can be made on the lands untill it is known to the incumbant who is the owner.

The late act of Assembly Directed Your Excellency to appoint Commissioners to Value our Cherokee lands which was Done; Your appointment was Considered to be a good Juditious one & gave General satisfaction to the Citizens of the County as they Considered the Commissioners to be men of honesty & Integrity, but it so happened that McDowell one of the Commissioners Could not serve from his bad health & want of Sight & hence resigned; It is supposed that you will appoint Charles McDowell of Burke instead of John McDowell Resigned; If you have or will make that appointment please Require of him a speedy acceptance or refusal; for it is believed that he has been advised to withhold his acceptance or refusal as long as he could in order to protract the business so that it might be again brought before the next Genl. Assembly, when an act could be passed to oppress the Cherokee people & exact from them more money to make the Western turnpike Road; as a part of that Road has been sold out at higher Rates than was wished for, by persons on the more Eastern parts of that Road, for that the Cherokee fund would be exhausted too soon for [*missing*] that part of the road that has been sold out; It was sold & purchased as might be expected; some lots were sold so that the purchaser made a profit, & others a loss, if they had to hire the labour & suport the Labourers; but most of the purchasers used their own hands & used their own provision without as much hiring or much actual outlay; as if they had to hire all; this is Considered as actual Gain by the more easterly Speculators; Your Excellency has Crossed the Mountains & know that a road Cannot be made across them without Great Labour; It is evident that the purchasers of the Road Did not make as good bargains of the State in the purchase of the Road, as the State made of the purchasers at the land sales in 1836, if one half of the sum that the land then sold for was remitted. With respect to the appointment of a Commissioner in place of John McDowell, if you have not already made one, or if you have appointed Charles McDowell & he Refuses to act, it would be the Desire of more than two thirds of Cherokee County that you would appoint Col. N. Edmiston[2] a Commissioner for that he was acquainted with the Cherokee lands before the sale, and since that time & knows their intrinsick Value; that he is an honest man & a man of unyielding integrity; this would be of great advantage to the Commissioners in placing a just Estimate on the lands. Be pleased to appoint a Commissioner in Lieu of McDowell as soon as Convenient & release the people of Cherokee from their State of Suspense.

---

[1]Robert Henry (1765-1863), a soldier in the American Revolution, was an early settler of Buncombe County and taught at the first school in the state west of the Blue Ridge, at Union Hill. He became a surveyor and an attorney, serving as county solicitor by 1806, and was the county's first physician. He developed and operated the early resort Sulphur Springs. Sondley, *Buncombe County*, 712, 769-770.

[2]Ninian Edmondston (1789-1868), a Haywood County farmer, served in the War of 1812, as sheriff of Haywood County, as a member of the House of Commons (1821-1822, 1823-1827, 1828-1834), and as a state senator (1834-1835). Allen, *Annals of Haywood*, 118-119; Cheney, *North Carolina Government*, 278-304 passim.

David S. Reid to Jacob Siler A&H-GLB

Executive Office
Raleigh.
September 24th/51

I enclose you a copy of a letter from the Attorney General in relation to questions submitted by you arising under the act of the last session of the General Assembly in relation to Cherokee lands.

I differ somewhat from the opinion given by the Attorney General. I believe that the words "*all persons*" used in the seventh section of Chapter XXV has reference to such persons as are capable of holding lands under the existing laws of this State.

I doubt whether Indians without special legislation answer this description, and therefore believe you ought not to issue *certificates of purchase to them.*

As this question however admits of some doubt you will in any preliminary action of yours on this subject afford any Indian applicant a fair opportunity for having his rights brought before the Judicial tribunals of the State for decision.

As to the question arising under the 5 section of Chapter XXIV it appears to me that you are required to deduct the payments which have been made by the purchasers to the state, on each tract, from the valuation thereof, and for the balance due if any take bonds as required by the act. The act makes no discrimination between payments made on account of *principle* and those made on account of *Interest.* with due defference to the opinion of others it does appear to me that this point does not admit of a reasonable doubt. To withhold the execution of the act upon the ground that the Legislature may have intended what they did not enact would in my opinion be unjust and inconvenient to all concerned. I would therefore act accordingly.

William K. Lane to David S. Reid RF

Pleasant Grove
Wayne County NoCa
September 27th 1851

As the time for appointing the Directory on the part of the State of the Wilmington and Raleigh Rail Road Co will soon arrive I take the liberty to make some suggestions on the subject

In the first place I would give it as my opinion that you should attend the anual meeting of the Stockholders and represent the State in person if you can possibly do so.

In the second place I would name as fit persons for Directors Mr James S Battle of Nash County Mr William T Dortch[1] of Goldsboro and Mr William C Bettencourt[2] of Wilmington.

I have taken the liberty of using the names of these Gentlemen without their knowledge or consent but I feel no hesitation in saying they would accept the appointment and having known them long and well I can safely say that the interest of the State would be safe in their hand.

In conclusion permit me to renew to you assurances of my highest regard & remain, Very Respectfully yours.

---

[1]William T. Dortch (1824-1889), a Goldsboro attorney, was a member of the House of Commons (1852-1855, 1858-1861, 1874-1875), speaker of the House (1861-1862), Confederate States senator (1862-1865), and state senator (1876- 1883). He was appointed a director of the North Carolina Railroad in 1853. Cheney, *North Carolina Government*, 322-328 passim, 456-461 passim; Reid, *Gubernatorial Campaigns*, 89; Jerome Dowd, *Sketches of Prominent Living North Carolinians* (Raleigh: Edwards and Broughton, 1888), 120-121, hereinafter cited as Dowd, *Sketches*; Powell, *DNCB*, II, 95.

[2]William C. Bettencourt, postmaster of Wilmington by 1841, was in 1851 a New Hanover County justice of the peace. He was appointed a director of the Wilmington and Raleigh Rail Road Company in 1851. *Register of Officers and Agents*, 300; David S. Reid to William C. Bettencourt, October 20, 1851, Governors Letter Books, Reid; *Wilmington Journal*, November 14, 1851.

Ebenezer Emmons to David S. Reid A&H-GP

Albany [New York]
Oct 4. 1851

I have the honor to acknowledge the receipt of your letter of the 25 inst. in which you remark, that I have not expressed myself in a manner sufficiently clear to be understood. Without referring to what I did say in the letter referred to, I now wish to say that while it appears that the appropriation is used up in Salaries, I propose to pay all the expenses of the survey including expenses of the laboratory out of it—that is all the expenses excepting those of publication of the report or reports.

The class of expenses are those of the field. Mostly travelling expenses & those incidental to this kind of investigation.—the laboratory, including apparatus & Chemicals—

My salary (as you wish me to speak of it) must be $2,500 It will be necessary to employ 2 assistants & I do not find that competent men can be obtained at salaries less than 1500 & 1000 pr ann. These assistants must be men of some experience if justice is to be done to the state; it must go straight forward for two years if it is the determination to complete it in that time. There are many young men who may volunteer for the Sake of the information to be obtained—but this class of assistant cannot be relied upon—

For the successful prosecution of the work I do not see that your Excellency as the Executive of the State, can have other guarantees than those of integrity & competency in the persons employed: & to sustain or acquire even a reputation a great deal of hard work has to be performed.—I say this because, not a few well informd persons in other matters regard a survey, to be made up of pleasant jaunts in pleasant weather, in pleasant company—

In conclusion I wish to be understood that under the item of salary, is included all the expenses of the survey up to the period of the publication of the reports, that two assistants will be required one whose salary may be fixed at 1500. the other at 1000.—

Samuel P. Hill[1] *to David S. Reid* A&H-GP

Yanceyville N C
Octo 8th 1851.

The county of Robertson in Tennessee has been settled almost wholy by persons from North Carolina and removals continue to take place to that and the adjoining counties. It often becomes important that conveyances should be executed there transfering the rights of property here; there is great delay and inconvenience experienced for the want of a Judge or other proper officer to certify the acknowledgments of the parties, and more especially where the rights of married women are to be transferred. They have no Judge near them, and the certificate of the Governor of Tennessee is not obtained without difficulty by reason of the distance to Nashville.

By a reference to the 21st chapter of the Rev. statutes I find that the Governor of the State is authorised to appoint one or more commissioners in each State as he may deem expedient to take the acknowledgments or proof of deeds for the conveyance of lands &c in this State. For the convenience of parties in this State and Tennessee and facilitating business transactions between them, I would suggest Miles S Draughan[2] of Springfield, Robertson, Co Tenn (or any other one that you may think advisable) as a proper person to receive the appointment of Commissioner. If you are not adverse to the appointment of such a Commissioner and should determine so to do, I would be pleased if the appointment should be made at an early date as possible and the commission forwarded to the appointee; I should also be glad to know his name and address.

I have nothing new—Mrs Douglas[3] passed through our village a few days since on her return home under the care of Mr Ellington[4]

---

[1]Samuel P. Hill, a resident of Yanceyville, was a member of the Caswell County Agricultural Society in 1854, a commissioner of the Alamance and Caswell County Plankroad Company in 1855, and a lieutenant in the Sixth Regiment North Carolina Troops during the Civil War. After the war he was active in promoting local railroads. Powell, *Caswell County*, 200, 476, 493, 501-504.

[2]This was likely M. S. Draughon, a 34-year-old attorney born in Tennessee and living in 1850 in Robertson County, Tennessee. A record of "Commissions Issued During Gov. D. S. Reid's Administration" indicates that this appointment was not made, but in 1854 Reid did appoint as Tennessee commissioners Alexander W. Campbell of Jackson and M. W. Alexander of Chattanooga. See, however, Hill's letter to Reid, April 3, 1852, Reid Family Papers, in which Hill mentions the tentative appointment of *Samuel* S. Draughon of Springfield. Seventh Census, 1850, Robertson County, Tennessee, Population Schedule, 61, 66, 67 (microfilm), Archives, Division of Archives and History, Raleigh; Governors Office Records, "Commissions and Resignations, 1841-1855."

[3]Martha Martin Douglas (Mrs. Stephen A. Douglas) made her home in Washington, D.C., with her husband until her untimely death on January 19, 1853. Reese and Fisher, *Settle Family*, 683.

[4]Probably a reference to John Waddell Ellington (1804-1886), who married Lucinda Settle and was, hence, Martha Martin Douglas's uncle. Reese and Fisher, *Settle Family*, 688.

Ebenezer Emmons to David S. Reid A&H-GP

Albany [New York]
Oct 22. 1851

I have the honor to acknowledge the receipt of the commission for the Geol & Agricultural Survey of North Carolina—In accepting of this trust, I hope I am actuated by a desire to promote the industrial pursuits of your State. It is my determination to satisfy the people as far as it is possible for me, in the brief period which can be devoted to the Survey. I know that expectations are always formed or created which cannot be realized; certainly to the satisfaction of some. Your State is rich in resources & a more direct attention to those resources, will ultimately make North Carolina one of the most independent States of the Union.—

I shall hope to receive your advice in all matters pertaining to the Survey, together with the distinguished Gentlemen, who with yourself have charge of it. To carry out the details of the Survey it is understood that two assistants will be required. As you made no reference to this part of the subject I found on referring to the act ordering this work that it seems to make it the duty of the Geologist to appoint the assistants, subject to your approval. With this understanding, I respectfully propose the name of David A. Wells[1] of Cambridge, Mass. & Ebenezer Emmons Jr. The first is a highly intelligent young man; one, who is becoming distinguished as the author of the American Year Book of Facts which has a larger circulation in Europe of any American book—He is a chemist of promise & was educated in the Lawrence Scientific Institute. Under Prof Horsford[2] & the distinguished man, Prof— Agassiz[3]—He has been in the employ of Ohio State Agricultural Society as its Analyst of the Soils & other products & is also a practical Geologist—My son was my assistant during the Geological Survey of this State with approval of Governor Marcy. His attention has been turned to Geology, & does not profess to have more than an ordinary acquaintance with Chemistry. He is an excellent artist especially in all that pertaines to illustrations in mining, geological phenomena etc. He is a more valuable assistant for combining the ability & experience both as a geologist in the field & for giving an accurate representation on paper of what he sees, Should you approve of the gentlemen I have named they will enter upon their duties with the expectation that the performance of those duties must satisfy your Excellency. It is the wish of my son to reside in N.C. during the entire period of the Survey, if he can arrange his affairs so as to leave without too much sacrifice.—I shall enter upon the duties of the survey at the earliest moment possible I have the impression from some source or other, that December is one of your worst months for outdoor work. Any delay which your Excellency may deem as lost time on my part I will cheerfully make up by additional assistants—

[1]David Ames Wells (1828-1898), a native of Springfield, Massachusetts, graduated from Williams College in 1847 and Lawrence Scientific School in 1851. Known primarily as an economist, he was chairman of the National Revenue Commission (1865-1866), special commissioner of the revenue (1866-1870), chairman of the New York State Tax Commission (1870-1876), and a member of the board of arbitration of the Associated Railways. He was also responsible for setting up the Bureau of Statistics. He was a prolific writer, and his works included *Our Burden and Our Strength*, which expounded the dynamic nature of northern economic life. *CDAB*, 1170.

[2]Eben Norton Horsford (1818-1893), a native of Moscow, New York, graduated from Rensselaer Polytechnic in 1838 and taught chemistry at Lawrence Scientific School from 1847 to 1863. He later did industrial chemical research. *CDAB*, 455.

[3]Jean Louis R. Agassiz (1807-1873), a native of Switzerland, established himself as a leading naturalist by his study of glaciers. He came to the United States in 1846 and by 1848 was a professor at Lawrence Scientific School. *DAB*, I, 114-122.

David S. Reid to William H. Thomas Duke-WHT
[Confidential]

Executive Mansion,
Raleigh,
October 22d, 1851.

I have the honor to acknowledge the receipt of your letter of the 10th ultimo, for which you will please accept my thanks.

The Attorney General was of the opinion that under the act of Assembly, Indians, who had complied with the terms of the act, were entitled to Pre-emption rights. I doubted whether they were, but wrote the Agent that in all preliminary movements to give them a fair opportunity to have their claims tested in the Courts of justice.

As to the construction of the act in relation to interest on Cherokee bonds the Attorney General thought the proper construction was to deduct the payments on acount of interest as well as on account of principal, but suggested that it would be the safer plan for him to have the question decided by the Supreme Court. For myself I have no doubt about the construction of the act in relation to this point. The payments on account of interest ought to be deducted as well as those made on account of principal. The construction of the act on this point is too plain for the agent to pursue a course to compel those interested to undergo the delay and expense of having the question settled by the Supreme Court before he acts in the matter, and I have so instructed him.

I think you know whether I have been favorable to such a course of policy in regard to Cherokee lands as would promote the interests of the people of that part of the state. Delay has necessarily attended the execution of the laws in regard to this subject, but I can assure you, and all concerned, that I have been actuated by no desire except to see them faithfully and promptly executed. But do as I may, there are many, you know, who will complain. It is their privilege to do so. Yet I doubt whether the policy of any administration has been more favorable than the present to the people of Cherokee—I mean, of course, *the State administration.*

I would like very much to see you and talk things over.

Please present me kindly to my friends in your part of the Country; and accept for yourself my respects and best wishes.

George Aaron to David S. Reid A&H-GP

Wilmington
October 22nd. 1851

I address to you these Few lines to let your honour know that I am A Coloured Man an English Subject Born at Barbee[1] an English Island in the west indies and came to London in Brig deblont and from there to New York and got my discharge from her and Sailed the remaining of my time in American Ships which I Joined a Boston Brig to go to Wilmington from there and Back to Boston[2] which I was taken out of her on Suspision of being A Runway Slave No tidings or any information from any Slave holder or Master to own has there property Seen the time I have been Exicuted in Wilmington for A runway Slave I have Benn going on 14 Months in Jail here and if No Releif from your honour I shall be sold at the expiration of one Month more[3] So it is to Excllency I apply for releif which I am Destitude of evry Necessary articles And I am a Mary Man in New York and A Wife and two children there which I should be very glad to see them[4]

---

[1]Probably a reference to the British island of Barbados in the West Indies.

[2]Aaron was likely a crew member of either the brig *Ellen Reed* of Boston, under the command of Captain Shipman, or the brig *Lodebar* of Boston, under the command of Captain Drew, both of which arrived at the port of Wilmington on September 1, 1850, with cargoes for local merchants. According to the "Marine Intelligence" table of ships arrived and cleared, no other Boston brigs stopped at Wilmington within two weeks before or after that date. *Wilmington Journal*, August 23, 30, September 6, 13, 20, 27, October 4, 1850.

[3]A newspaper advertisement, dated September 15, 1851, carrying the signature of New Hanover County sheriff Owen Fennell, announced that George Aaron, charged with being a runaway slave, had been imprisoned in the county jail for twelve months and that, pertinent state laws having been complied with, Aaron was to be sold at auction at the courthouse on December 8, 1851, the opening day of the December term of county court. The county court had ordered in September that Aaron be sold "to pay for his jail food." September term 1851, Minutes of the New Hanover County Court of Pleas and Quarter Sessions (microfilm), Archives, Division of Archives and History, Raleigh, hereinafter cited as New Hanover Court Minutes; *Wilmington Journal*, October 31, December 5, 12, 1851.

[4]There is no surviving correspondence in the David S. Reid private manuscript collections or in the Governors Office Records or Governors Letter Books to indicate that Reid responded to this request for relief. It is possible that Aaron's claim to having a family in New York is true. In 1850 a white woman named Mary Aaron, age 58, was living with her two sons, Victor, 12, and Michael, 10, an "idiot," in Ward 10 of New York City, next door to a free black seaman and his wife. Mrs. Aaron and her sons were all born in Poland and came to America sometime during the 1840s. They are the only persons named Aaron in New York City listed in the 1850 census. There is no further mention of Aaron in New Hanover County Court records. Seventh Census, 1850, New York City, Ward 10, Population Schedule, 126 (microfilm), Archives, Division of Archives and History, Raleigh.

John O. Campbell[1] *to David S. Reid* A&H-DSR

Weldon, N.C.
Nov. 3d, 1851

As one of your constituents, I take the liberty of addressing you on a subject in which I, as well as a very large number of your political friends, feel an abiding interest—one in which the *state* has a deep interest—and one in which, *I* feel assured, you feel all the concern which your position calls for. I will only add, that I am a democrat—have always been one, and expect to live and die one, and that my vote and the little influence I possess, was in your favor at the last and previous election.

There seems to be a general belief along the line of the Wilmington Rail Road, *and in Wilmington,* that a strong effort will be made to displace the present most capable and efficient President of the road. I have just recd. a letter from one of the strongest democrats of Wilmington, which, with rumors to the same effect, induce the belief that it is the intention of the state's proxy to cast the 500 votes of the state against General MacRae.[2] What foundation there is for this rumor, I am unable to say, but the known caution and sound sense of the writer, justifies the belief that there is cause for apprehension. After stating the belief that Mr. Fennell[3] would throw the vote of the state against the General, the writer adds: "The fate of Gen. MacRae is uncertain. A change is not desired by the great mass of democrats here and elsewhere," &c. an opinion established by the anxiety of Democratic stockholders in this part of the country.

To do away with all doubt, there is a hope that the state's proxy will be instructed, or, at least, advised to vote *with the majority of the individual stockholders*—those whose position best qualify them to judge of the prudence of a change.[4] I will here give an extract from a letter just recd. from a member of the Board of Internal Improvements, in answer to one from me—Thos. Bragg, Esq. He says:—"I was sorry to hear that an effort would be made to displace Gen MacRae. I should think it impolitic and unjust so to do, and have no doubt that the interests of the state and of the stockholders, from what I have understood, would be promoted by retaining him in office. I sincerely hope he will not be removed.x x x x x x x As an individual member of the Board of Internal Improvements, I have no hesitation in expressing such a wish. Of course no instructions could be given except by the whole Board. If I have time I would have addressed Gov. Read on the subject. I feel sure that he would not desire the removal of Gen. McR. on any *political* ground, and I know of no *personal* objection which he can have to his being retained." Mr. Bragg was under the impression that the meeting was to be the first of this week, instead of Thursday (13th) of next week.

Is the removal of Gen. MacRae *prudent*? When *he took charge of the road*, it was in wretched order, passing the trains at slow speed, and much risk. The motive power was not sufficient to transport the freight offered. The travel was leaving it for other, and then better routes. The credit of the company was at the lowest ebb. The stock was selling at $5, and never higher than about $10, per share, and gloom and despondency was felt as to its fate. How is it now? The road is pronounced by travellers to be among the best in the U. States. The road is well furnished, giving every desired facility. Freight has increased—travel has increased—until the nets are almost doubled. The credit of the company is restored. Stock is selling, when offered, at $50 per share—and a general feeling of satisfaction, to say the least, is felt by the individual stockholders. Is it a time to make a change? Just as he has brought about this gratifying result, to remove the head and executive? Would it be *politic*? These are questions which I submit with deference, but with confidence, to your sound discretion.

Could you not make this an occasion for a visit to that section of the state? Your strength lies in a great degree, along the entire line of the road. It is *democratic ground, all the way*. I have written in much haste, but hope in language sufficiently connected to be intelligible. I ask for the subject such reflection and action as it merits.

---

[1]John O. Campbell was postmaster of Weldon by 1841. *Register of Officers and Agents*, 299.

[2]Alexander McRae, previously identified.

[3]Owen Fennell, sheriff of New Hanover County in 1851, was a state senator from 1854 to 1857. In the Civil War he was a second lieutenant in the First Regiment North Carolina Troops and rose to the rank of captain. Cheney, *North Carolina Government*, 322, 324; Sprunt, *Cape Fear*, 321; *Wilmington Journal*, October 31, 1851.

[4]With the approval of the Board of Internal Improvements, Reid appointed Owen Fennell of Wilmington as the state's proxy for the general meeting of the stockholders of the Wilmington and Raleigh Rail Road Company. On November 13, 1851, when the meeting took place in Wilmington, Fennell opposed the reelection of McRae and cast the state's votes for John Campbell. Fennell did not canvass individual stockholders, however, and made no attempt to influence how any votes other than those he controlled would be cast. Consequently, McRae was reelected president by a vote of 6,486 shares to 4,324 shares. Reid had not given Fennell strict instructions but had advised him that it would be best to agree with the wishes of the majority of individual stockholders. Apparently personally opposed to McRae, Fennell rejected the governor's advice. This unpopular action perhaps led to Fennell's defeat when he sought reelection as county sheriff the following spring. David S. Reid to Owen Fennell, October 20, 1851, Governors Letter Books, Reid; *Wilmington Journal*, November 14, 21, 1851.

Frank I. Wilson to David S. Reid RF

Rutherfordton, N.C.
Nov. 28th 1851

Enclosed I send you my account for advertising the Fall Distribution, &c., of the Literary Fund. This you can retain, and I will forward you $5 soon to make up the $25—your share of the rent of the Press.

You have doubtless learned that our mutual Friend, Hayden,[1] is no more. His death has left a vacuum in our community not easily filled; for few men possess the clear judgment, the business tact, and honest heart that he did. He told me some weeks ago that he had recd a letter from you, in which you expressed your satisfaction with the course of the Banner. If afforded me much pleasure to hear it, and I hope I shall continue to give general satisfaction, though I cannot expect to commit no errors. The coming year will test my enterprise, but I believe I shall bear my Banner in triumph through the strife; or if defeated, that I shall be entitled to the honors of war. My subscribers generally, both whig and democrat, have renewed their subscriptions; and except a few old *fixtures* the whig party, in this county at least, is virtually dissolved. What "cohesive attraction" may be applied to bring the fragments together I cannot tell; but the Star's U.S. Bank and High Tariff will not have that effect. I believe I can fight Fillmore more successfully in this District than almost any other man likely to be brought out by the whigs for President. But my best policy now is to say but little. When the proper time arrives I think I can persuade the people here that they would be acting very inconsistently to support almost any whig.

Since I took possession of the Banner I have added about 250 new subscribers to my list. I think that the political excitement of the coming year will be an advantage to me. I have now upon my books about $500 for job work and advertising, though a considerable portion of it is against persons having demands against me. With the money received I have supported my family and paid the expenses of the office with the exception of about $50, which I can pay at almost any time, by making a few collections that I can call in at any time. In another year I hope to be able to refund the money paid for the press. I have already paid about $100 of it in advertising and subscriptions. If my health, and that of my family, is spared a year or two longer I shall be *even* with the world, or a little *ahead* of it. I now have $26 worth of job-work to do, and it shall be done in a week from this time if nothing happens. I have been rather scarce of help for a few weeks, but have made arrangements for a *new start* after Christmas. I have force enough at present, but one of my hands has heretofore been in the habit of going on a "bust" occassionally, and I only employed him for a short time, as I cannot put confidence in him. Taking all things together I think I am doing, as the old phrase has it, "as well as could be expected."

For your generous aid in establishing me in business I cannot permit the opportunity to pass without returning my thanks and acknowledging my gratitude. Hoping to hear from you soon I remain

---

[1]Thomas A. Hayden, previously identified, died in Rutherfordton on November 21, 1851. He established the *Mountain Banner* there in 1848. W. W. Holden, in a brief obituary, described Hayden as a "practical printer," who had for fifteen years been foreman of the *Charleston Mercury* office. *North-Carolina Standard*, December 3, 1851.

Ebenezer Emmons to David S. Reid A&H-GP

Albany [New York]
Dec 11 1851

I am Sorry to See in the Standard (News Paper) that therein exists complaints which must occasion more or less annoyance to yourself on account of my appointment to the Survey of your State—I was fearful of it, but I hoped after receiving the commission there was a degree of unanimity sufficient at least to fully sustain your Excellency in the measure—I shall soon (or at least hope to) enter upon the duties required & I trust it will turn out that you have not misplaced your confidence—It certainly will be my object to conciliate all parties as it regards politics it has been my course to keep aloof from & not offend either party though it has been known that my real sentiments placed me in the Democratic party—yet I possessed the full confidence of Gov Seward[1] although he is ultra in his feelings.—I need not dwell upon this subject I feel that my duties call me entirely to the development of the resources of the State & I take this time & opportunity to assure you that my time will be devoted to that object that I have been disposing of my engagements north in such a manner that I may & can devote myself to the survey I hope to leave Albany on or before the first of January—I have a matter of considerable importance in a pecuniary point of view, which I hope to get adjusted soon—On the Score of objections to my appointment I cannot of course answer to the one which is made in your State & which is heard on the ground as I understand, of being "a Northern Man, or not resident. Should other objections arise I shall be happy to meet them. I shall hope to meet your Excellency in Raleigh ere long & receive that advice in conducting the work which your better judgement & acquaintance with the State may dictate.

I propose now however to commence the work along the southern part of the Seaboard most respectfully

[1]William Henry Seward (1801-1872), a native of New York, served as Whig governor of that state from 1838 to 1842. An attorney, he served also in the New York state Senate (1830-1834), United States Senate (1849-1861), and as secretary of state (1861-1869). After 1855 he was a Republican. While secretary of state he negotiated the treaty with Russia for the purchase of Alaska, referred to by his political enemies as "Seward's Folly." *Biographical Directory of Congress, Bicentennial Edition*, 1792.

William Glazer[1] *to David S. Reid* A&H-GP

Palmetto Armory,
Columbia, S.C.,
Dec 17 1851

We have erected in this place an Armory for the Manufacture of Arms for the State of South Carolina, and are prepared to Manufacture Muskets, Rifles, Pistols & Sabres on terms equal to any establishment of the kind in any of the Northern States, and as ours is an Individual enterprise established by Southern men and Southern Capital We look to our Sister Southern States for a share of that patronage which every year, finds its way North, our establishment is the first of the kind and the only private institution in the whole Southern States, and to them we look for a permanancy which is desirable not only to ourselves but to all the Slave holding States, We are also prepared to Alter Muskets from Flint and Steel Locks to percussion on the plan adopted by the United States, We have a Contract to alter all the State Muskets of our State, and our Work we are happy to Say meets the unanimous approbation of our State Board of Ordinance as well as our prominent Military Officers and members of both Houses of Legislators, our terms for altering will be made known on application to us, We Would be pleased to hear from you at your earliest convenience

[1]William Glazer was the coproprietor of the Palmetto Armory of Columbia, South Carolina, which was established to manufacture arms.

Calvin Graves to David S. Reid RF

[Caswell County]
30. Decr. 1851.

Say to Caroline[1] that we were expecting a letter from her, and that because she makes the Executive Mansion her residence during her visit it does not follow that she, or her Cousin Caroline[2] is to make the Governor her Amanuensis.

We shall expect a letter once a week during her absence.

We are all well, and if our Corn Cribs were as well filled as our Ice houses, we should feel prety jolly in regard to supplies during the Coming year.

You will doubtless be surprised to be informed of the death of James N. Fuller[3] Esqr. late of Yanceyville, he died on Monday of last week. I am told, of Scarlet fever, after a very few days illness. That disease appeared about the first of November in Yanceyville in the family of Mr. Mitchell,[4] beyond which I understand it did not extend. Mr. Fuller left Yanceyville, saying, if he remained he should take the disease and die,—took lodgings at Mr. James,[5] Mr. James' having spent most of his time recently in traveling about the Country. And a few days ago while at Mr. James' he was attacked and survived but a short time.

Our love to all your family

---

[1]Caroline Graves, daughter of Calvin Graves, in 1857 married David S. Reid's brother Hugh.

[2]Caroline Settle, daughter of Thomas Settle and Calvin Graves's sister Henrietta Graves, became Hugh Reid's second wife in 1866. Both of Hugh Reid's wives were his first cousins.

[3]James N. Fuller (1824-1851), an attorney, was clerk and master in equity for Caswell County. At the time of the 1850 census he lived in Ann L. Graves's hotel in Yanceyville. He died December 22, 1851. Seventh Census, 1850, Caswell County, Population Schedule, 174; *Raleigh Star*, January 7, 1852.

[4]This is probably a reference to A. A. Mitchell (b. 1817), a native of Virginia and a house carpenter, whose house was near the hotel in which Fuller lived. Seventh Census, 1850, Caswell County, Population Schedule, 174.

[5]Wiley James (b. 1776), a native of Warren County, was an elderly farmer living near Yanceyville. Seventh Census, 1850, Caswell County, Population Schedule, 182.

1852

Thomas J. Mims to David S. Reid A&H-DSR

Robeson County NC
Near Floral College
January 2nd 1852

I have not the honour of a personal acquaintance with you, neither have I had the pleasure of merely seeing you. Yet I hope the subject of my letter will plead sufficient excuse for the liberty I take in writing to you.

I see that by a late act of the state Legislature which authorizes your Excellency to have a Geological Survey of the State made, you have engaged the Services of Prof Emmons of New York to accomplish the survey, and Prof E is authorized by said act of the Legislature "to employ such agents and assistants—to be approved by the Governor as may enable him (Prof E) to accomplish the survey" &c Perhaps clerks may be wanting, or if I am in any respect qualifyed to attend to any duty as an "agent or assistant" I would like exceedingly well to get employment in the survey. Perhaps my extensive acquaintance in the State (having been in about sixty NC Counties) would give me some advantage.

At present I will offer no reccommendation of myself, except a pledge—faithfully to attend to whatever I shd undertake, and for further information concerning my ability to be of any assistance in the survey I refer you to Hon Jas C Dobbin, Warren Winslow Esq Genl John Winslow[1] and John Waddill[2] Esqr of Fayetteville. I was raised in Fayetteville, and if any man is entitled to your partiality in asking your influence in getting employment it is me. It is needless to say that I am a Democrat, one who expressed (long before you were last nominated as a Candidate for Gov) a refusal to vote at the last Governor election unless you were the candidate; and when the day for voting arrived, I was "at my post" scouring the town of Fayetteville for delinquent and lukewarm voters.

While my pen is in hand let me express a wish that you may again be Elected Gov *Many of the whigs* in this County regret their last vote for Governor and are ready to support you next time, my individual second choice for Gov is Hon J C Dobbin or Col Geo Bower of Ashe—I lived two years with Col Bower. Col Bower is no more a scholar than myself, but his extraordinary correct judgement and his very apt &

sound common sense fits him to favably fill any office, with credit to the state, that the voters of the state could give.

If I have intruded—I beg your Excellency to excuse. Shd I got employment as above mentioned: then in expectation of the pay, and in view of a pleasant and yet perhaps arduous or laborious trip over the State I shall be highly well pleased, and under many weighty obligations to your excellency for the notice you may take of me and my application for Employment, I can write a very brisk and plain fist if I had conveniences which I have not tonight—in great haste

PS.

If ocasion requires you may address me at Floral College Robeson County NC

---

[1]John Winslow, an attorney from Fayetteville, served on the Council of State from 1849 to 1851. Oates, *Fayetteville*, 104, 305.

[2]John Waddill, a merchant from Fayetteville, was appointed to a town committee of vigilance in 1847. Oates, *Fayetteville*, 265. 432.

Braxton Craven[1] *to David S. Reid* A&H-DSR

Normal College
[Randolph County]
Jan 10. 1852

You are aware of the existence of Normal College, an Institution chartered by the last Legislature, and specially designed for the education of School Teachers. The Institution is under the direction of the first men of the State, is in a flourishing condition, and is considered by all to be very important to the whole country. The Trustees have done nobly indeed, but are not able to complete the necessary buildings. The public gentlemen of the state have commenced forming a company, of 50 to give $10 each. This will be but a small sum, but with the other resources it will render available, will place the Institution upon a firm basis Morehead, Badger and others approve the plan and have sent us the $10 each Your *name*, Sir, will be far more valuable than the money, and will doubtless enable us to succeed without difficulty By this small donation, you will do much for a State Institution of general interest, and will add many more to your already numerous friends. The remittance may be by mail, and will be promptly acknowledged and reported Shall I have the honour to hear from you at your earliest convenience?

---

[1]Braxton Craven (1822-1882), an educator from Randolph County, attended New Garden Boarding School and received degrees from Randolph-Macon, the University of North Carolina, Andrews College in Tennessee, and the University of Missouri. He became the assistant teacher at Union Institute, Randolph County, in 1841, and the next year he was named principal. Interested in improving teacher training for the common, or public, school system, he published *Theory of Common Schools* in 1850 and edited an education journal, the *Southern Index*. In 1851 Union Institute was rechartered as Normal College and was eligible for state funds. By 1856 Craven's experiment of a state teachers college had failed, and in 1850 the institution became the Methodist-sponsored Trinity College, which later became Duke University, *DAB*, IV, 516-517; Powell, *DNCB*, I, 455-456.

Elisha Mitchell to David S. Reid A&H-GP

University of N Ca
Janry 15th 1852

A report on the parcels left with me in June last has been too long delayed. I might offer several reasons why the examination was postponed. An analysis of a soil to be of any value requires two or three days at least of incessant labour and during the session it is not often that I have that much time to spare from duties that require my earnest and constant attention. Should your Excellency have any other work of the same kind to be executed hereafter I am happy to inform you that I am now better supplied than I was last summer, with the necessary apparatus and reageants and so long a delay need not be apprehended. Only I will mention that where a *soil* is to be examined it is desirable that one have as much as a pound Avoirdupois of it at command—7000 grains. The parcels handed me fell very far below this.
1. Parcel labelled "From the head of North River" Appears to be composed almost exclusively of vegetable matter reduced very nearly to the condition of peat—with pieces of clan coal or something like it in one or two places—also with roots as of grass running through it. Weight 536½ grains.

In reducing to powder 10 grains were lost adhering as a kind of gummy or resinous matter to the mortar and pestle.

Loss by heating to 212 for some time 57 grains. One hundred grains of the dried mass heated in a platinum capsule, burnt at first with flame and finally left 8½ grains only of ashes of a white color apparently

fine silica or sand. It resulted from this trial that there were only about forty grains of earthy matter in the whole parcel "from the head of North River—a quantity too small to operate upon with the view of ascertaining with such accuracy as would render the analysis valuable what might be the agricultural capabilities of the spot from which it was taken. This substance may be useful to the grounds near the spot where it is found if hauled out and applied to them as a manure.
No. 2. Parcel labelled "From the head of the Oyster Creek."
Weight—1067 grains.

Has a higher specific gravity than the last—dark and peaty in its appearance with grains of tolerably fine sand scattered through it also with some grass roots running through it. Picked out some of the larger pieces and put them aside. Proceeded to operate on the smaller matter (The whole parcel was finally used up) Weight—466 grains. Loss in pounding-adhering to the mortar Etc 5 grains. Loss by drying 30 grains. Burnt off the organic matter of one hundred grains in a platinum capsule. It burnt with flame leaving a light coloured powder with the appearance of powdered flint or quartz weight of the residuary matter—mean of three trials 46.486 grains—so that more than half of this parcel also or 53.514 parts in a hundred are vegetable matter.

Took one hundred grains of this residuary powder and proceeded to operate upon it for the purpose of ascertaining the constitution of the *soil* as distinct from the vegetable matter contained in it. Boiled for several hours in hydrochloric acid and filtered weight of the silica 93.05 grains leaving 6.95 grains in the solution. The substances consituting these 6.95 grains were one by one thrown down, collected dried and weighed affording the following results.

Silica as already stated 93" 05 grains.

Alumina—	3"27
Oxide of Iron—	31
Phosphoric Acid—	17
Lime—	1"23
Magnesia—	49
Potash and Soda—	71
Sulphuric Acid Chlorine and loss	47.-100" grains
	or taking the parcel as it came into my hands water excepted
Organic Matter-vegetable—	53" 514
Silica—	43.255.
Alumina—	1" 520
Oxide of Iron—	"144
Phosphoric Acid—	"079
Lime—	"711

Magnesia— "228
Potash and Soda— "330
Sulphuric Acid Chlorine and
loss— "219-100

This composition would indicate rather a light soil but such as may be expected to produce well—at least until the vegetable matter shall have been exhausted. I am very respectfully your Excellencys Humble Servant

---

John R. J. Daniel to David S. Reid RF

House of Reps.
January 22/52

I have received a letter from Charles Brown[1] of Philadelphia fomerly a member of Congress & whom I presume you well know, expressing a wish to procure employment on some of our Public works, for William Findlay Shunk,[2] his brother in law & son of the late gov. Shunk[3] of Pennsylvania as sub asst Engineer. Mr Shunk has been engaged for a year or so in the survey & location of R Roads, is said to be well educated, possessed of considerable theoretical knowledge in engineering, as well as some practical experience from his employment upon the Pennsylvania R Roads, and of good moral character. All that Mr Shunk asks, is a subordinate situation in some corps of Engineers, or employment as asst Engineer, until he can become acquainted, & have an opporunity of recommending himself by his qualifications & habits. If you are aware of any position that can be procured for him, you will very much oblige me, by letting me know it, & exerting your influence to procure it for him, & by so doing, you will confer a great favor upon our old friend Charly, and an important benefit upon Mr. Shunk, the son of an honest & worthy Sire.

---

[1]Charles Brown (1797-1883), a Philadelphia teacher and businessman, was a city councilman, state legislator, and Democratic representative in Congress (1841-1843, 1847-1849). *Biographical Directory of Congress*, 606.

[2]William Findlay Shunk (1830-1907), civil engineer, born in Harrisburg, Pennsylvania, was a midshipman in the United States Navy (1846-1850) and worked for the Pennsylvania Railroad (1851-1856) and the United States Coast Survey (1856). Except for service (1861-1865) as a clerk with the State Department in Washington, he spent the remainder of his career in various engineering positions. *Who Was Who in America, 1897-1942* (Chicago: Marquis Who's Who, 1943), 1123.

[3]Francis Rawn Shunk (1788-1848) was an educator, lawyer, and public official, serving as Democratic governor of Pennsylvania from 1845 to 1848. *CDAB*, 956.

Opposition View of "FREE SUFFRAGE REID" NCC

Raleigh
January 30, 1852

CANDIDATES FOR GOVERNOR.[1]

We have seen the names of the following distinguished gentlemen, among others, suggested to the Whig State Convention, either by public meetings or by the newspapers, as the candidate of our party for Governor, namely:—John A. Gilmer, of Guilford; John Kerr, of Caswell; Wm. H. Washington, of Craven; Kenneth Rayner, of Hertford; R. B. Gilliam,[2] of Granville; David A. Barnes,[3] of Northampton; and Alfred Dockery, of Richmond. This is a goodly list; and a standard-bearer may be selected from among them, under whose lead the Whigs of the State may rally, with quite a prospect of wrenching the government from the present "unlineal hands."

As the Convention will meet here on the 26th of April, it is right for every one to express their choice, and canvass, if they please, the merits of their favorites, that the Convention may be better prepared to select the man who, to competent qualifications and weight of character, may be deemed able to join the all-important faculty *that he can be elected.* Though the Presidential question will, of course, enter into the campaign, it would be idle for the Whigs to expect a canvass upon national issues alone; and our situation as to State policy is such, that there are interests which it is *highly important to consult* in the choice of a nominee,—interests of such weight as, in our judgment, *of themselves* to settle the question of his election, without reference to his opponent, who will doubtless be GOV. REID.

As a good Whig, whatever we have to say shall be said previous to the meeting of the Convention; for, when the candidate is fairly nominated, we recognize the duty of supporting him fully, by all means in our power, whether our individual choice (if we have one,) shall be gratified or not. But we like to see a prospectus of success ahead,—we must have *hope*, to inspire our exertions,—our cause must be such as to awake zeal and enthusiasm—and to keep us alive and active.

Upon what platform are we to stand as to our State policy?— for recollect that it is FREE SUFFRAGE REID we are to oppose.— Will the Convention "*skip*" this question?—and leave their candidate and every other man to his own devices upon it? We admit that nothing is wanting but union and organization. How are they to be brought about?

It is mighty useless for any body of men in North Carolina— supreme folly in any portion of the public press—to attempt to *ignore* the Convention movement in the State.—We defy the art of man to keep it out of the canvass. The Democrats take the field with "Reid and Free Suffrage by Legislative enactment," upon their banner—and what is our candidate to say to it? Is he to stand "mum" when it is flaunted into his eyes at every gathering in the State? Is he to approve it, and go for it too? Then the people would be very apt to take the "real simon pure" at once, and discard the imitations.

And yet we see some papers in the State trying to make it appear that this is a very small matter, and no bar whatever to "union and organization." Unless they mean to give up the contest, they will think better of it, and take their ground openly and fairly upon the subject. But one straight forward course will carry us safely through, leaving the Eastern Scylla on one hand and the Western Charybdis on the other; neutralizing everything like sectional influences, and uniting the Whig party upon the broad Republican ground of *popular rights*, their false position upon which broke them down in the last canvass. Will they take that course?

---

[1]This editorial commentary appeared on January 30, 1852, in the *Raleigh Times*, designated as the official Whig party campaign newspaper during the 1852 governor's race. This sample of its editorial expression reveals something of the opposing party's estimation of Reid's strength and also lists the leading contenders for the Whig gubernatorial nomination.

[2]Robert Ballard Gilliam (1805-1870), respected attorney, four-time speaker of the North Carolina House of Commons (1840-1841, 1846-1847, 1848-1849, and 1862), also represented Granville County two other terms as a Commoner (1836-1837, 1838-1839). A delegate to the Constitutional Conventions of 1835 and 1865-1866, he later served as a superior court judge. He was elected in 1870 to the United States House of Representatives but died before qualifying. Cheney, *North Carolina Government*, 307, 309, 310, 315-317, 329, 695, 746.

[3]David Alexander Barnes (1819-1892) was an 1840 graduate of the University of North Carolina. An attorney, he represented his native Northampton County in the House of Commons for three terms (1844-1845, 1846-1847, 1850-1851). Barnes was a delegate to the Secession and Constitutional Conventions of 1861-1862. During the Civil War he was a member of the military council of Governor Zebulon Vance. He served as a provisional judge of the superior court in 1865-1868, and he was an unsuccessful Democratic candidate for Congress in 1868. Governor W. W. Holden appointed him a trustee of the University of North Carolina in 1868. In 1872 Barnes moved to Hertford County. Cheney, *North Carolina Government*, 314, 315, 319, 362, 372n, 387, 825; Elections Returns, Congressional,

1790-1900, State Board of Elections, Archives, Division of Archives and History, Raleigh; Powell, *DNCB*, I, 98; Raper, *William W. Holden*, 295n; Raleigh *Sentinel*, November 5, 1868.

Nimrod S. Jarrett to David S. Reid A&H-GP

Aquone
2d Feb. 1852

Your letter dated 20th Inst. is at hand. In answer I would recommend Jessee Hyate[1] as a suitable person at the Holly Bridge and the Revt. Wm Holder[2] at the Murphey Bridge to collect the Toll. and as to the rate of Toll I would think it about right to collect half a cent per mile for a man on horse Back and all vehicles & stock in proportion. It is common on all the McAdamized roads that I have Traveled to pay one cent per mile for man on horse Back therefore I think the experiment might be made on our road at the above mentioned rate of Toll

as to the Salery of gate keepers I would think 20 percent about right as say not more than fifty Dollars per year for keeping a gate they will have to be fixed at particular points in order to catch the Toll without regard to distance only observing to collect the right amount of Toll per mile, as there are many roads running in and out this is the only way the Toll can be collected.

Should you deem it expedient to leave to me to contract with gate keepers I will do the Best I can for the State, and I will consult the cort & see if they will appoint overseers; the road needs some attention now in side deging [*sic*] it is on account of the freeze falling in the drane ditches and that Turnes the watter out in the road and washes gullies. Should the cort refuse to appo overseeers I must take the responsibility of calling out the hands for the present and put the road in order so that It will not damage I am very respectfully your most obt. Svt.

[1]Jesse R. Hyatt, a Burke County miller, had a cotton gin and mill on Paddy's Creek on the Catawba River by 1827. Phifer, *Burke*, 208.

[2]William Holder lived in Murphy, Cherokee County, in 1850. Seventh Census, 1850, Cherokee County, Population Schedule, 13.

Abraham Featherman[1] *to David S. Reid* A&H-DSR

Weston, Missouri,
February 3, 1852

You may think it strange to receive a letter from me, for many years have passed, since I first made your acquaintance, and the time, which intervened, since I last saw you, may have entirely obliterated my name from your memory. But your kind and disinterested friendship towards me, while living in the vicinity of your home, gives me the boldness to address you, not as the governor of the State of North Carolina, which has changed your social position, but not your feelings, but, not being accustomed to ceremony and formal phraseology, I shall couch my letter in the language of an old acquaintance. I shall sum up the object of this letter as briefly as possible, that I may not too long intrude upon your time and exhaust your patience. After having studied and practised medicine in this country, I went to Paris about 5 years ago, where I frequented the University and the Medical School for two years; having thus increased my knowledge in the sciences and my profession I returned to this country in 1849, without means however to set up for myself. I reached this town, on the Missouri river with about 2,000 inhabitants, pennyless, and was therefore compelled to assume the Editorship of a Democratic paper called the Platte Argus, which after 8 months successful operation, I sold out, in order to give it up into the hands of practical printers, who could make it more profitable than myself.

I commenced practising medicine and have done tolerably well last summer, but my lungs being slightly affected, and riding on horseback not agreeing with me, I am obliged to give it up again.

Some of my friends, here, advised me to make application in Washington, for a professorship of Mathematics in the Navy, and they assured me the cooperation of Senator Atchison,[2] who is a citizen of this county, and Mr Hall[3] representative from this district, and also the influence of Mr Cass[4] to whom I am known as Editor of the Argus, having besides a letter or recommendation to him from James Birch,[5] late judge of the Supreme Court of Missouri, who knows Mr. Cass personally. In order still to increase this co-operation from another quarter, knowing that you are acquainted with, and somewhat related to Senator Douglass[6] from Illinois, I request you, if you can do so, to ask him to exercise his influence in my favor, and act conjointly with Cass and Atchison. As far as competency and moral character are concerned, they will be sufficiently substantiated by testimonials from this section. I am a citizen of the United States, a Democrat of the Jacksonian school and Anti-Benton, but opposed to Disunion.

I do not know, whether you could exercise a direct influence upon Mr Graham,[7] Secretary of the Navy, he being a Whig, and you Democratic Governor of a Whig State, but if you could do so, my cause would be still in better hands.

Please write me as soon as possible, informing me whether you have done any thing, or whether you are able to do any thing in the matter.

Politics here have rather been in a state of confusion, the Democratic party having been divided between Benton[8] and Anti-Benton, but we have fine prospects for a fusion of these factions at the ensuing August election, and all will be safe.

I am Sir with the highest consideration your most obedient servant.

---

[1]Abraham Featherman (b. 1815), a native of Germany, was a physician and editor residing in 1850 in the town of Weston, Missouri. He was not a resident of North Carolina in 1840. Seventh Census, 1850, Platte County, Missouri, Population Schedule, 288 (microfilm), Archives, Division of Archives and History, Raleigh.

[2]David Rice Atchison (1807-1886), a native of Kentucky, was an attorney from Liberty, Missouri. He was a state legislator, county judge, and Whig member of the United States Senate from 1843 to 1855, serving as president pro tempore a number of times during his term of office. *Biographical Directory of Congress*, 493-494.

[3]Willard P. Hall (1820-1882), a native of Virginia, was an attorney in Sparta, Missouri. He was a lieutenant in the Mexican War, Democratic representative in Congress (1847-1853), Union delegate to the state Constitutional Convention of 1861, lieutenant governor (1861-1864), governor (1864-1865), and brigadier general of the state militia. *Biographical Directory of Congress*, 993.

[4]Lewis Cass, previously identified.

[5]James H. Birch (b. 1804), a St. Louis editor and attorney, was a native of Virginia. He was editor of the *Enquirer* and the Fayette *Western Monitor*, clerk of the state House of Representatives, register of the land office, judge of the state supreme court from 1849 to 1852, and a delegate to the state constitutional convention of 1861. Walter B. Davis and Daniel S. Durrie, *An Illustrated History of Missouri* (St. Louis: A. J. Hall and Company, 1876), 471-472.

[6]Stephen A. Douglas, previously identified.

[7]William A. Graham, previously identified.

[8]Thomas Hart Benton, previously identified.

Ebenezer Emmons to David S. Reid A&H-GP

Fayettville,
Feb. [6], 1852.

I have executed the preliminary examination of the Chatham CoalField which your Excellency proposed when I visited Raleigh. The results of this examination are highly satisfactory. I began it at Farmersville[1] the most easterly point where coal has been discovered, & have been able to trace it in its outcrop seventeen or eighteen miles. Along this outcrop, it rises to the surface at nearly an uniform dip & strike, & pursuing nearly a direct line from point to point, & maintaining withal through the whole distance, an average thickness of at least six & half feet. The principal bed exceeds seven feet at one or two points. A two foot bed lies below the main one with ten or twelve inches of slate only between them. Another 3 foot bed lies 13 feet beneath with bituminous slate intervening. The thickness of the main bed is all that can be wished, inasmuch as it is more profitable than one of 9 or 10 feet.

As there can be no question then as to the length of the line of outcrop & the thickness of the respective beds, the important question is will these beds thin out & become lost in the shales, or will they preserve their present average thickness This question, though it cannot be decided positively still if we may place confidence in geological principles, we may feel a great degree of assurance that they will prove as permanent as the beds of coal of Virginia and Pennsylvania. In the first place, diluvial action as it is sometimes called has never been felt here. There is no drift. The beds of pebbles are not transported masses, like our northern drift, but simply the remains of an old sea bottom. Beds of coal have not therefore been swept away. In the 2d place we find all the usual accompaniments of coal, as shale, fire clay, fossils, beds of the hydrous peroxide of iron. In the 3d place, there is a sufficient breadth & depth to the coal series; though the amount of coal is not always in proportion to the breadth & depth of strata; thus in the coalfield of Nova Scotia which I examined in 1835 I found only one bed of coal of four feet in strata whose aggregate thickness is fourteen thousand feet.

In the 4th place there is an uplift or an undulation of the strata by which the main bed of coal is brought to the surface at 1 ⁵371/2⁵38 or 2 miles south from the first outcrop, which last is within the outer rim of the basin. There can scarcely be a doubt therefore that there is a breadth of coal of 2 miles at least & which extends 17 or 18 miles continuously. I have however no idea that the coal field is thus restricted either in length or breath.

There is only one place where a bed thins out & this is the effect of a local disturbance common to all formations. From the facts & phenomena then of the Chatham coal field we have little reason to fear its early failure. It is proper for me to observe in this connetion that I do not regard this coal field as extensive as many others in this country. The Appalachian, the Illinois & Michigan coal fields are much longer & wider—the former being nearly 900 miles long & from 150 to 200 broad.

The quality of the coal of Chatham is excellent. It is adapted to parlor use, but particularly to the manufacture of gas for lighting houses & streets & also for coke, which may be employed in the manufacture of the best kinds of bar iron. I see no reason why it may not supersede the foreign bituminous coals. It is remarkably free from sulphuret of iron This mineral however is disseminated through the black shales, an important fact to be borne in mind when large quantities are to be sent to market for if this shale is mixed with the coal in considerable quantities, it may produce spontaneous combustion.

It becomes my duty to inform you that I have appointed Dr. McClenahan[2] of Pittsboro an Assistant in place of Mr. Wells[3] whose health is such as to forbid his participating in the duties of the survey at present. Dr. McClenahan being a native of this state; a man of energy & withal taking a deep personal interest in the work will bring to the survey many advantages. He is to give his whole time to the work—has already joined me & is to receive $1200 per an. He has been extremely valuable to me in facilitating my examination of the Chatham Coal field—

[1]Probably Farmville (later known as Coalglen) a community in southern Chatham County on the Deep River. It was the site of the Carolina Coal Mine. Powell, *North Carolina Gazetteer*, 111.

[2]Dr. Spence McClanahan of Pittsboro, Chatham County, was appointed assistant geologist for the state survey. *The Report of the Comptroller of Public Accounts, of the Receipts and Disbursements at the Public Treasury of the State of North Carolina, During the Fiscal Year Ending on the 31st Day of October, 1853* (Raleigh: W. W. Holden, 1854), 35, hereinafter cited as *Comptroller's Report*.

[3]David Ames Wells, previously identified.

Calvin Graves to David S. Reid RF

Locust Hill, N.C.
Feby 14, 1852.

I had the pleasure to receive your letter of the 5 Inst. a few days ago, informing us of the safe arrival of the girls[1] and Thomas[2] in Washington City. It was especially acceptable to us as we had heard nothing from them for a long time—be pleased to accept our thanks for your kindness in this regard.

By yesterdays mail we received letters from Judge Settle[3] of the 7th and Caroline[4] of the 8th Inst. informing us of their return to Raleigh, and of their expectation to reach Mason Hall, on Monday next, on the way homeward. I shall send a Conveyance to meet them there to bring on the bagage. We are all of opinion that it is quite time *the Wanderers* were at home.

We are sorry to learn that Henriettas[5] health is delicate. Tell her to be of good Cheer, it is (doubtless) a sickness unto life—rather than unto death: these things must be so. The family send love to you all—all well

[1]Caroline Graves and Caroline Settle, first cousins.

[2]Thomas Settle, Jr., nephew of Calvin Graves and first cousin and brother-in-law of David S. Reid.

[3]Thomas Settle, Sr., father of Caroline Settle and Thomas Settle, Jr., brother-in-law of Calvin Graves, uncle of Caroline Graves, and uncle and father-in-law of David S. Reid.

[4]Caroline Graves.

[5]Henrietta Settle Reid, wife and first cousin of David S. Reid, daughter of Thomas Settle, Sr., niece of Calvin Graves, first cousin of Caroline Graves, and sister of Caroline Settle and Thomas Settle, Jr.

Nimrod S. Jarrett to David S. Reid A&H-GP

Aquone
17th Febr. 1852

I wrote you on the 2d Febr. and have not recvd the answer. I now drop you this line to know what I shall do with those persons who have not finished their work according to contract, the time was out on the 15 Dec. there is one man or perhaps two that is not yet done nor they will not be before our cort in Cherokee which is to come on monday week was it not for those two late in the mountain road would all be open from this to the georgia line. must I sue them on their Bonds or wate longer on them

the road is verry muddy now on account of the hard winter our mountains are covered in snow at this time and have not been entirely clear since December.

C. H. Jordan[1] *to David S. Reid* RF

Person [County] N.C.
26th Feby 1852

When I last saw you (in Dec.) you spoke of Prof Emmons' wish to have his son and son in law appointed assistant geologists. You mentioned your own wish to make these appointments in N.C.; the propriety of which step appeared to me unquestionable. I have recently seen by the papers that Dr. McClannahan[2] is appointed one of the assistants; if you have not made the other and it can be dispensed with until July, I should feel under many obligations to you if you would give it to a son[3] of mine now at Hampden Sidney College who will graduate about the middle of June, and would be at your service as soon as he reaches home. *He is a good boy* and would be flattered by the appointment.

It would afford me pleasure to entertain Prof E—while he remains in this county and hope you will communicate my invitation to him to come to my house. I intend if professional duties do not prevent to accompany him to the different portions of the county and shew him things, that might be overlooked, of interest to the geologist.

Please inform me when the Prof will be here.

---

[1]C. H. Jordan (b. 1805), a native of North Carolina, was a physician living in Person County in 1850. Seventh Census, 1850, Person County, Population Schedule, 465.

[2]Spence McClanahan, previously identified, of Pittsboro.

[3]Edward C. Jordan (b. 1830). Seventh Census, 1850, Person County, Population Schedule, 465.

Ebenezer Emmons to David S. Reid A&H-GP

Goldsborough,
March 6, 1852

In view of the improvements which are in progress on Cape Fear river & also in expectation of finding deposits important to the agriculturists upon its banks & in the upper country on Deep river, I deemed it proper & best to make explorations on its course & banks while its waters were low. I have accordingly made numerous examinations of the formations on this river & am able to state facts of considerable importance as to its geology, but more particularly of the deposits of marl which abound upon its banks & at a distance from its course. Probably no substance has been discoverd which is so important to interest of agriculture of the lower counties of North Carolina as marl. The lands especially those in which sand predominates have been worn out I might perhaps say, more than once. Now it is by means of marl employed as the basis of a fertilizer, that these lands may be cheaply renovated. On the poorest however of these lands, it is not to be expected that this substance can supply *all* that is wanting to impart to them their original fertility, inasmuch, as in the progress of long cultivation & the production of a variety of crops the soil is exhausted of those elements which marl by itself does not contain. There are 2 kinds of marl upon Cape Fear river; One is known as shell marl & belongs rather to the upper parts of the river, or I may rather say it is in thicker beds at distant points from the ocean. The other marl is known as the "blue marl & is found at points nearer the ocean than the former. The shell marl reaches to a point at least twelve miles above Elizabeth[1] & is usually well exposed at different points on the banks of the river. So also it is often met within ravines at points distant from the river, hence it becomes more accessible to planters & requires less expense in hauling it. These beds vary considerably in extent. Some are visible ¼ of a mile on the banks; others appear to have been deposited in insulated patches. Their thickness varies from a foot to 7 feet in thickness. They are not continuous deposits. The composition of the shell marl is to the eye calcareous varying however from a very sandy marl to a perfect lime deposit, consisting of carbonate of lime. Many analyses should be made of this marl as it is only in this way that its real value can be determined.

The blue marl is a different substance from the shell marl. It is, by the way, the substance known as the green sand in New Jersey & has long been in use there & to the very great advantage of farmers. It belongs to the cretaceous formation of Geologists. The upper bed of this marl I now believe extends above Elizabeth. It is however quite sandy & I was unable to find at this point its characteristic fossils. Farther down the river however at Browns bluff & Robinson bluff, I found in what I now regard as the upper green marl the characteristic fossils, the *Exogyne costata* & at Sykes landing, the *Belemnite*. At Black rock however the lower green marl is in great force & I believe at many other points it would be easy to expose it, so that an inexhaustible supply of this substance might be obtained for the use of Planters on the Cape Fear & Deep rivers.

From the foregoing, it will probably be perceived that the banks of the Cape Fear & the numerous runs which enter it from the South are rich in these fertilizers, & it only requires an additional spirit of improvement on the part of the Planters to double the products of their plantations. It is proper to observe here that the marl deposits are found mainly on the left or South bank of the river. I am well satisfied that the time is not distant when these rich deposits will be fully employed, & that their value will be well understood. It is true that experience will be necessary to determine some points in its use. For instance, the most economical mode of preparing it in order to adapt it to the varieties of soil on which it is proposed to employ it. The blue marl especially requires an analysis in order to determine its composition. The Jersey marl contains potash & this substance is regarded as the principal fertilizer in it, & I hope it will be found that potash, & also phosphate of lime are elements of the marls of this State. These two, are the expensive fertilizers & are above all others to be sought for, for without them, the cereals would cease to produce perfect seed.

I have not attempted to give a detailed account of our examination upon the Cape Fear, but simply a statement of a few facts which I supposed may interesting to your Excellency, or so far as to satisfy you that the work is in progress. I am pleased with the attentions & intelligence of the Gentlemen whom I have met & the facilities which all wish to render, & especially the anxiety which is manifested in regard to the work. I am sometimes rather distracted to know where to go, the applications for examinations being so numerous.[2]

Dr. McCalahan the Bearer, will explain the character of our work & what is proposed to be done & will also receive any instructions which your Excellency may deem necessary to give.

---

[1]Elizabethtown.

[2]The *North-Carolina Star* of Raleigh gives the following account, reprinted from the *Goldsboro Republican*, of Emmons's visit to Goldsboro: "The State Geologist, Prof. Emmons, and his Assistants, spent several days of last week in our place, during which various parts of the county were visited and explored by the scientific

gentlemen. They left on Monday for some of the more Eastern counties. On Friday and Saturday nights, Prof. E. delivered his first lectures in North Carolina to the citizens of this County in the Court House. The general subject was Agricultural Chemistry. We took some notes, which however a want of time to write them out and the crowded state of our columns, prevents us from laying before our readers—The Lectures were quite well attended, and much interest was felt in the subject discussed by the learned lecturer." *Goldsboro Republican*, March 9, 1852, reprinted in Raleigh *North-Carolina Star*, March 17, 1852. The text of Emmons's letter to Reid was printed in the *Raleigh Register*, April 17, 1852.

James C. Dobbin to David S. Reid RF

Fayetteville
March 8th 1852

Some of the Officers of "The Fayetteville Independent Light Infantry Company" have just called on me and among other things mentioned that they had sent to your Excellency two communications asking your assistance in procuring for the company, from the United States, about sixty of the "Original Percussion Muskets" and that they had received no reply to either.

I took the liberty of suggesting althoug you had not replied to them—I had no doubt you were making the proper efforts at headquarters to get the War Department to furnish them.

This is an ancient time honored company. It was organized in 1793 and is now the oldest in the United States. They desire the improved Musket & think on your application at the proper Department they can be gratified. You will appreciate my dropping you this line as your attention may prevent the growth of a little complaint sometimes occasionally by small matters. I congratulate you, my Dear Sir, on your *unquestioned popularity*: Your administration is *cordially approved* and I really think your reelection as certain as any future political event can be.

Henry R. Shorter[1] *and others to David S. Reid* A&H-GP

Univ of No. Ca.
March 11th 1852

A large number of Students desirous of taking lessons in dancing meet with but one obstacle; the want of a room.

We have precured the services of Mr. Frensley[2] a gentleman of fine reputation to instruct us in the art of dancing, and all things are ready to proceed to business were it not for want of a proper place.

We applied to Gov Swain[3] for permission to use the lower part of the ball-room, a place peculiarly fitted for our purposes and the only one, but we were refused on the ground that the Gov would assume none of the responsibilities attending the granting of his permission, but refered us to your Excellency as the proper person to whom we must apply.

The dangers to be apprehended from our use of the room, arise from the use of cigars so near such a quantity of combustible matter as must always be near a new or unfinished building.

That there would be danger in most cases we do not deny, but if the room is granted to us we promise on our part, to prevent any smoking in or near the building, nor will we allow any person to chew tobacco so as to deface the appearance of the building. This all the class have promised and as for the rest of college their own sense of what is right and proper will prevent any intrusion on their part.

So confident are we of this, that we promote on their part the same that we ourselves have promised. In consideration of these things we a committee appointed by the class respectfully request Excellency as Chairman of the Executive Committee to grant us the use of the room in question.

---

[1]Henry Russell Shorter (1833-1898) of Eufala, Alabama, graduated from the university in 1853 and became a lawyer. Grant, *Alumni History*, 562.

[2]By 1850 Mr. Frensley was the first regular instructor of dancing at the university. Battle, *History of the University*, I, 590, 705.

[3]David Lowry Swain, previously identified, a former governor, was president of the university.

David L. Swain to David S. Reid A&H-GP

Chapel Hill
March 15th 1852.

Your note of the 12th to Mr. H. R. Shorter and others has just been shown me.

Some days ago Mr. S applied to me for the use of the room to which your letter alluded. I refered him to the contractors Mesrs Berry[1] and Richards,[2] and informed them that if their consent could be obtained, the Faculty would interpose no objections. The result was that the room was given up to Mr. Frensley[3] the next night. The following day Capt Richards showed me the enclosed advertisment, and remarked that the young men had informed him, that I had agreed to assume the responsibility if any accident should occur from fire. I replied that I had not done so, and had no power to do so, that by the terms of the contract, the responsibility rested upon the contractors until the building was delivered. He stated that he would not risque it, and gave immediate notice to the managers that they must use it no longer. It is due to the managers, to state, that they assured me, that the impression of Capt Richards, that they represented me as assuming any liability was founded entirely in misconception on his part, and such I am satisfied is the fact. With proper precaution, the risque cannot be great, and the advertisment by the managers will enable you to judge of it as accurately as I can. It is for the Executive Committee to determine whether they will for the purpose proposed absolve the contractors from their liability.[4]

---

[1]John Berry, previously identified.

[2]Henry Richards (b. 1813), a native of Orange County, was a Hillsborough brickmason. Seventh Census, 1850, Orange County, Population Schedule, 182.

[3]Mr. Frensley, previously identified.

[4]Smith Hall, donated by Governor Benjamin Smith and designed by architect A. J. Davis, was completed at a cost of $10,303.63. Designated as a library, it was nevertheless known in its early years as the "Ball Room." In later years it became the Playmakers' Theatre. Archibald Henderson, *The Campus of the First State University* (Chapel Hill: University of North Carolina Press, 1949), 144, 364, hereinafter cited as Henderson, *Campus of the First State University.*

Ebenezer Emmons to David S. Reid A&H-GP

Newberne
March 21 52

I am weather bound in a storm of snow at this place to day. Tomorrow I hope to be able to proceed to Carteret Co agreeably to your instructions.—Having made the necessary explorations I will communicate again with you. I hear conflicting accounts of those lands some declaring them worthless; others, that they are valuable. I shall be under the necessity of making up my mind on an independent examination.—

I now believe it will turn upon the actual composition of the soil as determined by an analysis.—

We have been engaged in Wayne & Edgecombe Counties for a few weeks. There is expressed everywhere an anxiety on the part of planters to have examinations of their individual property & to be followed by analyses of soils & marls. I have already an accumulation of specimens for that purpose. I shall be governed by your views in the matter. This is the only whole day but one I believe during which I have been confined to the house or unable to go on with out door work. My son has employed himself in making geological sections & drawings of the different objects illustrative of the work when detained indoors—So that some progress is making in all the departments of the work I regret hower to state that my son is under the necessity of returning to Albany in a day or two when some little works is finished which I left him to complete in Edgecombe, after receiving your instructions We received a letter stating the sickness & death of an only son & child, which, taken in connextion with other matters of a personal nature seemed to require his presence at home—We both designed going home sometime in April. We believe we can make greater progress in the survey by employing our private conveyance from place to place. We shall therefore take measures immediately or as soon as the survey of a few counties in this direction is completed to procure this additional facility. I propose entering upon an examination of the northern tier of counties in May. I shall be under the necessity of drawing upon the Treasury & it will diminish my expenses provided I can receive a Draft here. that is if it is unnecessary for me to visit Raleigh. As quarterly payments will be attended with less trouble than at irregular intervals, I will propose this. I hope to receive a communication on my return from Carteret & also farther instructions. My son E Emmons Jr wishes me to draw his salary at this time in his name if not objectionable—

Henry K. Craig[1] *to David S. Reid* A&H-GP

Ordnance Office
Washington,
March 22nd 1852.

I have the honor to acknowledge the receipt of your letter of the 18th inst. In accordance with your special request for a portion of the quota of arms, due to the state of North Carolina, to be supplied in percussion muskets originally so made, and not altered from flint lock, I shall order Capt. Dyer,[2] commanding North Carolina Arsenal, to issue *such* muskets *for the use of the Fayetteville Light Infantry company*, as soon as I am informed of the person, who is duly authorized to receive and receipt for them. Please inform me also of the exact number of muskets required to arm the company. Your letter states about sixty; another letter on the same subject, received through the Hon. JW Ashe,[3] states the number at sixty-four. This information is requisite, because the order to Capt. Dyer must be specific.

So far as regards their qualities for service, the altered muskets are in all respects as good as the original percussion. The former are usually, indeed almost always, issued to supply the quotas of the states; because they were made from that fund, and for that purpose, and were altered when the system was changed for all small arms from the flint to the percussion lock. In a special case, like the present, and to limited extent, the latter kind may be supplied.

---

[1]Henry Knox Craig (d. 1869), a native of Pennsylvania, entered the army as a first lieutenant in the artillery in 1812. Promoted to captain in 1813, he transferred to the ordnance branch, eventually rising to the rank of colonel and chief of ordnance (1851-1861). He was brevetted lieutenant colonel in 1846 for gallantry in action at Monterey, Mexico. He retired in 1863 and was promoted to brigadier general in 1865. Heitman, *Historical Register and Dictionary of the Army*, I, 333.

[2]Alexander Brydie Dyer (d. 1874), a native of Pennsylvania, was a graduate of West Point in 1837, when he became a second lieutenant in the artillery. He transferred to the ordnance branch by 1838 and was promoted to captain in 1853. He was brevetted captain for gallantry in action at Santa Cruz, Mexico, in 1848. By 1864 he was chief of ordnance with the rank of brigadier general, and the next year he was promoted to major general. Heitman, *Historical Register and Dictionary of the Army*, I, 392.

[3]Probably William S. Ashe, congressman, of New Hanover County, who in 1852 was representing District 7, which included Fayetteville. Ashe (1813-1862), a Wilmington rice planter and attorney, was a state senator (1846-1848, 1859-1861), a Democratic representative in Congress (1849-1855), and president of the Wilmington and Weldon Railroad from 1854 to 1862. He was a delegate to the 1861 state

Constitutional Convention and served as a Confederate army major. He was killed in a train accident near Wilmington. *Biographical Directory of Congress*, 491; Cheney, *North Carolina Government*, 684.

David S. Reid to Jacob Siler UNC-JS

Executive Office,
Raleigh,
March 22d, 1852.

Your Report of the 1st of January 1852 has been received and filed.

During the past year I informed the Commissioner, Mr. Jarrett,[1] that the act of the last Session of the General Assembly entitled "An Act to provide for a survey of a Rail Road from Salisbury to the Tennessee line" made an appropriation out of the first moneys collected by you, after the 1st day of January 1852, on Cherokee bonds and for the sale of Cherokee lands, and instructed him to make the contracts for building the Turnpike with a view to this appropriation.

I desire you inform me at your earliest convenience, what amount you have already in hand applicable to the before mentioned appropriation, and at what time you will probably have the whole amount—twelve thousand dollars—in hand.

These facts are necessary to enable the Board of Internal Improvement to determine at what time the survey shall commence.

My respects and best wishes.

---

[1]Nimrod S. Jarrett, previously identified.

Ebenezer Emmons to David S. Reid A&H-GP

Newberne
March 28, 1852

I have the honor to inform your Excellency that immediately on receiving your instructions I proceeded to Carteret County & entered as soon as possible upon the examination of the open ground Prarie belonging to the State. In order to qualify myself the better to give an opinion respecting this remarkable variety of Soil I have examined similar soils wherever I could find them especially where they have been under cultivation. Notwithstanding I have pursued this course I am not ready to report infull inasmuch as I have not been able to make analyses of the specimens of soils I have taken. I will hower express my views as far as they have been formed & then as soon as possible furnish you with the analysis when made—

These lands are situated in the neighborhood of Beaufort. They lie between Wards Creek & the North river at their northeastern terminus. I entered upon them at the head of Wards Creek. My landing was near what is called the *Chincopin ridge* which leads directly to them towards the North It terminates in a belt of prickly evergreens some 80 rods in breadth. These evergreens gradually diminish toward the grounds though they do not entirely disappear.—The grass increases as these diminish & finally at about the distanc of half a mile the open grounds proper are reached This open ground is spongy & wet, though, less so than I expected for at Newbern & Beaufort & surrounding country 4 days prior to my visit there had been a fall of snow previous to which there had been also a heavy rain. There were places slighly [*sic*] elevated which were comparatively dry. Numerous small pools of water are scatterd over this ground, which are supposed to have been made by Deer breaking up the turf & moss.

I began my examinations at the outer rim of these grounds in the belt occupied by the briers. The following results I obtaind by numerous soundings Many of which however I did not record inasmuch as the characters obtaind accorded with those I have given.

No. 1. Chincopin ridge. Depth of soil 3½ feet consisting of vegetable matter mixed with sand and clay, bottom hard though sandy.—2. Evergreens. depth of 5 feet soil vegetable mixed with sand—some logs beneath 3. 2½ feet. veg. matter mixd with sand. 4. 5 feet veget. with a very trifling quantity of sand. 5. depth 9 feet & no bottom. veget matter. 6.7 feet do 7:8 feet & at the depth of 4½ feet. logs. 8. 10 feet much as the preceeding. 9. Sounded 7½ feet no bottom. Some sand & clay mixd with the vege. matter. 10 7½ & no bottom. 11. 6½ feet of veg. matter. The preceeding soundings carried me fully into the open grounds, where the surface is grass & moss at its roots. Common spagnum of swamps. 12. 6½ feet. veg matter a small quantity of sand & clay intermixed. 13. 5 feet do. 14 5½ fe. 15. 5½. 16 5½ feet sand at bottom. 17. 4 feet struck a log. 18. 6 feet bottom sandy. 19. do. 20. 5 feet & logs 3½ feet[.] It will be observed from the forgoing that the depth of the soil is at least 5½ feet consisting mainly of vegetable matter changed into a black peaty substance intermixed with living roots. The bottom is sandy & hard & difficult to be penetrate by the Sound. I continued my examination for a long time until indeed I satisfied myself & the Gentlemen who accompanied me that the tract is uniform some of them having seen the same characters at those distant points still.—

The impressions which have been made upon my mind respecting this tract are favorable upon the whole that is, when thoroughly drained it will be productive. Of the feasibility of draining it I have not the least doubt. The water flows from it with quite a ripple at some places into Wards creek. This opinion of its value is founded upon the point 1st that it has produced trees—trunks of which remain. Sow if a soil has fertilizing matter sufficient to bear & mature trees with their leaves & fruit, it is a fair inference that it will produce corn. To in the grass with which it is coverd, there is silicate of the alkalines. In the leaves & seeds of fruits we have the phosphate of lime iron & magnesium. It is true that in the stump of the bay which are scattered over the ground, it is supposed we have the indications of a cold acid soil. Yet if so, draining becomes an effectual remedy. This whole tract is cold & bleak now from the great extent of evaporating surface. 2d I have examined lands of this character which have been quite productive for 16 years though there is this difference, the latter evidently contain more sand, but it is coarser than that of the open grounds; Still, I wish to determine the amount of actual soil, sand & clay etc., which this veg matter contains before I shall feel confident of certain results.

I feel that it is very desirable that these lands should be reclaimed. They are situated in a very favorable position easily accessible & should they prove as productive as the Hyde county land, would furnish more corn annually than the whole state of N. York ever produced—But I do not expect they will be as productive though that the outer rim, will, be, I have no doubt, when it is bearing the thickest of the brambles. The state may very properly take a prospective view of the matter. Draining will essentially change the soil, the surface will sink & the whole mass will become compact & more solid & will in process of time at least, be fitted for a successful cultivation.—

Nimrod S. Jarrett to David S. Reid A&H-GP

Aquone
29th March 1852

Your communication dated 9th Inst came to hand on the 21st In obedience to your directions I have proceeded to set up Toll gates at Notley Bridge and at the Murphy Bridge and have fixed the rate of Tolls as follows

For 6 horse waggon 3½ cents per mile
5 horse Do 3 cents per mile
4 horse Do 2½ cents per mile
3 horse Do 2 cents per mile
2 horse Do 1½ cents per mile
1 horse Do 1 cent per mile
2 horse carriage Barough or Buggy 2 cts pe m
1 horse Do 1 person 1 cent per mile 2 or more persons 1½ cts pe m
man on horse Back ½ cent pr mile
Loose horses & mules ¼ cent pr mile
cattle 2 cents per head for 20 miles Travvel on the road
sheep & hogs 1 cent a head for 20 miles Travvel

Should you deem the above rates of Toll proper you will so inform me. If not give such Instructions as you may think proper and It will be attended to forth with. I have found It nesesary to set another gate at Henry Moss' Esqr you will please confirm his apt. The road will be all finished to Franklin By the 15th Apl or shortly after as the Bonds are out at that time.

The Tolls will not Increase as was anticipated on account of the Georgia Legislature failing to pass the Bill to continue the road on to Roame or some point on the Georgia rail Road Its failure was caused By the bad management of the member from Gilmer County

I in complyance with your views had overseers appointed By the county cort of Cherokee & to be Instructed By the Agt. as to the manner of the work to be done By the two mill hands. Judge Manley[1] who was presiding on Superior Cort Bench & the Bar approvd this course as the act was so lame

[1]Matthias Evans Manly (1801-1881), an attorney from New Bern, was a member of the House of Commons (1834-1835), superior court judge (1841-1859), state supreme court justice (1859-1865), and speaker of the state Senate (1866-1867). In 1866 he was elected United States senator but was denied his seat. Hamilton and Williams, *Graham Papers*, I, 152n; Cheney, *North Carolina Government*, 335, 361, 832, 1109.

Archibald M. Campbell[1] *to David S. Reid* A&H-GP

Fayetteville,
March 29, 1852

Dear Sir: I have just been shown your letter to D. G. McRae, Esq., and also a letter from the Ordnance Department, to your Excellency, requesting me to specify the number of "Original Percussion Muskets," required by my Company.

The number requisite for the use of the Corps, is
Sixty four (64) muskets and bayonets
Sixty four (64) Screwdrivers
Sixty four (64) wipers
Six (6) Spring vices
Six (6) ball screws and two thousand (2,000) percussion caps.

Permit me, sir to tender you the hearty thanks of the members of my Company, for the interest you have taken in the prosperity of the Corps, and the prompt measures you have adopted to place in their hands the "Original Percussion Musket."

[1]Archibald M. Campbell, an auctioneer and commission merchant from Fayetteville, was town clerk, postmaster (1853), member of the Committee of Safety (1862), county register of deeds, and major commanding the Fayetteville Independent Light Infantry. Oates, *Fayetteville*, 161, 190, 238, 241, 269, 317, 749.

Nathaniel J. Palmer to David S. Reid RF

Milton, N. C.
March 30th 1852

Through your kindness I received from the Governor of Tennessee the appointment of Commissioner of Deeds. I have received similar appointments from the Governors of Virginia and Arkansas. I would like also to receive similar appointments from the Governors of Mississippi and Alabama and will esteem it as a singular favor if you will write a note to each of them recommending me for the appointment. I have written to them but did not send any recommendation. I find the office of Commissioner of Virginia one of some profit.

We are going to have a Democratic Meeting at Yanceyville to-day. We shall nominate you for re-election and I hope Judge Douglass[1] for the Presidency and Judge Strange[2] for the Vice Presidency. Our brother Hill[3] is for William R. King[4] but I hope he will yield to the generally expressed wishes of the party throughout the State The Whigs will hold a meeting and nominate Mr. Kerr. I do not know whether or not he will accept. He ought to know that he cannot succeed if he should it will be disastrous to his interests and that of his family. Kind regards to Mrs Reid

---

[1]Stephen A. Douglas, previously identified.

[2]Robert Strange, previously identified.

[3]Probably Samuel P. Hill of nearby Yanceyville.

[4]William Rufus King (1786-1853), a native of Sampson County, graduated from the state university in 1803 and became an attorney. He was in the House of Commons (1807-1809) and a representative in Congress (1811-1816). After serving as secretary to the United States legation in Naples, Italy, and St. Petersburg, Russia, he moved to Alabama in 1818. Active in forming the state constitution, he was elected one of the first United States senators from Alabama, serving from 1819 to 1844. From 1844 to 1846 he was minister to France. He again served in the Senate, from 1848 to 1852, and in 1852 was elected vice-president of the United States. *DAB*, X, 406-407; *Biographical Directory of Congress*, 1168.

Samuel P. Hill to David S. Reid RF

Yanceyville N C
April 3d 1852

I recd a letter from Mr Samuel S. Draughn[1] of Springfield, Tenn, whom you appointed a Commissioner of Affidavits, stating to me that he had taken the oaths of office and forwarded the papers to your office, but had recd no reply as to whether they were satisfactory or perhaps they were sent to the Secretary of State. He is unwilling to act untill he learns whether he has complied with the Law properly: He also stated that he had addressed your Private Secty to inform him on these points. May I ask the favor of you to have Mr Draughn letter answered.

You will see from the papers that we have had Douglass[2] nominated in our County; I found that among a *few* that Mr Buchanan[3] or Cass[4] would be more acceptable though they would support Mr Douglass very cheerfully. I regret exceedingly that the meeting was not called some months ago; as I believe a lead of that sort would have had great influence in the county meetings throughout the State coming from any County. He is without question the strongest man we could put forward in the coming contest, and the friends of Mr Buchanan will find it an uphill business to enlist the people warmly in his favour; they no doubt will support him cheerfully but we want more than *mere acquiesance* we will want a candidate that will call forth our energies and rouse up enthusiasm. The Tariff notions of Mr Buchanan do not stand upon such a footing as will give him any strength either North or South. As for Genl Cass we have tried him and we know the result.

It is to be hoped that our State convention will not endorse the claims of any one, unless they can unite with more harmony upon some man than there is a probability of. Our delegates to the Baltimore convention had best be untramaled, there will have to be more sacrifice of private preferences there, than at present we are aware of and for our State convention to endorse Mr Buchanan would serve to embarass our delegates and even give to him a prominence that would hardly be warranted if the feelings of the masses were accurately known.

I should be pleased to attend the State convention and take a part in it, but I do not think that it will be possible for me so to do. I need not say to you how much I should be pleased to see you consent again to bear our flag triumphantly throughout the State. Never were the indications of your success more palpable than they are at present. The Whigs are divided and the Democrats are united. Even my friend and neighbour Mr Kerr cannot unite them and I think there is very little doubt but he will make the effort if the nomination is given him. Let them nominate Scott and the State is ours by an overwhelming majority.

When I sat down to write I intended only a short letter yet I have been insensibly led to fill almost three pages. I should be pleased to hear from you and let me conclude by hoping that you will respond favourably to the unanimous call that is being made for you throughout the State.

---

[1]See Hill's letter of October 8, 1851, to Reid regarding this appointment, which may never have been completed. Draughn's name does not appear in any list of Reid's appointments. Governors Office Records, "Commissions and Resignations, 1841-1855."

[2]Stephen A. Douglas, previously identified.

[3]James Buchanan, previously identified.

[4]Lewis Cass, previously identified.

Calvin R. Finch[1] *to David S. Reid* RF

Nash County N. Ca
April 3d 1852

to the onerable David. S. Reid Our governor Captain general. and Commander in Chief Whear as my Companny Dst No 7 Wishes a Flag from you With your name On it We Want it By the 20th of May When We Intend to have a Large meeting Our Company Will Pay for the Flag if We Can get it Plase your honer if I Can get it send it to Stan hope & send the Cost & I Will see that you shall have the monny for it I Wish it not to Cost more than $10.00

your Verry Best Frind & a Tru Dmocrat as Ever Livd hears old Nash Bless the Land that Bore the Canne that Fed the goose that Bore the quil that first Rote the name of David S Ried Governor

---

[1]Calvin R. Finch (born circa 1818), militia captain, was a merchant living near Stanhope in Nash County in 1850. A postal route map for North Carolina shows that a rural post office named Finch was in operation three miles southeast of Stanhope as of June 1, 1896. Seventh Census, 1850, Nash County, Population Schedule, 255; T. E. Ricks (ed.), *Nash County Historical Notes: A Bicentennial Tribute* (Rocky Mount: Dixie Printing & Publishing Company for the Nash County Bicentennial Commission, 1976), 150, hereinafter cited as Ricks, *Nash County Historical Notes.*

Orlando B. Ficklin[1] *to David S. Reid* RF

Washington
4th April 1852

I had intended for the last two months or more to do myself the pleasure of writing to you as well for the purpose of saying something in regard to our former friendship, as with the additional view of making suggestions in regard to the coming Presidential campaign.

Appreciating the delicacy of your position, and the conflict in yr. own breast between inclination on the one hand to take a bold and decided stand in favor of Judge Douglas,[2] and duty upon the other to preserve your position as Executive of the old North State from any well grounded imputation of improper interference between rival candidates; Notwithstanding the existence of these facts I have felt that it would not be out of place in an old friend to write you of the signs of the times and of the prospects of Douglas.

Events have already sufficiently developd to render it certain that Genl Cass[3] is the man we shall have to beat and it is almost equally certain that if beaten at all, it must be with Douglas. The antecedents of Mr Buchanan,[4] and his proclivities together with those of his State in favor of a protective tariff render him unacceptable, not to say highly obnoxious to the West and he is certainly not a favorite in New England; whilst his strength in the South is based very much upon his supposed kind feeling towards the peculiar institution of the Slave states.

To defeat Genl Cass we must have a man to divide with him the West and New England; this can be done more effectually by Douglas than by any other person. Remove Douglas from the contest and the more numerous troops of Cass will overpower those of Buchanan and give the former the nomination even under the two third rule. Buchanan cannot possibly be the compromise candidate, nor can he in any event be nominated. I say this because I feel that it is certainly true beyond all possible question. I might also add, that in running him we should make a fancy race not a winning one; but it is unnecessary to say this as it is quite certain that he will never be nominated. If North Carolina therefore is opposed to the nomination of Genl Cass, the road is a plain one; that is to appoint Douglas delegates to the Baltimore Convention; and if she is so partial to Mr Buchanan as to desire to compliment him by giving him her first vote, let her do so, but it will be better to come up for Douglas from the start. The Democrats who desire the success of the party should see that the delegates are good Democrats and sound Douglas men. If we present a formidable front at the beginning, Douglas will divide with Cass in all the New England and most of the Western States; if not, Cass will receive the floating vote; therefore the necessity of having firm, original Douglas men *from the first*. The prospects for Douglas are very fair in most of the States and all admit his preeminent availability. I send you Douglas and Marshall's[5] speeches and we think of republishing the speech upon remitting the fine of Genl Jackson which you heard delivered.

I can send you any number of either or all of these documents for distribution; perhaps you had better have a Douglas Club organized to whom they could be directed and by whom distributed. Hoping that I may hear from you soon; that you may be re-elected Governor and come on to see us, I am your sincere friend

---

[1]Orlando Bell Ficklin (1808-1886), an attorney from Charleston, Illinois, was a native of Kentucky and an 1830 graduate of Transylvania University. He was a county militia colonel, state legislator, and Democratic representative in Congress (1843-1849, 1851-1853). *Biographical Directory of Congress*, 884-885.

[2]Stephen A. Douglas, previously identified.

[3]Lewis Cass, previously identified.

[4]James Buchanan, previously identified.

[5]Perhaps a reference to Democratic Congressman Edward C. Marshall (1821-1893), of California, an attorney who at the time this letter was written was serving in the Thirty-second Congress. A Mexican War veteran, he was a native of Kentucky. *Biographical Directory of Congress, Bicentennial Edition*, 1425.

Robert R. Heath[1] *to David S. Reid* A&H-DSR

Elizabeth City NCa
22 April, /52

Previous to the sitting of Pasquotank Superior Court, I spent a couple of days, with our mutual friend, Dr G. C. Marchant,[2] of Currituck Co.—As was natural, the approaching election, for Governor came up: we had a *long* conversation, in regard to it, and both mutually promised to write you: that promise, thus made, I now proceed to perform. It is neither flattery, nor presumption, to assume, that you, Sir, will be the honored Standard bearer of the Democracy, in the contest.—all true hearted and right minded Democrats will rejoice to see this, and will use their utmost endeavors to secure success.

It is quite certain, that the Democrats of the East are in a minority: yet a truer Set of men cannot be found: we lack strength and want—need—aid: in the two preceding canvasses, you have visited the west, and middle portions of the State; but you have never been with the Democracy of the East. We wish you to visit this section, previous to the election, if the Candidates, as we hope they will, canvass the State. A visit, at this time, would do much good: it would arouse our friends, to greater exertions, and would, no doubt bring into our rank many of our opponents, among whom there is much lukewarmness, no enthusiasm, and considerable disaffection. A visit from you, Sir, would do much to strengthen us, and weaken the power opposed to us: "Come over and help us" and rest assured the result will be highly favorable to our cause and principles.

The Superior Courts will be over: the County Courts sit as follows: Chowan first Mondy of May: Perquimens & Bertie 2d Mondy of May—Washington & Gates, 3d Mondy of May: Hertford 4th Mondy of May—Currituck last Mondy of May—Pasquotank 1s Mondy of June—Camden 2 Mondy of June:—perhaps your arrangements may be made to meet some of these Courts: at all events come: make your appointments *public, early*, so the people may know *when* and *where* to meet you, and I pledge you, the Democracy will give a Shout that shall ring from the SeaBoard to the mountains. Come down & see us: we can take no excuse; none!— I regretted very much that I could not see you, when at Raleigh: my engagements were constant: the weather was *cold*: on the night of your party, I was too ill to go out, and though I called two or three times afterwards to see you, to use an Irishism, I *found* you *out*: you were not *in*.

Hoping and trusting you will show yourself to the Democracy of the East, I remain

---

[1]Robert R. Heath of Edenton was a state superior court judge from 1858 to 1865. He received an honorary masters degree at the 1859 University of North Carolina commencement. Cheney, *North Carolina Government*, 362; Battle, *History of the University*, I, 703.

[2]Gideon C. Marchant, a physician from Indian Town, Currituck County, was postmaster in 1843. He served on the Council of State in 1858 and 1859. Cheney, *North Carolina Government*, 179; *Register of Officers and Agents*, 286.

J. B. Ferguson[1] *to David S. Reid* A&H-DSR

Fayetteville N.C.
May 3d 1852

At a regula [*sic*] meeting of the Fayetteville Independent Light Infantry Co held on the 1st May the following resolution was unanimously passed

Resolved That the thanks of the officers & members of the Fayetteville Independent Light Infantry Co are due & hereby tendered to His Excellency Gov Reid for the interest he has manifested in their behalf in procuring for their use from the National Government a supply of the original percussion muskets

Resolved That the Secretary be requested to forward a copy of the above resolution to His Excellency as an expression of the sentiment of our corps

In transmitting the above resolution expressing our thanks for the interest you have taken in procuring our muskets allow me to add my own & wishing you much success.

---

[1]J. B. Ferguson was the secretary of the Fayetteville Light Infantry Company.

Calvin Graves to David S. Reid A&H-DSR

Locust Hill, NC
May 3. 1852

Will you be pleased to send me a Copy of the Minutes of the Wake County Agricultural Society?

I want the form of their Constitution, and likewise to see what their *lecturers*, have to say to the farmers of Wake—especially so practical a man as Dr. Mason.[1]

I have this moment received through the Greensboro Patriot tidings of the proceedings of the Whig Convention. My predictions are verified,—the policy is, to dodge the responsibility of any given proposition to amend the Constitution, but to make a flourish of the right of the people *to decide everything.*

This pretended Comp. by the East & West will, (I think) insure the acceptance of Mr. Kerr.[2]

Caroline[3] has just returned from a visit to Judge Settles,[4]—your friends all well. The family send love to you & wife—

[1]Probably a reference to the Rev. Dr. Richard Sharpe Mason (1795-1874), native of Barbados, who was rector of Christ Episcopal Church in Raleigh from 1840 until his death. Archives, Episcopal Diocese of North Carolina, Raleigh.

[2]John Kerr, previously identified, was, in fact, Reid's eventual gubernatorial opponent.

[3]Caroline Graves, daughter of Calvin Graves.

[4]Thomas Settle, Sr., neighbor and relative of Reid's parents in Rockingham County.

Joseph C. Norcom[1] to David S. Reid A&H-DSR

Plymouth NC
May 19. 1852

Mr. Kerr.[2] the would be Whig Governor was at Gate[s]ville in Gates County on yesterday and was to address the people there to day, and from what I can learn from your friends in these parts it is thought advisable that you would visit this part of the state at once, and meet Mr Kerr. (presuming you to be the Democratic nominee) It is said that he intends canvassing the Edenton district thoroughly before he leaves this part of the State & perhaps intends visiting the whole of the Eastern part of the State at this time. I am of the opinion that he will do himself no good in the Edenton district If he is in favour of an open convention & If he is attacked on that point he will be routed—he may be of more service to himself in Stanly district[3] than any where else, but, if you can give him your attention in Tyrrell, Washington Hide & Beaufort, he cannot make much for himself in these counties. I have been interupted Several times since I commenced writing this letter and have but a moment to conclude hoping you will soon be seen & heard amongst us.

---

[1]Joseph C. Norcom of Plymouth represented Washington County as a delegate to the Constitutional Convention of 1835 and as a member of the House of Commons (1842-1843). Cheney, *North Carolina Government*, 312, 818.

[2]John Kerr, previously identified.

[3]Edward Stanly, previously identified Whig congressman, in 1852 represented the 8th Congressional District, which consisted of Wayne, Greene, Lenoir, Pitt, Jones, Craven, Carteret, Beaufort, Hyde, Washington, and Tyrrell counties. Cheney, *North Carolina Government*, 684.

Abraham W. Venable[1] *to David S. Reid* A&H-DSR

Washington [D.C.]
May 19th 1852

Perceiving as we all knew would be the case that you have been nominated with great unanimity as the candidate of our party I trust that you will permit a sincere friend to give some advice as to the campaign—I think it most desirable that you canvass the Eastern portion of the state fully and at once—I would avoid going to the [trial?] with Kerr.[2] Let him go and speak he cannot [rearrange] old party lines and there is no disposition to do so now with a large portion of the Whig party there at this time—I speak by the card—Now I respectfully suggest that the last of the canvass be made there by yourself— This conclusion has been adopted upon mature consideration. Kerr will do himself most harm when left to himself this I know by experience

---

[1]Abraham Watkins Venable (1799-1876), an attorney from Oxford, was born in Virginia and educated at Hampden-Sydney and Princeton. He moved to North Carolina in 1829 and was a Democratic representative in Congress (1847-1853)

and a member of the Confederate House of Representatives (1862-1864). *Biographical Directory of Congress*, 1753.

[2]John Kerr.

David S. Reid to Council of State DU-DSR
[Draft copy]

Executive Office,
Raleigh,
May 19, 1852.

[I have received your communication of this date informing me that the Counsellors of State had convened agreeably to my request and are ready to receive any communication I may think proper to make.][1]

The construction placed on 2d Clause of the 1st Section of the 3rd Article of the Constitution of the United States requires the vote for President and Vice President in 1852 to be according to the Census of 1850. This construction has been generally acquiesced in, and will, I presume, be adopted by all the states. Altho I have not been officially informed of the fact yet it is well understood that North Carolina according to the late apportionment will only be entitled to ten Electoral votes in the next election. The act of the General Assembly of this State at the Session of 1842-3 divided the state into eleven Electoral districts. Therefore the act of Assembly provides for the election of eleven Electors, while the State under the late apportionment will only be entitled to ten Electoral votes. The next election for President and Vice President will take place before the regular period appointed by law for the meeting of the General Assembly. It is provided by law that "the Governor may, with the advice of the Council of State, call a meeting of the General Assembly, if the same shall be absolutely necessary, at a sooner day than the same may stand adjourned to or appointed to meet." I submit to your consideration, whether it does not become necessary under the circumstances to convene the General Assembly at an earlier day than is provided for its regular meeting, to have further legislation to avoid illegality in the election for President and Vice President.

If your body should advise the General Assembly to be convened for the purpose I have mentioned, the question then arises as to the most appropriate time for the meeting. It occurs to me that it should not be called together till after the next August election. The Constitution provides that "The Senate of this State shall consist of fifty representatives, biennially chosen by ballot, and to be elected by districts; which districts shall be laid off by the General Assembly, at its first session after the year one thousand eight hundred and fifty-one." It is also provided that the apportionment of the members of the House of Commons "shall be made by the General Assembly, at the respective times and periods when the districts for the Senate are herein before directed to be laid off." If the General Assembly should be called together before the regular period, it would of course be a *session*, and the "first session after the year one thousand eight hundred and fifty-one;" The language of the Constitution is not the first regular or biennial session, but "*at its first session*" It would seem therefore that if the Legislature is convened the Constitution requires the Senatorial districts to be laid off and the members of the House of Commons to be apportioned. If the General Assembly is convened before the next August election it will be composed of the members chosen in 1850, who, I presume, were not elected with a view to legislation on the subject of laying off the Senatorial districts and apportioning the members of the House of Commons.

[I submit to legislation upon this subject I of to which laying off the Senatorial districts and apportioning the members of the House of Commons.][2] I therefore submit whether a due regard for the public interest and respect [for] public opinion does not require that the time of convening the General Assembly should be postponed till the [*blank*] Monday in [*blank*] next. The legislature then called together would be fresh from the people and fully prepared to reflect their will upon these questions. The next Session of the General Assembly will in all probability be one of more than ordinary length. The Laying off the Congressional and Senatorial districts, apportioning the members of the House of Commons and acting upon the Report of the Commissioners appointed to revise the Statutes, together with the ordinary business of legislation will protract the Session.

[The might meet at the time I have designated and pass an act to provide for the election of Electors.][3] The people might in primary meetings select their candidates for Electors, and the General Assembly when convened might pass the necessary act in time for the Presidential election. The legislature then could proceed to lay off the Senatorial districts and apportion the members of the House of Commons; repeal, for the session, the act fixing the third Monday in November as the time for the meeting of the Assembly, and then act upon the Report of the Commissions appointed to revise the Statutes or any other subject of legislation. In this way it seems to me that the expense and inconvenience of an extra Session might be avoided.

[I have made this communication][4]

This communication you will observe is predicated upon the fact th[at] the term of the members of the Legislature Commences at the [August election][5] regular annual election in August. [While I have heard some reasons expounded why the fact ought][6] Upon this point I think there can be no doubt. [for we all know that a reason against the][7] It has been said that this construction would opperate as an inconvunce, for if the office of Governor were to become vacant after the election in August there would be no speaker of the Senate to fill the vacancy. [Even if this were][8] Even admitting this to be true it argues nothing; for we all know that an inconvenunce exp[erienced] from a provision in the Constitution does [alter the Constitution][9] authorize us to change its construction. [All membrs to ch][10] The Constitution provides that membrs of the Assembly shall be beanially chosen. All seem to admit they are elected for a term of two years. In 1835 the Constitution was amended and instead of each County having a senator and t[wo] members of the Commons [an entirely][11] a different mode of representation was provided. Altho the amended Constitution was ratified in Nov. 1835 an ordinance of the Convention postponed its opperation till the 1st January 1836. The Constitution which went into effect on that day abolished the Assembly that had been chosen at the preceeding election. Consequently the first Assembly under that Constitution was elected at the [August][12] Summer elections of that year. The term of the members of that Assembly most clearly Commenced from the election. If the term Commenced at the election then [the Constitution not having been changed since][13] it must be so now, the Constitution not having been changed since.

I respectfully ask you to advise me on this subject.[14]

[1-13]These words, sections, or passages were crossed out of this draft.

[14]According to an Elizabeth City newspaper, "Gov. Reid and his Council of State . . . agreed to call an extra session of the Legislature, on the first Monday in October, to re-arrange the Electoral districts according to the new apportionment." *Old North State* (Elizabeth City), June 5, 1852, hereinafter cited as *Old North State*.

David S. Reid to Jacob Siler UNC-JS

Executive Office,
Raleigh,
May 20, 1852.

In reply to your letter I have to state, that it would seem that the moneys collected after the 1st January 1852 are applicable to the survey of the Rail Road and to no other purpose. Further legislation on this subject will probably be necessary at the next session.

Willis F. Riddick[1] *to David S. Reid* A&H-DSR

Gatesville,
Gates Co. N.C.
May 20th. 1852

The whigs of this District held a Convention at this place on Monday last to appoint Delegates to their National convention, an Elector sub-electors, &c—after which Mr. Kerr your opponent, addressed the people—quite a large crowd (being Court day.) Immediately thereafter, a number of Democrats, warm friends of yours, desired me to write, forthwith to you, requesting you to visit this county, and the whole eastern part of the state; but this county, in particular. This place, being now the head-quarters of the two parties in the district. It is all-important that you come and come in time. Have your appointments published in the "Standard", "Pioneer" and other Democratic papers, sufficiently early, so that the people living all over the country, and in the woods, may hear of them, and have an opportunity of hearing you. Let me not only request you, but urge you, and insist upon your coming. Hoping you will visit us and pardon the liberty taken by a Stranger

[1]Willis F. Riddick of Gates County was a local Democratic leader and postmaster of Middle Swamp in 1843. *Register of Officers and Agents*, 289.

Spier Whitaker[1] *to David S. Reid* A&H-DSR

Cottage, near Enfield N.C.
May 24. 1852

I see from the papers that Mr Kerr will be at Weldon, about twenty miles from this, on the 2nd June to address the people; whether you will meet him or not or whether you design and when to leave Raleigh as yet we have no notice. If you intend to meet with Mr Kerr and to be in Halifax at all, to do so at Weldon is very desirable although I think there will be but a few to hear you. I wish to hear from you as if you can not be with him, it is not at all agreeable to me for Mr K to be stepping so near my own toes and crowing on my own walk so probably I will be at Weldon myself and if allowed will say something to the good people then and there assembled.

On the first of June we fill up our nominations—the whigs on the fifth—as yet—no person but myself is in nomination for this county.[2] write to me at Halifax care of Geo W. Barnes.[3]

---

[1]Spier Whitaker (1798-1869), an attorney from Halifax County and Davenport, Iowa, was a member of the House of Commons (1838-1839) and state attorney general (1842-1846). Grant, *Alumni History*, 661; Cheney, *North Carolina Government*, 182, 1157.

[2]Halifax County was represented in the Assembly of 1852, which sat from October 4 to December 27, by Andrew Joyner in the Senate and by James D. Perkins and Richard H. Smith in the House of Commons. Joyner, a Whig, defeated Whitaker, 244-199, for the Senate slot. Perkins and Smith, both Whigs, garnered 610 and 592 votes, respectively, to defeat Democrats L. W. Batchelor, with 522 votes, and W. H. Tillery, who received 460 votes, according to unofficial returns published by contemporary newspapers. Cheney, *North Carolina Government*, 319, 321; *North-Carolina Standard*, August 11, 1852.

[3]George W. Barnes (born 1802), a native of Halifax County, was a wealthy farmer. Seventh Census, 1850, Halifax County, Population Schedule, 45; Eighth Census, 1860, Halifax County, Population Schedule, 810, Slave Schedule, 422.

William B. Pope[1] *to David S. Reid* A&H-DSR

Halifax
May 27th 1852

You doubtless have seen a notice of Mr. Kerr's appointment to speak at Weldon on Wednesday the 2nd June. If you can possibly meet him at that time it would be gratifying to your friends and promote the advancement of our cause in this county. At that time it will be known who will be our candidates for the legislature, we have great difficulty in getting candidates My Colleague Mr Clanton[2] is in very bad health and it is impossible for me to become a candidate this year without great prejudice to my private interests—I feel a great interest in our success this year, and am fearful that if we fail in getting a strong ticket all my labours two years since will avail nothing,[3] but I hope to see you before long and talk all these matters with you—

Let me know by return mail if you can be at Weldon on the 2nd June and I will immediately let it be known among our friends The situation of things at present require that you should meet Mr Kerr if you possibly can[4]—you can come very easily on the rail road & very directly; If you come I would be glad if you would first come to Halifax a day or two before hand and be sure to come to my house and spend the time with me and I will locate you comfortably I give you all the points &c Mrs Pope's & my best wishes & regards to Mrs. Reid & sister[5] I have written hastily let me hear from you forthwith

---

[1]William B. Pope of Halifax County was a member of the House of Commons (1850-1851, 1860-1861). Cheney, *North Carolina Government*, 1157.

[2]Dudley C. Clanton of Halifax County was a member of the House of Commons (1850-1851). Cheney, *North Carolina Government*, 1157.

[3]William W. Holden, on the eve of the election, reported: "Messrs. Pope and Clanton we have also classed as Whigs, because they were elected as independent Whigs, though they also gave some good Democratic votes. They were and are both for Reid; and we think we are safe in saying they are *both* for Pierce and King." *North-Carolina Standard*, August 4, 1852.

[4]Although Whigs won the single Senate and two Commons seats from Halifax County, the gubernatorial vote was extremely close. Unofficial returns showed that Kerr outpolled Reid by only 10 votes, 551 to 541. *North-Carolina Standard*, August 11, 1852.

[5]Probably a reference to Caroline Settle.

David S. Reid to Henrietta S. Reid RCC

Greenville, Pitt Co. N. C.,
Sunday, May 30, 1852.

I addressed the people at Snow Hill on yesterday. No one replied, and every thing passed off well. Last night I staid 9 miles this side of

Snow Hill with a Mr. Carr[1] a political freind. This morning I came 13 miles which brought me to this place. Having been here before, I knew a good many persons. After dinner I walked down to the river which is about two hundred yards from the Hotel and saw twenty-nine of Mr. Reynoldsons[2] converts baptised. He has been preaching about two weeks here and a great many have professed. I had some hope that I should meet father Settle here on his way home, and I may do so yet as I learn that he is still below. They say he is well.

Mr. Kerr reached here about an hour since and stopped at a different Hotel. I went over and called on him and have just returned to my room. The Conversation we had was in public and I did not get any of the particulars from him. From what I hear he has not damaged me much. Tomorrow I shall know his points, if possible. In all the counties I hear from my friends think I will get fully as good a vote as I did two [years] ago. But these things are uncertain, you know. I am never very sanguine. The political atmosphere will be getting warmer and warmer till the election. My friends here are in fine spirits and will be active.

My health is as good as usual. I feel much better than I did the day I left Rockingham. I hope dear that you and all the rest are well. My impression at present is, that Kerr can not beat me, but as I before said these things are uncertain. My speech at Snow Hill yesterday had some effect. My friends said they saw whig tears shed under its influence. *This however as well as many other things I write, is for my dear wife & for no one else.* I shall go from here to Weldon and thence to Raleigh on the 4th and then pursue Kerrs appointments.

In my travels I have beheld beautiful fields and neat mansions and they constantly bring to my mind the happiness of a private and rural life.

You are almost constantly the subject of my thoughts and not unfrequently the theme of my conversation. Really I feel much relieved when an opportunity offers in conversation to speak of you. Oh how I would like to see you this sabbath afternoon! When I attended the baptizing to-day I saw a large concourse of persons. I stood silently on the hill and surveyed the assemblage to see if I could behold any one who bore a resemblance of you. But none could I find.

My dear wife be careful of your health. Give yourself no uneasiness about me for you know that I am apt to do the best I can under the circumstances that surround me. I do not mean by this that I would have you forget me or to feel indifferent about my welfare, but I mean that I do not wish you to be distressed on my account. I hope I shall have my health, but if I should get sick you shall know it. Give my love to all, and accept for yourself all my love. May God bless and preserve you and them.

PS. I enclose you a specimen of the kind of tickets, a friend of mine in Greene sent me the other [day], which he is preparing to be used at the election.

---

[1]Elias Carr (born 1829), a prosperous young farmer of Olds Township in northeastern Greene County, was likely an older cousin of the better-known Elias Carr (1839-1900) of Edgecombe County, who later served (1893-1897) as governor of North Carolina. At the Democratic party convention at Snow Hill in Greene County on February 10, 1852, Elias Carr was appointed a delegate both to the district and state party conventions. *North-Carolina Standard*, February 21, 1852; Powell, *DNCB*, I, 328-329; James M. Creech, *History of Greene County, North Carolina* (Baltimore: Gateway Press, 1979), 274, 283, hereinafter cited as Creech, *History of Greene County*.

[2]The Reverend John Smith Reynoldson (1812-1854), born at Bromley, a village near London, was a well-educated but unruly youth who ran away from an apprenticeship with a chemist and went to sea. Successful for many years as a mariner, he was attracted to and joined a Baptist church that he visited in Portsmouth, Virginia. Abandoning his sailing career, he began teaching school in a destitute region of western Virginia. In 1841, Reynoldson was ordained and launched a new career as a missionary and traveling evangelist with an unusual gift for preaching. According to the Reverend J. B. Jeter's commemorative address: "In *spirit*, his preaching was singularly affectionate and fervent . . . In *style*, [it] was easy, original, and striking." From 1849 to 1851 he was pastor of Market Street Church, Petersburg. Reid may have heard him during one of the numerous "protracted meetings" that Reynoldson conducted throughout the region. Reynoldson lost his life aboard the iron steamer *City of Glasgow* when it disappeared in the icy north Atlantic on a voyage from Liverpool to Philadelphia. James B. Taylor, *Virginia Baptist Ministers*. Series II. (Philadelphia: J. B. Lippincott, 1859), 401-416 passim.

David S. Reid to Henrietta S. Reid RCC

Fayetteville,
June 7, 1852.

I left Raleigh at 4 pm. Saturday and reached here at 2 pm. yesterday. Last night attended the baptist church and heard Mr McDaniel[1] preach a very good sermon, but I do not regard him as equal to Mr. Reynoldson.[2]

Mr. Kerr reached here on saturday evening and was received with much pomp and parade. My friends made arrangements to give me a brilliant reception, but to avoid it I telegraphed them that I would reach here on sabbath. I did not wish any formal demonstrations on my arrival. My friends have shown me every respect and attention that I could desire and even more.

We addressed the people in the market-house to-day commencing at 11 am and closing after 5 pm. I made the opening speech of two hours and he replied in a speech of two hours. When he made his speech his friends appeared much deleghted but as we proceeded towards the close they were evidently less pleased with the result. The further we proceeded the worse it was for him till we closed.[3] My friends are deleghted with the result, and I do not think his friends claim a triumph for him, tho' I suppose Mr. Hale[4] will say in his paper that I was demolished. There were perhaps 1000 persons present and the assemblage was really imposing. This evening arrangements were made for me to receive my friends in a large Hall in the Hotel. Several hundred persons called on me. In receiving them I have had to stand on my feet several hours shaking hands and conversing with them. While they were calling on me they had rockets and fire-works going on in the street opposite the Hall and occasionally I could hear out in the streets loud Huzzahs for Reid. About 11 Oclock the crowd assembled in the Hall gave three cheers for Reid which were loud and hearty, and then passed by, every one shaking hands with me, and dispersed. I then retired to my room and after conversing a while with some particular friends they left and I commenced writing this letter to my dear wife. My friends think Mr. Kerr has not damaged me here. I think however that I made a better speech in Raleigh than I did to-day. Genl. Pierce[5] of N.H. and W. R. King, of Al. are the nominees for P. & V. President. I think a strong ticket.

I had expected to receive a letter here from you, but have been disappointed. I leave in the morning for Bladen. I am well but I can assure I am very tired. Tell father Settle that I have met the land question[6] both in Raleigh and here in a most triumphant manner.

You can not immagine how much I wish to see you my dear. I feel lonely without my dear wife. I hope your health is good and that you are taking good care of yourself. I wish the Canvass was over. Give my love to all the family. Accept for yourself my love and prayers for your health and happiness. Good night my dear wife.

PS. Mat[7] and the horses are in good plight. The horse travel finely. Mr. Kerr is now travelling in his own conveyance. It is court week here, but Dobbin,[8] Strange,[9] and W. Winslow[10] are absent.

---

[1]The Reverend James McDaniel, pastor of the Fayetteville Baptist Church for thirty years, was known as a "real pulpit orator." A native of Cumberland County, he was one of the seven ministers present when the Baptist State Convention was organized in 1830 at Greenville. Recording secretary from 1835 to 1841, he served as president of the Convention for eighteen years, 1849-1867, longest term ever served by one man in that post. M. A. Huggins, *A History of North Carolina Baptists, 1727-1932* (Raleigh: Baptist State Convention of North Carolina, 1967), 215, 228, 229, 391, hereinafter cited as Huggins, *History of North Carolina Baptists*.

[2]The Reverend John Smith Reynoldson, previously identified.

[3]The Fayetteville Democratic party newspaper, the *North Carolinian*, made frequent comments contrasting the speaking styles and deportment of Reid and Kerr following their debates in Fayetteville, on June 7, 1852; in Lumberton, on June 12, 1852; and in Troy, on June 19, 1852. "Gov. Reid makes no attempts at flights of oratory—no efforts to keep in the back ground the real points in controversy by empty declamation," it reported of his Fayetteville visit. At Lumberton, wrote the paper's correspondent, "Gov. Reid replied in his usual calm, dignified, statesman-like manner . . ." whereas Kerr "spoke as though he considered his fellow-citizens of Robeson a set of ignoramuses, entirely incapable of discriminating between sound, statesman-like, dignified reasoning, and ridicule, clap-trap, humbugging demagoguism. However popular his manner and matter may be in other portions of the State, it evidently did not take with our citizens. We have yet to learn that an orator dignifies and adorns his subject by comic actions, dodging, squatting, winking significantly, bending back and forward so as to exhibit his fine proportions, speaking of the b'hoys, believing the *devil* named Harry, and taking the name of God in vain irreverently, such as 'great God, good God, in the name of God, on God's earth,' about one hundred times in two hours. This manner brought forth cheers and applause from the boys and the less intelligent of his party, but did not receive countenance or encouragement from those who were judges. His party manifested much more enthusiasm before than after the discussion. I have heard several of them remark that he would make a capital clown in a circus. I have no doubt that he would dignify that office more than the one he now asks the people to confer upon him." At Troy, the paper reported, "Mr. Kerr led off with a great flow of eloquence, without much substance. He walked up and down while speaking, making quite an independent appearance." In contrast, "Gov. Reid must and certainly will make a good impression, wherever he goes, by his gentlemanly, dignified and mild deportment. His courteous and polite manner of speaking has gained the admiration of both whigs and democrats." *North Carolinian*, June 12, 19, July 3, 1852. [NOTE: The "b'hoys," is a reference to a popular "local color" story, "Uncle Sam and His 'B'hoys," about an eccentric old man with more than thirty sons, whom he called his "b'hoys." It was published in a national magazine, the *Democratic Review*, and reprinted widely in southern newspapers. *Mississippi Palladium* (Holly Springs, Mississippi), May 9, 1851 (microfilm), library, Mississippi State University, State College, Mississippi.]

[4]Edward Jones Hale (1802-1883) of Fayetteville, a strong Whig, was editor of the *Fayetteville Observer*, a newspaper that supported Kerr. Ashe, *Biographical History*, VIII, 173-179; Powell, *DNCB*, III, 3-4.

[5]Franklin Pierce (1804-1869), an attorney from New Hampshire, was a state legislator, representative in Congress (1833-1837), United States senator (1837-1842), and president of the United States (1853-1857). During the Mexican War he served as colonel and was promoted to brigadier general in 1847. *DAB*, XIV, 576-580.

[6]Among "A Few Plain Questions" addressed to Reid by the *Raleigh Register* was the following: "Is he in favor of dividing the proceeds of the public lands amongst the States, whereby North Carolina may get her just share in the same for purposes of Education and Internal Improvement?" Whigs complained that the western public lands were being given away to railroad companies, to the detriment of the "old" states. Reid countered, according to press reports, that "not a foot of land could be given away by Congress except with the [Whig] President's signature."

On the same question, when the two candidates spoke a few days later in Wadesboro, the local paper reported: "The Democratic Party, Governor Reid said, was not in favor of giving the lands away to the States. They (the Democrats) were for letting the land remain in the hands of the Government, and for having their proceeds to come into the public Treasury, whence they might be drawn to defray the expenses of the general Government. He was as much opposed to the Homestead bill recently passed by the House of Representatives as any person." *Raleigh Register*, quoted in the *Fayetteville Observer*, June 8, 1852; *Fayetteville Observer*, June 15, 1852; *North Carolina Argus* (Wadesboro), hereinafter cited as *North Carolina Argus*, quoted in the *People's Press*, June 26, 1852.

[7]Mat, coachman for the governor's own "private conveyance" in 1852, was one of the 30 slaves owned in 1850 by Reid's father-in-law Thomas Settle. Reid's father Reuben Reid owned 17 slaves in 1850. David S. Reid, who was enumerated in the 1850 census in his father's household, was not listed then as a slaveholder. Settle's will, dated March 19, 1856, provides for bequests of several slaves to his daughter Henrietta Settle Reid, including "Matt and his wife Mariah and all the children they now have or may hereafter have." In a codicil dated May 4, 1857, Thomas Settle stated: "I have assented to the sale made by Governor Reid of the boy Matt given by me to my daughter Henrietta, Governor Reid, and their children and bequeath the boy Jesse who was substituted in the place of Matt, to be held by them in the same way that they held the other slaves which I have bequeathed to them." David S. Reid owned 22 slaves in 1860. Seventh Census, 1850, Rockingham County, Population Schedule, 26, Slave Schedule, 111-112; Will of Thomas Settle, Rockingham County Wills, Book C, 258 (microfilm), Archives, Division of Archives and History, Raleigh, hereinafter cited as Settle Will; Settle Will, 260; Eighth Census, 1860, Rockingham County, Slave Schedule, 31.

[8]James Cochrane Dobbin, previously identified.

[9]Robert Strange, previously identified.

[10]Warren Winslow, previously identified.

Romulus M. Saunders to David S. Reid A&H-DSR

Raleigh
June 8th. '52

I have just reached home—We have given you an excellent nomination which have been well received—It was made by the Southern States—Virginia taking the lead & Kentucky concurring—Genl Pierce was in the H Rep in 36 '37—in the Senate in '43—next a volunteer in the Mexican War—a Col then Genl.—fought from Vera Cruz to Mexico—Polk offered him a [*illegible*] He is as sound as the Soundest on the Slavery question—His opinions known before he was named for the Presidency—John Kerr has been using my name freely—says he wishes to meet more so I am certain I vex him—Cannot you gratify us—By saying so at Ashboro & let us meet at Pittsboro & Graham—allamance—I suppose by the time you get there you would like to see your wife—or if any other point would suit you better—let me know—

Obituary of Ann Augusta Holden[1] NCC

Raleigh
June 25, 1852

DIED.[2]

In this City, on Sunday evening, the 20th of June, 1852, after a brief illness, ANN AUGUSTA, the beloved wife of WILLIAM W. HOLDEN, in the 34th year of her age.

Although, in general, we object to obituary notices, yet there are occasions when they are proper; for it is a reproach when "the righteous dieth and no man layeth it to heart." It is due to the memory of the dead, that their virtues should be praised—to the living that their examples should be held up for imitation.

The sudden death of this amiable lady has cast a gloom over our community.—Modest and unassuming in her disposition, the world knew her not, but her friends appreciated her worth, and deeply deplore her loss. On Saturday, she was walking about, apparently but slightly indisposed. Sunday evening her spirit was recalled to God who gave it. Her sun has gone down at midday. She has been cut off in the midst of her usefulness, and a void is made in many hearts; yet like the moon-beam, softened by intervening mists, the night of their sorrow is cheered by the remembrance of her pious life, and numerous virtues. "Blessed are the meek.***Blessed are the pure in heart, for they shall see God."

Her affectionate and sorrowing husband, and four little children,[3] now unconscious of their loss, feel, and in years to come will realize, that " 'tis a fearful thing to love what death can touch"—to lean upon an arm of flesh. May God grant to them those consolations which sympathising friends may pray for, but He only can give.

C.[4]

---

[1]Ann Augusta Young Holden (circa 1818-1852), daughter of John Wynne and Nancy Peace Young of Raleigh, was married to William W. Holden on November 3, 1841. Raper, *William W. Holden*, 9; *Raleigh Register*, November 5, 1841.

[2]This obituary was printed in the *Raleigh Times*, June 25, 1852.

[3]Laura, Joseph William, Ida Augusta, and Henrietta Reid (nicknamed variously Etta or Ettie). Raper, *William W. Holden*, 9.

[4]The author of this obituary was likely Charles C. Raboteau, poet and editor of the *Raleigh Times*, here laying aside his normal role as a Whig partisan.

William W. Holden to Henrietta S. Reid RCC

Raleigh
June 26, 1852.

You have no doubt heard, ere this, of the death of my dear and most beloved Wife. She had been complaining for some three or four days, but no apprehensions were indulged until the morning of the 20th, the day on which she died. On Saturday the 19th she was at breakfast and dinner, as usual, and in the evening she walked through the new house, up and down stairs. She complained of a slight weakness soon after, and about midnight she grew worse. Dr. McKee[1] was sent for. He prescribed, seemed to regard the case as an ordinary one, and left. He called again after breakfast on Sunday, said she was quite indisposed, prescribed again and returned home. As she did not seem to improve, I sent for him again in the course of an hour; and from that time, with Dr. Johnson,[2] he labored until a short time previous to her dissolution. No skill, no efforts could revive her sinking powers. About eight o'clock on the 20th, her pure spirit returned to God who gave it. In the midst of such grief, I feel that words are idle. My only consolation is that she lives evermore in Heaven. I can go to her, but she cannot come to me. Pardon me, madam, for this obtruding my sorrows upon your attention.

The object of this letter is this: Many kind friends had been endeavoring for several days, without success, to secure a suitable nurse for little *Etta Reid*,[3] now something over four months old, and a servant of yours, Sally,[4] hearing of our efforts, called yesterday and offered her services. I know, had you been here, what course you would have pursued, and I did not, therefore, hesitate. The girl is now at my house, and little *Etta* will no doubt do well. She will have nothing to do, of course, but to nurse and attend to the two children. Little *Etta* has not been at all sick, but is fat and hearty. The other children are well.

I feel confident, madam, that I am not going too far in hoping and believing that this arrangement will meet your approbation.

I heard from Gov. Reid but a few days since. He was in good health and spirits. I have just written him at length to Graham, Alamance. I have no doubt of his triumphant re-election.

---

[1]William H. McKee (1814-1875) was a physician residing in Raleigh in 1850. He was a member of the Committee of 50 appointed by the City of Raleigh and Wake County to prepare for the visit of President James K. Polk in 1847. Seventh Census, 1850, Wake County, Population Schedule, 272; *Daily Sentinel* (Raleigh), April 24, 1875, hereinafter cited as *Daily Sentinel*; William Dallas Haywood to James K. Polk, May 8, 1847, James K. Polk Papers, Presidential Papers, Special Collection 189, Manuscript Division, Library of Congress, Washington, D.C., hereinafter cited as Polk Papers, Library of Congress.

[2]Charles E. Johnson (1812-1876) was also a physician residing in Raleigh in 1850 and a member of the aforementioned Committee of 50. Seventh Census, 1850, Wake County, Population Schedule, 263; *Daily Sentinel*, April 1, 1876; William Dallas Haywood to James K. Polk, May 8, 1847, Polk Papers, Library of Congress.

[3]Henrietta Reid Holden (born 1852), fourth child of Ann Augusta Young Holden and William W. Holden, was named for Henrietta W. Settle Reid, wife of David S. Reid. She married Fred G. (Fritz) Mahler. Raper, *William W. Holden*, 9, 259.

[4]Sally Settle (circa 1810-circa 1875), the Reid servant who nursed little Etta Reid Holden after Etta's mother's death, was a slave bequeathed to Henrietta S. Reid and David S. Reid by Henrietta's father Thomas Settle. Jointly owned slaves were listed under the husband's name in slave schedules, and in 1860 David S. Reid is listed as owner of 22 slaves. She may be the black Sallie Settle, age 60, who is listed as residing in Wentworth Township, Rockingham County, in 1870 in the household of Dan Settle, 45, black farmer. Daniel, who would have been 31 in 1856, was a slave bequeathed to Thomas Settle, Jr., by Thomas Settle, Sr. The household included ten children, ages 1-18, probably her grandchildren, except possibly for John, age 18. In the 1880 census John Settle, black, age 28, is still a resident of Wentworth, but Sallie Settle and Dan Settle are absent. Settle Will, 258, 259; Seventh Census, 1850, Rockingham County, Slave Schedule, 111-112; Ninth Census, 1870, Rockingham County, 22; Tenth Census, 1880, Rockingham County, 175.

Matt W. Ransom[1] *to Daniel Shine Hill*[2] A&H-AB

Franklinton
July 5. 52

I have just time to say to you that the Raleigh Whigs expect you here on Wednesday. I promised Gales[3] to send you word. Great news from the North & North West—All up for Scott & Graham. We had a glorious Barbecue in Raleigh, Saturday. *Make a sally for Kerr*. A Writer from Washington in a private letter says that the Loco-foco party will do every thing to carry the State for Reid—the first blow in the Canvass—Look out for Slanders—

[1]Matt Whitaker Ransom (1826-1904), born in Warren County, graduated from the state university in 1847. Originally a Whig, he was nominated as a presidential elector for Scott and Graham in 1852. Later in 1852, although he was still only twenty-six, he was elected attorney general of the state by the Democratically-controlled Assembly, defeating veteran Democratic attorney William Eaton, Jr., also of Warren County. Ransom became a Democrat in 1855, partly because of his opposition to Know-Nothingism, and moved to Northampton County, which he represented in the House of Commons, 1858-1861. During the Civil War he served as a brigadier general and was wounded at Malvern Hill and Drewry's Bluff. He served as United States senator (1873-1895) and minister to Mexico (1895-1897). Cheney, *North Carolina Government*, 182; *DAB*, VIII, 379; Ashe, *Biographical History*, I, 420-421.

[2]Daniel Shine Hill (1812-1873), a native of Franklin County, was a teacher, planter, merchant, magistrate, and Confederate comptroller for Franklin County during the Civil War. He was a substantial slave owner, who rented numbers of his surplus slaves to planters in Mississippi during the 1840s and 1850s. He was a son of the Reverend Charles Applewhite Hill of Warren and Franklin counties, who was a four-term state senator (1823-1827) and unsuccessful sixth district congressional candidate in 1827. Hill assisted his father in the operation of Midway Academy between Louisburg and Warrenton until 1831. He was secretary of the board of trustees for Louisburg Male Academy in 1855 and a trustee of Louisburg Female Academy in 1857. In penciled notes on the reverse of Ransom's letter, Hill, apparently preparing to make, as Ransom requested, "a sally for Kerr," had jotted the following pro-Whig rhetoric: "You have been told that if the Whigs [remain] in power ruin ruin. Look at the prosperity of the Country under this abused Whig administration. Who ever saw labor buy such high reward[?]" Although not of the same generation, Ransom and Hill were cousins, both related to the Edward Jones family of Warren County. Ransom affectionately addressed Hill in this letter as "My Dear Kinsman." Daniel S. Hill to James Seddon, April 25, 1864, Private Collections, Mrs. Albert Bauman Collection, PC 1497, Archives, Division of Archives and History, Raleigh, hereinafter cited as Bauman Collection, PC 1497, State Archives; Cheney, *North Carolina Government*, 281, 283, 285, 287; Edward Hill Davis, *Historical Sketches of Franklin County* (Raleigh: Edwards & Broughton, 1948), 51-52, hereinafter cited as Davis, *Historical Sketches*; George-Anne Willard, *Louisburg College Echoes: Voices from the Formative Years, 1787-1917* (Louisburg: Louisburg College, 1988), 43, 45, 47, hereinafter cited as Willard, *Louisburg College*.

[3]Probably Seaton Gales, editor (1848-1856) of the *Raleigh Register*. Powell, *DNCB*, II, 269.

Samuel J. Person[1] *to Thomas D. S. McDowell*[2] UNC-TMcD

Wilmington
July 6th 1852

Your very flattering letter has just reached me, and I make haste to return my thanks for your kindness to me personally, and to the people of Bladen for the honor they have done me, though a stranger. Several of the Counties in this district have expressed a like preference, and gratitude, to say nothing of my deep concern for the success of our party, would not permit me to decline the service desired of me, but whenever that expression shall be made by the district in a way to authorize me to accept the office of elector. This is as far as I can now go, but I have no doubt but that I shall have the pleasure of seeing you in the fall in the discharge of the duties which that station will impose.

Your letter to Owen D. Holmes[3] Esqr has been properly directed, and will reach him very soon. The fact will also be announced in the "Journal"[4] of today. I am glad to hear that you are for the Senate in place of Gen'l McKay[5] as he was said to be in favour of an open convention. The advocacy of such doctrines now would only produce division in the democratic party, and perhaps cause their defeat in the State Elections.

We ought to go heart & soul with Govr. Reid for "free sufferage" by act of the Legislature, and against a change of the basis of representation and the distribution of the School fund, and here in the east as a corollary to the foregoing against an open convention. You can very easily shew from the debates & proceedings of the last legislature that the question of Convention was started by the original enemies of free sufferage not that they desired or thought a convention necessary, but for the insincere purpose of defeating that great measure of reform indirectly. Mr. Rayner & many others who advocated the submission of that question to the people declared that they would vote in the negative at the polls, and Mr. Kerr after eulogising our constitution as the most perfect on the Earth and declaring his opposition to all changes in the fundamental law has the effrontery to say that he would vote to call an open convention. And what for? By his own showing to amend what is already perfect, or more correctly, that a convention of the people shall meet at an expence of 30 or 40 thousand dollars for the purpose of declaring that our constitution is perfect and needs no amendment. But at the same time he is willing to let the people have free sufferage if they want it, *the dear people*, altho it will mar the beauty & destroy the symmetry of our most *perfect constitution*. What does all that mean? Demagougism &

duplicity. The want of the patriotism & manliness to oppose what is wrong though the dear people shall want it. The cutting "between wind & water" for the purpose of being elected governor. And the defeat of "free sufferage" by holding out prospects "pleasant to the eye," but which will "turn to ashes upon the lip"—And above all the discomfiture of the Democratic Party, a result for which no price is too great. Come to the rescue my friend, draw the sword and fling away the scabbard and do battle manfully in the cause of truth & democracy against the wicked hosts of demagougs and deceivers of the people. And you will not be without helpers from the former ranks of our opponents. Our friend Samuel Langdon[6] Esqr of Smithville is against Kerr and convention & being a gentleman of much influence in that County he will help us much. You will no doubt find many others to agree with him. He is also anti Scott & for Pierce openly, as is Dr John H Hill[7] the candidate for the commons & many others in that County. I don't know the doctor's views about the Governor. There are several good Whigs here who will oppose both Scott & Kerr. Our prospects are bright. Let us work like men & we will surely triumph. I have written at much greater length than I intended when I sat down, but the prospect of fixing North Carolina in the Democratic faith warms me up whenever I think about it.

I don't know your lady, but present my compliments. I hope to have that pleasure before very long.

I should be glad to hear from you again soon. I may be of some service to you as I spend one or two days of the week in Smithville where our family are spending the summer. Do husband[8] yourself for the vigorous presentation of democratic truths, make the people comprehend & they will surely embrace our faith.

---

[1]Samuel J. Person (d. 1868), a Wilmington attorney, graduated from the state university in 1843. He was a member of the House of Commons from Moore County (1848-1851) and from New Hanover County (1854-1855, 1860-1865) and a superior court judge (1854-1858). Tolbert, *Ellis Papers*, II, 474n; Cheney, *North Carolina Government*, 317, 319, 323, 328, 330, 331, 362.

[2]Thomas D. S. McDowell (1823-1898) of Bladen County graduated from the state university in 1843. He was a member of the House of Commons (1846-1851), state senator (1852-1855, 1858-1859), delegate to the state Constitutional Convention of 1861, and representative in the Confederate States Congress (1861-1862). Wheeler, *Reminiscences*, 38; Cheney, *North Carolina Government*, 315-325 passim, 388, 824; Grant, *Alumni History*, 388.

[3]Owen D. Holmes was a Wilmington attorney. Sprunt, *Cape Fear*, 586.

[4]The Democratic party newspaper, the *Wilmington Journal*.

[5]James Iver McKay, previously identified.

[6]Samuel Langdon of Smithville was a local Whig leader who defected to the Democrats. Smithville, incorporated in 1805, was county seat of Brunswick County from 1808 until 1978. Its name was changed to Southport in 1889. Powell, *North Carolina Gazetteer*, 466.

[7]John H. Hill (1807-1893), a Brunswick County planter and physician, was a member of the House of Commons during the 1850-1851 session. He later moved to Goldsboro. Cheney, *North Carolina Government*, 318; Sprunt, *Cape Fear*, 63.

[8]Used here in the sense of "conserve," that is, "save up your strength."

A Whig Satire Directed at David S. Reid NCC

Raleigh
July 9, 1852

Excerpt from "A Good Time Coming"[1]

One of the private Secretaries of Governor David Settle Reid has been instructed to announce that his Excellency, *de jure*,[2] in behalf of himself and party, proposes to give a free and universal Barbecue on Thursday, the 5th of August next,[3] weather permitting, in the town of Wilson, in the patriotic county of Edgecombe, in the rear of Tossnot depot,[4] to which all the voters in North Carolina are most cordially invited, without distinction of sect or party.

. . . .

Major Green W. Caldwell will act as the second assistant Marshal.[5] He will be expected to wear a pair of black casimere [*sic*] pants, tightly strapped down over high-heeled calfskin boots, with a vest of a pink color, and a round Robin[6] made of the finest blue cloth, with two rows of gilt eagle buttons in front, and 30 of the same quality in the form of two stars on the lower extremity of the coat, directly over the two suspender buttons, and behind his *ears*. He will also be required to furnish himself with a well trimmed Panama hat, with a blood red ribbon upon it for a band, on which he will have the most eloquent portion of his famous secession speech in the last Legislature. It may not be improper for the gallant Major to wear as a sash, the flag presented to him by the ladies when he was acting as captain of a volunteer company in Charlotte.

. . . .

Gov. Reid[7] has been so fortunate as to secure W. W. Holden, Esq.,[8] of the Humbug Brass Band, to discourse sweet music to the crowd during the day. Mr. Holden will perform on an enormous Tin Horn—the Editors of the Wilmington Journal on French Horns—the Editor of the Pioneer on the Trombone—the Fayetteville Carolinian on the Clarionette— the Republican and Patriot on the Triangle—the Roanoke Republican on the Octave flute—the Mountain Banner and Lincoln Republican on small Tin Whistles—and should everything at the *free barbecue* go off as well, and terminate as happily— for the Democracy of this State as is hoped for, by his Excellency, the band are instructed to play in double quick time the following *beautiful* march, written by a personal friend of the Governor, and is now being set to music by a distinguished German Professor of this City, to be furnished to the band on the August occasion alluded to:—

THE MARCH.

Hail, thrice hail to the Chief who in triumph advances,
Like a hog with his tail curled to a big pile of corn;
When grim hunger is pinching, how gaily he prances,
With a heart full of devil and eye full of scorn:
Behold he cares not a whit for the fences and ditches,
But goes looming ahead like a fair maid in her prime;
When she is reviewed by a long regiment in breeches,
Where every brave heart fills with joy as her feet keep the time.
High diddle dump, high diddle day,
Go it, Davie!
Hurrah! onward he goes like a rat when the weasels
Are all chasing him hard round an old barn for his life;
Or a poor little child when it runs from the measles
Or an old widower when he's in search for a wife:—
Progressing along as if old Nicholas was after him,
He cares not a fig what he says or does in the race;
If he only gets through with his life and a whole skin,
He knows well that his party will provide him a place;
High diddle dump, high diddle day,
Go it, Davie!
Thus with the banner of party unfurled to the breeze,
In which the motto is stamped 'to the victor the spoils';
He goes into hard work all his *drill* sergeants[9] to please
And does all that he can and is well paid for his toils;
Why need he care for people, constitution or trade,
For rapine or carnage, for war, trouble or care,
When working for party he knows his jack will be made,

If once more he gets seated in the Governor's chair:
High diddle dump, high diddle day,
Go it, Davie!

Done this 29th day of June, at the office in the City of Raleigh and State of North Carolina, by his Private Secretary,

DAVID REID PROGRESS.[10]

---

[1]This lengthy satirical article by an unknown Whig author appeared in the *Raleigh Times*, July 9, 1852.

[2]The Whig press frequently referred to Reid as governor *de jure*, that is, governor in name only.

[3]Election day.

[4]The town of Wilson, incorporated in 1849, developed from an early community that grew up around Toisnot Baptist Church, established in 1803. Tosnot [*sic*] Depot was established on the railroad about 1840. The reference to the rear of the depot is perhaps an allusion to the large and well-known Toisnot Swamp located nearby. Until 1855, when Wilson County was formed, the town of Wilson was in Edgecombe County. Powell, *North Carolina Gazetteer*, 494, 537, 538.

[5]The article writer proposed that Reid appoint twelve marshals to help put on the "barbecue." These, of course, were the leading Reid supporters across the state, and each was ridiculed as Caldwell is here. Chief marshal was to be Gen. Romulus Mitchell Saunders, whom the Whig press delighted in referring to as "Old Roan." The other assistants, as designated, were "Col. James Dobbin of Cumberland, Col. W. W. Avery, Col. George Bower, Col. Albert Waugh of Forsythe, George S. Stevenson, Esq., of Newbern, Lt. Uriah W. Swanner of Washington county, Dr. Ballard of Gates, Marshall Dickerson of Pitt, Gen. Thomas A. Person of Northampton, and Corporal Curtis H. Brogden of Wayne." *Raleigh Times*, July 9, 1852.

[6]A round robin is a complaint or petition with the signatures arranged in a circle so that it is impossible to determine who signed first.

[7]A favorite Whig nickname for Reid was "Dainty Davey."

[8]Holden was designated by the Whig press as "governor *de facto*," that is, the real governor of the state, because of his supposed influence over Reid.

[9]A reference to W. W. Holden and other powerful Democrats.

[10]Reid had more than one private secretary during his four years as governor. "David Reid Progress" is likely a critical reference to Reid's hiring of his first cousin Thomas Settle, Jr., who was his secretary during his first term. Reid's teenaged nephew Samuel F. Adams, Jr., served as his secretary in 1853. Democratic editor William B. Gulick also was Reid's secretary in the 1850s.

David S. Reid to Henrietta S. Reid RCC

Lenoir, Caldwell Co: N. C.
Sunday night, July 11th, 1852.

Well; how do you do my dear wife?

My health has improved since I saw you and I now feel fully as well as usual. The weather is very warm. I thought last Wednesday that the heat was more oppressive than I ever felt it.

We spoke at Wilkesboro on yesterday and things passed off pretty smoothly. My friends in Wilkes say they will give me as good a vote as they did at the last election, and perhaps better. I left Wilkesboro this morning and arrived here this afternoon. The route was through a dreary and lonely part of the Country, that presented but little of interest except some mountain scenery and occasionally a nice corn field. Genl. Patterson,[1] as usual met us at Wilkesboro and invited us to his house. I declined and Mr. Kerr accepted. My acquaintances that I have seen since I arrived are all whigs and, of course, I have not received any reliable information in regard to my prospects in this County. We speak here tomorrow, but I brought this evening the first news they had here of the appointment. It so happens however that Mr. Hewlett[2] has an appointment lecture here tomorrow on Temperance and I suppose we shall have a crowd. By the way you will see that we are to speak in Rutherfordton on *Sunday*! While at Salem Mr. Blum[3] sent me word to know whether he should publish that I would attend Mr. Kerrs appointments.[4] I wrote him a note that I would attend them, but I did not know where they were and would thank him to send me a list of them. He accordingly sent me the list as I sent it to you, including Rutherfordton *the 18th*!

Suppose you speak to some of our friends to save us some Apple-Tree Scions of the choicest kinds, and to have some Peach seed planted. I have been in Rockingham so little that I could not think of these things. Take care of the grape vines and send word to Barber[5] to see what has become of the one we planted there. I have received no letter from you here, but the mail comes tomorrow and I may receive one then. Every day that passes seems to lighten the burden of the Canvass. I am very anxious to see the end of it, I can assure you. But I knew what it was before I undertook it, and do not find Kerr on the stump a more troublesome customer than Manly, whatever may be the result of the election. It is like drawing eye teeth to get him to tell in this part of the State that he is against a change of the Basis of Representation and in favor of dividing School Fund according to federal population.

On my way to this place to day I called to see an old friend Col. William P. Waugh[6] who is in a low state of health and I fear can not survive long. What a change two years brings round! What a number of those whom I knew two years ago have been "gathered to their fathers"—and oh! my dear Father, my good Father, of the number! May Heaven bless his immortal spirit![7]

My thoughts to-day have been almost entirely occupied about you. This warm weather, especially when the air is not damp keep the windows in your chamber up so that your chamber may be well ventillated while you sleep. A want of fresh air while sleeping is enervating and unhealthy. Eat heartily but temperately and be careful about fruits and vegetables. Be careful about the use of ice. I do not think it advisable to make a practice of using ice water regularly, and more especially when we can get pure water. The degree of a good spring is doubtless the most wholesome temperature for water. Be cheerful. But above all pray, and endeavor to lay up an inheritance in Heaven! You know my dear that I have often expressed to the great joy and consolation it would afford me to know that you had experienced Christian Grace. I again repeat that such an event would fill my heart with inexpressible joy. When will you have more leisure? When will be a more opportune moment to attend to this important matter? I entreat you not to suffer your mind to be distressed too much on this subject, for I believe in a Religion founded upon faith, works, and philosophy. It does seem to me that if you were a good Christian that I should feel so much encouraged by your example that my chance of gaining the immortal salvation of my soul would be greatly increased. Much reflection on the subject brought my mind to the conclusion many years ago, that of the two sexes Woman was the peculiar guardian of Religion upon this Earth. Her example ever has, and ever will do much. Upon this subject she is within her proper sphere and the extent of her influence is incalculable. How happy would be the idea, how consoling the assurance that when separated on Earth that *we* are to be united in Heaven! My dear, do not lose sight of these things. They have engaged much of my thoughts from early youth to the present day. In the busy conflict in which I am engaged I regret that I do not bestow that time to this subject which its importance demands. I trust however that it is otherwise with you. Nothing good nor nothing truly great is inconsistent with the true principles of Religion. Any thing in our thoughts or actions which conflicts with this great principle ought to be abandoned. Will you the dear wife of my affections, seek, diligently seek Religion, and give your dear Husband the light of your example and the aid your prayers that we may both make our calling and election sure? At the moment I pen these lines (10½ Oclock at night) I feel certain that some friend is praying for the immortal salvation of my soul.

Oh dear Wife how I would like to see you! I wonder how you look. Do not wear your clothes too tight this warm weather, and especially your shoes—wear large ones. My friends here and at Wilkes say I look much better than I did two years ago. I have had a very good appetite for several days. Eating and speaking however do not go very well together, for much eating is apt to produce bad speaking.

As I travelled over that lonely road to day I looked frequently to see if I could not find some pretty little flower or leaf to send you as a little token of much affection, but really I could find nothing worth sending. I however clip a lock of hair from my head which I send in exchange for your rose. If you should find any gray hairs in it, *excuse haste*, for it is night and I can not see to pick them out.

I wonder what sort of work you are doing. You are sufficiently industrious I know.

My love to all the family. I hope this may find you and them in good health.

My dear wife my letters to you are very hastily written and the style is such as I would not use in writing to any one else. Yet I would not write differently to you. It would seem hypocritical not to write just as I may think at the time I write, and to express my thoughts in just such language as may occur in the hurry of the moment.

Accept my dear wife—and I will use that endearing expression as often as I please—renewed assurances of my profound love.

---

[1]Samuel Finley Patterson (1799-1874), a native of Rockbridge County, Virginia, moved as a young man to Wilkesboro. He held many public offices during his long career, including that of state treasurer and clerk of the state Senate (1829-1834). He was elected to the state Senate (1846, 1848, 1864) and House of Commons (1854). He was a delegate from North Carolina to the Philadelphia Peace Convention in 1866. He was a trustee of the state university and served as brigadier general and major general of the state militia. Patterson, a Whig in 1852, was influential in the formation in 1841 of Caldwell County, where his home, "Palmyra," was for many years a center of hospitality for visitors. Ashe, *Biographical History*, II, 328-333.

[2]Hewlett, probably not a North Carolina resident, was likely a traveling lecturer employed by the Sons of Temperance. The Grand Division of North Carolina hired what was reported as its first native traveling lecturer, the Reverend Peter Doub (died 1869), a Methodist circuit rider from Stokes County, on November 13, 1852, as the result of complaints that "the introduction of foreign lecturers is productive of a vast amount of prejudice which is not enlisted against one of our own citizens." Doub reported after eleven months of employment that he had delivered 150 "stated Lectures" and had preached sixty-four times, "many of these sermons, directly or indirectly, upon the subject of Temperance." The organization at this time employed one lecturer, who traveled throughout the state. As early as 1844, however, the *Greensborough Patriot* reported that Edward S. Cotten of Warren County

had been "appointed Temperance Lecturer for this State." *Proceedings of the Grand Division of North Carolina, Sons of Temperance*, October Session, 1853 (Raleigh: A. M. Gorman, Printer—Spirit of the Age Office, 1853), 10, 23; *Milton Chronicle*, September 2, 1869; Diary of Peter Doub, January 8, 1830, January 17, 1832, Manuscript Department, Duke University Library, Durham; *Greensborough Patriot*, April 6, 1844.

[3]John Christian Blum established *The People's Press*, a politically independent newspaper, on February 8, 1851, in Salem and was its editor through 1853. Wescott and Ramage, *Duke Newspaper Checklist*, 700.

[4]Blum already had been publishing the candidates' appointments. A previous article headed "Gubernatorial Candidates" noted: "We notice that Gov. REID has made his arrangements to meet Mr. KERR, at the times and places mentioned last week, to wit:—At Greensborough, June 29th; Salem, July 1st; Huntsville, July 3rd; Wilkesborough, July 6th." The meeting of Reid and Kerr in Wilkesboro did not actually take place until Saturday, July 10, however, as noted above. *People's Press*, June 12, 1852.

[5]Possibly one of two farmers named Barber— John, age 49, or Reuben, age 61, who lived in western Rockingham County in 1850 within reasonable distance of the Dan River plantation given by Thomas Settle to Henrietta and David Reid. Seventh Census, 1850, Rockingham County, Population Schedule, 61, 64.

[6]William Pitt Waugh (circa 1787-1852), merchant, a native of Adams County, Pennsylvania, emigrated in 1803 with his brothers John, James, Andrew, and David, to Wilkes County, North Carolina. Two years later they were joined by their nephew Major John Finley. Finley and Waugh were pioneers in the establishment of chain stores carrying a complete line of general merchandise. Their holdings extended throughout western North Carolina and into Tennessee, Virginia, and other states nearby. Waugh built a brick mansion at Moravian Falls between the Taylorsville and Lenoir roads. He resided there until his death on August 14, 1852. Waugh, who never married, became a justice of the peace in 1811 and a trustee of Wilkesborough Seminary in 1837. The value of his real estate in 1850 was estimated at $53,721. He left a very large estate, which was disputed for several years. Hayes, *Land of Wilkes*, 71, 72, 88, 198; Seventh Census, 1850, Wilkes County, Population Schedule, 361; *Raleigh Register*, September 1, 1852.

[7]Reuben Reid (1787-1852), father of David S. Reid, died June 22, 1852, in Rockingham County. A farmer, he was listed as 64 years old in the 1850 census. *Raleigh Register*, July 3, 1852; Seventh Census, Rockingham County, Population Schedule, 26; Reese and Fisher, *Settle Family*, 678.

David S. Reid to Henrietta S. Reid RCC

Marion, McDowell Co:
July 16, 1852.

I reached here yesterday in the afternoon and we addressed the people here to-day. I am well. Hope you are well my dear wife. The result of the speaking to-day I learn was not unfavorable, and the prospect is by no means discouraging. My friends in this county think they can give me a better vote that I received here two years ago.[1] From all I can learn Scotts nomination is not well received in this county. The Whig leaders are evidently alarmed at the signs of the times. Mr. Gaither[2] had to catechise me to-day while speaking. I took it all in good part and he made nothing by it. Kerr is scared and is making a desperate effort. He is getting more and more *Western* as he gets farther up. He has the ingenuity to do the most of it by insinuations and in such a way that it is hard to get hold of him. He is now getting more on the defensive and the discussions are easier for me. He tells them that altho he is against a change of the basis when they get a convention they can have such amendments as they want! To day he resorted to the pitiful expedient of telling them that he thought the western part of the State ought to have a United States Senator, and he was for their having one! He advocates a Convention *strong* but says he himself does not want any change of the Constitution except to carry out free suffrage and to abolish the land qualification for Governor and members of the Assembly. He reminds me more and more of Manly every day.

After the discussion this evening I took tea with Mr. Carson[3] a whig who I suppose will vote for me. I think Avery[4] will be elected, and perhaps Davis,[5] a Clingman whig.

Tomorrow I go to Rutherfordton and speak there on Monday. I hope I shall get to rest on Sunday. He states in his speeches that Geo. Williamson[6] who voted for free suffrage in the last Assembly is publicly out against it.

I hope my dear that you are doing well. Oh how I would like to see you! Nothing would give me so much pleasure. You occupy my thoughts by day and dreams by night. I will close this letter and go to bed.

Give my love to all the family—and accept for yourself my dearest wife, renewed assurances of the pure love and affection of your devoted husband. May God bless you my dear wife.

P S. The Geranium blossom will bring you many kisses from your dear Husband

---

[1]McDowell County was formed in 1842 from Rutherford and Burke counties. Its vote totals in gubernatorial contests were not reported separately until 1854, however. McDowell returns were filed with Burke in 1850 and 1852, where Reid's total improved by 145 votes. Powell, *North Carolina Gazetteer*, 306; Cheney, *North Carolina Government*, 1398, 1419.

[2]Burgess Sidney Gaither, previously identified.

[3]Probably William M. Carson, a Whig who represented Burke County in the House of Commons in 1838. Phifer, *Burke*, 413.

[4]William Waightstill Avery, previously identified, was a states' rights Democrat. He was reelected in 1852 to a seat in the House of Commons, representing Burke County, Powell, *DNCB*, I, 71. See also John Hill Wheeler to David S. Reid, April 19, 1847.

[5]Presumably, Champe T. N. Davis, a Whig elected to represent the 46th senatorial district in 1854. Winner of the second House seat from Burke in 1852 was John S. Erwin, a Whig. Phifer, *Burke*, 414.

[6]George Williamson, a Yanceyville miller and farmer, was a member of the Council of State (1834 and 1835) and the state Senate (1850-1851). He served in the Mexican War and was later active in railroad promotion and the state agricultural society. He was a trustee of Dan River Institute, on the board of the Bank of Yanceyville, and a member of the state Farmers' Alliance. Powell, *Caswell County*, 118-119, 136, 269-271, 345, 369, 502, 507; Cheney, *North Carolina Government*, 176, 1088.

Thomas Settle to David S. Reid A&H-DSR

Rockingham County N.Ca.
July the 16th 1852

Henrietta has received your letters regularly up to Wilkesboro and that inclusive and We were all highly gratified to hear that your health was improving and your political prospects not discourging

We are all in good health and your Misses health is quite good Your Mother[,] Hugh[1] and the rest of the family are in good health I have been up to Barbers[2] and the Island[3] and find they have unusually good crops. Will is pressing on rapidly with your house[4] he has the wood work nearly completed and has his brick and other materials hauled to build the chimneys and under pin the house. He has also laid in his points. I have advanced to him upwards of one thousand dollars but have observed your directions and took his bond. I feel much oblidged to you for advancing for me the one hundred dollars for the fifth instalment of my stock in the central rail road.

Your Uncle Calvin Graves has been in Raleigh lately and wrote me from that place stating that your prospects were good and still brighting and that he had seen a letter from Marcus Erwin[5] stating that Kerr had been renounced and denounced in their Whig meetings for the doctrines he had advanced in the East and his competition Mr. Woodfin[6] had been forced to state if Kerr did advance the doctrines imputed to him in the East he Woodfin would not support him.

I have just received a letter from Holden, he says your prospects there and in the East are good and brighting and he has no doubt of your reellection. He says he hears of certain Democratic Reid and Pierce gaines & no losses

We all wish the canvass was over and that we could see you and none so much as your Dear wife. We all hope you good health and success and that you will take good care of your health. We have here the best prospects for fine crops that we have had for several years. I would have written to you before but your Wife would say Father I will write this time and you can write the next letter until this morning when I told her I would not be put off in that way any longer so I write this letter directed to you at Hendersonville. We all join in our love to you generally and your Wife in particular and may the Lord guard guide protect & bless you and yours is the prayer of your affectionate Father

---

[1]Hugh Kearns Reid, previously identified, brother of David S. Reid.

[2]Likely either John Barber or Reuben Barber, both previously identified. Neither is listed in the census as an overseer, however.

[3]"The Island" was one of at least three large tracts that Thomas Settle acquired along the Dan River in Rockingham County. His 1856 will states: "I will and devise to my son Thomas Settle my tract of land on Dan River called and known by the name of the Mulberry Island tract." To his son David A. Settle, Thomas Settle, Sr., bequeathed another Dan River tract that he had purchased from his late brother-in-law, Robert Martin. Adjoining land belonging to Robert Martin was a third plantation, of 699 acres, located on the south bank of the Dan River northwest of Wentworth and frequently referred to as "the River" (to distinguish it from "the Island"), that Thomas Settle had purchased for $4,100 from William D. Bethell and James M. Scales. He deeded it to David S. Reid and Henrietta S. Reid in 1853. Thomas Settle to David S. Reid and Henrietta S. Reid, July 5, 1853, Rockingham County Deeds, Book 2T, 326; Settle Will, 259.

[4]The house under construction was at the "River" plantation.

[5]Marcus Erwin (1826-1881), an attorney from Asheville, was a native of Burke County and graduated from Transylvania University. During the Mexican War he served with the Texas troops. By 1848 he had settled in Asheville and for a time edited the *Asheville News*. He was a solicitor, member of the House of Commons (1850-1851, 1856-1857), and state senator (1860-1861). An advocate of secession, he entered Confederate service and rose to the rank of major. After the war he was a United States assistant district attorney. Sondley, *Buncombe County*, 775-776.

[6]Nicholas W. Woodfin (1810-1876), an Asheville attorney and farmer, was a Whig member of the state Senate (1844-1854) and a delegate to the state Constitutional Convention of 1861-1862. Sondley, *Buncombe County*, 774.

Abraham W. Venable to David S. Reid A&H-DSR

Washington
18th July 1852

Permit me to call your attention to a difficulty as to the coming election of electors for President and Vice President. By the constitution (Hickeys Constitution Article 2 Sec. 1) it is provided that each state shall be entitled to as many electors as the whole number of Senators and Representatives of the Congress" by same Book page 291 the act of 1792 provides that each state shall be entitled to the number of Senators and Representatives to which they shall be entitled when the President and Vice President thus chosen shall come into office. Now as the President and Vice President shall come into office after the 4th March 1853 and the apportionment shall be complete before that time I call your attention to the subject intending to write you again in a few days after we shall have fully consulted upon this matter. I would respectfully suggest that the matter be kept out of the papers until it is ascertained what shall be necessary as to the preservation of the elective vote of the State even should the Legislature have to [meet]. With my best respects to Madame

---

Daniel W. Courts to David S. Reid A&H-DSR

Raleigh NC
July 22 1852

We think all is well here, that Wake will give you an increased vote. Had a democratic meeting at the Court house Saturday night. It was enthusiastic, especially when your name was mentioned. The Times & other papers say you wrote the letter from Greensboro[1]; give them Jesse,[2] They say too that you carried your election two years ago by the Rockingham lie.[3] I would ask Kerr publicly the character of the Whig figures, Galloway[4] Dillard[5] Aiken,[6] Mebane[7] &c Tell your friends to spread themselves. Saunders is fighting hard.[8] I should not be mealy mouthed, they will beat you if they can by any sort of means

[1]The "Greensboro letter," a report signed by "A Democrat" and carried by Holden's *North-Carolina Standard* of July 7, 1852, caused a prolonged controversy during the remainder of the campaign. Calling the report "a most gross perver-

sion and false representation" of the June 29 debate between Reid and Kerr, Whig papers complained that Kerr's positions on several issues were misrepresented. This was not the first time that such an accusation had been made in the Whig press, as early as in May the *Raleigh Times* had referred to the "Tell-lie-graphic" dispatch man of the *Standard*'s distorting the truth in political reports. The *Fayetteville Observer* charged that Reid himself either wrote or dictated the "Greensboro letter," and that as a result of this "dishonorable duplicity" he would "sink to an infamy from which there would be no political resurrection." *Fayetteville Observer*, July 20, 1852; *Raleigh Register*, July 7, 10, 1852; *Raleigh Times*, July 9, 23, 1852.

[2]"Jesse" is an expression, designated by *Webster's Seventh New Collegiate Dictionary* (1972) as "chiefly dialectal," referring to the biblical rod of Jesse. A "jesse" is a severe scolding or beating.

[3]The "Rockingham lie" is a reference to the Whig charge that Reid in his 1850 campaign against Manly also distorted his opponent's positions in order to achieve victory. During that campaign one Whig paper warned its supporters of rumors circulated by Democrats: "One of these rumors, for instance, represents him [Manly] as having taken very strong ground in the West in favor of altering the present basis of representation, & c. We have ample reasons for believing that many of these slanderous reports have been sent down here from Reid himself . . . If LYING can beat Gov. Manly, he is to be beaten." Again, in 1852, referring to the "Greensboro letter," a Fayetteville Whig noted: "It is precisely the same kind of fraud which helped to elect Reid two years ago." *Raleigh Register*, July 10, 1850; *Fayetteville Observer*, quoted in the *Raleigh Times*, July 23, 1852. See also William W. Holden to David S. Reid, July 10, 1850.

[4]Thomas S. Gallaway (1809-1879), a Rockingham County planter and Whig leader, ran unsuccessfully against Reid in 1838 for a seat in the state Senate. The county was predominately Democrat, and Gallaway never held public office. In 1860 Gallaway owned ninety-two slaves and was one of the largest slaveholders in the county. Mon Vue Cemetery; *North-Carolina Standard*, August 15, 1838; Eighth Census, 1860, Rockingham County, Slave Schedule, 6-7.

[5]John Henry Dillard (1819-1896), previously identified, of Rockingham County and law partner of Thomas Ruffin. Although a Whig, he took little part in politics and after the decline of the Whig party became a Democrat. Powell, *DNCB*, II, 69; see also John H. Dillard to David S. Reid, August 13, 1838.

[6]George L. Aiken was a Rockingham County planter in 1850 and a local Whig leader. Seventh Census, 1850, Rockingham County, Population Schedule, 2.

[7]Probably a reference to William Nelson Mebane (1809-1859), Presbyterian minister at Madison, whose son, William Nelson Mebane, Jr., later represented Rockingham County in the House of Commons (1874-1875) and state Senate (1876-1877). Will of William Nelson Mebane, February 22, 1859, Rockingham County Wills, Book C., 303 Archives, Division of Archives and History, Raleigh, hereinafter cited as Mebane Will; Cheney, *North Carolina Government*, 1257, 1258; Seventh Census, 1850, Rockingham County, Population Schedule, 105.

[8]After serving from 1846 to 1850 as "envoy extraordinary and minister plenipotentiary" to Spain, Judge Romulus Mitchell Saunders, a native of Caswell County and a faithful Democrat, previously identified, returned to his adopted home in Raleigh where he "entered warmly into political action," representing Wake County in the House of Commons in 1850 and 1852. Ashe, *Biographical History*, III, 391.

David S. Reid to Henrietta S. Reid RCC

Burnsville, Yancy Co:
Monday, July 26, 1852

I reached this place last night in good health, and addressed the people here to-day. Nothing extraordinary occured. My friends here think that my vote will be as good or better than it was two years since in this county. I do not know how it will be. Almost every body in this county is for dividing the School Fund according to the white population and in favor of changing the basis of representation. Kerr goes it strong on demagougism and I endeavor to show him up.

There was one thing that occured to day during the discussion that afforded me great amusement as it did every body else. While Kerr was speaking there was an old fellow in the crowd who would occasionally interrupt him by saying, "That is a fact." "I believe in that doctrine". "You are the man for me" &c &c. To all of which Kerr would reply most pleasantly & good naturedly, by saying he knew he was fond of truth and that he was a man of discrimination. After a while the old man exclaimed, Well: I be d—ned if I ain't for Reid! Whereupon Kerr fired up and got quite vexed and declared that enough of a thing was enough! That Gov. Reid had not been interrupted, and he did not wish to be! The thing was so plain that every body saw it.[1]

My dear, I am very well and hope that your health is good, and that all the rest are well. I wish very much to see my dear wife. Often, often indeed do I think of you. You occupy my thoughts by day and dreams by night. If there is any truth in the saying, your ears must burn very often, for I talk about you whenever I get a chance. Before we were married I thought you the prettiest woman in the State or out of it, and my travels this summer have more fully confirmed that openion. Take care of yourself my sweet wife. Oh! how very anxious I am to find you in good health.

Kerr and my self keep on ordinary terms. Since I saw you I think the Canvass up to this time has worsted Mr. Kerr more than my self. I am now standing the Canvass much better than I did in the East. I am getting some what anxious to beat Kerr, not because I desire to be Governor for another term, but because I think he merits, richly merits a beating.

I have a pretty good appetite these days. I eat no vegetables. Bacon and chicken constitute most of my food. Give my love to all, if you please. What else can I write? The Canvass is near the close, yet I have much bad road to encounter and many mountains to cross and recross. I encounter all these things with more alacrity than I would do if it were not for you. Under all circumstances I hold you in fond and bright remembrance; loving purely and devotedly the dear partner of all my joys and all my woes. My love, dearest. May God deal to you his choicest and richest blessings till we meet. Good night, dear wife.

---

[1]Following the June 29, 1852, debate between Reid and Kerr at Greensboro, public attention centered on a controversy regarding authorship of the "Greensboro letter," a news account of the debate that placed Kerr in an unfavorable light. A more lighthearted exchange toward the close of that debate was also reported by the press, however. The anecdote, printed originally by the *Greensborough Patriot*, was reprinted by other Whig newspapers. As reprinted by an Elizabeth City editor, it was prefaced: "The discussion at Greensborough was closed by an amusing and spicy colloquy concerning the Presidential candidates. This is the substance as reported in the Patriot—Mr. Kerr said that Gov. Reid's gunpowder taunt upon the Whigs for bolstering up their cause with a 'General' came with a poor grace from him, when his party had found it necessary to try a 'General' too. There was this difference, however, in this gunpowder game; the Democrats could start a *pocket pistol*, while the Whigs had a *twenty pounder*, which had many a time jarred the continent by its tremendous reports.

"Reid. 'A pocket pistol sometimes does great execution, particularly in close quarters; and I doubt not the gentleman's 24 pounder will be found to do as much execution at the breech as at the muzzle.'

"Kerr. 'Exactly! That's the way with the old piece—it killed Polk and Marcy at one end, and the Mexicans at t'other.'" *Old North State*, July 17, 1852.

David S. Reid to Henrietta S. Reid RCC

Franklin, Macon Co:
Sunday, August 1st, 1852.

I am well. This day ushers in a new month, and one somewhat interesting to politicians.[1]

I left Scotts Creek this morning and crossing the Cowee Mountain reached here about four Oclock this afternoon. The Road was in the worst condition I ever saw it, but I got along safely and without detention except slow travelling. I have eat my dinner and chatted a little and gone to my room to write you this letter. As I started up to my room I stepped into the yard and gathered the enclosed from the Swannana[2] vine. Two years ago I carried some of the seed home and gave them to sister Henrietta, and I think I gave you some of them.

Politically I hear no bad news. I speak here to-morrow and then go over the Nantahala and other mountains to Murphy, distant 50 miles. Got no letter from you at this place. Mails are tardy & unfrequent here.

I hope your health continues good my dear wife. As I came on to day, Sabbath brought to mind many things. Often, often have I thought of my dear wife. Almost every one I see asks me something about you, and it affords me pleasure to answer their questions. I hope you have employed this Sabbath day in Holy thoughts. Last night I dreamed I saw you and that you exclaimed that you had made your "calling and election sure," and the pleasure it afforded me is indescribable. I never saw you more beautiful and lovely before in all my life.

I wonder how you look my dear. I wish to see you so much. Have so many little things to tell you, but then I am afraid I shall forget them before I see you. Of course I would like very much on some accounts to be elected, but be the result what it may I shall be perfectly satisfied.

I have travelled over many hills and seen many faces since I left you. The farther I get from you the better I love you, if possible to love you better than I did before.

Please give my love to all.

My dear sweet wife accept my true and unchanging love for yourself. May God bless, guard and protect you is my most earnest prayer.

---

[1]This is an allusion to the fact that August was election month.

[2]The Swannanoa vine was apparently a flowering plant native to western North Carolina. This middle nineteenth-century common name does not appear in contemporary books on North Carolina or Appalachian wild flowers or native plants, so that it is not possible to identify it more specifically.

David S. Reid to Henrietta S. Reid RCC

Murphy, Cherokee Co:
Wednesday, Aug: 4, 1852.

I left Franklin yesterday morning and traveled trough the rain over the Nantahala and Valley River Mountains and staid at the head of Valley River seventeen miles from this place. This morning it rained in torrents and I reached this place about 11 Oclock. We had a long discussion which I hope was not unfavorable. I hope I shall gain in this county, but these things you know are uncertain. My friends are in good spirits. The discussion was warm to-day and I bore down on Kerr pretty hard. After the discussion the mail came in and brought your letter of the 25th with the postscript of Father (for he is the only father I now have). I was much gratified to hear from you and him and to learn that all were well. Thank God for that. Tomorrow the election takes place. I can not write you the vote as the mail leaves early in the morning. My dear I am well. Hope this will find you well and all the rest. I shall be at this place tomorrow at the election.

Oh my dear how I wish to see you. Ten thousand kisses and all my love to yourself and all the rest. May God bless you my dear wife. I will now go to bed and be ready for the election tomorrow. Good night dear wife.

William W. Holden to David S. Reid A&H-DSR

Raleigh,
Aug. 10. 1852

Knowing your anxiety to hear from the election, I drop you some items in relation thereto. We have heard from the Counties of Caswell, Person, Granville[,] Bertie, Hertford, Northampton, Craven, Jones, Richmond, Lenoir, Greene, Martin, Brunswick, Iredell, Stanly, Washington, Pasquotank[,] Perquimans, Chowan, Camden, Gates, Anson, Burke, Bladen, Cumberland, Columbus, Chatham, Cleavland, Davidson, Davie, Duplin, Edgecombe, Franklin, Guilford, Halifax[,] Johnston, Lincoln, Moore, Mecklenburg, Nash, New Hanover, Onslow, Orange[,] Pitt, Robeson, Rowan, Rutherford, Randolph, Sampson, Surry, Forsythe, Wake, Warren, Wayne—54 in all. In these Counties Mr Kerr gains 2,107, and you gain 3,300, making your clear gain 1,193. Your majority, I think, must reach 5,000. You have lost but 52 votes in Washington—Reid 297, Kerr 247; and we have saved the Commoner, Phelps,[1] in that County. You have gained 78 in Chowan, 16 in Perquimons, and 70 in Gates. You have gained 109 in Richmond, 89 in Iredell, and 63 in Jones, and lost 68 in Stanly, 28 in Brunswick, and 31 in Pasquotank, and 10 in Greene. These are returns not included in those of the Standard, which you will receive by this mail. I will keep this letter open until we receive the Western Mail to-night, Tuesday.

You will see you have lost in Caswell. I am glad Mr. Williamson[2] is beaten. In Person we have lost a Commoner! and there is no doubt of a loss in Perquimans and Chowan. Wilson[3] was beaten 11 votes and Johnson[4] 32. If we have lost in Wilkes and Buncombe, we shall be in a bad [box], unless we have gained in Carteret, or Caldwell, or Davie, or Macon. The Whigs claim a loss of two in Surry, which I doubt, and also two in Stokes, which is highly improbable. Dr. Mills,[5] you will see, is beaten. We have no news for Camden and Currituck but I have my fears. Craven and Jones have done nobly; but our losses in Johnston, Orange, and Lincoln and Person, to say nothing of Bladen and Robeson, are totally inexcusable The rumor here is that we have gained a Commoner in Tyrrell! The Canvass is in great doubt, but we are sure of the Senate by four, and quite sure, I think of a majority on joint ballot.

Your triumph is indeed a brilliant one. The Feds here, who were so bitter but a few days ago, now hang their heads and say Free Suffrage did it. They have been foiled only for the moment. Politically, they deserve no quarters.

By the way, I made another good guess as to the Wake vote, though I did not publish it. Several days before the election I made out the supposed vote for yourself, Kerr, Saunders,[6] Wilder,[7] and Allen.[8] I gave you 1560 votes in Wake—you got 1561, but I missed considerably in every other calculation. I gave Kerr for instance, 1043—he got 1102. The Sheriff's election has come in one of defeating us generally in the County. But for that I feel sure we should give you 100 gain.

I am worn down and exhausted by the labors of the campaign, but I shall get better as soon as I can get enough sleep. My children are well, and little *Etta Reid* especially. She has not been sick an hour.

Your friends here expect you soon, and will be glad to see you. Please let me know what day you will arrive.

Please present my kindest regards to Mrs. Reid and Judge Settle's family, and accept for yourself, Sir, assurances of my unalterable attachment and friendship.

P.S. Our news by the Western Mail is not as full as I expected. We have lost a Commoner in Wilkes, also in Buncombe— also in Stokes, Joel F. Hill[9] beaten No news from Caldwell or Macon: We have not gained in Davie, You have lost 43 in Stokes, 21 in Cabarrus, and your loss in Surry is not 291, as first reported, but 165. Your clear gain is still 1200, not counting Buncombe, where it is thought you have gained over 200. The news for the great part comes in with provoking slowness. I fear we have lost the Legislature on joint ballot. As matters now stand, we have certainly lost the Commons.

---

[1]Charles Phelps of Washington County was a member of the House of Commons (1833-1834, 1852). Cheney, *North Carolina Government*, 1303-1304.

[2]George Williamson, previously identified.

[3]Thomas Wilson of Perquimans County served in the House of Commons (1828-1832, 1833-1834, 1838-1845, 1850-1851, 1866-1867) and as a delegate to the state Constitutional Convention of 1865-1866. Cheney, *North Carolina Government*, 832, 1239.

[4]Lucius Johnson (born 1830), Democrat, an Edenton attorney, was beaten by Hugh W. Collins, a Whig. *Old North State*, August 7, 1852.

[5]Columbus Mills, previously identified.

[6]Romulus M. Saunders, previously identified, was one of three victorious Wake County Democratic candidates for the House of Commons in 1852. Cheney, *North Carolina Government*, 321.

[7]Gaston H. Wilder, previously identified, a victorious Democratic candidate from Wake County for the House of Commons in 1852. Cheney, *North Carolina Government*, 321.

[8]William A. Allen, also a Democrat, was elected to represent Wake County in the House of Commons in 1852. Cheney, *North Carolina Government*, 321.

[9]Joel F. Hill of Stokes County was a member of the House of Commons from 1854 to 1859. Cheney, *North Carolina Government*, 1275.

Asa Biggs to David S. Reid A&H-DSR
[Confidential]

Williamston
Augt 23, 1852

On monday after the election I left here with my family on a visit to my brother at Norfolk. On the road I ascertained the very gratifying fact that you were triumphantly elected. I happened to be in company at the time with our mutual friend Stallings[1] of Gates and you can perhaps imagine our hearty congratulations. I returned home on Saturday last and I avail myself of the first mail to congratulate you upon your and our success. I am free to say that your majority is much larger than I anticipated. I felt great confidence when I left Raleigh 10th July that your election was sure but I did not expect as large a majority. The only regret I have about the election is that our Democratic friends in some of the counties should have permitted local causes to render our majority in the Legislature doubtful considering the importance of the next General Assembly, but with this draw back our success is important and cheering beyond calculation upon the approaching Presidential election. I trust the redemption of the Old North State from the counsels of the Whigs may be completed in November.

Before you receive this you will no doubt have been advised (much to your suprise I expect) that the Commission to revise the Statutes[2] will not report to the Legislature, I remained in Raleigh nearly 10 days after I reached there before we had a meeting. Before we met I was astonished at a proposition of Mr. Moore to postpone a report. To this proposition I decidedly objected. We met and commenced a review of the titles assigned to Genl. Saunders. We did not get through his part. Mr. Moore was called off to attend the Supreme Court and I am ascertained it was impossible in the state of the commission to force a report. Several objections were interposed but none of them in my opinion sufficient to justify us in not reporting. I considered the duty imperative so much so that I expressed my readiness to lose my fall courts and stay at Raleigh until the revision was completed although it would subject me to great inconvenience and loss.—I was for a report. Mr. Moore was opposed to it and Genl Saunders was neither for one or the other because he expected to resign any way about 1st August. The result is very unpleasant to me because I have a great aversion to undertake any thing especially the performance of a public duty and fail in meeting the public expectation especially when I think a satisfactory excuse cannot be rendered. But so it is this time but I have the consolation to know and I have taken some pains to be prepared to show that the default is not justly attributable to me for my work was completed as far as practiable without a joint revision. I feel that the matter will be the subject of remark when the Assembly meets and what I more particularly regret is that I fear it will be made the subject of attack upon your administration without an opportunity being afforded to make public the real cause of the default. I can only hope that the facts may be so well understood that the censure may fall upon the proper head. I was urged to run for the Senate and I would very willingly have been in the next Legislature but my conclusion was that having accepted the Commission I was precluded from running for the Legislature. I acted upon this conclusion and the result shows its correctness for had *both* the Democratic Commissioners been members of the Legislature and no report made the denunciations would have been loud and long. Much more I could say and will say on the subject when we meet. I thought it necessary to say what I have to set myself right and to apprise you how things stand.

The election in this state has produced great Consternation among the Whigs throughout the country and the Norfolk Whigs with whom I met cannot account for it, except they say your free suffrage has done the business.—If Clingman comes out now publicly as I have no doubt he will against Scott, if Caldwell[3] does the same as I hear he probably will, if Outlaw[4] remains as he is (what he will do I cannot ascertain with any satisfaction) I feel entire confidence we will carry the State in November.

Present my best respects to Mr. Holden & say to him that in my opinion he has fought the battle manfully.

My kindest regards to Mrs. Reid. Accept for yourself the assurances of the highest esteem of yr. obt servt.

[1]Whitmel Stallings, previously identified, was a member of Reid's Council of State.

[2]The commission to revise the state statutes was appointed on May 8, 1851, and consisted of Biggs, Romulus M. Saunders, and Bartholemew F. Moore. Reid, *Gubernatorial Campaigns*, 49.

[3]Joseph P. Caldwell, previously identified, of Statesville, was at this time a Whig representative in Congress.

[4]David Outlaw (1806-1868), a Windsor attorney, graduated from the state university in 1824. He was a member of the House of Commons (1831-1834, 1854, 1858), a delegate to the state Constitutional Convention of 1835, a militia colonel, a Whig representative in Congress (1847-1853), and a state senator (1860, 1866). *Biographical Directory of Congress*, 1414-1415.

Jesse G. Shepherd[1] *to David S. Reid* A&H-DSR

Fayetteville
August 28th. 1852.

I need not say how much of joy I feel in the result of our late elections in this State. Until I saw you in June, I had fears that with a full Whig vote in the East and the Convention lobby in the West, Mr Kerr would run beyond the vote of Gov' Manly in 1850. My subsequent reflection to which your conversation led my mind induced me to think that your vote would improve in the West and especially in Ashe, Cherokee, Haywood & Yancy. Such was the development but beyond my thought or hope except in the county of Cherokee where I knew you could use with great effect the relief bill of the last legislature which Mr Kerr in Surry was so indiscreet as to compare to the Bankrupt law of 1841. The Whigs in this section are more disappointed than any set of men I ever saw—1850 is not be to mentioned in the same day with 1852. Altho' your vote in this county was increased 78, the addition to Mr Kerr's vote was large for reasons given by Mr Dobbin in a private letter to Mr Holden—the week after the election. Your vote was the largest ever given in the county in a Presidential, gubernatorial or any other election between a whig and a democrat. Mr Dobbin's highest vote was in 1850—1340—yours in 1852—1388. We are to have on the 7th of September, a jubilee which we hope to make of the first order. Will you please to sign early next week—two commissions for Wm G. Matthews[2] and A McPherson[3] as notaries public in this town. They are both very clever men. Officers in the Bank of Fayetteville.

[1]Jesse George Shepherd, a Fayetteville attorney, was a native of Virginia. He served as a member of the House of Commons (1854-1857, 1862-1865), speaker of the House (1856-1857), superior court judge (1858-1860), and member of the Council of State (1866-1867). Cheney, *North Carolina Government*, 180, 324, 362, 371n, 1113-1114; Oates, *Fayetteville*, 547, 861.

[2]W. G. Matthews sold dry goods, groceries, and guns in Fayetteville in 1849. Oates, *Fayetteville*, 749.

[3]Alexander McPherson was elected Fayetteville town treasurer in 1868. Oates, *Fayetteville*, 277.

David S. Reid to Henrietta S. Reid RCC

Executive Mansion,
City of Raleigh,
Sunday, Aug. 29, 1852.

The first night after leaving you I staid at Uncle Calvins, the next at Hillsboro, and arrived here on Monday evening last, leaving Rebecca[1] at St. Mary's. We encountered mud and rain on the route, but reached here safely and in health. Found all well and every thing going on as well as I expected. The crop of grass large, and Cabbage small. On Wednesday or thursday Sally[2] Called. I suppose she is pleased with her position, tho' I asked her but few questions. Mr. Holden called to see me the night I arrived here and I have seen him almost every day since that time. I have not seen his poor little Babe, tho' he informs me that she is doing remarkably well.

My friends here met me with great cordiality. There were but two persons holding office in the Capitol who voted against me, and they were E. B. Freeman[3] and James F. Taylor,[4] both of whom I learn made themselves exceedingly active against me. The leading Whigs here were utterly astonished at my election. I was surprised to learn that they had not the most distant idea of such a result! Dr. Hill[5] voted for me and gave me some of the Cigars he won on my election.

I have not seen Rebecca since we reached here. I sent Dave[6] up yesterday and he informed me she was well. Father Settle arrived here on thursday before dinner, and left on friday morning, in good health. He complained of the muddy roads, but appeared in good spirits. He visited Rebecca while here. Dave is well and makes himself quite easy here. Sq. and Tony & Maria[7] are all very well. Sq. and Rollo recognised me as old friends and cling to me like they would be the last to desert my standard or to disown me.

Our bacon was not at all injured. I find house-keeping infinitely less trouble than I expected, or it may be that I have seen so many *big troubles* this year that I have become somewhat indifferent to *little ones*. Tomorrow will be a week since I reached here and yet I do not remember to have rung a bell or scolded a servant during the time. Mrs. Henry[8] and Mrs. Roulhac[9] have tendered me any advice or apertance I may need in the way of house-keeping. Both of them as well as Mrs. J. B. Hinton[10] & others send love to you. No one here expected your return as they all seemed to have heard long before it was known to me that you did not expect to return with me.

To-day in the forenoon I attended service in the Baptist Church and heard an interesting sermon from the text, "What profit is it to a man to gain the whole world and lose his own soul?" In the afternoon by special invitation I attended service in Dr. Hintons church,[11] where I found a large congregation, the largest I believe that I have seen in any church in Raleigh, and heard an eloquent and interesting sermon preached from Ezekiel Ch 3 v. 5 & 6.

I am overwhelmed with business in consequence of a protracted absence from this city. I have had a severe head ache every day since I reached here, save one. Yesterday I laid down & took a nap and dreamed I visited you and found you gone to Mr. Perkin's.[12] I know no language, my dear wife, adequate to the expression of my great anxiety to see you. I hope you will be cheerful and meet the impending crisis with courage and fortitude. I have an abiding confidence that in the goodness and mercy of God all will be right. Dr. Williamson[13] left for home the day before yesterday. My love to Mother Settle,[14] sisters Caroline[15] and Fannie[16] and to Thomas[17] & David[18] if there. Receive my dear wife the ardent love of your affectionate husband. May God bless and preserve you, is my most earnest prayer.

PS. Mr. Wm. H. Haywood, jr.[19] & lady have gone North. Mr. H. has a cancer under his tongue, & the object of his visit is to procure medical aid. Serious doubts are entertained whether he will ever return. Miss Mag. Henry[20] has been sick at the springs.

P.S. High-water or some other cause prevented the western mail from arriving yesterday.

---

[1]Rebecca W. Settle (ca. 1838-1853), sister-in-law of David Settle Reid, was the daughter of Thomas Settle and Henrietta Graves Settle of Rockingham County. She "was much beloved by her school-companions and friends, for her gentle and amiable disposition." Settle Family Cemetery, Reidsville; *North-Carolina Standard*, March 2, 1853; student records for the 1852-1853 academic year at St. Mary's School, now St. Mary's Junior College, are no longer extant.

[2]Sally was the Reids' servant who had been lent to W. W. Holden, following the death of his wife, to care for the Holden children. William W. Holden to Henrietta S. Reid, June 26, 1852. Rockingham Community College Historical Collection.

[3]Edmund B. Freeman (1795-1868) was secretary of the state Constitutional Convention of 1835. A Massachusetts native, in 1829 he published the Halifax *Minerva*, whose name was changed in 1830 to the *Roanoke Advocate*. He sold his interest in the paper and moved in 1834 to Raleigh, where his uncle the Reverend George Washington Freeman was rector, 1829-1840, of Christ Church. An advocate of southern rights, Edmund B. Freeman served for twenty-five years, 1843-1868, as clerk of the state supreme court. Cheney, *North Carolina Government*, 817; Powell, *DNCB*, II, 237-238.

[4]James F. Taylor (born circa 1823), resident of Raleigh in 1850, was state librarian. Seventh Census, 1850, Wake County, Population Schedule, 261.

[5]This was probably John H. Hill, Brunswick County physician and legislator. Cheney, *North Carolina Government*, 318; Sprunt, *Cape Fear*, 63.

[6]Probably Dave Settle, a slave, as David A. Settle, the governor's 12-year-old brother-in-law, is mentioned below as being elsewhere.

[7]Mariah Settle was a slave, identified in Thomas Settle's 1856 will as the wife of Matt, the governor's coachman. Settle Will, 258.

[8]Margaret Haywood Henry (born circa 1801) was widow of Louis D. Henry (1788-1846) of Fayetteville, state leader in the Democratic party and unsuccessful Democratic candidate for governor in 1842. *Raleigh Register*, January 5, 1821; Seventh Census, 1850, Wake County, Population Schedule, 281; Wheeler, *Sketches*, 129.

[9]Probably Catherine Roulhac (born circa 1811), second wife of Joseph Blount Gregoire Roulhac (1795-1856), who represented Bertie County in the state Constitutional Convention of 1835. His first wife was Frances Gray of Bertie County. He was a merchant in Raleigh during the 1840s and 1850s. Cheney, *North Carolina Government*, 817; *Raleigh Register*, January 30, 1856; Moses N. Amis, *Historical Raleigh with Sketches of Wake County and Its Important Towns* (Raleigh: Commercial Printing Company, 1913), 77; Seventh Census, 1850, Wake County, Population Schedule, 256.

[10]Margaret G. Hinton (1801-1856), wife of Dr. Joseph B. Hinton of Raleigh. Gravestone inscription, Raleigh City Cemetery; *Raleigh Register*, December 17, 1856.

[11]Joseph B. Hinton, previously identified, was pastor of the Christian Church in Raleigh from 1847 to 1860. See P. J. Kernodle, *Lives of Christian Ministers* (Richmond: Central Publishing Company, 1909), 224-227.

[12]Probably Abraham Perkins, a neighbor of the Thomas Settle family in Rockingham County. A Virginia native, Perkins, 78 years old in 1850, was patriarch of a large family. His son Constant Perkins (b. ca. 1814), a farmer, also lived nearby. Seventh Census, 1850, Rockingham County, Population Schedule, 24, 27.

[13]James E. Williamson, previously identified.

[14]Henrietta Williams Graves Settle (1799-1886) was a daughter of Azariah Graves and Elizabeth Williams of Caswell County, and sister to Calvin Graves. She married Thomas Settle of Rockingham County on September 21, 1820, but outlived her husband by more than twenty-eight years, dying January 14, 1886, at the home of her son-in-law Hugh K. Reid in Reidsville. One obituary noted: "She was greatly beloved and revered for her great qualities of heart and intellect. She raised a large family, all very superior people." *North State* (Greensboro), January 21, 1886; Powell, *DNCB*, II, 342; Reese and Fisher, *Settle Family*, 674.

[15]Caroline L. Settle, previously identified.

[16]Fannie K. Settle (b. 1833) married John W. Covington of Richmond County. After his death she married Oliver H. Dockery. Reese and Fisher, *Settle Family*, 676.

[17]Thomas Settle, Jr., previously identified.

[18]David A. Settle (1839-ca. 1906), youngest son of Thomas and Henrietta Settle. Reese and Fisher, *Settle Family*, 676.

[19]William H. Haywood, Jr., returned home to Raleigh, where he died on October 7, 1852. *Raleigh Register*, October 9, 1852.

[20]Margaret H. Henry (born circa 1837) was an unmarried resident of Raleigh in 1850 and member of the household of Mrs. Margaret Henry, identified above. She eventually married Edward Graham Haywood of Raleigh, who was the only one of William H. Haywood, Jr.'s, three sons to survive the Civil War. Seventh Census, 1850, Wake County, Population Schedule, 281; Ashe, *Biographical History*, VI, 302-303.

Thomas Settle to David S. Reid A&H-DSR

Williamston
Martin County N.Ca.
August 31st 1852

I arrived here on sunday evening[1] safely and in good health. I held Court on yesterday and got through the State Docket which was unusual for Martin. Your friends here are much rejoiced at your success and make many inquiries after you. I hope to hear from you often and hear that you and your wife are well. I have written to my wife this morning and hope to get a letter from home at Greenville next week. I am compeled to make this letter short for it is near the time for the court bell to ring. May the Lord protect and bless you and yours is the prayer of your affectionate Father

P.S. I fear the rains have been heavy up the country from the rain in the Roanoke

[1]August 29, 1852.

David S. Reid to Thomas Settle UNC-TS

Executive Mansion,
Raleigh
Sep. 8. 1852.

We are all well here, except Rebecca; she has been slightly indisposed to-day. I went up to St. Marys this afternoon and found her up. She will no doubt be entirely well in a day or two. I presume she has been eating too freely of fruit.

I received a letter from my dear wife on Saturday last, dated six days ago, and they were all well then.

They have had high freshets up the country. The Yadkin has been higher than in 1850, and the damage no doubt great. Dan River I learn was not as high by three or four feet as in 1850. I can get no very correct account of the devastating effects of the freshet in Rockingham. I suspect the loss amounts to about a third of the corn on the River, and a good deal of the Tobacco destroyed. I suppose you have more correct accounts from home of the extent your loss than I have received, tho' I have no idea that it is at all to be compared to what it was in 1850.

I am overwhelmed with business, and in my present situation feel quite uneasy and lonely—Never so much so, in all my life.[1]

I hope your health continues good and that you are having an agreeable circuit. Do not be uneasy about the freshet, for I trust you will have a bountiful crop after all.

Accept my love and best wishes. May God bless you.

PS. Mr. Haywood returned to this city on yesterday, quite feeble. No hopes are entertained of his recovery, and it is not supposed that he can survive more than a few weeks at farthest.[2] How uncertain are the things of this life!

---

[1]Not only was Reid without his wife, Henrietta, who had gone home during the latter part of her first pregnancy to stay with her mother in Rockingham County, but his father Reuben Reid had recently died. The *Raleigh Register* of July 3, 1852, reported his passing: "DIED. In Rockingham county, on Tuesday the 22d instant, Reuben Reid, Esq., aged about 68 years, the father of the present Governor of the State."

[2]See David S. Reid to Henrietta S. Reid, August 29, 1852, Rockingham Community College Historical Collection, note 19.

This picture of David S. Reid, Henrietta Reid, and David S. Reid, Jr. (born on September 10, 1852), may have been the inspiration for William W. Holden's poem on page 453. Original photograph courtesy of Lucile Reid Fagg; copy from the Division of Archives and History.

The Executive Mansion, residence of North Carolina governors from 1816 until the Civil War, stood at the south end of Fayetteville Street on the site now occupied by Memorial Auditorium. The photograph, from the Albert Barden Collection, was taken around 1865. It contrasts sharply with Emma Morehead Whitfield's painting [*above*], dated 1922, which portrays the mansion of 1841. Photographs from the files of the Division of Archives and History.

Thomas Settle, Jr., to Henrietta S. Reid RCC

Richmond Hill.
Septr. 23. 1852.

I received a letter from Sister Caroline a day or two since informing me of the important fact that I was an uncle.

I did not know that I would feel so proud of a nephew, I would give most any thing to see him.

I hope you are both doing well, I wish I could hear every mail how you are coming on.

Make some of them give me a description of your boy. Whom does he favor. Has he his fathers knack at getting along in this world, Any thing they could write to me about "His diminutive Excellency" would be very interesting.

I see from Sister Carolines letter that you have named him David S. Jr. A good and lucky name. I suppose the Governor has been up before this. give him my best love and tell him that I wish him much happiness with his boy.

I hope to see you all this winter. God grant that it may be in health and happiness. Your boy will then be of a more interesting age.

I have enjoyed very good health since I left you, and am studying tolerably well. I hear nothing of interest in these parts. In fact nothing of interest occurs.[1]

I was rejoiced to learn that Uncle Josiah[2] had given his consent for cousin Fannie[3] to marry I. H. Graves.[4] I hope it is a prudent match and that he will do something "*very clever*" for them.[5]

Sid Smith[6] of Raleigh (old Bens son) who is here reading law received a letter last evening from his father[7] stating that W. H. Haywood was expected to die in a few days. The ravages of his Cancer seems to have been very rapid.

I wish some of you would write to me very often. I am always glad to hear from any of you, but I am particularly anxious just at this time to hear how you and D. S. Jr. are coming on. I can say nothing about myself except that I am well &c. but any of the thousand little things which occur in the family circle would deeply interest me, so write *very* often.

I had almost forgot to say tell the Governor that the Author of the Doweltown letter[8] or rather the letter giving an account of the Doweltown discussion is Samuel M. Lowrie,[9] of Mecklenburgh. a law student of Judge P.[10]; who obtained a County Court license last August in Morganton. A good democrat. My love to Mother all the rest.

[1]Thomas Settle, Jr., previously identified, was a student at the Richmond Hill law school conducted from 1847 to 1877 at Richmond Hill, the Yadkin County home of Judge Richmond Mumford Pearson, also previously identified. Located in an isolated section of what is now Yadkin County, some five miles or more northwest of the present-day town of East Bend, the school was forty miles from the nearest railroad, at High Point. Until the North Carolina Railroad was completed there was no rail connection. From Rockford, a nearby village, Judge William Horn Battle in an 1851 letter to his wife wrote: "I shall certainly not be very sorry to leave here, as I think the place has as few attractions as any I have seen." In 1849, John M. de Berniere described Richmond Hill: "of all the lonesome places this gets worse. . . ." William Horn Battle to Lucy M. Plummer Battle, March 8, 1851, and John M. de Berniere to Kemp Plummer Battle, September 3, 1849, Battle Family Papers, Southern Historical Collection, University of North Carolina Library at Chapel Hill, hereinafter cited as Battle Family Papers. Samuel R. Wooten, "A History of Richmond Hill Law School" (unpublished master's thesis, Appalachian State Teachers College, 1963), 21, 44, hereinafter cited as "A History of Richmond Hill Law School."

[2]Josiah Settle (1799-1869), brother of Thomas Settle, was born in Rockingham County. On June 3, 1826, he married Frances L. Graves, sister of Henrietta Graves Settle and Calvin Graves, in Caswell County. Reese and Fisher state incorrectly in the Settle family history that after the death of his wife on October 7, 1829, Josiah sold his land in North Carolina and moved to Ohio. He never remarried while living in North Carolina, but as late as 1850 he owned 38 slaves and still lived with his daughter Fannie in Rockingham County on a plantation adjacent to those of his brother Thomas Settle and David S. Reid's father Reuben. Apparently, Josiah did not leave the state until after Fannie's marriage in late 1852 or early 1853. By September 1853 he was living in Tishomingo County, Mississippi, and then sold his Rockingham County plantation to Hugh K. Reid. In a final and seemingly extraordinary act for the uncle of an antebellum southern governor and United States senator, Josiah Settle removed to the free state of Ohio and in 1860 lived in Hanover Township, Butler County, in a household with a 45-year-old black woman, Nancy Settle, and seven children, all named Settle and all of whose color is listed as mulatto. One child, a 10-year-old boy, was named Josiah Settle, Jr. Seven-year-old Josephine was born in Mississippi, but Nancy and the other six children were born in North Carolina. No other nonwhite people and no other individuals born in either North Carolina or Mississippi were living in Hanover Township in 1860. There was no real estate listed for Josiah Settle, age 60, but Nancy Settle owned real estate valued at $8,000, an indication at least that he had signed property over to her. Robert Settle, one of the children, was still living in Hanover Township in 1870 and owned real estate worth $1,000, suggesting that he had by then inherited his one-eighth share of the property. The 1833 will of David Settle, Josiah's father, mentions among his slaves a "negro girl named Nancy . . . [and] her brother, named Bob," for whom Robert may have been named. Josiah Settle's will, probated September 29, 1869, in Butler County, Ohio, provided for his black and white children, and his estate papers refer to Nancy Settle as his widow. In return for a cash settlement of $1,000, his two white children, Elizabeth Settle Howard and Fannie Settle Graves, released all claims on any of Josiah Settle's estate in Ohio in favor of Nancy Settle and her children. Reese and Fisher, *Settle Family*, 686; Settle family cemetery, Reidsville Township, Rockingham County; Seventh Census, 1850, Rockingham County, Population Schedule, 26, Slave Schedule, 112; Josiah Settle to Hugh K. Reid, September 19, 1853, Rockingham County Deeds, Book 2D, p. 70; Eighth Census, 1860, Butler County, Ohio, Population Schedule,

162; Ninth Census, 1870, Butler County, Ohio, 184; Will of David Settle, Rockingham County Wills, B, 73; Estate papers of Josiah Settle, 1869-1870, Probate Court, Butler County, Ohio.

[3]Fannie Hamin Settle was born circa 1829 in Rockingham County, the daughter of Josiah Settle and Frances L. Graves. In 1850 she was living on her father's plantation in Rockingham County. Reese and Fisher, *Settle Family*, 686; Seventh Census, 1850, Rockingham County, Population Schedule, 26.

[4]I. H. Graves, "of Georgia," was likely a relation of the extended Graves family of Caswell and Rockingham counties, although he has not been further identified. Reese and Fisher, *Settle Family*, 686.

[5]This appears to be an allusion to dowry gifts. Henrietta had recently received a 699-acre plantation from her own father. The phrase "*very clever*," both in quotation marks and underlined, appears to indicate Thomas's approval of this practice and his wish that his and Henrietta's cousin Fannie will be the recipient of similar generosity from her own father.

[6]Sidney Smith (b. circa 1831) was in 1850 a resident in the Raleigh household of John Hutchings, age 54, who owned real estate valued at $14,000. Sidney A. Smith of Wake County was licensed in December 1853 by the state supreme court to practice law in the county courts. Sidney A. Smith, age 30, then a resident of Johnston County, enlisted in Wake County on March 18, 1862, as a private in Company D, 47th Regiment, North Carolina Troops, served briefly as a second lieutenant but was reduced to ranks and detailed as a nurse by reason of permanent disability for field duty. He may be the same Sidney Smith who enlisted as a private in Company F, 45th Regiment, North Carolina Troops, at Camp Holmes near Raleigh on November 5, 1863, for the duration of the war, although there were at least five men named Sidney Smith from North Carolina who served in Confederate military units. Seventh Census, 1850, Wake County, Population Schedule, 267; *North-Carolina Standard*, January 4, 1854; Manarin and Jordan, *North Carolina Troops*, III, 367, VI, 598, XI, 80, 283, 291, 303.

[7]Benjamin Smith was a member of the Committee of 50 appointed by the City of Raleigh and Wake County to prepare for the visit of President James K. Polk in 1847. William Dallas Haywood to James K. Polk, May 8, 1847, Polk Papers, Library of Congress.

[8]The "Doweltown letter," like the previously mentioned "Greensboro letter," was a Democratic party-slanted press report of a campaign debate between Reid and Kerr. Dowellton, located in central Yadkin County in the vicinity of modern Harmony Grove Church, was the site of the first court held in the newly created county in 1851. The gubernatorial candidates spoke at Yadkin Court House on Tuesday, July 6, 1852. The "Doweltown letter" is a reference to an article in W. W. Holden's *North-Carolina Standard* titled "Discussion at Yadkin Courthouse," by a correspondent identified only with the pseudonym "Ho Demos." *North-Carolina Standard*, July 28, 1852; *People's Press*, June 26, 1852; Powell, *North Carolina Gazetteer*, 148.

[9]Samuel J. Lowrie, born about 1829 in Mecklenburg County, was practicing law there at the outbreak of the Civil War. Settle gives his middle initial as "M," but most sources cite it as "J." He was appointed a first lieutenant in the "Charlotte Artillery" in 1861 and evidently also served later in the Confederate Navy. Manarin and Jordan, *North Carolina Troops*, I, 63, 546; IX, 586.

[10]Richmond Mumford Pearson, previously identified.

Fanny Settle to Thomas Settle [Jr.] RCC

Rockingham Co.
Sept 30th 1852

Sister Henrietta received your most welcome letter this morning, and requests me to answer it. We are all well. Sister H and her little boy continue to improve. You asked for a description of him; he is decidedly the prettiest little creature you ever saw, He has black eyes, brown hair, very fair skin & a high forehead just like his Father's. I have [been] quite beside myself since his advent, if I can't hold him all the time, I hang around his cradle to look at him. I am bad enough on any pretty little baby, so you can well imagine what a terrible time of it this little fellow has with me. Sister Caroline is as bad or worse than I am about him. Sister Henrietta received a letter from Gov Reid this morning. We also had one from Father & Becca[1] a day or too since; they were all very well. Aunt Lucinda Ellington[2] & cousin Rhoda Scott[3] have both been dangerously ill when we heard from them last, they were improving. Sister Caroline & myself went to church last Sunday, and heard Mr. Roberson[4] preach a very good sermon. He had quite a large congregation. Cousin Cornelia Graves[5] was married a week or too since to Mr Lewis Tuberville[6] of Virginia, & I suppose is doing very well. I have not received a letter from Minna Haywood[7] in a good while, nor can I expect it; they must be in great distress. We are driving on just like we were when you left. Sister Caroline[,] Drape[8] & myself take sprees occasionally in the old buggy. They are so busy in the crop, that we can get the driver & horses only on Sunday for church. What is Lizzie Pearson[9] about now a days? has she come out for a grown lady? Give my best love to her. Mother intends sending for Davy[10] the last of this week, you would have been amused to have seen Davy feeling in the little baby's mouth for his teeth the first time he ever saw him, he did it to make us laugh. Brother you have no idea how much we miss you, & how we want to see you; do let us hear from you often. Mother, Sisters Henrietta & Caroline & little David S. Reid jr join me in much love to you. Write soon, dear Brother, to your affectionate Sister

P. S. I send you a lock of little Davy's hair. Sister H says, she hopes to be able to write to you soon.

---

[1]Rebecca Settle, previously identified.

[2]Lucinda Ellington (1806-1852), daughter of David and Rhoda Mullins Settle, died in Rockingham County in October 1852. She was married on July 2, 1830, to John Waddell Ellington of Rockingham County. Reese and Fisher, *Settle Family*, 688-689.

[3]Rhoda Scott, previously identified, was the wife of William Scott and a sister of David S. Reid.

[4]John Robertson (born 1805) was a Missionary Baptist minister residing in the western division of Rockingham County in 1850. He was pastor in 1860 of Hogan's Creek Baptist Church. Seventh Census, 1850, Rockingham County, Population Schedule, 65; Huggins, *History of North Carolina Baptists*, 205.

[5]Cornelia W. Graves (born 1835) was a daughter of William Graves of Yanceyville and his wife Ann L., whose maiden name was also Graves and who was a sister of Henrietta Graves Settle. Hence, Cornelia was first cousin to both the writer and the recipient of this letter. Seventh Census, 1850, Caswell County, Population Schedule, 174; Will of Elijah Graves, Sr., Caswell County Wills (microfilm), Book R, 359, Archives, Division of Archives and History, Raleigh, hereinafter cited as Elijah Graves, Sr. Will; William Graves Will; Will of Azariah Graves, Caswell County Wills (microfilm), Book Q, 373, Archives, Division of Archives and History, Raleigh, hereinafter cited as Azariah Graves Will.

[6]Lewis W. Tuberville (also spelled Turbeville) was issued a marriage license on August 30, 1852, in Caswell County, and he and Cornelia W. Graves were married there on September 14, 1852. Caswell County Marriage Bonds, 1780-1868, unpaginated (microfilm), Archives, Division of Archives and History, Raleigh, hereinafter cited as Caswell County Marriage Bonds.

[7]Minerva Haywood, nicknamed "Minna," was one of the six daughters of former Democratic United States senator William Henry Haywood, Jr., previously identified, of Raleigh. He was terminally ill and died one week after the date of this letter. Powell, *DNCB*, III, 89-90.

[8]Draper Settle was a Negro slave listed in the 1857 inventory of the property belonging to the estate of Thomas Settle filed in the November term 1857 Rockingham County Court of Pleas and Quarter Sessions. Rockingham County Inventory Docket of Accounts and Sales, 1855-1865, p. 242 (microfilm), Archives, Division of Archives and History, Raleigh.

[9]Elizabeth Pearson, daughter of Judge Richmond M. Pearson, was married in Yadkin County on May 24, 1860, to John H. Bullock. Yadkin County Marriage Bonds, unpaginated (microfilm), Archives, Division of Archives and History, Raleigh.

[10]Davy Settle, a slave, previously identified, who was at this time with Governor Reid at the governor's residence in Raleigh.

Sarah J. Hale[1] *to David S. Reid* A&H-DSR

Philadelphia,
Oct. 2d 1852

Mr. Godey[2] sent you, by yesterday's mail, a copy of the Lady's Book; in the Eds. Table are some suggestions respecting the Annual Thanksgiving.

I feel sure that a gentleman of your good sense will not regard these less because made by a woman. The Festival is social and domestic, prepared and presided over by ladies; and could it become the occasion of promoting sectional peace and harmony, the happiness of my own sex would be both extended and secured.

Will you, Sir, take this subject into consideration?[3] Should it seem good, will you aid, by your influence and example, the permanent establishment of the *last Thursday of November* as the true American day of Thanksgiving?

---

[1]Sara Josepha Buell Hale (1788-1879), editor and author, was literary editor of *Godey's Lady's Book* and a strong advocate of education for women. *CDAB*, 384.

[2]Louis Antoine Godey (1804-1878) published, among other magazines, *Godey's Lady's Book*. *CDAB*, 347.

[3]Reid was already aware of and interested in this movement, as he had in November the previous year issued a Thanksgiving proclamation. *North-Carolina Standard*, November 26, 1851.

Special Message of David S. Reid to the General Assembly A&H-GLB

Executive Department,
Raleigh
October 4, 1852

The meeting of the Legislature affords a fit occasion for the expression of deep-felt gratitude to an all-wise Providence for the many blessings bestowed upon us as a Republic, as a State, and as a People.

With the advice of the council of State, it was deemed absolutely necessary to call a meeting of the General Assembly at an earlier day than was provided for the regular meeting thereof, for the purpose of having legislative action in relation to the election of President and vice President of the United States. This necessity arose in consequence of the action of congress apportioning the Members of the House of Representatives among the several states, according to the census of 1850, by which the state of North Carolina will be entitled to only ten electoral votes, while the present Act of Assembly provides for the election of eleven electors. The communication of the Executive to the council of State, and the proceedings of that body thereon, and the officeal certificate of the Secretary of the Interior in relation to the appointment under the seventh census, are herewith transmitted.

Laying off the state in districts would impose the necessity on the people of making new nominations of candidates for Electors; which, for want of intervening time, would operate very inconveniently at the ensuing election. It is therefore recommended that an Act be passed, providing for the election, on the Tuesday after the first Monday in November next, of ten Electors of President and vice President; that the existing laws prescribing the qualification of voters, the manner of holding the election and making returns, as well as the penalty imposed for illegal voting be continued in force.

The constitution requires the Senatorial districts to be laid off by the General Assembly "at its first session after the year one thousand eight hundred and fifty one," and that the apportionment of the House of Commons shall be made by the General Assembly at the respective periods when the districts for the Senate are directed to be laid off.

In regard to amendments to the constitution by Legislative enactment, it is provided in the constitution, that: If after such publication, the alteration proposed by the preceeding General Assembly shall be agreed to, in the first session thereafter, by two-thirds of the whole representation in each House of the General Assembly, after the same shall have been read three times on three several days in each House, then the said General Assembly shall prescribe a mode by which the amendment may be submitted, to the qualified voters of the House of Commons throughout the state &c.

It is respectfully submitted whether public convenience will not be promoted by repealing for the session, the law requiring the meeting of the General Assembly on the third Monday in November, and proceeding to act on the ordinary business of legislation, thereby having but one instead of two sessions. Should the General Assembly decide to adopt this course, when informed of that fact, my regular Message will be communicated accordingly.

Biennial Message of David S. Reid to the General Assembly A&H-GLB

Executive Department
Raleigh,
Oct 14th 1852

Biennial Message

To the Honorable the General Assembly of the State of North Carolina;

Favored by a bountiful Providence with Peace and Plenty, the present would seem a most auspicious period for directing our thoughts and energies to such objects of legislation as are calculated to advance the great interests of the State, and to perpetuate the blessings of liberty.

Government was instituted for the security of the rights of persons and of property, and for the promotion of the substantial prosperity and happiness of the people. These objects, controlled by constitutional limitations, constitute the great political chart to guide Legislative and Executive action.

Among the subjects which claim the consideration of the General Assembly, is the question of Constitutional Reform. At the Session of 1850-'51, the General Assembly passed, by a constitutional majority, a bill to amend the Constitution, so as to extend to every freeman, who now has the right to vote for the Commons, the right to vote also for the Senate. The Executive Proclamation on this subject, was published agreeably to the requirements of the Legislature. I earnestly recommend that said amendment be passed by the constitutional majority of the present General Assembly, and submitted to the voters of the state for ratification.

The Constitution, as it now stands, prohibits every man who does not own fifty acres of land from voting in the Senate. This provision, it is believed, disfranchises in the Senate about one half of the free white men of the state, and embraces in its proscription a large class, who, in point of merit, intelligence and patriotism, are not inferior to any portion of our population. The proposition is not to take from the landholders their just rights but to elevate another meritorious class of our people to equal priveleges at the ballot-box. It is a marked feature in the progress of this reform, that a great portion of the free-holders, with a commendable disinterestedness, regarded this as a question of principal, and of right, and among them were found its earnest advocates and most zealous supporters.

A large majority of the people, in every portion of the state, are in favor of Equal Suffrage, and prefer the Legislative mode of effecting it. The greater part of the expense necessary to attain Equal Suffrage has already been incurred; and now to abandon the legislative mode, and to rely upon the Convention mode, would not only cause delay, but an increase of expenditure. The Convention mode is impracticable. The constitutional majority cannot be obtained in favor of a Convention; and, if the fate of this question is made to depend upon calling a Convention—its defeat may be regarded as certain. The Legislative mode is not only expressly provided for in our State Constitution, but is also recognized in the Constitution of the United States, as one of the modes for ratifying amendments, by the states, to the Federal Constitution.

This mode affords time for examination and reflection in relation to the amendment proposed, and finally, when it shall have passed two successive Legislatures, it cannot be adopted without the sanction of a majority of the voters of the state at the ballot-box. "A free, open and unrestricted Convention" could have no such restriction upon its power. Hence, a well founded apprehension exists in the minds of many ardent friends of constitutional reform, against the convention mode of effecting it. A Convention is impracticable and inexpedient, and I regard the Legislative, as the safe and only practicable mode, at this time, of amending the constitution.

A change of the Basis of Representation would be fraught with mischief. Even the agitation of the subject is calculated to destroy that harmony among the various portions of the State, which is so essential to prosperity and happiness. Let us unite in directing our attention to objects that may produce more beneficial results.

It is a circumstance gratifying, and at the same time highly complimentary to the State, that however much the people may desire constitutional reform, they promptly reject any other than a constitutional mode to attain it.

The election of Judges and Justices of the Peace, by the people, and for terms less than for life, are questions of constitutional reform, which I recommend to the favorable consideration of the General Assembly.

There is no object of more general importance than Common Schools, nor is there any question more worthy of the favorable consideration of the General Assembly and the people of the State.

It is contended by some that the present mode of dividing the School Fund, is unjust, and that it ought to be divided according to white instead of federal population. The present basis of distribution has met the approval of many successive Legislatures, and I do not see any good reason to recommend a change in this respect. No mode can be devised that will operate with equal benefit to all the counties.

It is submitted, whether the appointment of a general superintendant may not tend to improve common schools, and to advance the cause of education. Such an officer could no doubt do much to produce uniformity in the system, and to diffuse a proper spirit on the subject throughout the state. It is believed that the present system has greatly diminished the number of private schools. In many instances, it would seem that a reliance upon the common school prevents the district from providing a private school; and it is often found that a district has a very imperfect school, and that only for a very short period during the year. The schools should, if possible, be of such a character as to make it the interest of all classes to patronize them; for they are intended alike for the poor and the rich.

The execution of the system is more defective than the system itself. One case why our schools are not in a more flourishing condition, arises from the fact that public attention has not been sufficiently aroused to the importance of the subject. Sparseness of population and, and the want of adequate means to employ suitable teachers, are the principal obstacles that impede the progress of the system. The question arises, whether it is better to endure the system, with its present limited but gradually increasing benefits, or to improve it at once, by a resort to an increase of taxation. I can immagin no object for which an increase of taxation would be more justifiable and commendable. Contributions for public education have been aptly compared to the vapor drawn from the earth, not to exhaust, but to be returned in fertilizing showers.

Our Common School system, however, imperfect as it is, is producing lasting and beneficial effects. It will improve as we advance in experience and increase in population. During the past year, upwards of one hundred and twenty eight thousand were distributed from the Literary Fund, among the several counties of the state, and an equal amount will be distributed during the present year. The principal of the fund is gradually but slowly increasing, and is becoming more productive.

As yet, there has been nothing actually received from escheats, but it is believed that the act passed upon this subject at the last session, will, in the course of time, greatly increase the Literary Fund.

The President and Directors of the Literary Fund will in due time submit a report, showing the condition of the fund, and the proceedings of the Board in relation to other subjects committed to their management.

A judicious system of Internal Improvements by the state, has ever been regarded as a subject of great importance, and entitled to the favorable consideration of the General Assembly. The want of cheap transportation is deeply felt by the agricultural, commercial, manufacturing and mining interests of the whole State. To overcome this inconvenience could not fail to increase the reward of every industrial pursuit, and add to the wealth and prosperity of the people of the State. Believing that the members of the General Assembly, coming from the various counties, will be fully prepared to give due consideration to the claims of every portion of the state, I do not feel called upon to decide between the particular merits of the many public improvements which demand the patronage of the state. Works of internal improvement necessarily involve a large expenditure, and should be undertaken with a due regard to their practicability, and to the adequacy of the resources and means necessary to complete them. The General Assembly, which authorises a work of internal improvement, ought, as a general rule, to provide for raising the means necessary for its completion. Whether public opinion, and the condition of the treasury will justify the state at this time in embarking in other and new objects of improvement, and if so, to what extent, is a question which is submitted to the prudence and wisdom of the General Assembly. A wise and prudent system all should approve; a wild and extravagant scheme all should deprecate.

The requisite amount having been subscribed according to the terms of the Act passed at the last session of the General Assembly to incorporate the Raleigh and Gaston Railroad Company, in the month of October last, the Commissioners on the part of the state, delivered over the Road and fixtures to the new Company. Since that time, the Road has ceased to be under the control and management of the state. Since the transfer to the new Company, the road has been undergoing an entirely new superstructure, which is nearly complete.

This improvement has already enhanced facilities to the state. The stock has been subscribed to form the connecting link between this Road and the Wilmington and Raleigh and Seaboard and Roanoke Railroads, and this important work is in course of construction.

At the last session a Resolution was passed, authorizing the President and Commissioners of the Raleigh and Gaston Railroad to anticipate the receipts of the road by the purchase of two hundred and fifty tons of iron, for the purpose of repairing the road, and authorizing them to pledge the receipts of the road for the iron thus purchased. It was provided that the state should, in no manner, or in any event, be held liable for the purchase money; and, when the new charter should be accepted, the iron should be sold for the binefit of the state. In pursuance of this resolution, the President of the road purchased two hundred and fifty tons of iron from Mr. Anderson, of Richmond, and it was applied to repairing the Road. A part of the iron has been taken up by the new Company, and a part of it, I presume, still remains on the road. The new Company has made no proposition to purchase the iron. Unless the Legislature shall otherwise direct, the iron will be sold for the benefit of the state.

It is believed that, after the settlement of the accounts and the payment of liabilities for the expenses of the Road, there will be little, if any thing applicable to the payment of the debt contracted for this iron. If the Legislature requires the proceeds of the sale of the iron to be placed in the Treasury, it would prevent Mr. Anderson from receiving any portion of his debt. Should the proceeds be applied to this debt they would not pay one half of it. I recommend that the General Assembly authorize the proceeds of the sale of the iron to be applied towards the payment of the debt contracted for its purchase; and it is submitted, whether an appropriation shall be made to pay the balance.

The Report of the President in relation to the affairs of the Road, while under the control of the state, will in due time be communicated to the General Assembly. In enrolling the Bill passed at the last session to incorporate the Raleigh and Gaston Rail Road Company, it is believed that some of the sections as it passed were omitted, which renders farther legislation on the subject necessary. One of the omitted sections authorized the appointment of four directors on the part of the individual stockholders and only three on the part of the state. The Board of Internal Improvements only appointed the number provided for in the omitted section. But the state owns one half of the stock, and it is believed she ought to have the appointment of one half of the Directors, and it is recommended that such provision be made by law.

An Engineer was employed to survey Neuse River, and the balance of the appropriation made under the act of 1850-'51, after paying the expenses of the survey, has been subscribed to the Neuse River Navigation Company, as directed by said act, and a part of the appropriation paid to the Treasurer of the Company. This is a work of importance, and its completion promises highly beneficial results. The Report of the Engineer appointed to make the survey is herewith transmitted.[1]

Three Commissioners were appointed under the act of 1848-'9, to superintend the improvement of Tar River. This is a desirable improvement, but it is doubted whether the appropriation is sufficient to accomplish the object for which it was intended.

The whole amount of subscription of the state, to the Cape Fear and Deep River Navigation Company, has been paid. The work is progressing, and promises to open new and valuable commercial advantages not hitherto enjoyed by the state.

Under a Resolution passed at the last session of the General Assembly, the Public Treasurer transferred two thousand shares of the stock owned by the state, in the Wilmington and Raleigh Railroad Company, to the Wilmington and Manchester Railroad Company, whereby the State became a stockholder in the important improvement under the charge of that Company. In directing the transfer of the stock, the resolution did not make any change in regard to the number of directors to which the state should be entitled in the Wilmington and Raleigh Railroad Company. Under the circumstances, the Board of Internal Improvements did not feel authorized to make any change in the number of directors appointed on the part of the state. The stock transferred, is represented by the state in the Wilmington and Manchester Railroad Company. If the Legislature intended that the number of directors on the part of the state, should only be in proportion to her stock, farther legislation on the subject would appear to be necessary.

The Wilmington and Raleigh Railroad, with energetic management has of late overcome, to a considerable extent, the early embarrassments this important work had to encounter. The Company has commenced paying dividends, thus enabling the Literary Board to distribute an increased amount for the support of Common Schools.

The North Carolina Railroad, it is believed, is progressing as rapidly as could be expected, considering the circumstances attending its commencement and prosecution. This improvement promises to afford new and increased means of transportation to a considerable portion of the state, heretofore deprived of such facilities. The President of the Company will, in due time, submit a report in relation to the progress and condition of the work.

It is probable that application will be made during the present year, or early in the next, for the first instalment of the States' subscription to the stock of this road. To raise the sum, state bonds are authorized to be issued and sold. It is believed that this loan, as well as all others required, by the state, can be procured upon better terms by authorizing the Publi[c] Treasurer to issue Coupon Bonds.

An Act was passed at the last session of the General Assembly, appropriating twelve thousand dollars, "out of the first moneys collected after the first day of January 1852, from the Cherokee bonds, and from the sale of Cherokee lands," for the survey of a Railroad route from Salisbury to the Tennessee line. The Agent states, that only a small sum applicable to this appropiration has been collected. It was not therefore in the power of the Board of Internal Improvements, to procure the execution of the survey. It is to be regretted, that this could not be done before the commencement of the present session of the Legislature, as the contemplated line runs through a portion of the state, where the people are deprived of the means of convenient transportation, and are therefore deeply interested in the subject. It is uncertain, under the present Act, when a sufficient sum will be collected to defray the expense of the survey. Should the Legislature desire it to be made at an early period an appropriation for that purpose will be the means by which it can surely be accomplished.

The Fayetteville and Western Plank Road is in course of extension. The whole amount of the state's subscription to this work has been paid. The stock has already been paying dividends into the state Treasury. This not only bids fair to be a valuable improvement, but the stock it is believed will be a good investment for the State. The Report of the President and Directors of the Company is herewith transmitted.

An Agent was appointed to superintend the construction of the Western Turn-pike road. A considerable portion of the Road has already been made, and other parts of it are under contract. The Agent, it is believed, has faithfully performed his duty in superintending the work. Toll gatherers have already been appointed on the portion of the road completed, but a report of the amount of tolls collected has not yet been received.

It is respectfully submitted whether legislative action is not necessary on the subject of public high-ways. This is a subject of general importance to the state, and has been too much neglected. Good roads will be found to advance the interests of all the industrial pursuits of the state. The mode of assessing the labor to build and repair public highways is unequal and unjust. The work done on the public roads is a tax paid in labor. It often occurs that a person of quite limited estate contributes in the course of the year a considerable amount of labor to Roads, while his nearest neighbor who has a large estate contributes but little or nothing at all for that purpose.

It becomes the duty of the present General Assembly to lay off the state into Electoral, Congressional, and Senatorial Districts; and apportion the members of the House of Commons among the several counties of the state.

It is respectfully submitted, whether public convenience and the ends of public justice do not require the formation of one or two additional Judicial Circuits, and the election of a corresponding number of Judges.

The fiscal year closes on the 31st day of October, when the Public Treasurer will submit his Report giving a detailed account of the operations and condition of the Treasury.

The state debt is as follows:

State bonds already issued	$1,224,000
Loans authorized by law for various works of Internal Improvement for which it is expected bonds will be issued during the next two years	2,140,000
Total,	$3,364,000

The Report of the Comptroller for the fiscal year, ending the 31st of October 1851, is herewith communicated. It will be seen that the taxes paid into the Treasury during the year 1851, amounted to the sum of $157,137 71. The Revenue Act, passed at the last session, will, it is believed, increase the revenue paid into the Treasury this year, about $20,000. Neither the demands on the Treasury, nor public convenience would seem to require any increase of taxation during the next two years. No more money should be collected from the people, than is necessary to defray the expenses of good and economical government. Taxation is indispensable, but it is one of the first duties of the statesman, to endeavor to equalize the burdens as well as the benefits of government.

For many years the demands upon the Treasury were so limited, that but little attention was paid to the subject of taxation. Of late years, Internal Improvements and other public objects have increased the expenditures, and our financial system has assumed a more important aspect. It will be perceived, that of the $157,137 71 tax, paid into the Treasury in 1851, $37,059 32 was collected on land and town property; $36,133 07 on polls; $25,007 87 on interest tax; and $12,822 61 on store tax; amounting in the aggregate to the sum of $111, 022 87, paid into the Treasury on these principal items of taxation; and $46,014 84, paid on all others. The land and poll tax amounted to $73,192 39. The tax for county purposes is collected entirely on land and polls; and the amount paid into the Public Treasury on these two items is small, when compared with the tax paid for County purposes. We have no returns to show the amount of county tax collected in the State.

It is believed, however, that not more than twenty percent of the whole amount collected on land and polls, goes into the Public Treasury, and I have based the estimate of the average amount paid on land accordingly. An examination into the existing revenue laws will show that the present system operates very unequally. At present, $1000, loaned at interest pays 180 cents, while $1000, hoarded against the public convenience and public policy, pays nothing at all; $1000 invested in land, pays 300 cents, while $1000 invested in trade, pays 100 cents. Other unjust discriminations might be shown.

As a general rule, it is believed that the tax upon the estate of each person should be in proportion to its value, subject to such exceptions only as circumstances and fundamental principals may justify. Inasmuch as property on the one hand ought, not to be made the test of public privileges neither on the other hand ought the absence of property to exempt the person from bearing an equitable share of the public burden. Therefore it is thought just and proper to impose capitation tax. Slaves are regarded to some extent as both persons and property. The following wise provision in our state Constitution, which ought not to be departed from, defines the power of legislation upon this subject;

"Section III.

1. Capitation tax shall be equal throughout the state upon all individuals subject to the same.

2. All free males over the age of twenty-one years, and under the age of forty-five years, and all slaves over the age of twelve years, and under the age of fifty years, shall be subject to capitation tax, and no other person shall be subject to such tax; provided that nothing herein contained shall prevent exemptions of taxable polls as heretofore prescribed by law in cases of bodily infirmity."

It will be seen that slave property must form an exception in forming a system of ad valorem taxation. White males alone are subject to a poll-tax, while a poll-tax is imposed on both male and female slaves, and the period of taxation commences nine years earlier and continues five years longer. Thus it will appear that by taxing both sexes the amount of revenue collected from the tax on slaves is double the amount collected on white-polls, in proportion to the population of the two races; and the difference in the duration of the period for which they are taxed is equivalent to one hundred percent more.

It is therefore obvious that in proportion to the whole number of each, the poll-tax on the slaves is three times as much as the poll-tax on the white population. So it will be found that this provision in the Constitution has imposed a tax on slaves in the two-fold character of persons and property, and that an ad valorem tax cannot be imposed on that species of estate.

Persons and property being the principal objects of taxation, they should bear a fair and just relation to each other, in a system of revenue. It is believed that, after excepting slaves, each person's estate, real and personal, including money, whether at interest or not, ought to be taxed alike, according to value. This would require every person to contribute in proportion to the value of his or her estate, and would equalize the public burden between the various classes, upon principals of justice. I know of no better rule to ascertain the ability of the owner to pay, or the degree of protection his estate requires from government, than by resorting to the actual value of such estate.

This system need not interfere with taxing certain employments, and the income on professions, as is now done. Such persons as do not possess personal estate of the value of one hundred and fifty dollars, ought to be exempt from property tax, and an exemption of a like amount might be made in favor of all others. A system of revenue, based upon these principals, is recommended to the favorable consideration of the General Assembly.

On the 18th of May, 1851, Asa Biggs, B. F. Moore and R. M. Saunders, Esquires, were appointed commissioners, under the act of the last session of the General Assembly, to revise the public statute laws of this state. On the 2nd day of August, 1852, R. M. Saunders sent in his resignation, which, in consequence of my necessary absence, did not reach me until the 24th of that month. This letter of resignation is herewith communicated. I have received no official report from the commissioners; but in the latter part of the month of August, it came to my knowledge that the commissioners, prior to the date of this resignation, had decided not to report the revisal to the present Legislature. Under all the circumstances, it was deemed advisable not to fill the vacancy until the subject was submitted to the General Assembly. It is due to state that the commissioners were appointed with the hope and expectation that they would be able to complete their labor by the usual time of the meeting of the Legislature. They will, no doubt, in due time, report directly to the General Assembly, when such action can be taken as may seem expedient.

Professor Emmons was appointed under the act passed at the last session to make a geological and agricultural survey of the state. The work is progressing, and it is believed, will in the end be productive of highly beneficial results to the agricultural and mining interests of the state. Agriculture has been too long neglected, but it is hoped it may receive a new impulse, that will lead to the increased reward of the husbandman. It is believed, that an additional appropriation, to supply a boring apparatus, and to justify the collection of specimans, to be deposited at some suitable place or places, would promote the objects of the survey.

A report in relation to the progress of the survey is expected in due time, and, when received, will be laid before the General Assembly.

Commissioners were appointed to value the Cherokee lands, under the act passed at the last session for that purpose. It is believed that they have completed their duties, but their official report has not yet been received.

I herewith communicate the report for 1851, on the agent of the state for the collection of Cherokee lands, and the sale of Cherokee lands.

The report of the Cape Fear Navigation Company is herewith transmitted. Also, the report of the Wilmington and Manchester Railroad Company.

Resolutions of the General Assembly of New Hamshire, is relation to an Agricultural Bureau, and resolutions of the General Assembly of Florida, on the same subject, are communicated.

I also, transmit Resolutions passed by the Legislature of Connecticut, in favor of the Compromise measures passed by Congress.

My Letter Book is ready for your inspection, and will, on request, be laid before you by my private Secretary.

It will afford me great pleasure to co-operate with the General Assembly in all such measures as are calculated to promote the honor and welfare of the State.

---

[1]See W. Beverhout Thompson, "REPORT Upon the survey of the Neuse River, together with the plans and estimates for the improvement of the same, by W. Beverhout Thompson, Civil Engineer, 1852." *North-Carolina Star* (Raleigh), March 17, 1852, reprinted from the *Goldsboro Republican.*

James R. McLean to David S. Reid A&H-DSR
[Confidential]

Greensboro
Nov. 29th 52

Col William Gott[1] is the travelling mail agent, for North Carolina, Tennessee & Kentucky with a salary of $2000. per annum.

He was appointed to that place through the instrumentality of Mr Jas. T. Morehead.

I am requested by Mr Wilson S. Hill,[2] to say to you that he greatly desires to obtain that place after the coming in of the next administration—He is better qualified than Gott and has always stood inflexably by democracy, whether in good or evil report—He has devoted his whole time this summer, in aiding to secure your election as well as Gen. Peirce's.

I thought that I would write to you in time, believing that at the proper time you could secure him that appointment and I am sure there is no friend of yours more deserving it, than he. Please to write to me your views on the subject at your earliest convenience. Hill doesn't desire his intention to be made known at all and only wishes to know of what service you can be to him & what steps it would be necessary for him to take—I hope to be able to be in Raleigh a few days before the adjournment—I rejoice to see that free suffrage has gone triumphantly through the House Wishing you great health & happiness

I remain your friend & obt servant

---

[1]William Gott, a Whig appointee, was Greensboro postmaster in 1850 and 1851. Hamilton and Williams, *Graham Papers*, IV, 129n.

[2]Wilson S. Hill, previously identified, a Democrat, was a postal employee in Greensboro "for many years" prior to and including Gott's tenure as postmaster there. During the December 1851 term of the state supreme court he was licensed to practice law in the county courts of the state. On December 22, 1852, he was elected by the legislature for a second time to the Council of State and qualified on February 17, 1853. Hamilton and Williams, *Graham Papers*, IV, 130; *North-Carolina Standard*, January 3, 1852; *Greensborough Patriot*, January 8, 1853; Cheney, *North Carolina Government*, 178.

John E. Kendall[1] *to David S. Reid* A&H-DSR

Washington D. C.
Decr 13th 1852

I am at a loss to frame words into sentences in addressing you considering the slight acquaintance existing between us and more particularly in consideration of the subject of my address; but, in casting around me for the influence needed, in addition to that which I know I can command here, and knowing of, the friendship existing between you and a distinguished Senator from the west and a deserving Candidate before the last Democratic Convention at Baltimore for a nomination to the highest office in the gift of a generous people, with a sincere desire for his and your future prosperity in the course marked out, I am induced to ask of you a great favor—one which I have not much reason to believe you will grant but hope for.

I intend to be a Candidate for the office of Postmaster of this City under the administration to be brought into power on the fourth of March next, and to fortify myself I desire a letter of recommendation in general or specific terms from you and your friendly offices in obtaining one for me also from Hon S. A. Douglass to Gen. F. Pierce President elect of the United States.

I am personally known to Senator Douglass and have no doubt a word from you in my favor would secure me his influence with the incoming administration for what I ask.

I fear you will think me troublesome and perhaps presumptuous in addressing you on this subject, or at all; but the friendly offices of persons in power and influence with political friends for others in a more humble position, is deemed necessary and it is hoped you will so look upon the matter and excuse this appeal to your friendship and believe me that whatever course you may choose to adopt in reply will not change my regard for you and good wishes for your future welfare, though I should regret a decision adverse to my appeal.

Mrs. Kendall[2] and myself often look back with pleasure to the time spent together in the house with you while you were in Congress and feel gratified at your success in the political world in being twise successful in the contest for the chief magestracy of the State of North Carolina, and still more at the prospect to your personal happiness in taking to yourself a helpmate and wife, who you are so well calculated to please and make happy also.

Believe me as ever your friend and very obedient Servt

[1]John E. Kendall (born circa 1815), a native of New Hampshire, was assistant postmaster, 1847-1849, of the city of Washington. He retired "of his own volition" sometime during the 1849-1853 tenure of Whig postmaster William A. Bradley. Kendall's campaign to become postmaster was unsuccessful, as, on May 27, 1853, another Democrat, James G. Berret, was appointed to the position. By 1860 Kendall was employed as treasurer for a local telegraph company. Berret, a Maryland native who was chief clerk of the Pension Bureau prior to his postal appointment, was elected mayor of Washington in 1858 and again in 1861. Soon after his reelection he was arrested as a southern sympathizer and resigned his office. Eighth Census, 1860, District of Columbia, Population Schedule, 190; Madison Davis, "A History of the City Post-Office," in *Records of the Columbia Historical Society, Washington, D.C.* Compiled by the Committee on Publication and the Recording Secretary (Washington: Columbia Historical Society, 1903), VI, 186-190 passim, hereinafter cited as *Records of the Columbia Historical Society*.

[2]Ellen Kendall (born circa 1822) was a native of Pennsylvania. The Kendalls resided during the late 1850s and the 1860s in Ward 4 on E Street between Sixth and Seventh streets. Eighth Census, 1860, District of Columbia, Population Schedule, 190; Henry E. Davis, "Ninth and F Streets and Thereabout," in *Records of the Columbia Historical Society* (1902), V, 249.

R. J. Powell to David S. Reid A&H-DSR

Washington, D.C.
14th December 1852.

Enclosed herewith I Send the bill of expenses for preparing the No Carolina Block of Marble for the Washington National Monument—

This bill although dated the 23d ult—was not handed to me till yesterday—

The work is done in a Satisfactory manner, and the price charged I think reasonable and fair. I have used every precaution to prevent imposition either in the work or price and hope I have been Successful—

Not knowing but that you might desire the bill put in som particular form. I have thought it best to send it just as it is, which if not in the desired form will be put in Such as may be desired—You can enclose the draft payable to my order and please inform me as to the form and manner you wish the receipt—and I will comply with your wishes in the matter.

It was necessary to Send out a number of Special Agents of the P.O. Depot. to bear the Presidents Message to the various Telegraphic points throughout the [Country]—after ascertaining that no *Whig* from N.Carolina desired the appointment[1] for that region of [Country], I made application, but *Whiggery* was inexorable, an *abolition Whig*, from New York, who had not applied for the place, was hunted up, and the appointment given to him.—hence I was disappointed in my anticipated visit to the good old North State. Whiggery will So Soon be no more, that I do not know that we ought longer to pray for its extinction—but Such glaring proscriptions, in So Small a matter as referred to above I do hope will be Suitably rewarded—

I exceedingly regret the State of things Still existing, when I last heard, in the Legislature—My Surprise has all the while increased that a Single Democrat, Should fail to Support Mr. Dobbin[2]—If he were a man in any way objectionable, I Should feel less regret—but as I conceive no one can have a Single valid objection to him, on the contrary he possesses every requisite for the exalted station—I can but regard the cause of those who Still persist in voting against him with astonishment and regret—

I know not what, if anything, has been done by Judge Strange's[3] friends, but I do hope his name will be properly placed before Genl Pierce for a place in his Cabinet.

If Such a course meets your approval, I design having the Block of Marble formally presented on the 22nd February next—by probably Mr. Venable.[4]

---

[1]The exact North Carolina postal appointment sought by Powell has not been ascertained.

[2]James C. Dobbin, previously identified.

[3]Robert Strange, a Fayetteville Democrat, served as United States senator (1836-1840). Although highly regarded, he did not receive a cabinet appointment. He died February 19, 1854. *Biographical Directory of Congress, Bicentennial Edition*, 1887.

[4]Abraham W. Venable, previously identified, was an incumbent Democratic congressman. On February 22, 1853, the block was presented by Congressman Venable to the board of managers of the Washington Monument Society. Venable "delivered a highly appropriate address, in the presence of a numerous and distinguished company" assembled at "Monument Place" to witness the ceremony. According to press accounts, "This beautiful block is of handsome marble, a production of the good old State which it represents, is four feet long and two feet high, with the arms of North Carolina handsomely Sculptured in bas relief, and the name of the State in conspicuous letters beneath it." *National Intelligencer* in the *North Carolina Whig* (Charlotte), March 2, 1853, hereinafter cited as *North Carolina Whig.*

Second Inaugural Address of David S. Reid to the General Assembly[1]

A&H-mn

Raleigh
December 22, 1852

Profoundly grateful for the approval of my administration in being again called to the Executive Chair of North Carolina, I shall enter upon a second term with the earnest invocation to the Great Ruler of the Universe to enable me to discharge the duties of the office with prudence and justice, and in an acceptable manner to the people of the State.

The principles avowed in my last Inaugural Address will govern my administration during the ensuing term. They are too well known to require repetition on this occasion.

The extension of the right of suffrage is a great question of popular right, founded upon the immutable principles of truth and justice, and is demanded by the voice of the people. This reform is essential to the preservation of the blessings of liberty, and I shall continue earnestly to urge its consummation.

Keeping constantly in view the fact that the place I occupy was bestowed for public convenience, it will afford me pleasure to cooperate with the Legislature and the people in all measures calculated to promote the cause of Education—to justly distribute the benefits and burdens of government—and to advance the Agricultural and other great interests of the State, to the end that industry and enterprise may be properly rewarded, and the people become more free, prosperous and happy.

---

[1]According to press reports, Reid delivered this address to both houses of the state legislature. His inauguration took place on a Wednesday, and the oaths of

office were administered by Wesley Jones, a justice of the peace for Wake County. *Greensborough Patriot*, January 8, 1853.

Samuel P. Hill to David S. Reid A&H-DSR

Yanceyville
Dec. 28th 1852

I intended to have a conversation with you before leaving Raleigh relative to the Superintendent of the Mint at Charlotte, but was prevented from so doing by leaving Raleigh soon after the adjournment of the Legislature. It seemed to be generally understood among our friends from all sections of the State during the Winter that the office should be bestowed upon Maj Caldwell,[1] and that there would be no other applicant for it if he desired it. *He does desire it.* Yet I do not know that he mentioned it to you or to any one else to make any effort to secure it for him; and of course it will not be given him unless his friends make an exertion for him. Your relations with persons who will have some influence with Genl Peirce if brought to his aid would assist much in securing him the appointment. Could you not secure the assistance of Judge Douglass for him? I conversed with the Major the evening before parting with him and I know he would be gratified if you would enlist the Judge in his behalf. He is however so modest that I would not be at all astonished if he remained quiet, and made no serious effort to secure the place. His means are limited and his services and character require that he should be *well* considered of in the distribution of gifts to North Carolina.[2]

Our Friend Col Wheeler[3] is armed with a strong recommendation the concluding prayer of which would include any office in the gift of the President; whether he would be disposed to make it refer especially to the Mint, can be best judged of by those who know the Col and his former relations with that office If you can aid the Major by all means do so; I believe his friends wil have to move for him as I fear he will not make the exertion usually required to obtain appointments.

Our friends everywhere I find felt a deeper interest in the election of a Senator than I had immagined; the causes of our failure are well understood, and it is to be hoped that the constituents of those Gentlemen who [were] defeated will give to them some slight token of their disapprobation

I should be pleased to hear from you

[1]Greene W. Caldwell, previously identified, was elected to Congress in 1841 and was appointed superintendent of the United States Branch Mint at Charlotte in 1844. Caldwell resigned this post to enter military service during the Mexican War, 1847-1848, and upon his return home was elected to the state Senate. Charlotte Democrat William Julius Alexander was appointed in 1846 to replace Caldwell at the mint and served until at least some time in 1851. Alexander was succeeded by the Whig appointee James W. Osborne. Following an unsuccessful bid for reelection to Congress, Caldwell resumed his medical practice in Charlotte. He was in March 1853 appointed a second time as superintendent of the Charlotte mint, displacing Osborne. Powell, *DNCB*, I, 19, 303; *North-Carolina Standard*, March 30, 1853.

[2]Democratic editor W. W. Holden commented that the appointment of Caldwell would be popular in Charlotte. Even the Whig newspaper in Charlotte spoke favorably of him: "We have no objections against the recipient of the appointment to urge, and the country will have none. Mr. Caldwell is a gentleman who deserves the favors of his party, for the sacrifices which he has made for its interests." But the paper complained against the "odious principle" of political appointments according to the spoils system, noting that whereas "The heads of the Whigs are [under the new Democratic administration] falling off on every hand," the former superintendent Osborne, although a Whig, retained "the sub-officers of the Mint . . . all Democrats, whom he found in their present places, when he was appointed Superintendent." Osborne was an "honest, competent, and faithful incumbent" who never tried to influence anyone's vote, the *Whig*'s editor maintained. *North-Carolina Standard*, March 30, 1853; *North Carolina Whig*, March 30, 1853.

[3]John Hill Wheeler, whose history of North Carolina was published in 1851, had been superintendent of the mint at Charlotte, 1837-1841, and then state treasurer, 1842-1843. Apparently, Wheeler was dissuaded from competing with Caldwell for the mint appointment, and the *New York Express* reported by mid-March, 1853, that Wheeler was to be named auditor of the Treasury, replacing Whig incumbent John Wilson Farrelly of Pennsylvania, at a salary of $4,500. When this appointment also fell through for Wheeler, the *North Carolina Whig* rather gleefully reported: "Wm. F. Phillips has been appointed Auditor of the Treasury for the Post Office Department in place of Farrelly. [This was the place assigned to Col. Wheeler of N. C. What is the matter? Is not the Colonel to have a sop, after all?]" Ashe, *Biographical History*, VII, 474; *North-Carolina Standard*, March 19, 1853; *North Carolina Whig*, April 27, 1853; *Who Was Who in America, Historical Volume, 1607-1896* (Chicago: Marquis Who's Who, Inc., rev. ed., 1967), 246.

Poem by William W. Holden[1] RF

[Raleigh]
[December 1852]

I.

Pictures in light! Sleep on, dear boy.
Two hearts beat close to thine,
Who love thee more than words can tell,
Or human thought divine.

II.

Fond arms are round thee, and fond eyes
Are looking on that face,
Where traced with sunbeams, sit serene
Both Innocence and Grace.

III.

Light and no darkness for thee, boy!
Light from the upper spheres!
And Hope and Love be theirs and thine
Now, and through endless years!

---

[1]This poem was written by William W. Holden when shown a picture of Reid's son, David Settle Reid, Jr., the Reids' first child, who was born on September 10, 1852. He died of illness on August 7, 1871. David S. Reid to Thomas Settle, Raleigh, January 2, 1853, Reid Papers, PC 1, State Archives; Greenview Cemetery, Reidsville.

APPENDIX 1

Official Gubernatorial Election Returns by County, 1848, David S. Reid (Democrat) vs. Charles Manly (Whig).[1]

County	*Reid*	*Manly*
Alexander	201	334
Anson	400	1,049
Ashe	782	551
Beaufort	512	857
Bertie	370	524
Bladen	516	281
Brunswick	194	301
Buncombe	644	921
Burke	396	1,299
Cabarrus	377	743
Caldwell	138	589
Camden	80	489
Carteret	365	407
Caswell	1,081	263
Chatham	781	935
Cherokee	217	582
Chowan	228	293
Cleveland	727	421
Columbus	440	174
Craven	730	742
Cumberland	1,023	578
Currituck	583	179
Davidson	669	1,096
Davie	391	542
Duplin	921	218
Edgecombe	1,406	104
Franklin	673	319
Gates	390	371
Granville	946	1,016
Greene	315	207
Guilford	442	1,567
Halifax	507	601
Haywood	430	412
Henderson	227	656
Hertford	173	330
Hyde	298	469
Iredell	257	1,042
Johnston	814	720
Jones	181	215
Lenoir	455	196
Lincoln	1,877	832
Macon	352	451
Martin	557	339
Mecklenburg	1,068	698
Montgomery	86	609
Moore	556	544
Nash	887	106
New Hanover	1,015	275
Northampton	500	512
Onslow	663	176
Orange	1,726	1,714
Pasquotank	176	471
Perquimans	265	366
Person	578	360
Pitt	571	589
Polk	128	228
Randolph	313	1,199
Richmond	68	345
Robeson	623	581
Rockingham	968	340
Rowan	696	827
Rutherford	311	1,057
Sampson	692	530
Stanly	26	746
Stokes	1,223	1,003
Surry	1,226	1,090
Tyrrell	106	336
Wake	1,293	991
Warren	630	172
Washington	182	358
Wayne	1,097	264
Wilkes	309	1,299
Yancey	634	357
TOTALS	41,682	42,536

[1]Extracted from Connor, *North Carolina Manual, 1913*, 995-996.

APPENDIX 2

Official Gubernatorial Election Returns by County, 1850, David S. Reid (Democrat) vs. Charles Manly (Whig).[1]

County	*Reid*	*Manly*
Alexander	213	270
Anson	502	1,043
Ashe	687	604
Beaufort	537	814
Bertie	431	526
Bladen	561	311
Brunswick	260	306
Buncombe	649	1,035
Burke	344	1,341
Cabarrus	412	693
Caldwell	147	640
Camden	85	497
Carteret	361	415
Caswell	1,144	263
Chatham	896	1,149
Cherokee	230	713
Chowan	223	281
Cleveland	820	297
Columbus	451	165
Craven	541	609
Cumberland	1,310	602
Currituck	457	185
Davidson	699	1,159
Davie	313	577
Duplin	1,035	226
Edgecombe	1,481	88
Franklin	694	311
Gates	367	397
Granville	974	984
Greene	342	317
Guilford	526	1,772
Halifax	536	485
Haywood	399	508
Henderson	272	664
Hertford	171	270
Hyde	316	422
Iredell	279	1,010
Johnston	849	633
Jones	182	221
Lenoir	477	255
Lincoln	1,992	690
Macon	390	484
Martin	595	313
Mecklenburg	1,152	670
Montgomery	171	631
Moore	589	671
Nash	909	80
New Hanover	1,187	278
Northampton	524	489
Onslow	715	186
Orange	1,855	1,634
Pasquotank	217	390
Perquimans	291	347
Person	577	329
Pitt	583	591
Polk[2]	——	——
Randolph	379	1,350
Richmond	141	680
Robeson	626	562
Rockingham	1,107	337
Rowan	649	890
Rutherford	937	500
Sampson	853	507
Stanly	66	834
Stokes	1,452	1,060
Surry	1,352	1,017
Tyrrell	131	353
Wake	1,450	979
Warren	689	183
Washington	291	189
Wayne	1,091	221
Wilkes	374	1,373
Yancey	632	456
TOTALS	45,080	42,337

[1]Extracted from Connor, *North Carolina Manual, 1913*, 995-996.

[2]Polk County votes in the 1850 gubernatorial election were reported with those of Rutherford County.

APPENDIX 3

Official Gubernatorial Election Returns by County, 1852, David S. Reid (Democrat) vs. John Kerr (Whig).[1]

County	*Reid*	*Kerr*	*County*	*Reid*	*Kerr*
Alexander	230	361	Johnston	883	733
Anson	513	1,088	Jones	240	214
Ashe	682	368	Lenoir	459	267
Beaufort	554	847	Lincoln	1,934	680
Bertie	420	527	Macon	432	451
Bladen	631	358	Madison	168	278
Brunswick	271	343	Martin	676	260
Buncombe	684	946	Mecklenburg	1,421	731
Burke	489	1,216	Montgomery	209	706
Cabarrus	441	714	Moore	646	615
Caldwell	196	600	Nash	1,030	84
Camden	122	488	New Hanover	1,342	350
Carteret	392	411	Northampton	586	504
Caswell	1,013	270	Onslow	696	167
Chatham	980	995	Orange	1,796	1,528
Cherokee	550	540	Pasquotank	247	453
Chowan	228	249	Perquimans	312	347
Cleveland	870	305	Person	550	341
Columbus	443	198	Pitt	649	636
Craven	698	597	Randolph	439	1,279
Cumberland	1,388	783	Richmond	194	624
Currituck	603	178	Robeson	760	693
Davidson	746	951	Rockingham	1,072	356
Davie	345	490	Rowan	712	776
Duplin	1,072	190	Rutherford[2]	590	1,106
Edgecombe	1,425	104	Sampson	905	509
Franklin	721	341	Stanly	80	896
Gates	406	363	Stokes	1,481	1,132
Granville	1,063	1,005	Surry	1,376	1,206
Greene	361	347	Tyrrell	114	282
Guilford	480	1,524	Wake	1,561	1,102
Halifax	541	551	Warren	697	162
Haywood	551	368	Washington	297	247
Henderson	340	762	Watauga	234	183
Hertford	246	360	Wayne	1,196	283
Hyde	408	368	Wilkes	393	1,345
Iredell	393	1,035	Yancey	694	336
			TOTALS	48,567	43,003

[1]Extracted from Connor, *North Carolina Manual, 1913*, 997-998.

[2]Includes returns from Polk County.

INDEX

B

C

D

E

G

H

Q

R

W